Aging as a Social Process

Aging as a Social Process

An Introduction to
Individual and Population Aging

BARRY D. McPHERSON
University of Waterloo

BUTTERWORTHS
Toronto

Aging as a Social Process
© 1983 Butterworth & Co. (Canada) Ltd.

Printed and bound in Canada
54321   34567898

Canadian Cataloguing in Publication Data

McPherson, Barry D.
Aging as a Social Process

Includes index.
ISBN 0-409-84830-1

1. Gerontology.   2. Aging.   3. Aged.   I. Title.
HQ1061.M36   305.2'6   C82-094792-X

The Butterworth Group of Companies

Canada
Butterworth & Co. (Canada) Ltd., Toronto and Vancouver

United Kingdom
Butterworth & Co. (Publishers) Ltd., London

Autralia
Butterworth Pty. Ltd., Sydney

New Zealand
Butterworth of New Zealand Ltd., Wellington

South Africa
Butterworth & Co. (South Africa) Ltd., Durban

United States
Butterworth (Publishers) Inc., Boston
Butterworth (Legal Publishers) Inc., Seattle
Mason Publishing Company, St. Paul

Contents

Foreword

For most of the years of its history, a history well described in this book, the quality of research and theory in social gerontology has been strained. Paradoxically, as if driven by the external demographic forces of population aging, the field has nonetheless expanded rapidly as an area of inquiry and, especially in North America, as an area of academic study. During the past five years a number of textbooks have sought to codify existing knowledge and to present it in a form suitable for teaching purposes; but until very recently the material available for codification has been highly unreliable, and many of the textbooks have been uncritical and far too skimpy in their coverage.

Methodologically, social gerontology has lagged behind general sociology in analytical and statistical sophistication. This may reflect the isolating influences of multidisciplinary programs, which have played an important part in gerontological research and training and which have tended to pull social scientists from their 'home' departments to work in multidisciplinary settings. Or it may reflect the compromises that result from attempts to work with other disciplines — compromises that seem to blend the worst aspects of each participating discipline.

Theoretically, the field of social gerontology has been dominated by one school of thought, structural functionalism; and the major debates, such as those centering on activity and disengagement theory in the social psychology of aging, or on modernization and its effects on the social status of the aged in the broader, more structural sociology of aging, have all been cast within the framework of society as an equilibrium system of linked status positions and role behavior, with social change viewed as incremental and social process seen as inherently self-regulating. Throughout the period of the rapid growth of social gerontology, its theory became increasingly archaic when contrasted with the critiques of structural functionalism and the growth of theoretical diversity in sociology.

The field, fortunately, has now caught up and has attained methodological rigor and theoretical sophistication comparable to other areas of sociology. The latest knowledge can be presented in a more technical way, and the received wisdom from the earlier period of social gerontology must now be critically evaluated against high standards. For these reasons, this book is called for, and for these reasons, it is a success.

Barry McPherson has brought together the most comprehensive review of the state of our knowledge in social gerontology that I have seen. But he has gone beyond that in calling the student's attention to the methodological problems of so much of this knowledge. The various chapters cover a wide ground. While concentrating on the North American situation, the book is, nonetheless, comparative across societies and in time. Students and instructors will find the explicit discussion of methodological concerns in social gerontology to be valuable and easy to digest. The discussion of the theory is prefaced by a helpful review of general theoretical perspectives. The eclectic approach to theory may displease some scholars who have strong preferences for one theoretical approach, but it is admirably suited to the student who must be exposed to the broad range of theories while simultaneously being encouraged to address each critically.

The book is, then, as comprehensive and contemporary as it can be, and it is reliable and constructively critical in its codification of knowledge. This also implies that it is not an easy book, and it will find its greatest appeal with students who are more challenged than entertained by social gerontology. There are other, lesser textbooks in the area which will 'entertain' more but which cover the field in a skimpy and often misleading fashion. From my own perspective, and that of many colleagues in the field, I think the book will also be much used for basic reference purposes, simply because of its comprehensiveness. I trust that the book will be valuable to students in serious courses in social gerontology, and serious students will appreciate its virtues. This is an important book and a welcome addition to the published resources in the field.

Victor W. Marshall
University of Toronto
February 1983

Preface

Because of the increasing proportion of adults who are in the middle and later stages of the life cycle, and because of social, economic, and political changes that have had an impact on the aging process, a number of occupations now consider the special needs of adults when planning and delivering services. Among those who need to acquire an understanding of the social processes of aging and the associated problems are health care personnel, psychiatrists, occupational therapists, immigration personnel, psychologists, architects, dietitians, recreation and media workers, social workers and agency administrators, kinesiologists, religious leaders, lawyers, economists, politicians, journalists, educators, policy planners, urban and regional planners, and engineers.

Before social policies and programs for the elderly are initiated, the existence of a potential problem must first be verified, why and how the problem arose must be understood, and solutions must be derived. Guesswork or hunches are not sufficient; rather, valid information on which to base decisions and plan programs must be available. The need to provide the professions listed above with valid information has led to an increasing concern with the problems of aging and the aged, and a concomitant interest in describing and explaining the process and product of aging from a social science perspective.

At first, studies were mainly descriptive. They sought to draw attention to a specific situation (such as the near-poverty status of many elderly citizens) or to provide a policy or a solution for some perceived social problem affecting the elderly. However, this approach often led to an exaggeration of the problem or to the creation and perpetuation of myths. Thus, throughout the 1960s and 1970s, sociologists, psychologists, economists, demographers, political scientists, anthropologists, and social gerontologists initiated research to explain, not just describe, phenomena associated with both the aging process and the status of being old. As a result, more reliable and valid information became available to assist in developing policies and in implementing social services. Moreover, this research refuted some myths about the elderly, thereby reducing to some degree prejudiced perceptions of the elderly.

This book is a synthesis of social science research concerning individual and population aging. The structure and content is based on an undergraduate course on the sociology and social psychology of aging that I have taught since 1971. Throughout, the emphasis is on identifying, describing, and explaining patterns, processes, and problems concerning individual and population aging, rather than on describing programs or providing prescriptions to assist the elderly. This approach permits students in a variety of programs to acquire basic knowledge essential to careers in fields related to gerontology, and to develop a better understanding of the aging process as it will influence them and their parents in the future.

Throughout the book, a variety of theoretical and methodological orientations are used to describe and explain the aging process. Although desirable, it is difficult to write a text from a single theoretical perspective since the literature on gerontology is highly eclectic and is based on a number of theoretical perspectives from various disciplines. The quality of the research also varies greatly. Therefore, the reader is exposed to a variety of research methods and theoretical frameworks that represent the state of the art in social gerontology.

This book does not contain the standard (and usually token) chapter on the biology of aging. Rather, recognizing that biological factors do influence social behavior, the reader is introduced to the effect of degenerative changes in the physical and sensory systems as these changes relate to social processes and interpersonal interaction. Similarly, there are no sections or chapters on death and dying, social policy, psychopathology, or social services for the elderly, since many of these topics are the focal points of separate courses and texts. Moreover, much of the material on social policy and social services is unique to a particular social system (city, state, or nation) and becomes dated very quickly. It is left to the instructor to introduce relevant local and regional information on legislation, social policies, and social services for the elderly.

In organizing the book, an attempt was made to avoid the social-problems orientation found in many other textbooks. In fact, the issue of whether aging constitutes a social problem for more than a minority of adults is questionable. Therefore, the material in this book is based on the premise that aging is a social process involving interaction between the personal system (the individual), various social systems that influence the behavior of the aging individual, and changing social, economic, and physical environments. Thus, although individual experiences vary, there are common patterns to the aging process. Individuals born at about the same time (an age cohort) are influenced by similar historical or social events (economic depressions, world wars, or changes in cultural value systems). Moreover, individuals with similar ascribed (race, sex) or achieved (educational level, social class, occupation) attributes also tend to exhibit common patterns of behavior throughout the life cycle. In short, how persons age as individuals is greatly influenced by the social structure and by social processes within particular social systems.

The objectives of this text are threefold:

1. To enable the student to understand the process of aging from a sociological and social-psychological perspective. Where possible, alternative explanations for specific aspects of the aging process are emphasized more than descriptions of the process or specific problems.

2. To provide the student with basic concepts, theories, and methodologies that can be used to understand social phenomena related to processes of individual and population aging.

3. To sensitize the student to the fact that aging is not just a biological process, but an equally complex social process. In fact, the reader may well be left with the impression that relatively little is known about aging as a social process. Herein lies a challenge to the curious, innovative student who may wish to pursue a career in the field of social gerontology.

The book is structured in four parts. Part One provides background information about aging as a social phenomenon, sensitizes the reader to some critical parameters that influence the aging process and the status of being old, describes aging and the status of being old in a number of cultural contexts, and introduces theory and methods that may be used to understand the aging process from a social science perspective.

Part Two presents a micro-level analysis of the aging process. The focus is on aging individuals who must adapt to changes in their physical and psychological systems. In Part Three, a macro-level analysis focuses on the social structure, related social processes, and the physical environment. All of these factors interact to influence the process of aging. Part Four is concerned with aging and social participation patterns, particularly within the family and the labor force, and at leisure.

To the Student

Each chapter begins with a general overview and concludes with a summary of major research findings. Within each chapter a large number of references are cited in the text. These serve a twofold purpose. First, they indicate that there is some theoretical or research support for the statement. Second, they serve as a teaching aid to help you find and use primary sources in the basic literature. These references will be particularly useful if you are required to write a term paper on a specific topic, or if you wish to acquire additional information about a particular area.

Attempts were made to include material from most of the social sciences, although sociology (the study of normative patterns of behavior in various social systems) and social psychology (the study of the interaction of individual differences and the social milieu) are the major disciplines represented. The material includes an analysis of the process of aging, as well as an analysis of the end product of that process — the status of being old in a particular society and in a particular physical environment. Throughout, information on the aging process is presented from both a micro (individual) and a macro (societal) perspective.

There has been a virtual information explosion in this field in recent years, and most of the material presented here is based on articles published within the past six years. Where possible, information is based on theoretical and research evidence from a number of societies, although much of the work in social gerontology has been done in North America.

As in any dynamic and rapidly growing discipline, information quickly becomes dated. Therefore, the reader who wishes to acquire the most recent information should regularly consult general reference sources, such as *Current Contents, Sociological Abstracts*, and *Psychological Abstracts*; and specific gerontology journals such as *Gerontological Abstracts, Aging, Black Aging, Journal of Gerontology, The Gerontologist, International Journal of Aging and Human Development, Research on Aging, Perspectives on Aging, Experimental Aging Research, Annual Review of Gerontology and Geriatrics, Educational Gerontology, Ageing and Society, Aging and Work, The Canadian Journal on Aging*, and *Journal of Gerontological Social Work*. In addition, there are a number of non-English-language journals such as *Acta Gerontologica Japonica* (Japan), *Acta Gerontologica* (Italy), *Gerontologie* (France), and *Zeitschrift fur Gerontologie* (Federal Republic of Germany).

The paucity of research in this field relative to other disciplines should lead you to question carefully and discuss with others the research findings presented in any single study. You will only acquire a true understanding of the aging process when you become a critical reader, able to decide whether conclusions are logical and valid. One published article on a particular subject does not represent the 'absolute' truth. This is especially true in the field of social gerontology since race, sex, ethnicity, education, place and type of residence, health, income, occupation, and personality can have a profound impact on the process and status of aging. Many studies in social gerontology reflect only one 'slice' of a particular social system (usually focusing on white, middle-class males) and other social, personal, or structural factors are seldom considered in the analysis of the results. In short, be skeptical, thorough, and knowledgeable in what you accept as fact. Finally, the test of how well a text serves as a learning resource is whether students find the material useful, interesting, clearly written, and comprehensive. Please provide feedback concerning this text to your instructor and to the author.

To the Instructor

The chronological order of the chapters in this book represents only one conceptual approach to introducing the student to knowledge in the field. For upper-level students who have had a course in research methods, a chronological approach from chapter 1 to chapter 11 is probably best. For lower-level students just being introduced to social gerontology and perhaps to the social sciences, one of the following sequences might be more appropriate: chapters 1, 3, 5 to 11, 2, and 4; or chapters 1, 5 to 11, and 2 to 4. For courses with a sociological orientation, the sequence might be chapters 1, 2, 3, 4, 7, 8, 9 to 11, 5, and 6; courses with a social psychological orientation could use a sequence consisting of chapters 1, 5, 6, 3, 4, 7 to 11, and 2.

Regardless of the sequence, local and regional demographic facts should be introduced where possible and information should be provided in class discussions about current public- and private-sector policies on health care, social and recreational services, retirement policies, public and private pension plans, and subsidized housing. These have not been included in the text because policies in these areas rapidly become dated (for example, monthly government pension rates), and because they are often unique to specific regions or communities. It is also important for the student to become familiar with and to be a critical reader of the basic literature in a given field. Textbooks seldom provide opportunities for this experience. Therefore, you may wish to supplement the information in each chapter by having students read and discuss one or two recent articles on individual or population aging from gerontology or social science journals. The list of references at the end of each chapter and the most recent issues of the journals mentioned above can provide a starting point for this educational experience.

Barry D. McPherson
Waterloo, Ontario, Canada
February, 1983

Acknowledgements

Behind every author there are a number of friends, colleagues, and relatives who provide invaluable support and assistance. So that those who provided direct or indirect assistance in the writing of this book will not remain anonymous, I wish to express my sincere thanks: to Gerald S. Kenyon and John W. Loy, friends and co-authors of earlier works, for encouragement and indirect conceptual input — may you 'age' with greater understanding; to Victor Marshall, for encouragement and feedback at all stages, for a thorough review of the completed manuscript, and for writing a thoughtful foreword; to Stan Eitzen and Dan Kubat for critical and constructive reviews of specific chapters; to Brenda Harvey, Betty Maes, Mark Tyndall, and Lorna Wenger who, when given the opportunity to 'turn the tables' and critique a professor's work, provided valuable feedback from the perspective of undergraduate students; to Barbara Brown, Jacqueline Frank, and Yasuo Yamaguchi for bibliographic assistance; to Kathy Johnson for her interest, efficiency, and professional editorial input; to Rick and Beth Beach of Waterloo Computer Typography for their patience, advice, and efficient typesetting; and to my worthy opponents at the Kitchener-Waterloo Racquet Club for keeping me mentally and physically fit after long days of writing (beware; now that I have put down the pen I will have more time for the racquet).

Deserving a special paragraph of recognition is Ms. Karri Deckert. Although classified as a secretary by the University of Waterloo, she has competently fulfilled a variety of other roles, including that of administrative assistant, slave driver, and cheerleader. She deciphered and translated my aging penmanship into an error-free manuscript; she frequently challenged me to write faster so that she would not be idle; she efficiently performed many administrative responsibilities on my behalf so that I could schedule blocks of time to read and write; and she remained dedicated and loyal to the project despite internal changes that placed extreme pressure on her time. I will never forget the look on her face when I informed her that she had entered over two million characters into the computer while typing this manuscript. Karri, a million thanks, times two.

Finally, to Liz, Jennifer, and David — 'the book' is finally finished. Thank you for your patience, time, and interest.

Grateful acknowledgement is also made to the following for permission to reprint or adapt excerpts from copyrighted material:

American Psychological Association for 'Aging and Skilled Problem Solving' by N. Charness © 1981 American Psychological Association; for an illustration from *Psychology of Adult Development and Aging*, edited by C. Eisdorfer and M.P. Lawton © 1973 American Psychological Association (adapted by permission of the author); for 'Person-Environment Dialectics: Implications for Competent Functioning in Old Age' by P. Windley and R. Scheidt in *Aging in the 1980s* edited by L. Poon © 1980 American Psychological Association.

Brooks/Cole Publishing Company for *Role Transitions in Later Life* by L. George © 1980 Wadsworth, Inc.

The Gerontological Society of America for 'Facts on Aging: A Short Quiz' by E. Palmore (in *The Gerontologist* 17(4/1977) © 1977 Gerontological Society of America; and for 'Facts on Aging Quiz: Part Two' by E. Palmore (in *The Gerontologist* 21(4/1981) © 1981 Gerontological Society of America.

Jossey-Bass Inc. for *From Thirty to Seventy* by H. Mass and J. Kuypers © 1974 Jossey-Bass Inc.

Prentice-Hall, Inc. for *Social Stratification: The Forms and Functions of Inequality* by Melvn M. Tumin © 1967 Prentice-Hall, Inc.; for *Aging and Modernization* by Donald O. Cowgill and Lowell D. Holmes © 1972 Prentice-Hall, Inc.; and for 'What Is a Grandma?' in *Growing Older* by Margaret Hellie Huyck © 1974 Margaret Hellie Huyck.

Social Security Administration, Office of Research and Statistics, for *Income of the Population 55 and Older, 1976* © 1979 U.S. Department of Health, Education and Welfare.

Travel, Tourism, and Recreation Section, Education, Science and Culture Division, Statistics Canada, for *Culture Statistics, Recreational Activities, 1976* © 1976 Statistics Canada.

United Nations Centre for Social Development and Humanitarian Affairs for 'Population Projection' © 1981 CSDHA.

Van Nostrand Reinhold Company for *Handbook of the Psychology of Aging*, edited by James E. Birren and K. Warner Schaie © 1977 Van Nostrand Reinhold Company.

PART ONE

An Introduction to Individual and Population Aging

Although aging has traditionally been considered a biological process, increasing research attention is being directed to the impact of sociocultural, historical, and environmental factors on the processes of individual and population aging. This increased interest has led to the development of a large body of research within the field of social gerontology.

Part I comprises four chapters that will equip the student to read, understand, and critique pertinent literature on individual or population aging. Chapter 1 introduces the concept of aging as a social phenomenon, outlines historical and contemporary developments in the field of social gerontology, alerts the student to some conceptual and methodological concerns, and introduces environmental and sociocultural variables essential to the study of individual or population aging.

Chapter 2 describes the process and product of aging in selected societies throughout history, analyzes the changing status of the elderly in preindustrial and industrial societies, especially following the onset of modernization, and examines, primarily within the North American context, the process and product of aging within indigenous, racial, ethnic, rural, and religious subcultures.

Chapter 3 provides the reader with information about demographic processes and indicators that describe the size, composition, and distribution of the population by age, and focuses on the social and environmental characteristics of older cohorts within a society, from both a historical and a contemporary perspective.

Chapter 4 introduces the goals and methods of scientific inquiry, as well as some specific methodological concerns that must be considered when studying the aging process. Most of the chapter discusses the major conceptual perspectives and social theories that have been used to stimulate, guide, and explain aging phenomena from a social science perspective. The section on social science perspectives and theories introduces the two general levels of analysis used throughout the book: the micro (or personal) level that pertains to individual aging, and the macro (or societal) level that pertains to cohort or population aging. These are not separate entities; there is constant interaction throughout adulthood between individual and population aging, and between the individual and the social structure.

1

Aging as a Social Phenomenon

Introduction

During the past twenty to thirty years, birthrates have declined and life expectancy has increased in most modern industrial societies. As a result, approximately 8 percent of the population in North America now is made up of people over 65. This proportion is expected to increase to about 12 percent by the year 2000, and to between 15 and 17 percent between 2010 and 2020 when the 'baby-boom' age cohort passes 65. This phenomenon, where an increasing percentage of the population is made up of older people, is known as 'population aging'.

In contrast, 'individual aging' refers to the structural, sensory, motor, behavioral, and cognitive changes in a given organism over time, especially with respect to how these factors influence life chances and lifestyle at various stages of the life cycle. An individual's reactions to these biological, physiological, and psychological changes and his or her behavior at different periods in the life cycle are closely related to the individual's past and present social context. The social processes and structure of a particular society can greatly influence the aging process for an individual or for a specific age cohort. In short, individual and population aging are social processes that may differ within various contexts.

Much of the early research in social gerontology sought to describe and improve the situation of the elderly (from a social problems perspective); more recently, the emphasis has been on explaining the process of aging during the middle and later years of the life cycle. This book reflects the latter focus.

This chapter provides an overview of the social process of aging, briefly outlines the development of the field of social gerontology, and alerts the reader to some of the methodological concerns and social and environmental factors that influence the aging process. Throughout, the universal biological and psychological processes, although somewhat independent of the social milieu, are seen to interact with social processes. These social processes are unique to a given culture or subculture in that they are influenced by social change and historical events. Moreover, they may vary owing to social and environmental factors such as sex, social class, income, education, race, ethnic background, nationality, and place of residence (urban or rural).

It will be apparent throughout this book that the study of aging and the aged is complex and involves many levels of analysis. These include physical, sensory, and motor changes within the individual; the impact of population aging on the individual and on society; the impact of social change on the status of the elderly; the patterns of aging unique to age cohorts or generations; the interaction among different age cohorts within a society; the culture-based patterns of aging; and the interaction of social and psychological processes with biological processes, especially with respect to how the latter influences the former at different stages in the life cycle.

The major aim of this book is to provide the student with valid knowledge about aging as a social process. It also illustrates the approaches and techniques used by social scientists and gerontologists to describe and explain how individuals and cohorts adapt to personal changes and to a changing social environment as they pass through stages in the life cycle. Throughout, the emphasis is on social phenomena — on identifying, describing, and explaining repeated patterns of events, behavior, and thought that occur as individuals or cohorts interact in various social and physical environments throughout their middle and later years.

Aging as a Social Phenomenon

For many years aging was considered to be mainly a biological process that was inevitable, universal, and irreversible. The process begins at birth and is characterized by ten to twenty years of growth, followed by a plateau or decline in the size and efficiency of the organism. This decline is evident in external signs such as skin wrinkles, change in hair color, loss of hair, and, more subtly, through internal changes such as a decline in vision, hearing, lung capacity, energy reserves, strength, and reaction time. However, not everyone experiences these changes at the same rate or to the same extent.

Although the average life span in earlier centuries was shorter than it is today,[1] some people lived long past their 'normal' life expectancy. These exceptions were studied carefully to determine a possible explanation for their longevity. Because these few examples showed longer life was possible, individuals searched for a magic potion or the Fountain of Youth many centuries ago.[2] Early explanations for longevity were based on genetic and hereditary factors over which the individual had little or no control.

Along with this interest in understanding and extending the life span, some societies were concerned with improving the quality of care for their elderly citizens, primarily to ensure that they were adequately housed, fed, and clothed. As a result, many practices initiated in the late nineteenth century in Western Europe and in the first third of the twentieth century in North America sought to prevent or relieve the physical suffering of the elderly. The few social policies that were initiated assisted the destitute elderly and the families who no longer could care for and cope with their elderly parents or grandparents.

In the late nineteenth and early twentieth centuries, the growth of disciplines such as psychology, sociology, anthropology, economics, and political science drew attention to the fact that a biological organism, regardless of its genetic background, does not age in a vacuum but within various social systems. Social scientists began to focus not only on the physical and social status of elderly citizens but also on the social, cultural, economic, and psychological factors that influenced the aging process. They were encouraged in this endeavor by the desire to understand a social phenomenon and by a realization of the need for knowledge to strengthen the scientific basis for professional practice and government policies relating to the elderly.

Recognizing that aging is not only a biological process, scientists sought to understand how sociocultural and environmental factors interact to influence individual and population aging. Aging is viewed as a social process characterized by health, economic, and social losses[3] that occur when the individual interacts within an age structure made up of numerous age strata.[4] As a result of the values and social expectations in a specific culture, interaction among age cohorts can enhance or destroy the status, rights, responsibilities, and power of individuals throughout the life cycle. In short, life chances and lifestyle are influenced by (1) physiological, sociological and psychological factors unique to an individual or age cohort; (2) the social structure of a given society; and (3) social, economic, and historical changes[5] that occur within a given sociocultural context.

In summary, longer life spans and a decline in birth rates and immigration have increased the actual number and the proportion of the elderly in the total population. Moreover, the elderly are becoming increasingly visible and vocal.[6] Thus, as a society's age structure changes with population aging, and as concomitant social and historical changes occur, the aging process both for individuals and cohorts may change. Aging is seen to be dynamic rather than static, and its influence on specific individuals and cohorts at one stage of the life cycle is related to experiences at earlier stages. Furthermore, aging is characterized by cultural norms that guide intergenerational and intragenerational interaction.

Aging involves interaction between biological, physiological, psychological, and social processes. While the social and psychological processes are the major areas of interest in this book, some attention is given to how and when biological processes influence behavior at later stages in the life cycle.[7]

Much of the initial research and writing in social gerontology focused on the status or the problems of being old; recently there has been increasing recognition of the need to develop a 'life span perspective' in order to understand the influence of earlier stages on later ones (Kerckhoff, 1976; Borland, 1978; Levinson, 1978; Dannefer, 1983). Beginning with the following two sections, this book will focus on the process and the product of aging as a social phenomenon.

The Aging Process

As we have seen, aging involves physical, psychological, and social change[8] and adaptation throughout the life cycle. These structural and behavioral changes and adaptations over the years within and between individuals and cohorts constitute the process of aging. While the aging process is not fully understood, there is common agreement that it is inevitable, universal, irreversible, and complex; that individuals and age cohorts experience different types and rates of aging; and that genetic, physical, psychological, environmental, and social factors are directly and indirectly involved. This section outlines various facets of the aging process and introduces concepts to facilitate an understanding of the process.

Types of Aging

Although the following facets of the aging process are introduced as distinct phenomena, interaction does exist between the various processes. For example, a decline in visual acuity[9] (a biological change) may lead to an inability to read or drive a car, thereby imposing some degree of intellectual or social constraint on a person's lifestyle. Similarly, forced retirement (a social act) may initiate psychological (depression), physical (decreased endurance), or social (absence of friends) losses that create problems for the individual and for society. Furthermore, with the exception of chronological aging, there is variation within and between individuals in the onset and degree of aging among the various systems. For example, an individual may appear physically 'old,' but his or her social or psychological behavior may be that of a younger adult.

Chronological aging.   Chronological aging (the passage of calendar time) determines status differentiation (often via legal statutes) and influences lifestyle. For example, chronological age, especially during childhood, determines when a person can join the Scouts, what teams to play for, and who to play with at school. However, the differences between individuals mean that chronological age provides only an approximate indication of normative structural growth and decline, psychological or physical performance, social and emotional development, and patterns of social interaction.[10] Chronological age can be deceiving; a 30-year-old may have the facial features of a 40-year-old, yet act and dress like a 20-year-old. Some may perceive this person to be 'old' for his age, while others who know him may perceive him as 'immature' for his age. This example illustrates that age and aging have a social meaning that is defined within a particular social or cultural context.

Throughout the life cycle, all members of a society, particularly adults, must obey laws pertaining to their rights and obligations as citizens. In many cases these laws refer to a specific legal age (Cain, 1976) before or at which a particular social function or right can or cannot be exercised. These include such rites of passage as beginning school, driving a car, being eligible to vote, being drafted for military service, being eligible to marry, and being required to retire. Unfortunately, many of these legal ages are established arbitrarily according to some preconceived norm as to what is the best or 'normal' chronological age for each right or obligation. In some cases legal age is based on the best available knowledge about chronological age norms — how most individuals behave in a given situation or perform a particular task at a specific chronological age.

Legal age may also be determined by 'functional' aging. This term refers to the relationship between chronological age and how well an individual can perform specific physical, social, or psychological tasks. In this sense, functional aging may be a more useful and meaningful construct than chronological aging. Functional aging takes into consideration individual differences and the fact that aging is a multifaceted process wherein an individual at a certain age may be 'older' or 'younger' than others. For example, mandatory retirement might be based on how well an individual can continue to perform job responsibilities, rather than on him or her reaching the chronological age of 60, 65, or 70. For example, a study of normative aging conducted in Boston identified and developed six nonchronological indicators of changes with age. These measures, which assess auditory and biochemical ability and personality, social, and anthropometric (measurement of the size and proportion of the body) changes in the individual (Bell, 1972), may be used by planners, policy makers, and personnel managers to assess the functional capacity of older persons.

The use of chronological age to determine legal age fails to account for individual or cultural differences in needs or abilities. While legal age introduces social order and control to a society, it may also impose constraints on individual rights and personal development. For example, legislation that makes retirement at age 65 mandatory implies that people become economically useless at that age (Cain, 1974, 1976). While some persons may no longer be able to perform their tasks or may not wish to continue working, others have the capacity and desire to continue contributing to the social system. Similarly, some may be ready to drive a car at age 16; others may be ready earlier, and others much later.

Examples of both intra- and intercultural discrepancies in the interpretation of the rights and responsibilities associated with legal age exist. One intracultural discrepancy is the legal requirement of compulsory military service at age 18 in some countries. Yet, those drafted are often not eligible to vote for those who make the laws until the age of 21. Cain (1974) refers to this discrepancy as 'age-status asynchronization.' An illustration of intercultural variation in the interpretation of legal age is mandatory retirement. The mandatory age may be 55 to 70 in industrialized nations; it may be whenever an individual is no longer functionally able to perform in less industrialized nations; or, in some societies, there may be no mandatory retirement age at all. (Interestingly, these same options can apply to the self-employed, since they are usually exempt from institutionally imposed social constraints on the right to work or retire.)

In summary, chronological aging provides a gross measure of the stage of growth and the expected pattern of behavior and change. It is most useful as a descriptive measure of changes within an individual. The following measures relate to functional aging and to an understanding of the type and rate of aging within individuals, between individuals within a society, and among individuals in culturally diverse societies.

Biological aging.   'Biological aging' refers to internal and external changes in the structure and functioning of the organism that influence behavior and longevity. One outcome of this process is senescence, wherein genetically and environmentally induced changes take place in the various systems of the organism, such as the muscular, skeletal, reproductive, neural, and sensory systems. Many are visible changes: loss of hair, change in hair color, change in skin texture, and change in stature, gait, and posture.

The rate and incidence of the internal biological changes influence the number of years an individual is likely to survive. Many of these changes and their accompanying adaptations also influence the social and psychological processes of aging. Similarly, the lifestyle of a particular social class, or stress or depression in an individual can either retard or accelerate the biological process. This facet of the aging process is beyond the scope of this book. The interested reader should consult the following references for more information on this subject: Shock, 1962; Finch and Hayflick, 1977; Shock, 1977; Rockstein and Sussman, 1979; McGaugh and Kiesler, 1981.

Psychological aging.   Psychological aging involves possible changes in personality, cognition, emotional arousal, psychomotor skills, learning, memory, motivation, or creativity. It involves interaction between cognitive and behavioral changes within the individual and environmental factors that affect his or her psychological state. For example, declining vision, memory, and attention span may lead to an abandonment of a lifelong interest in reading. This in turn can dramatically alter the leisure lifestyle of an individual and lead to boredom and depression.

Similarly, stressful events such as losing a spouse through divorce or death, declaring bankruptcy, or losing a job may alter the behavioral and mental processes of an individual at any chronological age. The degree to which an individual adapts often depends not only on personal psychological processes and capacities, but also on the amount of support and assistance received from significant others within the family and community.

There is also interaction between the biological and psychological systems. For example, a change in the endocrine system may lead to changes in emotional behavior or mental processes. Similarly, the loss of appetite that may accompany prolonged depression can result in a general deterioration of health. Psychological aging also involves cultural and subcultural differences in the process. These cultural factors enable us to ascribe a social meaning to age and aging that is unique to our culture.

Social aging.   'Social aging' represents regular patterns of behavior in individuals or groups as they interact with others within a specific social system. This may be a microsystem (such as the nuclear family) or a macrosystem (such as a nation or a region of the world). Aging as a social process varies considerably within and between cultures. Unlike the biological or psychological aging processes, which are relatively similar from one culture or subculture to another, social aging involves reciprocal interaction between the social system and the aging individual. An identical twin separated at birth from his or her sibling and raised in a different family, community, or country would exhibit aging patterns similar to those in his or her own social situation rather than that of the sibling.

Aging occurs within a social structure that provides a degree of order and stability. Within this structure, individuals occupy a number of status positions at socially determined and appropriate stages in the life cycle. These include the status of child, sibling, nephew or niece, friend, student, apprentice, spouse, parent, neighbor, colleague, boss, grandparent, aunt or uncle, retiree, widow or widower, and great-grandparent.

This structure of differentiated social positions forms an age-status system. Associated with each of these positions are role expectations or norms relating to how one should behave with others who occupy a specific position. Because these positions tend to be occupied at particular stages in the life cycle, much social behavior is influenced by age-related norms. Social systems are characterized by age-grading, wherein responsibilities or expectations are related to chronological age or social positions. At each age level, individuals are expected to conform to age-based norms associated with these social positions (see chapter 7).

Although learning and adopting patterns of social interaction by age is an important element of the social aging process, the importance of the social structure cannot be ignored, as Linton (1936) noted many years ago. The age structure of a society is stratified in a way similar to a ladder. While some societies distinguish among many strata (infancy, early childhood, preadolescence, adolescence, young adulthood, middle age, old age, very old age), others have only a few (childhood, adulthood, old age). Subjects in many studies have identified anywhere from two to fifteen subjective age categories during adulthood (Fry, 1976).

Regardless of the number of stages, the behavior and status of the members of each stratum are influenced by the expected rights and responsibilities assigned on the basis of age and by attitudes toward specific age groups. For example, some societies value the elderly (Japan); other societies (Canada and the United States) often devalue them and consider them less attractive, less interesting, and less worthwhile than younger people.

Within each culture, social timetables define the approximate chronological age when one enters or leaves various stages and occupies social positions (Fry, 1980). In fact, institutionalized rites of passage are sometimes initiated to provide continuity and to announce the transition from one position to another. Some examples include graduation, marriage, Bar Mitzvah ceremonies, and birthday celebrations. Special social events may signify a new status. In preindustrialized societies this might involve becoming a warrior or elder; in more developed societies, special status is accorded to individuals who marry, purchase their first car or home, or receive a promotion. For example, Musgrove and Middleton (1981) found that acquiring a mortgage was the most symbolic and emotional rite of passage among three distinct groups of adults: professional soccer players, teachers, and Methodist ministers.

The meanings attached to membership in an age stratum or to specific events are subject to change. In your parents' or grandparents' day, a woman who had not married by her mid-20s was often stigmatized and labelled an 'old maid.' In contrast, a single woman in her mid-20s is today viewed as 'liberated.' She is praised for protecting her future by not rushing into marriage and for pursuing an education and a career. In fact, in many instances she may be envied by her age-peers who are preoccupied with raising young children and meeting mortgage payments.

Within age cohorts the meaning and significance attached to similar rites of passage and to a particular age may vary by social group. For example, marriage may have more significance for lower-class women than for upper-class women, while a job promotion may have more significance for an upper-middle-class executive than for a blue-collar laborer.

The composition of the age structure also has an impact on the social definition of aging. The population in any society is made up of subgroups known as cohorts. These are made up of all persons born during a particular five- or ten-year period, or who enter an institution such as a university, marriage, the labor force, or the armed forces at about the same time (Ryder, 1965; Rosow, 1978). Over time, the number in any cohort at a particular stage in life may increase or decrease, creating unique problems for society or for members of the cohort. For example, those born between 1945 and the early 1950s composed one of the largest birth cohorts ever, and were part of the postwar 'baby boom.' The arrival of this cohort led to an urgent need for more schools during the 1950s and 1960s, and to a dramatic growth of suburban housing in the 1960s. By about 2010, this cohort will form the largest group ever of retirees, creating a unique economic drain on public and private pension funds.

The relative size of each cohort is not the only factor to have an impact on the aging process. The unique background, the shared experiences of economic, political, and social events, and the common sequencing of life events also influence cohorts (Elder and Liker, 1982). These commonalities influence values and lifestyle and differentiate a given cohort from other younger or older cohorts who experience the same phenomena, but at different stages in life. For example, during the early 1980s, a period characterized by inflation and high unemployment, cohort A in figure 1.1 was approaching its peak career years, and was probably coping reasonably well with the prevailing social and economic conditions. In contrast, cohort B was about to enter the labor force during a period of high unemployment, and therefore many members likely experienced difficulty in obtaining employment. Finally, cohort C was just entering the life cycle and was less likely to be directly affected by the prevailing economic climate. Thus, inflation and high unemployment in the early 1980s should have a different impact on these three distinct age cohorts now and in the future.

Figure 1.1 Cohort Differences and the Aging Process

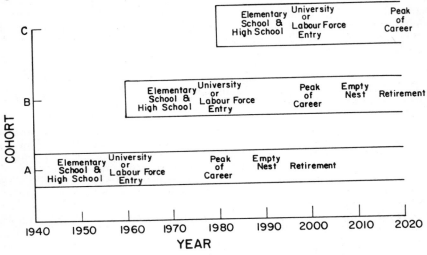

The aging process is also influenced by age cohort interaction. These intercohort relations can be described in terms of rules and expectations (Riley et al., 1972) that have the potential to promote cooperation or conflict between generations. This potential is often related to social differentiation within a culture — different age strata will have greater or lesser status, and therefore greater or lesser power. In societies where the elderly are valued, intergenerational relations are positive and the movement of a cohort from one stratum to the next is done without fear or regret. In contrast, in societies where youth is valued more highly than old age, intergenerational rivalry and conflict is more likely to occur, especially if the elderly resent the loss of status and power that they once held.

Conclusion.   The aging process involves individual and social change from the cellular to the societal or cultural level (Kiesler, 1981; Pampel, 1981). While each process functions independently and at its own rate, there is also interaction between the biological, psychological, and social processes. Consider an individual who experiences a social or physical loss such as widowhood or loss of vision. One outcome of the loss may be depression, which in turn may trigger biochemical changes and may lead to additional mental or physical problems. There is a need to study the aging biological and psychological organism within the social context; scientists know less about the social and cultural aspects of aging than about the biological and psychological processes. Similarly, there is a need to understand the reciprocal relationship between individual aging and social change. As society changes because of wars and economic cycles of growth and recession, individuals in various cohorts age in different ways.

The Product of the Aging Process: The Middle-aged and Elderly Adult

In the previous section the focus was on the aging process. This section emphasizes the outcome or product of that process, namely, the status of being middle-aged or elderly. Although these periods are not the end of the process (as is frequently assumed), they do represent unique stages of development for the individual and for society. Until recently, because of the increase in the number and visibility of the elderly, social gerontologists focused on the problems associated with the post-retirement stage in life, rather than on the process of aging per se. As a result, many biological, psychological, and sociological facts have been discovered; but they have seldom been verified in a variety of social contexts.

In order to assess knowledge of some of the verified social facts and to sensitize individuals to the prevalence of social myths and stereotypes concerning the later years, Palmore (1977, 1980a, 1981) and Miller and Dodder (1980) developed versions of a true-or-false 'Facts on Aging' quiz. The items in the test are based on documented research. The following questions are taken from the original Palmore quiz (1977) and the more recent version (Palmore, 1981). They provide you with an opportunity to assess your current level of knowledge and to clarify possible misconceptions about the elderly. See notes at the end of the chapter for the correct responses.[11]

T F   1. Older people tend to become more religious as they age.

T F   2. Most old people are set in their ways and unable to change.

T F   3. The majority of old people are seldom bored.

T F   4. The health and socioeconomic status of older people (compared to younger people) in the year 2000 will probably be about the same as now.

T F   5. Older persons have more acute (short-term) illnesses than persons under 65.

T F   6. The majority of old people are seldom irritated or angry.

T F   7. Older workers have less absenteeism than younger workers.

T F   8. The aged have higher rates of criminal victimization than persons under 65.

T F   9. The majority of the aged live alone.

T F 10. Older persons who reduce their activity tend to be happier than those who remain active.

Myths about the Elderly

In the absence of scientific knowledge about the aging process, personal observations or folk myths become the basis for social, psychological, or biological beliefs about old people. Although most of these beliefs are unfounded and negative in orientation, they tend to be accepted as facts. As a result, myths may negatively influence the behavior and expectations of middle-aged and elderly individuals — the self-fulfilling prophecy. In addition, they may influence the behavior and attitudes of others toward all older people or to anyone who happens to have a supposed 'middle-aged' or 'aged' characteristic. For example, men who are prematurely bald at age 25 may be considered 'old'; if they are prematurely gray at 30, they may be viewed as 'middle-aged.'

Stereotypes based on limited observations or on untested opinions are frequently present at all stages in life. For example, a visit to a shopping center after school hours might lead one to believe that all adolescents spend their leisure time smoking and 'hanging out.' Of course, this is a myth; only a small percentage of adolescents engage in this behavior on a regular basis, if at all. Nevertheless, young people may be stereotyped as lazy because of such observations. Similarly, through personal observation and (to some extent) through the role of the media in presenting and perpetuating stereotypes, certain myths about the elderly have become institutionalized and thereby accepted as fact. For example, the elderly are believed to be physically infirm, inactive, poor, senile, asexual, irritable, lonely, isolated, obsolete, irrationally afraid of aging and death, set in their ways, and in need of institutionalization.

Because of the prevalence of these myths, older people are often stigmatized. They may attempt to counteract this discrimination: some of the coping strategies that may be adopted include the use of facial creams, hairpieces, hair tints, faddish clothes, or cosmetic surgery, or adopting the language, values, and lifestyle of younger generations. In short, the middle-aged and elderly have recognized that chemical, surgical, and behavioral adaptations can be initiated to avoid conforming to a cultural definition of 'old age.'

The Social Reality of the Middle and Later Years of Life

Contrary to prevailing myths, only a minority of the elderly experience poor health, institutionalized living, poverty, loneliness, isolation, or senility. However, the greater the longevity of an individual, the greater the likelihood that one or more of these conditions will have some impact on the individual's life. These problems are mainly experienced by the very old (those over 75). If the elderly have certain ascribed or achieved characteristics, they are more likely to experience one or more of these problems. For example, as we will see later in this chapter, such factors as being female, being a member of a lower social class, being black, being a member of a native group, and having less education than one's age peers will influence not only the process of aging but also one's social, economic, health, and psychological status.

The aging process leads to individual differences among both the middle-aged[12] and the elderly, who must continuously adjust and adapt to changes in their unique social world. How an individual thinks and behaves at one stage is partly determined by what he or she was like at an earlier stage in life. The individual who is cautious, conservative, and introspective when young is likely to exhibit these same characteristics in the middle and later years.

Contrary to prevailing stereotypes or myths, old age is not characterized exclusively by economic, health, psychological, or social losses and problems. Rather, many of the apparent problems are societally induced outcomes rather than biological outcomes. Although aging is frequently viewed as a social problem, many advantages accrue to both society and the individual from aging and being older. Palmore (1979) lists the following advantages of aging for the individual: less criminal victimization, fewer accidents, availability of pensions and other guaranteed income, tax benefits, payment of medical expenses, reduced rates on consumer goods and services, and freedom from child-rearing and work. Some of the advantages to society cited by Palmore include lower criminal activity, greater political participation, increasing participation in voluntary associations, and increasing quality and quantity of work abilities.

Accounting for Behavioral, Cognitive, and Attitudinal Differences by Age: Aging Effects and Cohort Effects

It is commonly observed that people at different stages of life exhibit not only different physical traits but also different cognitive, emotional, and social behavior as they interact with others. While there are individual differences in both appearance and behavior within a given age cohort,[13] the differences are most pronounced between members of different generations. For example, people who are now in their 60s and 70s are generally more religious and more conservative than younger age cohorts. There appear to be two possible explanations to account for these generational differences.

First, differences may result from changes with age within the individual as he or she matures and develops. An obvious example is the external physical changes that occur in an individual from birth on, and which are reflected dramatically after about 40 years of age (such as changes in hair coloring and facial contours). Because aging is a dynamic rather than a static process, we all change and adapt to some extent as we occupy different social positions within a variety of social systems. For example, an authoritarian, autocratic individual who is promoted to a supervisory position in an organization might find that he or she must become more democratic and communicative in order to reach younger workers who may respond more productively to this style of leadership. Behavioral changes can occur over time, and the behavior of an individual at age 50 may be somewhat different from that exhibited at age 25. This is especially so if the expectations associated with a particular social position change or if new social positions are acquired.

Second, changes within the individual (aging effects) are not sufficient to account for apparent behavioral differences among various age cohorts. Rather, the impact of specific historical events unique to each cohort must also be considered (cohort effects). As noted earlier, a society consists of a series of successive age cohorts that pass through the life cycle as if on an upward bound escalator (Ryder, 1975; Riley et al., 1972). Each cohort may experience particular events differently from the preceding or following cohorts. For example, the onset of double-digit inflation in the early 1980s has had an influence on all cohorts, but it is perhaps most traumatic for the elderly who live on a fixed income, and least traumatic for children and teenagers who are still financially dependent on parents. Similarly, a depression, a war, an energy crisis, social or political unrest, or high unemployment can have a differential impact on different cohorts at a specific time. The event can have a lasting effect on the cognitive and behavioral processes of a specific cohort.

In summary, the outcome of the aging process for the individual and for society is dependent on changes within the individual over the life cycle, on different social experiences and historical events encountered by members of each cohort, and by the interaction of these two processes. However, it must be continually recognized that there are individual and cultural differences in the aging process, both within individuals and within cohorts. It is because of this interaction of individual differences and cross-cultural differences that the aging process is relatively difficult to understand.

The Field of Social Gerontology: Historical and Contemporary Perspectives

A historical approach to a topic is often considered by students to be uninteresting, trivial, or irrelevant. However, a historical analysis enables us to better understand our current situation through an appreciation of our 'roots.' With an understanding of the past we may be in a better position to predict and control the future if we see similar events or patterns evolving at a later stage in history. This section presents a general overview of how and why the field of gerontology, and particularly social gerontology, has evolved.[14]

Early History

Throughout history mankind has been preoccupied with the search for two major improvements to the quality of life — wealth and the prolongation of life and vigor. The latter goal is evident in the earliest writings of philosophers and historians who described the status and treatment of the aged in many societies. For example, those who lived a longer-than-normal life span were often held in awe and were sometimes feared, since it was believed that they possessed some magic power.

The fact that some people lived longer than others led to the creation of myths and folk tales to explain this longevity. The earliest literature was characterized by three themes (Gruman, 1966). The 'antidiluvian theme' was based on the belief that people in the past had avoided death by various means and had lived perhaps as long as 900 years. According to the 'hyperborean theme,' there are unique cultures in which people experience exceptional longevity. This was thought to occur because of such factors as social isolation, diet, genetics, high levels of physical activity, and special treatment of the aged. Examples of cultures in which individuals are thought to live at least 100 years (centenarians) are the Vilcabambans of Ecuador (Leaf, 1975), who reportedly have 1,100 centenarians per 100,000 population, and the Abkhasians of Georgia in the U.S.S.R., with a reported sixty centenarians per 100,000 population (Benet, 1974). By comparison, in many industrialized societies there may be fewer than three people per 100,000 who live to the age of 100. However, the extreme longevity among the Vilcabambans and Abkhasians has not been substantiated since birth records are rarely available (Medvedev, 1974; Mazess and Forman, 1979). Moreover, individuals in these societies may exaggerate their age to attain high status, to escape military duty when they are young, or to pretend to be something they are not in order to gain attention from visiting scholars, journalists, or tourists — a practice that has long been of concern to social and cultural anthropologists.

The 'rejuvenation theme' was symbolized by the search for the Fountain of Youth. The modern equivalent involves the use of mineral baths, special nutrients, hot tubs, exercise, health spas, cosmetic surgery, or hormones and chemicals to present a younger physical appearance and to promote a longer life span.

Social Gerontology in the Twentieth Century

Although anthropologists had previously documented the status and treatment of the elderly in a number of preindustrialized tribes and agrarian societies, until the 1920s interest in the aged was limited to providing social welfare programs and developing social policies. This interest resulted from the increased visibility of the elderly as a group — a group that was forming a larger percentage of the population. Most early research was motivated by an attempt to ameliorate a perceived social problem rather than by the desire to understand the process of aging. This is illustrated by the publication in 1922 of a book by Abraham Epstein (*The Challenge of the Aged*) in which he advocated income maintenance, employment, and social welfare for the elderly.

Prior to the 1920s, the literature dealt chiefly with the study of childhood and adolescence, since these were viewed as the essential developmental stages in the life cycle. However, two exceptions were *Senescence, The Second Half of Life*, published in 1922 by the psychologist G.S. Hall, and *Problems of Aging*, published in 1939 by E.V. Cowdry. This latter book presented the results of the Stanford Later Maturity Project. These influential works stimulated social scientists to examine the interrelationships between social structure, social institutions, and individual and group behavior as they are related to aging and the elderly.

It was not until the early 1940s, however, that sociologists began to study age as a possible explanatory factor in social behavior. During this period Chen (1939) discussed the social significance of old age, Landis (1940) studied the attitudes and adjustment of aged rural residents in Iowa, and Cottrell (1942) published an inventory of propositions concerning adjustment to age and sex roles. Similarly, Parsons (1942) noted the importance of age and sex in the social structure, while Linton (1942) stressed the importance of age as a social category and the need to understand the formation and function of age norms.

By the 1940s, then, the field of knowledge comprising social gerontology was beginning to evolve from three perspectives: (1) studies concerned with programs of welfare and social policies for the aged; (2) studies by social scientists who were primarily interested in using age to gain a better understanding of social behavior in general; and (3) studies by social scientists whose main objective was to understand and explain the aging process and the status and behavior of the aged. It was this last group that began to label themselves social gerontologists, in addition to their identification with other disciplines such as psychology, sociology, anthropology, political science, or economics.

Table 1.1 presents a time line that outlines key events in the development and growth of the field of social gerontology since 1940. While it is not possible or necessary to list every relevant publication, contributor, or event, the time line does indicate the emergence of major publications and professional associations devoted to the study of aging and the aged as a social phenomenon.

In summary, it appears that most of the impetus prior to World War II was in the biological and medical domain; that much of the early work was concerned with solving a social problem; that the period from 1945 to the mid-1950s was characterized by theoretical essays and a few empirical investigations,

Table 1.1 A time line depicting the development of the field of social gerontology since 1940

Date	Event

The Normal Stage (up to 1945)

1940   Publication of the journal *Geriatrics*.

The Network Stage (1945–56)

1945   L. Simmons, *The Role of the Aged in Primitive Society*. A major review of the anthropological literature on the status and treatment of the elderly in primitive societies. It showed a negative relationship between status and the growth of technology in society.

1945   The Gerontological Society of America was established and held annual meetings thereafter to promote the scientific study of aging from multidisciplinary perspectives, and to stimulate communication among scientists, researchers, teachers, and professionals.

1945   The first issue of the *Journal of Gerontology* was published.

1946   The American Psychological Association added a 'Maturity and Old Age' section.

1948   O. Pollack, *Social Adjustment in Old Age*. A significant study that shifted the focus from the problems to the process of aging. It also identified the University of Chicago as a leading research center in social gerontology.

1948   The International Association of Gerontology was founded in Liege, Belgium. This organization hosts international seminars on aging every three years.

1948   R. Cavan et al., *Personal Adjustment in Old Age*.

1952   The Gerontological Society organized a 'Psychology and Social Sciences' section. This reflected the growing interest in and acceptance of this perspective for the study of aging phenomena.

1953   R. Havighurst and R. Albrecht, *Older People*.

1956   J. Anderson (ed.), *Psychological Aspects of Aging*. This book included the papers from a 1955 conference by the APA Maturing and Old Age section.

1959   L. Cain (ed.), 'The Sociology of Aging: A Trend Report and Bibliography,' *Current Sociology*, 1959.

1959–60   a) J. Birren (ed.), *Handbook of Aging and the Individual: Psychological and Biological Aspects*.

  b) C. Tibbitts (ed.), *Handbook of Social Gerontology: Societal Aspects of Aging*.

  c) E. Burgess (ed.), *Aging in Western Societies*.

  These three handbooks represent the state of knowledge in gerontology in the late 1950s.

The Cluster Stage (1961–75)

1961   *The Gerontologist*: a second journal published by the Gerontological Society to focus on the more applied and professional interests of those working with and for the aged.

1961   E. Cumming and W. Henry, *Growing Old: The Process of Disengagement*. The first attempt to develop a social gerontological theory to account for satisfaction in the later years.

1961   First White House Conference on Aging. These conferences are held every ten years in the United States to draw scientists and professional workers together to make recommendations for consideration by Congress.

Table 1.1 (continued)

Date	Event
1962	The 'Aging in the World' series was composed of papers published from the Fifth Congress of the International Association of Gerontology held in 1960. These volumes included: a) C. Tibbits and W. Donahue (eds.), *Social and Psychological Aspects of Aging.* b) J. Kaplan and G. Aldridge (eds.), *Social Welfare of the Aging.* c) N. Shock (ed.), *Biological Aspects of Aging.* d) H. Blumenthal (ed.) *Medical and Clinical Aspects of Aging.*
1965	A. Rose and W. Peterson (eds.), *Older People and Their Social World.*
1967	E. Youmans, *Older Rural Americans.* One of the few studies to consider aging in a rural context.
1968	M. Riley and A. Foner (eds.), *Aging and Society. Volume One: An Inventory of Research Findings.* This landmark volume presented and interpreted the empirical findings of social science research to this date.
1968	E. Shanas et al., *Older People in Three Industrial Societies.* A cross-national comparative study of the social situation of older people in Denmark, Great Britain, and the United States.
1968	B. Neugarten (ed.), *Middle Age and Aging: A Reader in Social Psychology.* The first collection of readings on the social psychology of aging.
1969	R. Havighurst et al., *Adjustment to Retirement: A Cross-National Study.*
1969	M. Riley et al. (eds.), *Aging and Society. Volume Two: Aging and the Professions.* A statement of the concerns and involvement of a number of professions in the care of the aging and aged.
1970	E. Palmore, *Normal Aging: Reports from the Duke Longitudinal Studies, 1955–69.* The first interdisciplinary longitudinal study.
1972	M. Riley et al., *Aging and Society. Volume Three: A Sociology of Age Stratification.* Presents a model of aging which stresses the interaction between history and the social structure as it affects various age cohorts.
1972	D. Cowgill and L. Holmes, *Aging and Modernization.*
1972	R. Atchley, *The Social Forces in Later Life: An Introduction to Social Gerontology.* The first textbook written exclusively for university students enrolled in undergraduate course in social geronotology.
1972	Canadian Association on Gerontology founded.
1973	*International Journal of Aging and Human Development* first published.
1974	National Institute on Aging established in the United States to promote research on all facets of gerontology.

The Speciality Stage (1975–)

Date	Event
1975	R. Rapaport and R. Rapaport (eds.), *Leisure and the Family Life Cycle.* The first examination of leisure within the family context across the life cycle.
1975	Association for Gerontology in Higher Education formed to facilitate leadership development for training programs which were being established in universities and colleges in the United States.
1976	J. Schulz, *The Economics of Aging.* A comprehensive economic analysis of the aging process.

Table 1.1 (continued)

Date	Event
1976–77	Three new handbooks published which represented the state of knowledge up to the mid-1970s.
	a) R. Binstock and E. Shanas (eds.), *Handbook of Aging and the Social Sciences* (1976).
	b) J. Birren and K. Schaie (eds.), *Handbook of the Psychology of Aging* (1977).
	c) C. Finch and L. Hayflick (eds.), *Handbook of the Biology of Aging* (1977).
1978	*Aging and Work* first published.
1979	*Research on Aging: A Quarterly Journal of Social Gerontology* first published.
1980	V. Marshall, *Aging in Canada: Social Perspectives*. This was the first reader presenting a collection of articles pertaining to aging and the aged in Canada.
1982	International Year of the Elderly.
1982	*Canadian Journal on Aging* was first published.

and the creation of specialized associations and journals; that the next decade was characterized by handbooks summarizing research to that date, and by increased theoretical and empirical work; that the late 1960s saw growing interest in longitudinal and cross-cultural research; and that the 1970s represented an explosion of knowledge that resulted in the appearance of many handbooks, journals, and textbooks on the subject, and the establishment of centers for undergraduate and graduate training in gerontology.

From a more analytical perspective, Mullins (1972, 1973) suggested that scientific specialties evolve through four stages of development: normal, network, cluster, and specialty. This model can help us understand the emergence of social gerontology as an area of specialization that is now accepted as a legitimate area of scientific inquiry (Sackmary, 1974).

The first or 'normal' stage is characterized by a low degree of organization, with only a few papers being published by individuals who have a range of scholarly commitments (Mullins, 1973:21). This stage reflects the development of social gerontology prior to 1945. Until then, only a few relevant publications existed, scholars were isolated from each other, there were no formal gerontology organizations, and few if any scholars devoted their careers exclusively to research on aging.

The second or 'network' stage is characterized by the initiation of frequent, regular communication among first-generation scholars via conferences, newsletters, and journals; by the formation of national and international associations; and by the appearance of theoretical and conceptual essays and empirical studies, often in anthologies and conference proceedings. This stage in social gerontology ran from the mid-1940s to about 1960, and was characterized not only by increasing scholarly interest in the field, but also by 'missionary' work to convince others that the area was a necessary and legitimate field of inquiry.

In the 'cluster' stage, which ran from about 1961 to 1974, a second generation of researchers was trained by first-generation gerontologists. Much of this training occurred at centers designed to focus on one or more aspects of gerontology. Thus, whereas the first generation tended to train in isolation in a department of sociology, anthropology, social work, or psychology (that permitted them to study aging as one aspect of a doctoral program), many of the second generation were educated at the Ph.D. level with other students within a gerontology program. This created a 'cluster' of scholars — faculty and students — who reinforced and stimulated one another's interests and thinking (Mullins, 1973:22–23). This stage was also characterized by increasingly sophisticated theoretical and empirical work, by the appearance of edited books of readings, and by the publication of the first textbooks.

The final or 'specialty' stage is attained when a field becomes recognized as a legitimate area of inquiry and when scientists identify themselves as specialists in the area. Since 1975, social gerontology has been increasingly accepted by policy makers, the public, and research agencies as a necessary and legitimate field of inquiry.[15] Students at both the undergraduate and graduate levels (the third generation) are electing to specialize in one aspect of the field or in social gerontology in general. There is now available a 'critical mass' of mature and productive scholars from the second and third generation,[16] both within the disciplines of psychology and sociology and within the more general field of social gerontology. This critical mass not only increases the opportunities for graduate work by aspiring fourth generation gerontologists, but also serves as a catalyst for increasing the quality of knowledge about social phenomena associated with aging and the aged.

In summary, the development of social gerontology as a field of study has evolved primarily since 1945. In the early years the emphasis was on a description and treatment of the status of the elderly. However, in recent years there has been increased interest in understanding the dynamics of the aging process and the status of the aged from the perspectives of disciplines such as psychology, sociology, political science, economics, family studies, leisure studies, and health studies. In addition, phenomena associated with aging can be studied by professions such as nursing, social work, architecture, urban and regional planning, recreation, and physical education, and from the perspective of the humanities and the arts through poetry (Lyell, 1980), the novel, music, sculpture, and painting.

This complex mix of disciplines, professions, and arts comprises the field known as social gerontology. It has two main components — the disciplines of scientific inquiry that seek to describe and explain the process of aging, and the professions that seek to solve the practical problems associated with aging. Generally, gerontology can be defined as the interdisciplinary application of knowledge by those affiliated with the biological sciences, clinical medicine, and the behavioral and social sciences and by social planners and practitioners in the field of human services.[17] However, since all fields of study are dynamic rather than static, perhaps the best way to identify and define a field is to examine the subject matter presented at conferences and to read articles published in the major journals.[18]

Factors Influencing the Process and Product of Aging

In the preceding sections overviews of the process of aging and of the historical development of social gerontology have been provided. The following sections describe and explain a variety of social facts and processes related to aging.

However, before beginning this more finite analysis, a number of caveats must be introduced in order to prevent later misinterpretations. The patterns and processes of aging vary among individuals and groups depending on social, environmental, biological, and psychological factors. In addition, a number of methodological and conceptual matters must be considered in the interpretation of research findings. This section provides a checklist of a number of methodological, theoretical, and conceptual factors that must be considered by the student when interpreting or applying findings from the literature in social gerontology.

Aging: A Multidimensional Process

Aging does not occur in a vacuum. Rather, aging involves an interaction of biological, psychological, social, and cultural factors, any or all of which may proceed at different rates for a specific individual or cohort. Such factors as rate of biological aging, changes in physical or mental health, changes in environment, and past and current economic status, can influence the aging process and the state of being old.

Conceptual and Methodological Concerns

Levels of analysis.   The aging process functions on three levels. The 'individual' level enables an investigator to identify and explain internal or external changes in the process, over time, within or between individuals. The individual approach is common in biology and psychology, where investigators try to account for individual changes or differences in such domains as physiological functioning, the physical structure of the organism, learning abilities, personality, memory retention, and life satisfaction.

Aging can also be studied from the perspective of the 'social system.' Here the focus is on understanding the influence of the structure of society on the individual aging process. This level of analysis is also concerned with the outcome of interaction between the individual and other individuals, groups, or social institutions. The social-system approach seeks to identify and explain common patterns of social behavior that are influenced by age (age norms) and by interaction between a succession of age cohorts in a particular society (Elder, 1975). This approach is concerned with understanding social processes such as age grading, age stratification, socialization, discrimination, and integration.

The third level of analysis is the 'comparative'; this approach concentrates on the search for cultural or subcultural differences in the process of aging (Gutmann, 1977; Palmore, 1980b; Cowgill, 1981). If the emphasis is on comparing entire societies, the approach is referred to as cross-cultural or cross-national research. However, comparative analysis can also be employed within a society in which subcultural differences are identified and explained. For example, many studies have compared the differences between whites, blacks, Hispanics, or native people with respect to the status of the elderly and the process of aging. Similarly, a comparison between religious, economic, or regional groups is a comparative subcultural analysis of aging. In short, the process of aging and the status of the aged may vary by subgroups because of cultural differences within or between societies.

Cross-sectional, longitudinal, and cohort analysis.   In chapter 4, research methods will be discussed in detail. Here, the reader will be alerted to some of the limitations associated with the most common research designs used to study aging phenomena. This section also reinforces the earlier point that we must learn to distinguish between age changes (aging effects) and age differences (cohort effects).

In the cross-sectional method of research, subjects of various ages are tested once and tables or graphs are derived that show a relationship between age and a particular social parameter. However, cross-sectional research designs can only indicate *differences* between age groups; they cannot be used to conclude that *changes* have occurred because of aging.

Longitudinal research designs involve repeated testing of the same subjects over a longer time, often ten years or more. A major difficulty with this method is that subjects move, die, or drop out of the study, and a considerably smaller sample may be left at the end of the testing period. Moreover, bias may be introduced because subjects are often volunteers, or because those who drop out of the study may differ in intelligence, class or health from those who remain in the study. Nevertheless, this method enables researchers to examine age changes over time.

A third method, which has some advantages over cross-sectional and longitudinal research designs, is known as cohort analysis. This method involves collecting the same information at different times, with different individuals in the same age cohort being studied each time. For example, some national surveys are repeated at regular intervals, with approximately the same number of respondents in each cohort. While the respondents at each time are usually different, they are representative of the same age cohort, and changes with age as well as differences between age cohorts may be inferred.

In summary, it is important, as you read research articles and newspaper accounts of studies completed on aging phenomena, that you understand the method used and the limitations of possible interpretations or conclusions that can be drawn. Differences owing to age can be drawn from cross-sectional studies, whereas changes related to the aging process may best be inferred from longitudinal studies or cohort analyses.

The Influence of the Physical Environment

We have noted that individual and cohort differences must be considered when the biological, psychological, and social aspects of the aging process are being examined. It must be remembered that current health status, health care utilization, and various psychological and biological processes can retard or hasten the aging process regardless of chronological age, and can greatly influence the social interaction and adaptation of an individual or cohort at any given time.

In addition to these personal factors, a number of external factors in the physical and social environment interact with age to influence the status and behavior of individuals at specific stages in the life cycle. These will be discussed throughout the text; the remainder of this chapter includes an overview of some social, cultural, and physical environmental factors that influence the behavior of the aging individual or cohort. In the following subsection the physical context in which people live and age is examined. Here, as Lawton (1980:16–17) notes, we must consider not only the conditions in the objective physical environment but also the meaning of the subjective environment as perceived and interpreted by an individual.

Geographical region.   The geographical environment includes climate, altitude, terrain, and the natural distribution of plant and animal life. While very little is known about the relationship between geography and the aging process, environmentalists are giving increasing attention to the impact of various ecological factors (such as air and water pollution) in specific regions, on both short- and long-term physical and mental health and for the quality of life in general. For example, in the United States, living in a highly industrialized northern city fosters a different lifestyle from living on a farm in the midwest, or in a small community in the southwest. Similarly, aging in the highly industrialized and densely populated cities of Manchester, England, or Frankfort, West Germany, represents a different physical environment from that encountered by those living on the Seychelle Islands in the Indian Ocean.

For many elderly people who are economically independent, climate and terrain seem to have a special subjective meaning. For example, in the United States some people over 65 have migrated from the heavily populated and colder northeast and midwest regions to the more temperate southeast and southwest regions. For some, this is a seasonal migration; for others, it represents a permanent move. The increasing density of the elderly population in an area has both a direct and an indirect influence on the process of aging for individuals, on the age structure of the region, and on the delivery of social services (Longino and Biggar, 1982; Monahan and Greene, 1982). For example, a high concentration of older people restricts most social interaction to those who are 60 to 80 years of age and stimulates the provision of consumer goods and services that meet the specific needs of an older population.

Type and quality of housing.   The individual who lives in an apartment in the core of a city experiences a different lifestyle from the suburban homeowner or the farmer. Similarly, in the later years, home owners, age-integrated apartment dwellers, retirement community residents, senior-citizen (age-segregated) apartment dwellers, and residents of partial or totally institutionalized dwellings will have different lifestyles, and will experience different problems and processes related to aging.

Rural/urban environments.   Since the time of the Industrial Revolution there has been a population shift from rural to urban and suburban areas, although the trend has been reversed somewhat in recent years. One outcome of this migration pattern has been the disruption of the relatively stable and predictable social and cultural patterns that characterized rural lifestyles. Not surprisingly, most studies concerned with this demographic shift have focused on the impact of this migration pattern on the urban milieu (Fischer, 1972, 1975) rather than on the rural milieu (Dewey, 1960; Ansello and Cipolla, 1980; Lee and Lassey, 1980; Wilkinson et al., 1982).

Urban sociologists and ecologists have sought to describe the structure, processes, and problems of urban social life. They have been particularly interested in the size, density, and heterogeneity of the urban population; the nature of social interaction and social relations; the similarities and differences within and between urban and suburban areas; and the demographic composition of residential neighborhoods (racial, ethnic, and class differences). They have also examined the impact of a particular social structure on social relations and on crime; and the influence of the physical structure (residential, commercial, and industrial sectors) of the community on interpersonal relations and lifestyles.

On a micro level of analysis, the more tangible characteristics of a neighborhood are also important factors in lifestyle and life satisfaction (Lawton, 1980:37–50). As Lawton (1980:38) notes, 'the neighborhood may be a source of aesthetic enjoyment, physical security, sensory variety, basic resources, help in emergencies, social interaction, interesting things to do, the feeling of territorial pride and many other satisfiers of human needs.' In short, the neighborhood has the potential to provide stability, familiarity, and identification, and, like the place of employment, serves as a central focus for daily social interaction.

Urban residents are generally overrepresented in gerontology studies. Among the elderly, the urban poor have been studied to a much greater extent than other elderly subgroups. To date, little attention has been directed to the aging process or the aged in a rural environment[19], or to comparing the process for a variety of urban, suburban, or rural lifestyles.

Since most research has been conducted in an urban social context, the reader must recognize that the process of aging may be different in small towns, in suburbia, and in farming communities. For example, in a town with few elderly citizens, the town council may allocate funds to a youth center rather than to a senior-citizen center. Moreover, although the rural elderly generally report higher levels of well-being, life satisfaction, or morale than urban residents, most objective dimensions of the quality of life (socioeconomic and health status, level of nutrition, availability of services, quality of housing) indicate that the rural elderly experience numerous disadvantages compared to urban residents (Lee and Lassey, 1980).

In summary, behavior at various stages in the life cycle is a function of the interaction between an aging individual and his or her social and physical environment. Therefore, the student must be alert to differences and similarities in the aging process related to the physical environment (see chapter 8). Specifically, geographical region, type and quality of housing, and size, density, and composition of the community and neighborhood, must be assessed to determine whether these factors have an impact on a particular process or problem associated with aging.

The Influence of Social and Cultural Differentiation

Throughout history, the status and power of individuals in most societies have been evaluated on the basis of biological or social characteristics such as age, sex, religion, wealth, race, marital status, ethnic background or national origin, education, or occupation. These attributes, which may be either ascribed (such as race) or achieved (such as education), are assigned different values within each culture. They influence the process by which individuals aspire to or are allocated to different social positions within that society. For example, in contemporary North America one is generally evaluated more positively if one is white rather than black, male rather than female, rich rather than poor, young rather than old, and educated rather than uneducated (Tumin, 1967:27).

Once these evaluations of social worth become institutionalized, they lead to the ranking of individuals and to systems of stratification. The outcome of this process of social differentiation is that some individuals have greater status and receive greater rewards than others. This in turn can lead to inequalities that influence life chances and lifestyle,[20] or to competition and conflict among occupants of the various social strata.

It would be considerably easier for the scholar to study stratification systems and the aging process if each dimension were a separate entity. However, the social world is more complex than this, and many of these dimensions interact with each other. Thus, although age is the social dimension of major interest in this text, a number of other social variables interact with age to determine who has access to social positions and the accompanying power, prestige, wealth, property, and psychic gratification (Tumin, 1967:39–42). These interactions are especially relevant for the processes of social integration and interaction in the later years of life.

The following subsections briefly describe the major stratification systems and illustrate how a number of social categories interact with age to influence both the process of aging and the state of being old. All of these categories will be discussed in more detail throughout the book. However, it is important for the student to be aware of these interacting factors when beginning to study aging as a social process.

Finally, as noted earlier, there is an age stratification system in which social and chronological age serve as criteria for acquiring or giving up particular positions within social institutions. This system also provides a structure for the pattern of social interaction that evolves within a variety of social systems at different stages in the life cycle. Thus, the reader must recognize that each age cohort is a heterogeneous mix of individuals who vary in economic, racial, ethnic, gender, religious, educational, health, and marital status dimensions (Marshall, 1981).

Social and economic stratification.   A society is divided, like a ladder, into a number of distinct social classes or social strata. The number of strata can range from a simple trichotomous division (professionals, white-collar workers, blue-collar workers) to a scale that involves at least six strata (upper class, upper middle class, middle class, lower middle class, upper lower class, and lower class). There appear to be common characteristics associated with each stratum within the social structure, characteristics that are often passed from generation to generation; these relate to values, attitudes, behaviors, and general lifestyle.

Many studies of social stratification are based on a self-rating or objective scale made up of such factors as education, annual income, or occupation (Blau and Duncan, 1967; Blishen and McRoberts, 1976; Treiman, 1977). The system of social stratification, although it does not act independently of the others, tends to have a greater influence than other stratification systems (for example, gender or racial) on life chances and lifestyles at all stages of the life cycle. This occurs primarily because there is inequality among social groups in terms of wealth, prestige, and education.

Although there are significant differences between age cohorts with respect to values and behavior, differences also exist within each age cohort. Each cohort is a heterogeneous group that includes members with different class, ethnic, racial, and religious backgrounds. As a result of these within-cohort variations in social characteristics, subgroups within each cohort experience different life chances and lifestyles with respect to how they think and behave at various stages in the life cycle.

These differences also influence the chronological age at which major life events occur. A man or woman from an upper-class family who attends a prestigious university or professional school will enter the labor force at a later age and with greater income and prestige than the son or daughter of a blue-collar worker who leaves high school at age 16 and immediately enters the labor force.[21] Throughout the adult years the processes of aging for these two subgroups will vary. Although both groups belong to the same age cohort, the aging process may differ dramatically with respect to life expectancy, incidence of illness, place of residence, adaptation to retirement, economic status, family and friendship interaction, volunteer activity, residential mobility, use of leisure time, and life satisfaction. Unfortunately, as noted earlier, many studies in social gerontology have been based only on white, middle-class, male respondents.

Like groups at earlier stages in the life cycle, the aged are a heterogeneous group. Although old age is often characterized by physical, psychological, and social losses not all individuals suffer these declines or experience them at the same rate. For example, it is commonly believed that one of the major problems of old age is the likelihood of being poor. However, as Henretta and Campbell (1976) noted, the factors that determine retirement income are the same as those that determine income before retirement, namely education, occupation and marital status.

If there is a disruption in the source and amount of income at retirement, a similar pattern of status distribution may also exist within the cohort. While all retirees experience some loss of economic status, those who had higher incomes prior to retirement will generally have a higher economic status in retirement. Similarly, Dowd (1980) argues that the lives of the elderly are largely dependent on the relative power resources they retain. While everyone may experience some reduction in salary and some loss of power (status, privilege, prestige) after retirement and thus be disadvantaged compared to younger age cohorts, not all members of a cohort will find themselves in an impoverished state, either immediately or in the long term.

In summary, the process of social stratification influences an individual's access to status, power, and wealth, and hence influences life chances and lifestyle. Although it is frequently noted that the elderly lose status, if sufficient income is available during retirement, status within the age cohort will likely be retained.

Racial and ethnic stratification. In multicultural societies such as the United States, Canada, South Africa, or Australia, the social structure may be stratified by racial or ethnic background across the society in general and within specific groups. The division of society into racial or ethnic groups is based on social perceptions or definitions of the relative superiority or status of certain groups. Differences tend to be exaggerated, and are considered more important if members of the group remain insulated within their community, either through self-segregation or through social isolation imposed by the dominant group.

These subcultures within society are often labelled as minority groups,[22] and because of prejudice, stereotyping, and ethnocentrism on the part of the majority group, their members often experience institutionalized discrimination. However, the mere possession of ethnic or racial characteristics does not necessarily imply discrimination. Rather, it is the relative ranking within a society that determines whether a particular group will be viewed as a 'minority' group and thereby experience discrimination from those ranked above them. This discrimination is more likely to come from persons in the groups immediately above them in the ranking structure. This occurs since the lower group may be perceived as a threat to the higher group's relative position in the social structure.

The differential ranking by ethnicity or race in North American societies is based on perceived social distance (Bogardus, 1967) from the ideal, which is generally considered to be white, middle-class and Protestant. Blacks, native people, and recent immigrants have always been ranked lower than second-generation whites. Although the relative ranking of racial and ethnic groups remains fairly constant over time, during periods of war or open-door immigration policies the lowest rankings can change dramatically. For example, in the United States the lowest ranking has been held by the Japanese (after World War II), by the Vietnamese (in the 1970s), and by refugees from the Third World (at present).

This ethnic and racial stratification system exists until there has been both structural and cultural assimilation by the minority group. Unfortunately for most members of minority groups such as blacks and native people, structural assimilation (by which equality of opportunity, authority, and power is gained in the major associations and institutions of mainstream society) has not occurred. Thus, like members of the lower class, members of many minority groups have fewer opportunities and privileges within a society, because of prejudiced attitudes or overt or subtle discrimination by members of the dominant group.

This process of social ranking by ethnic or racial background can be further complicated by the inevitable relationship between class and racial or ethnic status. Not all members of a minority group have the same levels of education, income, or ability. Gordon (1964) devised the concept of 'ethclass' to refer to a group having a specific ethnic background and class position. For example, in the United States, recently arrived upper-class Vietnamese physicians or scientists may have greater social status and opportunities than lower-middle-class blacks. This element of social reality exists despite the fact that blacks in general have a relatively higher ranking than recent Vietnamese immigrants.

With respect to the process of aging, patterns appear to vary by racial or ethnic group (Holzberg, 1982). These variations exist because of language and cultural differences, emigration patterns, and degree of assimilation.[23] However, we still know very little about these subcultural variations because, until recently, most studies of aging and the aged have focused on white, Anglo-Saxon, Protestant males.

One outcome of subcultural differences in life chances and lifestyle is that the status of the aged can vary greatly by race, ethnicity, and religion. This is reflected in how the aged view their own position within the minority group and within mainstream society; in how they are treated by their own subgroup; and in how their situation compares to the aged in the dominant group and in other minority groups. Thus, the status of the elderly Jew or Mennonite may be relatively higher than that of the elderly Protestant, while the relative status of the elderly black within his or her own social group may be superior to that of the elderly white because of apparent closer family ties among blacks. Similarly, the status of the elderly person living in Japan is generally superior to that experienced by his or her Japanese age peer living in North America. This occurs because acculturation has led to changes in the values of Japanese living in North America and their perceived obligations to elderly members of the family.

In summary, the process of ethnic and racial stratification in multicultural or pluralistic societies influences the process of aging and the status of the aged. This variation occurs because of the relative ranking of the minority group and because of its subcultural values. As you study social gerontology, be aware that the stratification process may vary by racial and ethnic groups within and between societies.

Gender stratification. Like age, gender is a universal biological fact that acquires a social definition within different societies and social systems (LaFontaine, 1978). In most societies, a system of gender stratification evolves in which men are considered to be superior to women.[24] Even today, with changing cultural and social conditions, this relative ranking holds within the psychological and social domains if not in the legal domain.

As a result of gender stratification, an ascribed attribute or social identity (being male or female) accounts for role behavior at specific points in the life cycle and facilitates (or impedes) a number of social processes. Normative criteria evolve for acquiring or relinquishing social roles, for entering or leaving particular social systems, and for determining appropriate or inappropriate behavior in a variety of social situations. Sexist attitudes may develop wherein individuals (usually women) are discriminated against in their lifestyles and life chances.

Although a definitive explanation for the existence and continuation of gender stratification is lacking, some insight can be gained by examining the following models and by considering the process of sex-role identification and socialization. Eichler (1973) suggested that three models can assist in understanding the phenomenon of gender stratification. The first suggests that women comprise a social caste. As a result, they are denied mobility because of an ascribed attribute (being female). The basic assumption of this model is that women are less valued in the labor market. However, Eichler argues that there are many exceptions to the caste rules with respect to the female role. For example, women do not socially avoid outsiders (males); they can be socially mobile when they marry outside their own class, and there are differences in social ranking among women that are as great as those between men and women. Furthermore, some women have higher status and higher skill levels than some men. Because there are many exceptions to this model, gender stratification should not be viewed as a caste system.

A second model considers women to be members of a minority group that experiences economic and psychological disadvantages emanating from a power struggle between the sexes. Eichler suggests that this model also fails to fit social reality, since these conditions should lead to the formation of 'gender consciousness,' which in turn should lead to social conflict and social change. Until recently, this process of conflict and change had not been evidenced to any great extent.

The third model suggests that women comprise a unique class based on their ability to compete in the labor market. In fact, early in the twentieth century sex status became the basis for a class-like struggle for equal rights that continues today. Eichler criticizes this view, however, because it does not distinguish between employed and unemployed women. She further argues that this model is not adequate to explain gender differences: there is a double standard of evaluation by which women as a group are divided into two categories — those who are economically independent (the employed), and those who are not (the unemployed or the housewife).

The system of gender stratification and its consequent inequality are perpetuated through the sex-role socialization process. Gender identification usually begins at birth, since a child's significant others compulsively attempt to 'make a girl a girl and a boy a boy.' Each society has definite ideas about what constitutes appropriate male and female behavior.

The parents are the most influential agents in maintaining these cultural expectations. In the past, when a young girl expressed an interest in organized sport she was often discouraged by her parents from participating so that she might present the socially sanctioned 'image' of a female. Despite the fact that recent research has failed to support most of the psychological and physiological myths surrounding female participation in sport, institutional and legal barriers still must be overcome in order to achieve equality. If opportunities to participate in what have hitherto been considered male domains are to increase, changes must be made in the values, norms, and goals of significant others responsible for the socialization of females. The most appropriate targets for change are parents and elementary-school teachers who serve as socializing agents during the early, critical years of gender socialization.

Throughout this book reference will be made to research that substantiates the existence of sex differences in the process of aging or in the status of the aged. However, it should be noted that there is a paucity of research evidence concerning aging as a social process for females,[25] and myths and stereotypes abound. This is not surprising, since women have seldom been the subject of study in almost all scientific disciplines. It is more remarkable that sex differences in the process and product of aging have not been studied extensively, since the demographic profile of most societies indicates that the ratio of women to men increases with age, particularly after about the age of 40. When concern is expressed about poverty, loneliness, lack of power, and widowhood in the later years, the subject of concern is more likely to be a woman than a man.

In connection with aging, the following situations merit special attention with respect to women: (1) because women have generally been excluded from full participation in society, they are dependent on men and may therefore lack the power to change this status; (2) a woman's social status has traditionally been derived from her father and later her husband; (3) aging in women is often characterized by role losses — the children leave home, the woman retires, she loses her physical attractiveness and is stigmatized (Posner, 1980), and her spouse and friends die; (4) aging women experience discrimination because of a double standard (Sontag, 1975); and (5) there are racial and ethnic variations among women in their adaptation to the aging process. The aging woman is sometimes depicted in journalistic reports as asexual, physically obsolete, a widow, poorly educated, and poor. Yet, not all older women live in poverty and isolation, as any travel agent will verify.

As in any other topical area within the social sciences, the study of older women must be analyzed by controlling for such factors as age, education, income, social status, and marital status. For example, there may be significant differences in the social situation of women who are 60 to 75, 75 to 84, or 85 and older (Chappell and Havens, 1980). While older females clearly constitute an ever-increasing majority of the elderly population, not all women experience the dual stigmatization of being both old *and* female — the 'double-jeopardy' phenomenon. However, some may experience triple jeopardy (being old, female, and poor) or multiple jeopardy (being old, female, poor, and a member of a disadvantaged minority group). In short, as with most other aspects of aging, a description of ideal, generalized patterns of aging by gender should be avoided. In this way stereotypes concerning the process of aging in women are less likely to be perpetuated.

Education, religion, and marital status.   Although these elements do not constitute a stratification system per se either alone or in combination, they represent three additional social factors that must be considered in the study of the aging process and of the status of the middle-aged and elderly person. The average amount of formal education attained by each successive birth cohort is increasing, especially for women and members of minority groups. The current middle-aged and elderly segments of the population have attained higher levels of formal education than previous generations, but less than later generations will attain.

Levels of educational attainment have been found to be positively correlated with such factors as type of occupation, income (McConnel and Deljavan, 1981), health, values, attitudes, a positive self-concept, life satisfaction, longevity, and adjustment to retirement. Education does not cause any of these events or characteristics, but it does provide an opportunity set by which a particular lifestyle is more likely to be adopted. For example, persons with college degrees are more likely to spend their leisure time reading, studying, joining clubs, doing volunteer work, attending concerts, and playing or watching sports. Of course, the amount of formal education attained varies within and between age cohorts, and can have a profound influence on lifestyles at various stages in the life cycle. The educational background of subjects used in gerontology studies should be carefully considered: the university-educated retiree will probably adapt to retirement differently from the retiree who left school at age 16.

Religious affiliation and degree of religious involvement or commitment also influence to some extent the process and the product of aging. Much of this influence derives from the tenets and philosophy of a particular religion and the effects these have on an individual's lifestyle. Religion also influences attitudes toward and the status of the aged. For example, religious groups such as the Jews, Mennonites, Hutterites, and Amish in North America provide high-quality care for the elderly within their groups. It is interesting to note that the last three of these groups form unique rural subcultures within and yet outside of mainstream society.

Marital status is another influential factor in the aging process. Whether one is never-married, married, separated, divorced, remarried, or widowed influences daily life throughout the life cycle. One's economic status, interaction with family and friends, degree of social isolation, mobility, availability of health care, and leisure activities are all affected to some extent by marital status. In most instances the lifestyle of the married 30-year-old is different from that of the single 30-year-old, just as the economic status of the still-married 65-year-old female is generally better than that of her widowed age peer. When one analyzes the aging process and compares individuals of a particular age cohort, variations in marital status should be considered as a possible explanatory factor in social behavior.

Summary and Conclusions

In this introductory chapter the reader has been introduced to the concept of aging as a social process influenced by the social and age structures of society, by a variety of social processes, and by social, political, and economic change within a given culture or subculture. These factors have an influence on both individual and population aging, and they interact with other factors that are more closely related to biological and psychological aging.

The reader has been alerted to the prevalence of myths concerning aging and the aged; to the difference between aging, cohort, and historical effects; to a number of methodological and theoretical matters that must be considered in the interpretation of research findings; and to cross-cultural and subcultural variations in the aging process, particularly with respect to the treatment and status of the elderly. In addition, the reader has been introduced briefly to a number of demographic, sociocultural, and environmental factors, and to some major stratification systems that have been found to influence the aging process. (These parameters are discussed in more detail throughout this book.) Finally, the chapter provides a brief descriptive and analytical discussion of the historical development of the relatively new field of social gerontology.

Based on the information presented in this chapter, it can be concluded that:

1. Chronological aging represents only an approximate measure of an individuals' normative development or changes. There is great variation in physical, emotional, social, and psychological development within and between individuals.

2. Functional aging is a more accurate measure, since it considers individual differences by age. Functional aging reflects the relationship between biological maturation or deterioration and how well, if at all, an individual can perform specific physical, social, or cognitive tasks.

3. Psychological aging involves the reaction to biological, cognitive, sensory, motor, emotional, and behavioral changes within an individual, as well as the reaction to external environmental factors that influence behavior and lifestyle.

4. Social aging involves patterns of interaction between the aging individual and the social structure. Many social positions are related to chronological age, and individuals are expected to conform to the age-based norms associated with these positions. Social aging is also influenced by the size and composition of the social structure as it changes over time, by change within a society, and by cultural and subcultural variations in attitudes toward aging and the aged.

5. A number of unsubstantiated beliefs about aging and the aged are accepted as fact. These myths may influence the behavior and expectations of aging individuals, as well as the attitudes of younger people toward older people, especially those outside the kinship system.

6. Aging as a social process can be studied on three levels of analysis: the 'individual' level, which is concerned with age changes within individuals and age differences between groups of individuals; the 'social system' level, which is concerned with the influence of the social structure on the aging individual and the influence of various social processes on aging individuals or age cohorts; and the 'comparative' level, which attempts to explain aging by searching for cultural or subcultural variations or similarities within or between societies.

7. Age differences between individuals or cohorts can be inferred from cross-sectional research studies, whereas changes with age may be inferred from a longitudinal study. Cohort analysis may be used to infer age changes and age differences.

8. The aging process is influenced by elements in the physical environment such as geographical region, type and quality of housing and neighborhood, and rural or urban residence.

9. Ascribed or achieved attributes of an individual (sex, race, religion, education, income, class, marital status, ethnicity) influence life chances and lifestyle, and are important factors in the analysis of aging as a social

process. These attributes acquire different social meanings or values within different cultures and at different points in the life cycle.

10. The evaluation of these attributes by means of social differentiation creates class, racial, ethnic, and gender stratification systems in many societies. These systems interact with age to influence both the process of aging and the status of being old. Individuals located near the least-valued end of these various stratification systems may be disadvantaged (the elderly, blacks, females) throughout life, and may experience increased discrimination, segregation, or isolation as they age.

Notes

1. For example, the average life span in early Greek and Roman societies was 20 to 40 years (Goldscheider, 1971).

2. Ironically, Ponce de Leon, while searching for the Fountain of Youth in the year 1512, discovered the coast of Florida. This state has one of the highest percentages of elderly residents and has become a common retirement haven. While neither a potion nor a fountain has ever been discovered, contemporary North Americans still pursue their cosmetic and physiological dream through the use of wrinkle creams, hair coloring, health spas, cosmetic surgery, and a variety of nutrient products.

3. These involve a loss at retirement of social status, identity, and power; and the loss of friends and spouse through retirement, separation, divorce, or death.

4. In chronological order, some stages of the life cycle have been defined as infancy, childhood, early and late adolescence, young adulthood, mature adulthood or middle age, and old age. For the purpose of research studies, chronological ages are frequently assigned as boundaries to these various stages (infancy, 0–2 years; elderly, 55–75; very old, 76 and older). However, for the intermediate categories numerous age boundaries have been used. This makes the research process confusing and the results difficult to compare. For example, middle age has been variously defined as 40 to 64, 35 to 55, or 30 to 60 years of age.

5. Some unique social, economic, and historical events that have had an impact on the aging process and the status of the elderly include the Depression of the 1930s, World Wars I and II, urbanization, the immigration and migration of young people, a declining birthrate, and greater life expectancy. Some present and future factors include the energy crisis, double-digit inflation, high rates of unemployment among those under 25, the need to retain the older worker in the labor force, the advent of automation in industry, computer-induced unemployment, and the birth-control pill.

6. Conflict between age groups has led to the increasing use of the label 'gray power' as more and more senior citizens and preretirement adults seek to improve their position by lobbying for changes in laws and social policies.

7. For example, as will be seen in chapter 5, sensory losses in vision and hearing can inhibit the type, frequency, and quality of social interaction as one ages.

8. The changes, although usually thought to involve losses, can be positive. For example, gray hair may be seen as a sign of distinction; retirement, which is often feared as a period of economic hardship, can be a rewarding experience that provides the opportunity to acquire new knowledge, skills, and friends. While changes are inevitable, whether they are viewed as positive or negative depends on the perception of the individual and the reaction of others in society.

9. Chapter 5 discusses the relationship between changes in the physical system and how the organism adapts to a changing social and physical environment.

10. 'Chronological age norms' are to be distinguished from 'social age norms' that define expected patterns of behavior and thought at specific stages in the life cycle. The two norms frequently interact when an individual is told to 'act your age'; that is, behave according to what is expected in this

society of a person of that chronological age.

11. The correct responses are 1-F, 2-F; 3-T; 4-F; 5-F; 6-T; 7-T; 8-F; 9-F; 10-F.

12. There is, in fact, a real paucity of information about the middle years, other than that which pertains to such phenomena as the 'midlife crisis' (which may be a myth), the change of careers in midlife, the reaction of women to the 'empty nest' after their children leave home, the re-entry of women into the labor force, and the onset of a decline in physical and mental energy (Borland, 1978; Tamir, 1982).

13. The last section of this chapter discusses the need to consider differences in a variety of ascribed and achieved characteristics whenever the aging process or a specific cohort is being studied.

14. The student who is intrigued with the historical development of this field should read the following works as well as the classical studies and books which are cited in this overview: Adler (1958), Birren (1959), Gruman (1966), Streib and Orbach (1967), Shanas (1971), Birren and Clayton (1975), Binstock and Shanas (1976:4–34), Riegel (1977), Freeman (1979), Oliver and Eckerman (1979), and Achenbaum (forthcoming).

15. However, gerontology programs and research are still highly dependent on the traditional disciplines of biology, psychology, and sociology. Thus, a totally separate and discrete professional identity may never develop.

16. For example, over 1300 scholars presented papers at the combined meeting of the Gerontological Society of America and the Canadian Association on Gerontology in November 1981.

17. Four disciplines are included within the Gerontological Society of America. The *biological sciences* section is for scientists interested in aging of animals and plants, senescence of isolated cells in culture, evolutionary aspects of life span limitation, and in the biochemical, structural, and functional aspects of aging biological systems. The *clinical medicine* section is for professionals (physicians, dentists, nurses) engaged in clinical research, education, or treatment relating to aging patients. The *behavioral and social sciences* section is for research scientists, educators, and practitioners in such fields as psychology, sociology, anthropology, ecology, economics, and political science. The *social research, planning, and*

practice section is for researchers, educators and practitioners in the human service field. Members include social workers, social planners, directors of facilities and service programs, public administrators, policy makers, and environmental designers and planners. The Canadian Association on Gerontology includes the following sections: biological sciences, health sciences, social sciences, psychological sciences, and social welfare.

18. See *The Gerontologist*, no. 5, each year for the program of the annual meeting of the Gerontological Society of America, as well as the annual index in the following journals: *Journal of Gerontology, The Gerontologist, International Journal of Aging and Human Development, Experimental Aging Research, Aging and Work, Research on Aging: A Quarterly Journal of Social Gerontology, Annual Review of Gerontology and Geriatrics, Canadian Journal on Aging, Ageing and Society, Journal of Gerontological Social Work*, and *Educational Gerontology*. In addition, Edwards and Flynn (1978) and Place et al. (1981) include a number of key resources in their bibliographies. Areco's *Quarterly Index to Periodical Literature on Aging* is also a useful resource.

19. The student who is interested in the structure and processes of social life in rural environments should consult the journal *Rural Sociology*. However, even here there are few studies pertaining to aging or the aged. Similarly, while many introductory sociology textbooks include a chapter on urban or rural sociology, the sociology of aging is seldom discussed.

20. 'Life chances' refers to the probability that an individual with given characteristics (race, sex, social class, religion, and ethnic background) will attain or fail to attain goals such as a certain level of income, education, or power (Theodorson and Theodorson, 1969:231). 'Lifestyle' refers to culturally induced patterns of thought and behavior that involve personal styles of dress, thought, and speech; type and place of residence; type of leisure pursuits; and number and type of friends. These personal expressions of the self are highly influenced by cultural values and norms and by experiences and opportunities earlier in the life cycle (Williams and Wirth, 1965).

21. The reader should be aware that the reverse comparison can also be made. That is, the youth from an upper class background who quits school early may lose the economic

support of the family and be forced to enter the labor force with little education at an early age; sons or daughters of a lower-class family might continue their education until they enter the labor force in their mid-20s as doctors or lawyers. In that case, social mobility has occurred, income, prestige and power have increased, and adaptation to the aging process will be more similar to the upper-middle-class group in their age cohort than to that of their parents.

22. 'Minority group' usually refers to a group having subordinate status in the social, political, or economic sense rather than in the numerical sense. Blacks in South Africa, although a numerical majority, are still considered to be a minority group.

23. It is important to recognize that the influence of these factors can change from one generation to another within the minority group because of acculturation and assimilation.

24. One explanation for this devalued female status is that the female role, as traditionally viewed, does not reflect the highly valued (by males!) attributes of achievement, aggressiveness, competitiveness, independence and productivity.

25. Recent exceptions are Barnett and Baruch, 1978; Dulude, 1978, 1981; Matthews, 1979; Seltzer, 1979; Block et al., 1980; Fuller and Martin, 1980; Holahan, 1981; Troll, 1981.

References

Abu-Laban, S. and B. Abu-Laban. 'Women and the Aged as Minority Groups: A Critique,' pp. 63–79 in V. Marshall (ed.). *Aging In Canada: Social Perspectives.* Don Mills: Fitzhenry and Whiteside, 1980.

Achenbaum, A. *Aging: History and Ideology.* Cambridge, Mass.: Winthrop Publishers Inc., forthcoming.

Adler, M. 'History of the Gerontological Society,' *Journal of Gerontology*, 13(2/1958), 94–100.

Anderson, J. (ed.) *Psychological Aspects of Aging.* Washington, D.C.: American Psychological Association, 1956.

Ansello, E. and C. Cipolla (eds.). 'Rural Aging and Education: Issues, Methods and Models,' *Educational Gerontology*, 5(4/1980), 343–447.

Atchley, R. *The Social Forces in Later Life.* 1st edition. Belmont, Calif.: Wadsworth Publishing Co., 1972.

Atchley, R. 'Selected Social and Psychological Differences between Men and Women in Later Life,' *Journal of Gerontology*, 31(2/1976), 204–11.

Barnett, R. and G. Baruch. 'Women in the Middle Years: A Critique of Research and Theory,' *Psychology of Women Quarterly*, 3(2/1978), 187–97.

Bell, B. 'Significance of Functional Age for Inter-Disciplinary and Longitudinal Research in Aging,' *Aging and Human Development*, 3(2/1972), 145–47.

Benet, S. *Abkhasia: The Long-Living People of the Caucasus.* New York: Holt, Rinehart and Winston, 1974.

Binstock, R. and E. Shanas (eds.). *Handbook of Aging and the Social Sciences.* New York: Van Nostrand Reinhold, 1976.

Birren, J. (ed.) *Handbook of Aging and the Individual.* Chicago: University of Chicago Press, 1959.

Birren, J. and V. Clayton. 'History of Gerontology,' pp. 15–27 in D. Woodruff and J. Birren (eds.). *Aging: Scientific Perspectives and Social Issues.* New York: Van Nostrand Reinhold, 1975.

Birren, J. and K.W. Schaie (eds.). *Handbook of the Psychology of Aging.* New York: Van Nostrand Reinhold, 1977.

Blau, P. and O. Duncan. *The American Occupational Structure.* New York: John Wiley and Sons, 1967.

Blishen, B. and H. McRoberts. 'A Revised Socioeconomic Index for Occupations in Canada,' *Canadian Review of Sociology and Anthropology*, 13(1/1976), 71–79.

Block, M. et al. *Women Over Forty: Visions and Realities.* New York: Springer Publishing Co., 1980.

Blumenthal, H. (ed.). *Medical and Clinical Aspects of Aging.* New York: Columbia University Press, 1962.

Bogardus, E. *A Forty-Year Racial Distance Study.* Los Angeles: University of Southern California, 1967.

Borland, D. 'Research on Middle Age: An Assessment,' *The Gerontologist*, 18 (4/1978), 379–86.

Burgess, E. (ed.). *Aging in Western Societies.* Chicago: University of Chicago Press, 1960.

Cain, L. (ed.). 'The Sociology of Aging: A Trend Report and Bibliography,' *Current Sociology*, 8(2/1959), 57–133.

Cain, L. 'The Growing Importance of Legal Age in Determining the Status of the Elderly,' *The Gerontologist*, 14(2/1974), 167–74.

Cain, L. 'Aging and the Law,' pp. 342–68 in R. Binstock and E. Shanas (eds.) *Handbook of Aging and the Social Sciences.* New York: Van Nostrand Reinhold Co., 1976.

Cavan, R. et al. *Personal Adjustment In Old Age.* Chicago: Science Research Associates, 1949.

Chappell, N. and B. Havens. 'Old and Female: Testing the Double Jeopardy Hypothesis,' *The Sociological Quarterly*, 21(2/1980), 157–71.

Chen, A. 'Social Significance of Old Age,' *Sociology and Social Research*, 23(July-August, 1939), 519–27.

Cottrell, L. 'The Adjustment of the Individual to His Age and Sex Roles,' *American Sociological Review*, 7(5/1942), 617–20.

Cowdry, E. (ed.). *Problems of Aging*. Baltimore: William and Wilkins, 1939.

Cowgill, D. 'Aging In Comparative Cultural Perspective,' *Mid-American Review of Sociology*, VII(2/1981), 1–28.

Cowgill, D. and L. Holmes. (eds.). *Aging and Modernization*. New York: Appleton-Century-Crofts, 1972.

Cumming, E. and W. Henry. *Growing Old: The Process of Disengagement*. New York: Basic Books, 1961.

Dannefer, D. 'Sociology of the Life Course,' in R. Turner (ed.). *Annual Review of Sociology*. Volume 9. Palo Alto: Annual Reviews, Inc., 1983.

Dewey, R. 'The Rural-Urban Continuum: Real or Relatively Unimportant,' *American Journal of Sociology*, 66(1/1960), 60–66.

Dowd, J. *Stratification Among the Aged*. Monterey: Brooks/Cole Publishing Co., 1980.

Dulude, L. *Women and Aging: A Report on the Rest of our Lives*. Ottawa: Canadian Advisory Council on the Status of Women, 1978.

Dulude, L. *Pension Reform with Women in Mind*. Ottawa: Canadian Advisory Council on the Status of Women, 1981.

Edwards, W. and F. Flynn. *Gerontology: A Core List of Significant Works*. Ann Arbor: The Institute of Gerontology, University of Michigan, 1978.

Eichler, M. 'Women as Personal Dependents,' pp. 36–55 in M. Stephenson (ed.). *Women In Canada*. Toronto: New Press, 1973.

Elder, G. 'Age Differentiation and the Life Course,' pp. 165–90 in A. Inkeles et al. (eds.). *Annual Review of Sociology*. Volume 1. Palo Alto: Annual Reviews Inc., 1975.

Elder, G. and J. Liker. 'Hard Times in Women's Lives: Historical Influences Across Forty Years,' *American Journal of Sociology*, 88(2/1982), 241–69.

Epstein, A. *Facing Old Age: A Study of Old Age Dependency in the United States and Old Age Pensions*. New York: A.A. Knopf, 1922.

Epstein, A. *The Challenge of the Aged*. New York: Macy-Masius, Vanguard Press, 1928.

Finch, C. and L. Hayflick. (eds.). *Handbook of the Biology of Aging*. New York: Van Nostrand Reinhold, 1977.

Fischer, C. 'Urbanism As A Way of Life: A Review and an Agenda,' *Sociological Methods and Research*, 1(2/1972), 187–242.

Fischer, C. 'The Study of Urban Community and Personality,' pp. 67–90 in A. Inkeles et al. (eds.). *Annual Review of Sociology*. Volume 1. Palo Alto: Annual Reviews, Inc., 1975.

Freeman, J. *Aging: Its History and Literature*. New York: Human Sciences Press, 1979.

Fry, C. 'The Ages of Adulthood: A Question of Numbers,' *Journal of Gerontology*, 31(2/1976), 170–77.

Fry, C. 'Cultural Dimensions of Age: A Multidimensional Scaling Analysis,' pp. 42–64 in C. Fry (ed.). *Aging In Culture and Society: Comparative Viewpoints and Strategies*. New York: Praeger Publishers, 1980.

Fuller, M. and C. Martin (eds.). *The Older Woman: Lavender Rose or Gray Panther*. Springfield, Ill.: Charles C Thomas, 1980.

Goldscheider, C. *Population, Modernization and Social Structure*. Boston: Little, Brown, 1971.

Gordon, M. *Assimilation in American Life*. New York: Oxford University Press, 1964.

Gruman, G. *A History of Ideas about the Prolongation of Life: The Evolution of Prolongevity Hypothesis to 1800*. Philadelphia: American Philosophical Society, 1966.

Gutmann, D. 'The Cross-Cultural Perspective: Notes toward a Comparative Psychology of Aging,' pp. 302–26 in J. Birren and K.W. Schaie (eds.). *Handbook of the Psychology of Aging*. New York: Van Nostrand Reinhold, 1977.

Hall, G.S. *Senescence, The Second Half of Life*. New York: Appleton, 1922.

Havighurst, R. and R. Albrecht. *Older People*. New York: Longmans, Green, 1953.

Havighurst, R. et al. *Adjustment to Retirement: A Cross-National Study*. Assen, The Netherlands: Van Gorcum and Co., 1969.

Henretta, J. and R. Campbell. 'Status Attainment and Status Maintenance: A Study of Stratification in Old Age,' *American Sociological Review*, 41(6/1976), 981–92.

Holahan, C. 'Lifetime Achievement Patterns, Retirement and Life Satisfaction of Gifted Aged Women,' *Journal of Gerontology*, 36(6/1981), 741–49.

Holzberg, C. 'Ethnicity and Aging: Anthropological Perspectives on More Than Just the Minority Elderly,' *The Gerontologist*, 22(3/1982), 249–57.

Kaplan, J. and G. Aldridge. (eds.). *Social Welfare of the Aging*. New York: Columbia University Press, 1962.

Kerckhoff, R. 'Marriage and Middle Age,' *The Family Coordinator*, 25(1/1976), 5–11.

Kiesler, S. et al. (eds.). *Aging: Social Change*. New York: Academic Press, 1981.

LaFontaine, J.S. (ed.). *Sex and Age as Principles of Social Differentiation.* New York: Academic Press, 1978.

Landis, J. 'Attitudes and Adjustment of Aged Rural People in Iowa,' Ph.D. thesis, Louisiana State University, 1940.

Lawton, M.P. *Environment and Aging.* Monterey: Brooks/Cole Publishing Co., 1980.

Lee, G. and M. Lassey. 'Rural-Urban Differences Among the Elderly: Economic, Social and Subjective Factors,' *Journal of Social Issues,* 36(2/1980), 62–74.

Leaf, A. *Youth In Old Age.* New York: McGraw-Hill, 1975.

Levinson, D. *The Seasons of a Man's Life.* New York: Alfred A. Knopf, 1978.

Linton, R. *The Study of Man.* New York: Appleton-Century-Crofts, 1936.

Linton, R. 'Age and Sex Categories,' *American Sociological Review,* 7(5/1942), 589–603.

Longino, C. and J. Biggar. 'The Impact of Population Redistribution on Service Delivery,' *The Gerontologist,* 22(2/1982), 153–59.

Lyell, R. (ed.). *Middle Age, Old Age: Short Stories, Poems, Plays and Essays on Aging.* New York: Harcourt, Brace Jovanovich, 1980.

Marshall, V. (ed.). *Aging in Canada: Social Perspectives.* Don Mills: Fitzhenry and Whiteside, 1980.

Marshall, V. 'Social Characteristics of Future Aged,' pp. 31–55 in B. Wigdor and L. Ford (eds.). *Housing for an Aging Population.* Toronto: University of Toronto Press, 1981.

Matthews, S. *The Social World of Old Women: Management of Self-Identity.* Beverly Hills: Sage Publications, 1979.

Mazess, R. and S. Forman. 'Longevity and Age Exaggeration in Vilcabamba, Ecuador,' *Journal of Gerontology,* 34(1/1979), 94–98.

McConnel, C. and F. Deljavan. 'The Educational Variable in Gerontological Research: An Economic Perspective and Aggregate Data,' *Educational Gerontology,* 7(4/1981), 339–54.

McGaugh, J. and S. Kiesler (eds.). *Aging: Biology and Behavior.* New York: Academic Press, 1981.

Medvedev, Z. 'Caucasus and Altay Longevity: A Biological or Social Problem?,' *The Gerontologist,* 14(5/1974), 381–87.

Miller, R. and R. Dodder. 'A Revision of Palmore's Facts on Aging Quiz,' *The Gerontologist,* 20(6/1980), 673–79.

Monahan, D. and V. Greene. 'The Impact of Seasonal Population Fluctuations on Service Delivery,' *The Gerontologist,* 22(2/1982), 160–63.

Mullins, N. 'The Development of a Scientific Specialty: The Phage Group and the Origins of Molecular Biology,' *Minerva,* 10(1/1972), 51–82.

Mullins, N. *Theories and Theory Groups in Contemporary American Sociology.* New York: Harper and Row, 1973.

Musgrove, F. and R. Middleton. 'Rites of Passage and the Meaning of Age in Three Contrasted Social Groups: Professional Footballers, Teachers and Methodist Ministers,' *British Journal of Sociology,* 32(1/1981), 39–55.

Neugarten, B. *Middle Age and Aging: A Reader in Social Psychology.* Chicago: University of Chicago Press, 1968.

Neugarten, B. 'Age Groups in American Society and the Rise of the Young-Old,' *The Annals of the American Academy of Political and Social Science,* 415(September 1974), 187–98.

Oliver, D. and J. Eckerman. 'Tracing the Historical Growth of Gerontology as a Discipline,' Presented at the 32nd Annual Meeting of the American Gerontological Society, Washington, D.C., 1979.

Palmore, E. (ed.). *Normal Aging: Reports From the Duke Longitudinal Studies, 1955–1969.* Durham: Duke University Press, 1970.

Palmore, E. 'Facts on Aging: A Short Quiz,' *The Gerontologist,* 17 (4/1977), 315–20.

Palmore, E. 'Advantages of Aging,' *The Gerontologist,* 19(2/1979), 220–23.

Palmore, E. 'The Facts on Aging Quiz: A Review of Findings,' *The Gerontologist,* 20(6/1980a), 669–72.

Palmore, E. (ed.). *International Handbook on Aging: Contemporary Developments and Research.* Westport, Conn.: Greenwood Press, 1980b.

Palmore, E. 'The Facts on Aging Quiz: Part Two,' *The Gerontologist,* 21(4/1981), 431–37.

Pampel, F. *Social Change and the Aged.* Lexington, Mass.: D.C. Heath & Co., 1981.

Parsons, T. 'Age and Sex in the Social Structure of the United States,' *American Sociological Review,* 7(5/1942), 604–20.

Place, L. et al. *Aging and the Aged: An Annotated Bibliography and Library Research Guide.* Boulder: Westview Press, 1981.

Pollock, O. *Social Adjustment in Old Age: A Research Planning Report.* Bulletin 59. New York: Social Science Research Council, 1948.

Posner, J. 'Old and Female: The Double Whammy,' pp. 80–94 in V. Marshall (ed.). *Aging in Canada: Social Perspectives.* Don Mills: Fitzhenry and Whiteside, 1980.

Rapaport, R. and R. Rapaport. (eds.). *Leisure and the Family Life Cycle.* London: Routledge and Kegan Paul, 1975.

Riegel, K. 'History of Psychological Gerontology,' in J. Birren and K. Schaie (eds.). *Handbook of the Psychology of Aging.* New York: Van Nostrand Reinhold, 1977.

Riley, M. and A. Foner. (eds.). *Aging and Society. Volume One: An Inventory of Research Findings.* New York: Russell Sage Foundation, 1968.

Riley, M. et al. *Aging and Society. Volume Two: Aging and the Professions.* New York: Russell Sage Foundation, 1969.

Riley, M. et al. *Aging and Society. Volume Three: A Sociology of Age Stratification.* New York: Russell Sage Foundation, 1972.

Rockstein, M. and M. Sussman. *Biology of Aging.* Belmont, Calif.: Wadsworth, 1979.

Rose, A. and W. Peterson. (eds.). *Older People and Their Social World.* Philadelphia: F.A. Davis, 1965.

Rosow, I. 'What Is a Cohort and Why?,' *Human Development*, 21(2/1978), 65–75.

Ryder, N. 'The Cohort as a Concept in the Study of Social Change,' *American Sociological Review*, 30(6/1965), 843–61.

Sackmary, B. 'The Sociology of Science: The Emergence and Development of a Sociological Specialty,' Ph.D. dissertation, Department of Sociology, University of Massachusetts, 1974.

Schulz, J. *The Economics of Aging.* Belmont, Calif.: Wadsworth Publishing Co., 1976.

Seltzer, M. 'The Older Woman: Facts, Fantasies and Fiction,' *Research on Aging*, 1(2/1979), 139–54.

Shanas, E. et al. *Old People in Three Industrial Societies.* New York: Atherton, 1968.

Shanas, E. 'The Sociology of Aging and the Aged,' *The Sociological Quarterly*, 12(2/1971), 159–76.

Shock, N. (ed.) *Biological Aspects of Aging.* New York: Columbia University Press, 1962.

Shock, N. 'Biological Theories of Aging,' pp. 103–15 in J. Birren and K.W. Schaie (eds.). *Handbook of the Psychology of Aging.* New York: Van Nostrand Reinhold, 1977.

Simmons, L. *The Role of the Aged in Primitive Society.* New Haven, Conn.: Yale University Press, 1945.

Sontag, S. 'The Double Standard of Aging,' pp. 32–33 in *No Longer Young: The Older Woman in America.* Occasional Papers in Gerontology, no. 11. Detroit: Institute of Gerontology, University of Michigan-Wayne State University, 1975.

Streib, G. and H. Orbach. 'The Development of Social Gerontology and the Sociology of Aging,' pp. 612–40 in P. Lazarsfeld, W. Sewell and H. Wilensky (eds.). *The Uses of Sociology.* New York: Basic Books, 1967.

Tamir, L. *Men in Their Forties.* New York: Springer Publishing Co., 1982.

Theodorson, G. and A. Theodorson. *Modern Dictionary of Sociology.* New York: Thomas Y. Crowell Co., 1969.

Tibbitts, C. (ed.) *Handbook of Social Gerontology: Societal Aspects of Aging.* Chicago: University of Chicago Press, 1960.

Tibbitts, C. and W. Donahue. (eds.). *Social and Psychological Aspects of Aging.* New York: Columbia University Press, 1962.

Treiman, D. *Occupational Prestige in Comparative Perspective.* New York: Academic Press, 1977.

Troll, L. 'Age Changes in Sex Roles amid Changing Sex Roles: The Double Shift,' pp. 118–43 in C. Eisdorfer (ed.). *Annual Review of Gerontology and Geriatrics.* Volume 2. New York: Springer Publishing Co., 1981.

Tumin, M. *Social Stratification.* Englewood Cliffs, N.J.: Prentice-Hall, 1967.

Wilkinson, C. et al. *Comprehensive Annotated Bibliography on the Rural Aged (1975–1981).* Morgantown: West Virginia University Press, 1982.

Williams, R. and C. Wirths. *Lives Through the Years.* New York: Atherton Press, 1965.

Youmans, E. *Older Rural Americans.* Lexington: University of Kentucky Press, 1967.

2

Aging from a Historical and Comparative Perspective: Cultural and Subcultural Variations

Introduction

The experiences and meaning of aging and the status of the elderly vary within and between cultures. Cultural variables that affect the status of the elderly (such as respect for the aged) are influenced by structural or social system variables (industrialization, a changing family structure). The continuing interaction between the cultural and structural levels of analysis must be recognized when one is searching for explanations of aging phenomena. The first part of this chapter illustrates the diversity in status and treatment of the elderly from a historical and comparative perspective. The second part considers subcultural variations in the status of the elderly, primarily within the North American context.

The Meaning of Culture

The culture of a society or of a subgroup within a society develops when a group shares a way of life at the same time and place. The culture provides a symbolic order and a set of shared meanings to social life, and is composed of nonmaterial and material elements. The nonmaterial elements include norms, customs, values, beliefs, knowledge, morals, and sanctions. These are symbolically represented through material elements or artifacts such as laws, language, art, dress, folklore, technology, literature, music, art, ceremonies, and games. Those products that are highly valued are transmitted from one generation to the next through the process of socialization.[1]

Of particular importance in understanding the social life and processes of a society are its values and norms. Values are the internalized criteria by which members select and judge their own and others' goals and behaviors in society. Values tend to be trans-situational in that they are reflected in all institutions within a society. They include principles such as democracy, equality of opportunity, freedom, achievement, competition, goal orientation, and respect for the elderly. Norms are derived from and closely interrelated to basic values. Norms serve as guidelines to acceptable behavior in specific social situations. For example, many norms concerning how we dress, how we spend our leisure time, or when we work are related to age or to the social positions we occupy.

In most societies there is a high degree of cultural integration or consensus about how people think and behave. This is reflected in the phenomenon known as 'ethnocentrism,' wherein members regard their mainstream culture as superior to all others. This ethnocentric tendency influences how we behave toward persons from other cultural backgrounds, including members of subcultures in our own society.

Some behavioral patterns, values, and social institutions are similar from one culture to another, although they may be expressed in different forms. For example, all societies have some form of political, social, and economic organization, a common language, and a way of socializing members. These processes evolve from systems of social differentiation — family units, the labor force, and educational systems.

The Historical and Comparative Approach to Understanding the Aging Process

Just as the biologist searches for similarities in structure and function among different species in order to arrive at generalizations or laws, the social scientist seeks to understand aging phenomena by examining the process of aging and the status of the aged in a variety of cultural contexts. The historian[2] examines the meaning of aging within a society at different historical periods. For example, a historical analysis shows that the status of the aged has not always been as low as it is at present. This type of information helps us to identify and understand present attitudes. Historians strive to identify patterns of thought and behavior that are repeated in a variety of contexts (cultural universals), as well as those unique to a culture or period (cultural variations).

A comparative historical analysis gives us a background to the present situation by illustrating how cultural factors influence the aging process. We are able to understand and appreciate what a symbol or pattern of behavior 'means' in another culture. By using this knowledge, solutions to problems in our own society may be found.

In the sections that follow, the process of aging and the status of the aged in a number of cultural contexts are described (Fry, 1980a; Holmes, 1980; Keith, 1980; Amoss and Harell, 1981; Holzberg, 1981). These sections present descriptive accounts of the aged in a specific society rather than an analytical comparison of different societies. Unfortunately, with few exceptions (Simmons, 1945; Barker and Barker, 1961; Gutmann, 1967, 1980; Shanas et al., 1968; Havighurst, 1969; Cowgill and Holmes, 1972; Myerhoff and Simic, 1978; Fry, 1980b; Keith, 1980, 1982), most scholars have only described variations within a single society. There has been little attempt at analysis and comparison across societies. Moreover, most of the anthropological studies have dealt with preindustrial societies where social structures tend to be homogeneous rather than heterogeneous. Thus, even where more modern societies have been studied, differences in aging patterns have seldom been examined for unique racial, ethnic, class, or religious subgroups. As we have seen, in North America white, middle-class males have been overrepresented in most gerontological studies (Achenbaum, 1974).

The Modernization Hypothesis and the Changing Status of the Aged

As noted earlier, scholars have sought to identify social factors that are thought to influence longevity and the status of the aged, however the 'elderly' may be defined in each society. Our knowledge of early societies is based chiefly on archeological evidence and on the few documents produced by philosophers or historians of the time (Laslett, 1976). Clearly, longevity was greatly influenced by climate, availability and type of food, natural disasters, disease, medical knowledge, and relations with other tribes or groups. Until about the middle of the seventeenth century, the average life expectancy seldom exceeded 40 years (although those with higher status generally lived longer).[3] Because there were few elderly citizens, those who survived were often held in esteem and awe, and received preferential treatment.

Prior to the Industrial Revolution, two major types of societies existed. In the primitive hunting-and-gathering societies where production was carried out by domestic groups, the oldest member was considered a source of knowledge about rituals and survival skills. In a society where social differentiation was based largely on age, authority was linked to age and elders held influential positions in the social, political, and religious spheres of life (Goody, 1976). For example, based on an analysis of seventy-one primitive societies, Simmons (1945, 1952) found that status and treatment of the aged was governed by tradition and rituals unique to each culture. The elderly were expected to contribute as much as possible by assisting with economic and household chores; by teaching the young people games, customs, songs, and dances; by serving as the repository of rites and traditions; by counselling the young about hunting, growing crops, and warfare; and by serving as chiefs or elders of the community.

Press and McKool (1972) noted that there were four prestige-generating components for the aged in the Mesoamerican era: the 'advisory' component, or the degree to which the advice and opinions of the aged were heeded; the 'contributory' component, or the degree to which the aged participated in and controlled ritual and economic activities; the 'control' component, or the degree of direct authority of the aged over people and institutions; and the 'residual' component, or the degree to which the aged retained prestige because of their earlier contributions to society. The second major type of preindustrialized society was the agrarian-peasant model. The aged owned or controlled the land, and were considered the heads of extended families made up of at least three generations. In these societies, the elderly had experience and knowledge of survival skills, husbandry, history, ritual, and law. The aged in most types of preindustrial societies held meaningful roles, as long as they were physically and mentally able to contribute to the family and community. They had considerable power over the social, religious, and economic life of the society. This gave them influence, security, and status. When the elderly were no longer able to contribute, they 'retired' and transferred control over family resources, usually to the oldest son. They were then cared for by the family and the community because of past contributions (the residual component of prestige), and because they were the major source of knowledge about the culture.

As Laslett (1976) concluded, the status of the aged probably varied between and within societies, depending on locale and period. For example, there were a few instances (such as in some Inuit societies) where the old were forced to die, by their own hand or by the hands of relatives, once they were deemed a burden to society. From an exchange perspective, when costs exceeded contributions, the old were forced to leave the community so others would have a better chance to survive.

With the onset of the Industrial Revolution, first in Great Britain and Western Europe and then in North America, societies experienced dramatic social changes as they moved from rural, agricultural societies to urban, technological societies. These changes were even more dramatic than the earlier shift from nomadic hunting-and-gathering societies to stable agrarian societies. As a result, new social structures, cultural values, political and social systems, and social processes began to evolve. These new structures had a profound impact on the lifestyle of all age cohorts, but particularly on the aged.

For the individual, industrialization generally resulted in a higher level of educational attainment; improvements in health care and living conditions, which increase longevity; independence from parents after late adolescence or early adulthood; greater personal wealth; and an increase in leisure time because of shorter working hours.

At the societal level, the Industrial Revolution led to at least six major changes in the social and economic system (Burgess, 1960; Cowgill, 1974a). First, there was a shift from home to factory production with the result that the family was no longer the center of economic production. This meant a separation of work and home and a dramatic increase in the number of people dependent on nonfamily employers for their economic security. Accompanying this shift in place of employment was a trend to increased migration to cities, especially by younger age cohorts. This urbanization resulted in greater social differentiation, the development of multiple social groups (family, work, neighborhood), exposure to new values and norms, and the establishment of public schools.

A third trend was the breakup of the extended family and the emergence of the nuclear, conjugal family, often in a different community (a neolocal) from that of the parents. A fourth trend was the rise of large organizations and the creation of new occupations requiring skills that the young could acquire through apprenticeship or formal schooling. Many of the skills possessed by the elderly became obsolete, mandatory retirement was invoked, and a certain level of formal education was increasingly demanded as a prerequisite to employment. Because new knowledge was being generated so rapidly, the knowledge acquired by the elderly through experience was no longer of much worth (Maxwell and Silverman, 1970).

The rapid shift to automation posed a threst to the individual because, while it created some new jobs, it also led to the loss of jobs and initiated the process of compulsory retirement which meant that the elderly were left with a 'roleless role' (Burgess, 1960). Automation also led to competition among age groups for jobs. For those who were employed, industrialization offered a promise of increased leisure time and a rise in the standard of living.

Finally, industrialization brought new technology to the medical field. The quality of medical care improved, thereby reducing infant and childhood mortality rates and prolonging adult life. The result was an increased life expectancy, a larger population, and a larger proportion of old people within the population. This combination of increased technology in the labor system, improved health care, increased urbanization, and compulsory public education is referred to as 'modernization.'

Despite these improvements in the quality of life, many have argued that the role and status of the aged declined after the Industrial Revolution. Modernization resulted in a worldwide pattern of declining relations between generations. As a result, the aged lost power, security, and status because they no longer had functionally essential social roles and were no longer looked to for knowledge and information. Also, because adult children no longer lived in the family home, many did not believe they had a moral, social, or legal obligation to support their aging parents.

To test the assumption that the status of the aged declines with the degree of modernization, Cowgill and Holmes (1972) reviewed the work of Simmons (1945) concerning the relationship between cultural traits and the status of the aged in preindustrial societies. They asked anthropologists to describe aging and the status of the aged in fifteen different cultures and subcultures. These ranged from preliterate societies, such as the Sidamo of southwest Ethiopia, to semi-industrialized societies, such as Thailand in the 1960s, to highly modernized societies, such as the United States.

Based on their analysis of these societies, they concluded that there were eight universal and twenty-two culture-specific propositions for which there was some evidence of support (Cowgill and Holmes, 1972:321–23). Some significant universal propositions were that:

1. The aged always constitute a minority within the total population.

2. In an older population females outnumber males; widows comprise a high proportion of the older population.

3. In all societies, some people are classified as 'old' and are treated differently because they are so classified.

4. In all societies, racial norms prescribe some mutual responsibility between old people and their adult children.

Similarly, some interesting culture-specific propositions were that:

1. Modernized societies have higher proportions of old people.

2. The status of the aged is high in primitive societies and is lower and more ambiguous in modern societies.

3. The status of the aged tends to decline as their numbers and proportions increase.

4. The status of the aged is inversely proportional to the rate of social change.

5. The status of the aged tends to decline with the increasing literacy of the population.

6. The status of the aged is lower in societies that favor the nuclear form of the family and neolocal marriage.

In summary, Cowgill and Holmes concluded that increasing modernization of societies accounts for the declining status of the aged. They found that the status of the aged is high in societies where they perform useful, valued functions. However, there were some cases that did not agree with the theory. For example, the elderly have an apparent continuing high status in Japan, Ireland, and Russia, all of which are modernized to various degrees. These exceptions were attributed to unique factors related to the stage of historical development within the society, or to rigid adherence to earlier cultural values, particularly those pertaining to older members of the family (Palmore, 1975b; Holmes, 1976).

In contrast, according to some reports the status of the aged has declined in China, even though modernization has occurred to some degree. Cherry and Magnuson-Martinson (1981) recently noted that the traditional authority of the aged in China has declined, not as a consequence of modernization, but because of a combination of the socialist revolution and the demands by urban youth for an end to age discrimination. These two factors led to a political cleavage between generations. However, this conflict is primarily restricted to urban regions. Since most Chinese live in rural areas, traditional father-son relationships still prevail, and the current status of the elderly in China still closely resembles that which existed in the nineteenth century.

Not surprisingly, as with most theories,[4] there have been many challenges to the assumption that the status of the aged changed because of the onset of modernization (Cowgill, 1974b; Dowd, 1981). Harlan (1964), in a study of three traditional villages in India, noted that the social status of the aged in preindustrialized societies is not always as high as is assumed. He argued that generalizations concerning the status of the aged must be based on a representative sampling of all socioeconomic levels. Greater care should be taken to distinguish between hypothetical ideal norms of family life with regard to the authority and prestige of the aged, and the actual relationships and behavior that occur.

Gutmann (1980:431) cautions that, while there may be acceptance of the cultural values pertaining to the aged, structural factors such as urbanization may inhibit putting these values into practice. Within the same society, the cultural ideas pertaining to the aged may remain constant (honor the elderly), but the actual treatment they receive from younger people may deteriorate as one moves from primitive to urbanized societies. That is, while the primitive, rural, and urban members are all familiar with the cultural values, the more urbanized citizens are less likely to accept and internalize these values or to demonstrate them in their behavior toward the elderly.

Laslett (1966) and Hendricks and Hendricks (1977–78), on the basis of evidence from historical demography, found that in spite of continuing stereotypes, the emotional, physical, and economic needs of the aged were not better met prior to industrialization. The status of the elderly in modernized societies is no lower and may actually be higher than it was prior to industrialization. Many examples from postindustrial societies can be given of how the aged are supported by their children, and of how mandatory retirement can relieve the aged of the burden of work and reward them with freedom and leisure time. In short, the assumption of a difference in treatment of the aged before and after modernization is misleading, and is not supported by Laslett's (1966) analysis of early demographic evidence.

More recently, Stearns (1976) suggests that in preindustrial France the elderly were held in disdain. This callous, pessimistic image of old age was held by all age groups in France, including the elderly themselves. These attitudes resulted from the cultural belief that old age is an unpleasant time, and that old people are nuisances. These views were held much longer in France than in the United States, despite the onset of modernization at about the same time in both countries.

A number of authors have felt that the before-and-after-modernization explanation may not be as simple as suggested. This view is based on the observation that the processes of modernization proceed at different rates and by different stages within various societies. Moreover, the elderly are a heterogeneous group and not all members of the older cohorts may experience a change in status (Dowd, 1981). Modernization can affect societies in different ways, since a particular event may not have an impact until as long as five decades after its occurrence (Achenbaum and Stearns, 1978).[5]

The process of modernization may have varying degrees of influence on different age cohorts and subcultural groups within a society because of their experience with and adherence to different value systems. An evaluation of the meaning of old age and the status of the aged may depend on the social environment and the value structures of various age cohorts. Burgess (1960) noted a number of differences between European nations and the United States that may have consequences for the way the aged are treated. For example, he reported that the aged are less concentrated and less visible in North America; that there is a more decentralized government in North America, which enables three levels (city, state, federal) of authority to be concerned about the aged; that there is greater cultural and regional diversity in values and lifestyle in North America; and that there are stronger historical and cultural ties between generations in Europe.

From a more empirical perspective, Palmore and Manton (1974) found that the relationship between the degree of modernization and the status of the aged in thirty-one countries could be represented by a bowl-shaped curve (curvilinear). Immediately after the onset of modernization, the status of the aged may decline. However, the long-term effect of social change is that the difference in status between the aged and non-aged decreases and the relative status of the aged rises. They suggested that in the more modernized nations the status of the aged is improving, although it may or may not rise to the level attained prior to modernization.

In the United States, the change in intergenerational relations occurred just after the American Revolution and before the onset of industrialization. Fischer (1977), for example, presents a historical analysis of the period from 1770 to 1820 when age equality became one of the bases for building a new society. Following the American Revolution, priority seating by age at town meetings was replaced with priority seating by wealth; a single style of dress was permitted for men of all ages (before the revolution, the elderly dressed in a different style); and a new vocabulary to express contempt for old people evolved (incorporating terms such as 'old fogy'). Once initiated, this devaluation of the elderly continued through the late 1800s and early 1900s, particularly after the Civil War (1861–65).

According to Achenbaum (1974, 1978), the image of the elderly as obsolete was fostered by a number of interdependent events. First, medical research suggested that the longer people lived, the more likely they were to suffer from incurable pathological disorders. Second, with the rise of bureaucracies, the work experience of the elderly was not valued as highly as the possession of newer job skills. A third factor was the acceptance of the view that the energy and strength of youth needed to be developed and exploited. Thus, the onset of technological change, the increase in bureaucratization, and changes in social values contributed to a loss of self-esteem, self-worth, and self-respect on the part of the elderly (Sheehan, 1976).

In summary, there is conflicting evidence concerning the status of the aged in preindustrial societies compared to modern, urban societies. Just as some earlier societies held the elderly in high esteem while others abandoned them, similar patterns can be found in contemporary societies. For example, just as the elderly were abandoned by some nomadic tribes, today they are often abandoned in institutions for the aged, where, because of advanced technology, they can be kept alive beyond the point where it may not be worth living (Maxwell and Silverman, 1981).

As we will see, there are some universal patterns in the process of aging and the status of the aged, but numerous cultural variations between and within societies do occur. While a definitive explanation for such variations is lacking, the rate and degree of social change (from a traditional, agricultural society to an industrialized urban society) does have some influence on the observed differences. Cultural traditions, changes in family kinship structure, the pressure from youth for age equality, and social change all seem partially to account for these cross-cultural differences.

The next two sections present brief descriptions of aging in various preindustrial and industrial societies. These societies, which are representative of many, provide only a general overview of the modal pattern. The descriptions are based on various accounts from each society at a given point in history. We see only a 'snapshot' of a specific period in a society's development, rather than a historical 'movie' of the society over a period of many years. The presentations also tend to overlook variations within the society among a variety of cultural subgroups.

Aging and the Aged in Preindustrial Societies

Preliterate Societies

Preliterate societies have no written languages; therefore knowledge, beliefs, and survival skills are found in the memories of those with the greatest experience, the elders. The economic system is based on production and consumption within domestic kinship groups. Inheritance and the dependency of children on their parents is linked to a degree of obligation toward the old in the family unit (Goody, 1976). Generally, preliterate societies are of two types. The least developed are nomadic hunting and gathering societies, as exemplified by some Inuit tribes. The more stable preliterate societies are subsistence agrarian communities, such as the Anasazi Indians who inhabited the Mesa Verde area in what is now southwestern Colorado from 550 to 750 A.D.

Regardless of the degree of development in a society, the interaction of economic conditions, religious beliefs, family structure, control of property, and system of government influence how the aged are treated. In societies where there is a surplus of food, where the oldest members control property, and where knowledge of survival, rituals, and customs is stored by the elderly, their status is high and they are protected. In societies where food is scarce, where property is nonexistent, or where leadership is based on perceived ability rather than on longevity or familial ties, the elderly may be abandoned or put to death (gerontocide), with or without ceremony. In both types of preliterate societies, older men commanded greater respect than older women.

Low status.   In nomadic tribes, abandonment of the aged was relatively common. Holmberg (1969:224–25) reported that the Sirino tribe in Bolivia abandoned their elderly when they became ill or infirm. The Yakuts of Siberia forced their elderly to become beggars and slaves. The Chukchee of Siberia ceremoniously killed the aged in front of the members of the tribe (de Beauvoir, 1972). However, within the Chukchee tribe, behavior differed, depending on whether the tribe lived in settled villages along the coast, or whether they lived a nomadic life herding reindeer. In the herding tribe, older people had knowledge about breeding and survival of the herds, and were therefore less expendable. Thus, in some preliterate societies, particularly nomadic societies, the aged were devalued if they became a burden and had no specialized knowledge or skills, if cultural values dictated that they were no longer worthy of life (for example, because of declining physical strength), or if children sought revenge on their parents.

High status.   In societies where the majority of the population was illiterate, face-to-face interaction was the primary means of teaching and ruling. Information and skills were acquired and retained through years of experience. The elderly were information banks for the society. Since survival and the passing on of the culture to the young depended on this information, the aged were held in high esteem. For example, Maxwell and Silverman (1970) examined twenty-six societies to determine the extent to which the aged were involved in the following six types of information processing: (1) as hosts of feasts, games, or visiting groups; (2) as consultants on survival skills or ritual; (3) as decision makers for the group; (4) as entertainers; (5) as arbitrators of disputes; and (6) as teachers of the young. They found a strong relationship between the amount of useful information held by the aged as expressed by their participation in information-processing activities, and the esteem accorded to them by other members of the society.

Other factors leading to a higher status for the aged in preliterate societies were stability of residence, a viable system of food production, the availability of low-skill functional roles, a nuclear family, and a system of religion in which the elderly were thought to be able to communicate with the gods. Simmons (1960), Rosow (1965), de Beauvoir (1972) and Goody (1976) describe such practices as the visits of aged Hopi Indians to one relative after another to obtain food; old chiefs conducting political or religious meetings; old Incas still making a contribution by serving as scarecrows; elders educating the children in the evenings; old Omaha Indians advising the young to leave the choice morsels in the kettle for them, lest 'your arrow twist when you shoot'; and old Aztecs having access to stimulants prohibited to others because it would 'warm their blood.' Thus, if the aged were members of a relatively non-nomadic, family-based society, and if they were assigned or had acquired special powers or functions, their status was generally high and they were accorded respect and good treatment until their death (Kagan, 1980).

Early Literate Societies

The ancient Hebrews.   This is one of the earliest societies for which there exist written records and well-preserved artifacts. It is also one of the first societies in which long life was viewed as a blessing rather than a burden. In the years between the 1300 B.C. and 100 A.D., the Hebrews were a nomadic desert tribe essentially made up of a large extended family. This family consisted of wives, concubines, children, sons and their wives and children, slaves, servants, and any others who attached themselves to the domestic group for protection. They were ruled by the eldest man, the patriarch of the family, who was the religious leader, judge, and teacher. He controlled all aspects of political, religious, economic and social life and was identified by his long gray beard — a sign of wisdom, experience, and authority. In this relatively stable yet nomadic culture, aging, at least for men, represented increasing wisdom, respect, and power.

The city-states of ancient Greece and Rome.   According to ancient Greek literature, there appeared to exist a dread and hatred of old age. The Greek gods were depicted as eternally youthful and beautiful, and much of the literature commented on the declining physical and mental strength of the aged. In ancient Greece, power was more likely to be associated with wealth than with age, and if an older man attained respect and power, it accrued to him because of his wealth.

Like the Greeks, elderly Romans lost power and influence as they aged, unless they could retain them through their wealth. This is not surprising, since evidence from burial remains indicates that life expectancy may have been only 20 to 30 years (Preston, 1977). The citizen-soldier was a dominant figure; death, even by suicide, was sometimes seen as preferable to suffering the indignities of physical, mental, and social deterioration. For most of the elderly, aging was hated and feared. This was especially true in the declining years of the Greek and Roman civilizations, when barbarism placed a premium on youth and strength. Survival of the fittest prevailed, and those who could not contribute to the society were abandoned or put to death.

Later Literate Societies

Japan.   It is difficult to find accurate and complete information about aging in preindustrial Japan. Plath (1972) indirectly provides some information. He notes that there is no evidence in over a thousand years of recorded history that the Japanese abandoned their aged as a matter of custom. Japanese citizens followed the Confucian precepts that demanded honor for all elders and for parents in particular. However, he also notes the high rate of suicide among Japanese elders, particularly among women, and wonders whether this is a pattern reflecting the earlier custom of self-sacrifice (a cultural norm dating back to early Samurai practices). Plath also draws attention to the recurring Obasute theme in Japanese folklore, where old people in a village are required to make a pilgrimage to Oak Mountain with a young kinsman during their seventieth year. Here, they are expected to wait for death or be pushed off the cliff.

England.   After the decline of the Roman civilization, the Roman church prevailed as the ruling authority throughout feudal England and Western Europe. Although one might expect the status of the aged to improve with the rise of Christianity, this was not the case. The Church was more interested in recruiting new members than in performing social work. However, by the sixteenth and early seventeenth centuries, longevity increased and such precepts as charity, hospitality, and care for one's fellow man began to be practiced as basic tenets of parish life. As a result, there was a growing concern for the treatment of the aged, especially if they were poor. For example, almshouses provided a form of institutionalized care. However, since manpower was scarce, all were expected to work as long as they were able, including the elderly. The state became involved in supporting the aged with the passage of the Elizabethan Poor Laws in 1603. As a result, prior to the onset of the Industrial Revolution, the elderly who did not have families to care for them were looked after by the parish, with some limited financial assistance from the state. These poorhouses were by no means seen as the ideal form of care for the elderly.

Colonial America. Although much of the information about preindustrial societies is based on early documents or on the interpretation of artifacts, there is greater reliability and validity in the written historical and census records of life in early America. It is on the basis of this evidence that Fischer (1977), in his classic work, *Growing Old In America*, chronicles the status of the aged from colonial times onward.

The rigors of colonial life placed a premium on strong, healthy adults, and the colonies were initially a young male-dominated society, with a median age of about 20 years. In fact, less than 2 percent of the residents were over 65. Being highly religious, the Puritans took their cue from the Bible and honored their elders by letting them occupy leadership positions and permitting them to sit in the most prestigious seats at town meetings. This status was not solely based on religious beliefs; it was also related to wealth, in that the elderly owned the land and resources and hence could command respect from their families. Because wealth played a role in acquiring status, those who were poor or destitute were scorned or driven from the town so they would cease to be an economic burden. As in many other societies, older women did not receive the same respect as older men.

After the French and American Revolutions, the status of the aged deteriorated as supporters of political and social equality argued that those who could pay and work were eligible to acquire power and status. As we saw earlier, this new order was reflected in the seating arrangements at town meetings, where prestigious seats were assigned to the wealthy or to those who had made exceptional contributions to the community.

As the settlement of the West began in the 1800s, emphasis was still placed on the strength, vigor, and vitality of young men. In many cases, the pioneers were sons of eastern colonials who decided to break from the family to seek their own fortune and lifestyle in their 'little house on the prairie.'

In summary, according to Fischer (1977), the declining status of the aged in North America began not with industrialization, urbanization, and greater literacy, but with the change in cultural values after the American Revolution. This led to an emphasis on equality based on performance and income, and a westward migration away from the influence and control of one's parents. As a result, many of the elderly were left in the eastern colonies to fend for themselves and ended their lives alone, often in poverty.

Summary

Before turning to an analysis of the status of the aged in industrial societies where machines play a major economic role, let us review the status of the aged in societies in which the means of production came almost entirely from plants, animals, and man (Cottrell, 1960). Although the evidence is weak, high status of the aged in preliterate societies seemed related to living in a society that had a food surplus, that was stable rather than nomadic, and that had cultural values which assigned religious, educational, social, or political leadership roles to the elderly. The position of the elderly was more secure if they had control of knowledge and wealth.

In these societies, retirement did not exist. Instead, older people were assigned less demanding chores as they became mentally and physically weaker. In many societies, especially nomadic ones, the elderly were abandoned when they could no longer contribute and were considered a burden. Thus, in static, preliterate societies, prestige accrued to the older men who had more 'time' to acquire the spiritual, mental, and economic resources that were needed and valued by all members of the society. Even in the face of declining strength and relinquished economic power, old people generally continued to dominate and perform kinship, political, or religious roles until death. They controlled cultural values and ideas that assisted them in maintaining their high status (Gutmann, 1980).

In literate, preindustrial Eastern and Western cultures, the status of the aged seemed to vary according to prevailing living conditions, religious beliefs, and cultural values. For example, the elderly appeared to have high status and power in the early years of the Hebrew, Greek, Roman, and American societies. They lost status as wars, migration, and changing values accorded higher status to youth and to those who acquired wealth and made functional contributions to the society, regardless of age.

Aging and the Aged in Industrialized Societies

With the onset of the Industrial Revolution, first in Great Britain and later in other societies, great economic and social changes occurred. Generally, these changes are referred to as modernization (or, for non-Western nations, as Westernization). Modernization has the potential to change the relative status and roles of all age cohorts within a society. The following sections outline the process of aging and the status of the aged in various modernizing or modern societies. Again, only a broad 'snapshot' is presented here.

The Impact of Modernization

Samoa.   The traditional authority of Samoan elders changed with the introduction of Western cultural values and a Western economic system based on the exchange of goods (Maxwell, 1970; Holmes, 1972; Watson and Maxwell, 1977: 46–58). The traditional culture was a subsistence society involving a number of extended families who lived in a seaside village headed by an elected chief. In each village there was sharing within and between families, and the aged were respected and cared for by the extended family.

In the early 1800s Christianity was introduced to the islands. Contact with Westerners increased when the United States took control of Eastern Samoa after 1900. During and after World War II transportation facilities were expanded; the literacy rate increased, and old people were no longer seen as important repositories of information; industries were established and provided employment and money; Western material goods (such as canned foods) were imported, and food sharing decreased; tourism was encouraged and led to even more contact with Westerners. As a result of these influences, the power and authority of the elders in the community decreased. At the same time, young people became independent wage earners. However, the elderly were still treated with respect within the family, and children contributed to the economic support of the elders in their extended family.

Thailand.   Cowgill (1968, 1972) describes the industrialization, urbanization, and Westernization of Thailand as a slow process that has had an impact mainly in the larger cities. This is illustrated by the tendency of the older people in the rural and urban areas to adhere to traditional beliefs, skills, customs, values, and dress, while the young become increasingly westernized. As a result, there is growing intergenerational tension and a lessening of respect for the aged.

Salt River Pima.   The inhabitants of this reservation near Phoenix, Arizona have changed their economy from individual subsistence as farmers to a wage and land-leasing system where large, mechanized farming cooperatives predominate (Munsell, 1972). Although elderly men still have relatively high status within their extended families, the traditional political leadership of the community by the aged has been usurped by younger, educated members. The nuclear family has become more prevalent, and this has lowered the status of the aged, particularly the men. In fact, Munsell (1972:132) suggests that older women have gained status relative to their traditional role, because they function as a parent substitute when a breakdown of the nuclear family occurs.

Rural Nepal.   Nepal is a poor, preindustrial country similar to many of the least developed countries of the Third and Fourth Worlds. For a study of a community of Sherpas living in the mountains of Nepal, Goldstein and Beall (1981, 1982) identified eight dimensions of status that must be considered when assessing the total situation of the elderly. These included biological, health, activity, authority, economic, household, psychological, and ritual status. The authors found that the elderly Sherpas were ranked highly on most of these dimensions. Yet, despite this apparent high status, many older persons reported low levels of life satisfaction, especially concerning living alone. The authors attributed this dissatisfaction to the indirect impact of modernization whereby many of the young migrated to work in India. As a result, many old people were left without the traditional presence of the youngest son. Although they were in good physical health, many reported low levels of psychological and emotional well-being.

Eastern European Industrialized Societies

The Union of Soviet Socialist Republics.   Although many societal resources are directed toward youth, the treatment and status of the aged in the Soviet Union reflects the traditional values of peasant societies. McKain (1972) reports that the status of the elderly is conferred not by age, but by attaining a new status such as retiring or becoming a grandparent (the grandmother, or *babushka*, is a respected Russian figure). Respect for the aged in modern Soviet society is derived from the role they play in teaching the young, from the grandparents helping to raise grandchildren in the home, from social conventions that require the aged to receive special assistance or preferred treatment in public, and from grandparents living with children and actively participating in daily decisions. Similarly, many political leaders are elderly men who represent experience and long-standing loyalty to Soviet policies.

Perhaps the key factor in the continued high status of the elderly is the shortage of housing and labor, and the fact that both the husband and wife are usually employed. The grandparents, particularly the *babushka*, help raise the children and perform domestic chores. Although Soviet senior citizens receive pensions, they are expected to contribute to society in some productive way by helping the family, working on the farm, or doing part-time work for the state. In return, they are provided with leisure opportunities and free medical care. Thus, the status of the aged in the Soviet Union is high and their situation is similar to other age cohorts. However, the question remains as to whether this status will persist if the socialist system advances to the stage where separate dwellings will be available for most nuclear families.

Industrialized Eastern Societies

In order to understand the present status of the aged in China and Japan, some basic Oriental philosophical and religious principles need to be introduced. While the two countries vary in many respects, some commonalities were reported by Piovesana (1979). First, there is a belief that age represents an accumulation of wisdom. Second, filial piety or respect for parents is a Confucian concept that is reinforced by the principle of ancestor worship. This practice maintains a link with the past, and ensures respect for parents who will be the next ancestors to be worshipped. Finally, within both societies, the unity of the family and the crucial role of the elderly are cultural norms that have persisted to the present. Thus, as Palmore (1975b) notes, a vertical system of relationships exists in Japan. According to this system, seniority and age are essential in determining the nature of interpersonal interaction in all social situations.

Japan.   Modernization began in Japan in the Meiji era (1868–1912), and the process was greatly intensified after World War II, when most of Japan was rebuilt. A detailed analysis of the status of the aged in industrialized Japan has been completed by Palmore (1975a, 1975b, 1975c). He found that the pension system was inadequate, and that less money was spent per person on older people than in any other industrial society; only a minority of the elderly Japanese are self-supporting. Over 75 percent live with their children and about 1 percent are institutionalized. Palmore reported that over 55 percent of Japanese men over 65, although forced to retire between 55 and 60, are still in the labor force, mainly in family businesses or as self-employed workers. He suggests that the tradition of filial piety and the remnants of a vertical social structure contribute to the integration of the aged into society and to the continuing respect received from younger age cohorts.

This vertical system of interpersonal relationships is determined largely by age rather than competence, as it is in Western societies. Thus, in the traditional family, the head or oldest person sits in the best seat, is served first, and takes the first bath (Nakani, 1972). Palmore (1975a) stresses the important domestic functions of the grandmother, and the fact that three-generation families are the preferred unit, except for the college-educated. In fact, Maeda (1975) states that many of the elderly consider it shameful not to live with their children.

Palmore (1975c) presents evidence that the status of the aged has not declined much since the onset of industrialization. As examples, he cites a number of factors, including the national holiday on September 15 called 'Respect for the Elders Day,' the special meaning and celebration attached to one's 60th birthday (Kanrecki), and the norm of giving up one's seat to an old person on a bus or train. However, perhaps in recognition that the status of the elderly was declining, the National Law for the Welfare of the Elders was passed in 1963 to perpetuate the traditional respect granted to the elderly. This law requires that the elderly be given respect, that they be given the opportunity to work, and that they be given the right to participate in social activities.

Although Palmore (1975b) argues that there has only been minimal loss of status by Japanese elders since industrialization, the evidence suggests otherwise. Sparks (1975) and Plath (1972) found that although children may care for their parents, an increasing number do so reluctantly. Indeed, some abandon their parents or pass them from one sibling to another to enable them to meet the minimal norm of filial duty. Plath cites the continuing high rates of suicide among the elderly as evidence of their dissatisfaction with life. He also indicates that even where elderly parents reside with the children, their quality of life may be low since they may not be included in family conversations and activity. In effect, the elderly are sometimes reduced to the level of domestic laborers or servants. Similarly, Maeda (1975) states that the elderly often live in a small room without privacy, that there is frequent intergenerational conflict between the mother and the daughter-in-law, and that the elderly are economically dependent on their children. As a result of these conditions, there has been rapid development of old people's clubs and federations, which give them a center in which to engage in social activities independent of their children.

China and Hong Kong.   The social structure and ideology of China is considerably different from that of Westernized societies. China was traditionally an agricultural state ruled by a series of emperors. At the local level, the organization of the community was based upon the kinship group where filial piety prevailed (Treas, 1979). Women of all ages, as well as young people, had low status. In short, the older generations had power, prestige, and authority in family and community life, both of which were highly related.

In the late nineteenth century, contact with the West led to an influx of industrial technology, the beginning of foreign trade, and the urbanization of youth. As a result, the young in urban areas demanded more formal eduation. Once this was acquired, they began to question traditional values such as the lower status of women and automatic leadership by the elderly. At the same time, rural peasants were distressed by the economic situation and sought to overthrow the political system. Modernization, along with internal political unrest, combined to bring the Communists to power in 1949 after the Socialist Revolution (Cherry and Magnuson-Martinson, 1981). As a result, through the political ideology, equalization of age relationships was advocated, with a resulting loss of status by the aged and an increase in status by other age groups.

Although there is now generational independence, filial piety still exists since the old are housed with the young, but only in exchange for domestic and child care assistance. As Treas (1979) notes, traditional intergenerational assistance and respect prevail to a greater extent in rural areas, where the regime has imposed less age equalization order in the hope of not alienating the broad base of political support. In the urban areas, mandatory retirement and pensions are being introduced, and many of the elderly, particularly women, engage in voluntary work to maintain the respect of the community.

China and Hong Kong represent societies that reflect intracultural variation in the status of the aged (Ikels, 1975, 1980; Treas, 1979). There are at least three distinct social, cultural, and political structures: traditional Chinese rural villages; traditional Chinese urban communities; and the urban, non-Communist, industrialized society of Hong Kong. In the traditional rural villages, the status of the elderly remains high and they are cared for by the family (or by the community if their children have migrated from the village). In the pre-modernized cities of mainland China, there are few elderly people, since many return to their native village when they grow old. However, those who remain have high status, especially if they have the skills and education to continue performing functional tasks. If they do not have these skills, they are 'encouraged' to retire as early as age 50.

In Hong Kong, the potential for generational conflict is high. The elderly who experience the most difficulty are those who do not have relatives, or whose relatives are themselves economically deprived. In this situation, old people may be cared for by other elders or by neighbors in the community.

In summary, the Republic of China cannot, as yet, be classified as a modern nation. However, the onset of modernization, combined with political turmoil and the introduction of socialism, has led to a cultural and political revolution. As a result, although the status of the aged has declined, especially in the larger urban areas, the elderly have experienced a rise in their standard of living. Modernization cannot account totally for the increased status of youth and women. Political questioning of the need for age equality was also a significant factor, as it was in the United States prior to the onset of modernization (Fischer, 1977). However, a major difference between the United States and China is the active role played by the Chinese government in promoting an age-equalization policy, especially in light of the cultural tradition of filial piety not inherent in American culture. In short, as Treas (1979) and Cherry and Magnuson-Martinson (1981) suggest, age-stratification systems and the relative status of age groups do not exist in a political or cultural vacuum.

Middle Eastern and Western European Industrialized Societies

Israel.   Israel represents another example of how the process of aging and the status of the aged varies in an emerging society (Talmon, 1961; Weihl, 1970, 1972). The State of Israel was formed in 1948, although the first kibbutz was established by Jewish immigrants in 1909. A relatively new state, Israel is largely composed of immigrants who are classified as 'veterans' or 'non-veterans' (Weihl, 1970). The veterans emigrated early in life and developed the society; the non-veterans arrived later in life and had to adapt to existing institutions and norms. About 95 percent of the population over 65 (about 9 percent of the total population) is foreign-born, and many arrived after the age of 50. Generally, these immigrants came either from Eastern European countries or from the Middle East and the Orient.

The non-European aged, in general, have had more difficulty in adjusting because of their higher illiteracy rates and because Israeli pension payments are based on length of residency and employment in the country (Weihl, 1970). Because of economic necessity and cultural tradition, a large percentage of non-Europeans live with their children. In general, Israel provides marginal economic security for the elderly through social programs that reflect the traditional feelings of respect and concern for parents. However, these programs are not adequate since approximately 40 percent of the elderly live below the poverty line and another 30 percent only slightly above it (Schneider, 1981).

A unique feature of Israeli society is the kibbutz. A kibbutz is a group of 50 to 1,000 people who live in a self-sustaining economic and household community (Feder, 1972; Wershow, 1973). For the most part kibbutzes are agricultural cooperatives (although some industries have been established) that emphasize common ownership of property and equality in production and consumption. All members of the kibbutz must work hard to produce sufficient food and goods for themselves. The oldest men and women in the kibbutz are called *vatikim*. In addition to receiving the same benefits as regular members, they are usually given better-quality housing. They also benefit from close family bonding, since three generations usually live within the kibbutz.

This bonding has been a source of support in the past. However, there is increasing intergenerational conflict between young members, who wish to see the farming become more mechanized and the *vatikim*, who adhere to the philosophy of manual labor to produce goods. Although the elderly oppose retirement because it reflects a life without purpose or meaning, they nevertheless engage in a process of gradual retirement which involves lighter tasks and reduced hours of work. In this way, they become more dependent on communal institutions, and as their numbers increase because of longevity, they become a greater economic burden. As a result, some *kibbutzim* have established industries where the elderly can be assigned to work at easy but tedious tasks, thereby enabling them to continue in some functional capacity. However, for old women in particular, this creates a problem; they cannot adapt to the repetitive factory chores to which they are assigned.

In summary, although the system is not without social strain, the Israeli kibbutz represents a model in which many of the basic problems of aging (economic security, family and community relations, health care, and retirement) have been addressed and partially solved. This situation has evolved because of a religious and social commitment to equality regardless of age.

Norway and Great Britain.   These countries have both undergone rapid industrialization, with an accompanying increase in urbanization and changes in family and social structures. Both countries have lost young people through emigration. As a result, they are among the countries with the highest proportion of the population over 60 years of age (about 20 percent). In addition, both countries have evolved into welfare states which, while providing some economic security for the elderly, also deprive them of meaningful work roles.

In Norway (Pihlblad et al., 1972), the status of the aged is related to changes in inheritance customs and to the onset of mandatory retirement. In the past, land was transferred from the father to the oldest son, who was required by contract to care for his parents. However, when children migrated to the cities, the extended family system declined and the elderly either were left in the rural areas or followed their children to the city at some later date. This led to the perception that the aged were a 'social problem,' and to the subsequent introduction of social welfare programs. For most Norwegians, retirement is mandatory at 70 years of age, when they become eligible for a government pension, medical and housing assistance, and club memberships to enable them to 'rest on their oars' (Pihlblad et al., 1972:232) after having 'pulled their weight' for many years.

In short, government services seek to ensure that the elderly do not suffer from economic deprivation as they do in some countries. There seems to be a unique moral obligation, based on respect for past contributions, that enables the elderly to maintain a Norwegian lifestyle. However, in spite of these efforts, the elderly are often bitter over the loss of their work roles. In addition, there has been a decline in the special meaning and function of the traditional role of Norwegian grandparent. This has come about because of intergenerational mobility and the accompanying psychological and physical distances between generations.

Great Britain provides a social welfare system comparable to those of most European countries, although in Britain an individual is eligible for a pension if he or she retires at age 65. In contrast to Norway, 42 percent of the elderly in

Great Britain live with one of their children, probably because of strong kinship ties and a shortage of housing (Wedderburn, 1970). However, as in Japan, despite being physically integrated into the family older people often feel socially isolated. Finally, although various social services are provided for them, the elderly are seldom consulted about their needs or interests.

North American Societies

As relatively new societies made up of numerous ethnic and racial groups, Canada and the United States represent unique social structures and cultures. For this reason, it is extremely difficult to describe a modal pattern of aging in each country. Nevertheless, some features of these societies make the status of the aged different from the societies described previously.

The aged population is increasing both in absolute numbers and in proportion to the total population. This changing age structure is due to declining birth and immigration rates, combined with increased longevity. The onset of industrialization in these countries led to lifestyles characterized by increasing individualism, by rapid social change, by affluence, by increased geographical and social mobility, by automation, by higher literacy rates for each succeeding generation, and by an increasing number of women in the labor force. There are few customs or ceremonies associated with aging, other than birthday celebrations at ages 16, 21, 40, and 65. In fact, although children are socialized to respect the elderly, there is little evidence that this respect is put into practice in these youth-oriented societies.

Since status is intimately linked to work (and for many women, to the husband's occupation) in North America, retirement is a significant factor in the loss of status after about age 65. There also seems to be continued interaction and interdependence between parents and adult children, but to a lesser degree than in many other countries, partly because people are more likely to live in different communities or regions. Moreover, much of this interaction occurs indirectly via telephone and mail rather than in face-to-face contact. Because of mobility and the great variety of lifestyles in North America, the elderly seldom live with their adult children, but live instead in various housing arrangements — their own homes, retirement villages, age-segregated apartments, or homes for the aged.

Although aging and the aged in Canada and the United States are relatively similar, there are some important differences. First, Canada is more socialistic, perhaps because of its historical ties to Great Britain. As a result, the aged tend to receive larger (but still inadequate) government pensions. They also receive greater health care benefits through subsidized medical plans operated by the public and private sectors. Second, although the historical and social development of the two countries has followed a similar pattern, Canada has generally been slower in adopting new ideas, values, and norms. Third, the climate in Canada is not conducive to retirement villages, and many Canadian retirees, or 'snowbirds,' winter in the southern United States. Finally, most Canadian cities and towns have fewer native, ethnic, and racial minorities, and except for the native Inuit and Indian groups, those that do exist may be less disadvantaged and more acculturated than blacks or Hispanics in the United States. Canada does have a large French-Canadian (Francophone) population (22 percent) with different social, religious, and political values from those of the dominant anglophone population.

In summary, there are some cultural differences in the aging process between North American societies and other modernized societies. There are also Canadian and American differences in the process that will be discussed throughout the book, particularly with respect to public-sector support, adoption of new values, and language.

Aging and the Aged in Subcultures

The Concept of Subcultures

Within heterogeneous or pluralistic national cultures, there exist various unique subcultures. These may be natural groups based on race or ethnicity, or they may be created when members of a subgroup acquire and adhere to a set of norms, values, customs, behaviors, and attitudes that are different from those accepted and used within the larger society (Arnold, 1970; Gordon, 1947; Fischer, 1975). In some instances the group may use a different language, and may be separated from mainstream society in such homogeneous environments as a reservation, ghetto, barrio[6] or retirement community.

Wolfgang and Ferracuti (1967) suggest that a subculture may form when values and norms differ in content and importance from those of mainstream society, when they cease to be a fad and become stable over time, and when they begin to regulate the behavior of individuals in the group. Once these values and norms are adopted by a number of individuals, who may or may not interact with each other, they begin to influence the existing occupational and leisure lifestyles, or they lead to the creation of new lifestyles. This sharing of norms, values, attitudes, language, behavior, and dress gives the subgroup a distinct social identity, regardless of existing or previous social or physical commonalities. In addition, social categories such as age, race, ethnicity, religion, and occupation often serve as the initial catalysts in the formation of a subculture.[7]

Subcultural traits can develop either from the members being physically isolated from mainstream society (on a reservation), or from their self-imposed isolation because of different behavior, beliefs, or economic opportunities (in ghettoes or barrios). Through this process of isolation, and the growth of in-group solidarity via language, dress, or behavior, the degree of communication and social interaction with outsiders in mainstream society varies greatly.

The most common, intact, ascriptive-based subcultures are those based on race or ethnicity. In North America, many of these subcultures are also labelled as minority groups (Kent, 1971; Jackson, 1980; Cuellar et al., 1981). Many of these subgroups experience discrimination in varying degrees, leading to different opportunity structures, rewards, and privileges within mainstream society.

The various ethnic and racial groups are also stratified within mainstream society. As a result, members of a specific minority group may have varying lifestyles and life chances compared to individuals in other racial or ethnic groups. For example, Blau et al. (1979) found that ethnicity is a more powerful factor than age or social class on such lifestyle factors as educational attainment, the timing of role exits, health, self-concept, morale, and economic dependency. Minority-group women generally experience discrimination to a greater extent than other women, while Mexican-Americans experience discrimination to a greater extent than blacks or whites. It is important that the common characteristics of all minority groups, and the unique characteristics of specific subcultures, be examined with respect to the aging process.

Moore (1971a) has outlined five characteristics of minority subcultures. First, each subculture has a unique history, and the cultural origins and the life history of the group within the dominant society must be considered. Second, this history is often marked by discrimination, stereotypes, and repression, by restrictions on place of residence, and by persistence in retaining the native language. Third, there is great variation within subcultures, between individual groups (different Indian tribes) and within a specific group (blacks living in New York City versus blacks living in the rural South). Subcultures are often a heterogeneous mix of people in which differences in sex, education, language, social class, or place of residence can have a profound impact on aging and the aged.

A fourth characteristic of minority subcultures is that they often develop their own coping substructures (church, clubs, family) in order to survive independently of mainstream society. Finally, many subcultures experience social change within the group that can influence their lifestyle in different ways. For example, older blacks may adhere to a philosophy of 'Uncle Tomism' in which they accept discrimination and second-class status. In contrast, younger blacks may be more likely to adhere to 'black power' values and ideals in which they seek equality in society, sometimes by the use of force or by legislation (Affirmative Action).

Although there is a need to understand the process of aging within the various subcultures, a number of problems are associated with obtaining this information (Ujimoto, 1981). First, like cross-cultural studies, analyses of subcultures have been primarily descriptive, qualitative studies of one specific social milieu. Structural characteristics and meanings may be described that do not apply across all strata within a particular subculture. Another problem is that of distinguishing subcultural boundaries from each other (the black subculture and the subculture of poverty), and from the dominant culture itself (a subcultural norm discrepant with a cultural norm may still lie within a tolerable range of behavior for those sharing the cultural norm). Sending children to a separate school where particular religious or social values are taught may be viewed as a discrepant subcultural norm still within the range of acceptable behavior for the society.

A third problem is identifying the extent to which the individual is influenced by or committed to the norms and values of the subculture; for example, the extent to which the lifestyles of elderly blacks are influenced by the black subculture. Another problem is the extent to which scientists, who are not members of the group, are able to obtain valid evidence from members of subcultural groups. If the scientists and the members of the group are unable to speak the language, or if the scientists are unable to understand the in-group jargon, the data may be misinterpreted. Similarly, members of the subgroup may be suspicious of researchers and may mislead them or present the 'ideal' response rather than describe the real situation. Finally, research of this type often depends on a convenience sample. Hence, the lower- and lower-middle-class segments may be neglected because of language difficulties or because of their reluctance to participate.

In order to appreciate these subcultural diversities in life chances (a social structural factor) and lifestyle (a cultural factor), the process of aging and the status of the aged in a number of subcultures will be described. Most of the subcultures are located in North America, and illustrate the cultural diversity of Canada and the United States.

Indigenous Subcultures

Indigenous people are those whose ancestors were the original inhabitants of a region or country. In most situations, these people have either been assimilated to varying degrees because of social, political, or technological change, or have retained their original identity by remaining isolated from the mainstream. The following subsection describes aging among two groups indigenous to North America, and one that is unique to the Soviet Union.

The Inuit of North America.   Although the native peoples of Northern Alaska and Northern Canada are increasingly experiencing modernization, many still belong to nomadic, premodernized tribes that live just outside, but in contact with, the modern world. In these societies the aged are not stigmatized, even though there are social labels for older men and women. In the Inuit society men are called *ituq* when they are about 50 years old. This labelling process occurs when they can no longer hunt year-round. Similarly, women are called *ninquiq* at about 60, when they give up the more strenuous domestic chores (Guemple, 1969). The definition of old age is related to biological aging, and is initiated by withdrawal of the elderly from active participation in economic or domestic work. This occurs because of declining strength or health. However, this labelling can be delayed by a 'renewal' process in which the older man works to complete his hunting in the spring and summer, or takes a younger woman as a wife. For the older woman, this renewal process involves adopting a child she hopes will take care of her in old age (Guemple, 1969).

The elderly are assured of constant care by two interacting social institutions, the extended family and the community (Guemple, 1980), both of which are based on communal sharing. As long as an individual can contribute in some way, he or she is considered a part of the community and receives assistance. However, if their children leave the community, as happens more frequently today, and if the elderly can no longer make a contribution, they may be viewed as parasites and abandoned or killed. This occurs not through indifference but through necessity. This early death is more likely to occur if modern assistance, such as federal pensions and health care, is not yet available. Interestingly, because of subcultural folklore, the elderly accept this imposed death. The Inuit believe that their names and social identity remain in an underworld at death and later enter the body of a newborn child. Because of this belief, they die willingly, knowing that their identity will live on in the community. With the increasing conversion of tribes to Christianity, however, this belief is becoming less prevalent.

North American Indians.   Unlike the Inuit, the Indian has interacted to a greater extent with white settlers, explorers, and government personnel. In this interaction they have fared badly, despite living in relatively close contact with modernized North America. The Indian is today among the least visible and most deprived of the minority groups in North America. At present, between 30 and 50 percent of Indians live on reservations in rural areas in Canada and the United States. Although there is great cultural diversity among tribes, generally their lifestyle and life chances lead to economic deprivation, an average life span of about 50 years, hunger and malnutrition, little educational opportunity, substandard housing, and difficulty in obtaining regular employment.

In short, members of this subculture are often alienated from traditional lifestyles, resentful and suspicious of mainstream society, and relatively powerless to change their social and economic conditions. Rogers and Gallion (1978), in their study of elderly Pueblo Indians, suggested that there are some characteristics common to most Indian tribes that make them different from mainstream society. These include a deep-rooted loyalty to and identification with the family and tribe, rather than loyalty to the self; a great respect for the elderly and their traditional values and lifestyle; a feeling of stress as a result of acculturation and contact with mainstream society; and a population that is increasing rapidly and in which the elderly make up a smaller and smaller percentage of the total Indian population.

Given the harsh living conditions of most Indians, it is easy to imagine that the plight of the elderly Indian is generally worse than that of the elderly person in mainstream society (Levy, 1967; Doherty, 1971; Goldstine and Gutmann, 1972; Jeffries, 1972; Murdock and Schwartz, 1978; Rogers and Gallion, 1978). However, even though over 50 percent of the Indian population over 65 years of age live on reservations, relatively little information is available on the aging process in this unique subculture.[8]

Like many premodern people, the elders, at least in the past, received respect and held power as long as they contributed to the society. However, with the onset of modernization on the reservations, with the migration of children to the cities, and with the necessity (in the United States) to transfer land to an heir in order to be eligible for federal assistance, the elderly have lost this culture-based respect and power. Moreover, even if their children live on the reservation, they generally have inadequate incomes and have difficulty supporting themselves, let alone their parents.

For elderly Indians who receive social and financial assistance, the total annual income is generally below the poverty line, which is the minimum amount needed for bare subsistence. In addition, many of these elderly Indians support unemployed children and their families on this limited income (Williams, 1980). The status of the aged Indian is lowered further by a lifetime of poor health compounded by a lack of access to health care facilities. Most reservations have no nursing care facilities, and elderly Indians who need regular health care must enter a nursing home away from the familiar lifestyle of the reservation. There, they will seldom have access to their native food, they may see family and friends infrequently, and will often experience cultural shock.

Indians who migrate to urban settings learn that marketable skills are necessary to survival. Those who are educated in the public school system and who adopt Christianity and the values of mainstream society generally show less respect for the aged. These young, educated Indians are increasingly occupying leadership roles, which in the past were held only by the elders. This shift in power and prestige results in intergenerational conflict (Williams, 1980).

In summary, the elderly on reservations experience poverty, malnutrition, loss of respect, and poor general health. Despite the intervention of federal health and financial assistance programs, the aged still suffer higher unemployment, more substandard living conditions, and greater poverty than any other minority group in North America. While other ethnic and racial groups have been assimilated into the dominant culture to some degree, the Indian, like the Eskimo, has remained both culturally and physically isolated. Because statistics indicate that Indians have a shorter life expectancy than whites, it has been argued that the eligible age for federal assistance should be lowered from 60 to 45 years of age. In this way, a larger number would then be eligible to collect assistance earlier in life.

The Abkhasians of the Georgian Republic. This society of collective farms in and around rural villages is located in the Caucasus Mountains in the southern U.S.S.R. It has become identified as a unique subculture because of the vitality and apparent longevity of its citizens. It is estimated that within this society 2.6 percent of the population is over 90 years of age, compared to only 0.1 percent throughout the rest of the Soviet Union (Benet, 1974; Pitskhelauri, 1982). In this society the elderly are highly valued, and their prestige increases with age. This is one reason birth records, if they exist at all, may be altered: people wish to appear older than they actually are and thereby acquire greater status.

The Abkhasians work at their own pace from childhood to death, and are never fully retired. Throughout there is stability in lifestyle, with an emphasis on the attitude that work is essential for everyone regardless of age. These people appear physically younger than their years, and they have the culturally induced expectation and the hope that they will live long lives.

Although an explanation for this longevity is lacking, heredity, combined with various sociocultural factors, seems to account for the extended life. Longevity in this subculture may be influenced by many factors: a system of folk medicine; a low-calorie, low-cholesterol diet of vegetables and milk; lack of competition among workers; and a strong bond with a large extended family, including nonrelatives who have the same surname. All of these combine to provide a serene, secure, and healthy lifestyle. However, as Benet (1974) notes, the younger generation is consuming more calories per day than earlier generations, and the Soviet government has introduced worker competition into the collective system. It will be interesting to observe whether these and other factors change the longevity and status of the elderly in the next century.

Racial Subcultures

Racial subcultures are those in which such ascribed physical features as skin color, eyelid fold, or physical stature predominate to make the members appear different from those in mainstream society. However, it is not the physical characteristics that set them apart socially, politically, or economically.[9] It is the social meanings assigned to these features by the dominant group which views itself as superior. Adherence to subcultural values and attitudes by members of the minority group will also set them apart. It must be stressed, however, that there is great variation within subcultures, just as there is within mainstream society (Fujii, 1980). For example, although a majority of blacks are located in the lower socioeconomic stratum, they are also found in the middle and upper levels. Thus, not everyone in the subculture ages or experiences the later years in a similar way. The next subsection examines how aging and the status of the aged among blacks differs from that of mainstream society.[10]

Black Americans. Although a number of articles about elderly black Americans have been written (Jackson, 1970, 1971; Wylie, 1971; Dowd and Bengtson, 1978; Davis, 1980a; Davis, 1980b), and although we know more about blacks than about other minority groups in North America, we still rely mainly on descriptive information for the inferences we make. It is more difficult to understand the process of aging in this subculture, because the group is more heterogeneous than others with respect to education, income, health, and occupational status.

Blacks comprise the largest minority group in the United States, with an estimated population of approximately 30 million, or about 14 percent of the total. Only about 8 percent of all blacks are over 65 years of age. While their life expectancy is less than that of whites up to age 65, it increases and surpasses that of whites after about 70. Of the 50 percent of blacks that live in the north, 60 percent live in the inner core of large cities, while those who live in the south tend to live in rural areas. This inner-city environment, combined with limited social participation and opportunities in American society, greatly influences the aging process for blacks.

In order to understand and appreciate the process of aging as experienced by a majority of black Americans, it is necessary to outline briefly the social milieu and the social structure in which they age. First, a high percentage of blacks are raised in slightly larger families than whites, although this tendency is decreasing each year. In many cases they live in substandard housing in urban ghettos or in impoverished rural areas, with inadequate nutrition or health care. In this subculture of poverty they encounter crime, receive inadequate schooling, and lack recreational programs and facilities.

In general, blacks have a lower level of educational attainment. This, combined with various forms of discrimination,[11] leads to unemployment or underemployment, and a perpetuation of their poverty. The pattern of labor-force involvement for blacks is often irregular and is characterized by high unemployment, periodic employment, or employment at low wages in less desirable occupations. This is especially true in southern rural areas. Not surprisingly, a higher percentage of black women at all ages seek employment. Moreover, elderly black women without husbands, or whose husbands are ineligible for public or private pension benefits, are often required to remain in the labor force longer and more regularly than black men in order to survive.

These employment patterns combine to lower the eligibility of blacks for private and public pension or assistance plans in old age. Also, this problem of unemployment and underemployment is more critical during times of double-digit inflation, when the gap between black and white income widens further, thereby worsening black poverty. Finally, the continuing tendency of young blacks to migrate from the rural south to the urban north places a greater stress on middle-aged and old blacks who must compete with these youths for scarce positions, many of which demand heavy physical labor.

In summary, throughout the life cycle many blacks have a lower quality of life than whites because of lower levels of education; high unemployment, irregular employment, or underemployment; physically demanding jobs; substandard housing; greater exposure to crime; and inadequate diet and health care. These problems are compounded in later life when income decreases further or ceases altogether, and when health declines (there is a higher incidence of illness and disability among the black population). At the same time many blacks must keep working as long as possible to supplement a low and often inadequate retirement income.

It is relatively easy to describe the status of the aging black American. First, between 35 and 40 percent of blacks may live at or below the poverty line, even if they are partially employed, and even if they receive some federal financial assistance (Fujii, 1980). This often occurs because they have not been in the labor force long enough or consistently enough to be eligible for partial or full benefits, or because their jobs were not included in private or public pension plans (Dowd and Bengtson, 1978). Moreover, the poverty that increases with age is more likely to occur in the urban areas, especially among black women, who generally live longer and often have no husband. Although the number of elderly blacks living in poverty has been decreasing since the late 1960s, the onset of double-digit inflation may reverse this trend in the 1980s.

The second most pressing problem for elderly blacks, and one that is related to poverty, is health. Compared to whites, aging blacks have higher death rates, greater incidences of illness and disability, less access to quality medical care and preventive health services, a lower standard of living, and inadequate diets. A large percentage have never been enrolled in a government or private medical insurance program.

For elderly blacks, the family is a primary source of assistance, since many homes include members from three generations. Also, because of congested living conditions in the inner cores of large cities, children often live near their parents. Elderly blacks rarely enter nursing homes, because of the cost, because their families prefer to provide support, or because there is discrimination in the treatment they receive. This pattern of strong family support among blacks is linked to such historically based values as ancestor worship, reverence for the aged, and support of the extended family (Wylie, 1971; Davis, 1980b).

Chinese and Japanese North Americans. Although they form two distinct subcultural groups, both the Chinese and Japanese in Canada and the United States have relatively similar cultural backgrounds. The first generation, who were foreign-born, were socialized to the traditional values of individual dependence on the family, the importance of the family for social support, and the necessity of obedience to and respect for the eldest members of the family and community. This first-generation group has had great difficulty in adjusting to growing old in a foreign culture (Kalish and Moriwaki, 1973; Ujimoto, 1981). While the problem is less severe for each succeeding generation born in North America, the problems of being part of a subculture remain. For example, each generation has experienced a degree of discrimination, although less so than Indians and blacks. The Chinese and Japanese in North America appear to adapt more easily to the post-retirement years than do blacks, Indians or Hispanic Americans. As with most subcultures, there are variations in economic, educational, and health status within each group. This is particularly so among the more recent generations that have experienced considerable social mobility. Thus, when examining the current status of the elderly Asian North American, it is important to distinguish between those who are foreign-born and those who are native-born.

It is also important to distinguish between elderly Chinese North Americans (Cheng, 1978) and elderly Japanese North Americans (Ishizuka, 1978). Although there are many similarities in the cultures and patterns of historical entry into North America, there are also significant differences. For example, among the Chinese, there are still a large number of elderly single males whose families or brides were never permitted to emigrate. Older Japanese women are well represented, because they live longer and because Japanese brides were permitted to emigrate. Thus, the early-generation Chinese elder is often a man with no family, and the elderly Japanese is more likely to be a woman with a family. In addition, the Japanese are generally more integrated within a community, while the Chinese are more likely to live in segregated Chinatowns within large urban centers, especially on the West Coasts of Canada and the United States. This living pattern has inhibited assimilation into the dominant culture.

The Chinese emigrated to North America in two major waves (Wu, 1975). The first to arrive were young, illiterate, unskilled male laborers who came during the 1850s to work as 'coolies' on the railways and in the gold mines. They came from Canton province, and most intended to make their fortune, buy land in China, and return to live on that land in their old age. However, this group stayed in North America, despite experiencing discrimination and hostility. As a result, many withdrew into the relative security of urban Chinatowns, or lived in small towns where they opened laundries or restaurants to serve mainstream society. The second wave of Chinese immigrants, the Mandarins, arrived after 1948 when the Communists occupied mainland China. Most of these immigrants were older Chinese who were permitted to leave. Because of their age, few learned English. This remains a problem since only about 1 percent of elderly Chinese speak or read English (Fujii, 1980). As a result, they often lack knowledge about services available to them within the community.

Throughout their lives both groups were employed in low-paying jobs, most of which did not include eligibility for private or government pension plans. For the first generation in each immigrant cohort, life was characterized by poverty, illiteracy, adherence to traditional cultural values, and generally poor health because of inadequate access to medical care (Carp and Kataoka, 1976). With each subsequent generation, the importance of an education has been emphasized, especially for boys. Consequently, many Chinese North American professionals and businessmen now serve both the Chinese and dominant cultures. Moreover, each succeeding generation has sought and generally achieved social mobility within the dominant social system.

The situation of the elderly Chinese North American is closely related to whether childhood socialization took place in China or North America. Those who were socialized in China are more likely to adhere to traditional Chinese values, which are often different from those of their children. The older Cantonese in North America are more likely to be men with no families who are in poor health, who lack access to recreational facilities, who use drugs frequently, and who have a high suicide rate. Kalish and Moriwaki (1973) refer to these individuals as 'geriatric orphans.' For both groups, even where a family exists the value of filial piety is seldom adhered to by subsequent generations. Because they are ineligible for many forms of government financial and social assistance, elderly Chinese people survive on a limited income, often by living with others in a single room, usually within Chinatown.

A major problem of the elderly Chinese has been their inability to afford adequate medical care and their inability to communicate their personal health problems to English-speaking medical personnel. This problem increases when they are institutionalized in nursing homes where they are often unable to communicate with English-speaking staff or fellow residents, and where they usually do not have access to their ordinary diet. They become even more isolated in this environment than they were in the larger society.

With the increasing level of education and income acquired by each succeeding generation, the status of elderly Chinese North Americans is improving, and will increasingly parallel the status of aging white Americans and Canadians. While elements of the subculture may always have some impact on the individual, this will be less traumatic as acculturation occurs among future generations. In fact, there is some evidence that cultural roots can be of special significance in enhancing the status of minority elders compared to the status of many elderly in mainstream society. This occurs when special institutions and services are established by and for members of the subculture, with or without government assistance (Wu, 1975).

Japanese North Americans appear to be a racial group that is more socially and economically advantaged, at all ages, than other minority groups. However, this was not always the case. Like the Cantenese immigrants, Japanese immigrants arrived in North America after the 1880s to seek their fortune and then return to Japan. Like the Chinese, the first wave (the Issei) were primarily unskilled laborers, many of whom were second or later-born sons who migrated because their older brothers had inherited the family land and wealth. Unlike the Chinese, however, they were permitted to bring their wives and families or to send for Japanese brides. They formed nuclear families (Osako, 1979), although, as Kitano (1976) has noted, they had a low birth rate.

The Japanese stressed the importance of learning English and attaining an education so that their children could obtain better jobs. Despite being imprisoned as possible traitors and being forced to sell their property during World War II, the first- and second-generation Japanese in North America have attained a higher socioeconomic status than most other minority groups. This is remarkable, because they did not have easy access to higher education, to jobs, or to the vote.

Most elderly Japanese North Americans are widows, are in good health, and live as independently as possible since housing is not generally a problem (Montero, 1980a, 1980b). Elderly Japanese of the first (Issei) generation know little English; the third (Sansei) and fourth (Yonsei) generations know little, if any, Japanese. While this creates intergenerational communication problems for some elderly people, it also reveals that the Japanese in North America are less tied to their cultural roots, although there is still respect and support for the family and elders.

Despite the social mobility and cultural assimilation experienced by second- and third-generation Japanese Americans, the quality of relationships with elderly parents has not declined. Osako (1979) notes that the old receive assistance from their children and adjust to a state of dependency and reduced authority without losing self-esteem. This occurs because both generations adhere to the tradition of group goal-orientation, rather than to an individualistic ethic emphasizing self-improvement.

Although relatively little is known about this racial subculture, there appear to be fewer unique problems associated with aging, perhaps because the Japanese North Americans have sought assimilation into the dominant culture. In fact, in recent years there has been a trend toward increased inter-racial marriage and greater suburbanization. These processes hasten assimilation and further weaken traditional values and the solidarity of the group (Kiefer, 1974; Osako, 1979). As a result, the meaning and experience of old age become similar to those of the dominant culture.

Ethnic Subcultures

Ethnic subcultures are those in which cultural characteristics such as language, religion, or national origin influence lifestyle and life chances. In the United States and Canada, many ethnic groups have emigrated at specific historical periods and been subsequently acculturated to varying degrees. Some common examples are the Irish in Boston, the Poles in Chicago, the Ukranians in Western Canada, the Scots in Nova Scotia, and the Italians in Toronto and Boston. In addition, large ethnic groups such as the French Canadians in Quebec have formed a distinct major culture with their own institutions within the larger society. These ethnic groups provide a framework of common values, identity, and history as well as a social network providing assistance and friendship. In short, ethnicity, like race, can influence how specific individuals adapt to the aging process (Gelfand and Kutzik, 1979; Gelfand, 1981, 1982; Holzberg, 1982).

Mexican Americans.   Other than demographic information, relatively little is known about aging within the Mexican American (Chicano) or Hispanic subcultures. These people, who make up the second-largest minority group in the United States, number about 7 million, and are found mainly in the southwestern United states. The two main groups are the descendants of those who occupied the land when the southwest was controlled by Spain or Mexico, and the recent immigrants from Mexico who cross the border to find work. Of these, many are illegal immigrants, and a high percentage are unable to read, write, or speak English.[12]

The current cohort of elderly Chicanos was raised in a rural environment. However, many now live in urban areas that foster different values, attitudes, and expectations (Maldonado, 1975). This contrasts sharply with younger Mexican Americans who have been socialized in urban barrios. Generally, it has been found that Mexican Americans have a high birth rate and a low life expectancy. Only about 4 percent of all Mexican Americans are over 65 years of age. The cycle of poverty may be a major factor in this low life expectancy. Language barriers and inadequate education force workers into low-paying, physically demanding jobs, if indeed regular employment is even obtained. Moreover, as Dowd and Bengtson (1978) have reported, the average income of Mexican Americans decreases by 62 percent between 45 and 75 years of age, compared with a decrease of 36 percent for white Americans. Because of this inadequate income Mexican Americans often have deficient diets and live in substandard housing. They have little, if any, access to Spanish-speaking physicians, especially in rural areas.

Given this life of low income and isolation from mainstream society, it is not surprising that approximately 35 percent of aged Mexican Americans live below the poverty line (Fujii, 1980). Many are ineligible for Social Security benefits, either because their employment was not covered or because they are illegal aliens. Furthermore, since many are unable to communicate in English, they may not be aware of available local or federal assistance programs.

Regardless of their impoverished status, most elderly Mexican Americans prefer to remain in substandard housing within their cultural group. In fact, this has been cited as a major factor in their underutilization of nursing homes and other health services, despite their need for institutionalized health care in the later years (Eribes and Bradley-Rawls, 1978). Most recently, Newquist (1981) identified a number of sociocultural barriers that may limit access to needed health care by older Mexican Americans: (1) group attitudes toward the need for treatment which are often influenced by religious and cultural beliefs and customs; (2) the availability of and cultural dependence on folk practitioners and folk remedies; (3) economic barriers created by expensive health care; (4) geographic barriers (the need to travel a great distance from the barrio for treatment); (5) language barriers; and (6) perceived discrimination in the treatment of minority-group patients.

Although it is often assumed that the aged are cared for by the extended family within the barrio because of cultural norms, this is not always the case. Although some aged parents live with their children in a barrio or on a farm, some studies have shown that the elderly have been abandoned in rural areas and that within urban areas there is an increasing gap between the young and old that discourages sharing and interaction (Moore, 1971b; Maldonado, 1975; Alvirez and Bean, 1976; Fujii, 1980). In fact, one study found that 61 percent of younger Chicanos did not believe the family had an obligation to support the elderly parents (Crouch, 1972).

Many of these changes in values have resulted from urbanization and a loss of attachment to the agrarian way of life, in which the extended family was essential for survival. With the movement to urban barrios, there has been more pressure for children to ensure that their own nuclear family survives. At the same time, the elderly have sought to remain independent so as not to burden their better-educated, socially mobile children. Even where support of aging parents may be a necessity and is still practiced, it may not be the preferred pattern (Alvirez and Bean, 1976). Furthermore, where this pattern of support exists, the quality of the relationship may be low in that not all of the physical, emotional, or psychological needs of the aging parents are met. Finally, Maldonado (1975) suggests that the failure of government agencies to provide services to aged Mexican Americans is based on the assumption that they are not needed because the elderly are cared for within the extended family. This assumption is increasingly being challenged, and more social and economic assistance is being directed toward the needy and abandoned aged within this subculture.

Rural and Religious Subcultures

Rural subcultures.   Although rural lifestyles changed dramatically with the onset of industrialization and the accompanying mechanization of farming, rural life is still quite distinct from urban life. Rural areas also differ greatly from each other: some are wealthy, some are impoverished; some are isolated, some are within commuting distance of metropolitan areas. In a rural environment, lifestyles are influenced by such factors as an agricultural economic base; low population density; geographical isolation; fewer social, health, and recreational services than in urban areas; an out-migration of young people to urban centers; a social life revolving around the family and community; later retirement; and limited public transportation facilities.

Rural life is often further influenced by homogeneous religious or ethnic traditions and values. As a result, a folk society tends to persist; there is an emphasis on traditions, roots, kinship, helping others in the community, independence, and rigid adherence to religious, ethnic, and community values (Youmans, 1967, 1977; Ansello and Cipolla, 1980).

In the early twentieth century, living in a rural environment in old age often meant a struggle to survive, especially before universal pension plans were introduced (Wershow, 1975; Synge, 1980). During this time a father held on to his land as long as he was able to work. When his health declined, control was passed either to the oldest son, or to all sons who stayed on the farm out of a sense of responsibility for the parents. Arensberg and Kimball (1940) found that farmers in rural western Ireland protected their positions by controlling land and information until it could be exchanged for perpetual support. The adult sons lived in the parent's house and were dependent on the father before they assumed control of the farm. Similarly, Synge (1980) notes that in rural Ontario the father maintained control, but that sons built their own homes on the family property and contributed to the welfare of the extended family.

The elderly were assured some degree of security by controlling information and wealth in the family and in the community (Maxwell and Silverman, 1970; Lozier and Althouse, 1974). Farmers who experienced the most difficulty in the later years were often those who were childless. They were almost totally dependent on neighbors or hired laborers for assistance (Synge, 1980). Thus, old age in the early twentieth century was not a time of retirement and leisure for most farm couples.

With the onset of rural modernization, however, and the out-migration of youth, the elderly in rural areas have been caught between traditional and modern cultures. Although there is great diversity within a rural culture (which may accommodate professionals, businessmen, farm owners, farm laborers, or industrial workers), there seem to be common patterns in the aging process. In many rural areas the incidence of poverty, substandard housing, and poor health is higher than in urban areas. Moreover, where there is a widely dispersed population it is difficult to deliver social or health services, particularly in-home health care. This lack of access to services is often compounded by the lack of transportation.

When their children migrate to cities or other regions of the country, the rural elderly are often isolated. They become highly dependent on other aging neighbors and on often inadequate social services. They are in many cases the victims of triple jeopardy — they are old, poor, and isolated. The end result is a restricted social life that often involves 'retirement to the porch' (Lozier and Althouse, 1975). This restricted lifestyle may not be conducive to their mental or physical health. Moreover, this pattern of infrequent intergenerational contact is foreign to their value system and to their past experiences.

Religious subcultures.   Although new religious subcultures (or cults) have arisen within urban centers in recent years, some of the established religious groups chose a rural, pastoral lifestyle many years ago. The Amish, the Mennonites, and the Hutterites are a few of the distinctive, separate religious subcultures that survive in rural areas throughout North America. In urban areas, Jews represent the epitome of a religious group that places a high value on the study of gerontology, and on the care of their elderly (Gelfand and Olsen, 1979; Cottle, 1980).

In the Middle East, the Druze are a minority religious sect (Gutmann, 1976). They live in highland villages in Syria and Israel, and follow a traditional way of life in an agricultural economy. In order to coexist with the dominant Muslim world from which they are separated, they raise their sons to be policemen and soldiers for the majority government. For the Druze, religion is central to their identity and way of life, particularly for men. The basic tenets of the religion are kept secret from the outside world, from all Druze women, and from young Druze males who are labelled *jahil*, or 'the unknowing ones.'

As a man enters late middle age, he is invited to become an *agil* and receive a copy of the secret religious text. If he accepts this invitation he gives up alcohol and tobacco and devotes a great deal of time to prayer. As men age, their lives become almost completely ruled by religious duties. Admittance to the religious sect gives men increasing power as they age, because they are thought to serve as a passive interface between Allah and the community. As Gutmann (1976:107) notes, the older Druze 'switches his allegiance from the norms that govern the productive and secular life to those that govern the traditional and moral life.' Religion enables men to continue being active in the community, but on a different level and for a different purpose from when they were younger.

The Poverty Subculture

A unique subculture is present in almost every large city. It is made up of homeless people who live in single-room dwellings or who sleep in parks, subways, or alleys on or near skid row. These individuals, primarily men, comprise a transient, impoverished subculture. They experience physical, social, and psychological disadvantages. In order to explain the existence of skid rows from a social-psychological perspective, Bogue (1963) theorized that men arrive on skid row for the following reasons, ranked in order of importance: economic difficulties, poor mental health combined with alcoholism, poor social adjustment, or physical handicaps. He also suggested that a skid row exists to provide a milieu in which homeless persons can be rehabilitated.

Tindale (1980) interviewed 60- to 75-year-old indigents who were 16 to 20 years of age during the Depression in the 1930s. He found that these men had a lifestyle of poverty before, during, and after the Depression and that they were never able to establish a regular pattern of employment. They often experienced marriage failure, drank heavily, and suffered from poor health. While the Depression made it difficult for them to get established, it was not the Depression per se that led them to a skid-row existence. As Tindale (1980:94) notes, they are 'both the product and the producers of their history.' Now that these old men no longer work, they have little if any contact with their family. They survive and cope with the aging process (except for the physical problems) because life after 65 is not very different from that before 65. The skid-row subculture provides a certain kind of security. Its residents are respected and unthreatened by their fellow indigents with whom they share money and goods in order to survive (Rooney, 1976).

Even with increased social assistance and urban renewal (Eckert, 1979), skid-row populations may not be decreasing. Indigent people may move to single-room occupancy (SRO) hotels in other parts of a city as skid-row areas are redeveloped. However, as Cohen and Sokolovsky (1980) report, many skid-row occupants, because of their previous occupational levels and patterns, have lower monthly incomes than the usual SRO dwellers and may be unable to pay the weekly rent. Thus, they truly become homeless. Also, by being unable to live in a SRO hotel they lose the benefit of assistance from hotel staff as their health deteriorates (Erikson and Eckert, 1977).

In summary, as Bahr and Caplow (1973) concluded, many of the characteristics of skid-row life result from the interaction of poverty, personality problems, and aging (Stephens, 1976). Skid row is often the net that catches single men and a few women (Lally et al., 1979), and locks them into what is essentially an institutionalized way of coping with aging across the life cycle.

Summary: Aging and Subcultures

In pluralistic societies such as Canada and the United States, there is a need to understand the culture and lifestyle of the various racial, ethnic, and other groups that comprise the heterogeneous population.[13] Subcultural groups often have a number of common social characteristics, such as poor education, high rates of unemployment, low incomes, inadequate health care, lack of facility in the English language, and substandard housing. However, there are also many differences between groups, differences that reflect unique cultural backgrounds and specific histories in North America. These differences influence the aging process for members of a particular subculture. This influence often depends on the extent to which the group is isolated from the dominant culture through discrimination or self-segregation. Similarly, the influence of the subculture on individual members depends on the extent to which cultural roots are rejected, and on the degree to which the person is assimilated into the structure and value system of the dominant culture.

For those who are now old, the indigenous, racial, or ethnic subculture appears to have a significant influence on lifestyle (Cantor, 1976). These elderly people have historically had less access to the life chances that were available to many of their age peers. Their disadvantaged situation does not improve, and indeed may worsen. Moreover, they are likely to adhere to their basic cultural values, customs, and beliefs, and are often unable to function in a rapidly changing world. Even their children become strangers when they adopt different values and lifestyles.

In short, to understand the aging process within subcultures, such factors as subcultural values, inadequate incomes, the culture gap between generations, lower life expectancy, and linguistic differences must be considered. These elements can create handicaps that influence life chances and lifestyles. They can be particularly influential when isolation, racial or ethnic discrimination, and age discrimination combine to influence the economic and health status of the aged.

Summary and Conclusions

This chapter has defined the concepts of culture and subculture, and indicated how the status of the aged and the process of aging varies across cultures and subcultures. The aging process and the status of the aged was described for a number of preliterate and literate preindustrialized societies, and for a number of industrialized and modernized societies. Particular emphasis was given to the impact of the process and rate of modernization on the function and status of the elderly. The status of the aged was described within a variety of indigenous, racial, ethnic, rural, and religious subcultures, primarily in a North American context.

Based on the information presented in this chapter, it can be concluded that:

1. The meaning of aging, the status of the aged, and the process of aging varies across cultures and subcultures, and at different historical periods.

2. While some universal patterns in the aging process and the status of the aged are observed, cultural and subcultural variations are numerous.

3. In hunting-and-gathering societies where there was a surplus of food, the older members (at least until they became infirm) generally held influential positions in the social, political, and religious spheres of tribal life. They were considered to be a source of knowledge of rituals and survival skills.

4. In rural, agrarian, and peasant societies where the elderly own or control the land, power and status are retained until the land is transfered to a son.

5. It is frequently assumed that the elderly lose power and status when a society becomes industrialized and modernized. To date, the evidence is conflicting. In some societies the status of the elderly declines following modernization; in some, their status declined before modernization, often after an industrial revolution; in some, their status remained at the pre-modernized level; in some, their status declined even without the onset of

modernization; and in some, their status declined initially following modernization, but eventually increased after social and technological changes had taken place.

6. Even where support of aging parents is a cultural or subcultural norm, it may not be the preferred pattern. As a result, the quality of the relationship may be low and the physical, emotional, or psychological needs of the aging parents may not be met.

7. The subculture of some racial, ethnic, and religious groups can have an influence on the process of aging, particularly on the status and treatment of the elderly. Subcultural factors can influence life chances and lifestyles, especially if there is a significant intergenerational cultural gap between aging parents and their children or grandchildren.

Notes

1. Generally, two levels of culture have been identified. High culture, which in Western society includes classical music, ballet, theatre, poetry, and the fine arts, has traditionally been considered the domain of the upper class or well-educated social elite. Mass or popular culture is made up of those cultural elements that are transmitted via the press, the electronic media, or other forms of mass communication. However, Gans (1974) has also derived five 'taste' cultures wherein age and social class strongly influence who identifies with each level. These include high culture, upper-middle culture, lower-middle culture, low culture, and quasi-folk culture.

2. Surprisingly, few historians have been interested in historical analyses of the aging process or the status of the aged. There is a need for demographic and socio-cultural historical approaches to the analysis of aging and the aged (Fischer, 1977; Achenbaum, forthcoming).

3. An interesting and thorough overview of aging throughout history is described by Hendricks and Hendricks (1981:29–80).

4. One of the most useful functions of any theory is to stimulate criticism and new creative work in the area. This will become more evident when the disengagement theory of aging is discussed in chapter 4.

5. Achenbaum and Stearns (1978) suggest that the concept of modernization may be more appropriate for tracing the development of the changing status of the aged in Britain, France, Germany, and North America, and that it may not be appropriate for Japan, Russia, Turkey, and Latin American nations.

6. A barrio is a Mexican American residential community within a large city in the southwestern United States, where Spanish is spoken almost exclusively, and a strong cultural identity is maintained.

7. Theories to explain the process of subcultural emergence and development have been proposed by Arnold (1970), Cohen (1955), Shibutani (1955), and Pearson (1979).

8. Little information is available because of the inaccessibility of many reservations, language problems, a general mistrust of outsiders, and a determination to keep Indian culture, lifestyle, social structure, and problems private.

9. Otherwise, why not differentially evaluate people by eye color, hair color (which can be changed to make one more socially acceptable), or shoe size?

10. Unfortunately, there is a paucity of information on this subject. That which is available is often based on stereotypes or inadequate samples.

11. For example, it is claimed that blacks are often paid less than whites who perform the same job; this is known as 'unequal pay for equal work.' Similarly, blacks may have unequal opportunities for advancement and therefore earn lower incomes.

12. This is perhaps a major reason why we know so little about their lifestyle. They are suspicious of social scientists and refuse to be interviewed, or they are unable to be interviewed because of a language barrier (Delgado and Finley, 1978).

13. The literature on aging in minority groups has given little attention to three subject areas, all of which are worthy of further research: transportation/mobility, leisure, and nutrition (Miller-Soule et al., 1981).

References

Achenbaum, W. 'The Obsolescence of Old Age in America, 1865–1914,' *Journal of Social History*, 8(Fall 1974), 48–62.

Achenbaum, W. *Old Age in the New Land: The American Experience Since 1790*. Baltimore: Johns Hopkins University Press, 1978.

Achenbaum, W. *Aging: History and Ideology*. Cambridge, Mass.: Winthrop Publishers Inc., forthcoming.

Achenbaum, W. and P. Stearns. 'Essay: Old Age and Modernization,' *The Gerontologist*, 18(3/1978), 307–12.

Alvirez, D. and F. Bean. 'The Mexican American Family,' pp. 271–92 in C. Mindel and R. Habenstein (eds.). *Ethnic Families In America: Patterns and Variations*. New York: Elsevier, 1976.

Amoss, P. and S. Harrell (eds.). *Other Ways of Growing Old: Anthropological Perspectives*. Stanford: Stanford University Press, 1981.

Ansello, E. and C. Cipolla (eds.). 'Rural Aging and Education: Issues, Methods and Models,' *Educational Gerontology*, 5(4/1980), 343–447.

Arensberg, C. and S. Kimball. *Family and Community In Ireland*. Cambridge: Harvard University Press, 1940.

Arnold, D. (ed.). *The Sociology of Subcultures*. Berkeley: The Glendessary Press, 1970.

Bahr, H. and T. Caplow. *Old Men Drunk and Sober*. New York: New York University Press, 1973.

Barker, R. and L. Barker. 'The Psychological Ecology of Old People in Midwest, Kansas, and Yoredale, Yorkshire,' *Journal of Gerontology*, 16(2/1961), 144–49.

Benet, S. *Abkhasians: The Long-Living People of the Caucasus*. New York: Holt, Rinehart and Winston, 1974.

Bengtson, V. et al. 'Modernization, Modernity, and Perceptions of Aging: A Cross-Cultural Study,' *Journal of Gerontology*, 30(6/1975), 688–95.

Blau, Z. et al. 'Aging, Social Class and Ethnicity: A Comparison of Anglo, Black and Mexican American Texans,' *Pacific Sociological Review*, 22(4/1979), 501–25.

Bogue, D. *Skid Row in American Cities*. Chicago: Community and Family Study Center, 1963.

Burch, E. *Eskimo Kinsmen: Changing Family Relationships in Northwest Alaska*. New York: West Publishing Co., 1975.

Burgess, E. (ed.). *Aging In Western Societies*. Chicago: University of Chicago Press, 1960.

Cantor, M. 'Effect of Ethnicity on Life Styles of the Inner-City Elderly in New York,' in M.P. Lawton et al. (eds.). *Community Planning for an Aging Society: Designing Services and Facilities*. Stroudsburg, Pa.: Dowden, Hutchinson and Ross, Inc., 1976.

Carp, F. and E. Kataoka. 'Health Problems of the Elderly of San Francisco's Chinatown,' *The Gerontologist*, 16(1/1976), 30–38.

Cheng, E. *The Elderly Chinese*. San Diego: Campanile Press, San Diego State University, 1978.

Cherry, R. and S. Magnuson-Martinson. 'Modernization and the Status of the Aged in China: Decline or Equalization?' *Sociological Quarterly*, 22(2/1981), 253–62.

Cohen, A. *Delinquent Boys*. New York: Free Press, 1955.

Cohen, C. and J. Sokolovsky. 'Homeless Older Men in the Inner-City: Skid Row and SRO,' Presented at the 33rd annual meeting of the Gerontological Society of America, San Diego, November, 1980.

Cottle, T. *Hidden Survivors: Portraits of Poor Jews in America*. Englewood Cliffs, N.J.: Prentice-Hall, 1980.

Cottrell, L. 'The Technological and Societal Basis of Aging,' pp. 92–119 in C. Tibbitts (ed.). *Handbook of Social Gerontology*. Chicago: University of Chicago Press, 1960.

Cowgill, D. 'The Social Life of the Aging in Thailand,' *The Gerontologist*, 8(3/1968), 159–63.

Cowgill, D. 'The Role and Status of the Aged in Thailand,' pp. 91–101 in D. Cowgill and L. Holmes (eds.). *Aging and Modernization*. New York: Appleton-Century-Crofts, 1972.

Cowgill, D. 'The Aging of Populations and Societies,' *The Annals*, 415(September, 1974a), 1–18.

Cowgill, D. 'Aging and Modernization: A Revision of the Theory,' in J. Gubrium (ed.). *Later Life: Communities and Environmental Policy*. Springfield, Ill.: Charles C. Thomas, 1974b.

Cowgill, D. and L. Holmes. *Aging and Modernization*. New York: Appleton-Century-Crofts, 1972.

Crouch, B. 'Age and Institutional Support: Perceptions of Older Mexican Americans,' *Journal of Gerontology*, 27(4/1972), 524–29.

Cuellar, J. et al. (eds.). *Minority Aging: Current Status and Future Directions*. San Diego: San Diego State University Center on Aging, 1981.

Davis, D. 'Growing Old Black,' pp. 356–68 in J. Quadagno (ed.). *Aging, The Individual and Society*. New York: St. Martin's Press, 1980a.

Davis, L. *The Black Aged in the United States: An Annotated Bibliography.* Westport: Greenwood Press, 1980b.

de Beauvoir, S. *The Coming of Age.* Warner Paperback Library, 1972.

Delgado, M. and G. Finley. 'The Spanish-Speaking Elderly: A Bibliography,' *The Gerontologist,* 18(4/1978), 387–94.

Doherty, E. (ed.). 'Growing Old in Indian Country,' in *Employment Prospects of Aged Blacks, Chicanos and Indians.* Washington, D.C.: National Council on the Aging, 1971.

Dowd, J. 'Industrialization and the Decline of the Aged,' *Sociological Focus,* 14(4/1981), 255–69.

Dowd, J. and V. Bengtson. 'Aging in Minority Populations: An Examination of the Double Jeopardy Hypothesis,' *Journal of Gerontology,* 33(3/1978), 427–36.

Eckert, J. 'Urban Renewal and Redevelopment: High Risk for the Marginally Subsistent Elderly,' *The Gerontologist,* 19(5/1979), 496–502.

Eribes, R. and M. Bradley-Rawls. 'The Underutilization of Nursing Home Facilities by Mexican-American Elderly in the Southwest,' *The Gerontologist,* 18(4/1978), 363–71.

Erikson, R. and K. Eckert. 'The Elderly Poor in Downtown San Diego Hotels,' *The Gerontologist,* 17(5/1977), 440–46.

Feder, S. 'Aging in the Kibbutz in Israel,' pp. 211–26 in D. Cowgill and L. Holmes (eds.). *Aging and Modernization.* New York: Appleton-Century-Crofts, 1972.

Fischer, C. 'Toward a Subcultural Theory of Urbanism,' *American Journal of Sociology,* 80(6/1975), 1319–41.

Fischer, D. *Growing Old in America.* London: Oxford University Press, 1977.

Fry, C. 'Towards an Anthropology of Aging,' pp. 1–20 in C. Fry (ed.). *Aging in Culture and Society: Comparative Viewpoints and Strategies.* New York: Praeger Publishers, 1980a.

Fry, C. (ed.). *Aging in Culture and Society: Comparative Viewpoints and Strategies.* New York: Praeger Publishers, 1980b.

Fujii, S. 'Minority Group Elderly: Demographic Characteristics and Implications for Public Policy,' pp. 261–84 in C. Eisdorfer (ed.). *Annual Review of Gerontology and Geriatrics.* Volume 1. New York: Springer Publishing Co., 1980.

Gans, H. *Popular Culture and High Culture: An Analysis and Evaluation of Taste.* New York: Basic Books, 1974.

Gelfand, D. 'Ethnicity and Aging,' pp. 91–117 in C. Eisdorfer (ed.). *Annual Review of Gerontology and Geriatrics.* Volume 2. New York: Springer Publishing Co., 1981.

Gelfand, D. *Aging: The Ethnic Factor.* Cambridge, Mass.: Winthrop Publishers, Inc., 1982.

Gelfand, D. and A. Kutzik (eds.). *Ethnicity and Aging: Theory, Research and Policy.* New York: Springer Publishing Co., 1979.

Gelfand, D. and J. Olsen. 'Aging in the Jewish Family and the Mormon Family,' pp. 206–21 in D. Gelfand and A. Kutzik (eds.). *Ethnicity and Aging: Theory, Research and Policy.* New York: Springer Publishing Co., 1979.

Goldstein, M. and C. Beall. 'Modernization and Aging in the Third and Fourth World: Views from the Rural Hinterland in Nepal,' *Human Organization,* 40(1/1981), 48–55.

Goldstein, M. and C. Beall. 'Indirect Modernization and the Status of the Elderly in a Rural Third World Setting,' *Journal of Gerontology,* 37(6/1982), 743–48.

Goldstine, T. and D. Gutmann. 'A TAT Study of Navajo Aging,' *Psychiatry,* XXXV(4/1972), 373–84.

Goody, J. 'Aging in Nonindustrial Societies,' pp. 117–29 in R. Binstock and E. Shanas (eds.). *Handbook of Aging and the Social Sciences.* New York: Van Nostrand Reinhold, 1976.

Gordon, M. 'The Concept of the Subculture and Its Application,' *Social Forces,* 26(1/1947), 40–42.

Gubser, N. *The Nunamiut Eskimo: Hunters of Caribou.* New Haven: Yale University Press, 1965.

Guemple, L. 'Human Resource Management: The Dilemma of the Aging Eskimo,' *Sociological Symposium,* 2(2/1969), 59–74.

Guemple, L. 'Growing Old in Inuit Society,' pp. 95–101 in V. Marshall (ed.). *Aging in Canada: Social Perspectives.* Don Mills: Fitzhenry and Whiteside, 1980.

Gutmann, D. 'Aging Among the Highland Maya: A Comparative Study,' *Journal of Personality and Social Psychology,* 7(1/1967), 28–35.

Gutmann, D. 'Alternatives to Disengagement: The Old Men of the Highland Druze,' pp. 88–108 in J. Gubrium (ed.). *Time, Roles and Self in Old Age.* New York: Human Sciences Press, 1976.

Gutmann, D. 'Observations on Culture and Mental Health in Later Life,' pp. 429–47 in J. Birren and R. Sloane (eds.). *Handbook of Mental Health and Aging.* Englewood Cliffs, N.J.: Prentice-Hall, 1980.

Harlan, W. 'Social Status of the Aged in Three Indian Villages,' *Vita Humana,* 7(1964), 239–52.

Havighurst, R. et al. (eds.). *Adjustment to Retirement: A Cross National Study.* Assen, Netherlands: Van Gorcum, 1969.

Hendricks, J. and C. Hendricks. 'The Age Old Question of Old Age: Was It Really So Much Better Back When?,' *International Journal of Aging and Human Development,* 8(2/1977–78), 139–54.

Hendricks, J. and C. Hendricks. *Aging In Mass Society: Myths and Realities*. 2nd Edition. Cambridge, Mass.: Winthrop Publishers, Inc. 1981.

Holmberg, A. *Nomads of the Long Bow*. Garden City, New York: Natural History Press, 1969.

Holmes, L. 'The Role and Status of the Aged in a Changing Samoa,' pp. 73–89 in D. Cowgill and L. Holmes (eds.). *Aging and Modernization*. New York: Appleton-Century-Crofts, 1972.

Holmes, L. 'Trends In Anthropological Gerontology: From Simmons to the Seventies,' *International Journal of Aging and Human Development*, 7(3/1976), 211–20.

Holmes, L. 'Anthropology and Age: An Assessment,' pp. 272–84 in C. Fry (ed.). *Aging in Culture and Society: Comparative Viewpoints and Strategies*. New York: Praeger Publishers, 1980.

Holzberg, C. 'Cultural Gerontology: Towards an Understanding of Ethnicity and Aging,' *Culture*, 1(1/1981), 110–22.

Holzberg, C. 'Ethnicity and Aging: Anthropological Perspectives on More Than Just the Minority Elderly,' *The Gerontologist*, 22(3/1982), 249–57.

Ikels, C. 'Old Age in Hong Kong,' *The Gerontologist*, 15(3/1975), 230–35.

Ikels, C. 'The Coming of Age in Chinese Society: Traditional Patterns and Contemporary Hong Kong,' pp. 80–100 in C. Fry (ed.). *Aging in Culture and Society: Comparative Viewpoints and Strategies*. New York: Praeger Publishers, 1980.

Ishizuka, K. *The Elderly Japanese*. San Diego: Campanile Press, San Diego State University, 1978.

Jackson, J. 'Aged Negroes: Their Cultural Departures from Statistical Stereotypes and Rural-Urban Differences,' *The Gerontologist*, 10(2/1970),140–45.

Jackson, J. 'The Blacklands of Gerontology,' *Aging and Human Development*, 2(3/1971), 156–71.

Jackson, J. *Minorities and Aging*. Belmont, Calif.: Wadsworth Publishing Co., 1980.

Jeffries, W. 'Our Aged Indians,' pp. 7–10 in *Triple Jeopardy – Myth or Reality*. Washington, D.C.: National Council on Aging, 1972.

Kagan, D. 'Activity and Aging in a Colombian Peasant Village,' pp. 65–79 in C. Fry (ed.). *Aging in Culture and Society: Comparative Viewpoints and Strategies*. New York: Praeger Publishers, 1980.

Kalish, R. and S. Moriwaki. 'The World of the Elderly Asian American,' *Journal of Social Issues*, 29(2/1973), 187–209.

Keifer, C. *Changing Cultures, Changing Lives*. San Francisco: Jossey-Bass, 1974.

Keith, J. 'The Best Is Yet to Be: Toward an Anthropology of Age,' pp. 339–64 in B. Siegel et al. (eds.). *Annual Review of Anthropology*. Volume 9. Palo Alto: Annual Reviews Inc., 1980.

Keith, J. *Old People as People: Social and Cultural Influences on Aging and Old Age*. Cambridge, Mass.: Winthrop Publishers Inc., 1982.

Kent, D. (ed.). 'The Elderly in Minority Groups,' *The Gerontologist*, 11(1/1971), 26–98.

Kitano, H. *Japanese-Americans: The Evolution of a Subculture*. Englewood Cliffs, N.J.: Prentice-Hall, 1976.

Koller, M. *Social Gerontology*. New York: Random House, 1968.

Lally, M. et al. 'Older Women in Single Room Occupant (SRO) Hotels: A Seattle Profile,' *The Gerontologist*, 19(1/1979), 67–73.

Laslett, P. 'Societal Development and Aging,' pp. 87–116 in R. Binstock and E. Shanas (eds.). *Handbook of Aging and the Social Sciences*. New York: Van Nostrand Reinhold, 1976.

Levy, J. 'The Older American Indian,' in E. Youmans (ed.). *Older Rural Americans: A Sociological Perspective*. Lexington: University of Kentucky, 1967.

Longino, C. 'Changing Aged Nonmetropolitan Migration Patterns, 1955 to 1960 and 1965 to 1970,' *Journal of Gerontology*, 37(2/1982), 228–34.

Lozier, J. and R. Althouse. 'Social Enforcement of Behavior Toward Elders in an Appalachian Mountain Settlement,' *The Gerontologist*, 14(1/1974), 69–80.

Lozier, J. and R. Althouse. 'Retirement to the Porch in Rural Appalachia,' *International Journal of Aging and Human Development*, 6(1/1975), 7–15.

Maeda, D. 'Growth of Old People's Clubs in Japan,' *The Gerontologist*, 15(3/1975), 254–56.

Maldonado, D. 'The Chicano Aged,' *Social Work*, 20(3/1975), 213–16.

Maxwell, R. 'The Changing Status of Elders in a Polynesian Society,' *Aging and Human Development*, 1(2/1970), 137–46.

Maxwell, R. and P. Silverman. 'Information and Esteem: Cultural Considerations in the Treatment of the Aged,' *Aging and Human Development*, 1(4/1970), 361–92.

Maxwell, R. and P. Silverman. 'Gerontocide,' paper presented at a conference on 'The Content of Culture: Constants and Variants,' Pomona College, Claremont, Calif., Nov. 30-Dec. 1, 1981.

McKain, W. 'The Aged in the USSR,' pp. 151–65 in D. Cowgill and L. Holmes (eds.). *Aging and Modernization*. New York: Appleton-Century-Crofts, 1972.

Miller-Soule, D. et al. 'Minority Aging Research: The State of the Literature,' paper presented at the annual meeting of the Gerontological Society of America, Toronto, Nov., 1981.

Montero, D. 'The Elderly Japanese-Americans: Aging Among the First Generation Immigrants,' *Genetic Psychology Monographs*, 101(1/1980a), 99–118.

Montero, D. *Japanese-Americans: Changing Patterns of Ethnic Affiliation Over Three Generations.* Boulder, Colo.: Westview Press, 1980b.

Moore, J. 'Situational Factors Affecting Minority Aging,' *The Gerontologist*, 11(1/1971a), 83–93.

Moore, J. 'Mexican Americans,' *The Gerontologist*, 11(1/1971b), 30–35.

Munsell, M. 'Functions of the Aged Among Salt River Pima,' pp. 127–32 in D. Cowgill and L. Holmes (eds.). *Aging and Modernization.* New York: Appleton-Century-Crofts, 1972.

Murdock, S. and D. Schwartz. 'Family Structure and the Use of Agency Services: An Examination of Patterns Among Elderly Native Americans,' *The Gerontologist*, 18(5/1978), 475–81.

Myerhoff, B. and A. Simic. *Life's Career-Aging: Cultural Variations on Growing Old.* Beverly Hills: Sage Publications, 1978.

Nakani, C. *Japanese Society.* Berkeley: University of California Press, 1972.

Newquist, D. 'Barriers to Western Health Care for the Mexican-American Elderly,' paper presented at the annual meeting of the Gerontological Society of America, Toronto, Nov., 1981.

Osako, M. 'Aging and Family Among Japanese Americans: The Role of Ethnic Tradition in the Adjustment to Old Age,' *The Gerontologist*, 19(5/1979), 448–55.

Palmore, E. 'The Status and Integration of the Aged in Japanese Society,' *Journal of Gerontology*, 30(2/1975a), 199–208.

Palmore, E. *The Honorable Elders: A Cross-Cultural Analysis.* Durham, N.C.: Duke University Press, 1975b.

Palmore, E. 'What Can The USA Learn from Japan About Aging?,' *The Gerontologist*, 15(1/1975c), 64–67.

Palmore, E. and K. Manton. 'Modernization and Status of the Aged: International Correlations,' *Journal of Gerontology*, 29(2/1974), 205–10.

Pearson, K. *Surfing Subcultures of Australia and New Zealand.* St. Lucia: University of Queensland Press, 1979.

Pihlblad, C. et al. 'Status and Role of the Aged in Norwegian Society,' pp. 227–42 in D. Cowgill and L. Holmes (eds.). *Aging and Modernization.* New York: Appleton-Century-Crofts, 1972.

Piovesana, G. 'The Aged in Chinese and Japanese Cultures,' pp. 13–20 in J. Hendricks and C. Hendricks (eds.). *Dimensions of Aging: Readings.* Cambridge, Mass.: Winthrop Publishers, Inc., 1979.

Pitskhelauri, G. *The Long-Living of Soviet Georgia.* New York: Human Sciences Press, 1982.

Plath, D. 'Japan: The After Years,' pp. 133–50 in D. Cowgill and L. Holmes (ed.). *Aging and Modernization.* New York: Appleton-Century-Crofts, 1972.

Press, I. and M. McKool. 'Social Structure and Status of the Aged: Toward Some Valid Cross-Cultural Generalizations,' *Aging and Human Development*, 3(4/1972), 297–306.

Preston, S. 'Mortality Trends,' pp. 163–78 in A. Inkeles et al. (eds.). *Annual Review of Sociology.* Volume 3. Palo Alto: Annual Reviews Inc., 1977.

Rogers, J. and T. Gallion. 'Characteristics of Elderly Pueblo Indians in New Mexico,' *The Gerontologist*, 18(5/1978), 482–87.

Rooney, J. 'Friendship and Disaffiliation Among the Skid Row Population,' *Journal of Gerontology*, 31(1/1976), 82–88.

Rosow, I. 'And Then We Were Old,' *Trans-Action*, 2(2/1965), 20–26.

Schneider, R. 'Growing Older in Israel,' *Perspective On Aging*, X(2/1981), 4–7.

Shanas, E. et al. *Old People in Three Industrial Societies.* New York: Atherton Press, 1968.

Sheehan, T. 'Senior Esteem as a Factor of Socioeconomic Complexity,' *The Gerontologist*, 16(5/1976), 433–40.

Shibutani, T. 'Reference Groups as Perspectives,' *American Journal of Sociology*, 60(6/1955), 562–69.

Simmons, L. *The Role of the Aged in Primitive Society.* New Haven: Yale University Press, 1945.

Simmons, L. 'Social Participation of the Aged in Different Cultures,' *The Annals of the American Academy of Political and Social Science*, 279(Jan. 1952), 43–51.

Simmons, L. 'Aging in Preindustrial Societies,' in C. Tibbitts (ed.). *Handbook of Social Gerontology.* Chicago: University of Chicago Press, 1960.

Sparks, D. 'The Still Rebirth: Retirement and Role Discontinuity,' in D. Plath and E. Brill (eds.). *Adult Episodes in Japan.* Leiden, Netherlands: Brill, 1975.

Stearns, P. *Old Age in European Society: The Case of France.* New York: Holmes and Meirer, 1976.

Stearns, P. 'The Modernization of Old Age in France: Approaches Through History,' *International Journal of Aging and Human Development*, 13(4/1981), 297–315.

Stephens, J. *Loners, Losers and Lovers.* Seattle: University of Washington Press, 1976.

Streib, G. 'Social Stratification and Aging,' pp. 160–85 in R. Binstock and E. Shanas (eds.). *Handbook of Aging and the Social Sciences.* New York: Van Nostrand Reinhold, 1976.

Synge, J. 'Work and Family Support Patterns of the Aged in the Early Twentieth Century,' pp. 135–44 in V. Marshall (ed.). *Aging In Canada: Social Perspectives.* Don Mills: Fitzhenry and Whiteside, 1980.

Talmon, Y. 'Aging In Israel–A Planned Society,' *American Journal of Sociology,* 67(3/1961), 284–95.

Tindale, J. 'Identity Maintenance Processes of Old Poor Men,' pp. 88–94 in V. Marshall (ed.). *Aging in Canada: Social Perspectives.* Don Mills: Fitzhenry and Whiteside, 1980.

Treas, J. 'Socialist Organization and Economic Development in China: Latent Consequences for the Aged,' *The Gerontologist,* 19(1/1979), 34–43.

Ujimoto, V. 'Theoretical and Methodological Issues in the Study of Aged Ethnic Minorities,' Presented at the 9th biennial conference, Canadian Ethnic Studies Conference, Edmonton, Alberta, Oct. 1981.

Watson, W. and R. Maxwell. *Human Aging and Dying: A Study in Sociocultural Gerontology.* New York: St. Martin's Press, 1977.

Wedderburn, D. 'Old People in Britain,' pp. 94–106 in E. Shanas (ed.). *Aging In Contemporary Society.* Beverly Hills: Sage Publications, 1970.

Weihl, H. 'Aging in Israel,' pp. 107–17 in E. Shanas (ed.). *Aging In Contemporary Society.* Beverly Hills: Sage Publications, 1970.

Weihl, H. 'Selected Aspects of Aging in Israel, 1969,' pp. 197–209 in D. Cowgill and L. Holmes (eds.). *Aging and Modernization.* New York: Appleton-Century-Crofts, 1972.

Wershow, H. 'Aging in the Israeli Kibbutz: Some Further Investigation,' *International Journal of Aging and Human Development,* 4(3/1973), 211–27.

Wershow, H. 'Days Beyond Recall: Subsistence Homesteading in the Rural South, Circa 1920,' *International Journal of Aging and Human Development,* 6(1/1975), 1–5.

Williams, G. 'Warriors No More: A Study of the American Indian Elderly,' pp. 101–11 in C. Fry (ed.). *Aging in Culture and Society: Comparative Viewpoints and Strategies.* New York: Praeger Publishers, 1980.

Wolfgang, M. and F. Ferracuti. *The Subculture of Violence.* London: Tavistock, 1967.

Wu, F. 'Mandarin-Speaking Aged Chinese in the Los Angeles Area,' *The Gerontologist,* 15(3/1975), 271–75.

Wylie, F. 'Attitudes Toward Aging and the Aged Among Black Americans: Some Historical Perspectives,' *Journal of Aging and Human Development,* 2(1/1971), 66–70.

Youmans, E. (ed.) *Older Rural Americans.* Lexington: University of Kentucky Press, 1967.

Youmans, E. 'The Rural Aged,' *The Annals of the American Academy of Political and Social Science,* 429(Jan. 1977), 81–90.

3

Demographic, Social and Environmental Aspects of Aging

Introduction

The universal phenomenon of aging has many cultural and subcultural variations. With the transition from predominantly agrarian societies to more industrialized, urban societies, there have been dramatic changes in the size, composition, and distribution of the world's population. This chapter provides an overview of population aging from a demographic perspective.

According to Hauser (1976), changes in the structure and size of societies have been characterized by four interrelated demographic elements. Many of these changes have subsequently influenced the aging process and the status of the aged. The first is a population 'explosion,' first in the more developed regions of the world and, after World War II, in the developing nations in Asia, Africa, and Latin America. The world's population increased from about 1 billion inhabitants in 1800 to about 4 billion in 1970 (Hauser, 1976:61) to about 4.5 billion in 1980 (*Bulletin on Aging*, 1981). United Nations projections indicate that if fertility rates remain relatively constant, by the year 2000 the world population will total about 7.9 billion, with 1.5 billion people residing in the more developed countries and 6.4 billion residing in the less developed countries.

This explosion has been explained by the 'demographic transition theory,' which holds that the age structure of a society changes in three distinct stages. In the preindustrial stage there is uneven population growth; high birth rates are accompanied by high death rates resulting from famine, epidemics, and wars. The second (or transition) stage is characterized by a continuation of high birth rates, but with mortality rates decreasing significantly, especially among infants and children. These decreases result from technology-related improvements to living conditions such as sanitary water, preventive medicine, consistent food supplies, and better and more accessible medical care. (This stage did not occur in the developing countries until after World War II). The third stage occurs when a nation becomes a modern industrialized society, and is characterized by low birth and death rates and, often, zero population growth (ZPG).

The second demographic element in the transition to an industrial society is known as the population 'implosion.' The population becomes concentrated in a relatively small area, primarily through urbanization. This trend can have different effects on elderly people both in developed and in developing nations. For example, the quality of urban life does not rise to the same extent in developing countries as it does in developed countries. This is partly because there is usually a higher population density in a smaller area, which can lead to crowded living conditions and competition for scarce resources such as jobs, housing, food, and water. Local elites may become dependent on their economic ties with wealthier nations, and may siphon off some of the profits from export sales. This prevents wealth from being disbursed throughout a society, and results in a low standard of urban living.

Population 'displosion' is the third demographic element in the transition from folk to modern societies. This process involves the appearance of greater heterogeneity in the population within a geographical location. This heterogeneity increases the likelihood of conflict between various social groups, which may occur when a subgroup seeks to attain social, economic, and political equality with other visible groups.

The final element is a 'technoplosion.' Technological development proceeds rapidly and leads to dramatic changes in the work and leisure lifestyles of people of all ages, although the elderly often have the greatest difficulty in accepting and adapting to technological change. When a technoplosion occurs, such as increasing computerization in the workplace and at home, it is often the elderly who are the last to adjust to the change, if indeed they ever do.

Scientists have tried to determine what causes population changes and what effect these changes have on different age cohorts in a population. Before we can begin to understand the social processes associated with aging, it is necessary to understand the age structure within which these processes operate. The purpose of this chapter is to paint a broad picture of the age composition and distribution of the world and of particular countries. This information will also provide a base of information for those in the service professions concerned with developing policies and programs.

The chapter begins with a brief nontechnical introduction to the field of demography. The remainder of the chapter presents a discussion of selected demographic patterns relevant to the aging process. Throughout, a few tables and figures are used to illustrate trends and patterns. It is important that you pay attention to the 'numbers' in these graphics, since they can provide you with valuable information not only about the past but also about your own future. For example, write down the year you were born, and add 25. You will probably be a full-time member of the labor force by that year. Add 40 to your year of birth; by this time you will probably be the parent of teenagers and established in a career. Add 65 and 70, respectively, to your birth year; this will give you the years when you and your birth cohort will retire. You now have an estimate of the demographic profile of your life for some common life events.

More important than the actual year at which these events will occur for you are: (1) the demographic and social characteristics of your birth cohort in relation to those who were born before and after you; (2) a demographic profile of the social, economic, and political conditions that prevail when you and others reach a particular stage in the life cycle; and (3) the impact of particular social and historical events on your cohort and on others at a given point in history. These are the general concerns of demographers who search for patterns of change over many decades and then, based on varying assumptions, provide projections for the future.

Some textbooks include pages of demographic statistics or facts. However, even as this book was being written, 'current' published statistical profiles were becoming dated. For example, there is almost always a two-year lag from when the information is collected from individuals through the census until it is published as aggregated population statistics.[1] Moreover, statistical summaries can be as confusing as they are illuminating because there is often variation in the sources and years of the data, in how the data are categorized in tables or figures, in how a cohort is defined, in how many age categories are used, and in how indices are computed.[2] For example, some tables present data for one-, five-, or ten-year cohorts. Similarly, some tables place all persons over 65 in one category; others use five-year (61–65, 66–70, 71–75, 76–80, 81–85) or ten-year intervals (60–69, 70–79, 80–89). Clearly, those aged 60 to 65 are different (in health and past experiences) from those who are over 75. Data involving the elderly should be divided into a number of categories in order to obtain a more accurate picture of age cohorts.

This chapter focuses on general trends and patterns of demographic and socioenvironmental changes in the population, rather than on statistics for a specific country or region of that country. Where actual statistics are presented, the reader should examine and interpret the trends, patterns, and implications revealed by the numbers, rather than simply memorize the numbers. Appendix 1 provides a general discussion of how to read a table or figure. You should read this appendix before beginning the next section of the chapter.

You should also visit the government publications section of your library to examine the most recent statistics and trends for your country, region, town, and neighborhood.[3] These trends should then be interpeted to determine their implications for you, your parents, and the older citizens in your geographic locale with respect to the social, political, economic, legal, labor force, and leisure domains. For example, you should be interested not just in those over 65, as are many gerontologists, but rather in the comparative characteristics of all age cohorts.

The study of aging does not only involve two dichotomous groups — those under 65 and those over 65. Rather, the interrelationships among age cohorts within the age structure must be considered. For example, in periods of high unemployment, if a large proportion of the population between 16 and 25 is unemployed, and a large proportion over 60 is also unemployed, it might be useful to look for elements of conflict between these two cohorts as they compete for a scarce resource, namely, a job that provides income.

In contrast, when there is consensus among age cohorts, social integration and cooperation should prevail. An increase in the number or proportion of one age group, such as the elderly, can result in a number of population-induced social changes that must be addressed. These might include: (1) in the economic domain, a need for higher pensions, or the onset of high rates of inflation that forces more elderly people to seek work after retirement; (2) in the political domain, a redistribution of votes in a region, the development of senior-citizen advocacy groups, and the election of elderly candidates; (3) in the educational domain, the need for adult education, the closing of elementary schools, and an increase in the use of educational television; (4) in the legal domain, an increase in the number of crimes committed by old people (such as stealing to obtain necessities), an increase in crimes against the elderly in urban core areas, and a need for legal assistance by the elderly; and (5) more generally, the creation and provision of services to an older client group by leisure, health care, and social workers in each community (Longino, 1982).

An Introduction to Demography

The situation of a specific age cohort at a particular time cannot be fully understood without an awareness of the antecedent experiences in their life history and the size and composition of other age cohorts in the society. This information is provided by demographers, who monitor the three basic processes related to population dynamics: fertility, mortality, and migration. At the macro level of analysis, aging is a demographic process that involves changes in the characteristics of the population over a period of many years. Demographers study changes in the size, composition, and territorial distribution of the population.

In order to describe the population and to identify the patterns and impacts of change, demographers usually report statistics by using a mean, median, or percentage. Based on patterns from the past, on current statistics, and on assumptions about the future, they make 'projections' of what might happen, rather than 'predictions' of what will happen. As assumptions or facts change, demographers constantly revise their projections. For example, early projections for the baby-boom cohort (Bouvier, 1980) born from the mid 1940s to the late 1960s indicated that members of this cohort would experience greater competition for jobs than any other cohort to date. Yet, when the first projections were made, demographers did not include as assumptions the impacts of an energy crisis and double-digit inflation on the economy. As a result, they vastly underestimated the high degree of unemployment or underemployment that would face this large cohort. Needless to say, their projections have been revised accordingly.

Employing census information[4] and vital-statistics registrations,[5] demographers use birth, death, and migration rates to determine the size and shape of the age structure. They collect and analyze statistics such as degree of labor-force participation and unemployment, crime rates relating to specific age groups, internal migration rates, and family size. They are also interested in the distribution of the population by geographical region, age, sex, income, occupation, race, religion, and ethnic background. However, they are not merely content with describing changes in the age structure. Rather, they search for possible explanatory factors (social, political, economic, or historical events) that may cause changes in fertility, mortality or migration rates, and examine the consequences of these changes in birth, death, and migration rates. Some of these consequences include significant political, social, or economic changes for the society at large, and significant lifestyle changes for its individual members.

In addition to these obvious descriptive variables through which they observe trends and make projections, demographers have also devised a number of demographic indicators. These are useful in analyzing patterns of change in population size, composition, and distribution. Some of the common indices that pertain to aging are introduced in the following subsections. Remember that demographic statistics represent generalizations and that in reality there is variation in the composition and distribution of the elderly population within and between countries. Furthermore, not all of this variation can be revealed by a particular table or graph because of the way in which the index was constructed; because a significant social, political, or economic fact was unknown or ignored; because the social situation has changed dramatically since the figures were calculated; because information was not available; or because not all of the available information was included in the table or figure.

Life Span

The life span is the theoretical maximum number of years an individual can live. Although there are individual differences, there seems to be a biological limit that has changed relatively little since ancient times.[6] Today, the life span for humans is about 100 years. Most die before this age, although in each society a few will attain centenarian status.

Life Expectancy

Life expectancy is the average number of years of life remaining for an individual at a given age. It is determined by recording the death rates for each age at a particular time. Then, 'life tables' are constructed, which make it possible to project the average number of years of life remaining for a person.[7] The two most frequently cited statistics are life expectancy at birth and life expectancy at retirement (or age 65).

Obviously, this measure is related to death rates; a low death rate for a certain age group means a correspondingly high life expectancy. Therefore, it is not surprising to find that as infant mortality has decreased over time, as the standard of living has increased, and as medical care has improved, the average life expectancy at birth for a particular cohort has also increased. In early Roman times, life expectancy at birth was 20 years; by 1900 in North America, it was 45 to 50; in the early 1980s, it had increased to about 73 years in Western industrialized nations, and to 45 to 50 years in less developed nations such as India and China (Laslett, 1976; Hauser, 1976; Siegel, 1981). It is projected (Siegel, 1981) that by 2000 life expectancy at birth in the less developed regions will increase to 61.9 years for men and 65.1 years for women (63.5 average), and to 69.8 for men and 77.0 for women (73.4 average) in the more developed regions.[8] The greatest gains are expected to be made in African and Asian countries.

Regional variations in life expectancy in each country may reflect differences in standards of living, climate, or migration patterns of particular groups. For example, the average life expectancy in different sectors of a metropolitan area may vary by as much as four years above or below the area average. This variation results from differences in the quality of life among different classes. Similarly, although there has been an increase in life expectancy at age 65, the increase has been considerably less than that at birth. Since 1900 in North America the average life expectancy at age 65 has increased only from about 12 years to 16.5 years.

The pattern of life expectancy throughout the world at any given historical point is influenced by the social and physical conditions that have an impact on an age cohort. Events such as famines, epidemics, wars, and depressions can have a profound impact on a specific age cohort in a specific country. At the same time, the event may have little or no influence on the life expectancy of another age cohort in that society, or on a similar age cohort in another country. For example, a lengthy war could have a significant influence on the life expectancy of those under 25, but considerably less impact on those over 40.

In addition to cross-national differences in life expectancy at birth, and differences between cohorts within a country, there are differences within cohorts according to race, sex, and geographical region (Brotman, 1977). The life expectancy at birth and at age 65 for the total population of the United States is 73.8 and 16.5 years respectively. The figures for males are 70.0 and 14.1 years respectively, and for females the figures are 77.6 and 18.5 years respectively (*Statistical Bulletin*, 1981a).

As a cohort ages, life expectancy at later stages in the life cycle is strongly influenced by such related lifestyle factors as marital status, education, occupation, and income. Studies show that those men and women who have achieved distinction in a particular occupation live longer, on the average, than men or women in the general population. To illustrate, the mortality rate of those listed in *Who's Who in America* was approximately 30 percent below that of their age peers in the general population (*Statistical Bulletin*, 1968:2–5; 1979:3–9). However, even within this group of elites, there are occupational differences. For example, women who were community service workers, government officials, librarians, curators, or scientists experienced the lowest mortality rates. Those who were physicians, surgeons, performers, or entertainers had higher mortality rates. For them, such factors as risk, stress, and atypical working hours may account for a lowered life expectancy.

In North America, whites have a higher life expectancy at birth than nonwhites; female rates are higher than those for males; those living in the North have a higher life expectancy than those living in the South; those in urban areas have higher rates than those in rural areas; and those with higher levels of education and higher incomes have higher rates than those who are less educated and those who have lower incomes. One interesting pattern that has been noted by demographers is the 'crossover' effect: after about age 75, the life expectancy of nonwhite males in North America is greater than that for white males. This suggests that if nonwhite males survive to age 75, they are likely to live longer than white males.

Although it is seldom used anymore, another measure of longevity is the average number of years until death. By using this measure, 'old age' is defined as the period beginning with the age at which a group would have a certain time to live (10 or 15 years). Thus, in those countries with a lower life expectancy, or in specific subcultures (such as North Americans Indians), old age begins sooner. If this index was used more widely, some groups might be eligible sooner for pension and health benefits; in fact, the use of this index has been requested by some native Indian groups in the United States.

In summary, life expectancy is closely related to such factors as sex, standard of living, and lifestyle, with women living longer in most countries. However, it must be remembered that life expectancy figures are averages, and are based on the assumption that age-specific mortality rates will be the same in the future as they are at present (Marshall, 1980). Thus, individuals within each birth cohort may die earlier or live longer depending on their own unique biological, psychological, and social aging processes. Similarly, there may be cohort differences because of period effects; a particular cohort may be more susceptible to higher (war or epidemic) or lower (discovery of a wonder drug) mortality rates.

Crude Birth and Death Rates

Crude birth and death rates record the number of births and deaths per one thousand people during a one year period. They provide a relative measure by which frequencies of births and deaths can be compared over time. Generally, in Western, industrialized nations, both rates have fallen since the early 1900s, with the exception of the baby-boom years in the late 1940s and throughout the 1950s. For example, in the United States, the crude birth rate has fallen 50 percent (from about 30 to 15 per 1000 people) from the year 1900 to the present.

This measure is subject to great fluctuation between and within countries, depending on religious beliefs, birth-control availability and use, and social norms concerning marriage and family size. Similarly, crude death rates vary (Myers, 1978) because of such factors as availability of preventive medicine, quality of sanitary services, quality of health care, and the incidence of degenerative diseases, war, or natural disasters. For example, the eradication of cardiovascular diseases, cancer, and other lifestyle-related diseases in industrialized countries could decrease crude death rates and increase life expectancies by about five years. This is similar to what happened when tuberculosis and influenza were virtually eliminated as causes of death.

The Sex Ratio

The sex ratio is the number of males per one hundred females in a given population. A ratio of 1.0 indicates an equal number, and a ratio of less than 1.0 indicates that there are fewer males than females in that particular age group. Figure 3.1 illustrates two patterns that are found in most modernized nations. Although males outnumber females at birth (about 106 male births per 100 female births), females outlive males as chronological age increases. This changing sex ratio results from a higher incidence of mortality among men, primarily because of accidents prior to early adulthood and to degenerative diseases in the middle and later years. As illustrated in figure 3.1, the sex ratio has decreased throughout history, as well as across the life cycle for a given cohort.

Figure 3.1 The decreasing sex ratio: historically by years and by chronological age. Adapted from reports by Statistics Canada and the United States Bureau of the Census.

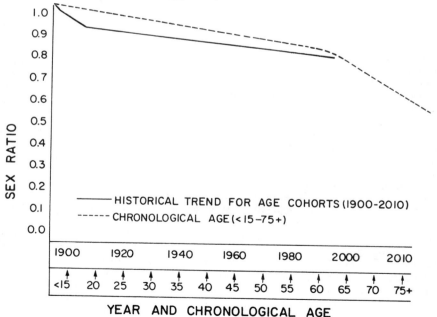

At present the sex ratio in Canada and the United States is 86 and 68 men per 100 women, respectively, for the population 65 years of age and older. It is projected that this ratio will decline to about 78 in Canada and about 65 in the United States by the year 2000. This will occur because of higher mortality rates among men, and increased longevity among women. Within a given generation, the sex ratio decreases as chronological age increases. According to Statistics Canada (1979:chart 3), the sex ratio in Canada at present is .89 at 65 to 69 years of age; it decreases to .83 (70 to 74 years), .71 (75 to 79 years), .63 (80 to 84 years), .59 (85 to 89 years) and .54 (90+ years).

One consequence of the changing sex ratio is that many older women are widows who in their later years may become physically and emotionally isolated. It is interesting to note that the ratio used to be higher in the North American west since the population of the 'old frontier' was largely male. However, this pattern has almost disappeared; in North America there is now little variation in the sex ratio by geographical region. However, there is still a higher sex ratio in rural than in urban areas, since women seem to be more inclined to migrate from rural to urban areas.

The Dependency Ratio

The dependency ratio indicates the number of nonworkers who must be supported directly or indirectly by those in the labor force. Clark et al. (1978) have divided the population into three categories that represent general estimates of the relative number of people who are workers and dependents. These categories are workers, young dependents, and old dependents. The total dependency ratio is an approximate measure of the economic support that must be provided by those who are in the labor force to those who are unemployed, or 'dependent.' The higher the ratio, the greater the number of dependent people in the population who must be supported by those in the labor force, and by health and economic assistance programs in the private and public sector. The dependency ratio is determined by identifying all those who are under 19 and over 65 years of age (the young and old dependents), and dividing this number by those who are 'eligible' to be in the labor force, namely, all those between 20 and 64 years of age.

In North America the dependency ratio has increased over time. This increase has occurred because the proportion of those over 65 years of age has increased, while the fertility rate has decreased, thereby lowering the number of eligible workers under 64 years of age. If mandatory retirement was delayed or eliminated and more older people remained in the labor force, the ratio would decrease. In the United States it is estimated that the current dependency ratio is approximately 114 (100 workers of all ages will support 114 dependents of all ages). It is projected that this ratio will fall to 106 in 2000 and rise to 112 after 2020 when the baby-boom cohort retires (Sheppard and Rix, 1977). When the dependency ratio is high, the potential for social and economic conflict between generations increases, since fewer workers must support more retirees.

The dependency ratio for the total population can be subdivided into 'young' and 'old-age' ratios (Kalbach and McVey, 1979; Siegel, 1980; Clark, 1981). The old-age dependency ratio is constructed by dividing the number of people 65 and older by the number of those 20 to 64 years of age. According to the United States Bureau of the Census, the old-age dependency ratio was .09 in 1930 (each person over 65 was supported by approximately ten persons in the labor force); it had increased to about .19 in 1980 (each person 65 and older is now supported by only about five people in the labor force). It is projected that the ratio will increase to about .25 by 2015, so that each older person will be supported by approximately four people in the labor force (Clark, 1981:302). Similarly, in Canada the old age dependency ratio in 1976 was 13 percent (thirteen pensioners were supported by one hundred workers). It is projected that the Canadian ratio will increase to 16 percent in 2000, and will increase dramatically to 29 percent by 2031 when you and your younger siblings are retired (Stone and Fletcher, 1980, 1981).

Dependency ratios may be constructed according to different criteria. Some include 15- to 64-year-olds in the labor force, while others include 18- to 64-year-olds or 20- to 64-year-olds. Similarly, some measures eliminate those 15- to 64-year-olds who are not in the labor force (such as students or prisoners), and include those over 65 who are still employed and who are therefore not 'dependent.' Dependency ratios can vary according to who is or is not included in the calculation. For example, late entrants to the labor force (college graduates) are seldom excluded, and adjustments are seldom made to account for unusually high periods of unemployment. However, as long as there is consistency within a country in constructing a particular ratio, a reasonably accurate picture of the past and a projection for the future can be attained. Today, most demographers compute 'young,' 'old,' and 'total' dependency ratios for both urban and rural populations. For example, Kalbach and McVey (1979:172) reported that the rural dependency ratio in Canada is 71.9 (100 members of the labor force supporting 71.9 dependents) compared to a ratio of 57.1 in urban areas.

Although dependency ratios are frequently used to provide an index of the economic burden placed on a society by its dependent members, they are estimates only (Denton and Spencer, 1980:17–19). Variations in age with respect to entry into (legal school-leaving age) and exit from (age of mandatory retirement) the labor force, along with variations in rates of labor force involvement by women, can distort the measure. Denton and Spencer (1980) argue that a more precise measure is obtained when the actual size of the labor force is used to compute the dependency measure.

Population Age

Like its individual members, the population of a nation may be viewed as 'young,' 'mature,' or 'aged.' Although the absolute number of elderly persons in the nation might indicate the age of the population, it is not sufficient. Decreased fertility and lower immigration rates will increase the proportion of the aged within the total population, and an increase in fertility and immigration rates will result in a decrease in the proportion of the aged population. Unlike the individual, who can only grow older, the age of a nation can increase or decrease over time.

In order to monitor changes in the age of a given population, the United Nations classifies nations as 'aged' if 7 percent of the population is over 60 or 65; as 'mature' if between 4 and 7 percent are over 60 or 65; and as 'young' if fewer than 4 percent are over 60 or 65 years of age. Table 3.1 illustrates the age of selected nations at three specific times. In this table, 60 years is the determinant of population age.

Generally, 'aged' nations are highly industrialized and have low birth and death rates and long life expectancies. 'Mature' nations are partially industrialized and have low death rates. 'Mature' nations still have high birth rates, and are characterized by increasing longevity, largely because of decreased infant

Table 3.1 Population age as reflected by the percentage of the population over 60 years of age. Adapted from United Nations' *Demographic Yearbooks* and *Bulletin on Aging*, 6(1/1981), 7–16.

United Nations Category	1970	Year 1980	2000 projected
Aged (7% over 60)			
German Democratic Republic	15.6	17.0	21.6
France	13.4	17.0	18.7
United States	9.9	15.6	16.1
Canada	8.1	12.9	15.1
Soviet Union	7.7	13.0	17.5
Japan	7.1	12.6	19.8
Mature (4–7% over 60)			
Israel	6.8	11.3	11.0
Cuba	5.9	10.3	12.2
Union of South Africa	4.1	6.4	7.0
Young (4% over 60)			
Hong Kong	3.9	10.1	13.4
Mexico	3.7	5.1	5.1
Peru	3.1	5.5	5.8
Zambia	2.2	4.3	4.6

mortality and better medical and health practices. A 'young' nation is one wherein there is little, if any, industrialization, and where there are high birth and death rates and short life expectancies.

As of 1980 there were approximately fifty-three 'aged,' one hundred 'mature,' and six 'young' nations throughout the world. In fact, since 1970, there has been a large increase in the number of nations that have moved from the 'young' to the 'mature' category. Not surprisingly, most of the 'aged' nations are the more developed nations in Europe and North America, while 'mature' countries are found in Africa, Central America, and South Asia (*Bulletin on Aging*, 1981). These changes in the proportion of the aged will result in more of the developing countries being classified as 'mature' or 'aged' nations by the turn of the century — unless the value of the percent used for defining each category is adjusted upward. Thus, an 'aged' nation may be defined as one where 12 percent of the population is over 60 or 65 years of age.

In terms of the absolute number of persons in the world 65 years of age and over, the total in 1980 was 244 million; of these, approximately 130 million lived in developed countries and about 114 million lived in the less developed countries. This figure of 244 million represents between 5 and 6 percent of the total world population (Siegel, 1981). However, as Siegel states, by the year 2000 the projections are for a population of 390 million persons over 65, with 167 million in the more developed countries and 223 million in the less developed countries.

The largest percentage increase will occur in the less developed countries (127 percent versus 41 percent in the more developed countries from 1975 to 2000), largely because medium or high fertility rates are projected to continue (Siegel, 1981). To illustrate this growth in another way, it is estimated that between 1975 and 2000 there will be approximately a 97 percent increase in the population over 60 years of age in the less developed regions, compared to a 40 percent increase in the more developed regions (*Bulletin on Aging*, 1980). These fluctuations over time in the number of elderly persons reflect changing birth rates rather than a decrease in death rates or a decrease in the volume of immigration, particularly in the less developed regions of the world.

Size and Composition of the Age Structure: Past, Present, and Future

In this and the following sections, enough statistics and statistical profiles could have been presented to fill the rest of the book. However, rather than produce a demographic fact sheet, the text and tables are limited to those facts that can best provide you with a working knowledge of the age structure of the world, and particularly of North America, as it has been, as it is, and, as it might be in the future. For the student who becomes intrigued with this approach to the study of aging, there are numerous publications that can be used as primary research sources to provide more specific information.[9] There are also numerous indices to measure demographic aging (Kii, 1982). What follows is a general overview rather than an in-depth analysis of the demographics of an aging population.

In each section a world view is presented first, followed by descriptions of Canada and the United States as representatives of industrialized Western nations. In addition, reference will be made to specific countries where anomalies or unique trends appear. Where possible, past information is presented to compare with the present and the future. Finally, it must be noted that there is variation by country in the definitions of 'elderly' or 'old.' For example, where life expectancy at birth is 45, a person becomes 'old' sooner than in a country where life expectancy is 70 years. Similarly, there are different ages for mandatory retirement; these ages range from about 55 years to 70 years. However, despite these variations, the United Nations, and most countries, normally use age 60 or 65 as the benchmark to determine who should or should not be included in the aged population. In the following sections, references to the aged population will usually mean those 65 and older. Again, it must be recognized that the aged are a heterogeneous group wherein there is variation within a specific cohort (65 to 70) and between chronological age groups (65 to 70 versus 75 to 80).

Number and Proportion of Elderly People in the Population

Since the early 1900s there has been a dramatic increase in each decade in the proportion of the elderly in the total population. For example, the population 65 years of age and over in Canada was seven times larger in 1976 than it was in 1901, whereas the general population was only four times larger (Statistics Canada, 1979). This worldwide trend is expected to continue into the next century, with especially large increases occurring in the elderly population in developing countries. For example, Siegel (1981) reports that in 1975 approximately 5.3 percent of the total world population of approximately 4.1 billion was 65 years of age or older (3.3 percent in the less developed regions and 10.5 percent in the more developed regions).[10] As noted earlier, some countries have a large proportion of people over 65 (for example, Austria, the German Democractic Republic, the German Federal Republic, Norway, France), while others have a low proportion (Indonesia, Zambia, Ecuador). According to Siegel (1981), by 2000 the proportion of people over 65 in the world will rise to about 6.1 percent, with a projected increase to 4.4 and 12.6 percent in the least and most developed countries respectively.[11]

The increase in the proportion of the elderly in the modernized nations will result from further declines in birth rates and from the aging of large birth cohorts born earlier, such as the baby-boom cohort which will reach 65 after 2010. Furthermore, some countries already have attained or are approaching zero population growth. If life expectancy increases in these countries, a proportion of 15 to 19 percent aged population may not be unusual in some countries. For example, Siegel (1981) projects that in the United States 14 to 17 percent of the population will be over 65 by about 2020, while Stone and Fletcher (1980) project that 18 percent of the population in Canada will be over 65 by 2031. In the less developed countries, a projected high fertility rate combined with reduced infant and child mortality will produce only moderate increases in the proportion of the elderly. Siegel (1981) states that this pattern is likely to be especially pronounced in Africa, where the proportion of the elderly is projected to rise from 2.9 percent in 1975 to only 3.2 percent in 2000. However, if fertility rates decline dramatically in developing nations, as some demographers assume, then the proportion of elderly in the total population will increase more rapidly.

In North America, the percentage of the elderly population increased from about 5 percent of the total population in 1900 to about 9 percent in 1980 (about 2.5 million in Canada and 25 million in the United States). It is projected that by 2000 there will be an increase to about 12 percent (3.0 to 3.5 million in Canada and 30.5 million in the United States), with a further increase to as high as 17 percent between 2010 and 2020 when the baby-boom cohort reaches 65. Also, because of increasing longevity, the proportion of the elderly who are over 75 and over 85 has increased dramatically. For example, in 1900, 29 percent of the elderly in the United States (National Council on the Aging, 1978) were 75 and over; by 1975 38 percent of the elderly population was over 75 years of age. Similarly, in the same time span, the proportion of those 85 and over increased from 3.9 to 8.4 percent.

It is important to note racial and ethnic differences among the elderly in North America. In the United States, 11 percent of the white population is 65 years of age or older, but only 2.4 percent of the black population and 3.6 percent of the Hispanic population is 65 or over (National Council on the Aging, 1978). Similar ethnic differences are observed in Canada. According to the 1976 mini-census, of the approximately 2.1 million Canadians over 65, 59 percent report that their mother tongue is English (anglophones), while 22 percent report that their mother tongue is French (francophones).

In summary, shifts in the age structure of the population have occurred and will continue to occur well into the next century. As a result, the relative size of both the middle-aged and elderly segments of the population are increasing at a faster rate than the younger segments. As different age groups increase or decrease relative to each other, stresses may be placed on the various services and institutions designed to meet the needs and demands of each group. For example, the most significant fluctuation in the age structure of North America was a result of the baby-boom, which lasted from 1945 to the early 1960s. This large bulge in the age structure placed tremendous pressure on the elementary and high schools in the 1960s and on the colleges and universities in the 1970s. These facilities were expanded rapidly to meet this need; but now, in the face of declining enrollments, some of these facilities may be closed.

Similarly, this baby-boom bulge has created problems in the labor force since 1970, when large numbers of young people began to compete for a limited number of jobs. The result has been high unemployment, mostly among 16- to 25-year-olds, from the early 1970s on, and limited opportunities for advancement because of the number of competitors for each position. While this bulge was followed by a relative 'baby drought' in the 1970s, the long-term implications of the boom will be directly or indirectly experienced by all age cohorts for many years to come. For example, there may well be a shortage of labor by the end of this century. This in turn may lead to later mandatory retirement and to an increase in immigration rates. More significant, however, will be the impact on pension schemes and on health and leisure services when the baby-boom cohort become a 'senior boom' that retires between 2000 and 2030. At that time and in the following fifteen years, this segment of the population may make unprecedented demands on public and private pension programs, and on social services. These pressures may affect the quality of life for everyone, retirees and workers alike.

The Aged-Dependency Ratio

The aged-dependency ratio, which represents the degree to which the nonworking elderly population is supported by those in the labor force, is higher (Siegel, 1981) in the modernized nations (16.2 persons 65 and over per 100 persons aged 15 to 64) than in the less developed nations (6.0 persons 65 and over per 100 persons aged 15 to 64). Siegel projects that by 2000 the ratio of those 65 and over in modernized nations will increase to more than 19 per 100 younger persons and to between 6.9 and 7.9 in less developed nations.

Siegel has also constructed a ratio of adult children (45 to 49 years of age) to elderly parents. This ratio provides an index of the amount of support for the elderly that is available within families (the family dependency ratio). Using 1975 data, he found that the child-to-parent ratio in the more developed regions of the world was 92 children (who were 45 to 49 years of age) per 100 parents (who were 65 to 74 years of age). In the less developed regions, this ratio was 163 adult children per 100 parents. Siegel projects that by 2000 these ratios will decrease to 86 and 149 respectively. These family dependency ratios are higher in the less developed countries because of higher birth and death rates. The ratio suggests that the few surviving elderly in less developed countries have more children to support them in the later years.

The Sex Ratio of the Elderly

A universal pattern is the increasingly greater number of women than men across the life cycle, with a particularly large increase in old age. As Siegel (1981) shows, in the modernized countries in 1975 there were sixty-four males per one hundred females aged 65 and over, compared to eighty-eight per one hundred in less developed countries. This trend is expected to continue, although with less differentiation by the year 2000. This ratio is subject to variation because of historical events or unusual mortality patterns. For example, the sex ratio in the U.S.S.R. and Eastern Europe was fifty-three men per one hundred women in 1975, partly because of the large number of male deaths during World War II. However, this ratio should climb to a projected value of sixty by the year 2000, and increase thereafter unless abnormal mortality patterns occur. Similarly, in countries where female death rates are higher at all ages (for example, India or

Pakistan), the ratio at age 65 may be more than ninety men per one hundred women.

In North America men outnumbered women in the early 1900s because of higher immigration rates for men. However, the trend, especially since World War II, has been toward a steady decrease in the number of men to women at all ages, but particularly after age 65. In 1976 the sex ratio in Canada for those 65 and over was eighty-six men per one hundred women, while in 1975 in the United States there were sixty-eight men per one hundred women (which decreased to fifty-eight per one hundred after 75 years of age). In the United States, by 1980 the ratio was sixty-six men per one hundred women for those 65 years of age and older. For those over 85, it decreased to fifty men per one hundred women (*Statistical Bulletin*, 1981b). It is projected that the U.S. ratio will be sixty-five men per one hundred women over 65 by 2000.

These trends can be accounted for by a number of combined factors. First, a shift in immigration patterns occurred: although there was a decrease in the actual number of immigrants to North America, more females than males immigrated in the 1930s and 1940s. Many of these people are now older widows. Second, although there have been significant medical advances in this century, the longevity of men has not increased significantly, since they experience a higher incidence of cardiovascular disease than women. Third, men of all ages tend to have higher accidental-death rates. Finally, compared to Canada, the lower ratio in the United States may be partially accounted for by greater involvement in foreign wars and, hence, a higher incidence of male deaths for particular age cohorts.

Summary

There has been about a twenty-year increase in the average human life span during the past century. Moreover, the absolute numbers of elderly people and the proportion of those over 65 have grown significantly. This 'graying' trend has resulted because of increasing longevity owing to better health care, decreasing birth and infant mortality rates, higher standards of living, and a decreasing immigration rate. Women have a higher life expectancy than men, and the ratio of men to women decreases over the life cycle. This pattern of increasing longevity and proportional growth of persons over 65 is most pronounced among whites and females, especially in more developed nations.

These trends are expected to continue into the twenty-first century, and will be most evident in the least developed nations, as well as in modernized nations when the baby-boom cohort becomes the senior-boom cohort. In North America, as the immigration rates decrease, the elderly population will become more homogeneous in cultural orientation and past life experiences. This is not to say that each cohort that passes 65 will be a homogeneous group: rather, they will be more comparable in terms of language, customs, values, and life experiences than the present over-65 age cohorts, many of which include members who were not born in North America.

Distribution of the Aging Population

This section presents information concerning the distribution of the aged population according to a number of demographic and environmental factors. This information enables us to understand better the lifestyles, status, and problems experienced by particular cohorts at specific stages in the life cycle. While the focus here is on the elderly of North America, the reader must remember that some (but not necessarily all) of these factors will apply to the elderly in every country. Some may not necessarily apply to all future elderly cohorts in North America. Whether a factor influences the aging population is very much dependent on historical events, cultural traditions, geography, population distribution, degree of modernization, and type of political system.

Demographic Factors and the Age Distribution of the Elderly Population

Educational status.   In the early part of this century, effort and ability were more important prerequisites than educational attainment in obtaining and advancing in a job. However, academic achievement has become increasingly essential to success. Today, a person's level of educational attainment influences attitudes, values, behavior, friendships, job opportunities, and income throughout the life cycle, particularly in modernized nations.

It was not until after World War II that educational opportunities increased, as did the value placed on attainment of high-school diplomas and college degrees.[12] The present cohort of older people has generally completed less formal education than younger cohort. Table 3.2 indicates the level of educational attainment of those under and over age 65 in Canada. The figures shown in table 3.2 are averages, and do not account for sex, ethnic, class, or racial differences. For example, in the United States, a lower percentage of blacks than whites complete a high-school or college education; and, while a higher percentage of women than men complete high school, a lower percentage of women complete college. As of March 1977 (McConnel and Deljavan, 1981) the median level of education for those 65 and over in the United States was as follows: men, 9.0 years (white men, 9.4 and black men, 6.2), and women, 9.8 years (white women, 10.2 and black women, 7.4). Statistics on educational attainment include many who were foreign born and who emigrated to North America when they were beyond high-school age. Many of those in the present cohort of older people were not educated in North America. Therefore, with the recent decrease in immigration rates, in the future a larger percentage of each age cohort will have completed at least some high school because of statutes requiring attendance until the age of 15 or 16.

Table 3.2   Level of educational attainment of those under and over 65 in Canada. Adapted from Statistics Canada, 1976 Census.

	Under 65	65 and over
Elementary School	23.9	58.9
High School	60.4	34.1
College Attendance	8.9	4.5
College or University Degree	6.8	2.6

As noted above, the level of educational attainment of the over-65 population is lower than that of younger age cohorts. However, with each new cohort the median number of years of formal education increases. These projections suggest that by the year 2000 approximately 50 percent of those over 65 in the United States will have attained at least a high-school education (Cutler and Harootyan, 1975), although the percentage completing a university degree will remain at less than 20 percent. Although the level of educational attainment of the elderly will increase, it is still expected to lag behind the under-65 population, at least until the relatively well educated baby boom cohort reaches age 65 after about 2010. However, the age-cohort gap in educational attainment could narrow faster because of the increasing trend for adults to enroll in college and university credit and noncredit courses. It also remains to be seen how educational television will influence the formal and informal educational pursuits of adults at all ages.

Marital status.   Quite simply, most older men are married and most older women are widowed. This discrepancy increases further with advancing age. To illustrate, between 75 and 80 percent of men over 65 in Canada and the United States are married, whereas only 40 percent of women over 65 are married. Thus, women who are widowed at 65 to 70 years of age may live alone for ten to fifteen years. This pattern of an uneven ratio between widows and widowers has resulted from a number of factors, including higher death rates for men, the social norm of men marrying younger women, a higher remarriage rate for widowers, an informal social norm that discourages elderly widows from remarrying, and the unavailability of older men should older women wish to remarry. The social consequence of this pattern is a large number of older widows who live alone.

Regardless of their sex, those who are married have a higher life expectancy than their single counterparts. For example, the 1976 Canadian mini-census showed that the life expectancy of married men is just over 72 years, whereas it is about 64 years for lifelong bachelors and 60 years for widowers and divorced men. Similarly, the life expectancy for married women is about 79 years, compared to 76 years for women who never marry and 73 years for widows and divorcees. It is suggested that this pattern occurs primarily because married couples have a different lifestyle from that of unattached persons: they live in better housing, they eat better, they take better care of themselves; in addition, a spouse is likely to make sure that prompt medical attention is received when illness occurs.

Labor-force participation.   Because fewer people are self-employed, especially in urban areas, and because of the introduction of mandatory retirement, the proportion of those over 65 in the labor force has declined steadily throughout this century, particularly in the past three decades. In 1900 about two of every three elderly males were employed; by 1975 only one in five was in the U.S. labor force. This ratio is expected to be about one in six by 1990 (National Council on the Aging, 1978:75). Thus, an increasing proportion of the elderly male population will be unemployed for the remainder of this century, despite a large number who want to work or need to work for economic survival. Moreover, for some retirement is occurring earlier than age 65, and an increasing number are becoming unemployed during the middle (45 to 64) years.

The average duration of unemployment increases with age. For the middle-aged and elderly, the earlier the unemployment, whether temporary or permanent, the greater the loss in income and the greater the number of years spent without sufficient income. This has a profound effect on the psychological adjustment of many, and on the quality and style of life for most. Recently, it has been argued in the United States that forced retirement at age 65 is discriminatory. As a result, the mandatory retirement age has been increased to 70 years for most occupational groups in the United States.

Labor-force participation by both men and women declines in the later years, although an increasing number of women have been entering the labor force when their families leave home or because of economic necessity if they are divorced or widowed. Many of these women remain employed until age 65 and after, often in part-time or low-paying occupations. Until the mid-1970s, about 8 percent of the women over 65 in Canada and the United States were employed. Since then there has been a slight decline, along with generally higher unemployment rates at all age levels. It is projected that the percentage of employed women over 65 will be about 7.5 percent by 1990 (National Council on the Aging, 1978:77). That is, the reduction in the number of employed elderly women will be less than that for men, perhaps because they have a greater need to earn income, especially if they are widowed or divorced.

In summary, most elderly people are retired. For some this status is voluntary. However, a growing number retire only because they cannot obtain or retain a job. Among those who are employed after 65, between 50 and 66 percent are only employed in part-time positions. Again, in some cases this is by choice. For others, part-time work represents the only type of employment they can obtain, or the maximum amount of time they can devote to earning an income without becoming ineligible for government pension benefits. In short, older employees who wish to work are generally found in low-paying occupations. For those who need to work, even obtaining a job does not guarantee that their economic needs can be met.

Economic status.   This subsection briefly describes the economic status of the elderly individual. (Chapter 10 presents a more extensive analysis of the economic impact of retirement.) The discussion begins with some caveats. First, with respect to this topic, perhaps more so than any other area statistics become obsolete very quickly. Therefore, the most recent and accurate statistics should be obtained from the government documents section of your library. Second, statistics that are reported in the media may be manipulated or misinterpreted in order to support a particular view.

Furthermore, as we shall see, sufficient information is seldom available. This is either because complete information was not collected from individuals, or because the statistics are aggregated and treat the aged as one homogeneous group. Aggregate data for those over 65 years of age may include the very wealthy who report little job-related income but who have large investments and equity; those who are employed full- or part-time; those retirees who receive social security and pension payments; and those retirees who receive minimal social security payments and no private pension payments. Thus, in order not to distort reality, statistics on the economic status of the elderly need to be presented (1) for the retired, the partially retired, and the full-time worker; (2) for the young-old and the very old; (3) for married couples, the separated and divorced, the widowed, and the never-married; (4) for racial and class groups; (5) for males and females; (6) for total assets, not just current income; and (7) for single versus dual pensioners (where both spouses receive private pension payments).

Researchers should also be aware that individuals may intentionally misrepresent the information they report about their assets, income, and expenditures. They do so because they view these topics, like sex, to be confidential matters. Or they may unintentionally provide incomplete or inaccurate information because they do not really know their economic situation apart from income from pension plans or employment. For these reasons, Henretta (1979) argues that the economic status of the elderly should be measured by net worth or wealth, rather than by annual income.

Finally, there does not appear to be agreement concerning the meaning of 'poverty,' 'inadequate income,' or 'inadequate standard of living' (Hogg et al., 1981), or the point at which social problems arise related to each of these categories. For example, the 'poverty index' in the United States is calculated as three times the annual amount of money income (before taxes) that is needed to purchase food to maintain a minimum adequate diet. A multiple of three is used because it is assumed that a family spends about one-third of its income on food. Yet family size is not considered as a factor (although marital status is). Moreover, the 'hidden poor,' who live with and are supported almost totally by relatives, are usually not included among those living below the poverty line. In 1982 the poverty line in the United States for a married couple with two children was approximately $9,200. In Canada, a person lives below the poverty line if more than 62 percent of income is required to provide the basic economic necessities of food, shelter, and clothing (The percentage figure varies according to region.) In 1981, the poverty line in Canada was about $8,400 for a married couple, and about $5,800 for a single person.

Schulz (1980:37–38) notes that in 1977, 14 percent of all elderly persons in the United States received money income that placed them below the poverty level, a decline from 35 percent in 1959. Thus, the economic status of the elderly appears to be improving because of the increased size and availability of public and private pension plans, because salaries and savings have increased, because of tax concessions and increased subsidies for the elderly (in-kind income such as subsidized housing, transportation, medical care, and food), and because families are more likely to provide income than services to aging parents. However, since the aged are not a homogeneous group, there are variations from this average. For example, only about 12 percent of elderly whites live below the poverty line, compared to about 35 percent of elderly nonwhites. Similarly, 24 percent of families with a female head (widows or divorcees) 65 and over live below the poverty line, compared to 9 percent of families with a male head. In Canada, the median income in 1976 of 65- to 69-year-old males was more than twice than that of females of a similar age (Stone and MacLean, 1979).

The poverty index is based solely on before-tax money income. Therefore, if in-kind income (such as health plans, food stamps, subsidized housing), transfer payments (government pensions or social security), tax benefits (income tax deductions or property tax relief), within-family transfers (cash from children), and an adjustment for underreporting of income are taken into consideration, an individual's actual financial status will often be higher than that reported. For example, Schulz (1980:37) quotes a 1977 Congressional Budget Office study showing that 58 percent of elderly families would fall below the poverty line if social insurance benefits were not included in total income. If they are included, only 19 percent fall into this category; If all sources of income, including 'in-kind' income, are included, the figure drops to 4 percent.

Let us now examine the median income levels for the United States as reported by a recent survey (Grad and Foster, 1979).[13] The median total family income for families of all ages was $20,000, whereas for families headed by persons aged 65 or over it was only $8,600.[14] Not surprisingly, the median income of elderly men ($11,000) exceeded that of women ($6,700). Of those with less than $5,000 median income per year, 78 percent are women. Finally, the median income of blacks, in families and unattached, was $5,000; for Hispanics it was $5,600.

In Canada, the situation is much the same. For example, in 1977 the average income for all families was approximately $21,000; for families headed by persons aged 65 to 69, $12,000;[15] for families headed by persons aged 70 and over, $9,000; for all unattached individuals, $9,000; for unattached individuals aged 65 to 69, $4,500; and for unattached individuals aged 70 and over, $4,000 (Stone and Fletcher, 1981). As in the United States, the incomes for families headed by a man and for unattached men exceeded that for women in all situations. Interestingly, the Canadian statistics reveal that since 1969 the relative difference in income between the elderly and other age groups has remained about the same.

Some attention has been directed toward introducing a more subjective component in assessing the standard of living or quality of life experienced by the elderly person. Unlike the purely objective measurements based on minimal survival needs, subjective approaches take into account a range of needs and wants related to the real standard of living of older persons. One such measure is the United States Bureau of Labor Statistics' Retired Couples' Budget. This index provides three different levels of modest but adequate standards of living.[16] The budget pertains to urban families only and is adjusted annually in response to changes in the Consumer Price Index. Although this index is not widely used, it does acknowledge that after retirement the standard of living can vary greatly because of three main factors: assets, expenditure patterns of disposable income, and the impact of inflation, especially on rental costs and fixed or decreasing incomes.

Although it is difficult to obtain complete and accurate information about assets held by the elderly, generally they have nonliquid equity in a home and some liquid assets such as cash, bank deposits, stocks, or bonds, which yield varying rates of interest. However, the longer one lives, the more likely it is these liquid assets will be converted to cash to maintain a minimal standard of living. Ultimately, nonliquid assets (such as a home) may have to be sold in order to pay for institutionalization or health care. As with other sources of financial support, whites, men, and the married generally have more assets during retirement.

Despite the persistence of the idea that the economic needs of the elderly are fewer than those of younger age groups, they still have a need for food, shelter, and health care. Moreover, while the need for these specific items remains constant or increases with age, they are highly susceptible to inflation. According to most studies, most elderly people spend a higher proportion of their budgets on food, shelter, and health care than do other age groups. For example, in 1973 (National Council on the Aging, 1978:66) those 65 years and over, compared to those 55 to 64 years of age, spent more on food (16.3 percent versus 12.3 percent), housing (23.0 percent versus 16.4 percent), health care (7.3 percent versus 4.3 percent), and transportation (19.7 percent versus 12.9 percent). The average annual income of those over 65 decreased by about 50 percent, but their consumption patterns did not decrease at the same rate. It is usually impossible to save money after retirement, and preretirement assets must often be used to maintain a comparable standard of living. This dependency on preretirement assets becomes particularly pronounced the longer one lives.

The expenditure pattern after retirement is further complicated by the double-digit inflation of recent years: the purchasing power of those with relatively fixed incomes is eroded even further and at a faster rate. Moreover, the 'real' dollar value of savings, investments, and private pensions has declined so that $1.00 earned twenty years ago is worth less than 50 cents when it is spent today. Although government pension plans are indexed to inflation, many private plans are not. Moreover, even where a government plan is pegged to inflation, the increase, like salaries for the employed, usually lags at least a year behind the real rate of inflation. Some argue that the elderly have a degree of protection against inflation (Schulz, 1980:42–46) because social security benefits are adjusted automatically for inflation. However, this source of income accounts for only about 50 percent of the retirement income of the elderly in Canada (Stone and Fletcher, 1981: chart 23) and the United States. The other 50 percent is derived from earnings, assets, and private pension plans, most of which are negatively influenced by inflation.

In summary, although the economic status of the elderly has improved in the past two decades relative to earlier retiree cohorts, their status relative to younger age groups has not changed significantly. Clearly, there is a curvilinear relationship between age and income that varies from near zero (a small 'allowance' from one's parents) in early childhood, to a maximum in the years before age 64 (if steadily employed), to a level that likely falls below or approaches that of the starting salary received by an individual upon entrance into the labor force as a full-time employee.

For most of the current elderly cohort, the major source of income is social security payments, although a larger percentage of each new cohort of retirees will have access to private pension plans.[17] The elderly are gaining increasing tax relief and public health assistance that compensates somewhat, but not entirely, for inflation. Thus, although only a small percentage of the elderly live in 'poverty' conditions, many experience a decline in their standard of living, either when they avoid using their savings or when they begin to draw on their savings. This erosion of savings has a particularly harsh effect on widows who usually outlive their husbands by many years.

Environmental Factors and the Age Distribution of the Elderly Population

Despite the prevailing myth that the elderly are institutionalized, only about 9 percent of those over 65 in Canada (Schwenger and Gross, 1980) and just over 5 percent of those over 65 in the United States live in institutions.[18] Most of those who are institutionalized are over 75, female (widows), and Caucasian. Thus, it appears that at least 90 percent of the elderly are still located in the community, although they are not randomly distributed by country, by region, by place of residence, by neighbourhood, or by type of housing. This section briefly outlines, from the macro to the micro level, where the elderly live. In chapter 8 more detailed information will be presented concerning the impact of ecological factors on the aging process and the housing, mobility, and migration patterns of the elderly.

Variation in geographical region.   The United Nations has subdivided the world into eight regions. According to the 1980 estimate as well as projections for the year 2000, the population of persons 65 and over is distributed throughout the world as outlined in Table 3.3. Table 3.3 indicates that the elderly comprise a higher percentage of the population in the more developed regions, particularly in Europe, North America, the Soviet Union and Oceania. It is projected that the greatest increase between 1980 and 2000 in the elderly population as a percent of the total will occur in East Asia, Europe, and the Soviet Union.

Table 3.3   Projected regional distribution of the world population, 1980 and 2000. Source: *Bulletin on Aging*, 6(1/1981), 7–16. [More developed regions = North America, Japan, Europe, Australia, New Zealand, Soviet Union; Less developed regions = Africa, Latin America, China, other East Asia, South Asia, Melanesia, Micronesia, Polynesia; Africa = Eastern, Western, Middle, Northern, Southern Africa; Latin America = Caribbean Islands, Central America, South America; North America = Canada and the United States; East Asia = China, the Koreas, Japan, Hong Kong, Mongolia; South Asia = Eastern South Asia (Burma, Indonesia, Phillipines, Singapore, Vietnam), Middle South Asia (Bangladesh, Afghanistan, India, Pakistan, Iran), and Western South Asia (Iraq, Israel, Saudi Arabia, Syria, Yemen); Europe = Eastern, Northern (including Great Britain, Northern Ireland, Iceland), Southern (Greece, Turkey, Italy, Portugal), and Western Europe; Oceania = Australia, New Zealand, New Guinea, Fiji.]

Region	Total Population (Millions)		Percent of the population aged 60 and over (per 1000 inhabitants)	
	1980	2000	1980	2000
World	4,415.0	6,199.4	8.4	9.4
More developed regions	1,176.0	1,341.6	15.2	18.2
Less developed regions	3,239.0	4,857.8	6.1	7.1
Africa	469.4	828.1	4.9	5.2
Latin America	368.5	608.1	6.2	6.8
North America	246.4	289.5	15.4	16.0
East Asia	1,135.9	1,406.1	8.9	14.4
South Asia	1,376.7	2,135.7	4.9	5.9
Europe	528.8	589.6	15.9	18.1
Oceania	22.8	29.7	11.4	12.5
Soviet Union	266.7	311.8	13.0	17.5

While we have relatively little choice in which country of the world we reside in, there is considerably greater freedom, at least after about age 15, to choose a region within a country, a rural or urban environment, a neighborhood, and a type of housing within that neighborhood. All of these factors provide clues about the needs of people, their lifestyles and the normative system that influences them. Like other age groups, most of the elderly in North America live in those states and provinces with the greatest population density. Thus, in absolute terms, in Canada, almost 75 percent of those 65 and over live in Quebec, Ontario, and British Columbia (Statistics Canada, 1979); in the United States approximately 45 percent live in the six most populous states (New York, California, Pennsylvania, Illinois, Texas, and Ohio) and in Florida.

However, the geographical distribution of the elderly in proportion to the total population reveals a different pattern. In Canada, Prince Edward Island (with 11.2 percent), Saskatchewan (11.1 percent), Manitoba (10.4 percent), British Columbia (9.8 percent), and Nova Scotia (9.7 percent), have the highest proportions of elderly citizens. With the exception of British Columbia, which has a high rate of in-migration by retirees, the other provinces are characterized by low incomes, high out-migration of the young, and high old age dependency ratios.

In the United States, after Florida (16.1 percent), South Dakota, Missouri, Arkansas, Kansas, Iowa, Nebraska, Oklahoma, and Rhode Island all report that over 12 percent of their populations are 65 years of age and over. Like British Columbia, Florida has a high incidence of in-migration by retirees, while the midwest states reflect out-migration by the young from farms to urban areas. As Lawton (1980:24) observes, the variation between states with respect to the proportion of the over-65 population is about 8 percent. This variation in the distribution of the elderly must be considered when establishing policies and providing services to meet the needs of specific age groups (Longino, 1982). There are also some significant within-state variations at the county level (Van Es and Bowling, 1978–79; Gillaspy, 1979). These too can have an impact on the distribution of state and provincial financial resources and social services.

Rural-urban distribution.   In both Canada and the United States, about 75 percent of those 65 years of age and over live in urban areas; the remaining 25 percent live in rural areas, usually on farms. Of those who live in urban areas, about 60 percent live in large cities; 40 percent live in communities with fewer than 25,000 inhabitants. In the United States, about 31 percent of all those 65 and over live in the central core of a large city.

There are racial differences in the distribution of the elderly within the central core areas of cities. About 55 percent of elderly blacks and 53 percent of elderly Hispanics live in the central city, compared with about 30 percent of elderly whites (Lawton, 1980:25). Thus, the age structure and the racial composition of a neighborhood must be determined when examining the status and interaction patterns of the elderly. The elderly person who lives in the central city experiences a different social and physical environment from one who lives in a suburban area, a small town, or on a farm. Residents of the central core may have poorer housing, may be more dependent on public transportation, may have higher living costs, and may be more susceptible to crime.

The current cohort of elderly persons is overrepresented in the central cities and in small rural towns with a total population of fewer than 2500 inhabitants. In the metropolitan areas, the elderly living in the central core usually own their homes. However, because of a lack of income, because of the lower value of homes compared to those in the suburbs, and because of strong attachments to the neighborhood, they tend to remain in the central area. This 'aging-in-place' phenomenon occurs even when the racial composition of the neighborhood changes, or when a home begins to need major repairs, some of which may not be affordable. In the small rural towns, the overrepresentation of the elderly is primarily a function of the out-migration of the young to larger centers and the in-migration of retired farmers.

This pattern of age segregation (Rosow, 1967) in specific sections of the larger cities reflects to some extent the age of a neighborhood. That is, the elderly are situated in the central core because this is where housing was located when they first purchased a home. Similarly, recent immigrant groups have tended to settle in core areas because housing is less expensive, because public transportation is available, and because the labor market is usually nearby.

The suburban fringe areas around cities expanded greatly after the 1950s. In the early years of a suburban development, the age of the occupants is generally under 40. With time, the population in the suburbs ages, since most individuals tend to remain in the same house throughout adulthood, with only a small percentage making a move after retirement. Thus, the suburbs that were constructed in the 1950s are increasingly likely to have a large proportion of elderly people, as children leave and the aging parents remain in the family home (Stahura, 1980). It is often not until the original owners grow too old to look after a home or until a spouse dies that the property is resold, often to a younger couple, thereby initiating a new cycle in the age structure of the neighborhood.

Within the next twenty years the suburban areas will include an increasingly larger proportion of older individuals. Whether the suburbs become age-segregated neighborhoods will depend on migration patterns between communities. For example, the onset of the energy crisis, combined with inflationary housing prices and the changing lifestyles of young adults, has led to a trend of younger couples moving into the central city for economic and social reasons. This pattern decreases the proportion of the elderly in the central core, and perhaps hastens age segregation in the suburbs. Similarly, with decreases in immigration rates, fewer immigrants are moving into the central core. The proportion of the elderly in the inner core may not change much in the future since the loss of immigrants may be offset by in-migration to the central core by younger, working couples. Finally, the higher proportion of younger inhabitants in the suburbs may not change if minority groups and second- and third-generation immigrants continue to migrate, first to the older suburbs and then to the newer suburbs as their economic situation improves.

In summary, while most elderly people tend to remain in the central core of large cities or in small rural towns, most neighborhoods are age-integrated (Cowgill, 1978). However, because neighborhoods are developed at different times, between-neighborhood variation in the average age of occupants is a common pattern. Cowgill states that growth is the prime determinant of internal age segregation within a metropolitan area. This internal community migration must be monitored by the public and private sectors in order to meet age-specific needs as demographic changes occur. If the proportion of the elderly increases in a suburban neighborhood, resources may need to be shifted from the youth sector to the senior sector of the population within that neighborhood. For example, community recreation departments may need to expend an increasing proportion of their human, physical, and financial resources to provide facilities and programs for middle-aged and elderly adults. Similarly, owners of business establishments may need to change the types of merchandise or services they offer.

Housing and living arrangements.   In North America, between 65 and 70 percent of the elderly heads of private households own their homes.[19] (Statistics Canada, 1979; National Council on the Aging, 1978; Stone and Fletcher, 1980, 1981). The percentage of homeowners increases for those who live in smaller urban areas and on farms (Struyk, 1977). In addition, more elderly men than women own their own homes. This is partially a reflection of the greater likelihood of a widow selling the family home and moving into an apartment or institution later in life. For the elderly, the home represents a major financial asset. In the United States, about 50 percent of the homes owned by those over 65 were constructed before 1940, and are currently subject to high maintenance costs. Thus, while a home is an asset, it can also become a financial liability in the later years, especially if maintenance costs cannot be met, resulting in structural deterioration and declining value.

In the past, many elderly people lived with an adult child or other relative. Today, the trend is for both generations to seek autonomy and independence.[20] More than 70 percent of men over 65 are married and living with a spouse. However, because of greater longevity and a tendency not to remarry, only 30 to 35 percent of all women over 65 live with a spouse. Thus, excluding those who live with someone in the extended family and those who live with a spouse, about 12 percent of elderly men and 33 percent of elderly women between 65 and 74 years of age live alone. This percentage increases to about 18 and 41 percent, respectively, after the age of 75 (National Council on the Aging, 1978:21). Living alone, especially if one is poor, ill, and without friends, can lead to social isolation, loneliness, and a further decline in physical or mental health. Finally, as noted earlier, only between 3 and 5 percent of the younger segment of the elderly population (under 75) in North America are institutionalized, although this percentage increases to between 7 and 10 percent after the age of 75, and to over 35 percent after about the age of 85.

Summary and Conclusions

In this chapter, the emphasis has been on population aging rather than on individual aging. The reader has been introduced to demographic indices and patterns that indicate the size, composition, and distribution of the age structure throughout the world, along with projections for the future.

Although the elderly are still a numerical minority, they comprise an increasingly larger proportion of the population in all countries because of declining fertility and greater longevity. This trend is likely to continue, so that by the beginning of the next century between 12 and 17 percent of the population in North America will be 65 years of age and over. Similar trends are likely to occur in other countries. However, the greatest increase will likely occur in the older, more developed nations, and in the developing nations as fertility controls are introduced and adopted. Thus, there is cross-national variation in the number and proportion of the aged compared to the total population. Within a country the elderly are not a homogeneous group, but vary greatly, especially with respect to health, economic status, sex, and class. These variations are likely to continue in the future, particularly where the society itself is experiencing population aging and considerable social change.

In conclusion, this demographic analysis of population aging has indicated that:

1. Population aging is a reflection of three basic demographic processes: fertility rates, mortality rates, and migration rates.

2. The life span represents the theoretical and biological limits to the maximum number of years an individual can live. At present, the life span for humans is about 100 years, although most will die before this age.

3. Life expectancy is the average number of years of life remaining for an individual at a given age. At present, the life expectancy at birth is about 73 years in the more developed nations, and about 45 to 50 years in the less developed nations.

4. Higher life expectancies are predicted for Caucasians, females, urban dwellers, the married, and those with higher levels of educational attainment and income.

5. There is a 'crossover' effect in life expectancy for nonwhite males: after about age 75, their life expectancy exceeds that of white males.

6. Although males outnumber females at birth, the sex ratio (males per 100 females) declines with age. At present, the sex ratio for the population over 65 years of age is eighty-six and sixty-eight males per one hundred females in Canada and the United States respectively.

7. The old-age dependency ratio represents the number of nonworkers over 65 years of age who are supported by those in the labor force who are 20 to 64 years of age. At present, each person over 65 in the United States is supported by approximately five people in the labor force; in Canada, the ratio is approximately one to eight. The ratio in the less developed nations is about half that in the more developed nations.

8. The population of a nation may be labeled as 'young,' 'mature,' or 'old,' depending on the proportion of people in the total population who are over 60 or 65 years of age. As of 1980 there were approximately fifty-three 'aged' (7 percent over 60 or 65), one hundred 'mature' (4 to 7 percent over 60 or 65), and six 'young' (less than 4 percent over 60 or 65) nations throughout the world. A majority of the aged nations are the most developed nations; the mature countries are found in Africa, Central America, and South Asia.

9. With declining birth rates and increased longevity, populations are increasingly moving from the 'young' to the 'mature' to the 'aged' classification.

10. At present, the elderly comprise a higher percentage of the total population in the more developed nations and regions of the world than in the less developed nations and regions.

11. Although it is increasing with each birth cohort, the level of educational attainment of the population 65 and over is lower than that of younger age cohorts.

12. Most older men are married, and most older women are widowed. This discrepancy widens for those over about 70 years of age.

13. The proportion of those over 65 in the labor force has declined steadily throughout this century in industrialized societies.

14. Of those who are employed after the age of 65, between 50 and 66 percent are employed in low-paying part-time positions.

15. The economic status of the elderly has improved in recent decades, but their relative economic status compared to younger cohorts has not changed significantly.

16. Only a small percentage of the elderly live in 'poverty' conditions, but many (especially older widows) experience a decline in their standard of living after retirement.

17. Those most likely to fall below the poverty line are elderly nonwhites and families headed by women.

18. Of those over 65 years of age, approximately 9 percent in Canada and 5 percent in the United States are institutionalized. Most of those who are institutionalized are Caucasian, female (widows), and over 75 years of age.

19. Within North America, the elderly generally live in those states and provinces with the greatest population density.

20. In North America, about 75 percent of those over 65 live in urbanized areas, with about 31 percent living in the inner core of large cities.

21. The racial composition of those living within the inner city varies. Only about 30 percent of elderly whites live in the central core, compared with over 50 percent of elderly blacks and Hispanics, who often live in racially homogeneous ghettoes.

22. The suburbs that were built in the 1950s are likely to have a large proportion of elderly people in the next few decades.

23. In North America, between 65 and 70 percent of the elderly heads of private households own their homes, especially in smaller urban areas and in rural areas. Also, more elderly men than women own their homes.

24. About 12 percent of elderly men and 33 percent of elderly women between 65 and 74 years of age live alone. This percentage increases to about 18 and 41 percent respectively after the age of 75.

25. Although the elderly are still a numerical minority, they comprise an increasingly large proportion of the population in each nation, especially where fertility rates have decreased and where longevity has increased. In the future, large increases in the proportion of elderly citizens can be expected in developing nations if fertility controls are introduced and adopted.

Notes

1. For example, complete results for the 1980 United States census should be available in late 1982; the results from the 1981 Canada census may not appear until late 1982 or early 1983.

2. For example, the old-age dependency ratio mentioned later has been variously compiled using the following ages in the denominator: 15 to 64, 18 to 64, and 20 to 64. Thus, the specific ratios for a given year may differ according to the source consulted. The trend over a number of years is most meaningful if the same denominator is employed from one study to another, and from one country to another.

3. Some useful statistical sources that are available in the periodicals or government publications sections of most libraries include: Publications from the United Nations Social Development Division, such as the annual *Demographic Yearbook* (New York) and the semi-annual *Bulletin on Aging* (Vienna); Reports of the United States Bureau of the Census (Washington); Reports of Statistics Canada (Ottawa); Reports of the World Health Organization (Geneva); Reports of the International Labor Organization (Geneva); Reports from the United Nations Educational, Scientific and Cultural Organization (Paris); Reports from The National Council on the Aging (Washington); Reports from city, state, or provincial social agencies; Journals such as *Demography, Social Indicators, Population Studies,* and the numerous gerontology journals; the monthly *Social Security Bulletin* (Washington, D.C.: U.S. Government Printing Office); the quarterly *Statistical Bulletin* (New York: Metropolitan Life Insurance Co.); Demography sourcebooks that concentrate on individual and population aging (Stone and Fletcher, 1980, 1981; National Council on Aging, 1978, 1981; Gutman, 1982).

4. Most countries now have a census every ten years, in which there is an attempt to count every citizen. For example, in the United States, a census is conducted in years ending in 0; in Canada, a Census is conducted in years ending in 1. In addition, there is often a mini-census taken halfway between the

complete censuses. Unfortunately, every census undercounts the population because of inaccuracies in reporting, because some people are not available to be interviewed or counted (including illegal aliens or those who cannot speak English (or in Canada, English or French), or are traveling. For example, the 1970 U.S. census reported an underestimate of approximately 5 million people, many of whom lived in the slums and core areas of large cities.

5. Registrations are required for such events as births, immigrations, deaths, marriages, obtaining a driver's license, buying a house, and paying income and property taxes.

6. It is difficult to determine the lifespan of earlier civilizations and generations because registrations of births and deaths were not recorded, or were inaccurate or incomplete until about the mid-nineteenth century (Laslett, 1976).

7. To determine your own life expectancy, after identifying yourself as male or female, Caucasian or nonwhite, you enter the row in a specific life table for your country and your year of birth. Move across to the column that matches your current chronological age. This figure indicates the average number of remaining years you can expect to live. Generally, if you were born in North America between 1960 and 1970 you can expect to live, on the average, about 68 years if you are a male and about 75 years if you are a female. The present life expectancy of 25-year-olds in North America is approximately 48 years for males and 54 years for females; for 20-year-olds it is about 52 for males and 59 for females.

8. According to the most recent statistics, the expectation of life at birth in the United States is 73.8 years, with the average expected lifetime for males being 70.0 years and for females 77.6 years (*Statistical Bulletin,* 1981a:14–15).

9. The primary sources should include *Demographic Yearbooks*, produced by the United Nations; the various reports of Statistics Canada, the United States Bureau of the Census, and the census bureaus in other countries; *Demography*; the United Nations *Bulletin on Aging*; and the publications of the U.S. National Council on the Aging (1978, 1981).

10. Siegel (1981) defines the 'most developed countries' as: Canada, the United States, those in temperate South America, those in

Europe, the Soviet Union, Japan, Australia, and New Zealand; the 'least developed countries' are those in all other areas of the world. For more detailed projections by country in each region of the world, see the tables in the United Nations *Bulletin on Aging,* volumes 3 to 6 (1978–81). These tables present the proportion of the population over 60 years of age in 1975 and 1980, and make projections for the year 2000.

11. Population projections (McFarland, 1978; Denton and Spencer, 1980:19–21) are made by taking the existing population in a given year, and then making assumptions about future fertility rates, mortality rates, and migration rates. Based on these assumptions it is possible to project, but not to predict, the size and proportion of the population in total and for age, sex, and race categories. Because they are projections rather than predictions, demographers often include low, medium, and high projections based on possible variations in the fertility, mortality, and migration rates. In this chapter, only the medium projection rates are reported.

12. This value on education was further heightened by the onset of the 'space race' in the late 1950s (Sputnik was launched on October 4, 1957) and early 1960s when it became apparent that North America needed to develop greater scientific technology and knowledge.

13. It must be remembered that the aged are not a homogeneous group, and statistics pertaining to income vary by subgroups. Schulz (1980) cautions that we must distinguish between the young-old and the old-old; the early retiree (before 65) and the late retiree (after 65); the retired and the non-retired; the never-married, widowed, or divorced, and the married; whites and nonwhites; males and females; and between those who are only eligible for social security and those who have both private and government pensions. In addition, the level of educational attainment has an impact on earnings, and education indirectly influences the assets and savings available for the post-retirement years.

14. The source of this income is social security, 39 percent; employment income, 23 percent; asset income, 18 percent; private pensions, 7 percent; government employee pensions, 6 percent; other sources, 5 percent (Grad and Foster, 1979).

15. The source of this income is employment income, 32 percent; investment income and

private pensions, 29 percent; transfer payments (Old Age Security, Guaranteed Income Supplement, Spouse's Allowance if one spouse is between 60 and 64), 39 percent (Statistics Canada, 1979).

16. In 1978 the levels were: $5,514, $7,846, and $11,596.

17. For example, even professional athletes with as little as five years of employment are eligible for a substantial private pension plan administered by the sport league.

18. According to Schwenger and Gross (1980), the higher rate in Canada is the result of such factors as a cultural norm to institutionalize 'deviant' citizens and a harsh climate. However, the major reason may be the socialized health insurance scheme, which makes it financially easy for the sick and dying elderly to enter hospitals and homes for the aged. The lower percentage in the United States can be accounted for by the higher personal cost of health care and fewer available beds in institutions, at least until recent years.

19. The elderly live in single-family dwellings, apartments, hotels that serve permanent and transient residents (especially the poor or social deviants), and mobile homes.

20. Although the generations tend to live in separate dwellings, at least one younger relative usually lives nearby (Shanas et al., 1968).

References

Brotman, H. 'Life Expectancy: Comparison of National Levels in 1900 and 1974 and Variations in State Levels, 1969–1971,' The Gerontologist, 17(1/1977), 12–22.

Bouvier, L. 'America's Baby Boom Generation: The Fateful Bulge,' Population Bulletin, 35(1/1980), 3–36.

Bulletin on Aging, 3–6 (1978–81) Published by the Social Development Branch, Department of International Economic and Social Affairs, Vienna International Centre, P.O. Box 500, A–1400, Vienna, Austria.

Bulletin on Aging, 5(2/1980), 10–12 ('Population Projections by Broad Age Group, by World, by Developed and Developing Regions and Major Areas for the Years 1975 and 2000').

Bulletin on Aging, 6(1/1981), 7–16 ('Population Projections').

Clark, R. 'Aging, Retirement and the Economic Security of the Elderly: An Economic Review,' pp. 299–319 in C. Eisdorfer (ed.).

Annual Review of Gerontology and Geriatrics. Volume 2. New York: Springer Publishing Co., 1981.

Clark, R. et al. 'Economics of Aging: A Survey,' Journal of Economic Literature, 16(September, 1978), 919–62.

Cowgill, D. 'Residential Segregation by Age in American Metropolitan Areas,' Journal of Gerontology, 33(3/1978), 446–53.

Cutler, N. and R. Harootyan. 'Demography of the Aged,' pp. 31–69 in D. Woodruff and J. Cirren (eds.). Aging: Scientific Perspectives and Social Issues. New York: D. Van Nostrand Co., 1975.

Denton, F. and B. Spencer. 'Canada's Population and Labor Force: Past, Present and Future,' pp. 10–26 in V. Marshall (ed.). Aging in Canada: Social Perspectives. Don Mills: Fitzhenry and Whiteside, 1980.

Fischer, C. 'The Study of Urban Community and Personality,' pp. 67–90 in A. Inkeles, J. Coleman and N. Smelser (eds.). Annual Review of Sociology. Volume 1. Palo Alto: Annual Reviews, Inc., 1975.

Gillaspy, R. 'Differentials in Survivorship of the Older Populations Among Areas Within a State: The Case of Pennsylvania,' Journal of Gerontology, 34(2/1979), 273–79.

Grad, S. and K. Foster. Income of the Population 55 and Older, 1976. Washington: Social Security Administration, 1979.

Gutman, G. (ed.). Canada's Changing Age Structure: Implications for the Future. Burnaby, B.C.: Simon Fraser University Publications, 1982.

Hauser, P. 'Aging and World-Wide Population Change,' pp. 59–86 in R. Binstock and E. Shanas (eds.). Handbook of Aging and The Social Sciences. New York: Van Nostrand Reinhold, 1976.

Henretta, J. 'Using Survey Data in the Study of Social Stratification in Late Life,' The Gerontologist, 19(2/1979), 197–202.

Hogg, S. et al. 'Concerning The Definition of Poverty in the Elderly,' pp. 165–84 in J. Crawford (ed.). Canadian Gerontological Collection III. Winnipeg: Canadian Association on Gerontology, 1981.

Kalbach, W. and W. McVey. The Demographic Bases of Canadian Society. Toronto: McGraw-Hill Ryerson, 1979.

Kii, T. 'A New Index for Measuring Demographic Aging,' The Gerontologist, 22(4/1982), 438–42.

Laslett, P. 'Societal Development and Aging,' pp. 87–116 in R. Binstock and E. Shanas (eds.). Handbook of Aging and the Social Sciences. New York: Van Nostrand Reinhold, 1976.

Lawton, M.P. Environment and Aging. Monterey: Brooks/Cole Publishing Co., 1980.

Longino, C. (ed.). 'Symposium: Population Research for Planning and Practice,' *The Gerontologist*, 22(2/1982), 142–69.

Marshall, V. *Last Chapters: A Sociology of Aging and Dying*. Monterey: Brooks/Cole Publishing Co., 1980.

Marshall, V. 'Social Characteristics of Future Aged,' pp. 31–55 in B. Wigdor and L. Ford (eds.). *Housing for an Aging Population: Alternatives*. Toronto: Program in Gerontology, University of Toronto, 1981.

McConnel, C. and F. Deljavan. 'The Educational Variable in Gerontological Research: An Economic Perspective and Aggregate Data,' *Educational Gerontology*, 7(4/1981), 339–54.

McFarland, D. 'The Aged in the 21st Century: A Demographer's View,' in L. Jarvik (ed.). *Aging into the 21st Century: Middle-Agers Today*. New York: Gardner Press, Inc., 1978.

Myers, G. 'Cross-national Trends in Mortality Rates Among The Elderly,' *The Gerontologist*, 18(5/1978), 441–48.

National Council on the Aging. *Fact Book on Aging: A Profile of America's Older Population*. Washington, 1978.

National Council on the Aging. *Aging in the Eighties: America in Transition*. Washington, 1981.

Rosow, I. *Social Integration of the Aged*. New York: Free Press, 1967.

Schulz, J. *The Economics of Aging*. 2nd edition. Belmont, Cal.: Wadsworth Publishing Co., 1980.

Schwenger, C. and M. Gross. 'Institutional Care and Institutionalization of the Elderly in Canada,' pp. 248–56 in V. Marshall (ed.). *Aging In Canada: Social Perspectives*. Don Mills: Fitzhenry and Whiteside, 1980.

Shanas, E. et al. *Old People in Three Industrial Societies*. New York: Atherton, 1968.

Sheppard, H. and S. Rix. *The Graying of Working America: The Coming Crises of Retirement-Age Policy*. New York: The Free Press, 1977.

Siegel, J. 'On the Demography of Aging,' *Demography*, 17(4/1980), 345–64.

Siegel, J. 'Demographic Background for International Gerontological Studies,' *Journal of Gerontology*, 36(1/1981), 93–102.

Stahura, J. 'Ecological Determinants of the Aging of Suburban Populations,' *The Sociological Quarterly*, 21(1/1980), 107–18.

Statistical Bulletin, 49(1/1968), 2–5 ('Longevity of Prominent Women').

Statistical Bulletin, 60(1/1979), 3–9 ('Longevity of Prominent Men').

Statistical Bulletin, 61(4/1980), 13–15 ('Expectation of Life in the United States at New High').

Statistical Bulletin, 62(2/1981a), 14–15 ('Decline in Life Expectancy').

Statistical Bulletin, 62(3/1981b), 2–4 ('Changes in the Age Profile of the United States Population').

Statistics Canada. *Canada's Elderly*. Ottawa: Ministry of Supply and Services, 1979.

Stone, L. and S. Fletcher. *A Profile of Canada's Older Population*. Montreal: Institute for Research on Public Policy, 1980.

Stone, L. and S. Fletcher. *Aspects of Population Aging in Canada: A Chartbook*. Ottawa: Ministry of Supply and Services, 1981.

Stone, L. and M. MacLean. *Future Income Prospects for Canada's Senior Citizens*. Montreal: Institute For Research on Public Policy, 1979.

Struyk, R. 'The Housing Situation of Elderly Americans,' *The Gerontologist*, 17(2/1977), 130–39.

Van Es, J. and M. Bowling. 'A Model for Analyzing the Aging of Local Populations: Illinois Counties Between 1950 and 1970,' *International Journal of Aging and Human Development*, 9(4/1978–79), 377–87.

4

Understanding Aging: The Use of Scientific Perspectives, Theories, and Methods

Introduction

This chapter initiates a shift in emphasis from description to explanation, an approach that will prevail throughout much of the book. In order to provide the reader with the necessary conceptual tools and methodologies, the threefold approach of this chapter is (1) to describe the goals and methods of scientific inquiry; (2) to describe the methodological approaches and concerns to be addressed when studying the process of aging; and (3) to illustrate the major theories and conceptual frameworks[1] that have been used to explain social phenomena associated with aging and the aged.

As will become readily apparent later in the chapter, there is not at present, nor is there likely to be in the future, a single theory that explains how individuals or populations age. A number of competing yet sometimes complementary perspectives have been proposed to provide understanding of social or physical phenomena related to the aging process.

Scientists are constantly striving to develop more complete and parsimonious explanations for social or physical phenomena. Although additional perspectives and theories will be developed in the future, a complete explanation for aging phenomena is unlikely to emerge.

As you read this chapter, learn the concepts, theories, and theoretical perspectives so that they can assist you in understanding the process of aging. Accept them as the best available information at this time, recognizing that as you read this book new explanations or models for aging are likely being developed and tested in a number of disciplines. In short, the theories and methods presented in this chapter represent the 'state of the art' in social gerontology. Because this state is likely to change over the next ten years, you must begin reading the major journals in order to remain current with respect to theory, methods, and substantive information.

The Purpose and Goals of Science: The Search for Knowledge

In order to help you to discover, describe, and understand social phenomena pertaining to the aging process, this and the following sections will discuss the purpose and process of the scientific approach to acquiring knowledge. It is hoped that by the end of this chapter you will understand, and be prepared to play, the 'science game' (Agnew and Pyke, 1978), regardless of whether you study aging or some other social or physical phenomenon. The scientific approach is concerned with formulating a relationship or hypothesis, obtaining reliable observations or facts to support or refute the relationship, explaining the observations, arriving at conclusions that separate fact from myth, and searching for order and patterns in events.

Regardless of the discipline, all scientists have three main goals: description, discovery, and explanation. The scientist observes and describes objects or events to obtain facts rather than opinions. In the field of sociology, scientists are interested in the structure and composition of social systems (which range in size and complexity from a married couple to the entire world), and in the interactions and changes that take place within and between social systems. The psychologist is interested in describing phenomena occurring within and between individuals, while the social psychologist studies the individual within a small social system or group.

Although the acquisition of facts is an important step in the scientific process, by itself it is not sufficient to advance knowledge. The scientist must then proceed to discover and test patterns of general relationships. This involves searching for and observing the regular and coincidental occurrence of events such as retirement and loss of status, or widowhood and changing patterns of interaction. The sociologist searches for repetitive patterns and relationships between properties of social systems, while the psychologist searches for relationships between characteristics of the individual (such as age and personality traits), or between individual characteristics and environmental stimuli (such as level of morale and quality of housing).

The final and most crucial goal of science is to account for observed relationships or patterns through scientific explanation. This not only enables us to understand why the relationship occurs, but also sometimes enables us to predict when and under what circumstances it will reoccur. In order to arrive at an explanation, a scientist constructs a logically related set of statements that can be tested (Rudner, 1966).

Nonscientists also pursue these three goals as they attempt to understand and guide behavior in everyday life. The major difference between the scientific and nonscientific approaches is the use by scientists of relatively standardized methods to discover and test relationships, and the degree to which they search for alternative or more complete explanations. The scientist is an intellectual craftsman (Mills, 1959; Ravetz, 1971; Nisbet, 1976) who has acquired the tools of a particular discipline, who employs these tools to gain insight into social or physical phenomena, and who remains convinced that there is always a more complete or a better explanation of the phenomenon under investigation. The nonscientist, in contrast, is usually satisfied with the simplest and most obvious explanation for a particular event. For many years, 'instinct' was widely accepted as the explanation for most human behavior. The ready acceptance of this one explanation tended to discourage the search for nonbiological explanations of individual and group behavioral patterns. However, with the growth of the social sciences, theoretical explanations for a variety of social phenomena have been proposed. For example, there are some generally accepted theories in social gerontology that help us to better understand aging as a social process.

In summary, the goal of science is to describe, discover, and explain repetitive phenomena. While scientists from different disciplines might ask different questions and employ different approaches to arrive at an understanding of a specific phenomenon, they all generally adhere to the principles and practices inherent in the scientific method of inquiry:

1. Science is a logical process which demands that explanations make sense. Both deductive (from the general to the specific) and inductive (from the specific to the general) logic are used to arrive at explanations.

2. For scientists, there must be a 'rational' (logical) explanation for every event, since it is assumed that behavior does not occur by chance.

3. Unlike the historian, who may be interested in explaining a specific event (for example, why and how World War I began), the scientist is interested in explaining general patterns regardless of time and place (for example, why and how do individuals acquire and lose status as they age?).

4. Science is characterized by adherence to objectivity and by the need to verify facts and observations. A given fact, relationship, or theory should be able to be tested and verified by any number of scientists who, although working in isolation, follow the same general procedures. In short, findings must be replicated and reproduced before they can be accepted as explanations.

5. Scientific evidence is always subject to revision and change. In fact, the history of any science generally shows that sooner or later what has previously been accepted as 'the' explanation is often subjected to revision or rejection because of new evidence. Science proceeds by the elimination of false (unsupported) hypotheses. For example, at one time most gerontologists accepted the theory that all older people 'disengage' as they grow older; increasingly, evidence suggests that this is not a universal or inevitable process. Similarly, it was once believed that the elderly could not and should not have sexual relations; but recent biological, psychological, and sociological evidence suggests that they not only can, but that many want to — and do.

Concepts, Propositions, and Theories

To provide descriptions of social or physical phenomena, it is necessary to use concepts, definitions, and classification schemes. A concept is an abstract generalized idea about an object or phenomenon. For example, 'aging' is a concept that expresses a dynamic change in the appearance and behavior of individuals. It represents a theoretical view of a social, biological, or psychological process. As such, it provides a common means of communication among scientists interested in a similar phenomenon. A concept is only a theoretical frame of reference. In order for it to be useful in generating knowledge, it must be measurable, either directly or indirectly. Each concept has associated with it one or more variables that can be used to measure the concept and to relate it to other concepts. For example, chronological age is a variable that represents the aging of an individual in years from birth. However, the concept of 'age' can be expressed by using other variables, such as 'functional age' or 'legal age,' which explain various facets of the aging process. In short, a variable is a symbol to which numbers may be assigned. Generally, these variables are related to each other either as an independent variable (a presumed cause, an antecedent event) or as a dependent variable (a predicted or presumed outcome, a consequence of an earlier event).

Scientists and students need to be precise and consistent about the meaning of the concepts and variables they use. Therefore, two types of definitions are necessary — theoretical and operational. The theoretical definition (or nominal definition, as it is sometimes called) gives the standard, general meaning of the concept. The operational definition specifies the procedures that are necessary to measure the variable. To illustrate, a theoretical definition of functional age might be 'an indicator of age that is based on level of performance in a variety of daily self-maintenance or job-related tasks'; an operational definition of this concept might be 'the level of performance in such tasks as adding speed, writing speed, perceptual motor speed and accuracy, reaction time and decision making.' All concepts must have both a theoretical and an operational definition; in this way, scientists can understand each other when they communicate, and they can use and measure the concepts in similar ways as they seek to explain phenomena.

Taken together, a number of concepts can be linked into typologies, taxonomies, or schemas that facilitate the analysis of individual or group phenomena. For example, as Loy et al. (1978:29) noted, a 'social system,' a key construct in sociology, is made up of a normative component called 'culture' (values, norms, sanctions), a structural component called the 'social structure' (social positions, social status, regular patterns of social interaction), and a behavioral component called 'interacting individuals' (persons with varying physical, social, and psychological characteristics). For each component there are sets of cultural, structural, and personal variables that can be measured, interpreted, and used to explain social behavior or social processes in large or small systems. This classification scheme for social systems may assist us in describing or understanding aging as a social process.

To this point we have discussed concepts, definitions, variables, and classification schemes. However, these pertain only to the first goal of science, description. In order to explain or predict social phenomena (that is, to discover relationships), a theoretical statement is needed that suggests a hypothesized relationship between two or more concepts or their variables. For example, we have moved from the descriptive level to the explanatory level when we generate and test statements such as the following:

1. As age increases, the level of health decreases.

2. The greater the age of an individual (at least until mandatory retirement), the higher the earned income.

3. There is an inverse relationship between the distance from the center of a metropolitan area and the age of the residents.

4. As the degree of modernization increases, the status of the elderly in a society declines.

The discoveries that result from scientific inquiry are stated as propositions. These can have varying degrees of explanatory power and empirical (research) support. Those that have some explanatory power and little empirical support are known as hypotheses; those with high explanatory power and strong empirical support are known as laws. However, as noted earlier, the social sciences in general, and social gerontology in particular, have few if any laws; most statements represent untested hypotheses.

In short, the goal of discovery involves a constant search to obtain support for relationships between independent and dependent variables. It is important to recognize that variables per se are not tested; rather, it is the relationship between variables that must be supported by research evidence.

Once again, however, it is not suficient to describe concepts, or to discover and test relationships between concepts. The ultimate goal of the science game is to account for the discovered relationships through scientific explanation. In short, this final step involves constructing a new theory or using an existing one to explain social behavior and organization as they apply to the aging process.

Although there is no universally accepted definition of a theory, it is generally defined as a set of interrelated propositions (made up of defined concepts or variables) that present a logical, systematic, and reasonably complete view of a phenomenon. This view is constructed by specifying the relationships among variables in order to explain and predict the phenomenon. In short, a theory is the product of scientific inquiry as well as a tool for scientific inquiry. As a tool, a theory serves as a conceptual scheme: (1) to provide assumptions and definitions; (2) to summarize and synthesize existing knowledge; (3) to translate facts into empirical generalizations; (4) to guide and stimulate thinking by raising questions and indicating gaps between theory and research; and (5) to serve as a stimulus to search for more complete or alternative explanations.

As a product of science, a theory provides a summary of existing or anticipated findings. It also identifies propositions that need to be tested, and it helps to provide explanations for unexpected findings. A theory represents a simpler model of how the complex social or physical world operates; it guides the development and implementation of policy; it provides a conceptual system to accept or reject, and therefore further stimulates the development and accumulation of knowledge; and it enables us to make predictions, and thereby introduce some element of control in our lives. Thus, we rely to a greater extent on theories or models as we move from description to discovery to explanation.

There are many types of theories (Loy et al., 1978; 47–49) and many theoretical perspectives, even within a given discipline. For example, in sociology we find the competing theoretical perspectives of conflict theorists, functional theorists, system theorists, social exchange theorists, symbolic interaction theorists, and phenomenological theorists (Warshay, 1975; Cohen, 1980). This variety enables sociologists to select theories and theoretical perspectives appropriate to the specific question or problem they wish to study. In short, as Ritzer (1975) has noted, sociology is a multiple-paradigm[2] science and 'no aspect of social reality can be adequately explained without drawing on insights from all of the paradigms.'

Just as different research methods are needed, so too are different theoretical perspectives and paradigms[3] necessary, since each is based on different assumptions and utilizes different concepts. However, one perspective usually proves to be superior to another in providing a more complete or valid explanation of a specific phenomenon. Later it will be seen that a variety of theoretical perspectives and a number of theories are employed to explain the aging process. One perspective cannot explain all social phenomena associated with aging or the aged (Marshall, 1981a). Ultimately it will be necessary to merge theories from psychology, biology (Sacher, 1980) and sociology.

This variety in theoretical approaches to a phenomenon may be initially confusing; however, the presence of competing theoretical perspectives is good for a discipline, as long as the competition does not become counterproductive. That is, as long as the competing theoretical perspectives introduce alternative views of the world, and thereby advance understanding of the phenomenon, they are useful and necessary. But if scientists begin to spend most of their creative time attempting to establish that their perspective is superior to another perspective (as has happened in some fields, although not as yet in social gerontology) internal theoretical debates will detract from the basic goal of advancing knowledge. Scientists, like other individuals, are competitive and seek to construct the best 'theory' yet available. When they find fault with one theory, this serves as a stimulus to discover and test a more complete explanation. Later in this chapter, a number of specific theories from the disciplines of sociology, psychology, and social gerontology are discussed.

Research Settings and Methods

Introduction.   In the previous subsection the more creative and intellectual aspects of the research process were described. Having developed concepts, propositions, and perhaps even a theory, the researcher now begins to make and record observations. This stage permits testing of the explanatory value and power of a proposition, or of a series of interrelated propositions — a theory.

This section briefly describes three settings (library, field, and laboratory) where research can occur, and four general techniques (survey research, secondary analysis, participant observation, controlled experiments) that are commonly used to answer questions about a specific phenomenon.[4] While these settings and techniques are used in all of the social sciences, including social gerontology, some are more applicable to specific disciplines or specific research questions. For example, survey research in the field is a common tool in sociology, while controlled laboratory experiments are more prevalent in psychology.

Since social gerontology tends to be a hybrid field made up of anthropologists, sociologists, psychologists, social psychologists, economists, and political scientists, all of the following settings and techniques have been used to answer questions about the aging process, or about age differences among individuals at specific stages in the life cycle. However, because of the nature of the process, social gerontology has a number of unique methodological concerns that create problems not only in the design of studies, but also in the interpretation of findings (Fry and Keith, 1980). These issues are addressed later in this chapter.

Just as the prescribing of medicine by a physician is guided by the patient's apparent symptoms, the choice of research setting and method is guided by the theoretical question that needs to be answered. That is, the research process involving observation and interpretation is not initiated randomly. This decision to examine the relationship between certain variables derives from a review of the existing literature, along with the creative insight of the scientist. Thus, if a scientist is interested in accounting for the level of life satisfaction among widows, he or she is unlikely to include such variables as eye color, maiden name, or zodiac sign. Rather, the existing literature and the logical process of deduction are used to construct a theory that includes such variables as income, perceived health, age, number of friends, or degree of participation in the labor force.

In short, the research process seeks to answer questions with more precision and understanding than would result were we to rely on common sense or chance. This is not to suggest that significant research findings have not occurred serendipitously, but it is certainly true that the chance of finding a significant and complete explanation, and finding it sooner, is greater if a scientific approach is used.

Library settings.   Both qualitative and quantitative data useful in answering some research questions may already be available and stored in public or private archives such as libaries, museums, and data banks. The research technique that uses this material is called secondary analysis (Henretta et al., 1977; George, 1979). The most common type of secondary analysis involves the use of existing data sets collected for some other purpose (Patrick and Borgatta, 1981). Thus, the use of existing opinion polls, census, or registration data represents a form of secondary analysis. For example, an analysis of the relationship between age and the leisure patterns of Canadians (McPherson and Kozlik, 1980) was based on a previous survey conducted to examine the frequency and type of leisure activities engaged in by the total adult population of Canada. The responses had not previously been analyzed to determine whether differences existed between the types of leisure activities of various age cohorts. A major weakness of secondary analysis is that the data set may lack essential independent or control variables that are needed to provide a complete explanation for a specific research question.

Another type of secondary analysis is known as content analysis. In this more qualitative and less systematic analysis, the research scientist searches for patterns and characteristics included in textual material (Holsti, 1969). For example, numerous studies have sought to examine the degree of prejudice or discrimination against the elderly that is indirectly presented in literature or the mass media (Roberts and Kimsey, 1972; Gaitz and Scott, 1975; Kingston and Drotter, 1981; Sheppard, 1981). Studies using content analysis have determined the type and prominence of roles played by elderly people; their personality, dress, and actions; and the beliefs and actions of younger age cohorts toward the elderly as described in children's books, school textbooks, the movies, and in television commercials and serials.

Field settings. A great deal of social research tends to be conducted in real-life settings rather than in artificial laboratory environments. These research situations can involve many people, such as a national sample of senior citizens, or they can involve only a few people, such as an interview with all physicians over 80 years of age who still practice medicine. Survey research is the most common method used in the field. This technique generally involves either the use of face-to-face or telephone interviews, or a questionnaire that is mailed or given to the respondent. The information collected can be used to describe a phenomenon (for example, the number of widows over 70 years of age who live below the poverty line), to test the relationship between variables (whether those over 65 are more likely to support one political party rather than another), or to determine attitudes, beliefs, or behavior before and after specific events (a questionnaire or interview with elderly individuals when they enter a nursing home might be repeated one year later to determine whether attitudinal or behavioral changes have occurred).

The major advantage of survey research is that it permits observations to be made for samples representing much larger populations. Unfortunately, this method can be very expensive and time-consuming. Also, when a questionnaire is used, much information may be lost because the investigator cannot probe the respondent to obtain a more detailed interpretation of what is meant by a particular response. Nor can it be determined whether the respondent correctly understood the question. There are also a number of disadvantages or limitations to using surveys with older respondents (Brown et al., 1981). For example, elderly people appear to be more prone to agree with statements regardless of the content; to use a smaller proportion of response categories on a given scale; to use the extreme response categories (high or low); and to give the same response to all questions in a set of questions that have similar response categories (Herzog, 1981). These factors do not appear to be related to level of education, but they may be related to fatigue (long questionnaires or interviews), to declining health, or to lack of experience with multiple-response instruments.

A second major form of field research is participant observation or ethnography. In this technique, investigators are involved as observers of, or participants with, the respondents as they engage in social interaction in one or more social settings over a period of time (Holmes, 1976; Fry and Keith, 1980). In some cases the role of researcher is unknown to the subjects in the study. This sometimes helps to prevent the intentional distortion or misrepresentation of information or behavior by the subjects. At other times, the purpose of the investigator's involvement is known, and he or she participates either as a regular member of the group or purely as a passive observer.

The major limitations of this method are that it often lacks the use of standardized instruments (such as a questionnaire), which makes it difficult to replicate the study exactly; it can be very time-consuming; and it requires special observational and conversational skills on the part of the participant observer. One recent example of a participant observation ethnography in sociology is Tindale's (1980) study of old, impoverished men who live on skid row. He worked as a volunteer in a hostel; having made contacts, he then began to spend time with the men in a park, in their rooms, in a bus terminal, and in a few bars. Similarly, Gardner (1981), employing anthropological field methods, described aging in a rural, self-contained farm community in Kentucky.

The third type of research method employed in the field is the field experiment. In this approach, one or more independent variables are manipulated by the experimenter under controlled conditions (Schaie, 1977). Although a major weakness of this approach is the inability to control all possible confounding factors, this is compensated for in part by the realism attached to the results, compared to the results from a laboratory experiment. An example of a recent field experiment in social gerontology involved a comparison of tenants living in high-rise apartment buildings who did, or did not, have access to an on-site public health nursing program (Flett et al. 1980). It was found that those in buildings with access to on-site nursing had better health and lower rates of hospital admission than the control group who did not have access to on-site nursing. Similarly, Bosse and Ekerdt (1981) administered a questionnaire concerning perceived leisure involvement to a group of employed men in 1975. Three years later a similar questionnaire was administered to those who had retired and to those who were still employed in order to examine changes in perceived leisure involvement.

Laboratory settings.   In psychology and in most of the physical and natural sciences, controlled experiments are completed in laboratories so as to eliminate extraneous factors that might influence the relationship being studied. Subjects are randomly assigned to groups, conditions of the experiment are randomized, variables are precisely manipulated, and accurate, reliable, and valid instruments are used to measure the effects of the experiment (Birren and Renner, 1977; Schulz, 1980; Mangen and Peterson, 1982).

For example, Bowles and Poon (1982), testing for age differences in recognition memory processing, had young and elderly subjects respond to a study list of 120 words. The words were displayed on a screen for two seconds. The subjects were then presented with 120 pairs of words and were asked to indicate which word in the pair had been on the original list. While no significant difference in accuracy was observed between the two groups, it was found that those older adults who performed at a higher level had better verbal ability as measured by a standard vocabulary test. Thus, within the controlled laboratory experiment, verbal ability was introduced as a control variable.

Summary.   There are many research settings and techniques available to scientists who wish to study social phenomena. Although these have been presented as separate approaches, in reality a social scientist may use more than one of these methods within the same study. The use of participant observation, archival data, and survey research within a study can provide unexpected information, as well as more complete data. The advantage of a multi-method study (Marshall, 1981b) can be illustrated by a study of the degree of social isolation among residents of a nursing home. The degree of isolation can be examined by observing the frequency of visits to public places in the home, by interviews with the residents and staff, and by an examination of daily staff reports which include anecdotal comments about the behavior of residents.

There are some unique methodological problems to be considered when studying the aging process. Some of these problems are outlined later in this chapter. The next subsection emphasizes the need to link theory and research so that the research process produces valid, complete, and reliable knowledge. If the information derived from the research process does not meet these criteria, then application of the knowledge in policy or practice is not valid.

Finally, although the situation is improving, there is still relatively little research being initiated by social scientists concerning the aging process, at least compared to other topics of interest in the social sciences. Moreover, there is very little, if any, replication of studies in social gerontology to insure that the findings are valid and reliable, and that they apply beyond the original sample that comprised the first study on a given topic.

The Link Between Theory and Research

As with the age-old question, 'Which came first, the chicken or the egg?' scientists and philosophers of science have debated whether theory or research, as interrelated facets of the science game, should be initiated first (Merton, 1957; Lastrucci, 1967; Snizek, 1975). To date, agreement has not been reached on this question, and may not ever be reached, since the priority of one over the other is very much related to the style, experience, and ability of the individual scientist.

Scientists do agree that both theory and research are necessary and that there is a strong relationship between the theoretical orientation and the preferred method of inquiry.[5] For example, Snizek (1975) found that sociologists who focus on the individual tend to stress deduction and to use empirical, quantitative techniques and procedures in their research. In contrast, those who focus on group characteristics tend to rely more upon induction, and to use an interpretive or intuitive analytical approach. That is, their research design is guided by the research question and the theoretical perspective. For example, symbolic interactionists tend to use participant observation as their major research technique, and to rely on qualitative rather than quantitative data (Chappell, 1978).

The interaction of theory and research seems to operate much like the problem of the chicken and the egg. Theory suggests ideas for research and helps to explain the research findings; the research process tests theories and stimulates the revision of existing theories. Research also facilitates the construction of new theories to fit the existing evidence. To put this idea in more scientific terms, the theoretical products of scientific inquiry are concepts, propositions (hypotheses), and theories. The methodological processes include the logical processes of induction and deduction, and empirical processes such as sampling, operationalization of the variables, instrumentation, observation, measurement, data analysis, and interpretation.

The process of developing a scientific body of knowledge can begin with observations, from which propositions and theories are derived (the first-research-then-theory approach). It can also begin with the construction of hypothetical propositions and theories that are later tested to determine whether the relationships are supported or refuted (the first-theory-then-research approach). Regardless of the starting point, the ultimate goal is to use research evidence to support or refute a hypothesis or theory. If the evidence fails to provide support, the hypothesis or theory needs to be revised, or more valid supporting evidence needs to be obtained.

In actuality, a composite approach is usually employed. That is, observations are not made without some preliminary theoretical work, and theory development does not proceed too far without testing at least some of the propositions in the postulated theory. At the present stage of development in social gerontology, the amount of research completed far exceeds the amount of theoretical work. Thus, a greater emphasis has been given to making observations, to collecting evidence to describe phenomena, and to testing relationships between variables. As a result, the development of hypotheses or theories that more adequately and completely explain aging as a social process has been neglected. This is a normal stage of development for any new field. However, if the scientific process continues as it has in other disciplines, we can expect that the knowledge derived in the next decade will be increasingly cumulative[6] rather than representing random, unrelated facts (Forscher, 1963; Seltzer, 1975; Henretta et al., 1977; McPherson, 1978). Moreover, the quantity and quality of theoretical development should increase as scholars become better prepared in this facet of the science game.

Methodological Concerns in Social Gerontology

Introduction

With the increasing emphasis on deriving more complete knowledge about the aging process rather than on dealing with aging primarily as a social problem, more attention is being directed to methodological issues. This emphasis is necessary in order to design better studies and to interpret more accurately data patterns and observations. In this section some of the more important methodological concerns are discussed, so that, as you read journal and newspaper articles, you will be better prepared to consider the reliability and validity of both the findings and the interpretations of the observations.

Research Designs and the Interpretation of Data

The production of valid knowledge involves not only asking the 'right' questions, but also answering the questions with the appropriate procedures. Not only must the study be designed correctly, but the interpretation of the findings must be accurate and must not be inflated beyond the information provided by the observations.

To date, most social gerontology research has either examined differences between age groups on a number of variables, or examined changes that occur within age groups or individuals as they pass through various stages in the life cycle. Both of these questions can be influenced by historical events and cultural differences. Thus, social scientists, and you as readers of their work, must be careful to distinguish among the effects of aging, cohort differences, and historical and environmental influences when studying the process of aging and the behavior of the elderly (Maddox and Wiley, 1976; Costo and McCrae, 1982). In order to answer research questions, social scientists have generally collected data using either a cross-sectional or a longitudinal design. In the following subsections, the issues raised by the use of each method are discussed, and an alternative design that has recently been used is introduced.

Cross-sectional designs. Because the cross-sectional design is the least costly in terms of time and money, it has been widely used by social scientists. This design involves recording observations or responses by individuals of different ages and then reporting the results according to age group. For example, in a study of the relationship between age and attendance at movies in 1980, the results might be as reported in Table 4.1.[7] While it appears that movie attendance declines with age, we cannot conclude that differences between age groups are due to growing old.

Table 4.1 The possible relationship between age and movie attendance: a cross-sectional design.

Age	Percentage attending three times or more per year in 1980		
	Males and Females	Males	Females
14–19	58	65	52
20–24	54	62	50
25–34	45	52	39
35–44	23	41	25
45–54	17	31	14
55–64	11	20	10
65–74	7	19	9
75 and over	3	12	6

Rather, we can only conclude that at one point in history (such as 1980) there were age differences in the frequency of movie attendance. The data indicate that younger age cohorts are more likely to attend movies three or more times per year. Furthermore, there are often variations within specific age groups in specific variables. These differences may be greater than those between age groups (Krauss, 1980). For example, it appears (Table 4.1) that males of all ages attend more movies than females. Thus, the low frequency of attendance by those over 55 might be a reflection of the fact that there are more females than males in that age group.

The differences between age groups, or age cohorts, might also suggest that there are generational or cohort differences in lifestyle that are revealed by sampling movie attendance at a particular point in history. For example, it is quite likely that those over 65 never attended movies to any great extent at any time in their lives. This pattern may have evolved either because movies were relatively unavailable in their early years, or because they were unable to afford to attend movies when they were young. In either situation, this cohort, unlike later generations, probably never adopted movies as a salient part of their leisure lifestyle. Similarly, they may not now wish to spend part of their limited and relatively fixed income on the ever-increasing price of admission to movies.

This design identifies differences between age groups, but does not permit us to adequately explain why this pattern varies by age. That is, the data pattern may reflect generational or cultural differences in lifestyle (immigrants may be less inclined to attend movies, and the over-65 group is made up of many who emigrated to this country in early adulthood), changes with age, or the unique impact of specific historical events (such as a depression or an energy crisis) on a particular age group at some point in their life cycle. Therefore, alternative designs must be considered to arrive at more complete and valid explanations of phenomena related to changes with age.

In summary, the cross-sectional design enables us to make observations regarding characteristics of various age strata in society at a certain time. However, it can rarely provide definitive information about the process of aging experienced by a given cohort. While this design alerts us to patterns of behavior that may vary by age, we must be careful not to misinterpret the results of studies using a cross-sectional design.

Longitudinal designs: the search for changes with age.   Longitudinal designs can give a more accurate and complete explanation of the aging process, because they follow the same individuals or groups for a number of years (a panel study). However, very few studies of this nature have been completed (Palmore, 1981; Mednick and Harway, 1982). The major reason for this paucity of longitudinal research in all fields is that it is expensive and time-consuming. Also, original subjects are often lost through death, relocation, or refusal to continue[8] (Schulsinger et al., 1981).

With this design it is possible to observe direct evidence of changes in individuals and groups as they age, either in prospective studies (where subjects are retested at regular intervals) or, although less desirable, in retrospective studies (where individuals respond to similar questions as they pertain to specific earlier stages in their life cycle). For example, Table 4.2 presents hypothetical data for a longitudinal study completed in the year 2005. These data indicate the frequency of movie attendance across the life cycle for 1910 and 1940 birth cohorts.

Table 4.2   The possible relationship between age and movie attendance: a longitudinal design.

Year	Age	Percentage of 1910 birth cohort attending three times or more per year	Year	Age	Percentage of 1940 birth cohort attending three times or more per year
1925	(15)	10	1955	(15)	58
1935	(25)	15	1965	(25)	62
1945	(35)	42	1975	(35)	60
1955	(45)	40	1985	(45)	57
1965	(55)	30	1995	(55)	52
1975	(65)	22	2005	(65)	40

As can be seen, few of the 1910 cohort attended movies prior to 1945. Yet, with soldiers returning from World War II, and with a more stable economy and increased marriage rates, a large percentage of this generation might have begun to attend movies in their leisure time. This effect on a particular age cohort at a particular point in their life cycle is known as a 'period effect.' It represents a change in behavior because of environmental events, rather than because of reaching a specific chronological age (age 45 in this case).

This table also illustrates the need to avoid 'cohort-centrism'; that is, making generalizations about the aging process and the status or behavior of the elderly on the basis of only one cohort. Since the life experiences of each birth cohort can vary, it is important that longitudinal studies include at least two age cohorts to control for possible differences in life experiences (period effects and socialization differences). For example, the results shown in Table 4.2 indicate that the 1940 birth cohort exhibits a higher frequency of movie attendance at all ages than the 1910 cohort. Furthermore, this cohort has a relatively stable pattern of movie attendance across the life cycle, with only a slight decline in attendance occurring in the later years.

Although longitudinal designs have some advantages over cross-sectional designs, there are some inherent limitations to their explanatory power. For example, unless the study is of sufficient duration, period effects at a particular stage may be missed. Similarly, unless more than one age cohort is included, possible between-cohort differences may be missed. Thus, generalizations on the basis of one cohort can be misleading.

Finally, as in cross-sectional designs, intracohort variations by sex, social class, marital status, ethnicity, educational attainment or other relevant variables must be considered and reported (Krauss, 1980). Unfortunately, these controls are often neglected in longitudinal studies since more emphasis is placed on changes or differences at subsequent times. That is, variation within a cohort may increase or decrease because of maturation or specific period effects. For example, frequency of movie attendance at age 35 may decrease significantly from that at age 25 for the large segment of each cohort who become parents, and therefore have less time or money for leisure (a maturation effect). Or, attendance may decrease at a certain point for all adult cohorts, regardless of chronological age, because the movie industry over a period of five years produces movies that primarily appeal to a teenage market (a period effect). Similarly, another shift in the themes of movies (about subjects such as single parenting or remarriage) at a particular point might result in an increase in movie attendance by adults in two or three adjacent cohorts who are separated or divorced. That is, they might be attracted back to movie theatres as part of the dating process, as well as by movies that depict themes related to their current situation.

Cohort analysis: a general model for isolating age changes and age differences. In response to the limitations in the use of cross-sectional and longitudinal designs for studying the aging process, cohort analysis has been developed (Schaie, 1965, 1967; Glenn, 1977; Palmore, 1978; Hastings and Berry, 1979; Glenn, 1981). This design accounts for maturational change, cohort differences, and environmental (period and cultural) effects, thereby reducing the confusion of age changes with age differences. In order to isolate possible explanatory factors, Schaie (1965) derived a general developmental model that obtains similar information about individuals who were born at different times and who are measured at different times.

While ideally this approach should involve a longitudinal, prospective study over three or more generations, most cohort analyses involve a retrospective, secondary analysis of information stored in archives. For example, national surveys (opinion polls, government census) often ask the same questions at regular intervals. However, at each interval different people represent the specific birth cohort. This eliminates the need for a longitudinal study where the same individuals must be followed for many years. For example, imagine we are in the year 2005 and have constructed a table based on one item (pertaining to movie attendance) that has been included in a national survey every ten years since 1935. Table 4.3 illustrates hypothetical patterns of movie attendance across the life cycle for three birth cohorts — those born in 1920, who represent your grandparent's generation, those born in 1940, who represent your parents' generation, and those born in 1960, who represent your generation.

Table 4.3 The possible relationship between age and movie attendance: a cohort analysis.

	Year of measurement percentage attending movies three times or more per year (age in years)							
Birth cohort	1935 (1)	1945 (2)	1955 (3)	1965 (4)	1975 (5)	1985 (6)	1995 (7)	2005 (8)
(a) 1920	10	12	33	30	21	11	4	—
(Your grandparents)	(15)	(25)	(35)	(45)	(55)	(65)	(75)	
(b) 1940	—	—	58	62	60	41	52	40
(Your parents)			(15)	(25)	(35)	(45)	(55)	(65)
(c) 1960	—	—	—	—	72	60	69	61
(Your generation)					(15)	(25)	(35)	(45)

In this type of analysis[9] it is possible to observe cross-sectional age differences (read down column 5 for the year 1975), to study age changes within a cohort over time (read across rows a, b or c), to compare patterns of movie attendance by cohorts of the same chronological age (at 35 years) at different points in history (compare cells 3a, 5b, and 7c), and to note whether patterns of attendance change across the life cycle from one cohort to another (compare rows a, b and c). For example, the hypothetical data in Table 4.3 suggests that, except for the 1920 cohort that was socialized to movies relatively late in life (compare cells 1a and 2a versus cell 3a), there seems to be increasing frequency of movie attendance by the later cohorts, both initially (cell 1a versus cell 3b versus cell 5c) and later in life (cell 4a versus cell 6b versus cell 8c). Moreover, despite increasing attendance by the younger cohorts, there is a decreased involvement among all cohorts after age 35 (cells 3a to 7a, cells 5b to 8b, cells 7C to 8c). For the two most recent cohorts this trend begins sooner in that the peak is reached at about age 25 and age 15 respectively (compare cells 4b and 5b, and cells 5c and 6c).

Through cohort analysis it is possible to compare the impact of period effects on each cohort. For example, to determine whether excessive inflation and high unemployment were significant factors in movie attendance around 1985, an investigator might note that there was a sharp decrease in attendance by the 1920 cohort. But this might be expected because of retirement, and the decrease might be similar to results for the 1915 and 1925 cohort when they reached 65 years of age. However, an examination of cells 5b, 6b, and 7b and cells 5c, 6c, and 7c suggests that both of these cohorts reported a decreased frequency of attendance in 1985, before rising slightly and then continuing the overall pattern of declining attendance by age.

Finally, in order to clearly demonstrate the necessity to control for the historical experiences encountered by a given cohort as they age (Cain, 1967), consider the following example of how changes in social institution, or a change in social structure can alter the behavior and status of the aged from one cohort to another. Cain (1981:91) reports that most of those who were 60 to 80 years of age in 1945 had rural or immigrant backgrounds, had only completed elementary school, were employed in blue-collar jobs, and had relatively poor nutrition and medical care throughout their life. In contrast, those 60 to 80 years of age in 1970 were more likely to be native-born, urban dwellers, white-collar workers, and to have had the advantage of full access to medical care, adequate nutrition, a variety of leisure opportunities, and higher income than their parents. Similarly, Glenn (1981) stresses that all 'side' information representing possible period effects must be considered before age effects are inferred from cohort analyses. Specifically, in an examination of patterns of alcohol consumption by age, Glenn (1981) stressed that before it can be concluded that consumption declines with age, an historical analysis of societal norms and laws concerning alcohol consumption must be completed.

Problems Associated with Selecting the Sample

In all research studies a representative sample of the population is required to insure the validity of the results. Unfortunately, when a given population has special characteristics, it is often difficult to derive randomly selected and representative probability samples. In many studies involving the elderly, it is difficult to obtain a sampling frame, because there is usually not a readily available list of individuals 65 years of age and over. As a result, investigators either draw a sample from those who are visible in church or senior-citizen groups, or they depend on volunteers, especially for longitudinal studies.

Moreover, even when a random sample is selected, it is often drawn from a large, readily available group. Therefore, the sample may not really be representative of the total elderly population in the region or country. To date, many gerontology studies have used white, middle-class males as subjects. Yet, as we have seen, the elderly, like other age groups, are heterogeneous. The end result of this tendency to study white middle-class subjects, some of whom are volunteers rather than random selections, is that the generalizability of the results can be questioned.

Similarly, because white middle-class males tend to be overstudied (as are college freshmen and sophomores by psychologists), women who are married or in the labor force, members of certain racial and ethnic groups, and those at the lower end of the socioeconomic strata have been highly underrepresented in gerontology studies. While there has been an increased emphasis in recent years on the study of blacks, women in the labor force, and blue-collar workers, the full range of the social spectrum has yet to be adequately studied because of inadequate sampling procedures. Furthermore, most studies have used samples unique to a particular community, region, or country, with few national or cross-national samples being included.

To offset some of these problems, gerontologists are striving to include people of different racial, ethnic, and social backgrounds when selecting their sample. For example, a two-stage sampling design seeks, in the first stage, to identify and describe elderly residents residing within a large probability sample of households in a region or country. The second stage involves drawing a representative sample to account for intracultural variations and obtaining the consent of those selected to participate (Lee and Finney, 1977).

Problems Associated with Collecting Data from the Elderly

Obtaining information from the elderly is somewhat similar to collecting information from very young children. It requires special skills, techniques, and instruments that are not normally needed for other age groups. For example, it is especially important to establish rapport, since older people may be skeptical of research and unsure of scientists or their staff, perhaps suspecting they may be some kind of government 'spies.' A second concern is that many of the current cohort of elderly people were not 'raised' on questionnaires or multiple-choice questions, and may therefore have difficulty responding to them. They may also be more likely, as are children, to respond in socially approved directions, to respond with a 'no opinion' or 'don't know,' or to be unwilling to admit the true state of their everyday moods or of their economic or health status.

Furthermore, in an interview situation, the reliability of the information collected may be lessened because of an inability to recall items (Ridley et al., 1979), because of hearing or visual deficiencies, or because of fatigue or a short attention span. This is most likely to occur with the very old, many of whom may be institutionalized (Schmidt, 1975). Once rapport is established, it may be difficult to restrict the conversation to the items in the interview, and to remain within the desired time limit. If an interview with a retiree is conducted in the household, the spouse may interject opinions or influence the responses of the interviewee.

As a final concern, there is a need to devote more attention to the process of aging and to the status of the aged among minority groups. If this is to occur, then questionnaires or interviews should be conducted in the language of the group, and members of the minority group should play a major role in the research process (in designing the study, as interviewers, as participant observers). This involvement will establish rapport and credibility with the respondents. It will also ensure that cultural factors unique to the minority group are considered in the design of the study and in the interpretation of the evidence (Bengtson et al., 1977).

Summary

While the research process is complex and can occur in many settings, the process follows four general steps: (1) by logical induction, a proposition or hypothesis is formulated from existing or newly created concepts; (2) in order to provide evidence to support or reject the proposed relationship, a scientist collects information from a valid sample on variables that represent the concepts in the hypothesized relationship, or makes and records observations in a field setting; (3) based on the evidence, explanations are derived to account for the observations, and conclusions are drawn as to whether the evidence supports or rejects the hypothesized relationship; (4) having accumulated a number of propositions that have some qualitative or quantitative support, an attempt is made to link these into a logical theory that will explain the social phenomena in as many social situations as possible.

Social Science Perspectives and Theories

Introduction

In this section of the text, a number of conceptual perspectives and theories for studying the aging process and the aged are introduced. While students often react negatively to the word 'theory,' it is important to recognize the use and value of theory before rejecting this way of thinking about social phenomena (Decker, 1978; Bengtson and Dowd, 1980–81). Thus, theories should be regarded as 'tools of the trade' that will help you to become better craftsmen — whether your goal is to become a practical, applied problem solver (social worker, policy maker or administrator) or a knowledge generator (a social or physical scientist), or whether you are mainly interested in a better understanding of yourself and others. Since no one conceptual perspective or theory is totally adequate to account for any social process or social problem, a number are included in this chapter. Those that are introduced represent the approaches that have been most frequently used to date.[10]

In their efforts to advance understanding, social scientists often strive for the simplest possible view of the world. As a result, theoretical and methodological approaches are often dichotomous or bipolar in nature. Scientists tend to use theoretical or empirical approaches to understanding a phenomenon; basic or applied research (Harris et al., forthcoming); qualitative or quantitative approaches to recording observations; dichotomous analyses of findings (male/female, worker/retired, old/young); or a conflict-or-consensus perspective. Moreover, new theories that describe social phenomena are often a mirror image of an existing theory.[11] In fact, much of the progress of science proceeds somewhat similarly to a basic law of physics; namely, for every action there is an equal and opposite reaction. Regardless of whether the reaction may be less than, equal to, or greater than the original theory in terms of explanatory power, the new theory or model serves as a useful conceptual device to stimulate thinking and to advance knowledge about the phenomenon.

In order to assist the reader in understanding the various approaches to aging, this chapter uses the dichotomous approach to some extent. However, it must be remembered that a social phenomenon is seldom black or white. Rather, there are gray areas where there is usually either convergence, overlap, or interaction between dichotomous categories or processes. Although social gerontologists have studied the 'aged' as opposed to the 'young,' understanding the process of aging requires an analysis of all stages of the life cycle, and of how the various stages interact with each other. The focus of study in social gerontology should be on both the dynamic process of aging and on the state of being old.[12]

To achieve this objective, social scientists working in the field of social gerontology use perspectives, theories, concepts, and methods from their basic discipline, and from those recently developed by social gerontologists. They approach the study of aging on one of two basic levels of analysis — the micro or the macro level.

At the micro level of analysis the concern is with changes in either the biological/physical system or the psychological/personal system, as well as with the interaction between these micro systems. In comparison, the macro-level approach is concerned with the impact of social structure, processes and problems as they relate to the aging population or individual. At the macro level we are also interested in individuals as they function within and as part of the various social systems, whether the system be a married couple, an extended family, an organization, a community, a society, or the world. For each level, different conceptual perspectives have evolved within the basic social sciences and social gerontology. Similarly, theories have been developed that are most applicable at either the micro level or the macro level of analysis.

In the next four subsections, conceptual perspectives and theories from the social sciences that help us to understand aging phenomena are described and discussed, first for the micro level of analysis and then for the macro level. It is important to recognize that the micro level of analysis has primarily involved a concern with the adjustment of the aging individual to society. This concern with the individual is reflected in a social psychological orientation to the study of aging. In contrast, the macro level of analysis focuses on stability and change in the age structure of an organization or society, and how this structure influences the aging individual. As a result, an historical and sociological orientation to the study of aging is utilized.

Relatively little attention has been directed to synthesizing findings or developing theoretical models to arrive at valid and complete explanations for various aging phenomena (Dowd, 1980:4; Riley, 1980). To date, social scientists interested in aging or the aged have generally resorted to the theories, concepts, and methods of the basic social science disciplines. However, with the growth of specialization in social gerontology, a few theories have been developed to explain various facets of individual or population aging. As the astute reader will note, the major emphasis, at least until recently, has been on explaining phenomena associated with the elderly themselves, rather than with the process of aging. Moreover, more emphasis has been placed on individual aging than on population aging.

Two General Sociological Perspectives

The sociologist Dawe (1970) identified two contrasting perspectives that have guided both general sociological research and gerontological research. The 'normative' perspective suggests that established rules (norms) and status hierarchies are present in society in order to provide social control or social order. This order is deemed necessary for the survival of the society. According to this perspective, it is assumed that individuals learn roles by internalizing shared norms and values through socialization. These roles are generally adhered to without question by the majority (conformity prevails). Where rules are broken (deviation from the norms), varying types of sanctions are imposed by significant others or by the formal agents of social control (in western democracies, the legislatures).

In summary, this perspective argues that social order is maintained by adherence to the norms of social institutions external to the individual. That is, we are like puppets who follow societally imposed rules; thus we have little, if any, control over our lives. This view of the social world is reflected in the life span or life course perspective that prevails at both the micro and macro levels, and in the structural-functionalist and age-stratification perspectives that will be described later.

In contrast, the 'second sociology,' or the 'interpretive' perspective (Marshall, 1980a), views individuals as social actors who, through processes of negotiation, define, interpret, and control their institutionalized roles. In this way, individual actors create the social order. As a result, institutions and structures can be changed when people engage in interaction. According to this perspective, individuals seek to give meaning to their lives by imposing their own definition of a situation. They control their destiny, and that of others, by introducing changes in societal institutions as they are perceived to be needed.

In summary, individuals create and then use norms through conflict, negotiation, and compromise with others during interaction, and thereby socially construct reality. As Marshall and Tindale (1978–79) suggest in their plea for a radical scholarship in gerontology, there is a greater need to consider the historical context in which individuals grow old. They argue that we need to study aging phenomena from the perspectives and realities of the elderly, rather than from that of scholars under 65 years of age. This 'interpretive' view is exemplified by symbolic interactionism, phenomenology, ethnomethodology, critical theory, neo-Marxism, and social exchange theory.

Micro-level Perspectives

The life-span developmental perspective.   Social scientists interested in human development have historically directed most of their attention to infancy, childhood, and adolescence. This emphasis evolved because most social, emotional, behavioral, and cognitive changes occur during these early stages of life. For years, the adult stages of the life cycle were ignored or, if studied, were considered as stages isolated from the earlier stages of life.

Although there is no general theory that accounts for social behavior at all stages in the life course[13] (Clausen, 1972), social scientists have increasingly recognized that human development is a lifelong dynamic process wherein the events, experiences, and roles of one stage in life are influenced by earlier stages. There appears to be a cyclical pattern to the process whereby individuals acquire prestige, power (social and physical), and independency as they age, at least up to a certain stage. Thereafter, at some later stage, prestige and power begin to decline and the individual may become, once more, a dependent being.

In order to provide some structure to the life-span perspective, the life cycle is divided into stages, and each stage, although interconnected with others, is studied as a separate entity. For example, one common breakdown is that proposed by the psychologist Erikson (1950). He identified eight stages of psychosocial development: early infancy, later infancy, early childhood, middle childhood, adolescence, early adulthood, middle adulthood, and late adulthood. Many other schemes have been proposed, including some that attach a chronological age span to each stage or period of development.

It must be recognized, however, that there are individual differences within a given stage or age range, and that development may begin late in one stage and overlap into the next. Moreover, some individuals may experience asynchronization of role or maturational development (Hogan, 1981). For example, those who receive a doctoral degree before age 25, those who are grandparents in their thirties, those women who have a child in their forties, those who retire in their forties, and those who initiate a second career in their forties or fifties all deviate from what are considered 'normal' ages at which these events should occur in the life course. As a result of individual differences and asynchronization, it is difficult to delineate precisely the temporal period at which stages begin and end. This same process may also occur at the cohort level of analysis. That is, because of an event such as war, disordered cohort flow may result in oversized or undersized cohorts (Waring, 1975). The appearance of these atypical cohorts may, in turn, induce change in age-graded institutions and may alter life chances. It must also be recognized that the overlap between stages, and the variation within stages, are to a great extent individual-, cohort- or culture-specific. Thus, the life-span perspective requires a comparison of the developmental patterns of different cohorts in different cultures, as well as within subcultures in a given society.

This life-span perspective was initially used by developmental psychologists who were interested in the growth and development of such personal characteristics as personality, behavior, attitudes, motor and perceptual skills, and intelligence. However, it is now recognized that an individual with various psychological, social, and physical attributes interacts with others within various social systems. Those who use the developmental perspective now study the elements and processes of both the personal and the social system. These include such factors as changes in personality and in physical, psychological and social maturation; patterns and meaning of interaction with significant others; the development of the social self; sequential role change (Rosow, 1976); socialization and adaptation to personal or social system changes; meanings attached to others and to specific events; and significant events and transition points for individuals. It is because of this complexity that investigators usually focus on only one stage in the life cycle. Moreover, most of the studies are cross-sectional rather than longitudinal.

One approach that has relevance for studying the aging process from a developmental perspective is to reconstruct the life script of individuals. In this way, retrospective interviews or questionnaires seek to identify crucial events and turning points at each stage of the life cycle, thereby providing a biography for a given individual. For example, significant sociocultural events (such as a war or a depression) may interact with significant personal events (the first job, the birth of a child). In this situation, the occurrence of a significant personal event at the time of a major sociohistorical event makes the event significant and salient to an individual, and thereby vividly remembered. Perhaps you might wish to interview a grandparent or an elderly neighbor in order to gain insight into personal and societal factors influencing their life history.

To date, the life-span perspective has primarily been of interest to psychologists interested in the 'personal' or micro-level system, particularly as it pertains to early socialization and adaptation in infancy, childhood, and adolescence. As a result, until recent years (Brim and Wheeler, 1966; Baltes and Willis, 1977; Baltes et al., 1980; Birren et al., 1981), relatively little attention has been given to adult development, especially in the later years of life. This lack of interest is surprising, because a more complete understanding of the total developmental process would result if the processes and characteristics of the later developmental stages were understood. Future work from a developmental perspective is likely to focus on how social age regulates an individual's behavior and social and psychological development, as well as the meaning of age in different social systems at different stages in the life cycle.

Similarly, although some early work was done by Cain (1964), until recently little attention has been paid to the impact of an aging population on the aging individual. Whereas the life-span perspective links the micro (developmental psychology) and macro (age-stratification theory) approaches to the study of aging (Elder, 1974, 1975; Riley, 1979; Marshall, 1981a).

This perspective involves an analysis of the interaction of earlier psychological, biological, and social processes and how these processes may have lasting, cumulative, or delayed effects at a later stage in life. Not all early events have a later impact; there are unique events that can occur only at a specific stage, and which can have an impact only at that stage. Therefore, the major goals of this perspective are to determine how and why earlier and later events in the life cycle are interrelated; how these processes and characteristics change or remain stable over the life cycle; and how specific events (such as an economic depression) at a specific stage of the life cycle have an impact on different age cohorts within different cultures.

The major assumptions underlying this perspective are:

1. That adults pass sequentially through all stages.

2. That individuals have certain goals or tasks to be accomplished within each stage, and most adults succeed in doing so.

3. That development is cumulative, orderly, and hierarchical, so that in most cases one stage must be completed before the next stage can begin.

4. That aging is a lifelong process which, if it is to be explained, involves understanding antecedent and consequent events.

5. That the process of aging involves the interaction of psychological, biological, and social processes.

6. That historical events and social and environmental change must be considered when studying the life course of an individual or cohort (Riley, 1979:4-5).

While these assumptions may apply to cognitive, motor, and maturational development, they may not be valid for all behavior and role sequences in adulthood. For example, mid-life career changes, divorce, childlessness, single parenting, delayed marriage, and homosexuality are life events that vary from the 'normal' stages and sequences of the 'normative' life cycle model. Thus, because of individual differences, there may be several 'normal' life-cycle patterns, especially during periods of rapid social change. The onset of these individual events or social changes can have degrees of influence on an individual depending on what stage he or she is at in the life cycle when the event occurs. Therefore, attempts to understand phenomena in later life using the life-span perspective must consider historical and personal events earlier in the life cycle, as well as demographic changes in the structure of an aging society.

The symbolic interactionist perspective. Whereas the life-span perspective was a subset of the normative perspective, symbolic interactionism (Manis and Meltzer, 1972; Hewit, 1976) is a subset of the interpretive perspective. The individual is considered to be an active participant in a specific social situation or setting. Through this process the individual defines and interprets a specific setting, in personal terms, as a result of interacting with significant others verbally or symbolically (through dress, gestures, language, mannerisms). In this way, social meaning is attributed to the symbols and behavior, and shared meanings of the situation are derived according to the meaning the situation has for each individual. Our interaction with others involves interpreting the meanings of their actions, and behaving in a way that reflects our own intended meaning.

Symbolic interactionists have identified three processes that lead to specific meanings and hence to cognitive or behavioral acts. First, an individual defines the social situation in terms of how it operates and what it means to him or her (Thomas, 1931).[14] Second, individuals observe and interact with others in order to examine and arrive at a definition of the 'self' (Cooley, 1902). In this process we as individuals consider how others see us and how others evaluate what they see in us. As a result of this evaluation and interpretation, which operates continuously, we arrive at a view of ourselves and a situation and behave accordingly.

The third process involves what Goffman (1959) refers to as 'the presentation of self.' Individuals define the situation and then decide how they will present themselves to others in terms of dress, manner and content of verbal interaction, and general and specific behaviors. For example, you as university students may present yourself differently to others depending on whether you are at an 8:30 a.m. class, at an interview for a job, at a bar late in the evening, at a dormitory with age-peers, or at home for a visit with your parents. Different dress, speech, and behavior patterns are selected in order to present a self appropriate to the specific situation.

In short, symbolic interactionism represents an analysis[15] of a specific social process or situation that occurs in everyday life. The focus, then, is on social interaction as a process, and the various meanings and interpretations each participant brings to that interaction. This perspective does not normally take into account the larger social system in which the specific setting is found, nor does it normally take into account past experiences or the impact of historical events. Rather, it is concerned with how each individual interprets and assigns meaning to a specific event, behavior, or situation. In recent years this approach has been used with older people to examine the meaning and lifestyle of living in nursing homes (Gubrium, 1975), retirement villages (Jacobs, 1975; Marshall, 1975a, 1978–79), age-segregated apartments (Hochschild, 1973) and single rooms on or near skid row (Tindale, 1980). This approach has also been used to study the process of labelling and stigma management among older women (Matthews, 1979). Finally, a recent text by Marshall (1980b) is an excellent example of interpretive sociology, which is primarily based on a symbolic interactionist approach to aging and dying.

The social exchange perspective.   At both the individual (personal) and collective (society) level, social interaction can be viewed as a process wherein all who are involved seek to maximize the rewards (gains) and reduce the costs (losses), whether they be material (money, goods, or services) or non-material (friendship or assistance). Social interaction involves reciprocity (give and take); each actor in the relationship strives to balance the costs and rewards. According to this view of the world (Emerson, 1976), interaction will be initiated and continued as long as it is rewarding to both parties, even though the rewards are unlikely to be equal. When one actor gains more than the other, and the interaction continues, power accrues to one side in the exchange relationship. That is, the actor for whom the cost is greater is 'in debt' to the other and is therefore subject to compliance in future interaction between the two actors.

In reality, most social relationships do not operate as if they were 'balanced' budgets. Rather, they include some degree of imbalance wherein one side cannot reciprocate equally. That side becomes dependent and is obligated to try to redress the balance in the future. In most exchange relationships participants strive to maximize their power, yet maintain a fair outcome. Not surprisingly, status characteristics can influence exchange rates (Dowd, 1980:53–54). For example, since status factors can influence our perceptions, possessing such valued characteristics as being white, male, highly educated, wealthy, and young can strengthen one's position in the negotiation process. Thus, to be black, female, illiterate, poor, or old can place one at a disadvantage in social interaction. To have two or three less highly valued status characteristics is to experience double or triple jeopardy in social exchange relationships. Later in this chapter we will see how aging is conceptualized as a process of social exchange wherein the elderly have few resources to exchange and are subject to compliance and lowered status in social relationships.

Micro-level Theories

Introduction. In the following subsections, we will look first at theories from the social sciences that have been used to explain aging phenomena at the individual level of analysis; these are followed by more specific theories that have been developed by social gerontologists to explain the aging process, or the status of being old, from the perspective of the individual. At the outset it must be recognized that none of these theories provides a complete explanation of aging. Some theories apply to growing old (the process), while others pertain to being old (the end product); some apply only to the individual, others to both the individual and to cohorts.

Role theory. The two basic concepts associated with role theory, 'status' and 'role,' were first introduced by the sociologist Linton (1936). While there has been continuing debate concerning the definitions of these concepts (Rosow, 1976:457–72) from both the structuralist perspective (which holds that normative roles are 'taken' as is) and interactionist perspective (roles are created and interpreted by the individual) (George, 1980), the following definitions are generally accepted by social scientists. Social status refers to a socially defined position within a given social structure that is separate from, but related to, other positions. Status can be achieved by an individual through personal choice, or by competition and use of training and abilities. Examples of acquired or achieved status positions include lawyer, father, employer, or spouse. Status positions may also be ascribed at birth (male or female, black or white), or they may be acquired at some later stage in life (widow or retiree).

Associated with each status position is a social role. This represents a social definition of the behavioral patterns, rights, and responsibilities expected from those occupying a specific status position. The definition results in a set of role expectations derived from what the individual expects while occupying that status, and, more important, what others expect of the individual in a given situation. These normative expectations serve as guidelines for behavior in specific situations. However, as interactionist theorists suggest, there is a wide range of permissible behavior for any given role, especially with respect to informal roles (such as that of college roommates) that are found outside the normative social structure. Inadequate role performance can be explained by deviant behavior (the individual ignores normative behavioral expectations), by an inadequate or incomplete socialization process, or by conflicting role expectations.

The earlier theorists assumed that status and role were inevitably linked (Linton, 1936); Rosow (1976) suggests that an individual may hold a status without a defined role. He also indicates that a role may be performed that is not intrinsic to a specific social status. He lists three major types of roles:

1. An 'institutional' role (role and status are both present) such as occupation, family, class, race, age, sex, or ethnicity.
2. A 'tenuous' role (status present, role absent) such as honorary position (professor emeritus, an honorary chairman of the board), nominal position (the executive who is 'put out to pasture' by being given a title with no

functional responsibilities), or amorphous position (the aged who are excluded from social participation such as widows and the chronically unemployed).

3. An 'informal' role (formal role and status are both absent) not linked to an institutionalized status (confidants; opinion, symbolic, or charismatic leaders; heroes and villains; deviant social types, such as blackmailers, pool hustlers and prostitutes).

To role theorists, social behavior can be explained by examining the various processes that result when roles are acquired, performed, and lost (Biddle and Thomas, 1966; Sarbin and Allen, 1968; Biddle, 1979). This dynamic process involves role learning, role change, and role transition.

Role learning often involves the acquisition of a new status and takes place through the process of socialization; role change involves a change in role expectations associated with the same status. For example, the status of 'child' remains intact as long as one's parents are alive, but the role expectations change as the individual moves through the life cycle.

The process of role transition results when an individual gains or loses a status position, and must thereby acquire or give up specific role behaviors (George, 1980). For example, the change of status from student to employee, or from being single to being a spouse, requires the acquisition of a new repertoire of behavioral standards, rights, and responsibilites, along with the loss of some rights and duties associated with the previous status (Rosow, 1976).

These processes of role learning, role change, and role transition can sometimes create role conflict for individuals. This occurs either because they are unsure about how they should behave in a given situation, or because two or more reference groups or significant others (parents and age peers) have contradictory expectations regarding role performance. For example, the recent widow may be unsure as to whether she should remain socially isolated and endure a long period of mourning, or whether, after a brief period of mourning, she should become socially active. This conflict may arise because her significant reference groups (children, the church, age peers) hold different beliefs concerning the behavior expected of a widow.

Inevitably, role changes have an impact on the individual's identity, self-image, and social behavior. In most cases, the impact is greatly influenced by the reaction of significant others and salient reference groups. Role changes pose a challenge to the individual and often require behavioral and cognitive adjustments and adaptation. Since many role changes are linked to chronological age or to reaching particular stages in the life cycle, it is not surprising that social scientists and social gerontologists have used role theory in an attempt to understand aging phenomena, particularly the status of being old.

The first use of this theory in gerontology was based on the premise that movement through the life cycle, especially in the later years, is characterized by a loss of or reduction in major social roles (worker, parent, or spouse). It was also based on the assumption that the process of aging involves major role transitions or role exits such as widowhood, retirement, the death of friends, and loss of independence (Marshall, 1980b:82). As a result of the prevalence of these role changes, old age was seen as a time of physiological, psychological, and social loss; as a period when new social relationships and roles typical of later life are adopted (Cavan et al., 1949); and as a period involving the acquisition of a devalued status with few meaningful roles, or, to use Burgess' (1950) concept, a 'roleless' role.

Because role loss was thought to be an almost inevitable process, early social gerontologists sought to explain the social adjustment process among the elderly (Cottrell, 1942; Cavan et al., 1949; Burgess, 1950; Phillips, 1957; Cumming and Henry, 1961; Blau, 1973; Lopata, 1973; Rosow, 1974). Role theory directed attention to the loss of meaningful institutionalized roles in later life; the devalued status of the aged and the occupancy of tenuous roles; the lack of an adequate socialization process for later-life roles (widow or retiree); and the impact of these processes on identity, self-concept, self-esteem, and social interaction.

While this role-loss perspective dominated the thinking within social gerontology for many years, more recently aging has been viewed as less problematic (Kalish, 1979; Palmore, 1979). That is, aging is increasingly viewed as a process of role transition and change wherein most individuals transfer successfully, and adjust effectively, to new role sets (George, 1980). Moreover, aging throughout the life cycle is viewed as a process that involves both gains and losses in a variety of interrelated roles. For some elderly people the transition may be stressful, and coping may be difficult; for others it will be uneventful and successful. It has been found that in most cases a change or loss of social roles is not usually sufficient to threaten one's identity or lower one's self-esteem (Larson, 1978).

In summary, the use of role theory has shifted from a problem-oriented to a process-oriented approach. As a result, the theory is a viable tool for helping us to understand social behavior. However, it must be remembered that norms and values vary by class, race, religion, ethnicity, sex, and age. The salience of specific roles within a role set (all the roles played by a particular individual — parent, spouse, employee, neighbor) and the interpretation of role performance may vary greatly between and within age cohorts, even for the same status position. Finally, although role theory has primarily been used to describe and explain role losses in old age, the theory also has the potential to describe and explain the processes of role acquisition, change, and transition at other stages in the life cycle.

Reference-group theory.   According to reference-group theory (Merton, 1957; Kemper, 1968; Hyman and Singer, 1968; Romeis et al., 1971), individuals identify with groups or significant others, and use them as a frame of reference for their own behavior, attitudes, values, beliefs, and feelings. Individuals normally adopt the standards of a group they perceive as positive, and reject those of a group perceived as negative.

Kemper (1968) suggests that there are three general types of reference groups that influence the socialization process and role learning. The 'normative reference group,' such as the family, provides guidelines for conforming behavior by establishing norms and espousing particular values. The 'comparison reference group' enables the individual to evaluate himself or his situation in comparison to others, and thereby make decisions and shape his attitudes and behavior in a particular role. The 'audience reference group' normally does not interact directly with the individual; rather, the individual attributes certain values and attitudes to the audience group, and attempts to behave in accordance with those values.[16]

At any given time, the reference groups for an individual can be past, present, or future (anticipatory socialization) groups; the individual does not have to be a member of the group in order for it to be salient. As we age, we selectively utilize a variety of reference groups that guide our behavior and either enhance or destroy our self-image. For example, Romeis et al. (1971)

hypothesized that well-adjusted aged individuals have high-quality (even if low-quantity) interaction with their reference groups, receive positive feedback about themselves (a positive self-image) from their reference groups, and have values and norms that agree with those of the reference groups.

The amount of influence a reference group has on the attitude formation, attitude change, or social behavior of an individual is closely related to the degree of identification with the reference group. Streib and Schneider (1971) suggested that an individual's pre-retirement orientation and degree of adjustment to retirement may be related to reference-group identification with family, friends, and peer cliques at work. All of these groups are significant to work and retirement decisions, and to personal adaptation. In an empirical test of this hypothesis, Cox and Bhak (1978–79) found that an individual's significant others, within and outside the family, are crucial to the development of positive preretirement attitudes and to a favorable postretirement adjustment. Similarly, Blau (1973, 1981) used reference-group theory to analyze the process whereby changes in age identity occur in the middle and later years of life.

Socialization and social learning theory [17].   Socialization is a lifelong process that enables an individual to participate in a society by learning appropriate symbols for communication, and by learning particular roles that will assist in developing a self-image or identity. Clausen (1966:250) defined socialization as both a process and an end product. As a process, socialization involves learning skills, traits, knowledges, attitudes, language, beliefs, norms, values, and shared behavioral expectations associated with present or future social roles. The process may vary because of such factors as gender, socioeconomic status, community or ethnic differences, cultural differences, and individual differences in the lifestyle and values of socializing agents.

The product (that is successful socialization) involves the demonstration of adequate and acceptable performance in specific social positions and the development of an identity, a self-image, and a sense of self-esteem associated with a position in a particular social group. This implies that socialization is a two-way process that involves the individual defining the self and acquiring new knowledge and skills through interaction with and feedback from others. These significant others, in turn, may be socialized by the process of interaction.

Most socialization occurs during childhood and adolescence, and socialization research has generally focused on those stages.[18] However, since the 1960s there has been an increasing recognition that socialization is a lifelong process, and that we cannot possibly be socialized in childhood for all the social positions we may occupy in later life. As we age, the socialization process tends to be concerned with learning more specific roles and behaviors, and tends to be more voluntary and interactive in nature than in the earlier years (Sewell, 1963; Clausen, 1968; Brim, 1966; Goslin, 1969; Mortimer and Simmons, 1978). Furthermore, there seem to be three basic differences between socialization processes in earlier and later life. These include (1) a shift in emphasis from values and motives to a concern with overt behavior; (2) a synthesis or revision of old knowledge rather than the acquisition of new material; and (3) an emphasis on learning specific role skills (such as those associated with being a parent) rather than on learning general behavioral traits (honesty, diligence, obedience).

Regardless of the stage in the life cycle, three factors influence the process of learning the requirements of full adult participation in society. (1) the social structure; (2) the stages and techniques of socialization; and (3) the socializing agents or significant others.

The social structure can lead to different socialization outcomes. For example, an elderly widow who is forced to give up her home will be socialized quite differently for her future roles depending on whether she moves in with a child, enters a senior-citizen apartment, or becomes totally institutionalized in a home for the aged. Wheeler (1966:60) suggests that because the individual and the social structure are interrelated, there are interrelated variables that influence the extent to which individuals are socialized. From society's perspective, these include the capacity of social organizations to establish clear goals and expectations, to provide facilities and resources for role performance, and to control performances through positive and negative sanctions. From the perspective of the individual, socialization involves the ability to learn the required norms, behaviors, and values, to perform as required or expected, and to be motivated to perform.

While most socialization early in life occurs within the family, school, and peer group, during adulthood work groups, peer groups, the mass media, and employment and voluntary organizations become more influential elements. Inkeles (1969:618) argues that four interrelated dimensions of social structure must be considered when analyzing the process of socialization. These dimensions include an ecological component (the size, density, physical distribution, and social composition of the population); an economic component (social forms for defining, producing, and distributing goods and services); a political component (the source and structure of power); and a value component (the values or culture of the setting).

The techniques used at various stages in the life cycle must also be considered in any analysis of the process of socialization. During infancy and childhood, the individual is greatly influenced by the family and school. The individual may be a passive actor who learns directly and indirectly the values, skills, and behaviors that are more formally taught. By late childhood and early adolescence, however, the individual becomes a more active participant in the process. Because of the influence of the media and the peer subculture, another view besides that of the family is presented, and the individual must make decisions as to what values and behaviors are to be internalized.

Throughout the adult years, with the possible exception of learning occupational roles, the process becomes more informal, voluntary, and specific, and may also involve less passive role taking (the structuralist view) and more active role making, negotiation, and accommodation (the interactionist view). The individual is more likely to shape the norms to which he or she will adhere through a continuous process of negotiation and accommodation with others in specific social situations (Marshall, 1980b:78). Adult socialization involves a continuous process of acquiring new values and behavior appropriate to adult status positions and group memberships. In order to better understand this process of adult socialization, three specific concepts need to be introduced: anticipatory socialization, desocialization, and resocialization.

Anticipatory socialization occurs when an individual accepts the beliefs, values, and norms of a status position to which he or she wishes to belong, or will belong, but to which he or she does not yet belong. In this way the individual is prepared for the new status (Albrecht and Gift, 1975). For example, to prepare for the large amount of leisure time available during retirement, an individual may begin to take longer vacations, or may work shorter weeks or fewer hours for a few years prior to retirement. Similarly, some individuals learn to cope with the inevitability of death through an indirect process of anticipatory socialization wherein they 'bury their peers' (Marshall, 1975).

Desocialization occurs when the individual experiences role loss or 'role emptying'[19] rather than the acquisition of new roles. Associated with this process is the frequent inability to give up the prestige or power associated with the role. Rosow (1974) suggests that desocialization is the reverse of the optimal conditions of socialization. He states that desocialization often leads to a devalued social position characterized by ambiguous norms, role discontinuity, and status loss. If this is the case, it is not surprising that some individuals deny aging or fight the process of desocialization in order to maintain their roles and status.

Resocialization involves a basic and often rapid change in lifestyle when an individual enters a new social status, such as widow or retiree, or a new social situation, such as a home for the aged. The individual must often informally learn the new expectations, values, and behaviors associated with the new status (Bennett, 1980). As Rosow concluded, there is at present little, if any, socialization to the status of old age, largely because there are few role models and few norms 'that effectively structure an older person's activities and general pattern of life' (1974:69). Personal definitions unique to the situation determine what is appropriate and desirable.[20]

The elderly sometimes are labelled as eccentric or deviant, perhaps because of an inadequate or incomplete socialization or resocialization process. Rosow concluded his book by noting that Hochschild's (1973) three-year participant observation study of working-class widows in a senior-citizen public housing project illustrates how successful socialization to a devalued status position (such as that of an elderly widow) can be accomplished. Rosow (1974:169) states that this process of resocialization to a new status in the later years is related to the presence of the following group functions: 'new group memberships, a new role set, clear role prescriptions, positive new reference groups, abundant role models, solid self-images, extremely strong group support and reciprocity, and the insulation of members not only from invidious external judgments, but also from the weakening of kinship and the external ties.' ('Widow-to-widow' programs are often based on these principles.) Similarly, new residents of a home for the aged might adapt more successfully and quickly if a structured 'resocialization' program were available to assist their transition to the institutionalized setting. After all, freshman are 'oriented' to college life, informally and formally, and formal orientation programs are used to integrate prisoners into penal institutions.

The third major element in the socialization process is the socializing agent. Socializing agents include parents and siblings within the family, distant relatives, neighbors in the community, teachers and peers within the school, leaders in voluntary associations, sport and entertainment stars, and peers in the workplace. While some of these socializing agents are more influential at one stage in the life cycle than at another, peers, voluntary association leaders, neighbors, and media personnel tend to be influential at all stages. In particular, the media have become significant socializing agents that teach or reinforce values and attitude, and serve as a source of norms and values.

Having briefly examined the process of socialization, let us turn now to an overview of one major socialization theory that can account for role change and role transition as we age — social imitation theory. While many theories have been proposed to account for social learning, including the classical stimulus-response-reinforcement models, social imitation theories argue that most social behavior is learned through observation, imitation, interaction, and emotional identification with significant others (Bandura, 1969; Gewirtz, 1969). No direct reinforcement is required for the learning to occur.

Since this process continues throughout the life cycle, there is a shift from a reliance on compulsory and exemplary role models (parents or teachers) during childhood and early adolescence, to a greater reliance on symbolic models (media figures) and specific role models (those occupying status positions into which an individual aspires or is required to move). These models are voluntarily selected by the individual from a wide variety of possible models in his or her social world. This theory is concretely illustrated by 'widow-to-widow' programs wherein a recently bereaved woman is encouraged to interact with another widow who assists her in becoming socialized to her new status. It is likely that both retirees and widows engage in some anticipatory socialization prior to moving into their new roles by observing the attitudes and behavior of those who have already successfully or unsuccessfully completed the passage.

Social exchange theory. The social exchange perspective is useful in explaining continuing patterns of interaction among individuals, in accounting for the allocation by age of roles and resources in social groups, and in explaining the acquisition of power and independence by some individuals. A basic assumption of this theory is that individuals search for social situations in which valued outcomes are possible, and in which their social, emotional, and psychological needs can be met. Since this goal may involve acquiescence and compliance by an individual or group, a fair exchange may not be readily apparent in every social relationship. Thus, knowledge of past experiences and of present personal needs, values, and options is required by social scientists prior to determining the equity of an observed social exchange. This is especially the case when this theory is used to explain the situation of the elderly (Maddox and Wiley, 1976:17–19).

While no one theory can explain all aging phenomena, social exchange theory is more useful than some since it can apply to both the individual and cohort levels of analysis. As a result, this theory has gained increasing acceptance as a viable explanatory mechanism for many facets of the aging process. The following studies illustrate the use of this theory in explaining selected facets of social interaction between generations, especially within the kinship network.

In one of the first studies to employ this theory, Martin (1971) argued that the 'complaining and trouble-recounting' of many elderly people is tolerated and rewarded by further interaction. This occurs because the listening is seen as not only a cultural expectation but as an obligation for debts incurred in past social exchanges. Thus, even though the present interaction may be viewed as unpleasant or a nuisance by the listener, it is often rewarded by increasing the frequency of interaction, especially where the older person is ill. Martin notes further that in some cases the complaining may be a conscious attempt to receive attention. In this way, complaining individuals force interaction with those who have neglected them.

The strongest proponent of this theory within gerontology has been Dowd (1975, 1978, 1980) who explains aging behavior as a process of social exchange. He suggests that the decreased interaction noted in the later years is the result not of an inevitable process of disengagement, but of a series of exchange relationships across the life cycle. As a result of these exchange relationships, relative social power diminishes as one ages. This forces compliance and an unbalanced relationship wherein the elderly experience greater costs and fewer rewards.

As one ages, few resources, other than experience, are available for exchange. This leads to conforming behavior and fewer interactions. For example, as the occupational skills of the older worker become outmoded or obsolete, he or she is forced to accept mandatory retirement in return for modest pension benefits (social assistance), and, in most cases, a reduced standard of living. Similarly, when individuals are perceived to be no longer able to care for themselves, they are institutionalized and cared for as a repayment for past debts.[21] As Dowd (1978:352) observes, 'old people, after decades of accumulated investment in society in the form of commitment to work and family, are frequently forced to reap such rewards as loneliness, prestige loss, and social and economic discrimination.' He notes that not all elderly persons experience these losses, that many do not see these losses as unjust, and that many are not even aware that the balance can be redressed. However, some elderly persons do actively seek to restore a more equitable distribution of resources. They perceive that the injustice is a source of lowered life satisfaction, and that a greater age consciousness is needed to restore equity (Dowd, 1978).

The relationship in modernized societies between older and younger age cohorts involves the aged experiencing varying degrees of increasing dependence, and a concomitant loss of power in relationships. Unless an attempt is initiated to restore some degree of balance, the relationship becomes institutionalized and the elderly are viewed as being dependent upon others (Dowd, 1975). According to Dowd, the aging process can be shown as a curvilinear relationship between chronological age and the amount of power. In general, there is increasing power, prestige, and privilege between about 20 and 50 years of age, with a decrease in these attributes thereafter. However, the slope and shape of the curve can vary by such personal factors as class, gender, race, level of education, and ethnicity.

The slope and shape of the curve can also vary by such structural factors as modernization, age-homogeneity of a social system, and by the initiation of social change wherein the elderly attempt to restore the balance of power by reducing the costs of interacting with younger age cohorts (Dowd, 1980). For example, Emerson (1962) suggests that a relationship can be balanced by four possible operations: (1) disengaging or withdrawing, thereby eliminating the relationship; (2) extending the power network by developing new roles, such as the Gray Panther activist who campaigns for social change; (3) reacquiring high status when obsolete skills are suddenly needed, or when there is a shortage of labor that creates a demand for the older worker; and (4) forming a coalition with other less powerful groups (such as unemployed youth), thereby gaining power against the middle-aged power bloc.

Labelling theory. Throughout life we are evaluated and 'labelled' by others as we interact within various social systems. In some instances the labels are formally attached (such as nicknames); in others they are unspoken but informally recognized by a variety of significant others with whom one interacts (a person is perceived to be intelligent, aggressive, or decisive, inefficient, or dishonest). Labels can be positive or negative, although they often tend to be negative.[22]

In the past, labelling theory has been used primarily to explain deviant behavior (Becker, 1973) and mental disorders (Scheff, 1974). According to this theory, primary labelling occurs when significant others perceive an individual's behavior to differ in quality or type from normative standards. As a result of this perception, an individual is labelled as 'delinquent,' 'unstable,' 'eccentric,' 'senile,' or 'charismatic.' That is, the labelling is a social judgment and represents an interpretation of the meaning of repeated patterns of behavior. The label is not an inherent property of the behavioral pattern. Rather, it reflects the meaning attributed by others to behavioral acts and is a product of a particular social system. D'Arcy (1980) noted that there was an increase in the number of persons over 70 years of age who were labelled mentally ill after the introduction of a policy of free hospitalization for mental illness in Saskatchewan. However, after the early 1960s, policy and legislative changes concerning the delivery of health care and the care of the aged broadened the alternatives for the care of the elderly. As a result, there was a dramatic decrease in the number of persons over 70 who were labelled as mentally ill. Thus, changes in the structure and processes for delivering psychiatric care in the province resulted in changes in the nature and frequency of labelling older persons.

If the process of labelling is repeated, it is often internalized within the individual's self-concept. People become dependent upon socially induced labels to understand and demonstrate who they are. As a result, secondary labelling occurs; the individual accepts the label and is indirectly socialized into playing the role of 'delinquent,' 'mental patient,' 'old person,' or 'charismatic leader.' In this way the cycle of socially induced behavior is reinforced. Obviously, not all individuals are labelled. For unknown reasons, labelling is more likely to occur for some individuals than for others, and moreso in some situations than in others.

Within the field of social gerontology, Kuypers and Bengtson (1973) were the first to suggest that this theory might assist in understanding the behavior of the elderly. They presented a 'social breakdown' model wherein the elderly are labelled as deficient, incompetent, or obsolete because they experience role loss, vague normative standards, and few reference groups as they grow older. They turn to societal sources for a definition of the self. However, society propagates stereotypical views of the elderly and they are labelled as useless, helpless, or incompetent.[23] Elderly people, in turn, may accept these negative labels. They are then socialized to particular roles, and may behave according to how they are expected to act. In contrast, Matthews (1979) indicates that many older women now fight back against the social forces that label them as useless or socially irrelevant.

In response to this process of 'social breakdown,' Kuypers and Bengtson (1973) proposed a 'social reconstruction' model wherein the individual, with the assistance of significant others within various social systems, could increase the level of competence. This process would involve eliminating the image that to be dependent (a nonworker) is to be incompetent; providing social services to improve adaptive capacity and coping skills; and giving the elderly greater control and power over their own social lives.

The social breakdown model implied that the process applies to most older persons, and that the phenomenon occurs because of the interaction between the society and the individual. However, George (1980:43) argues that 'negative self-evaluation in later life is the exception rather than the rule.' Most older people have the personal resources and coping skills to maintain a positive self-image, and thereby adjust to role transitions as they age. It is also likely that this process of social breakdown via labelling would be less likely to occur in an age-homogeneous environment (such as a retirement community or senior citizen apartment complex), where a subculture of the elderly can foster positive rather than negative labels.

Activity (substitution) theory.   Activity theory was the first theory in North America to attempt to provide a description of, and a prescription for, successful or ideal aging in the later years of life. The idea of slowing down but keeping active in order to adjust successfully to aging was first suggested by Havighurst and Albrecht (1953). Later, Burgess (1960) suggested that old age should not be viewed as a 'roleless role,' but that individuals should replace lost roles or social activities with new ones. This theory argued that individual adaptation involved continuing an active lifestyle of social interaction in order to maintain the self-concept and hence a sense of well-being or life satisfaction. The maintenance of this active lifestyle involved replacing lost roles, by either re-engaging in earlier roles or engaging in new roles.

The basic assumptions of this theory are (1) that the middle-aged and the aged have identical psychosocial needs; (2) that individuals will resist giving up roles in order to stay active; (3) that successful aging involves a substitution of lost roles (spouse, friend, or worker) or lost activities (work, childrearing, or sport) with new roles or activities in order to maintain the self-identity; and (4) that suitable roles or activities are available and that the individual has the capability to become involved in these new domains. Thus, the basic hypotheses of the theory are that high activity and maintenance of roles is positively related to a favorable self-concept, and that a favorable self-concept is positively related to life satisfaction (or adjustment, successful aging, well-being, morale). In short, a high degree of social activity and role involvement is positively related to life satisfaction in the later years of life.

For a number of years this theory was accepted without question and, in fact, was the basis for much of the social programming and services provided to the elderly — that is, keep them busy by providing a range of activities and social roles, and they will age 'successfully.'[24] However, with the appearance of disengagement theory in 1960 (Cumming et al., 1960), scientists and practitioners began to question the validity of the activity theory of aging. The appearance of a second theory within social gerontology stimulated questions and led to research studies that sought to support or refute either theory. As a result, a number of studies were initiated, with a variety of samples, to seek support for the proposition that life satisfaction among the elderly is positively related to high levels of role and activity involvement. While some studies have supported the proposition (Palmore, 1968), and others have failed to find support, few have refuted the theory by finding support for the opposing hypothesis - namely, that high activity is related to low levels of satisfaction.

However, the evidence to support the theory has not been overwhelming and, hence, a number of criticisms and reservations about the theory have been raised. For example, in a classic study by Lemon et al. (1972), which was the first formal statement and test of activity theory, the relationship between five types of social activity[25] and life satisfaction was examined for those who had recently purchased homes in a California retirement community. They found that only informal social activity with friends was related to life satisfaction, and hence little if any support for the theory was provided. In a more recent test of the theory in England, Knapp (1977) also found limited support. However, in the most recent study, Longino and Kart (1982) replicated the work of Lemon et al. (1972) and concluded that there was strong support for the theory. To provide for greater variation in the background characteristics of the subjects they drew probability samples from three distinct types of retirement communities. Specifically, they found that informal activity (such as that found in primary relationships) was positively associated with life satisfaction, whereas formal activity was negatively associated with life satisfaction. They concluded that activity theory has some merit as an explanatory model, but that it needs to be tested in a variety of theoretical contexts to enhance the relevance of the theory.

Opponents of activity theory have suggested that activity levels can decrease without a loss of morale; that some individuals have never been socially active in their lives, yet exhibit satisfaction; and that not all individuals have the economic or interpersonal resources to replace lost roles. Moreover, there has been virtually no consideration of the quality or meaning of the activity that serves as the substitute. To keep busy at mundane, repetitive, socially sanctioned tasks may not result in a high sense of morale or life satisfaction if the activities or roles have little intrinsic meaning to the individual. Another criticism is that the theory is not a theory at all. Rather, it represents a set of assumptions that may apply only to some individuals as they age. It has also been noted that activity theory might illustrate the chicken-and-egg dilemma. Are older people satisfied because they are active, or are people who are satisfied more likely to be involved in social roles and activities?

In summary, activity theory may explain the situation of some older people, especially those who have adhered to a lifelong pattern of high interaction. In reality, as will be seen in the next subsection, aging is an individual process that involves selective replacement of and selective disengagement from some roles and activities. More important, as suggested recently (Longino and Kart, 1982; McClelland, 1982), self-conception may be an important intervening variable between social activity and life satisfaction, especially for those who prefer to interact with age peers. In short, the pattern that constitutes 'successful' aging for a given individual is likely to be closely related to his or her personality, self-concept, health, economic resources, and previous lifestyle, and to whether he or she lives in an age-homogeneous or age-heterogeneous environment. The greater opportunity provided by an age-homogeneous environment may facilitate an adaptation process wherein high activity is necessary for high levels of satisfaction.

Disengagement theory.   The presentation of disengagement theory in the early 1960s (Cumming et al., 1960; Cumming and Henry, 1961) represented a landmark in social gerontology. There was now an alternative to activity theory as an explanation for social aging. Although the development of disengagement theory was supposedly not motivated by a specific attempt to refute activity theory, it is often seen as the antithesis of activity theory.

Disengagement theory derives from both the developmental and the functionalist perspectives. Old age is viewed as different from middle age, and change and adaptation in the later years are seen as functionally necessary both for the individual and for society. Because of the inevitability of death, because of the probable decrement in ability as one ages, because of the value placed on youth, and because of the need to ensure that tasks are efficiently completed and roles filled, both individuals and society demand disengagement. A mechanism must be available whereby youth can enter and advance in the labor force, whereby roles can be filled by those who are generally more competent, and whereby the death of an individual is not disruptive to the functioning of the social system. Faced with these necessities, normal aging is viewed as a functional and voluntary process that involves the inevitable withdrawal or disengagement of the individual from society and of the society from the individual. In reality, however, many forms of disengagement are not voluntary, for example, widowhood or mandatory retirement (Shanas et al., 1968).

Disengagement results in decreased interaction between an individual and others in society, and is hypothesized to be a universal process that is satisfying to both the individual and society. Disengagement is believed to be satisfying to the individual because it provides release from normative constraints: the individual is released from pressures to behave as expected (for example, expectations of high performance on the job are reduced), and is given more freedom to deviate from societal expectations without negative sanctions being invoked. What is ordinarily viewed as 'eccentric' behavior is considered socially acceptable among the elderly.

From the perspective of society, disengagement permits younger members to enter functional roles, thereby facilitating turnover without intergenerational conflict. It also ensures that equilibrium and stability will be maintained, since members are replaced in the functional roles of society before their death. For example, without mandatory retirement most leaders and workers would die while still employed, and the social system could lose equilibrium until they were replaced. In short, disengagement is seen as a process wherein individuals, supported by societal norms and customs, voluntarily and gradually withdraw from social roles and decrease their social interaction. As a result, the individual is thought to experience a high level of satisfaction, well-being, or morale in the later years of life.

The construction of disengagement theory, like activity theory, resulted in many studies that sought to support or refute this explanation of social aging, including some revisions and clarifications of the theory by the original authors (Cumming, 1963; Henry, 1964). The major criticisms were directed at the idea that the process was universal and that everyone withdraws from his or her previously established role set. Clearly, a comparison of preindustrialized societies (with no retirement and with high status of the aged) with modern industrialized societies (with mandatory retirement and a lower status of the aged) suggests that the process is not universal.

Similarly, a number of empirical studies within the same society have indicated that withdrawal is not a typical pattern. Moreover, there may be different types of disengagement, and people in different social situations may disengage to varying degrees. For example, an individual may be socially engaged in a work role but psychologically disengaged[26] from it (it no longer has interest, meaning, or value for the individual). Similarly, as Mindel and Vaughan (1978) noted in a study of the religious behavior of elderly persons, an individual may be disengaged organizationally (he or she may no longer attend religious services) but engaged nonorganizationally (he or she may engage in private prayer or may listen to religious services on radio or television). Moreover, individual differences in health or economic status, and the loss of friends through death or migration, may account for disengagement, rather than age per se.

Disengagement might also occur at early stages in the life cycle, which often happens for those who live on skid row. Or, because of personality differences, it may occur at different periods in the life cycle, or take different forms. For example, Cumming (1963) suggested that there were two styles of adapting to the environment — 'impingers' and 'selectors' — and each would react differently to disengagement. For example, the impinger continues to seek and initiate interaction, the selector is reluctant to initiate interaction and might appear withdrawn and apathetic. In fact, some individuals are socially or psychologically 'disengaged' throughout the life cycle, while others are fully engaged[27] in social interaction until death, although the nature of the activities may change as they adjust to the aging process.

Another criticism of the theory is directed at the cause-and-effect relationship: is the process initiated by the individual or by society? The individual may be socialized to disengage, to see this as an expected pattern of behavior in the later years, and to conform voluntarily by behaving as expected. In contrast, it may be that the society withdraws from the individual; because youth is more highly valued (at least in many modernized societies), the elderly may be forced to withdraw because there is a lack of access to social roles, to power, or to interaction.

Other criticisms of disengagement theory have commented on the logical weakness of the theory and on the methodology used to test the theory (Youmans, 1969; Maddox, 1964, 1970; Hochschild, 1975, 1976; Markson, 1975; Sill, 1980). Most of the studies have been cross-sectional, and no attempt has been made to control for age versus cohort effects; the theory has been tested mainly from the perspective of the individual rather than from that of the society;[28] and chronological age has been used as the major independent variable when, in fact, decreased health status, perceived imminence of death (Marshall, 1975b; Sill, 1980), or economic hardship may lead to disengagement.

Another concern is that the definition of disengagement has been variously interpreted to imply isolation, loneliness, or passivity, and that disengagement has been interpreted as the antithesis of activity when in fact an individual can be disengaged but still active in a number of smaller roles. Finally, disengagement theory, as originally postulated, did not examine the importance of psychological commitment to or the meaning of involvement in social interaction. The conscious thoughts and feelings of individuals concerning their own conceptions of aging have seldom been considered as factors in the occurrence of disengagement.

In summary, there is little empirical support that decreased role involvement and social interaction is universal and inevitable, or that this decreased interaction or disengagement is related to life satisfaction or morale. While some individuals disengage, others remain highly active. Whether, why, and to what extent these two patterns lead to more or less life satisfaction is not clear. In all likelihood, the way in which an individual behaves in the later years may be related to maintaining role flexibility. That is, some roles are continued, some are discontinued, some are intensified, some are reduced, and some are played for the first time. In order to achieve this role flexibility, a combination of structural disengagement (from work, family, or organizations) and continued interaction with age peers, in age-appropriate activities, may enhance life satisfaction.

Finally, although it is yet to be tested, Hochschild (1975) proposed an alternative theory which hypothesized that disengagement varies according to type of society (preindustrial, industrial, or postindustrial). Focusing on internal variations in engagement in an industrial society, she suggests that social class and sex roles account for variation in engagement. Hochschild (1975:565–67) argues that, for men, orientation and access to work during the middle years is class-related. This orientation, in turn, influences engagement in other social spheres (such as the family and leisure).[29]

Furthermore, engagement is seen to be of two types: 'social' engagement, which refers to interaction with others at work, in the family, and in leisure pursuits, and 'normative' engagement, which refers to the emotional importance and meaning attached to interaction. The social and normative engagement patterns adopted during middle age generally remain part of one's lifestyle in the later years.

Whether, and in what manner, an individual disengages in later life might be predicted and explained by knowledge of his or her social and normative engagement pattern, which in turn is related to class. Hochschild (1975:566) hypothesizes that older men who have access to work (those in the highest social class) and a history of valuing work highly (normative engagement) will demonstrate a higher level of social and normative engagement in their work than in their family or leisure. Alternately, those who are prevented from working (mandatory retirement), but who enjoyed their work would be socially disengaged but normatively engaged in work; socially rather than normatively engaged in the family; and socially and normatively engaged in a leisure pursuit that resembles an occupation (such as making and selling crafts). In short, engagement in work strongly influences engagement in the family and leisure domains during the middle and later years.

Continuity theory.   Through the early-life socialization process, the individual learns and internalizes habits, commitments, preferences, and dispositions that become part of the personality and lifestyle. These tend to persist as an individual grows older, and to remain prominent factors in social interaction unless there is a reason for change. Continuity theory argues that as individuals age, they strive to maintain continuity in their lifestyle (Williams and Wirths, 1965). According to the theory (Atchley, 1971), individuals adapt most successfully to aging if they maintain a lifestyle similar to that developed in the early and middle years. Thus, it is unreasonable to predict that an individual who has always prefered to live alone will adjust to retirement by joining voluntary associations or by travelling with a group. Similarly, an individual who has adhered to a very expressive and instrumental lifestyle, in which he or she is highly engaged in people and activities, will not likely disengage unless there is a radical reason for a change (such as failing health).

In short, continuity theory suggests that the pattern of adjustment to aging, and whether it is successful or not for the individual, is highly related to maintaining consistency in the established lifestyle. As a result, planning for the later years should involve knowledge of and adherence to a lifestyle established by the middle years. This is especially important with respect to establishing a variety of meaningful and satisfying leisure activities in the middle years that can be pursued in the later years.

While this theory has generally been supported by research evidence, two recent critiques have raised doubts about the validity and completeness of the theory. First, Covey (1981) notes that whereas most conceptualizations of continuity theory focus on the individual level of analysis, continuity in lifestyle can only occur where there is compatible interaction between individual characteristics and the social structure. For example, a social structural factor such as mandatory retirement leads to discontinuity in the occupational role. Covey concludes that structural constraints can be overcome, and continuity can be maintained when the individual has a high level of personal resources (wealth, power, health) that can be used to prevent or delay the impact of social structural forces that require role exit.

The second critique (Fox, 1981–82) represents a review of the strengths and limitations of continuity theory. Fox indicates a number of conceptual and measurement problems associated with the theory, and concludes that there is little evidence that continuity is an adaptive form of behavior in the later years. In fact, it is suggested that continuity in lifestyle can be maladaptive if an individual adheres to outmoded values and behaviors.

Macro-level Perspectives

Introduction.   This section introduces perspectives and theories that focus on the systems and structures of society and on population aging. These views do not imply that the individual is neglected or unimportant; rather, they suggest that the behavior of individuals is influenced by the social environment, and specifically by the social structure — that is, the relatively stable and enduring system of norms, values, and social relationships that occur in social groups and social institutions.[30] The following subsections describe macro perspectives and theories and provide some additional conceptual tools to enable you to better understand how the social system, whether small (a married couple) or large (a country), influences behavior as we age.

The structural-functionalist perspective.   The structural-functionalist perspective, characterized by the work of Parsons (1951), Merton (1968), and Sztompka (1974), focuses on the relationships between social structures and social institutions and the resulting influence on the individual. For example, a functionalist might ask what function the family, as a social institution, serves in society; what influence does it have on individual behavior in each society? Clearly, not only the function but the structure of the family varies cross-culturally, particularly when primitive tribes and highly modernized societies are compared.

This view of the world argues that there is a commonly accepted, agreed-upon order (a structure) to society, that most efforts are directed toward maintaining the existing forms and functions of social institutions (the family, the political system, or the economic system), and that each element of the structure (such as the family) can be analytically viewed as having a manifest (intended, purposeful) or latent (unintended) function (Merton, 1968). Social action by an individual is determined and regulated by a formal yet abstract set of rules derived from the structure of the society.

From this perspective, aging is seen as a process whereby the individual adjusts to role changes (such as retirement or widowhood). A major concern is with how the individual fulfills his or her functions in given social institutions (Bengtson and Dowd, 1980–81). An individual's failure to adapt indicates an inability to fit into the existing social structure, not that the structure is ineffective or inappropriate for that period in history.

It must also be recognized that not all social relationships are functional; some are dysfunctional and detract from the stable functioning of society. For example, with the proportion of the population over 60 years of age increasing, mandatory retirement may become a dysfunctional institution. That is, an ever-growing segment of the population will become economically dependent on an ever-shrinking labor force that must contribute an increasing percentage of its income to support the older generations. At the same time, the policy of mandatory retirement might also be dysfunctional for the society in that it eliminates from a number of institutions individuals who have a great deal of experience and knowledge.

To summarize, this perspective assumes that all components of the social structure are necessary, are interrelated, and have some useful function in maintaining the equilibrium of the social system. Moreover, the interrelationship between the elements of the structure has consequences for the opportunities and behavior of individuals. For example, the societally imposed (institutionalized) act of mandatory retirement deprives the older individual of a major social role in order to realize a specific societal function, namely, to permit younger people to enter the labor force. As a result, the older worker is required to adapt to this loss of role. In order to facilitate this adaptation, society legitimates the nonwork role of retiree, and in many societies provides an economic reward (in the form of a pension). The individual is expected to comply with this process and 'fit in' to the existing, stable order without reacting negatively.

The conflict perspective.   Functionalism perceives the social world to be normative and static; the conflict perspective (Dahrendorf, 1959; Collins, 1975) views society as dynamic and changing. According to this perspective, conflict is inevitable. Society is composed of competing groups who either presently control the resources (such as authority, power, money, goods, or services), or who believe that they are deprived, exploited, or manipulated. The latter group believes that change must be initiated in order for them to obtain an equal share of the resources. Those who adhere to the conflict perspective believe that social interaction involves negotiation and compromise to resolve conflict.

Conflict theorists search for and identify power groups, and attempt to explain how they manipulate or control other social groups (Tindale and Marshall, 1980). For example, it has frequently been mentioned that modern, industrialized societies are controlled by white, middle-aged males. This has led to conflict between youth, who have yet to gain power, and the middle-aged; and more recently, to conflict between the elderly, who have lost power and authority, and the middle-aged. In fact, it has been suggested that a voting coalition of the young and the elderly may form in the years ahead if the economic status of these two disadvantaged groups does not improve. Conflict between age strata will evolve because of perceived inequities in power, and inadequate access to valued resources.

The system perspective.   The system perspective is adapted from engineering and the biological sciences, and is closely related to functionalism. The system approach to understanding social phenomena (Kuhn, 1974) focuses on a description and analysis of the structure and composition of social systems (their boundaries, elements, and environments); the functions (integration socialization), processes (stratification, social change, or social control), and problems (conflict or discrimination) of social systems; and the interrelationships between a variety of social systems (large versus small, simple versus complex, groups, organizations, institutions). An older couple, a family, a nursing home, a retirement community, or a society can be analyzed as distinct social systems, or as social systems that interact with other social systems.

A social system is made up of a group of individuals who interact with each other according to a shared set of beliefs, values, and norms (Wiseman, 1966). More specifically, a social system consists of three subsystems: a normative subsystem, a structural subsystem, and a behavioral subsystem (Loy, 1972). The normative subsystem, or culture, includes beliefs, folkways, laws, norms, sanctions, and values. The values represent the goals of the system, the norms indicate the preferred pattern or method to achieve the goals, and the sanctions represent the rewards or punishments for conforming or deviating from the norms. The structural subsystem (or social structure) consists of regular, patterned interaction among a set of social positions. For each social position (such as father) there is a social role, status, and rank. The behavioral subsystem involves the social (age, sex, or race), physical (height, weight, or motor ability), and psychological (personality or attitudes) characteristics of the members of a social system that influence the way in which they play specific roles.

In social gerontology, systems analysis can be used to study the social structure within which individuals age, and to study the way in which individuals or groups adapt. It can also be used to study how the possession of particular social, physical, and psychological attributes can influence goals, behavior, and cognitions at specific stages in the life cycle. Obviously, this analysis can involve the study of a simple dyad (the retired couple), a specific group (the members of a senior-citizen center), a particular institution (the extended family), or a specific society (Canada or the United States). Moreover, each of these systems can be studied as separate entities, or as they relate to other social systems within that community or nation, or, perhaps, even with systems in other societies (cross-cultural research).

Macro-level Theories of Aging

Age stratification. Most of the micro-level theories of social gerontologists focus on how the individual adjusts to being old; the theory of age stratification is concerned with aging relative to all stages in the life cycle. Thus, the elderly are studied, not in isolation, but in relation to other age strata. This theory focuses on how the structure of society affects the aging individual, and on differences between age strata rather than on conflict between them (Marshall, 1981a).

As originally described and explained by Riley and her colleagues (Riley, 1971; Riley et al., 1972), this model of aging is based on the premise that chronological age determines behavior in two general ways. First, it controls to a certain extent the maturation or development rate for physical, mental, and psychosocial capacities. Second, society allocates the opportunity to play specific social roles (and their accompanying rights, privileges, status, and power) on the basis of age. Therefore, society is said to be divided into age strata[31] (as it is into class strata). Each stratum is made up of individuals who have some similar characteristics because they are at the same stage in the life cycle (the life-course dimension). Each stratum consists of those who have had similar experiences[32] because they have shared a common history (the historical dimension).

In the conceptual development of this model, Riley (1971) introduced a structural analogy between class strata and age strata, and a process analogy between social mobility and aging. She proposed four commonalities pertaining to class or age stratification systems. First, relatively similar behavior and attitudes can be expected from those at a specific position in the age or class structure because they have had a common history and lifestyle. Second, whereas movement through the class structure is possible, but not inevitable, movement through the age structure is inevitable and occurs in one direction only. Third, in both the age and class structures, interaction can occur among individuals within and between strata (intergenerational relations, class dominance or conflict). This interaction is governed by social norms, and may be influenced by the development of stratum consciousness, which in turn may lead to class or age-related consensus or conflict. Finally, the type and frequency of interaction within and between strata in both age and class structures is related to the degree of social, political, or economic change in a given society. Change may be initiated by, or may specifically affect, members of one stratum more than members of another. For example, as the structure of society changes because of modernization, the status of the aged may change. Riley et al. (1972) developed a two-dimensional model (at the societal and personal levels) to account for behavior at different stages in the life cycle.

At the societal level of analysis, the theory of age stratification argues that the population is divided into age strata because of cohort flow. That is, fertility, migration, and mortality determine the size and composition of each stratum.[33] Through the process of role allocation or age grading, individuals gain access to social roles and to their accompanying rewards on the basis of chronological, legal, or social age. Age is the criterion for entry into, and exit from, institutions within a given society. Moreover, age norms control the number who can play a given role at a specific point in history. For example, the legal school-leaving age can be raised or lowered, as can the age of mandatory retirement, in order to achieve equilibrium in the size of the labor force (Waring, 1975). From the societal perspective, social systems are made up of age-related roles whereby those of a particular stratum have certain role expectations and are accorded certain rights, privileges, and status. An age-related status system evolves, and inequality between the strata is usually inevitable.[34]

On the personal level, the theory of age stratification proposes that chronological aging involves first an increase and later a decrease in social, physical, and cognitive capacities, and in the development of psychosocial skills deemed essential to a specific society. As individuals age they have the capacity and opportunity to acquire new roles, to relinquish old roles, and to interact with role players within their stratum and other strata. This interaction is facilitated by age-related norms. It is assumed that individuals have relatively little input into the system, that they must passively adhere to societally induced norms, and that they must accept the allocated social roles and implied social inequality.

This theory, which first appeared in the early 1970s, was widely accepted as a viable explanation of changing behavior and status across the life cycle, despite the fact that few research studies explicitly tested the theory. Nevertheless, the theory was not without criticism, especially from those who adhered to an exchange or a symbolic interactionist perspective of social phenomena. Generally, the criticisms have involved two related concerns: the degree to which there is conflict between strata, and the failure of the theory to account for the interaction between age and other social categories such as race, ethnicity, and particularly class.

Interaction between members of different social or age strata can be characterized by cooperation (either voluntary or through compliance and conformity) or conflict, with varying degrees of perceived and actual inequality being observed. In many societies throughout history, some degree of class conflict has been inevitable. This conflict is either controlled for the benefit of society (a functionalist perspective), or it becomes overtly manifested in varying ways in order to bring about change for the betterment of the individual and the society (the conflict perspective). Age conflicts also appear to be present in some societies. These occur because structural inequalities produce different views of the way in which rewards are allocated. Age conflict is enhanced when members of subsequent birth cohorts have unique attitudes, opportunities (such as better education) and beliefs, based on their particular social and historical experiences. Each stratum becomes cohort-centric; it interprets events in the social world through its own unique experiences. This cohort-centrism makes it difficult to see and accept the view of other cohorts and, hence, to resolve differences. Cohort-centrism also creates the possibility that some level of age-stratum consciousness may be developed. However, as Foner (1979:235–36) suggests, except in college students in the 1960s, age-stratum consciousness has yet to be developed to the stage where it fosters open and serious age-strata conflict. In this respect it will be interesting to observe whether the 'Gray Power' movement increases or declines in the next decade.

Implicit in the discussion of age-related inequality is the view that some of this inequality is also class-related. Within each stratum there is also a system of social stratification similar to that which operates across the entire society. Tindale and Marshall (1980) suggest that conflict between generations occurs because those with a specific class background experience significant social-historical events in a way different from that of others in the age cohort. As a result, they develop a combined age- and class-related consciousness that may induce conflict. For example, in North America, the radical youth movement of the 1960s primarily involved a middle- or upper-middle-class college-age cohort. This cohort, or generational unit, rebelled against the power it perceived to be held by the middle-aged and the elderly in society.

This interaction of perceived age and class inequality has also been studied by Dowd (1980). He noted that the elderly at the bottom of the class structure experience more problems than the elderly in other social strata. Using an exchange and symbolic interactionist perspective, Dowd views aging as a process of negotiation or exchange among individuals. Conflict occurs when there is a perceived or actual unequal distribution of resources. As a result, one group seeks to redistribute resources to restore equity and balance to the system. Dowd argues that as we age we lose control over our lives because we lose access to sources of power, and with advancing age we are unable to negotiate a fair exchange. The elderly acquire low status and lose power, unless they are members of the upper classes and have residual sources of power. Most of the elderly seem to accept this devalued status and subordinate position in the age stratification system. Dowd suggests that rather than passively accepting this situation, the elderly must reject the status quo as the best solution for society or for themselves. That is, they must strive to remain engaged in meaningful social positions in order to improve their negotiating position relative to those in other age strata. Although it is unlikely that the class position of an elderly individual can be improved, by cooperation and the development of an age-stratum consciousness the overall position of all elderly people might improve.

The subculture of aging.   A subculture is a distinct social subsystem that arises within a larger social system. It is characterized by a unique set of beliefs, attitudes, values, norms, customs, and language. Once these characteristics become accepted by a number of individuals, who may or may not engage in face-to-face interaction, they begin to influence the lifestyles of those who identify with the subculture. Generally, a subculture may arise (Gordon, 1947; Arnold, 1970; Fischer, 1975; Pearson, 1979):

1. In response to some problem, interest, deprivation, or opportunity that is common to a group of people (such as the aged), to some common characteristic unique to the members (race, religion, or social class), or to a specific environment (a retirement community).

2. As a result of interaction between those with common cultural and historical experiences (such as limited access to resources, social segregation of the aged in retirement).

3. When a common reference group (such as senior citizens) guides the thoughts and behavior of a number of individuals.

4. When a social group (such as the Gray Panthers) is created to initiate or facilitate social change.

Adapting this framework to the process of aging, Rose (1962, 1965) argued that the social identity and self-concept of the older person was maintained or enhanced by membership within an age-based subculture. That is, individuals interacted more frequently with others of the same age rather than with other age cohorts in the society. In this way, age-related roles were established and a subculture evolved. He noted that the likelihood of an aged subculture forming, and thereby facilitating individual adjustment, is quite high, since elderly people have similar backgrounds, experiences, and needs, and are therefore attracted to each other for support and interaction. In addition, the elderly are often excluded from interaction with other age cohorts in mainstream society.

Rose and others have identified a number of conditions that may act as catalysts in the formation of an aged subculture:

1. People are living longer and healthier lives. Therefore, there are not only more aged individuals, but they are also more visible.

2. The elderly tend to be more visible because a large number are concentrated in the rural areas and inner cities, primarily because there is an out-migration of the young to the suburbs.

3. The elderly foster self-segregation by moving to age-homogeneous retirement communities.

4. A number of special social services are available for the elderly (voluntary associations, social security or welfare payments) that increase their visibility as a distinct social group.

5. Increased mobility and the development and use of the media facilitate and increase interaction among the aged. This interaction provides a catalyst for the development of an age-group consciousness (an awareness of values, needs, and lifestyles different from those of other age cohorts).

The outcome of creating an aged subculture may have both positive and negative effects on the individual and on society. On the positive side, for the individual it may lead to the development of an age-group consciousness that results in social action to improve opportunities and lifestyles. On the negative side, this action may create intergenerational conflict as various age cohorts compete for scarce resources. This age-consciousness may also reinforce the individual's self-concept of being old and devalued, thereby leading to dissatisfaction with life. In addition, it may foster social isolation from friends and relatives, especially among those in the lower social classes who are foreign-born or black (Rutzen, 1980). Yet, a subculture formed within a retirement community may lead to higher levels of social integration. This in turn can help to develop a positive self-image because identity is primarily based on age-related status elements, such as high levels of mobility and health (Longino et al. 1980).

As with all theories, a number of criticisms have been raised concerning the subcultural view of aging. First, it has been argued that the theory is not really a theory but rather a concept that facilitates a description of the behavior of some elderly people, and that serves as a guide for social action. Second, it was assumed by Rose that there was a general subculture of the aged to which all elderly people belonged. However, there is great variation within the elderly population, not only in terms of their personal characteristics, but also in terms of their reference groups and social environments. For example, elderly derelicts and elderly millionaires do not interact with each other, and each type is differentially integrated into mainstream society (Streib, 1976).

The type of environment in which elderly people live also influences their normative system. For example, an age-segregated versus an age-integrated environment would have a different impact on the interaction pattern of an elderly person. Similarly, being a member of a religious or ethnic group that places a high value on the status of the aged represents a different social environment from that encountered by the elderly living on or near skid row. Moreover, as Longino et al. (1980) noted, the meaning of living in a particular type of retirement community must be considered when analyzing the impact of a subculture on the individual. They found that, contrary to the prevailing myth, residents of some retirement communities were not seeking an activist lifestyle; they had moved to the community in order to obtain services or to enjoy the environment, not to seek the company of other old people. Thus, the impact of a specific subculture on the behavior of an elderly person can vary according to the type of community, the motivation for living in that community, the saliency of other subcultures in which the individual interacts, the availability of organizations to facilitate social interaction among the elderly, and the extent to which a given aged subculture is integrated with or segregated from other age cohorts.

In summary, all age cohorts are made up of individuals with heterogeneous characteristics and with varying patterns of social interaction and feelings of age-consciousness. To date, there is little, if any, evidence to suggest that there is a subculture of the aged to which all individuals beyond a particular chronological age belong.

The aged as a minority group. The process of aging may vary among members of minority groups (Holzberg, 1982). It has also been suggested that the aged are themselves a deprived group in society (Barron, 1953): the elderly become victims of differential and unequal treatment compared to other age cohorts because they are labelled as 'old,' 'obsolete,' or 'dysfunctional.' As a result, they are devalued and perceived to be a minority group that exists on the periphery of society, like blacks and women. Moreover, a large proportion of the elderly are women who experience double jeopardy (Dowd and Bengtson, 1978; Chappell and Havens, 1980).

As a result of Barron's (1953) view that the aged comprise a minority group, a number of authors have sought either to support the view that they are a minority group and therefore the object of discrimination, or to establish that they do not meet the criteria for minority group status.[35] Some of the arguments (Barron, 1953; Levin and Levin, 1980) in favor of the aged being identified as a minority group are that:

1. They have unique, visible physical characteristics.
2. They have little power and low social and economic status.
3. They are objects of prejudice and stereotyping.
4. They are often socially and physically isolated.
5. There is a group consciousness based on a negative self-concept and the need for collective action to obtain equitable access to rights and rewards.
6. If they are employed, they are perceived as a threat to other age groups.
7. To protect their rights it has been necessary to pass special legislation, similar to that initiated to protect the rights of certain ethnic or racial groups.

It has also been argued (Streib, 1965; Abu-Laban and Abu-Laban, 1980; Holzberg, 1982) that the aged do not have minority status because:

1. They are overrepresented in power positions (business or government).
2. They are not socially isolated, but rather are part of the family system.
3. They lack distinctive cultural traits.
4. They have no common group identity or age group consciousness.
5. Although they are subject to stereotypes concerning work performance, sexual interest and capability, learning ability, etc., these can be refuted by scientific evidence.
6. If they are disadvantaged in the later years, they were also likely disadvantaged in the earlier years.
7. They are only discriminated against if they possess particular personal characteristics, such as having a low level of education or being a member of a minority group.
8. They are not prevented by segregation from living in an integrated society.

Abu-Laban and Abu-Laban (1980) suggest that the application of the minority-group concept to the aged, and especially to women, has created controversy because it has been used for ideological reasons to draw attention to social problems. It has also been used to make comparisons in social experiences between groups, even though women and the aged could not create their own unique society (as could an ethnic group if it so desired). Abu-Laban and Abu-Laban suggest that some of the conceptual problems with the minority-group concept can be alleviated if it is recognized that there are similarities and differences between disadvantaged groups in both their historical experiences and in where they fit into the social structure. These variations in meaning and structure need to be considered before a group is labelled as a minority group. They argue that there is little, if any, evidence to support the view that the aged, in general, comprise a minority group. At best, it may be that an aged minority group is made up of those elderly people who experience double or triple jeopardy because of their ascribed or achieved membership in an economic, racial, gender or ethnic minority group.

In summary, while minority-group status may be a useful conceptual tool, and while it may be used for ideological purposes to draw attention to the status of the aged, research support for the utility of the concept is equivocal (Abu-Laban and Abu-Laban, 1980). This has resulted from major conceptual problems with the definition and measurement of two major aspects of the concept: subcultural membership and group consciousness. These have not been directly measured in most studies. The arguments for or against the existence of minority group status for the aged have been based on inferential evidence from selected studies.

Because of within-cohort differences in health, wealth, class background, race, and ethnicity, not all older people may perceive themselves to be members of a unique group, or experience aging from the perspective of a minority group. For example, Abu-Laban and Abu-Laban (1980) argue that while older women may possess minority-group status because they experience discrimination, they may not formally or informally be members of a minority group. Perhaps all that can be concluded at this time is that some elderly members of society may be labelled as members of a minority group, perhaps especially if they are already a member of a visible minority group (blacks, native people or Hispanics).

Modernization theory. Modernization theory seeks to explain aging phenomena from a structural perspective rather than from the perspective of the individual. It is based on a comparative analysis of societies, and an emphasis is placed on historical and cultural factors. The theory was first described in detail by Cowgill and Holmes (1972) in a cross-cultural study that analyzed the status of the aged in fourteen different societies. These societies ranged in degree of modernization from a gerontocratic tribe in Ethiopia to the highly industrialized United States. The major hypothesis of this theory was that the role and status of the aged varies inversely according to the degree of modernization in a society.[36] As social change occurs and societies become more modernized, older people lose functional roles, become devalued, and subsequently lose status and security. Cowgill and Holmes based their argument on three premises concerning primitive societies:

1. There are only a few social roles and little role differentiation; hence, the elderly remain socially integrated and functional, at least as long as they are physically and mentally able to contribute to the society.

2. Social stability is the rule and social change the exception; hence, the experience and wisdom accumulated by the elderly is needed and valued.

3. Because little, if any, technology exists, human resources are highly valued; the elderly are seen to possess these needed resources.

In addition to the qualitative comparative evidence presented by Cowgill and Holmes (1972), recent cross-cultural and intracultural empirical studies have also supported the theory. For example, Palmore and his associates (1971, 1974) developed an Equality Index to measure the relative socioeconomic status of the aged (over 65) compared to the non-aged (25 to 64). Their findings, based on comparisons within thirty-one countries that varied in level of economic development, found that the status of the aged declines from approximate equality in non-Western societies to about one-half equality in more modernized countries (Palmore and Whittington, 1971). However, in a later paper (Palmore and Manton, 1974) it was found that there was considerable variation between employment status, occupational status, and educational attainment within the more modernized societies.[37] While employment status declines steadily with modernization, the occupational and educational status of the aged experience the greatest decline in the early stages of modernization. However, after a country has been modernized to a certain level the rate of change levels off. Then, the differences between the aged and non-aged narrow as the status of the elderly in the occupational and educational domains begins to rise.

As with many of the other theories described above, criticisms were raised as to the validity of this explanatory model. First, the authors were criticized for failing to precisely define 'modernization.' In particular, their use of the concept applied only to the societal level of analysis.[38] In an effort to clarify the meaning of the relationship between increasing modernization and a declining status of the aged, Bengtson et al. (1975) stressed that there must be a clear distinction between 'modernization' (a societal or macro-level process) and 'modernity' (an individual or micro-level process whereby individuals in developing nations are exposed to technology, urbanization, and industrial experience).

Bengtson and his associates argued that 'modernity' and 'modernization' may not result in negative perceptions of the aged and in a devaluation of status, as is commonly asserted. They suggested that perceptions of the aged may also vary within a society. Using a sample of 5,450 males in six 'developing' nations, who were employed within three different occupational groups, they found that negative perceptions of aging are related to increasing societal 'modernization.' In contrast, individual 'modernity' is not related to negative perceptions of the aged, or to negative attitudes toward one's own aging. In short, negative views and declining status of the aged do not seem to accompany 'modernity.' Thus, when discussing the impact of social change on the status of a particular group, both 'societal' (modernization) and 'individual' (modernity) levels of analysis need to be considered.

A second, but related, criticism was that the authors made little attempt to explain the intervening process between the onset of modernization and the loss of status by the aged. Cowgill (1974), in a revision of the theory, identified four salient aspects of modernization and indicated how they result in a lower status for the aged:

1. The introduction of modern health technology increased longevity and led to intergenerational competition and retirement.

2. The development of modern economic technology made the jobs of the aged obsolete and led to new occupations in urban environments.

3. The onset of urbanization led to migration, and to social segregation by age and socioeconomic status.

4. The increased level of educational attainment with each subsequent generation enabled children to be better educated than their parents and grandparents.

In addition, Cowgill stressed that these technological and social changes led to an increase in the status of youth and young adults, and to an increase in the emphasis and value placed on work.

Other scholars suggested that the changing status of the elderly was not due to modernization per se, but rather to the technological and social changes that were introduced at various rates into specific societies. For example, Press and McKool (1980) argued that with increasing economic, social, and technological development, greater heterogeneity in status evolves within the society, and the elderly become less positively evaluated than younger age groups. Similarly, Maxwell and Silverman (1980) suggested that the elderly lose control of information with modernization, and that this loss of control subsequently results in a loss of authority and power within the society.

Most recently, Dowd (1981) argued, from an exchange perspective, that the possession of prestige and power resources (land or information) places the individual in a favorable exchange situation regardless of age. In agrarian economies the elderly controlled the ownership of land and thereby enjoyed a favorable exchange rate. In contrast, in modern societies the elderly are excluded from labor force participation and lack a favorable exchange rate; they have less esteem, prestige, and status than the elderly in more primitive societies.

A third criticism of the theory was that the explanation implied a universal, linear relationship which applied to all elderly people, and that modernization affected all cohorts of people at the same rate (Achenbaum and Stearns, 1978; Quadagno, 1980). For example, Cowgill (1974) and Palmore and Manton (1974) suggest that declining status of the elderly may be more rapid during the early stages of modernization when there is rapid social change, but may 'bottom out' in the more advanced stages. That is, in the later stages of modernization the status of the aged may rise again, although never to the same level as in the more primitive stage of development. In short, the relationship may be curvilinear over time rather than linear. For example, Cohn (1982) examined the age-specific occupational distributions in thirty countries and concluded that these distribution patterns may be a temporary phenomenon that results from the dynamic relationship between the level and rate of economic development and the changing age structure of the population. He noted that the decline in status of the elderly early in the modernization process results from a rapid increase in the number of professional and technical occupations and the subsequent occupancy of these positions by recently trained younger workers.

Despite the evidence of Bengtson et al. (1975), the impact of modernization may affect various social groups in different ways. For example, Myles (1980) noted that the status of the aged is also related to the structure of inequality in a society, which in turn is based on gender, race, and class variations within and between age cohorts. Thus, within 'postmodernized' or 'rapidly modernizing' societies, the status of the elderly is related to the degree of structured equality within that society.

A fourth criticism, mainly from historians, suggests that the onset of declining status for the elderly, if it occurs at all, may have occurred prior to or after industrialization. For example, the social historian Fischer (1977) has argued that in the United States the social values of libertarianism and equalitarianism, introduced during the French and American Revolutions, resulted in changes in attitudes and behavior toward the elderly between 1770 and 1820. The declining status of the aged and the increased power of the younger age cohorts preceded rather than followed industrialization. Similarly, the historian Laslett (1976) suggested that it is a myth that the aged have experienced a significant decline in status in modern societies. He concludes that the treatment of the aged in preindustrialized societies was not superior to the treatment they presently receive. More recently, Stearns (1981) argued that negative attitudes toward the elderly in France persisted long after modernization was initiated, and that modernization per se was not responsible for a change in the status of the aged in France.

Some authors have recently proposed that there are limits to the generalizability of modernization theory. For example, Hendricks (1980) noted that societal development does not occur at the same time or at the same rate across societies or within a single society. In fact, societal development occurs first, and perhaps exclusively, in a core area of a country, or in core countries throughout the world. Beyond this regional or international core is a peripheral region that fails to modernize at the same rate, or perhaps at all. In short, there are variations within and between societies in the onset and rate of modernization.

As an alternative explanation for the all-or-none view of modernization, Hendricks (1980) proposed an 'internal colonialism' or 'dualistic developmental' model. According to this model, power and control over resources resides in the metropolitan regions of a nation, and these regions control the development, if any, of the hinterland. As a result, the degree of declining status of the elderly within a nation varies by residential location. Those living closer to the core metropolitan area are the first to lose status, especially if they are members of an already devalued group.

Another view of the process of modernization has been suggested by Hendricks (1980) and by Tigges and Cowgill (1981). According to this macro view of development, a decline in the status of the aged as societies modernize may not occur if the least-developed or peripheral societies (Third World countries) have their development controlled by the most developed nations (the core countries). These authors argue that within the world economic system, the relation of the elderly to the means of production, and the position of the family in the production process, will vary. This results in varying degrees of status for the elderly, depending on whether they are found in a peripheral, semi-peripheral, or core nation. In the peripheral nations, or in the hinterlands of a nation, the elderly may be still involved in the production of goods within the extended family. Consequently, the elderly retain status or lose it at a different rate from those who live in more urbanized, nuclear-family-oriented environments.

Environmental theories.   The foregoing theories have sought to explain aging or the status of the aged on either the personal or social-system level. In an environmental theory of aging, the concern is with the impact of the social or physical environment on the individual. This perspective represents a direct attempt to account for the interaction between the personal system, the social system, and the environmental system.

Environmental factors impinge on the individual in two major ways throughout the life cycle. First, they may influence how an individual passes through the life course, and how long he or she lives; second, they influence the development and expression of the characteristics of individuals and cohorts as they age. The major thrust in examining the relationship between the aging individual and the environment resulted from a growing interest in aging in the late 1960s on the part of human ecologists.[39] They sought to integrate knowledge from a variety of disciplines, relating man to his resources, his social and cultural patterns, and his social and physical environment (Lawton and Rich, 1968; Bruhn, 1971).

The initial research sought to demonstrate a relationship between environmental factors and physical diseases or various facets of psychological or social behavior. More recently, the theories have focused on explaining how the interaction of personal and environmental characteristics influences the coping and interacting behavior of the individual in old and new environments. These environmental theories, which are discussed in detail in chapter 8, stress that the interaction between the individual and the environment must be considered in attempts to understand the aging process and the status of the elderly. They also stress that individual differences in experiences and perceptions must be examined when decisions are being made about which environment is most effective for a specific individual or for specific age cohorts.

Summary and Conclusions

In this chapter the reader has been introduced to the purpose and process of scientific inquiry, particularly with respect to research settings, research methods, conceptual perspectives, and theoretical frameworks that are used in the study of individual or population aging as social phenomena. The major focus of the chapter was on describing and critiquing research methods, perspectives, and theories that seek to explain the aging process and the status of the elderly, from either the individual or societal level of analysis.

In conclusion, it is noted that:

1. At present, no single theoretical, conceptual, or methodological perspective is prevalent within social gerontology. Rather, the field is still characterized, as are most new fields, by eclecticism in theory and methods.

2. The structural-functionalist perspective dominated the early work in social gerontology, but the symbolic interactionist and exchange perspectives are more widely used at present.

3. Social theories developed in the early stages of social gerontology were primarily concerned with how the aging individual adjusted to society (the micro or individual level of analysis). More recently, macro-level (societal) theories (age stratification theory and variants of modernization theory) have stressed the impact of a changing age structure throughout history and across cultures on the aging individual.

4. Compared to many other disciplines, as well as other areas within gerontology, the quality and quantity of conceptualization, theoretical development, and methodological rigor in social gerontology needs to be increased in order for the level of knowledge to advance beyond the descriptive and speculative stage.

5. The continued development of knowledge in social gerontology will depend on the initiation of theory and research directed at interaction between the individual and societal levels of analysis, as well as between the normative and interpretive perspectives.

Notes

1. In the literature, terms such as 'theory,' 'model,' 'perspective,' and 'framework' are often used interchangeably. Generally, 'theories' or 'models' are considered to be similar; they are a set of hypotheses or propositions that express relationships between variables. 'Perspectives' and 'frameworks' often represent more general, and sometimes untested, views of a phenomenon. In this text a 'theory' or 'model' refers to a formal, specific explanation of some facet of the social world; 'perspective' or 'framework' is used as a more global term to refer to groups of theories or models that can be categorized according to a more general concept. These perspectives are sometimes labelled as schools of thought (functionalism, symbolic interactionism) that represent competing orientations to the study of how social behavior or societies function. They provide a general orientation for raising research questions and interpreting findings.

2. Ritzer (1975:7) defines a paradigm as 'a fundamental image of the subject matter within a science. It serves to define what should be studied, what questions should be asked, how they should be asked, and what rules should be followed in interpreting the answers obtained.' According to Ritzer, a paradigm has four components: (1) an exemplar, or a piece of work that stands as a model; (2) an image of the subject matter; (3) theories; and (4) methods and instruments.

3. 'Perspectives' and 'paradigms' are virtually synonymous. It must be noted that theories are *not* paradigms in themselves, but rather components of broader paradigms, perspectives, or schools of thought.

4. For more detailed information about research settings and research methods in the social sciences, see Babbie (1975).

5. For a visual representation of the components and process of science, see Wallace (1969).

6. For example, Seltzer (1975), in an analysis of articles dealing with psychological aging and related processes, found that sampling frames were dissimilar, that operational definitions for the same concept varied widely, and that much of the data could not be compared from one study to the next. She concluded that although science is supposed to be cumulative, there is little evidence that research into the psychological aspects of aging proceeds in an orderly and cumulative manner.

7. The data reported in tables 4.1, 4.2, and 4.3 are fictitious. These hypothetical results are presented only to illustrate research designs and interpretation of the data. In reality, a recent survey in the United States found that

42 percent of those 18 to 64 years of age had attended a movie in the past month. In contrast, only 7 percent of those over 65 years of age had attended in the past month (Harris et al., 1981).

8. Because of the loss of subjects, the question can always be raised as to whether the final sample is similar to the original sample. For example, in a longitudinal study of movie attendance those who no longer wish to be in the study may be those who no longer attend because of such factors as low income, declining vision, or loss of mobility.

9. Ideally, this type of analysis must be completed for males and females and for other relevant variables (race, income, education, or religion) pertaining to the phenomenon. However, to simplify the explanation of cohort analysis, only patterns for the total population are included in Table4.3.

10. Additional perspectives or theories are introduced throughout the text to assist in explaining specific aging phenomena.

11. For example, as noted later, in this chapter activity theory is the conceptual antithesis of disengagement theory.

12. In reality, a content analysis of the literature would likely reveal that the major emphasis has been on studying the elderly, rather than the process of aging. However, in recent years, with better training, increased research funds, and a greater commitment to the field, more emphasis is now being placed on the study of the process of aging itself.

13. The terms 'life span,' 'life course,' and 'life cycle' are often used interchangeably in the literature.

14. A closely related perspective is phenomenology, which seeks to analyze how individuals perceive their social world. We perceive and interpret our world selectively, and different people react in different ways to the same event or setting. Our current perceptions are influenced by our past socialization experiences. Individuals can be expected to vary their perceptions, and thereby behave differently, with respect to such events as retirement, entrance to a nursing home, the presence of an economic depression, or the loss of a spouse. These perceptions may be influenced by such factors as past experiences, class background, amount of anticipatory socialization, degree of social support from family and friends, and physical and mental health.

15. This perspective makes extensive use of participant observation and in-depth face-to-face interviews in order to provide an 'ethnography' of a specific social setting.

16. For example, an after-dinner speaker might write a different speech depending on whether he or she was addressing a church group, a college fraternity group, an all-male group, an all-female group, a group of businessmen and politicians, or a group of unemployed laborers.

17. There are many socialization theories (Goslin, 1969). This subsection introduces the concept of socialization, presents a general model of the process, and briefly discusses the social learning theory of socialization.

18. See Zigler and Child (1969:451–68) for an excellent overview of the various theoretical approaches to early life socialization. They discuss the following theoretical approaches: social anthropology, psychoanalysis, a combination of social anthropology and psychoanalysis, normative-maturational, developmental-cognitive, genetic and constitutional, and learning.

19. Rosow (1976:465) describes 'role emptying' as a process 'wherein responsibilities and normative expectations within a position simply dwindle away.' This results in few normative expectations for the elderly and, hence, there is a wide range of possible interpretations as to how one ought to behave in the later years. This lack of normative guidelines may foster eccentricity and even deviant behavior.

20. Throughout the adult years, 'retroactive' socialization may also occur wherein members of older age cohorts are socialized by younger age cohorts with respect to new social norms or modes of lifestyle.

21. Many social scientists have employed this 'repayment of past debts' theme to explain the helping relationship between generations within a kinship group (Sussman, 1976).

22. Interestingly, negative labels seem to derive more from societally induced evaluations by others, while positive labels are more likely to be initiated by the individuals themselves.

23. They are viewed by society as helpless and incompetent, and therefore in need of special assistance, because some play no instrumental roles after they are forced to retire at a specific age; because some are economically dependent on society; because elderly widows live alone; and because many need

long-term care or institutionalization. Decisions must be made for them by government agencies, further reinforcing the label of being helpless and incompetent (Brown, 1980).

24. Some practitioners sought to facilitate social interaction among the aged by advocating age-homogeneous voluntary associations (senior-citizen centers) or retirement communities so that they could more easily define and play their own social roles.

25. The five types of activities, which involved different role relationships, were informal activity with friends, relatives, or neighbors; formal activity in voluntary associations; and solitary activity (single leisure pursuits, household maintenance tasks).

26. 'Psychological disengagement' refers to an increasing concern with the self and a tendency to be more passive. This form of disengagement usually occurs prior to social disengagement, and is often a symptom of impending decreased social interaction.

27. The presence of some individuals who are still engaged late in life has been variously explained by stating that they are unsuccessful disengagers, that they are out of sequence in their timing of disengagement, that they are biological or psychological exceptions to the norm, or that they have had an exceptionally favorable opportunity structure.

28. Although the discussion of disengagement theory might be considered as both a micro and a macro theory, it has been included in this section dealing with the micro level since most discussion and empirical tests of the theory have been initiated on that level.

29. Those in the higher social classes generally attach more meaning and importance to their work than to the family or leisure. As a result, they gain more satisfaction from their work and are more likely to want to continue working in the later years. Additionally, they generally have access to work in old age, either because they have the skills to continue working independently, or because they control the labor market.

30. Ritzer (1975:159) indicates that these 'social facts' have a coercive effect on the individual.

31. The size, proportion, and composition of the population within a given stratum may change over time within and between societies. For example, as noted in chapter 3, the proportion of those over 65 years of age has increased dramatically in recent years. Similarly, because of higher mortality rates for men and members of minority groups, the older age strata generally include more women than men, and more whites than nonwhites.

32. Although all members of a particular stratum may have encountered a specific event (a depression or a war) at the same stage in their personal life cycles, they may have experienced the event in different ways. For example, the Vietnam War had a differential impact on men between 18 and 25 years of age depending on whether, how, and where they served in the U.S. armed forces. Some resisted the draft and never served; others fought and were wounded or killed. This not only had profound effects on the individual, but also on the sex ratio in this stratum.

33. The size of the cohort influences life chances in that a small cohort may lead to low unemployment, while a large cohort (such as the baby-boom cohort) may lead to high unemployment and severe competition for limited positions, especially during periods of economic recession.

34. In that the theory as developed by Riley et al. (1972) was based on a functionalist perspective, this inequality is viewed as necessary and essential for the stability of society.

35. Arguments for and against minority-group status for the aged are summarized in Table 2 in Abu-Laban and Abu-Laban (1980:70).

36. 'Modernization' refers to a shift from an agricultural to an industrialized economy, or from a 'traditional' primitive, rural social system to a 'modern,' industrialized, urban social system.

37. 'Employment status' means employed or not employed; 'occupational status' refers to the prestige of the current or former occupation.

38. Surprisingly, only the end product (the status of the aged) rather than the process of aging has been accounted for by this theory.

39. As Lawton (1977:276) notes, the original stimulation for this approach within gerontology was provided by Kleemeier (1959). He stressed the importance of man-environment interactions, especially the impact of the social and physical aspects of housing and institutionalization on social behavior.

References

Abu-Laban, S. and B. Abu-Laban. 'Women and the Aged as Minority Groups: A Critique,' pp. 63–79 in V. Marshall (ed.). *Aging in Canada: Social Perspectives.* Don Mills: Fitzhenry and Whiteside, 1980.

Achenbaum, A. and P. Stearns. 'Old Age and Modernization,' *The Gerontologist,* 18(3/1978), 307–12.

Agnew, N. and S. Pyke. *The Science Game.* 2nd edition. Englewood Cliffs, N.J.,: Prentice-Hall, 1978.

Albrecht, G. and B. Gift. 'Adult Socialization: Ambiguity and Adult Life Crises,' pp. 237–51 in N. Datan and L. Ginsburg (eds.). *Life-Span Developmental Psychology: Normative Life Crises.* New York: Academic Press, 1975.

Arnold, D. (ed.). *The Sociology of Subcultures.* Berkeley: The Glendessary Press, 1970.

Atchley, R. *The Social Forces In Later Life.* 1st edition. Belmont, Calif.: Wadsworth Publishing Co., 1971.

Babbie, E. *The Practice of Social Research.* Belmont, Calif.: Wadsworth Publishing Co., 1975.

Baltes, P. and K.W. Schaie. (eds.). *Life-Span Developmental Psychology: Personality and Socialization.* New York: Academic Press, 1973.

Baltes, P. and S. Willis. 'Toward Psychological Theories of Aging and Development,' pp. 128–54 in J. Birren and K.W. Schaie (eds.). *Handbook of the Psychology of Aging.* New York: Van Nostrand Reinhold Co., 1977.

Baltes, P. et al. 'Life-Span Developmental Psychology,' *Annual Review of Psychology,* 31(1980), 65–110.

Bandura, A. 'Social Learning Theory of Identificatory Process,' pp. 213–62 in D. Goslin (ed.). *Handbook of Socialization Theory and Research.* Chicago: Rand McNally and Co., 1969.

Barron, M. 'Minority Group Characteristics of the Aged in American Society,' *Journal of Gerontology,* 8(3/1953), 477–82.

Becker, H. *Outsiders: Studies in the Sociology of Deviance.* New York: The Free Press, 1973.

Bengtson, V. et al. 'Modernization, Modernity and Perceptions of Aging: A Cross-Cultural Study,' *Journal of Gerontology,* 30(6/1975), 688–95.

Bengtson, V. et al. 'Relating Academic Research to Community Concerns: A Case Study in Collaborative Effort,' *Journal of Social Issues,* 33(4/1977), 75–92.

Bengtson, V. and J. Dowd. 'Sociological Functionalism, Exchange Theory and Life-Cycle Analysis: A Call for More Explicit Theoretical Bridges,' *International Journal of Aging and Human Development,* 12(1/1980–81), 55–73.

Bennett, R. (ed.). *Aging, Isolation and Resocialization.* New York: Van Nostrand Reinhold, 1980.

Biddle, B. *Role Theory: Expectations, Identities, and Behaviors.* New York: Academic Press, 1979.

Biddle, B. and E. Thomas. (eds.). *Role Theory: Concepts and Research.* New York: John Wiley and Sons, 1966.

Birren, J. et al. *Developmental Psychology: A Life-Span Approach.* Boston: Houghton Mifflin, 1981.

Birren, J. and V. Renner. 'Research on the Psychology of Aging,' pp. 3–38 in J. Birren and K.W. Schaie (eds.). *Handbook of the Psychology of Aging.* New York: Van Nostrand Reinhold, 1977.

Blau, Z. *Old Age in a Changing Society.* New York: Franklin Watts, 1973.

Blau, Z. *Aging in a Changing Society.* New York: Franklin Watts, 1981.

Bosse, R. and D. Ekerdt. 'Change in Self-Perception of Leisure Activities with Retirement,' *The Gerontologist,* 21(6/1981), 650–54.

Bowles, N. and L. Poon. 'An Analysis of the Effect of Aging on Recognition Memory,' *Journal of Gerontology,* 37(2/1982), 212–19.

Brim, O. 'Socialization Through the Life Cycle,' pp. 3–49 in O. Brim and S. Wheeler (eds.). *Socialization After Childhood.* New York: John Wiley & Sons, 1966.

Brim, O. and S. Wheeler. (eds.). *Socialization After Childhood.* New York: John Wiley & Sons, 1966.

Brown, A. 'The Elderly and Labeling Theory,' paper presented at the 33rd annual meeting of the Gerontological Society of America, San Diego, November 21–25, 1980.

Brown, K. et al. 'Improving Surveys of the Elderly with Particular Reference to the Choice of Residential Accommodation,' paper presented at the annual meeting of the Canadian Association on Gerontology, Toronto, November 1981.

Bruhn, J. 'An Ecological Perspective of Aging,' *The Gerontologist,* 11(4/1971), 318–21.

Burgess, E. 'Personal and Social Adjustment in Old Age,' pp. 135–56 in M. Derber (ed.). *The Aged and Society.* Champaign, Ill.: Industrial Relations Research Association, 1950.

Burgess, W. *Aging in Western Societies.* Chicago: University of Chicago Press, 1960.

Cain, L. 'Life Course and Social Structure,' pp. 272–309 in R. Faris (ed.). *Handbook of Modern Sociology.* Chicago: Rand McNally and Co., 1964.

Cain, L. 'Age Status and Generational Phenomena: The New Old People in Contemporary America,' *The Gerontologist,* 7(2/1967), 83–92.

Cain, L. Book review of *In Search of the New Old: Redefining Old Age in America, 1945–1970* by R. Calhoun (1978), in *Contemporary Sociology,* 10(1/1981), 91–92.

Cavan, R. et al. *Personal Adjustment in Old Age.* Chicago: Science Research Associates, 1949.

Chappell, N. 'Senility: Problems in Communication,' pp. 65–86 in J. Haas and B. Shaffir (eds.). *Shaping Identity in Canadian Society.* Scarborough, Ont.: Prentice-Hall, 1978.

Chappell, N. and B. Havens. 'Old and Female: Testing the Double Jeopardy Hypothesis,' *The Sociological Quarterly,* 21(2/1980), 157–71.

Clausen, J. 'Research on Socialization and Personality Development in the United States and France: Remarks on the Paper by Professor Chombart de Lauwe,' *American Sociological Review,* 31(2/1966), 248–57.

Clausen, J. *Socialization and Society.* Boston:Little, Brown & Co., 1968.

Clausen, J. 'The Life Course of Individuals,' pp. 457–514 in M. Riley, et al. (eds.). *Aging and Society. Volume III: A Sociology of Age Stratification.* New York: Russell Sage, 1972.

Cohen, B. *Developing Sociological Knowledge: Theory and Method.* Englewood Cliffs, N.J.: Prentice-Hall, 1980.

Cohn, R. 'Economic Development and Status Change of the Aged,' *American Journal of Sociology,* 87(5/1982), 1150–61.

Collins, R. *Conflict Sociology: Toward An Explanatory Science.* New York: Academic Press, 1975.

Cooley, C. *Human Nature and the Social Order.* New York: Scribner's, 1902.

Costa, P. and R. McCrae. 'An Approach to the Attribution of Aging, Period, and Cohort Effects,' *Psychological Bulletin,* 92(1/1982), 238–50.

Cottrell, L. 'The Adjustment of the Individual to His Age and Sex Roles,' *American Sociological Review,* 7(5/1942), 617–20.

Covey, H. 'A Reconceptualization of Continuity Theory: Some Preliminary Thoughts,' *The Gerontologist,* 21(6/1981), 628–33.

Cowgill, D. and L. Holmes. (eds.). *Aging and Modernization.* New York: Appleton-Century-Crofts, 1972.

Cowgill, D. 'Aging and Modernization: A Revision of the Theory,' pp 123–46 in J. Gubrium (ed.). *Late Life: Communities and Environmental Policy.* Springfield, Ill.: Charles C. Thomas, 1974.

Cox, H. and A. Bhak. 'Symbolic Interaction and Retirement Adjustment: An Empirical Assessment,' *International Journal of Aging and Human Development,* 9(3/1978–79), 279–86.

Cumming, E. 'Further Thoughts on the Theory of Disengagement,' *International Social Science Journal,* 15(3/1963), 377–93.

Cumming, E. and W. Henry. *Growing Old: The Process of Disengagement.* New York: Basic Books, 1961.

Cumming, E. et al. 'Disengagement: A Tentative Theory of Aging,' *Sociometry,* 23(1/1960), 23–35.

D'Arcy, C. 'The Manufacture and Obsolescence of Madness: Age, Social Policy and Psychiatric Morbidity in a Prairie Province,' pp. 159–76 in V. Marshall (ed.). *Aging In Canada: Social Perspectives.* Don Mills: Fitzhenry and Whiteside, 1980.

Dahrendorf, R. *Class and Conflict in Industrial Society.* Stanford: Stanford University Press, 1959.

Dawe, A. 'The Two Sociologies,' *British Journal of Sociology,* 21(2/1970), 207–18.

Decker, D. 'Sociological Theory and the Social Position of the Aged,' *International Journal of Contemporary Sociology,* 15(3 and 4/1978), 303–17.

Dowd, J. 'Aging as Exchange: A Preface to Theory,' *Journal of Gerontology,* 30(5/1975), 584–94.

Dowd, J. 'Aging as Exchange: A Test of the Distributive Justice Proposition,' *Pacific Sociological Review,* 21(3/1978), 351–75.

Dowd, J. *Stratification Among the Aged.* Monterey, Calif.: Brooks/Cole Publishing Co., 1980.

Dowd, J. and V. Bengtson. 'Aging in Minority Populations: An Examination of the Double Jeopardy Hypothesis,' *Journal of Gerontology,* 33(3/1978), 427–36.

Elder, G. *Children of the Great Depression: Social Change in Life Experience.* Chicago: University of Chicago Press, 1974.

Elder, G. 'Age Differentiation and the Life Course,' pp. 165–90 in A. Inkeles et al. (eds.). *Annual Review of Sociology. Volume 1.* Palo Alto, Calif.: Annual Reviews, Inc., 1975.

Emerson, R. 'Power-Dependence Relations,' *American Sociological Review,* 27(1/1962), 31–41.

Emerson, R. 'Social Exchange Theory,' pp. 335–62 in A. Inkeles (ed.). *Annual Review of Sociology. Volume 2.* Palo Alto, Calif.: Annual Reviews, Inc., 1976.

Erikson, E. *Childhood and Society.* New York: W.W. Norton, 1950.

Fischer, C. 'Toward a Subcultural Theory of Urbanism,' *American Journal of Sociology,* 80(6/1975), 1319–41.

Fischer, D. *Growing Old in America.* London: Oxford University Press, 1977.

Flett, D. et al. 'Evaluation of the Public Health Nurse as Primary Health-Care Provider for Elderly People,' pp. 177–88 in V. Marshall (ed.). *Aging in Canada: Social Perspectives.* Don Mills: Fitzhenry and Whiteside, 1980.

Foner, A. 'Ascribed and Achieved Bases of Stratification,' pp. 219–42 in A. Inkeles et al. (eds.). *Annual Review of Sociology.* Volume 5. Palo Alto: Annual Reviews Inc., 1979.

Forscher, B. 'Chaos in the Brickyard,' *Science,* 142 (1963), 3590.

Fox, J. 'Perspectives on the Continuity Perspective,' *International Journal of Aging and Human Development,* 14(2/1981–82), 97–115.

Fry, C. and J. Keith (eds.). *New Methods for Old Age Research: Anthropological Alternatives.* Chicago: Loyola University, Center for Urban Policy, 1980.

Gaitz, C. and J. Scott. 'Analysis of Letters to 'Dear Abby' Concerning Old Age,' *The Gerontologist,* 15(1/1975), 47–51.

Gardner, M. 'Caring and Sharing,' *Perspective on Aging,* 10(1/1981), 4–7.

George, L. et al. 'Symposium: Survey Research in the Study of Aging: Possibilities and Problems in the Use of Archival Data,' *The Gerontologist,* 19(2/1979), 196–219.

George, L. *Role Transitions in Later Life.* Monterey: Brooks/Cole Publishing Co., 1980.

Gewirtz, J. 'Mechanisms of Social Learning: Some Roles of Stimulation and Behavior in Early Human Development,' pp. 57–212 in D. Goslin (ed.). *Handbook of Socialization Theory and Research.* Chicago: Rand McNally and Co., 1969.

Glenn, N. *Cohort Analysis.* Beverly Hills: Sage Publications, 1977.

Glenn, N. 'Age, Birth Cohorts, and Drinking: An Illustration of the Hazards of Inferring Effects from Cohort Data,' *Journal of Gerontology,* 36(3/1981), 362–69.

Goffman, E. *The Presentation of Self in Everyday Life.* New York: Doubleday, 1959.

Gordon, M. 'The Concept of Subculture and Its Application,' *Social Forces,* 26(1/1947), 40–42.

Goslin, D. (ed.). *Handbook of Socialization Theory and Research.* Chicago: Rand McNally and Co., 1969.

Goulet, L. and P. Baltes. (eds.). *Life-Span Developmental Psychology: Research and Theory.* New York: Academic Press, 1970.

Gubrium, J. *Living and Dying at Murray Manor.* New York: St. Martin's Press, 1975.

Harris, C. et al. *Applied Research in Aging.* Cambridge, Mass.: Winthrop Publishers Inc., forthcoming.

Harris, L. et al. *Aging in the Eighties: America in Transition.* Washington, D.C.: National Council on the Aging, 1981.

Hastings, D. and L. Berry (eds.). *Cohort Analysis: A Collection of Interdisciplinary Readings.* Oxford, Ohio: Scripps Foundation, 1979.

Havens, B. 'Differentiation of Unmet Needs Using Analysis by Age/Sex Cohorts,' pp. 215–21 in V. Marshall (ed.). *Aging in Canada: Social Perspectives.* Don Mills: Fitzhenry and Whiteside, 1980.

Havighurst, R. and R. Albrecht. *Older People.* New York: Longmans, Green, 1953.

Hendricks, J. 'The Elderly in Society: Beyond Modernization,' paper presented at the annual meeting of the Gerontological Society of America, San Diego, November, 1980.

Henretta, J. et al. 'Survey Research in Aging: An Evaluation of the Harris Survey,' *The Gerontologist,* 17(1/1977), 160–67.

Henry, W. 'The Theory of Intrinsic Disengagement,' pp. 415–18 in P. Hansen (ed.). *Age with a Future.* Philadelphia: F. Davis Co., 1964.

Herzog, R. 'Measurement Effects in Surveys: Age Differences,' paper presented at the annual meeting of the Gerontological Society of America, Toronto, November, 1981.

Hewit, J. *Self and Society: A Symbolic Interactionist Social Psychology.* Boston: Allyn and Bacon, 1976.

Hochschild, A. *The Unexpected Community.* Englewood Cliffs, N.J.: Prentice-Hall, 1973.

Hochschild, A. 'Disengagement Theory: A Critique and Proposal,' *American Sociological Review,* 40(5/1975), 553–69.

Hochschild, A. 'Disengagement Theory: A Logical, Empirical, and Phenomenological Critique,' pp. 53–87 in J. Gubrium (ed.). *Time, Roles and Self in Old Age.* New York: Human Sciences Press, 1976.

Hogan, D. *Transitions and Social Change: The Early Lives of American Men.* New York: Academic Press, 1981.

Holmes, L. 'Trends in Anthropological Gerontology: From Simmons to the Seventies,' *International Journal of Aging and Human Development,* 7(3/1976), 211–20.

Holsti, O. *Content Analysis and the Social Sciences and the Humanities.* Reading, Mass.: Addison-Wesley, 1969.

Holzberg, C. 'Ethnicity and Aging: Anthropological Perspectives on More Than Just the Minority Elderly,' *The Gerontologist,* 22 (3/1982), 249–57.

Hyman, H. and E. Singer. *Readings in Reference Group Theory and Research.* New York: Free Press, 1968.

Inkeles, A. 'Social Structure and Socialization,' pp. 615–32 in D. Goslin (ed.). *Handbook of Socialization Theory and Research.* Chicago: Rand McNally and Co., 1969.

Jacobs, J. *Older Persons and Retirement Communities: Case Studies in Social Gerontology.* Springfield, Ill.: Charles C. Thomas, 1975.

Kalish, R. 'The New Ageism and the Failure Models: A Polemic,' *The Gerontologist,* 19(4/1979), 398–402.

Kemper, T. 'Reference Groups, Socialization and Achievement,' *American Sociological Review,* 33(1/1968), 31–45.

Kingston, A. and M. Drotter. 'The Depiction of Old Age in Six Basal Readers,' *Educational Gerontology,* 6(4/1981), 29–34.

Kleemeier, R. 'Behavior and the Organization of the Bodily and the External Environment,' pp. 400–51 in J. Birren (ed.). *Handbook of Aging and the Individual.* Chicago: University of Chicago Press, 1959.

Knapp, M. 'The Activity Theory of Aging: An Examination in the English Context,' *The Gerontologist,* 17(6/1977), 533–59.

Krauss, I. 'Between- and Within-Group Comparisons in Aging Research,' pp. 542–51 in L. Poon (ed.). *Aging in the 1980s.* Washington: American Psychological Association, 1980.

Kuhn, A. *The Logic of Social Systems.* San Francisco: Jossey-Bass, 1974.

Kuypers, J. and V. Bengtson. 'Social Breakdown and Competence: A Model of Normal Aging,' *Human Development,* 16(3/1973), 181–201.

Larson, R. 'Thirty Years of Research on the Subjective Well-Being of Older Americans,' *Journal of Gerontology,* 33(1/1978), 109–25.

Laslett, P. 'Societal Development and Aging,' pp. 87–116 in R. Binstock and E.Shanas (eds.). *Handbook of Aging and the Social Sciences.* New York: Van Nostrand Reinhold, 1976.

Lastrucci, C. *The Scientific Approach.* Cambridge, Mass.: Schenkman, 1967.

Lawton, M.P. 'The Impact of the Environment on Aging and Behavior,' pp. 276–301 in J. Birren and K.W. Schaie (eds.). *Handbook of the Psychology of Aging.* New York: Van Nostrand Reinhold, 1977.

Lawton, A. and T. Rich. (eds.). 'Ecology and Gerontology,' *The Gerontologist,* 8(2/1968), 76–119.

Lee, G. and J. Finney. 'Sampling in Social Gerontology: A Method of Locating Specialized Populations,' *Journal of Gerontology,* 32(6/1977), 689–93.

Lemon, B. et al. 'An Exploration of the Activity Theory of Aging: Activity Types and Life Satisfaction Among In-Movers to a Retirement Community,' *Journal of Gerontology,* 27(4/1972), 511–23.

Levin, J. and W. Levin. *Ageism: Prejudice and Discrimination Against the Elderly.* Belmont, Calif.: Wadsworth Publishing Co., 1980.

Linton, R. *A Study of Man.* New York: Appleton-Century, 1936.

Longino, C. and C. Kart. 'Explicating Activity Theory: A Formal Replication,' *Journal of Gerontology,* 37(6/1982), 713–22.

Longino, C. et al. 'The Aged Subculture Hypothesis: Social Integration, Gerontophilia and Self-Conception,' *Journal of Gerontology,* 35(5/1980), 758–67.

Lopata, H. *Widowhood in an American City.* Cambridge, Massachusetts: Schenkman, 1973.

Loy, J. 'Sociology and Physical Education,' pp. 168–236 in R. Singer et al. (eds.). *Physical Education: An Interdisciplinary Approach.* New York: Macmillan, 1972.

Loy, J. et al. *Sport and Social Systems.* Reading, Mass.: Addison-Wesley, 1978.

Maddox, G. 'Disengagement Theory: A Critical Evaluation,' *The Gerontologist,* 4(2/1964), 80–83.

Maddox, G. 'Fact and Artifact: Evidence Bearing on Disengagement Theory,' pp. 318–28 in E. Palmore (ed.). *Normal Aging.* Durham: Duke University Press, 1970.

Maddox, G. and J. Wiley. 'Scope, Concepts and Methods in the Study Of Aging,' pp. 3–34 in R. Binstock and E. Shanas (eds.). *Handbook of Aging and the Social Sciences.* New York: Van Nostrand Reinhold, 1976.

Mangen, D. and W. Peterson. (eds.). *Research Instruments in Social Gerontology. Volume 1: Clinical and Social Psychology.* Minneapolis: University of Minnesota Press, 1982.

Manis, J. and B. Meltzer. (eds.). *Symbolic Interactionism: A Reader in Social Psychology.* Boston: Allyn and Bacon, 1972.

Markson, E. (ed.). 'Disengagement Theory Revisited,' *International Journal of Aging and Human Development,* 6(3/1975), 183–228.

Marshall, V. 'Socialization for Impending Death in a Retirement Village,' *American Journal of Sociology,* 80(5/1975a), 1124–44.

Marshall, V. 'Age and Awareness of Finitude in Developmental Gerontology,' *Omega,* 6 (2/1975b), 113–29.

Marshall, V. 'No Exit: A Symbolic Interactionist Perspective on Aging,' *International Journal of Aging and Human Development,* 9(4/1978–79) 345–58.

Marshall, V. 'No Exit: An Interpretative Perspective on Aging,' pp. 51–60 in V. Marshall (ed.). *Aging in Canada: Social Perspectives.* Don Mills: Fitzhenry and Whiteside, 1980a.

Marshall, V. *Last Chapters: A Sociology of Aging and Dying.* Monterey, Calif.: Brooks/Cole Publishing Co., 1980b.

Marshall, V. 'State of the Art Lecture: The Sociology of Aging,' pp. 76–144 in J. Crawford (ed.). *Canadian Gerontological Collection III.* Winnipeg: Canadian Association on Gerontology, 1981a.

Marshall, V. 'Participant Observation in a Multiple-Methods Study of a Retirement Community: A Research Narrative,' Mid-American Review of Sociology, 6(2/1981b), 29–44.

Marshall, V. and J. Tindale. 'Notes for a Radical Gerontology,' International Journal of Aging and Human Development, 9(2/1978–79), 163–75.

Martin, J. 'Power, Dependence and the Complaints of the Elderly: A Social Exchange Perspective,' Aging and Human Development, 2(1/1971), 108–12.

Martin, W. 'Activity and Disengagement: Life-Satisfaction of In-Movers into a Retirement Community,' The Gerontologist, 13(2/1973), 224–27.

Matthews, S. The Social World of Old Women: Management of Self-Identity. Beverly Hills: Sage Publications, 1979.

Maxwell, R. and P. Silverman. 'Information and Esteem: Cultural Considerations in the Treatment of the Aged,' pp. 3–34 in J. Hendricks (ed.). In the Country of the Old. Farmingdale, N.Y.: Baywood Publishing Co., Inc., 1980.

McClelland, K. 'Self-Conception and Life Satisfaction: Integrating Aged Subculture and Activity Theory,' Journal of Gerontology, 37(6/1982), 723–32.

McPherson, B. 'Avoiding Chaos in the Sociology of Sport Brickyard,' Quest, 30(Summer, 1978), 72–79.

McPherson, B. and C. Kozlik. 'Canadian Leisure Patterns by Age: Disengagement, Continuity or Ageism?,' pp. 113–22 in V. Marshall (ed.). Aging In Canada: Social Perspectives. Don Mills: Fitzhenry and Whiteside, 1980.

Mednick, S. and M. Harway (eds.). Longitudinal Research In The United States. Boston: Martinus-Nijhoff, 1982.

Merton, R. Social Theory and Social Structure. Glencoe, Ill.: The Free Press, 1957.

Merton, R. Social Theory and Social Structure. New York: The Free Press, 1968.

Mills, C.W. The Sociological Imagination. New York: Grove Press, 1959.

Mindel, C. and C. Vaughan. 'A Multidimensional Approach to Religiosity and Disengagement,' Journal of Gerontology, 33(1/1978), 103–8.

Mortimer, J. and R. Simmons. 'Adult Socialization,' pp. 421–54 in R. Turner et al. (eds.). Annual Review of Sociology. Volume 4. Palo Alto: Annual Reviews, Inc., 1978.

Myles, J. 'The Aged, the State and the Structure of Inequality,' pp. 317–42 in J. Harp and J. Hofley (eds.). Structural Inequality In Canada. Toronto: Prentice-Hall, 1980.

Neugarten, B. 'Age Groups in American Society and the Rise of the Young-Old,' The Annals of the American Academy of Political and Social Science, 415(September/1974), 187–98.

Nisbet, R. Sociology as an Art Form. New York: Oxford University Press, 1976.

Palmore, E. 'The Effects of Aging on Activities and Attitudes,' The Gerontologist, 8(4/1968), 259–63.

Palmore, E. 'The Status and Integration of the Aged in Japanese Society,' Journal of Gerontology, 30(2/1975), 199–208.

Palmore, E. 'When Can Age, Period, and Cohort Effects Be Separated?,' Social Forces, 57(1/1978), 282–95.

Palmore, E. 'Advantages of Aging,' The Gerontologist, 19(2/1979), 220–23.

Palmore, E. Social Patterns in Normal Aging. Durham: Duke University Press, 1981.

Palmore, E. and K. Manton. 'Modernization and Status of the Aged: International Correlations,' Journal of Gerontology, 29(2/1974), 205–10.

Palmore, E. and F. Whittington. 'Trends in the Relative Status of the Aged,' Social Forces, 50(1/1971), 84–91.

Parsons, T. The Social System. New York: The Free Press, 1951.

Patrick, C. and E. Borgatta (eds.). 'Available Data Bases for Aging Research,' Research on Aging, 3(4/1981), 371–501.

Pearson, K. Surfing Subcultures of Australia and New Zealand. Queensland: University of Queensland Press, 1979.

Phillips, B. 'A Role Theory Approach to Adjustment in Old Age,' American Sociological Review, 22(2/1957), 212–17.

Posner, J. 'Old and Female: The Double Whammy,' pp. 80–87 in V. Marshall (ed.). Aging in Canada: Social Perspectives. Don Mills: Fitzhenry and Whiteside, 1980.

Press, I. and M. McKool. 'Social Structure and Status of the Aged: Toward Some Valid Cross-Cultural Generalizations,' pp. 47–56 in J. Hendricks (ed.). In the Country of the Old. Farmingdale, N.Y.: Baywood Publishing Co., 1980.

Quadagno, J. 'The Modernization Controversy: A Socio-Historical Analysis of Retirement in Nineteenth Century England,' paper presented at the annual meeting of the American Sociological Association, New York, August 1980.

Ravetz, J. Scientific Knowledge and Its Social Problems. New York: Oxford University Press, 1971.

Ridley, J. et al. 'Recall and Reliability of Interview Data from Older Women,' Journal of Gerontology, 34(1/1979), 99–105.

Riley, M. 'Social Gerontology and the Age Stratification of Society,' The Gerontologist, 11(1/1971), 79–87.

Riley, M. 'Introduction: Life Course Perspectives,' pp. 3–13 in M. Riley (ed.). *Aging from Birth To Death: Interdisciplinary Perspectives.* Boulder: Westview Press, 1979.

Riley, M. 'Age and Aging: From Theory Generation to Theory Testing,' pp. 339–49 in H. Blalock (ed.). *Sociological Theory and Research: A Critical Appraisal.* New York: Free Press, 1980.

Riley, M., M. Johnson, and A. Foner. 'Elements in a Model of Age Stratification,' pp. 3–26 in M. Riley, M. Johnson and A. Foner (eds.). *Aging and Society. Volume 3: A Sociology of Age Stratification.* New York: Russell Sage Foundation, 1972.

Ritzer, G. 'Sociology - A Multiple Paradigm Science,' *The American Sociologist*, 10 (August/1975), 156–67.

Ritzer, G. *Sociology: A Multiple Paradigm Science.* Boston: Allyn and Bacon, 1975.

Roberts, J. and L. Kimsey. 'How Does It Feel to Grow Old? Eleven Essayists Answer,' *The Gerontologist*, 12(4/1972), 389–92.

Romeis, J. et al. 'Reference Group Theory: A Synthesizing Concept for the Disengagement and Interactionist Theories,' *International Review of Sociology*, 1(1/1971), 66–70.

Rose, A. 'The Subculture of the Aging: A Topic for Sociological Research,' *The Gerontologist*, 2(3/1962), 123–27.

Rose, A. 'The Subculture of the Aging: A Framework For Research in Social Gerontology,' pp. 3–16 in A. Rose and W. Peterson (eds.). *Older People and Their Social World.* Philadelphia: F.A. Davis, Co., 1965.

Rosow, I. 'The Social Context of the Aging Self,' *The Gerontologist*, 3(1/1973), 82–87.

Rosow, I. *Socialization to Old Age.* Berkeley: University of California Press, 1974.

Rosow, I. 'Status and Role Change Through the Life Span,' pp. 457–82 in R. Binstock and E. Shanas (eds.). *Handbook of Aging and the Social Sciences.* New York: Van Nostrand Reinhold, 1976.

Rudner, R. *Philosophy of Social Science.* Englewood Cliffs, N.J.: Prentice-Hall, 1966.

Rutzen, S. 'The Social Distribution of Primary Social Isolation Among the Aged: A Subcultural Approach,' *International Journal of Aging and Human Development*, 11(1/1980), 77–87.

Sacher, G. 'Theory in Gerontology, Part I,' pp. 3–25 in C. Eisdorfer (ed.). *Annual Review of Gerontology and Geriatrics.* Volume 1. New York: Springer Publishing Co., 1980.

Sarbin, T. and V. Allen. 'Role Theory,' pp. 488–567 in G. Lindzey and E. Aronson (eds.). *Handbook of Social Psychology.* Reading, Mass.: Addison-Wesley, 1968.

Schaie, K.W. 'A General Model for the Study of Developmental Problems,' *Psychological Bulletin*, 64(2/1965), 92–107.

Schaie, K.W. 'Age Changes and Age Differences,' *The Gerontologist*, 7(2/1967), 128–32.

Schaie, K.W. 'Quasi-Experimental Research Designs in the Psychology of Aging,' pp. 39–58 in J. Birren and K.W. Schaie (eds.). *Handbook of the Psychology of Aging.* New York: Van Nostrand Reinhold, 1977.

Scheff, T. 'The Labelling Theory of Mental Illness,' *American Sociological Review*, 39(3/1974), 444–52.

Schmidt, M. 'Interviewing the Old Old,' *The Gerontologist*, 15(6/1975), 544–53.

Schulsinger, F. et al. *Longitudinal Research: Methods and Uses in Behavioral Sciences.* Volume 1. Hingham, Mass.: Kluwer-Nijhoff Publishing, 1981.

Schulz, R. 'Experimental Social Gerontology: A Social Psychological Perspective,' *Journal of Social Issues*, 36(2/1980), 30–46.

Seltzer, M. 'The Quality of Research Is Strained,' *The Gerontologist*, 15(6/1975), 503–7.

Sewell, W. 'Some Recent Developments in Socialization Theory and Research,' *The Annals of the American Academy of Political and Social Science*, 349(September 1963), 163–81.

Shanas, E. et al. *Old People in Three Industrial Societies.* New York: Atherton Books, 1968.

Sheppard, A. 'Response to Cartoons and Attitudes Towards Aging,' *Journal of Gerontology*, 36(1/1981), 122–26.

Silk, J. 'Disengagement Reconsidered: Awareness of Finitude,' *The Gerontologist*, 20(4/1980), 457–62.

Smith, M. 'The Portrayal of Elders in Magazine Cartoons,' *The Gerontologist*, 19(6/1979), 408–12.

Snizek, W. 'The Relationship Between Theory and Research: A Study in the Sociology of Sociology,' *The Sociological Quarterly*, 16(3/1975), 415–28.

Stearns, P. 'The Modernization of Old Age in France: Approaches Through History,' *International Journal of Aging and Human Development*, 13(4/1981), 297–315.

Streib, G. 'Are the Aged a Minority Group?,' pp. 311–28 in A. Gouldner and S. Miller (eds.). *Applied Sociology.* Glencoe, Ill.: The Free Press, 1965.

Streib, G. 'Social Stratification and Aging,' pp. 160–85 in R. Binstock and E. Shanas (eds.). *Handbook of Aging and the Social Sciences.* New York: Van Nostrand Reinhold, 1976.

Streib, G. and C. Schneider. *Retirement In American Society.* Ithaca, N.Y.: Cornell University Press, 1971.

Sussman, M. 'The Family Life of Old People,' pp. 218–43 in R. Binstock and E. Shanas (eds.). *Handbook of Aging and The Social Sciences*. New York: Van Nostrand Reinhold, 1976.

Sztompka, P. *System and Function: Toward a Theory of Society*. New York: Academic Press, 1974.

Thomas, W. 'The Definition of the Situation,' pp. 41–50 in W. Thomas (ed.). *The Unadjusted Girl*. Boston: Little, Brown and Co., 1931.

Tigges, L. and D. Cowgill. 'Aging from the World Systems Perspective: An Alternative to Modernization Theory?,' paper presented at the annual meeting of the Gerontological Society of America, Toronto, November 1981.

Tindale, J. 'Identity Maintenance Processes of Old, Poor Men,' pp. 88–94 in V. Marshall (ed.). *Aging in Canada: Social Perspectives*. Don Mills: Fitzhenry and Whiteside, 1980.

Tindale, J. and V. Marshall. 'A Generational Conflict Perspective for Gerontology,' pp. 43–59 in V. Marshall (ed.). *Aging In Canada: Social Perspectives*. Don Mills: Fitzhenry and Whiteside, 1980.

Wallace, W. *Sociological Theory*. Chicago: Aldine, 1969.

Waring, J. 'Social Replenishment and Social Change: The Problem of Disordered Cohort Flow,' *American Behavioral Scientist*, 19(2/1975), 237–56.

Warshay, L. *The Current State of Sociological Theory*. New York: D. McKay, 1975.

Wheeler, S. 'The Structure of Formally Organized Socialization Settings,' pp. 53–116 in O. Brim and S. Wheeler (eds.). *Socialization After Childhood*. New York: John Wiley and Sons, 1966.

Williams, R. and G. Wirths. *Lives Through The Years*. New York: Atherton, 1965.

Wiseman, H. *Political Systems*. New York: Praeger, 1966.

Youmans, G. 'Some Perspectives on Disengagement Theory,' *The Gerontologist*, 9(4/1969), 254–58.

Zigler, E. and I. Child. 'Socialization,' pp. 450–589 in G. Lindzey and E. Aronson (eds.). *The Handbook of Social Psychology*. Volume 3. Reading, Mass.: Addison-Wesley, 1969.

PART TWO

A Microanalysis of the Aging Process: The Aging Individual

Part Two comprises two chapters describing some of the incremental and decremental changes that occur with age in the physical and psychological systems of the human organism. Chapter 5 presents information about the way in which changes in the physical structure and in the physiological, sensory, and motor systems influence social, emotional, and cognitive behavior in the later stages of life. The chapter also illustrates patterns of involvement in physical activity and exercise at various stages in the life cycle, and briefly analyzes individual health problems and the use of the health care delivery system. In chapter 6, the focus is on changes in the sensory, perceptual, cognitive, and personality systems that occur within the aging individual, and on how these changes influence social and cognitive behavior.

Part Two includes a brief non-technical description of changes that occur in the physical and psychological systems in the middle and later years. This serves as the basis for a more detailed discussion of how these changes may influence the behavioral and cognitive processes of the older individual as he or she interacts with a changing social and physical environment.

5

The Aging Process:
Adaptation to Physical Changes

Introduction

It is commonly believed that the process of aging involves degenerative changes in the physical and psychological systems of the organism. These in turn are presumed to lead to inevitable physical, emotional, and intellectual losses. For example, myths and stereotypes often portray aging and the aged in negative terms. As a result, it is often assumed that the elderly are slower; have less strength, endurance, and energy; are chronic complainers about their acute or chronic illnesses; are uninterested in or incapable of sexual activity; are forgetful or senile; and are handicapped at work and in social interaction by deterioration in vision and hearing.

Until recent years these deficiencies were attributed almost exclusively to the inevitable, genetically based biological decline of the organism; the possible influence of historical events or social experiences on the aging process was neglected. A generalized model of inevitable biological decline was accepted, with little concern for individual differences resulting from social or environmental factors. As Charness (1981:22), a psychologist, recently noted: 'Aging research should become more concerned with an individual difference approach. In fact, one of the few unchallenged assertions in gerontology is that individual differences increase with age (Carroll and Maxwell, 1979).'

As noted earlier, there has been a tendency to confuse age differences with age changes. This has resulted from a reliance on cross-sectional research designs that compare members of different age cohorts on various physical or psychological variables. In this type of study older people are generally found to be inferior to younger people, especially in the accomplishment of intellectual and physical tasks. However, the observed differences between the young and the old in cross-sectional studies might also reflect differences in educational attainment, in lifestyle opportunities, in attitudes toward testing situations, in experience as subjects in experiments, in motivation to perform, or in meaningfulness of the test material.

In order to separate myth from fact, this chapter summarizes recent research evidence concerning the physical capabilities and performance potential of the older person. (In chapter 6 the psychological components of the organism are examined in a similar manner.) This chapter describes changes observed in the physical structure, physiological systems, and sensory and motor processes of older people. In addition, there is a brief discussion of changes in physical and mental health in the later years, and the need for and utilization of health care.

Throughout chapters 5 and 6 the information is presented from a social science perspective: special attention is directed to the influence of physical or psychological changes on social and intellectual behavior.

In summary, all individuals can expect some decline in health and some gradual loss of physical, motor, or mental efficiency and ability as they age. These losses, which are a result of inevitable biological changes, occur at different rates in different individuals. Most people, at least until very late in life, do not experience functional losses that seriously change or affect their social or cognitive behavior.[1] Most of us will not spend most of the later years as senile or physically decrepit old people. Rather, we will likely experience varying degrees of physical, perceptual, or cognitive losses that will require some degree of adaptation. This process of adaptation will be influenced by a variety of past and present social and environmental factors, such as previous lifestyle; personality structure and coping style; support from significant others; socioeconomic status; race; gender; and marital status. The process of adaption to changes in the physical and psychological systems will also be influenced by historical events and social changes (wars, depressions), and by unique personal events or transitions (divorce, involuntary retirement, or widowhood) that have occurred throughout the life cycle of a given individual or cohort.

Aging, Physical Structure, and the Physiological Systems

Introduction

As biologists and physiologists have frequently noted, the structure and function of the human organism attains full maturity and its greatest strength and energy sometime before twenty years of age. From early adulthood on, there is a gradual and progressive decline in the structure and function of the body's various components and a resulting decrease in the general activity level of the organism.

While some of these changes are external and highly visible (such as elasticity and texture of the skin), most are internal, and may or may not influence social behavior or work performance. Moreover, there are differences in the rate of decline for each organ or system (Clarke, 1973). For example, an individual who has reached a chronological age of 65 years may have the strength and energy of a 40-year-old, and the external physical appearance of a 50-year-old. Yet the same individual may have hearing or visual problems more commonly experienced by an 80-year-old. Furthermore, this interaction of physical and physiological aging has a unique impact on the behavior, attitudes, and performance of an individual. This is reflected in the dynamic interplay between the personality or personal coping style of the individual; the attitudes, perceptions, and interaction of others; and the individual's subsequent 'presentation of self' and type and frequency of social participation.

In summary, external physical and internal physiological changes occurring with age may have varying degrees of influence on the attitudes, social participation, and performance of specific individuals. The impact of these changes may be closely related to the severity of the change, the degree to which other changes occur at the same time or rate, and the extent to which the changes are perceived by the individual as threatening or limiting. Their impact is also influenced by the coping style of the individual, by the extent to which exercise is an integral facet of the individual's lifestyle, and by the reaction of significant others toward the individual (for example, social support, discouragement, lack of interest, decreased interaction).

The following sections illustrate some of the more common age-related changes in the physical structure and physiological functioning of the human organism, as well as the possible reactions to these changes. The influence of exercise and physical activity on the aging process is also examined. Throughout, it must be remembered that modal patterns are presented, and that there are system differences within and between individuals. These differences are related to such genetic and environmental factors as sex, socioeconomic status, diet, race, ethnicity, occupation, geographic location, marital status, body type, and age cohort. Unfortunately, these factors are seldom controlled in experimental situations.

Changes in the Structure and Composition of the Organism

External changes.   As we age, visible changes occur in the skin, the hair, and in the shape and height of the body. For example, during middle age the skin becomes dry and wrinkled as it becomes thinner and loses its elasticity and subcutaneous fat. Similarly, hair becomes thinner and loses its original color. Because of the negative connotations frequently associated with wrinkles and gray hair, some individuals actively fight a 'cosmetic battle' to change their physical appearance and thereby appear younger than their chronological age. Not surprisingly, a profitable cosmetics industry has evolved to meet this social need, as has a new specialty in the medical profession, the 'cosmetic surgeon.' In addition to changing one's appearance, the loss of hair and subcutaneous fat in the middle and later years leads to greater heat loss and to increased susceptibility to 'feeling cold.' This in turn may initiate a shift from outdoor to indoor activities, and perhaps even a move to a warmer climate if this is economically feasible.

For many adults, especially women, body weight increases up to about 50 years of age, although there is often a decline thereafter because of a change in body metabolism. This increase in weight is due to an accumulation of fat and a reduction in muscle tissue which appears most frequently in the abdominal area for men, and in the limbs and abdominal area for women. As a result, body shape may change from a lean and youthful appearance to a more portly, rotund, or mature appearance.

This visible change in shape sometimes results in a social labelling process whereby the individual is perceived by others to be older than his or her actual or desired chronological age. Attempts may be initiated to mask these physical changes with a particular style of dress. In fact, the fashion industry has capitalized on this recent concern with looking young by designing clothes that make one look slimmer. In reality, a combination of regular exercise and appropriate diet is a healthier behavioral adaptation to these changes in body composition. However, many individuals are unwilling to invest time and energy in these remedies.

Another visible sign of aging is the shortening of stature that begins in late middle age. This is related to changes in the structure and composition of the spine: vertebrae may collapse or intervertebral discs may become compressed. These changes are visibly reflected in an increased 'bowing' of the spine and the loss of a few inches in height.

In summary, external visible changes with age can influence how an individual perceives the self, and how others perceive and interact with the individual. For those who are secure and who live in a supportive social environment, these physical changes are seldom traumatic. However, for those whose identity and social interaction are closely related to their physical appearance, attempts to alter the presentation of the physical self may become a time-consuming battle, particularly if they are separated or divorced and anxious to attract another mate.

Internal changes.   Internal physical changes tend to have more of an impact on the performance of physical tasks than on social perceptions, attitudes, or behavior. These changes include a decrease in muscle mass and elasticity; a decrease in water content and an increase in fat cells relative to muscle cells; a decrease in bone mass and minerals so that bones are more brittle, which increases the likelihood of fractures; and a deterioration in the range, flexibility, and composition of the articulating surfaces and joints, which can enhance the likelihood of fractures or arthritis, particularly among those who live past the normal life expectancy. Many of these changes lead to decreased mobility and to an inability to perform household tasks in the later years.

Changes in the Physiological Functioning of the Organism

Over time, most physiological systems become less efficient and less capable of functioning to the maximum capacity of the earlier years of life. Decremental functional performance is usually experienced during strenuous or stressful work or leisure activities. However, as noted in a later subsection of this chapter, it is possible to maintain a fitness or training program as we age. This training process can retard the impact of physiological age-related changes, and can enhance performance in the later years. For example, Spirduso (1980) found that with increased levels of physical fitness, reaction times and movement times were faster. If physiological systems function efficiently, especially under physical or mental stress, the self-image of the individual may be enhanced. As a result, physical tasks that are often thought to be beyond the capacity of the older individual may be performed (such as skiing or participating in a marathon), and an active social life in the community may be sustained well into the later years.

The central nervous system.   The central nervous system begins to slow down with age, as evidenced by a longer response or reaction time, by the earlier onset of fatigue, by the appearance of hand tremors, and by a general slowing of the autonomic nervous system. Changes in the autonomic nervous system may lead to changes in metabolism, in the structure and function of a number of organs, and in the activities of nervous receptors, processors, and reactors. Some of these changes may be reflected in the slower execution of a task (although, contrary to popular myth, the quality of performance seldom decreases). More will be said about the impact of aging on the sensory processes in the next major section of this chapter. In the meantime, it is important to recognize that changes in the autonomic nervous system can significantly influence emotions and behavioral reactions. As Frolkis (1977:187) notes, 'With aging, essential changes are taking place in all links of the autonomic nervous system. These changes lead to shifts in the reflectory regulation of inner organs, to a decrease in the organism's adaptive capacities, to a decrease in reliability of homeostatic regulatory mechanisms, to an easier disruption of regulatory mechanisms, and to the development of pathology in old age.'

The muscular system.   Age-related changes in the muscular system result in a decrease in strength and endurance, although the rate and degree of loss seems to be related to the frequency and intensity of physical activity pursued by the individual (Clement, 1974; deVries, 1975). In addition, the time it takes for a muscle to relax or contract, and the time required before it can be restimulated, increase in later life. This is partly because of changes in the contractile tissue in the muscle, and partly because of neurological changes. These changes have an impact on the ability to engage in endurance tasks or in tasks requiring repeated actions of the same muscle group (such as digging in the garden or washing windows). In addition, a decline in muscular endurance can also reduce the efficiency of other body systems, such as the respiratory system. Furthermore, a decrement in the muscular-skeletal systems can lead to a greater likelihood of falls: there may be reduced leg lift when walking, which increases the chance of tripping, or there may be greater difficulty in regaining balance after stumbling. As will be noted later, the efficiency of the muscular system can be enhanced in the later years by regular exercise and physical activity; it is possible to retard the onset of muscular changes with age, and thus improve performance in daily tasks.

The cardiovascular system.   Among the many physiological changes that occur with age, the most visible (and the most significant for behavior) are those within the cardiovascular system: there is a decrease in the maximum heart rate attainable, a decrease in the maximum cardiac output and stroke volume, and an increase in blood pressure. All of these factors combine to lower the efficiency of the system and to hasten the onset of fatigue during various levels of physical activity. These outcomes, in turn, may limit the duration and type of work and leisure activities that can be pursued with enjoyment. However, these cardiovascular changes are not inevitable; it is possible, with a regular and sufficiently intense exercise program, to lower the resting heart rate, to increase the maximum heart rate during work, and to increase the cardiac output.

It is more difficult, however, to retard the onset of arteriosclerosis and atherosclerosis. Arteriosclerosis (or 'hardening of the arteries') is a loss of elasticity in the arterial walls, which restricts the flow of blood to the muscles and organs, thereby lessening endurance in work or play. Atherosclerosis is characterized by a hardening and narrowing of the arterial walls, resulting from the accumulation of fatty deposits that partially or completely block the flow of blood. These cardiovascular diseases, which are especially prevalent among men, are difficult to prevent or treat because their pathology is still not fully understood. However, adherence to low-cholesterol diets and maintenance of a regular exercise program throughout life seems to be related to a lower incidence of these diseases.

The respiratory system.   The efficiency of the respiratory system decreases with age because of a combination of factors. These include decreases in elasticity of the lungs; in vital capacity (the amount of air that can be forcibly exhaled after a full inspiration); in diffusion and absorption capacities; and in maximum voluntary ventilation and oxygen intake. These changes reduce the efficiency of intake and transportation of oxygen to organs and muscles.

The coordination and efficiency of both the respiratory and cardiovascular systems are highly interrelated in determining the physical fitness capacity of a given individual.[2] Unless individuals engage in regular endurance exercise throughout the adult years, by 60 to 75 years of age there may be as much as a 50 percent decrease in physical work capacity from the maximum value attained in early adulthood (deVries, 1975; Clarke, 1977; Shephard and Sidney, 1979; Smith and Serfass, 1981; Montoye, 1982).

In the absence of training, the cardio-respiratory systems normally function close to their maximum capacity. Hence, the less fit individual has few reserves for emergencies, and during stressful situations fatigue begins earlier and the recovery period is longer. Obviously, these physiological deficiencies can limit the type, intensity, and frequency of some forms of social behavior (sports, physical play with children or grandchildren, walking or hiking, gardening, or shoveling snow).

Summary.   Increasing age brings changes in the composition and structure of the body, and there are losses in functional capacity and efficiency at the cellular, tissue, organ, and system levels. Some of these changes can be delayed or offset by regular exercise programs. Deficiencies become most apparent under stress, as in physical work, exercise, or reaction to disease or accidents. As with other changes with age, there are differences within and between individuals with respect to the onset and degree of loss in the various systems. Moreover, the impact on behavior of changes in the physiological systems is most profound when deterioration occurs in more than one system at the same time; interacting changes between the central nervous system and the sensory-motor processes are likely more significant for the individual than changes experienced in only one of these systems.

Involvement in Physical Activity by Age

Introduction.   Exercise and physical activity provide a number of beneficial outcomes for the aging adult. For example, many studies over the years have found a positive relationship between the amount of participation in physical activity at work or play and the level of physical and mental health. Similarly, it has often been demonstrated that there is an inverse relationship between level of physical activity at work or play and mortality rates. Yet, as many studies have indicated, involvement in physical activity declines with age, especially among women and among those with lower levels of formal education. This pattern appears to be virtually universal, although it varies somewhat from nation to nation and from cohort to cohort.

In the following two subsections the pattern of involvement by age in physical activity is described, and some possible explanations for this universal pattern are discussed. (Later, in chapter 11, it will be seen that a similar pattern exists for most nonphysical leisure activities.) Once again, it must be remembered that most of the evidence is based on cross-sectional rather than longitudinal or cohort analysis research. Hence, it cannot be definitely determined whether the pattern reflects changes with increasing chronological age, cohort differences, or period effects for particular cohorts.

Patterns of physical activity across the life cycle.   A large number of children in most modernized nations are involved to some degree in institutionalized or informal sport or exercise programs at school or in the community. However, some never become fully socialized into this type of leisure behavior, either because their parents do not place a high value on physical activity, or because they do not have an opportunity to become involved at an early age. In addition, of those who were fully socialized to incorporate sport or physical activity into their lifestyle at an early age, many are no longer participating by the age of 15 or 16. This withdrawal during adolescence occurs because they no longer enjoy physical recreation, because they develop more salient interests, or because they have been involuntarily removed by adult coaches (who have decided they lack the skill to continue competing at a specific level).

This almost universal pattern of declining involvement in physical recreation begins relatively early in life. In fact, in North America it often occurs before individuals have even had an opportunity to adopt physical activity as an integral facet of their leisure lifestyle. Many children have withdrawn from involvement in physical activity because of unpleasant experiences in sport programs, because there is no alternative to elite sport for those who are less skilled, because they have experienced failure or loss of identity, because there is an overemphasis on performance rather than participation, or because facilities or programs are not available.

For those who remain involved past childhood, physical activity may have a lower priority as adolescents search for personal identity, assimilate into the youth culture, and rebel against adult values, including those that advocate physical activity or sport as part of a leisure lifestyle. The time of leaving formal schooling represents another significant transition point; for example, Boothby (1980) found a significant decrease in the amount and frequency of physical activity at high school-leaving age. This decrease was especially pronounced for women and for those from the lower socioeconomic classes.

Renson (1978) offers a number of possible explanations for this tendency of young people to drop out from physical activity at this stage of life. He suggests that physical education or sport is no longer compulsory; that they may leave a peer group that participates in and values sport and enter a peer group that has other primary interests or values; that there may not be an opportunity to participate in facilities outside the school setting; that they become more oriented toward an adult lifestyle and value system that may view participation in sport and physical activity as childish; and that occupational or family responsibilities may become too time-consuming. In short, social experiences rather than lack of ability or interest may account for declining involvement in physical activity after leaving high school.

A number of studies have found that watching sport is a major life interest of adults, especially men; but active participation in various forms of physical activity appears to be inversely proportional to age (McPherson, 1978). This trend is surprising in that there is increasing scientific evidence that physical activity can enhance longevity and the quality of life. In addition, there have been many direct attempts by government agencies and health-related professions to develop favorable attitudes among adults concerning the need and value of participating in regular physical activity (President's Council on Physical Fitness and Sports, 1982).

This pattern of less involvment by successively older cohorts seems to be more pronounced among the less educated, among those who have lower incomes, among those who live in rural areas and small towns, among those who are engaged in manual occupations, and among females (especially if they are married and have pre-school-age children). Studies in Denmark (Anderson et al., 1956), France (Dumazedier, 1973), Canada (Milton, 1975; McPherson and Kozlik, 1980; Perrin, 1981; Canada Fitness Survey, 1982), the United States (Kenyon, 1966), Finland (Kiviaho, 1977), Czechoslovakia (Kreipel, 1977), Norway (Fasting, 1979), and Great Britain (Birch, 1979) have all noted that a small proportion of adults are engaged in any type of regular physical activity. Numerous cross-sectional studies have indicated that participation rates vary dramatically among cohorts older than 20 years of age. Table 5.1 indicates age differences in the reported participation rates of Canadian adults in a variety of forms of physical activity. Interestingly, sharp decreases in participation rates are reported after 19 years and 64 years of age. These stages approximately represent entrance into, and departure from, the labor force. That is, a transition into and out of the labor force may initiate changes in patterns of physical recreation similar to those that occur in other dimensions of the lifestyle. The significant percentage decrease in involvement by those 65 years of age and older is also accounted for by the fact that this age category includes the very old (those over 80).

Table 5.1 The percentage participation in sport and exercise programs by age. Adapted from Culture Statistics, Recreational Activities, 1976. Statistics Canada, Catalogue 87–501.

Age	Sport[†]	Exercise[‡]	Jogging[‡]	Golf[†]	Swimming[†]
15–16	82.0	86.9	53.4	16.9	60.5
17–19	73.3	75.4	34.6	15.3	53.3
20–24	66.3	63.4	19.9	15.0	44.7
25–34	61.3	62.3	12.2	12.9	38.4
35–44	51.2	53.3	9.2	11.1	30.7
45–54	37.2	50.1	5.3	8.9	20.4
55–64	24.5	45.7	2.4	6.7	11.7
65 and over	9.7	37.0	4.0	2.5	3.6

[†] Participated at least once in the past year.
[‡] Participated at least once in the past month.

In summary, active participation in physical activity is inversely proportional to age after adolescence. However, this decline is less prevalent among males, among the better educated, among those with higher incomes, among those who live in medium-sized cities, among those in non-manual occupations, and among those who live in countries where physical activity is highly valued (as in Eastern Europe). Although this pattern of decreasing involvement with age may be slightly less dramatic with each successive cohort that passes age 20, the pattern is of serious social concern to those in the leisure and health care professions. An increasing percentage of the aging population is made up of sedentary adults who, although retired for a longer period of time, may lack the physical capacity to participate in a variety of social and physical activities that should be possible in the later years.

Explanations for varying degrees of involvement by age cohorts.   Clearly, there are cohort differences in the type and frequency of participation in physical activity. While some of these differences might be accounted for by declining energy reserves, there are also a number of possible sociological and psychological explanations.

First, individual attitudes toward physical activity may be a factor in low participation rates. Because of unpleasant experiences early in life, adults may have a negative attitude toward exercise. This attitude may be reinforced by a belief in stereotypes or myths, namely: that the need for exercise decreases with age; that the elderly do not have, or have lost, the skill to perform most physical activities; that physical activity is dangerous to one's health; and that older adults should 'take it easy' as they age (Conrad, 1976). Even among adults who do exercise, many perceive their current amount of exercise to be beneficial when, in fact, it is often insufficient to develop or maintain adequate fitness levels (Sidney and Shephard, 1977).

In addition to attitudes, an individual's commitment to a particular form of leisure behavior may influence his or her degree of involvement in exercise or sport programs. If a limited amount of leisure time is available, physical activity may have a low priority relative to more highly valued and established role commitments (the job, a hobby, or the family).

Moreover, there are individual differences in the type of role commitments at different stages in the life cycle, particularly with respect to differences by gender, race, age, socioeconomic status, stage in the family life cycle, and nationality. For example, Snyder (1980:10–12) suggests the following possible reasons for commitment to a given role or activity: the degree of intrinsic enjoyment or 'flow' (Csikszentmihalyi, 1975) in the activity itself (such as health and fitness, pleasure or pride in performance); the type or number of extrinsic rewards associated with participation or success (prizes, prestige, or power); the amount and type of social support received from significant others (approval, praise, or encouragement) and the degree of social interaction that enhances self-esteem and mutual compatibility; and the opportunity to use leisure, work, community, or family roles to maintain or enhance a consistent self-identity.

While each of these factors may strengthen a commitment to a particular form of leisure, they may also be perceived as a cost to be avoided. That is, there may be a lack of commitment to physical activity compared to other social roles or leisure activities.[3] In short, the degree of commitment indicates the time, energy, and economic resources that adults are willing to invest in physical activity. If this commitment is a by-product of socialization in the early years, and physical recreation is an integral facet of the lifestyle, then negotiation of role alternatives with respect to physical activity is less likely to occur in later life. Where there is a commitment to physical activity, work, the family, and other leisure roles enter the negotiation process with respect to how time, energy, and economic resources are to be expended.

From the perspective of society, the myth that the older adult is beyond help (Butler, 1977–78) often discourages the initiation of physical activity programs for the elderly segment of the population. Because of age grading and the creation of normative age criteria, facilities and programs are seldom provided to enable adults to be physically active on a regular basis. 'Acting your age' as an adult, at least for many cohorts, implies that participation in sport or physical activity is not considered to be socially acceptable behavior. These age norms interact with gender-related norms to create greater social barriers for women. However, as Ostrow et al. (1981) recently noted, age is perceived to be a more potent norm than gender with respect to imposing social barriers to participation in physical activity. This age-based social norm may also lead to a self-fulfilling prophecy or stereotype that implies that the middle years and beyond are sedentary stages of life.

This process of age grading, or ageism, is facilitated further when physically active role models are not available (McPherson, 1978; Ostrow, 1980, 1982). However, the increasing presence in recent years of physically active adults of all ages has resulted in a weakening of the restrictive age norms concerning involvement in physical activity in the middle and later years, for both men and women. Moreover, there is increasing scientific evidence that physical fitness is possible at all ages, and, more important, is beneficial to the physical and mental health of the individual. As a result, 'Master,' 'Veteran' or 'Senior' competitions by age group are now available for a number of sports and physical activities,[4] including competition in a marathon (twenty-six miles).

Another possible explanation for lower levels of participation among older cohorts is that they have been differentially socialized compared to more recent age cohorts. For any given age cohort (for example, ages 25 to 34), the values, opportunity set, and childhood and adolescent experiences in sport and leisure may have been considerably different from those of another age cohort (for example, ages 55 to 64). For most of those who are 65 years of age and over in the 1980s, the early socialization period featured an average work week of approximately fifty hours, a high value on work and a lower value on play and leisure, few vacations, little education beyond elementary school, and few opportunities to engage in any form of leisure in the late adolescent or early adult years. Moreover, many occupations demanded high levels of physical strength and endurance, thereby precluding the need for physical activity in the limited leisure time available.

For many in this age cohort, leisure was a time to restore the energy needed for work. Thus, most members of the cohort, especially women, never placed a high value on, or acquired experience with, physical activity during their leisure time. It is easy to understand why, at age 65 and beyond, they report little involvement in physical activity compared to younger cohorts. If longitudinal data were available, it is quite likely that this cohort would have reported low levels of involvement in physical activity at all stages of the life cycle.

Similarly, projecting ahead, it might be hypothesized that, except where declining physical ailments inhibit involvement in an activity, the cohort that is 25 to 34 years of age in the 1980s will report high levels of involvement in physical activity throughout the adult years, including during retirement. This is particularly likely to happen since they were socialized during the 'fitness boom' of the 1970s. When we discuss socialization and the patterns of involvement in physical activity over the life cycle, it must be recognized that the saliency of physical activity varies by age cohort. For example, between 1974 and 1981 the percentage of those under 65 years of age in the United States who were involved in jogging, walking, or other kinds of exercise increased from 22 to 31 percent, while participation by those over 65 years of age remained unchanged at 25 percent (Harris, 1981).

In addition to between-cohort differences, there are also individual differences within a given cohort that are based on sex, class, and education. However, since socialization is a lifelong process, resocialization into a pattern of regular physical activity, while difficult, may be possible. Physical activity is increasingly becoming a more socially acceptable and desirable leisure activity for adults of all ages, and resocialization may retard slightly the prevailing tendency toward declining involvement by age.

In summary, the frequency and type of involvement in physical activity begins to decline in late adolescence and continues thereafter. This pattern is more likely to be found among women, the less educated, lower income groups, and rural residents. This trend (with minor variations) is found cross-culturally, although the pattern appears to be more pronounced in North America than in other industrialized societies. While a number of alternative explanations for this pattern of declining involvement by age have been proposed, a definitive explanation is lacking. Nevertheless, it appears that the salient factors involve some combination of inadequate early life socialization and, during the adult years, a lack of opportunity, a lack of commitment for a variety of reasons, a lack of role models, and, because of ageism, the presence of cultural norms that devalue physical activity in adult lifestyles.

Outcomes of Exercise by Age

Physiological and health outcomes. Research evidence suggests not only that exercise is beneficial to physical and mental health at all ages, but also that a lack of regular, vigorous exercise may hasten the onset of physiological aging processes (Wiswell, 1980; Smith and Serfass, 1981). Exercise has the potential to slow or reverse some components of physiological aging, thereby enabling the aging individual to engage in leisure and work activities with greater efficiency, energy, and enjoyment. However, despite this research evidence, a pattern of increasing sedentary lifestyles with age prevails, and four out of five Americans are not advised by their physicians to engage in exercise (Butler, 1977–78).

From the perspective of the individual, an improvement in physical fitness not only increases the likelihood of good health, but it may lead to greater longevity, to a longer period of independence, to a higher quality of life, and to a faster and more complete recovery from some diseases. From the societal perspective, a physically active adult population has a higher fitness level, which in turn may indirectly lower the cost of health care. Thus, from both an individual and a societal perspective, there appear to be both immediate and long-term benefits to increasing the proportion of adults who are regularly involved in physical activity.

To date, there is considerable evidence concerning the degree of improvement in physical fitness among middle-aged men who participate in graduated and regular endurance exercise programs. While little information is available about adult women, or about adults over 60 years of age, the evidence is accumulating that training outcomes similar to those in the earlier years can be realized. In fact, adults over 60 can be trained to high levels of fitness and performance by graduated programs of walking, jogging, running, and swimming (Adams and deVries, 1973; deVries, 1975, 1978; Clarke, 1977; Harris and Frankel, 1977; Shephard, 1978; Smith and Serfass, 1981; Cunningham et al., forthcoming). The following are some of the possible physiological and health benefits that can be derived from participation in physical activity programs of sufficient intensity:

- increased blood flow through the capillaries
- increased muscular endurance
- decreased percentage of body fat and a lower body weight
- increased flexibility
- increased cardiovascular endurance

- decreased systemic blood pressure
- less loss of strength with age
- increased and more efficient blood flow from the extremities to the heart
- increased maximal oxygen intake and physical work capacity
- lowered resting and exercising heart-rate
- more rapid heart-rate recovery following strenuous exercise
- more rapid oxygen debt repayment following strenuous exercise
- increased utilization of anaerobic energy reserves
- increased neural regulatory control, including faster reaction time

All of the above may be developed or changed, regardless of the degree of physical activity in the earlier years (deVries, 1975:263). Through adherence to a regular, graduated exercise program (Clarke, 1977:17–23; Harris and Frankel, 1977; Shephard, 1978:176–203), adults in the later years of life can improve their level of physical fitness, thereby slowing the physiological aging process and enhancing their potential for a higher quality of life. It is also possible to train older adults to compete in athletic events, including marathons and distance events in swimming. While Olympic times will not result, the physical benefits of training for the individual may be relatively greater than for the younger Olympic athlete.

Psychological and social outcomes.   Many claims have been made concerning the impact of exercise on mental health. However, compared to the physiological area there is much less evidence concerning the psychological and social outcomes of exercise programs, and their impact on the mental health of adults. While a large number of studies have examined the relationship between certain personality traits and involvement in sport or exercise programs, relatively few have analyzed the specific psychological or social benefits of participation in an exercise program. Those studies that have attempted to determine the psychological or social changes that accompany exercise have reported that there is an increased sense of well-being, a relief of tension, a decline in manifest anxiety, greater self-confidence, greater emotional stability, less depression, an improved self-concept, higher fluid intelligence,[5] and an improved body-image (McPherson, 1965; Elsayed et al., 1980; Ostrow, 1980).

Research results are equivocal concerning whether personality traits change as a result of involvement in an intensive exercise program. However, there is some evidence that mood states and state anxiety, which are less stable than personality traits, may change for a time following the completion of an exercise session (McPherson, 1965; McPherson et al., 1967). Spreitzer and Snyder (1974) have suggested that one outcome of an exercise program for older adults is a more positive perception of their personal health. This, they argue, may in turn lead to an improved self-concept and greater life satisfaction.

The psychological and social outcomes from exercise may be greater, and both more meaningful and permanent, for those who engage in regular, supervised exercise programs following a heart attack. For this group of atypical adult men, physical activity may relieve anxiety and fear, increase self-confidence, reduce tension, relieve depression, alleviate the fears of significant others, and improve their sense of well-being and their general mood (McPherson et al., 1967).

While a number of studies have found a moderate relationship between involvement in physical activity and psychological changes, a satisfactory explanation for these outcomes is lacking. For example, Michael (1957) suggested that the euphoria or sense of well-being following exercise may be emotional in nature and may result from an adjustment of the autonomic nervous system. He further noted that regular exercise not only increases an individual's sense of well-being but increases the capacity for enduring nervous stress, disappointments, and frustrations. More recently, Elsayed et al. (1980), in noting that the high-fit group in their study had a higher fluid intelligence score, suggested that exercise may improve the process of energy production and transfer of oxygen to the brain, leading to improved performance on psychological tests. This explanation may be valid only if the exercise program is of sufficient intensity and frequency to induce physiological changes (Sidney and Shephard, 1977). It may also be the case that psychological changes are dependent on a high degree of motivation and favorable attitudes by the individual toward exercise and physical activity. For this reason it is important to develop an early commitment to physical activity so that it is incorporated into the adult lifestyle, rather than being a forced remedy reluctantly adopted to retard the aging process as the level of physical or mental health deteriorates.

Aging and the Motor and Sensory Systems

Introduction

In the previous section it was briefly noted that changes in the central nervous system occur with increasing chronological age. The most noticeable of these changes is a general slowing of motor, cognitive, and sensory processes. A number of alternative explanations for this observable phenomenon of 'slowing' have been proposed, including loss of neurons which are not replaced; decrease in size and weight of the brain; diseases such as manic-depressive psychosis, coronary heart disease, strokes, or depression; changes in neural impulse transmission; hormonal changes; oxygen deficiency resulting from cardiovascular disease or changes in fitness; changes in some or all of the sequential stages in information processing;[6] or loss of motivation or concentration.

Regardless of the cause or causes, there does appear to be a general decline in behavioral speed that is readily observed in psychomotor performance, in cognitive tasks, and in sensory and perceptual processes. This pattern is compounded when the required behavior becomes more complex. This occurs in abstract reasoning or when making rapid decisions while performing a motor task, such as in sport events, industrial jobs, or driving a car. This observable slowing can have a direct impact on a number of specific social behaviors and can lead to some characteristic behavioral reactions, many of which become generalized as stereotypes of the aged. For example, with advancing age there may be a slowing of speed, especially in complex tasks or movements, and a sacrifice of speed for accuracy. This 'cautiousness,' a generalized tendency to respond slowly or not at all because of the possible consequences of a mistake, occurs in many decision-making situations (Calhoun and Hutchison, 1981).

For many years it was suggested that this pattern of cautiousness was the result of older people being more rigid and conservative, or becoming more so with advancing age; but recent evidence suggests that they become more cautious in order to avoid mistakes. That is, cautiousness is a learned behavior in reaction to a neurobiological slowness. Regardless of the underlying mechanism, this behavioral slowing can offset the chances of survival when fast reaction is required (as in a traffic situation). It may also limit complex thinking because the mediating processes slow to the point where some of the elements, or even the goal of the task, may be forgotten (Birren et al., 1980:303). The following subsections indicate some of the motor and sensory changes that occur with age, and examine their impact on individual behavior, attitudes, social interaction, and interaction with the environment.

Motor Performance

Motor performance in a multitude of daily tasks (on the job, at home, while driving, or at leisure) depends on a complex process that involves perceiving and evaluating information from the sensory organs, storing and processing this information, and responding through the voluntary muscles (Welford, 1958, 1977, 1980a, 1980b). The most significant changes in motor performance with age are a loss of speed in decision making and a concomitant increase in reaction time. These changes are most evident when a complex decision is required and when the individual must respond rapidly. This loss is compounded if the situation is stressful (such as driving under dangerous conditions, or writing a test with implications for present or future employment).

Reaction time, which is the period from perception of a stimulus to reaction, is a complex phenomenon and not easily understood. It has been explained as a physical problem resulting from a number of possible physiological processes. These include an inevitable decline in signal strength as neurons and nerve cells die; an increase in reflex time for skeletal muscles; a loss of efficiency in central processing mechanisms wherein more time is required to monitor incoming signals (Simon and Pouraghabagher, 1978); and a general deterioration in the sensorimotor mechanisms. Cerella (1980:332) states that more complex information-processing tasks result in even greater performance decrements as one grows older. He suggests that this decrement involves two levels — a slight slowing of reaction time on sensorimotor tasks and a more severe slowing on tasks that involve mental processing. However, this physical decline may not be inevitable. For example, Birren et al. (1980:301) found that after a three-month training program, subjects showed improved speed on psychomotor tasks. Among adults, those who follow a regular exercise program may have faster reaction time than those who do not (Spirduso, 1980).

A loss of reaction time can be offset by changes in the strategy of performance, by practice (Grant et al., 1978), and by a high motivation to achieve at the required task. The most apparent change in strategy involves spending more time monitoring the input stimuli before a response is made. For example, the elderly become more cautious and demonstrate a desire for accuracy rather than speed in performance. This suggests that learning and practice of a task may offset the effects of slower reaction times, although the evidence that practice reduces reaction time is equivocal. However, not all situations permit unlimited reaction time and errors may result if sufficient time is not available. As Welford (1958:491) notes, the increase in traffic violations and in road and industrial accidents with age is attributed more to a slowing of the decision-making processes than to sensory or motor impairment. With unlimited time to perform a task, older people will perform about as well as they did when they were younger. In fact, with unlimited time to monitor stimuli, the older person may demonstrate greater accuracy than a younger person.

Given that this slowing appears to be a universal and to some extent an inevitable phenomenon (Gottsdanker, 1982; Salthouse and Somberg, 1982), how does it influence social behavior? If a job demands speed in decision making and in performance, then the older worker may be somewhat handicapped, more so than if the job requires merely physical strength. Although speed and accuracy in work may level off or decline slightly with age, experience, can compensate for the onset of slowness. Of those who cannot continue to perform, many voluntarily or involuntarily leave the job. This may create problems of unemployability, a loss of prestige, and a lower level of income because of a loss of seniority or a shift to a lower occupational level.

In the social domain, a slowing of reaction time and decision making, especially if accompanied by some of the sensory changes noted in the next section, may reduce the frequency, quality, and type of interaction with others and with the environment. That is, perception of the social world may change, and individuals may be perceived by others to be slow, old, or incompetent. This may lead to less social interaction and further sensory deprivation, resulting in emotional and behavioral problems such as loneliness, isolation, depression, and decreased mobility. In short, in situations where a fast reaction time is essential, most older people do not perform as well as they did when younger. This slowing, in turn, may directly or indirectly influence the frequency and quality of social interaction.

Sensory Processes

Introduction.   In order to interact with the physical environment and with other people, an individual must be able to send and receive information. This ability depends largely on sensory receptors, which have a minimum threshold that permits information to be received and transmitted to the brain. As one ages, this threshold increases and greater stimulation is needed in order to send information to the brain (Colavita, 1978).

This subsection examines the impact on the individual of biological changes with age in the threshold and function of the major sensory receptors and processors. These changes in efficiency may reduce the quality and quantity of information available to the organism. If the impairment is not severe, the organism may be able to compensate for the decrement by a variety of means. Some of these mechanisms include using a different sense modality to a greater extent (lip reading to compensate for a hearing impairment), intensifying (with a hearing aid) or correcting (with eyeglasses) the stimulus, and using experience to predict or identify the stimulus (knowing the shape of a stop sign). If two senses decline simultaneously, as vision and hearing often do late in life, the individual may be seriously limited in job performance, mobility, and general social interaction.

While many of the ramifications of sensory losses may appear obvious, it is essential to be aware of the impact of these changes on the individual, and to adjust our interactions to assist older individuals to continue a lifelong pattern of meaningful social relationships. It must be recognized that there are individual differences in the age of onset, and in the severity of and reaction to these decrements. By recognizing these differences, myths and stereotypes are less likely to be applied to all elderly persons.

Vision.   After middle age, structural and functional changes occur in the eye that may have an impact on social behavior (Fozard et al., 1977; Hoyer and Plude, 1980; Corso, 1981). These changes include a thickening of the lens and a decrease in the diameter of the pupil, both of which limit the amount of light reaching the retina; less flexibility in the lens (presbyopia), which decreases the ability to focus on objects at varying distances; a decrease in threshold adaptation to darkness, glare, and rapidly changing light levels; and a yellowing of the lens that filters out green, blue, and violet at the shorter wave-length end of the spectrum. In addition, loss or impairment of vision may be experienced by persons suffering from glaucoma (less than 5 percent of the population) or from some degree of cataract development (as much as 60 percent of the aged population).

As a result of these changes, an individual may require greater light intensity for reading and working, and may experience difficulty in adapting to changes in illumination when driving at dusk or when moving from well-lit to darkened areas. Some may also have difficulty reading road signs because of the glare in bright daylight or snow, and may be unable to perceive blue, green, and violet tones in the spectrum. As a result, the elderly person may have difficulty coordinating clothing colors or appreciating art or color television. While none of these changes are totally disabling, they can create problems and annoyances in daily living. For example, loss of color perception may influence aesthetic enjoyment of life; decreased visual acuity may prevent reading for work or pleasure; and a higher threshhold of light adaptation may prevent driving at night, or at all, thereby limiting mobility and increasing dependence on others.

Although visual losses (except in the extreme case of blindness) interfere less with social interaction than do hearing losses, conditions should be improved as much as possible in order to increase efficiency on the job, and to create a safer and more enjoyable environment elsewhere (Fozard, 1981). Despite the energy crisis which has led to the lowering of light levels, more illumination should be provided for the elderly in work and traffic areas. In addition, living environments need to be redesigned (for example, with increased illumination, reduced glare, larger lettering on signs and in books). In this way, the environment will be safer for older adults, they will be more efficient in processing information at home and at work, and they will maintain a greater interest in themselves and others.

Audition.   Along with vision, the auditory system is a major mode of receiving information from the environment. However, unlike visual problems that can be observed and more easily corrected, auditory impairment is less noticeable to oneself and to others. The older person may be unaware of an auditory deficit, and this may result in communication problems (Tamir, 1979). A major hearing problem is the progressive inability to hear higher frequency sounds in music and speech (presbycusis). This impairment, caused by the loss of fine hair cells in the inner ear, appears after about the age of 50 and is experienced more frequently by men, especially those who have had long exposure to industrial noise (Corso, 1977, 1981). As a result of this impairment the individual may have difficulty hearing certain consonants during conversation, especially when background noise is present (such as a radio, television, at parties, in crowds). The speaker may have to repeat the conversation or shout, thereby making the listener self-conscious and less likely to seek out or enjoy social interaction.

In a recent study, Norris and Cunningham (1981) found no significant relationship between bearing loss and frequency of interaction. However, they did suggest that hearing loss may lower the quality of interaction. Moreover, a hearing impairment may affect performance on the job, and the ability to interact safely and efficiently with the environment (for example, if one is unable to hear doorbells, telephones, or car horns). Presbycusis can create stress in social situations, inhibit communication, decrease the quality of social interaction, decrease the enjoyment of life (for example, if one misses the punchline in jokes), cause fear and embarrassment, and lead to depression (Warren et al., 1978). While hearing aids may provide partial compensation for hearing losses, the individual must resort to other means such as facing the speaker, lip reading, interpreting nonverbal communication (facial and hand gestures), and overcoming the fear and embarrassment of asking for information to be repeated (Fozard, 1981). If these compensating mechanisms are not used, hearing-impaired individuals run the risk of being labelled senile or antisocial if they do not respond to the spoken word. They may also misinterpret instructions or statements, and if their subsequent behavior is different from that expected, they may be labelled as senile or stubborn.

Taste, smell, pain, and touch. By about the age of 60, there is a higher taste threshhold (Murphy, 1979; Weiffenbach et al., 1982) for all four taste sensations: salt, sweet, bitter, and sour. In addition, there is a decreased saliva flow and a decrease in the number of taste buds (Engen, 1977). These changes may be compounded by smoking and by wearing dentures. Furthermore, a decline in absolute sensitivity to olfactory stimulation (ability to detect or identify odors) occurs with age (Schiffman et al., 1976; Schiffman, 1979; Schiffman and Pasternak, 1979; Corso, 1981; Schemper et al., 1981). Therefore, when changes in taste and smell decline concurrently, there may be a decrease in food intake, a decline in nutrition, and a loss of enjoyment in eating. For example, although Moore et al. (1982) found a minimal loss of sensitivity with age in sucrose taste thresholds, the thresholds were highly variable among the elderly. They suggested that those who experience a decline in sucrose threshold either might lose interest in certain foods or might compensate for the loss in sensitivity by greatly increasing their level of sucrose intake by eating foods with a high sugar content. Either of these adaptations may lead to dietary or medical problems.

In severe losses of taste and smell the individual may be unable to taste spoiled foods or to smell dangerous odors (Schiffman and Pasternak, 1979; Corso, 1981). Moreover, as Schemper et al. (1981) noted, some elderly persons not only have both a poor sense of smell and taste, but also weaker cognitive tools to identify odors. In short, from a behavioral perspective, changes in taste and smell may result in mealtime no longer being an enjoyable social or culinary experience. In addition, a person who is widowed and living alone may be less inclined to prepare food, especially if it no longer provides pleasure. This may lead to an improper or deficient diet, and to the onset of medical problems.

There appears to be a loss of sensitivity in touch and to vibration in some, but not all, parts of the body with advancing age (Kenshalo, 1977; Corso, 1981). Although complaints about pain seem to increase with age, the research evidence is unclear as to whether pain thresholds remain constant or decrease with age (Kenshalo, 1977; Harkins and Warner, 1980). Part of this confusion stems from a failure to separate the physiological variable of the pain threshold from the social and psychological elements of pain. Are observed age differences in pain perception related to the processing capacity of the central nervous system, to changes in the peripheral receptors, to the source of the pain, to the personality and motivation of the person experiencing the pain, to changes in cognitive processes interpreting the source and nature of the pain, or to a combination of some or all of these factors?

While pain thresholds may or may not increase with age, it appears that pain tolerance is at least partially related to motivational and cognitive factors; hence, no valid conclusions can be drawn concerning changes in pain threshold or pain tolerance with age. Some older persons may experience pain and may frequently report the presence of pain; others may experience pain but stoically live with it and not report its presence; others will not experience pain to any greater extent than younger people. For some, the social situation, the source of the pain, and the motivational and cognitive processes may influence whether pain is perceived or reported. Some individuals may complain even about minimal levels of pain in order to receive attention from others, particularly from their adult children.

Summary. Physiological changes with age in the sensory processes can have behavioral manifestations for the older person (Corso, 1981:201–19). A reduction in the efficiency of the sense modalities reduces the quantity and quality of information available. This in turn may reduce the ability and willingness of the individual to interact with the environment and with other people. In most cases the impairments experienced by the elderly are not severe, and the individual is able to compensate for the deficit through various forms of behavioral modification or rehabilitation (Corso, 1981:219–25).

Aging and Physical and Mental Health

Introduction

For many years interest in health and aging was based on a 'medical model' wherein the focus was primarily on the incidence, cause, treatment, and medical response to illness or disease among the elderly. This model also included the internal physiological and external physical changes in the organism that were influenced by personal health and environmental conditions. More recently, however, a number of journal and review articles (Shanas and Maddox, 1976; Aho, 1979; Siegler, 1980) and books (Kart et al., 1978; Hickey, 1980; Coburn, 1981; Wantz and Gay, 1981) have utilized a 'functional model' to study health and aging. The emphasis has been on describing and explaining how people cope with age-related chronic disabilities, how acute and chronic illnesses influence social behavior, and how the older person functions socially and psychologically when faced with increasing dependency because of physical or mental illness. This interest has resulted in a growing number of articles on the psychological and social limitations and capacities related to the objective state of health, on the economic and social aspects of health care, and on the impact of the perceived and objective state of health on participation in such domains as the family, work, and leisure.

One outcome of this research interest has been the debunking of the myth that the elderly are frail and sickly, and that they are incapable of performing tasks or participating in social life. This does not imply, however, that health is not a central concern for the elderly and a major factor in their quality of life. Rather, despite increasing longevity, changing social norms, and improved and more readily accessible health care, the physical, mental, and social well-being of the aging adult is intimately related to his or her personal reaction to the onset of acute and chronic disease and to the onset of varying degrees of disability. The sections that follow discuss the relationship between social participation and such health-related factors as acute illness, chronic illness, long-term disabilities, perceived state of health, utilization of the health care system, nutrition, sexuality, stress, and mental disorders.

It must be reiterated that the elderly are not a homogeneous group with respect to physical or mental health. Rather, there is a wide range of individual differences in the onset and severity of acute and chronic conditions, in the availability of and access to health care, and in the physical, social, emotional, and cognitive reactions to varying degrees of declining health. Some of these differences reflect former and current lifestyles, as well as environmental factors (for example, rural versus urban residence; pollution; amount of exercise or use of alcohol, tobacco, or drugs; or nutrition). Others are more directly related to heredity, and to achieved or ascribed characteristics such as sex, race, ethnicity, level of educational attainment, socioeconomic status, marital status, and income. For example, a recent survey in the United States found that over 62 percent of elderly Americans who were members of a racial or ethnic minority group viewed their personal health as only fair or poor. In contrast, only 37 percent of elderly white Americans rated their health status as fair or poor (Harris, 1981). Moreover, there is great variation in physical and mental health between the middle-aged, the recently retired, and the very old. Similarly, older women, in general, remain in general good health about five years longer than men (Marshall et al., 1982).

Health is not just a biological or medical concern, but also a significant personal and social concern. For example, with declining health, individuals can lose their independence, lose social roles, become isolated, experience economic hardship, be labelled or stigmatized (as 'frail,' 'sick,' 'disabled,' 'senile,' or 'obsolete'), change their self-perception, and be institutionalized. From the perspective of society, declining health leads to absenteeism, loss of productivity, and loss of experienced workers when disability forces an early retirement. In addition, the poor health of the elderly increases the dependency ratio, and the accompanying economic burden must be absorbed by those in the labor force. This in turn increases the cost of health care in the nation.[7] An age-related decline in health has an impact on both the individual and the society. Social scientists must be aware of the relationships between health, behavior, and aging, and must include personal health status as an independent and intervening variable in the social process of aging.

Physical Health, Aging, and Behavior

Acute and chronic conditions.[8]   The health of the elderly population is improving in most segments of most industrialized societies. This improvement has occurred because of advancements in lifelong nutrition, environmental and housing conditions, health standards, and health care. Nevertheless, even in the United States, it is estimated that approximately 86 percent of those over 65 years of age suffer from one or more chronic illnesses (Harris, 1978), a rate much higher than that found among younger people. In contrast, the elderly generally have a lower incidence of acute conditions. However, when acute conditions do occur among the elderly they may require a longer period of recovery,[9] and, when combined with a chronic illness, may sap the physical or mental reserves of the elderly individual. The onset of an apparently minor acute illness can have major consequences for the general health and adaptation of the older person.

Paul + Betty

The most prevalent chronic conditions that affect the daily physical health of older persons in the United States are arthritis (38 percent), hearing impairments (29 percent), vision impairments (20 percent), hypertension (20 percent), and heart conditions (20 percent). The major causes of death are coronary heart disease, cancer, and strokes (Harris, 1978). The poor, the nonwhite, and those with lower levels of education are more susceptible to poor health, particularly as they age. These subcultural differences seem to be related to nutritional problems, to lifestyle, to a lack of knowledge about health care, to inferior environmental conditions at work and in the home, and to a lack of access to medical care, often for economic reasons. While some of these subcultural conditions may be present for some of the elderly population, they have the greatest impact on those for whom these conditions have been present throughout the life cycle.

The impact on the individual of acute and chronic diseases or illnesses varies greatly, depending on the severity and duration of the illness, combined with the coping reaction of the individual. Most acute illnesses involve only temporary restrictions or changes in lifestyle. However, chronic conditions, which can range from minor aches and pains to long-term physical or mental disability, can severely restrict social interaction, mobility, job performance, the ability to care for oneself, and the fulfilling of family responsibilities.

A discouraging medical prognosis can dramatically alter lifestyles in the later years. A person's reaction to such a prognosis is a social and psychological process. This reaction may be positive, and involve preventing the chronic condition from changing a lifestyle to any appreciable degree; or it may be negative, and lead to 'giving up the fight to live,' because of an inability to tolerate pain, to be patient during the recovery period, to accept the changing self-image, to become dependent on others, or to cope with the physical and mental stress associated with the ailment (Hickey, 1980:15–17). Thus, the social reaction can range from little or no change in lifestyle, to some minor restrictions, to some degree of disability, to loss of independence, and, ultimately, to institutionalization.

According to Harris (1978), approximately 40 percent of the elderly in the United States are limited to some extent in carrying out their daily activities, and about 18 percent report that they have limited mobility because of a chronic condition. The chronic conditions causing the greatest restrictions are heart problems, diabetes, asthma, and arthritis. Gutman (1980) suggests that an independent lifestyle, even in the face of debilitating chronic conditions, can be maintained by the presence of a confidant, by assistance with shopping and domestic chores, by making transportation readily available, and by accessibility of needed services. Finally, as noted in chapter 3, most of the elderly population are not totally dependent; less than 10 percent are ever institutionalized in long-term care nursing homes.

In summary, despite a greater probability of chronic health problems with age, most older people function reasonably well in their daily activities. However, the onset of chronic and acute conditions does in some cases lead to a change in patterns of social participation. Some people may become increasingly or totally dependent on others, thereby severely curtailing their independence and mobility. Whether these changes occur, and to what degree, depends to a great extent on past and current personal styles of adapting and coping with physical stress, and on the level of social support and assistance from significant others in the family and community.

Perception of health, use of the health care system, and social behavior.
Despite the presence of diagnosed acute or chronic ailments, over 60 percent of
the elderly subjectively report that their health is good or excellent. These self-
perceptions correlate highly with objective physiological and medical evaluations. The self-ratings are more likely to be favorable for those with higher levels
of income and educational attainment (Ferraro, 1980; Graney and Zimmerman,
1980). Interestingly, Shanas et al., (1968) found that there were cross-cultural
differences in self-perceived health. They noted that if an illness is defined as
'normal' for the elderly in a nation, it is more likely to be accepted and ignored
when reporting the state of one's health. They found that Americans were more
concerned about the limitations imposed on them by illness than were British or
Danish citizens. With the onset of an illness, American respondents were more
likely to report their health as 'poor' or 'declining,' while those in the other
countries might consider the illness to be the norm for persons their age, and
therefore might not perceive or report a change in health.

There appears to be a relationship between a positive view of one's health
and higher levels of social involvement. For example, Graney and Zimmerman
(1980) found that favorable self-reports of health were positively related to a
higher degree of involvement in general activity, sexual activity, hobbies, clubs
and voluntary organizations, with friends. In short, the adaptive behavior to
changing health is influenced by self-perception. Just as age is socially defined,
so too may health status be socially defined by the individual. If the personal and
social meanings of the symptoms portray a composite picture of 'functional
adequacy' (Hickey, 1980:52), then perceived health status will be reported as good
or excellent. This perception is influencd by the level of health expectation for
persons of a particular chronological age.

Perceived health status is also influenced by the reaction of significant others, particularly by those in the medical profession. At present, health care
systems, although used more by the elderly than the young, are designed more
for treating acute rather than chronic or degenerative diseases. In addition, few
medical personnel at any level are trained for, or specialize in, the care of older
patients. Moreover, some health care personnel have negative attitudes about
working with elderly patients. If this negative attitude is perceived by elderly
patients (for example, if medical personnel appear to avoid them or to show little
interest in their condition), they may come to view their situation as hopeless.

Finally, quality and availability of medical care for the elderly varies greatly
from nation to nation and from community to community. For example, rural
areas or the central cores of large cities may lack physicians and facilities to
adequately serve the predominant clientele in the area, namely, the elderly. In
short, it appears that medical and sociocultural factors interact to influence both
actual and perceived health. A positive perception may be a significant factor in
the social and psychological adjustment of chronically or acutely ill individuals.

Nutrition.   Changes in diet may occur in the later years for physiological reasons, such as denture problems, diminished senses of taste and smell, and
problems in digesting certain foods. However, a number of situational factors
(such as widowhood or lack of income) may also intervene to change the diet of
an elderly person, thereby leading to potential health or social problems (Weg,
1977).

Although the individual nutritional needs of older persons can vary greatly
according to their biochemical processes and energy expenditure patterns, a
balanced diet is essential. Yet older people may dislike preparing meals and

eating alone; they may have insufficient income to pay for essential foods, especially during times of inflation; they may be less mobile and therefore unable to shop; and they may be susceptible to fad diets that are advertised as nutritious and efficient.

These factors may lead to changes in eating habits, resulting in lower energy reserves or greater susceptibility to illness. It is for this reason that many community service agencies now make an effort to monitor the nutritional status of elderly people, especially the very old who live alone (Wantz and Gay, 1981:289–93). One of the most successful programs is 'Meals-On-Wheels,' where at least one nutritious hot meal per day is delivered to the home by a volunteer. In addition, the volunteer usually visits with the recipient while the meal is eaten. In this way mealtime regains some meaning and pleasure as a setting for social interaction.

Sexuality. Although formerly a taboo subject, the study of the sexual interests, needs, and behavior of the older person has increased dramatically since the so-called sexual revolution began in the late 1960s. Just as premarital sex became a major interest of scholars in many disciplines, so too did the sexuality and sexual behavior of the aged. (Solnick, 1978; Comfort, 1980; Corby and Solnick, 1980; Ludeman, 1981; Szasz, 1981; Wharton, 1981; Thomas, 1982).[10] Most men and women are physiologically capable of engaging in sex into their 80s or 90s. However, there are individual differences in interest and actual sexual behavior, often owing to social, cultural, or psychological factors (Roff and Klemmack, 1979). Sexual interest and behavior in the later years often parallels earlier patterns; that is, those who were more active earlier in life are generally more interested in being active in the later years.

It is difficult to determine how many older adults engage in sex, and how frequently, because many refuse to discuss the topic. However, it appears that cultural norms and attitudes are changing, with a concomitant increase in the number of older adults who report that they are sexually active. Those most likely to be active are those in good physical health, those who have a high sense of esteem or self-identity, those who are happily married, those who have continued a high level of sexual activity throughout adulthood, and those who live independently in a noninstitutionalized setting. In fact, a current dilemma faced by nursing-home personnel is whether and how to provide for the sexual needs of older residents.

Mental health and behavior

Contrary to the prevailing myth, the majority of old people are not senile,[11] nor are they mentally ill. In fact, it has been estimated that only about 15 percent[12] of the North American population over 65 experience any form of diagnosed mental illness, with less than 5 percent of these being institutionalized. Nevertheless, this time of life represents one of the most difficult periods of mental and emotional adjustment in the life cycle (Schwartz, 1975; Butler and Lewis, 1977; Birren and Sloane, 1980). This period is more difficult than others because it is compounded by existing lifelong physical and mental concerns that may become more pronounced or salient in old age; because individuals experience a number of personal crises to which they must react (retirement, widowhood, or institutionalization); because it is seen as a time of physical, social, psychological, and emotional loss; and because they may no longer have the support and assistance of personal friends and loved ones during crisis events.

There are three general categories of mental health that pertain to the elderly, and each represents a serious problem for the individual and for society. Harris (1978) has estimated that there may be as many as seven million Americans living under one of these conditions, thereby making them more susceptible to mental illness. First, there are transitory, periodic, emotional reactions such as depression, anxiety, fear, and frustration that may result from personal feelings about adjusting to old age. These include a noticeable decline in vision, hearing, or energy that leads to changes in leisure patterns and social interaction. They may also occur in reaction to specific life events such as retirement, the death of a spouse, or the departure of the children from the home. The effect of these events on the individual appears to be exaggerated by poverty, declining physical health or serious illness, and social isolation.

In addition to individual crises, collective crisis events in the community may be more stressful for the elderly than for other age groups (Miller, 1980; Chiriboga, 1982). For example, widespread poverty or unemployment or the occurrence of a natural disaster, events that have an impact on the mental health of the total community, may be more traumatic for the elderly, and may lead to temporary or permanent mental health problems. In short, individual or collective crisis events can initiate emotional or mental stress that can lead to anxiety states, depression, and fear.

A second category of mental health problems encountered by the elderly are those labelled as functional disorders (Hickey, 1980; Wantz and Gay, 1981). Harris (1978) estimates that 13 to 15 percent of those over 65 years of age will experience some type of functional disorder before they die, such as schizophrenia, affective psychoses (manic-depressive reactions, or melancholia), psychotic depressive reactions, or paranoid states (irrational fears). These disorders result from a combination of many factors, such as irrational or excessive reactions to crisis events, social isolation after the death of a spouse, or personal reaction to a chronic physical illness. These conditions are also likely to be triggered by an inappropriate emotional reaction to stress related to personal experiences, by long-standing emotional or personality problems, or, by inappropriate individual coping or adapting strategies. These disorders do not involve an impairment of brain function, but they do require treatment and sometimes hospitalization when they influence daily behavior negatively.

A third category of mental illness is an organic disorder wherein brain damage occurs, either because of a hardening of the arteries in the brain or because the brain cells atrophy or become diseased (senile dementia). For example, Alzheimer's disease is responsible for about 75 percent of the senility characterized by declining memory, judgment, and learning ability. It is also often accompanied by severe personality changes. To date, there is no known cure for this progressive, fatal disease that is thought to result from cell damage in the hippocampus area of the brain cortex. While the progression of some of these organic disorders may be slowed through drug treatment, ultimately most individuals are no longer able to care for themselves or to interact socially. Hence, institutionalization becomes necessary.

Despite the need for treatment (for functional disorders) or hospitalization (for organic disorders), the mental health system is underused by the elderly for a variety of reasons. These include the reluctance of children to send their parents for professional treatment; a fear that real improvements are unlikely; a societal belief that health care resources should not be 'wasted' on the elderly; a tendency of the elderly to view their problems as being physical rather than psychological; and a lack of knowledge about the availability of services to treat the mental and emotional concerns of older adults (Gatz et al., 1980:5–18). However, if the services were used more extensively, it would soon become apparent that the health care system in most nations is inadequate, inappropriate, and expensive. This might further discourage old people or their families from seeking assistance in coping with mental and emotional illness.

Mental health is greatly influenced by stress (Renner and Birren, 1980). Some individuals seem to be 'stress-prone' (Lowenthal and Chiriboga, 1975), and to be highly susceptible to stress at any age. Moreover, earlier stressors seem to be predictive of later stressors (Chiriboga and Thurnher, 1981). The social or physical environment may also induce stress. Recently, Chiriboga and Thurnher (1981) suggested that there are three levels of stressors: the micro, the mini, and the macro. The micro-stressors involve daily occurrences (for example, lost keys, a bottle or can that will not open, or running out of shampoo in the shower); the mini-stressors are perceived problems within life events (stress at work) and transitions between events (children leaving home, retirement, loss of job, or widowhood); while the macro-stressors are characterized by major societal events that impinge on the individual, partly as a result of collective stress on the social system (an economic depression, a war, or an earthquake). Palmore et al. (1979), however, have found that many potentially stressful transition events have less serious long-term outcomes than is commonly assumed.

It is the ability or lack of ability to cope with stressful events at all three levels that significantly influences mental health in the later years (Birren and Moore, 1975; Chiriboga and Cutler, 1980; Horowitz and Wilner, 1980; Stagner, 1981; McCrae, 1982). In general, it appears that adult women across all age categories are more stressed than men, and are generally less able to cope with the stress. For elderly women, the major sources of stress appear to be the social isolation following widowhood and an inability to adjust to retirement (Levy, 1981). McCrae (1982) suggests that differences in coping with life events can be examined by the type of stress encountered rather than by age per se. However, he did find that older persons are less likely to employ hostile reactions or escapist fantasies in coping with the stress of life events.

While some individuals strive to avoid stress, others seek stress. In fact, behavioral problems in later life for those with a high need for stimulation may result from boredom and a lack of intellectual or physical stimulation. Unfortunately, very little is known about why changes in life events induce short-term or long-term stressful reactions among some older persons. Instruments are being developed to measure not only the degree of stress inherent in certain life events (Holmes and Rahe, 1967; Horowitz and Wilner, 1980), but also the coping strategies employed by various groups of individuals (Horowitz and Wilner, 1980). From what little is known, it appears that women, the less educated, those with lower incomes and socioeconomic status, and members of some minority groups may be more susceptible to stress. Regardless of these subcultural differences (Gutmann, 1980), the mental health needs of the elderly appear to warrant greater attention since the incidence of suicides, alcoholism, and drug abuse among the elderly appears to be increasing in North America.

In summary, the mental and emotional health of the elderly needs to be understood more completely by scientists and better serviced by the health care system (Wells, 1982). It appears that most mental health problems evolve from the interaction of both environmental and personal factors, which can be compounded by long-lasting personality or physical characteristics that create difficulties in adapting to stressful events later in life. Among the factors that may precipitate an emotional problem are living alone; loss of physical health, which restricts activity and mobility; loss of self-esteem following a heart attack; forced retirement; loss of income; death of a spouse or close friend; marital unhappiness; sickness of a spouse; and a forced change in the place of residence. While any one of these factors may be sufficient to cause an emotional problem, in combination they can be traumatic and lead to functional disorders. For those who are poor, socially isolated, less educated, or in poor health, when a potentially stressful event occurs the severity of mental illness can be quite pronounced and can lead to clinical depression. Most older adults will not become senile or experience a diagnosed mental illness. Nevertheless, for those who do, there is a need to provide adequate counselling and treatment to stem the increasing incidence of functional disorders, suicides, alcoholism, and drug abuse among the elderly population.

Summary and Conclusions

This chapter has examined the impact on social, emotional, and cognitive behavior of changes with age in physical structure; in physiological, sensory, and motor processes; and in perceived and objective physical and mental health. These changes in the physical systems of the organism affect not only the individual but also how others interact with him or her, and how society reacts to those who lose their independence and mobility. This chapter has discussed some of the physical, social, and psychological outcomes of regular exercise, adequate nutrition, and stress in the middle and later years of life.

Based on the research evidence presented in this chapter, it can be concluded that:

1. After early adulthood, the physical and psychological systems of the human organism become less and less efficient in perceiving, processing, and reacting to stimuli in the physical and social environment. This loss of efficiency can influence social, emotional, and cognitive behavior in the later years. Moreover, this loss of efficiency can be compounded by declining physical or mental health.

2. There is variation within and between older individuals in the rate and degree of change in the physical and psychological systems. In effect, most individuals, at least until very late in life, do not experience functional losses that seriously change or influence their social, physical, or cognitive behavior.

3. External visible changes with age may influence how an older individual perceives himself or herself as well as how others perceive and interact with the individual.

4. After adolescence, the frequency and type of involvement in physical activity during leisure declines with age, especially among women and among those with lower levels of educational attainment.

5. Exercise is beneficial to physical and mental health for persons of all ages. A lack of regular, vigorous exercise may hasten the onset of physiological aging processes.

6. From the perspective of the aging individual, an increase in the level of physical fitness improves physical and mental health. It may also lead to a faster and more complete recovery from some diseases, to increased

longevity, to a longer period of independence, and to a higher quality of life.

7. From the perspective of society, a more physically active adult population may increase productivity and lower the health care costs of a nation.

8. Adults over 60 years of age can be trained to high levels of fitness and performance by graduated and supervised programs of walking, running, and swimming.

9. With advancing age there is a general slowing of motor, cognitive, and sensory processes. This is normally reflected in a loss of speed in decision making and a concomitant increase in reaction time.

10. Given sufficient motivation, practice and time to perform a task, older people will generally perform about as well as they did in when they were younger.

11. Structural and functional changes in vision and audition, especially if they occur at about the same time, may lower the quality of interpersonal interaction, may reduce the quantity and quality of information available to the individual, may lower job performance, and may reduce the ability to interact safely and efficiently with the physical environment.

12. Although most older people function reasonably well in their daily activities, the onset of chronic or long-term acute health conditions may lead to a change in interpersonal interaction and in patterns of participation in various social institutions.

13. The adaptive reaction to a changing health status is influenced by the individual's self-perception of health status, and by the reaction of significant others (if they are labelled or perceived as sick, infirm, dependent, or incompetent).

14. Contrary to common belief, the majority of old people are not senile or mentally ill. However, some older people experience a decline in mental health, and may be classified in one of three general categories. First, they may be subject to periodic emotional reactions such as depression, anxiety, or fear. Second, they may experience functional disorders such as schizophrenia, affective psychoses, or psychotic depressive reactions. Third, and most seriously, they may be susceptible to organic disorders wherein brain damage occurs (senile dementia or Alzheimer's disease). While the prognosis for the first two categories is positive if treatment begins early, the prognosis for organic disorders is poor, and ultimately the individual may need to be institutionalized.

Notes

1. This does not imply that gross behavior changes do not occur because of organic deterioration or the reaction to physically or mentally stressful events. Rather, it suggests that, contrary to the prevailing myth, most elderly people do not encounter such problems. In fact, you will recall that less than 10 percent of the elderly are ever institutionalized, and, when they are, it is most often very late in life.

2. One measure of this cardio-respiratory efficiency in physical working capacity (PWC) is maximum oxygen intake, which is sometimes referred to as aerobic power. This measurement indicates the rate at which oxygen is moved from the atmosphere to the

working muscles and tissues, including those used by the heart and the respiratory mechanisms. The maximum oxygen intake can be determined by having an individual work to exhaustion (a maximal test on a treadmill or stationary bicycle), or by predicting the value from submaximal exercise tests in a laboratory or field setting (Shephard, 1978:85–107; Montoye, 1982; Cunningham et al., forthcoming).

3. This perspective is somewhat similar to the exchange theory of aging, wherein individuals attempt to minimize the costs and maximize the rewards when determining how to spend their leisure time.

4. For example, the National Senior Sports Association (1900 M St. N.W., Washington, D.C.) was created in 1980 for men and women over 50 years of age. This organization facilitates group travel to participate in organized recreational or competitive sports, or to attend spectator events with age peers. Similarly, in the United States there are now regional, state, and national 'Senior Olympic' competitions for men and women in five-year age categories (55 to 59, 60 to 64, 65 to 69, 70 to 74, 75 to 79, etc.). These competitions include 'skill' events (archery, badminton, free-throw basketball, bowling, casting, horseshoes, etc.) and 'Olympic' events (handball, racquetball, squash, tennis, walking, bicycle races, swimming, track and field events, etc.).

5. Fluid intelligence refers to intellectual development in perceiving, reasoning, and abstracting due primarily to biological factors. It reflects the functioning of neurological structures.

6. Birren et al. (1980:293) note that there can be changes with age in all five information processing stages that act between stimulus acquisition and the response. These include peripheral processing, central processing, sensory storage (iconic memory of visual events), short-term memory, and long-term memory.

7. For example, in 1975 approximately 30 percent of the national health care expenditures in the United States were for the elderly, who made up only about 10 percent of the population (Harris, 1978).

8. 'Acute' conditions are of a limited duration (such as flu or colds). 'Chronic' conditions persist over time and may be treated to reduce symptoms, pain, or trauma, but are less likely to be cured (heart disease, cancer, diabetes, or arthritis).

9. For example, in Canada, the average hospital confinement is 25.2 days for those over 65 years of age; the national average for all age groups is 11.3 days.

10. Biologists, psychologists, sociologists, social workers, and medical personnel have studied such topics as sexuality and aging; sexual identity in the later years; the physiology of sex and age; sexual liberation; sex and the institutionalized elderly; love in later life; male versus female differences among the elderly in needs, interests, and activity; and sexual problems unique to the elderly.

11. Senility, or senile dementia, refers to chronic brain damage which is caused by circulatory problems such as hardening of the cerebrovascular arteries, or to disease states in the brain (Alzheimer's disease). When the brain cells do not receive sufficient oxygen and nutrients, they atrophy and die. Senility should not be confused with forgetfulness or with functional disorders such as depression, anxiety, or paranoid reactions.

12. This percentage is only an estimate. It is probably slightly higher, since diagnostic services and counselling for the elderly are generally inadequate. Moreover, many of the elderly are unable or unwilling to seek professional help.

References

Adams, G. and H. deVries. 'Physiological Effects of an Exercise Training Regimen Upon Women Aged 52 to 79,' *Journal of Gerontology*, 28(1/1973), 50–55.

Aho, W. 'Participation of Senior Citizens in the Swine Flu Inoculation Program: An Analysis of Health Belief Model Variables In Preventative Health Behavior,' *Journal of Gerontology*, 34(2/1979), 201–08.

Anderson, H. et al. 'Sport and Games in Denmark in the Light of Sociology,' *Acta Sociologica*, 2(1956–57), 1–28.

Birch, F. 'Leisure Patterns, 1973 and 1977,' *Population Trends*, 17(1979), 2–8.

Birren, J. et al. 'Behavioral Slowing with Age: Causes, Organization and Consequences,' pp. 293–308 in L. Poon (ed.). *Aging in the 1980s: Psychological Issues*. Washington, D.C.: American Psychological Association, 1980.

Birren, J. and J. Moore (eds.). *The Relation of Stress and Age: A Selected Bibliography*. Los Angeles: Andrus Gerontology Center, University of Southern California Press, 1975.

Birren, J. and K.W. Schaie (eds.). *Handbook of the Psychology of Aging*. New York: Van Nostrand Reinhold, 1977.

Birren, J. and B. Sloane (eds.). *Handbook of Aging and Mental Health*. Englewood Cliffs, N.J.: Prentice-Hall, 1980.

Boothby, J. 'Experience of Physical Education and Its Influence on Later Sports Activity: A Study in North-East England,' *Durham and Newcastle Research Review*, 9(Spring, 1980), 57–66.

Butler, R. 'Public Interest Report No. 23: Exercise, the Neglected Therapy,' *The International Journal of Aging and Human Development*, 8(2/1977–78), 193–95.

Butler, R. and M. Lewis. *Aging and Mental Health*. St. Louis: C.V. Mosby, 1977.

Calhoun, R. and S. Hutchison. 'Decision-Making in Old Age: Cautiousness and Rigidity,' *International Journal of Aging and Human Development*, 13(2/1981), 89–98.

Canada Fitness Survey. *Canada's Fitness: Preliminary Findings of the 1981 Survey*. Ottawa: Ministry of Fitness and Amateur Sport, 1982.

Carroll, J. and S. Maxwell. 'Individual Differences in Cognitive Abilities,' pp. 603–40 in M. Rosensweig and L. Park (eds.). *Annual Review of Psychology*, Volume 30. Palo Alto: Annual Reviews, Inc., 1979.

Cerella, J. et al. 'Age and the Complexity Hypothesis,' pp. 332–40, in L. Poon (ed.). *Aging in the 1980s: Psychological Issues*. Washington, D.C.: American Psychological Association, 1980.

Charness, N. 'Aging and Skilled Problem Solving,' *Journal of Experimental Psychology: General*, 110(1/1981), 21–38.

Chiriboga, D. 'An Examination of Life Events as Possible Antecedents to Change,' *Journal of Gerontology*, 37(5/1982), 595–601.

Chiriboga, D. and L. Cutler. 'Stress and Adaptation: Life Span Perspectives,' pp. 347–62 in L. Poon (ed.). *Aging in the 1980s: Psychological Issues*. Washington, D.C.: American Psychological Association, 1980.

Chiriboga, D. and M. Thurnher. 'Antecedents of Change In Adulthood,' paper presented at the annual meeting of the Gerontological Society of America, Toronto, November 1981.

Clarke, H. (ed.). 'Individual Differences, Their Nature, Extent and Significance,' *Physical Fitness Research Digest*, 3(4/1973), 1–12.

Clarke, H. (ed.). 'Exercise and Aging,' *Physical Fitness Research Digest*, 7(2/1977), 1–16.

Clement, F. 'Longitudinal and Cross-Sectional Assessments of Age Changes in Physical Strength as Related to Sex, Social Class and Mental Ability,' *Journal of Gerontology*, 29(4/1974), 423–29.

Coburn, D. et al. *Health and Canadian Society: Sociological Perspectives*. Toronto: Fitzhenry and Whiteside, 1981.

Colavita, F. *Sensory Changes in the Elderly*. Springfield, Ill.: Charles C. Thomas, 1978.

Comfort, A. 'Sexuality In Later Life,' pp. 885–92 in J. Birren and R. Sloane (eds.). *Handbook of Mental Health and Aging*. Englewood Cliffs, N.J.: Prentice-Hall, 1980.

Conrad, C. 'When You're Young at Heart,' *Aging*, (April 1976), 11.

Corby, N. and R. Solnick. 'Psychosocial and Physiological Influences on Sexuality in the Older Adult,' pp. 893–921 in J. Birren and R. Sloane (eds.). *Handbook of Mental Health and Aging*. Englewood Cliffs, N.J.: Prentice-Hall, 1980.

Corso, J. 'Auditory Perception and Communication,' pp. 535–53 in J. Birren and K.W. Schaie (eds.). *Handbook of the Psychology of Aging*. New York: Van Nostrand Reinhold, 1977.

Corso, J. *Aging Sensory Systems and Perception*. New York: Praeger Publishers, 1981.

Csikszentmihalyi, M. *Beyond Boredom and Anxiety*. San Francisco: Jossey-Bass, 1975.

Cunningham, D. et al. 'Determinants of Self-Selected Walking Pace Across Age 19 to 66 Years,' *Journal of Gerontology*, forthcoming.

deVries, H. 'Physiology of Exercise and Aging,' pp. 257–76 in D. Woodruff and J. Birren (eds.). *Aging: Scientific Perspectives and Social Issues*. New York: Van Nostrand Reinhold, 1975.

deVries, H. 'Physiology of Exercise,' pp. 79–109 in F. Landry and W. Orban (eds.). *Physical Activity and Human Well-Being*. Miami: Symposia Specialists, 1978.

Dumazedier, J. 'Report to a Symposium on Sport and Age,' pp. 298–99 in O. Grupe et al. (eds.). *Sport In The Modern World – Chances and Problems*. Berlin: Springer-Verlag, 1973.

Elsayed, M. et al. 'Intellectual Differences of Adult Men Related to Age and Physical Fitness Before and After an Exercise Program,' *Journal of Gerontology*, 35(3/1980), 383–87.

Engen, T. 'Taste and Smell,' pp. 554–61 in J. Birren and K.W. Schaie (eds.). *Handbook of the Psychology of Aging*. New York: Van Nostrand Reinhold, 1977.

Fasting, K. *Physical Activity in Leisure Time: Factors Predicting Participation*. Oslo: Norges Idrettshogskole, No. 62, 1979.

Ferraro, L. 'Self-Ratings of Health Among the Old and the Old-Old,' *Journal of Health and Social Behavior*, 21(4/1980), 377–83.

Foner, A. 'Ascribed and Achieved Bases of Stratification,' pp. 219–42 in A. Inkeles et al. (eds.). *Annual Review of Sociology*. Volume 5. Palo Alto: Annual Reviews Inc., 1979.

Fozard, J. 'Person-Environment Relationships in Adulthood: Implications for Human Factors Engineering,' *Human Factors*, 23(1/1981), 7–27.

Fozard, J. et al. 'Visual Perception and Communication,' pp. 497–534 in J. Birren and K.W. Schaie (eds.). *Handbook of the Psychology of Aging*. New York: Van Nostrand Reinhold, 1977.

Frolkis, V. 'Aging of the Autonomic Nervous System,' pp. 177–89 in J. Birren and K.W. Schaie (eds.). *Handbook of the Psychology of Aging*. New York: Van Nostrand Reinhold, 1977.

Gatz, M. et al. 'The Mental Health System and the Older Adult,' pp. 5–18 in L. Poon (ed.). *Aging in the 1980s: Psychological Issues*. Washington, D.C.: American Psychological Association, 1980.

Gottsdanker, R. 'Age and Simple Reaction Time,' *Journal of Gerontology*, 37(3/1982), 342–48.

Graney, M. and R. Zimmerman. 'Health Self-Report Correlates Among Older People In National Random Sample Data,' *Mid-American Review of Sociology*, 5(2/1980), 47–59.

Grant, E. et al. 'Incentive and Practice in the Psychomotor Performance of the Elderly,' *Journal of Gerontology*, 33(3/1978), 413–15.

Gutman, G. 'The Elderly at Home and in Retirement Housing: A Comparative Study of Health Problems, Functional Difficulties and Support Service Needs,' pp. 189–200 in V. Marshall (ed.). *Aging In Canada: Social Perspectives*. Don Mills: Fitzhenry and Whiteside, 1980.

Gutmann, D. 'Observations on Culture and Mental Health in Later Life,' pp. 429–46 in J. Birren and B. Sloane (eds.). *Handbook of Mental Health and Aging*. Englewood Cliffs, N.J.: Prentice-Hall, Inc., 1980.

Harkins, S. and M. Warner. 'Age and Pain,' pp. 121–31 in C. Eisdorfer (ed.). *Annual Review of Gerontology and Geriatrics*. Volume 1. New York: Springer Publishing Co., 1980.

Harris, C. (ed.). *Fact Book on Aging: A Profile of America's Older Population*. Washington, D.C.: National Council on the Aging, 1978.

Harris, L. et al. *Aging in the Eighties: America in Transition*. Washington, D.C.: National Council on the Aging, 1981.

Harris, R. and L. Frankel (eds.). *Guide to Fitness After Fifty*. New York: Plenum Press, 1977.

Hickey, T. *Health and Aging*. Monterey: Brooks/Cole Publishing Co., 1980.

Holmes, T. and R. Rahe. 'The Social Readjustment Rating Scale,' *Journal of Psychosomatic Research*, 11(2/1967), 213–18.

Horowitz, M. and N. Wilner. 'Life Events, Stress and Coping,' pp. 363–74 in L. Poon (ed.). *Aging in the 1980s: Psychological Issues*. Washington, D.C.: American Psychological Association, 1980.

Hoyer, W. and D. Plude. 'Attentional and Perceptual Processes in the Study of Cognitive Aging,' pp. 227–38 in L. Poon (ed.). *Aging in the 1980s: Psychological Issues*. Washington, D.C.: American Psychological Association, 1980.

Kart, C. et al. *Aging and Health: Biologic and Social Perspectives*. Reading, Mass.: Addison-Wesley, 1978.

Kenshalo, D. 'Age Changes in Touch, Vibration, Temperature, Kinesthesis, and Pain Sensitivity,' pp. 562–79 in J. Birren and W.K. Schaie (eds.). *Handbook of the Psychology of Aging*. New York: Van Nostrand Reinhold, 1977.

Kenyon, G. 'The Significance of Physical Activity as a Function of Age, Sex, Education and Socio-economic Status of Northern United States Adults,' *International Review of Sport Sociology*, 1(1966), 41–54.

Kiviaho, P. 'Physical Activity of the Finnish Adult Population,' pp. 52–69 in *Yearbook of the Research Institute of Physical Culture and Health*, Jyvaskyla, Finland, 1977.

Kreipel, J. 'Sports Activity of the Population of Czechslovakia as Shown by the Results of Two Country-Wide Surveys Carried Out in the Years 1967 and 1973,' *International Review of Sport Sociology*, 12(4/1977), 69–76.

Levy, S. 'The Aging Woman: Developmental Issues and Mental Health Needs,' *Professional Psychology*, 12(1/1981), 92–102.

Lowenthal, M. and D. Chiriboga. 'Responses to Stress,' pp. 146–62 in M. Lowenthal et al. (eds.). *Four Stages of Life: A Comparative Study of Women and Men Facing Transitions*. San Francisco: Jossey-Bass, 1975.

Ludeman, K. 'The Sexuality of the Older Person: Review of the Literature,' *The Gerontologist*, 21(2/1981), 203–8.

Marshall, V. et al., 'Concerns About Parental Health,' in E. Markson (ed.). *Women and Aging*. Lexington, Mass.: Lexington Books, 1982.

McCrae, R. 'Age Differences in the Use of Coping Mechanisms,' *Journal of Gerontology*, 37 (4/1982), 454–60.

McPherson, B. 'Psychological Effects of an Exercise Program for Post-Cardiac and Normal Adult Men,' M.A. thesis, University of Western Ontario, 1965.

McPherson, B. 'Aging and Involvement in Physical Activity: A Sociological Perspective,' pp. 111–25 in F. Landry and W. Orban (eds.). *Physical Activity and Human Well-Being*. Volume 1. Miami: Symposia Specialists, 1978.

McPherson, B. and C. Kozlik. 'Canadian Leisure Patterns by Age: Disengagement, Continuity or Ageism?' pp. 113–22 in V. Marshall (ed.). *Aging in Canada: Social Perspectives*. Don Mills: Fitzhenry and Whiteside, 1980.

McPherson, B. et al. 'Psychological Effects of an Exercise Program for Post-Infarct and Normal Adult Men,' *Journal of Sports Medicine and Physical Fitness*, 7(2/1967), 95–102.

Michael, E. 'Stress Adaptation Through Exercise,' *Research Quarterly*, 28(1/1957), 50–54.

Miller, F. 'Measurement and Monitoring of Stress in Communities,' pp. 383–88 in L. Poon (ed.). *Aging in the 1980s: Psychological Issues*. Washington, D.C.: American Psychological Association, 1980.

Milton, B. *Social Status and Leisure Time Activities: National Survey Findings for Adult Canadians*. Canadian Sociology and Anthropology Association Monograph Series, B. Bernier and J. Rainville (eds.). Montreal, 1975.

Montoye, H. 'Age and Oxygen Utilization During Submaximal Treadmill Exercise in Males,' *Journal of Gerontology*, 37(4/1982), 396–402.

Moore, L. et al. 'Sucrose Taste Thresholds: Age-Related Differences,' *Journal of Gerontology*, 37(1/1982), 64–69.

Murphy, C. 'The Effect of Age on Taste Sensitivity,' in S. Han and D. Coons (eds.). *Special Senses in Aging: A Current Biological Assessment*. Ann Arbor: Institute of Gerontology, University of Michigan, 1979.

Norris, M. and D. Cunningham. 'Social Impact of Hearing Loss in the Aged,' *Journal of Gerontology*, 36(6/1981), 727–29.

Ostrow, A. 'Physical Activity as It Relates to the Health of the Aged,' pp. 41–56 in N. Datan and N. Lohmann (eds.). *Transitions of Aging*. New York: Academic Press, 1980.

Ostrow, A. 'Age Role Stereotyping: Implications for Physical Activity Participation,' in G. Rowles and R. Ohta (eds.). *Aging and Milieu: Environmental Perspectives On Growing Old*. New York: Academic Press, 1982.

Ostrow, A. et al. 'Age Role Expectations and Sex Role Expectations for Selected Sport Activities,' *Research Quarterly*, 52(2/1981), 216–27.

Palmore, E. et al. 'Stress and Adaptation in Later Life,' *Journal of Gerontology*, 34(6/1979), 841–51.

Perrin, B. *Physical Activity Patterns in Ontario*. Toronto: Ministry of Culture and Recreation, 1981.

President's Council on Physical Fitness and Sports. *A Synopsis of the National Conference on Fitness and Aging*. Washington, D.C., 1982.

Renner, V. and J. Birren. 'Stress: Physiological and Psychological Mechanisms,' pp. 310–36 in J. Birren and R. Sloane (eds.). *Handbook of Mental Health and Aging*. Englewood Cliffs, N.J.: Prentice-Hall, 1980.

Renson, R. 'The Dynamics of the Sports Socialization Process - Some Belgian Data,' pp. 21–33

in *Seminar on Sport For Young School Leavers*. Stockholm: Swedish Sports Federation, 1978.

Roff, L. and D. Klemmack. 'Sexual Activity Among Older Persons,' *Research on Aging*, 1(3/1979), 389–99.

Salthouse, T. and B. Somberg. 'Isolating the Age Deficit in Speeded Performance,' *Journal of Gerontology*, 37(1/1982), 59–63.

Schemper, T. et al. 'Odor Identification in Young and Elderly Persons: Sensory and Cognitive Limitations,' *Journal of Gerontology*, 36(4/1981), 446–52.

Schiffman, S. 'Changes in Taste and Smell with Age: Psychophysical Aspects,' pp. 227–46 in J. Ordy and K. Brizzee (eds.). *Sensory Systems and Communication in the Elderly*. New York: Raven Press, 1979.

Schiffman, S. and M. Pasternak. 'Decreased Discrimination of Food Odors in the Elderly,' *Journal of Gerontology*, 34(1/1979), 73–79.

Schiffman, S. et al. 'Thresholds of Food Odors in the Elderly,' *Experimental Aging Research*, 2(5/1976), 389–98.

Schwartz, A. (ed.). *Psychological Adjustment to Aging: A Selected Bibliography*. Los Angeles: Andrus Gerontology Center, University of Southern California, 1975.

Shanas, E. et al. *Old People in Three Industrial Societies*. New York: Atherton Press, 1968.

Shanas, E. and G. Maddox. 'Aging, Health, and the Organization of Health Resources,' pp. 592–618 in R. Binstock and E. Shanas (eds.). *Handbook of Aging and the Social Sciences*. New York: Van Nostrand Reinhold, 1976.

Shephard, R. *Physical Activity and Aging*. London: Croom Helm, 1978.

Shephard, R. and K. Sidney. 'Exercise and Aging,' pp. 1–57 in R. Hutton (ed.). *Exercise and Sport Sciences Reviews*. Volume 6. Philadelphia: The Franklin Institute Press, 1979.

Sidney, K. and R. Shephard. 'Attitudes Towards a Health and Physical Training Program,' *Medicine and Science in Sports*, 8(4/1977), 246–52.

Siegler, I. et al. 'Health and Behavior: Methodological Considerations for Adult Development and Aging,' pp. 599–612 in L. Poon (ed.). *Aging In The 1980s: Psychological Issues*. Washington, D.C.: American Psychological Association, 1980.

Simon, J. and A. Pouraghabagher. 'The Effect of Aging on the Stages of Processing in a Choice Reaction Time Task,' *Journal of Gerontology*, 33(4/1978), 553–61.

Smith, E. and R. Serfass (eds.). *Exercise and Aging: The Scientific Process*. Hillside, N.J.: Enslow Publishers, 1981.

Snyder, E. 'A Reflection on Commitment and Patterns of Disengagement from Recreational Physical Activity,' paper presented at the North American Society for the Sociology of Sport, Denver, October 1980.

Solnick, R. (ed.). *Sexuality and Aging*. Los Angeles: Andrus Gerontology Center, University of Southern California Press, 1978.

Spirduso, W. 'Physical Fitness, Aging and Psychomotor Speed: A Review,' *Journal of Gerontology*, 35(6/1980), 850–65.

Spreitzer, E. and E. Snyder. 'Correlates of Life Satisfaction Among the Aged,' *Journal of Gerontology*, 29(4/1974), 454–58.

Stagner, R. 'Stress, Strain, Coping and Defense,' *Research on Aging*, 3(1/1981), 3–32.

Szasz, G. 'The Sexual Consequences of Aging,' pp. 234–77 in J. Crawford (ed.). *Canadian Gerontological Collection III*. Winnipeg: Canadian Association on Gerontology, 1981.

Tamir, L. *Communication and the Aging Process*. Toronto: Pergamon Press, 1979.

Thomas, L. 'Sexuality and Aging: Essential Vitamin or Popcorn?' *The Gerontologist*, 22(3/1982), 240–43.

Wantz, M. and J. Gay. *The Aging Process: A Health Perspective*. Cambridge, Mass.: Winthrop Publishers Inc., 1981.

Warren, L. et al. 'Binaural Analysis in the Aging Auditory System,' *Journal of Gerontology*, 33(5/1978), 731–36.

Weiffenbach, et al., 'Taste Thresholds: Quality Specific Variation with Human Aging,' *Journal of Gerontology*, 37(3/1982), 372–77.

Weg, R. (ed.). *Nutrition and Aging: A Selected Bibliography*. Los Angeles: Andrus Gerontology Center, University of Southern California Press, 1977.

Welford, A. *Ageing and Human Skill*. London: Oxford University Press, 1958.

Welford, A. 'Motor Performance,' pp. 450–96 in J. Birren and K.W. Schaie (eds.). *Handbook of the Psychology of Aging*. New York: Van Nostrand Reinhold, 1977.

Welford, A. 'Motor Skill and Aging,' pp. 253–68 in C. Nadeau et al. (eds.). *Psychology of Motor Behavior and Sport – 1979*. Champaign, Ill.: Human Kinetics Publishers, 1980a.

Welford, A. 'Sensory, Perceptual and Motor Processes In Older Adults,' pp. 192–213 in J. Birren and R. Sloane (eds.). *Handbook of Mental Health and Aging*. Englewood Cliffs, N.J.: Prentice-Hall, Inc., 1980b.

Wells, T. *Aging and Health Promotion*. Rockville, Md.: Aspen Systems Corporation, 1982.

Wharton, G. *Sexuality and Aging: An Annotated Bibliography*. Metuchen, N.J.: Scarecrow Press, Inc., 1981.

Wiswell, R. 'Relaxation, Exercise and Aging,' pp. 943–58 in J. Birren and R. Sloane (eds.). *Handbook of Mental Health and Aging*. Englewood Cliffs, N.J.: Prentice-Hall, 1980.

6

The Aging Process: Adaptation to Psychological Changes

Introduction

Just as the aging individual must adapt to changes in the physical organism (chapter 5) and in various social systems (chapters 7 to 11), so too must he or she respond to changes in the various components of the psychological system (Schaie and Zelinski, 1975; Birren and Schaie, 1977). From a life-span developmental perspective (Hultsch and Deutsch, 1981), an understanding of changes in the cognitive, learning, and personality processes involves observing and explaining behavior within the same individual over time (aging effects), or between individuals at a specific time (individual differences).

These changes, which may be incremental or decremental, and which may or may not be observed in given individuals, occur at different rates and at different stages in the life cycle. From a systems perspective, the various elements within the larger psychological system interact in their influence on the individual. More significantly, changes within the psychological system are related to changes in the physical organism and in the physical and social environments (Thomae, 1976).

The following sections examine some common myths and stereotypes and briefly outline the influence of biological aging on cognition, learning, memory, and personality. The way in which adults may adapt to these psychological changes when and if they occur is also presented. As a result of the empirical evidence given here, readers should increase their awareness of possible behavioral and cognitive adapations within themselves and others as they age. In this way, aging is viewed as a process requiring not only adaptation to the social structure and processes, but also to possible changes in the psychological processes within the individual.

In summary, aging involves adaptation to changes that may occur in the physical and psychological systems. However, these changes, which occur at different rates and times, are more than mere facts. They interact with changes in the physical and social environments to influence behavior and adaptation at different stages in the life cycle. Thus, aging should not be viewed as a process of inevitable physical, biological, and psychological deterioration. Instead, it is a process of adaptation to specific changes.

Cognitive Processes and Aging

Conventional wisdom suggests that as people age they experience a general and inevitable decline in mental capacities and function. As a result, it is often thought that older people become less intelligent, are incapable of thinking, lack creativity, are forgetful, and are unable to learn new information or skills. Yet, case studies and recent empirical evidence suggest that the decline in cognitive processes may be less rapid and less severe than changes in sensorimotor or physical abilities. This section presents information concerning the rate and type of change with age in intelligence, learning, memory, forgetting, and creativity (Sprott, 1980; Craik and Trehub, 1981; Horn, forthcoming).

Throughout, the reader must remember that there are individual differences within a particular age cohort for each cognitive component. Moreover, most of the evidence is based on cross-sectional studies, which suggest that there are age differences between cohorts rather than that changes occur over time. Thus, inferences based on cross-sectional data can be misleading. This is especially true if the test items or instruments are based on abilities that are more salient in the earlier years, such as nonverbal psychomotor elements that emphasize speed. Furthermore, disease, educational attainment, class background, and past and present lifestyle can influence abilities and performance in the later years. Thus, cohort differences are almost inevitable, since each successive cohort will generally have received more and better education. As a final caveat, it should be remembered that the following subsections concern individuals who are 'normal' and who do not suffer from a chronic disease such as senility.

Intelligence

Intelligence is a multidimensional construct that consists of a number of primary abilities such as verbal comprehension, reasoning, abstracting, perceptual speed, numerical facility, problem solving, and word fluency (Willis and Baltes, 1980). However, psychologists have been unable to agree on the number, meaning,[1] or measurement of the many possible primary abilities.[2] Moreover, as Scheidt and Schaie (1978) note, it is important to distinguish between competence and intelligence: intelligence refers to underlying abilities that can be applied across many general categories of situations, and competence refers to adaptive behavior unique to a specific situation or class of situations.

As a result of this conceptual and methodological uncertainty, the terms 'fluid intelligence' and 'crystallized intelligence' have been used frequently in discussing adult intelligence (Cattell, 1973; Horn, 1978). Fluid intelligence is influenced by physiological and neurological capacity, and represents incidental learning that is not based on culture. Fluid intelligence represents the ability to adjust one's thinking to the demands of a specific situation and to organize information to solve problems. It is measured by performance tests (novel problem solving, such as filling in a space with pieces from a puzzle, inductive reasoning, or matching symbols to numbers) that are scored according to accuracy and speed.

Crystallized intelligence is the product of education, experience, and acculturation wherein individuals acquire specific knowledge and skills unique to their culture or subculture. Because crystallized intelligence is based on learning and experience, there are individual differences that vary by level of educational attainment, socioeconomic status, and race. This component is measured by verbal comprehension tests that stress vocabulary and the continual addition or restructuring of information within the cognitive system (defining the meaning of words or expressing mechanical knowledge).

Results from a number of studies and reviews (Schaie, 1975; Botwinick, 1977, 1978; Horn, 1978; Willis and Baltes, 1980; Horn et al., 1981; Hultsch and Deutsch, 1981), using both cross-sectional and longitudinal methodology, have confirmed that fluid intelligence, after reaching a peak during adolescence, declines with age. In contrast, crystallized intelligence increases with age. The loss in fluid intellectual abilities may range from three to seven IQ units per decade between 30 and 60 years of age (Horn et al., 1981). This decrease in fluid intelligence may be related to a deterioration in cerebral blood flow (Hertzog et al., 1978), to neurological losses, to slower performance with age on speed tests, or to less daily use of the novel-problem-solving function as one ages (intellectual demands may not be placed on the aging individual, and experience is used more than creative problem solving). In addition, a decrease in fluid intelligence may be related to deficits in the ability to organize information, ignore irrelevant information, concentrate, and recognize and use new information.

Increases in crystallized intelligence result from a continuing process of socialization (via formal education or experience) wherein new information is acquired. At the same time, existing verbal information is constantly being used and reinforced, especially by those who are highly verbal and reflective in their daily living.

In general, the 'classic aging pattern' with respect to intelligence indicates that, although there are individual differences, there is little significant decline until the 50s, with a more rapid decline beginning sometime after 60, especially in fluid intelligence. Where good health is maintained, verbal scores are consistently higher than perceptual-motor performance scores (speed) on all tests. This pattern holds whether the subjects are male or female, black or white, institutionalized or noninstitutionalized, or from upper or lower socioeconomic backgrounds (Botwinick, 1977). Moreover, studies suggest that continuity in performance is likely, although the performance levels of earlier years are not generally good predictors of the onset, direction, or degree of change in intelligence in later years.

Given that intelligence appears to decline less rapidly and frequently than previously assumed, what are some of the possible explanations of the individual differences in measured intelligence during the middle and later years of adulthood? Recently it has been generally concluded that it is not chronological age per se (at least up to the early 70s) that leads to a decline in performance. Rather, there is a complex interaction of biological decrements (such as general physiological and neurological decline, loss of physical health, reduced blood flow to the brain), sensory losses such as hearing (Granick et al., 1976), and environmental factors. In fact, increasing emphasis has recently been placed on the role of environmental factors. For example, Baltes and his colleagues (Baltes, 1979; Willis and Baltes, 1980) have suggested that there are three sets of environmental elements that interact with the individual to produce developmental differences: (1) age-graded influences, such as specific socialization practices and events unique to each cohort; (2) historical influences, such as economic depressions or wars that force early school-leaving; and (3) personal life events that create crises for an individual (death of a spouse, unemployment, divorce, or a traumatic medical event).

Similarly, Labouvie-Vief and Chandler (1978) developed a theoretical framework wherein both sociocultural and situational factors were hypothesized to have considerable impact on cognitive functioning. They argue that decrements appear most frequently after retirement and may be due to the policy of mandatory retirement and to the consequent loss of social function. They suggest that the decline may also be related to physical, structural, or personality factors within the testing situation (for example, fatigue, cautiousness, lack of reinforcement and practice, low motivation, unfamiliar or meaningless test items, and test anxiety), or to cultural and subcultural differences that influence ability or performance (such as socioeconomic status, race, English as the second language, birth order, or availability of reading material).

In the absence of physiological or medical trauma, much of the observed difference in intellectual performance can be accounted for by a variety of past and current social and environmental factors. Some of these factors that may either increase (+) or decrease (−) test performance include:

1. The amount of experience, motivation, and training concerning the material in the tests (lack of ecological validity) (+).

2. The level of education completed[3] and the number of years since leaving school (+).

3. The absence of stress and fatigue in test situations (Cunningham et al., 1978) (+).

4. The use of appropriate and meaningful test items (+).

5. The use of feedback, instruction, and practice in taking tests (+).

6. The presence of stereotypes that define the elderly as incompetent, thereby leading to a low level of test motivation (−).

7. The presence of an environment in the adult years that is conducive to intellectual stimulation (+).

8. A decreased emphasis on speed of performance (+).

9. The lifestyle during the adult years[4] (+ or −).

10. The onset of and adaptation to personal crises, including dramatic changes in job, marital, or health status (−).

These environmental explanations for the decline in intelligence with age have led to the initiation of remedial programs, and to attempts to change elements of the environment in order to modify both crystallized and fluid intelligence (Labouvie-Vief and Gonda, 1976; Plemons et al., 1978; Baltes and Willis, 1979).

In summary, among the elderly there is a range of demonstrated intelligence. First, and most important, as with all cohorts there are individual differences in intelligence from birth onward. This pattern is reflected in the later years, regardless of the losses encountered by specific individuals. Second, while some individuals experience little or no decline throughout adulthood, others experience severe intellectual loss. Moreover, while some elderly persons perform at a slower rate on some intellectual tasks, or encounter difficulty with novel tasks or situations (such as the use of computer banking), the normal aging process does not significantly diminish the ability to solve problems. In fact, the elderly are usually able to use their accumulated knowledge and experience to offset any loss of speed in intellectual tasks.

Finally, assuming normal health, apparent differences in intelligence may be more closely related to educational and cohort differences than to chronological age. The greater intelligence demonstrated by younger cohorts is a reflection of more and better education, of more experience in test situations, of higher-quality health care during infancy and childhood, and of a greater likelihood of having acquired learned skills or familiarity with material that appears on intelligence tests. Given a stimulating and supportive environment, gains rather than losses in intelligence might be the more typical pattern, at least until the last few years of life when nearness to death is often revealed by a decline in intellectual functioning. In fact, this decrease in intelligence test scores in the last few years of life is often referred to as the 'terminal drop' phenomenon.

Learning and Memory

Introduction. Learning and memory are complementary processes that illustrate the classic 'chicken-and-egg' dilemma. Learning involves the acquisition of information or behavior, while memory involves the storage and retention of the learned behavior. In order for material to be acquired and stored in memory it must be learned. Similarly, in order to demonstrate that material has been learned, it must be recalled from memory before the material can be used in response to a test. This illustrates the importance of distinguishing between learning and performance. When it is not possible to perform what was supposedly learned earlier, it is difficult to determine whether the material has not been learned; whether the material has been learned but not remembered; or whether the material has been learned and stored in memory, but cannot be retrieved for performance. In addition, lack of ecological validity[5] (where tasks and material are not meaningful or relevant to the individual), high anxiety in a test situation, temporary physiological or psychological states (fatigue, lack of motivation, or depression), and the requirement to perform or demonstrate learning in a short period of time can all influence performance rather than learning or retrieving per se.

Learning. The belief that 'you can't teach an old dog new tricks' is still widely held. However, empirical evidence suggests that while there are individual differences within and between age cohorts in learning ability, the elderly can learn if adequate personal and situational conditions are present (Arenberg and Robertson-Tchabo, 1977; Woodruff and Walsh, 1977; Waugh et al., 1978a). As we saw in chapter 5, there is a general slowing of the central nervous system with age. This influences the learning process as well. Older persons have the capacity to learn but it seems to take them longer to search for, code, recall, and produce the required response. Under conditions of self-pacing, where individuals can set their own rates of speed, learning is more likely to occur.[6]

Learning potential may also be restricted because of a decreased ability to distinguish relevant from irrelevant information (Hoyer and Plude, 1980). This problem may be especially acute for women since it has been found that they are more likely than men to attend to irrelevant stimuli (Laszlo et al., 1980). This age-related change in attentional selectivity also affects other cognitive processes, such as problem solving. Therefore, it is important to eliminate distractions in the environment for the older learner, and to enhance the learning environment with supportive instructions and guidance to enable the learner to focus only on relevant stimuli.

In addition to cognitive factors, a number of noncognitive factors also influence the ability to learn at all ages. First, there must be a willingness to use one's physical and mental capacities (Welford, 1976; Bolton, 1978). The level of motivation is most likely to be high for meaningful and relevant tasks. However, overinvolvement or overarousal, resulting in an excessive drive state, may detract from performance among the elderly more than among the young (Elias and Elias, 1977). Second, the learner must not only have a sufficient level of intelligence to acquire the information, but must have experience in learning situations; learning capacity involves acquiring and using the habits and skills of learning (Hultsch, 1974). Thus, older adults who have been involved in learning, education, or retraining throughout the adult years are more likely not only to want to learn but to be able to do so more efficiently. A third personal factor is health. Generally, individuals who are in good physical and mental health (especially those without cerebrovascular disease or severe uncorrected visual or auditory problems) are able to acquire new information with greater ease.

In summary, the existing evidence suggests that there are individual differences at all ages in learning performance. However, most elderly people appear to be at a disadvantage when the time to learn and respond is short. Given sufficient motivation, time, and good health, and continued and recent experience in learning situations, the performance of a 70-year-old can be relatively similar to that of younger adults. Moreover, most of the learning studies have been based on cross-sectional rather than longitudinal or cohort-sequential studies. Thus, the observed age differences may reflect generational differences in years of schooling and in the desire or opportunity to use learning capacities during the adult years.

Memory.   Memory is a complex process that is involved in almost all stages of information processing. One view of how memory works is illustrated by the three stage model proposed by Murdock (1967). The first stage involves receiving information and temporarily storing this information in 'sensory stores.' For example, auditory information (such as the sound of a siren) is stored in the 'echoic memory,' while visual information (the facial features of someone you have just met) is stored in 'iconic memory.' If this information is considered important, and is not interrupted by competing stimuli, it is transferred in the second stage, by the 'attention' process, to 'short-term memory.' From here, the information is transferred by additional rehearsal of the stimuli to a more permanent 'long-term memory.' Information can be lost in the first stage (sensory storage) by decay or replacement, at the second stage (short-term memory) by forgetting if the information is not repeatedly rehearsed, and in the third stage (long-term memory) through a failure of the retrieval system to find what has been stored. For example, there appears to be a decline with age in both recall and recognition[7] tasks, thereby suggesting that both acquisition and storage processes may change with age (Harkins et al., 1979; Rankin and Kausler, 1979; Bowles and Poon, 1982; Parkinson et al., 1982).

More recent theories suggest that there are specific types of memory. For example, Tulving (1972) describes 'episodic' memory as that which operates for specific events unique to the individual (a specific trip, the first love, or a meaningful event in the life course), while 'semantic memory' represents common knowledge, vocabulary, or concepts that are shared by most people (stop signs are red, 'caution' signs mean be careful, or a round object rolls). Another dichotomy (Winograd, 1975) distinguishes between 'declarative knowledge' (memory for general knowledge) and 'procedural knowledge' (memory for how to behave or perform in specific situations).

With respect to aging and memory, the evidence suggests that a progressive decline in memory performance is not inevitable, nor is it irreversible when it does occur (Craik, 1977; Waugh et al., 1978a, 1978b; Hartley, 1980; Fozard, 1980;

Hines and Fozard, 1980; Poon et al., 1980; Schonfield, 1980; Winograd, 1982). The older person seems to be able to remember and recall distant events (episodic memory) better than recent material.[8] However, as in learning experiments, the older person seems to require more time to retrieve information from both short- and long-term memory, especially when faced with many stimulus-response alternatives (Waugh et al., 1978a, 1978b; Madden and Nebes, 1980), or when stored material must be manipulated or reorganized before responding. These effects are found regardless of the familiarity with the material. However, the speed of retrieval is faster for familiar objects, regardless of age (Poon and Fozard, 1978).

The apparent reasons for 'memory loss' or slower and less efficient recall are not clearly understood. However, it appears that such factors as a low level of intelligence, lack of use of information, interference in the process because of the learning of new information (retroactive interference) and the large amount of information already stored (proactive interference), lack of motivation (a self-fulfilling prophecy that the elderly are forgetful), a low level of verbal ability (Bowles and Poon, 1982), and neurochemical changes in the brain cells or loss of brain cells may all contribute to changes in memory performance.

Since the explanation for slower and less efficient memory processes is not totally biological, it is possible to diagnose the problem and improve the efficiency of the memory process in the later years through practice (Taub, 1973) and intervention (Fozard, 1981). Memory can be enhanced by adopting procedures that facilitate memorization; by providing more time for the acquisition, rehearsal, and retrieval of information; by using meaningful material to be learned and remembered in experimental situations; by relying more on recognition than on recall; by reducing interference during the learning process; and by informing older adults that 'forgetting' and 'memory loss' are not inevitable, and that they do have the capacity to remember, although it might take longer to do so.

Thinking, Problem Solving, and Creativity

'Cognitive style' refers to the characteristic way that individuals conceptually organize the environment, manipulate the knowledge they possess, and make decisions or approach problems that have to be solved (Goldstein and Blackman, 1978; Cohen and Wu, 1980; Peterson and Eden, 1981). It is directly observable through conversational style, through the characteristic modes of perceptual and intellectual functioning, and through an evaluation by others of creative acts. Two contrasting cognitive styles have been labelled 'field-dependent' and 'field-independent.' The individual who is 'field-dependent' appears to be more perceptive of the social environment, more people-oriented, and generally more conventional in dress and behavior. In contrast, the person who is 'field-independent' is more analytical, more internally directed, and less constrained in behavior by tradition and convention. With respect to thinking, an individual may be reflective (a longer response time and fewer errors is the norm) or impulsive (a fast response time with less accuracy is the norm). There is some evidence that where the stimulus is familiar and unambiguous, older subjects are more impulsive than younger subjects (Coyne et al., 1978).

Cognitive style may also be revealed by the approach utilized when the decision involves some risk. Older adults have generally been found to be more rigid and cautious in their thinking (Botwinick, 1978:111); they are sometimes reluctant to make difficult decisions, especially when the situation is ambiguous, when speed is required or when they have a fear of failure. Thus, in some situations they react by substituting accuracy for speed (cautiousness); in others they may resort to prior learning or experience, even if it is no longer appropriate (rigidity). Furthermore, it appears that if given the option of not responding, or of not making a decision, many will select this alternative (Calhoun and Hutchison, 1981). It is not clear whether this rigidity and cautiousness among the elderly is an aging phenomenon, or whether it is a cohort and historical factor wherein these traits have been part of a lifelong cognitive style.

In chapter 5 we saw that there is a characteristic slowing of behavior with age as noted by a longer reaction time. This slowing is also evident in a general progressive decline in cognitive speed and verbal processes, which may limit complex thinking. This is likely the result of a general slowing of behavior because of changes in the central nervous system; to a loss of speed in all stages of information processing; and to a change in health, particularly with the onset of coronary heart disease or cerebrovascular disease (Birren et al., 1980; Cunningham, 1980). The slowing may also be due to deficits in attention. These may be either 'divided-attention' deficits (difficulty in processing currently relevant information, such as trying to listen to two conversations), or 'selective-attention' deficits (difficulty in ignoring irrelevant information, such as a conversation on the radio while talking to another person). According to a recent study by Madden and Nebes (1981), age differences in attention are more likely to be 'divided-attention' deficits rather than 'selective-attention' deficits.

As a result of this slowing and decline in speed of information processing, individuals attempt to compensate by relying more on past experience and knowledge, by employing memory aids, by learning to eliminate irrelevant stimuli and by using strategy hints from others. Charness (1981) has suggested that the individual differences noted in cognitive aging may be due either to 'hardware' (processing mechanisms) or to 'software' (strategies and learning controlled by the performer) changes. Since hardware changes are generally decremental (loss of speed or decline in memory), deficits in problem solving will occur unless software changes are learned and used. These compensating mechanisms are particularly important in problem-solving or decision-making tasks. Thus, with increasing age, adults become not only less accurate in problem solving but also slower.

It appears that problem solving ability may decline with age because of a general slowing of behavior, and because of an unwillingness or inability to incorporate newer, more efficient strategies that might lead to a solution or decision. However, the decline also appears to be related to the level of educational attainment and to the type of task. For example, less decline in ability is seen among the better-educated and for tasks similar to those used in one's occupation.

Charness (1981) has recently suggested that elderly people may be inferior to the young in problem solving not because of a decline in ability, but because they have always been less effective. That is, a cohort effect is present because they may not have acquired the skill when younger, and they may have had less use of the skill during their lifetimes. He further noted that, in his study of highly skilled chess players, 'despite decreases in efficiency in encoding and retrieval of information, older players can match the performance of younger players' (Charness, 1981:37). The older players have always had a high level of skill, and have used this skill consistently throughout life. In short, experience can offset loss of efficiency. Charness also found that the highly skilled older chess players actually took less time to select a good move than less skilled older or younger players. Again, this illustrates the range of individual differences within and between cohorts.

In addition to age differences in problem-solving ability, changes in intellectual capacity and style are revealed through patterns of creativity across the life cycle (Kogan, 1973). Like intelligence, this is a difficult concept to define and measure; like a piece of art, the significance of a creative endeavor is often dependent on the evaluation of others. Creativity may involve such accomplishments as the creation of a unique cultural product (a work of art, or literature, or an invention), the development of a new concept, the creation of a new approach to solving an old problem, a solution to an old problem, or the identification of a new problem.

In order to measure the concept, 'creativity' has been defined as either the total productivity (quantity) throughout one's career (the number of articles published by a university professor), or the point in the career at which the highest-quality work was completed (the age at which Nobel prize-winning work was initiated or completed). To date, the study of creativity has been primarily based on retrospective studies of the career profiles of various occupational groups, or on case studies of those elderly persons who have been defined as highly creative individuals (for example, Grandma Moses or George Burns).

According to Rabbitt (1977), creative 'potential' peaks at about age 40, with a decline appearing after about age 50. However, there are individual differences by occupation. For example, the peak of creativity in mathematics and chemistry occurs in the 30s or 40s, while in literature and history, where experience and a larger investment of reflective time in a single project is necessary, the peak occurs in the 60s. Furthermore, the highest-quality work appears to be produced at the time when the largest quantity of work is produced. The pattern of creativity also seems to be influenced by such factors as health, motivation, energy, personal lifestyle, competing interests, expectations by significant others, and the social environment. For example, it is likely that many aging individuals have a capacity for creativity, but lack the social environment that can provide the stimulation to question and to create, or the opportunity set to pursue ideas to completion.

In light of significant accomplishments by those in their 60s, 70s, or 80s, it appears that, given an appropriate environment, some elderly people are capable of highly creative work well into the later years of life (Rowe, 1976; Cole, 1979; Alpaugh, 1982). For example, McLeish (1976) stresses that later life can be viewed as a challenge and an adventure that can be realized through creative efforts. This motivation to create and to continue at a high level of intellectual functioning is aptly illustrated by the following lines from Tennyson's poem, *Ulysses:*

How dull it is to pause, to make an end,
To rust unburnished, not to shine in use!

And this gray spirit yearning in desire
To follow knowledge like a sinking star.

Death closes all: but something ere the end,
Some work of noble note, may yet be done.

... but strong in will
To strive, to seek, to find and not to yield.

Personality Processes and Aging

Introduction

In an attempt to explain changes in behavior with age, social scientists have sought to determine the relative influence of personality factors (Shanan, 1982; Costa and McCrae, forthcoming). Perhaps nowhere else is the interaction of the personal system with the social system more evident than when personality is considered as a factor in the aging process. Personality involves traits, characteristics, moods, cognitive styles, and lifestyles that are unique to the individual, but that interact with a variety of social system variables.

As with the concepts of 'socialization' and 'intelligence,' most of the interest in personality has focused on the early developmental years of childhood and adolescence. As a result of this interest, many perspectives,[9] designs,[10] and methods[11] have been used to describe and explain the characteristic way in which particular individuals think (cognitive style) and behave (lifestyle). Employing these various methods, theories, and concepts, two interacting questions have dominated the personality literature, regardless of the perspective held by a particular scientist. The first is whether behavior is internally (personality traits) or externally (the social situation) determined. The second question considers the extent to which personality is stable or subject to change over time. Interest in these two questions has been further intensified by the need to understand the impact of personality on behavior throughout middle and later adulthood.

Social behavior: a function of personality traits or the social situation?   Is behavior primarily determined by personality traits or by the social environment? According to the 'trait' approach, individuals, through a combination of heredity, early socialization practices, and interaction with significant others, develop personal traits and characteristics, a cognitive style, and a temperament. These behavioral dispositions are thought to be stable over time; they enable an individual to respond consistently and predictably to the social and physical environments.

In contrast, the 'situational,' 'behavioral,' or 'state' approach argues that behavior is determined by the social situation, and that individuals learn and perform social roles appropriate to a given situation. According to this latter perspective, a 'personality' per se does not exist. Or, if it does, it has little stability since the behavior of an individual is determined by externally induced social norms and sanctions unique to specific situations (for example, at work, at home, or at leisure).

As with many bipolar views of the world, neither position has received overwhelming support in the research literature. Rather, an interactionist perspective has evolved as a more realistic view. According to this perspective, behavior results from continuous two-way interaction between the person (with his or her unique cognitive and emotional traits) and the particular social situation (Endler and Magnusson, 1976; Epstein, 1979). Thus, an individual's personality influences behavior and adaptation to specific situations, while the situation itself influences what traits from the available repertoire will be expressed, and in what way.

It is through this dialectical process between the personal and social system that individual and group lifestyles evolve. For example, based on the longitudinal study of successful aging in Kansas City, Williams and Wirths (1965) identified six types of lifestyles that reflect an individual's values, interests, and preferences: (1) an emphasis on the 'world of work'; (2) a primary interest in the family ('familism'); (3) a major interest in the spouse ('couplehood'); (4) a preference for 'living alone'; (5) a propensity to be fully involved in daily life in a variety of ways ('living fully'); and (6) a tendency to be as uninvolved as possible in all activities ('living with minimal involvement').

Individuals were classified (a) as to which lifesyle they preferred, and (b) how successfully they aged in it. Individuals who exhibited characteristics of one lifestyle often also demonstrated characteristics of a similar and related lifestyle. As a result, Williams and Wirths (1965:170) further identified two general sets of lifestyles. The Gemeinschaft[12] set includes familism, couplehood and living fully. These lifestyles involve high role activity, high personal interaction of an affective nature, and little alienation or isolation. In contrast, the Gesellschaft[13] set includes characteristics from the world of work, living alone, and moving through life with minimal involvement. These lifestyles are characterized by minimal role activity, few close personal relationships, alienation, and isolation.

Many other typologies have been constructed to describe patterns or characteristic ways of behaving during the adult years, either in general or in specific situations. Some of the typologies that are based on personality studies will be described later in the chapter. It must be recognized that all typologies are only modal patterns and that there are individual differences in the behavior and traits demonstrated for each 'type.' Moreover, typologies never, in principle, present complete and permanent pictures of social beings and social reality.

Personality: stable or changeable over the life cycle?   There has been some controversy as to whether behavior is influenced by internal (personality traits) or external factors (such as change and variety in social situations, significant life events, or entering specific stages of life, such as middle age[14]). While this controversy has not been completely resolved, the available evidence, especially from longitudinal studies[15] (Maas and Kuypers, 1974; Costa and McCrae, 1980, forthcoming; McCrae et al., 1980; Costa et al., 1981), suggests that after early adulthood individuals demonstrate consistency in such personal characteristics as presentation of self, attitudes, values, temperament, and traits (Schaie and Parham, 1976; Neugarten, 1977a; Siegler et al., 1979; Costa and McCrae, 1980; Costa et al., 1980; Thomae, 1980). This pattern of stability is especially pronounced among highly educated men (McCrae et al., 1980). In fact, many individuals make a conscious effort to increase consistency in the behavioral and cognitive presentation of self. Because of the possibility of errors in measurement at a given time, when measures of behavior and personality are averaged over a large sample of situations, stability is the normative pattern in the absence of confounding health problems (Epstein, 1979).

Yet research evidence from surveys and individual case studies indicates that some personality changes do occur at or beyond middle age for some individuals. For example, a longitudinal study found that changes in personality traits may occur in two ways (Haan and Day, 1974; Haan, 1976). First, most of those in a cohort will change over time in some trait, but the relative position within the group for any one individual will not change. That is, the most dependable person at age 20 will be the most dependable person at age 40, even though the average score for the cohort may decrease or increase. In the second type, all members of a cohort may change but some will change relatively more than others. Thus, the person who was the most defensive at age 20 may no longer be the most defensive at age 40.

Although there have been few personality studies of women, this pattern of personality change over the life cycle may vary by sex. For example, Neugarten and Gutmann (1958) found that women are more likely to accept and use their egocentric and aggressive impulses as they age, while men are more likely to be nurturant and affiliative in the later years. Similarly, Maas and Kuypers (1974) found that women are more likely to change their lifestyles as they age, and men are more likely to change their personalities. A recent study (Ryff, 1982) found that older women are more likely to perceive a change with age in some elements of the personality structure (such as values).

Troll and Parron (1981) suggest that there is a 'double shift' in sex-role behavior during the adult years. This double shift results from changes within the individual and within society. They report that some women become more autonomous and some men become more expressive as they enter the later years. It is thought that the emergence of this sex-role change results from the interaction of biological changes, the onset of unexpected major life events, later-life socialization processes, and cultural changes in normative sex-role behavior.

How might these changes be explained? Unfortunately, no theory considers personality processes across the developmental life span of an individual. We depend on speculation and inferential evidence from research to explain why personality changes occur in later life.

First, demonstrated changes may reflect underlying latent needs and characteristics that have not been expressed earlier in life. Second, as social situations change with age, the individual may be less inclined to present the self in a particular way. For example, the striving, achievement-oriented individual may devote less time to work, may become more relaxed in interpersonal situations, and may demonstrate a different presentation of the self in all social situations. This may be more likely to occur if career goals have been attained, especially if at an earlier age than expected. Alternatively, according to the cognitive theory of personality (Thomae, 1980), there may be a perceived change rather than an objective change in the self. This perceived change may lead to observed behavioral changes in the later years. That is, the older person may perceive changes in health or in any number of personality traits, and then behave accordingly. For example, Fisseni (1976) found that subjects in the Bonn Longitudinal Study who perceived less change in their personal situations (especially in health) reported greater life satisfaction and less stress than those who perceived more change.

A third factor leading to an apparent change in personality may be a lack of opportunity to demonstrate certain traits. For example, the need to be aggressive or achievement-oriented may continue, but the social opportunities to do so may no longer be as readily available. In addition, the physical and psychic energy needed to continue a pattern of aggressive and achievement-oriented behavior may no longer be as available as it once was. Normative expectations as to how one is supposed to behave or think at a particular age may change with age. This would imply that age-related normative behaviors are clearly understood and accepted by the elderly. However, there appears to be little consensus concerning whether age-appropriate norms are present, and, if so, whether they influence the behavior of elderly persons (Sills et al., 1980).

Finally, since personality factors interact with a changing social environment, the personal system may interact differently with the social system during the later years. For example, there may be a shift from a concern with the external world to matters of importance to the personal system. That is, the individual may be more likely, for a variety of personal reasons, to accept rather than challenge the external environment,[16] to voluntarily relinquish some social roles, and to turn inward and show a greater interest in and concern for the self and those in the immediate family (Neugarten, 1977b).

In summary, while most people do not show marked personality changes with age (Costa and McCrae, 1980:27; Costa and McCrae, forthcoming), some appear to be less concerned with normative behavior and do change their patterns of interaction with the social world. Similarly, others are aware of the changing norms of younger cohorts and may change their behavior or cognitive pattern to fit in with contemporary lifestyles. Some of these changes have been hypothesized to be related to physiological or cognitive changes. However, they may also reflect latent character traits, a shift toward an increased interest in the self, a decreased opportunity set, a changing social environment, or a voluntary or involuntary loss of roles. In addition, changes may be induced by the onset of a significant personal life event wherein a change of lifestyle is seen to be the most appropriate coping mechanism (for example, a forced retirement, divorce, a demotion, widowhood, or departure of children from the home).

In the subsections that follow, personality traits, personality types, and personality disorders demonstrated in the later years of life are described. Throughout these sections, it must be noted that although women comprise an increasingly larger proportion of the adult population, most of the evidence is based on studies of white men prior to or following retirement (Atchley, 1976). Moreover, most of the information about personality types has been derived from cross-sectional rather than from longitudinal or cohort studies (Woodruff and Birren, 1972; McCrae et al., 1980).

Personality Traits

Many cross-sectional studies have measured single or multiple personality traits[17] to determine to what extent differences exist by age, or to determine if age is a more significant factor in personality differences than other social variables (such as sex, socioeconomic status, race, ethnic background, or birth order). Some of the more common traits[18] that have been measured include aggressiveness, anxiety, attitudes toward aging, authoritarianism, cautiousness, conformity, conservatism, creativity, decision making, dogmatism, egocentrism, ego strength, emotionality, extraversion, happiness, introversion, irritability, morale or life satisfaction, need achievement, passivity, perceived locus of control, reminiscence, rigidity, risk taking, self-concept or self-image, self-esteem, and sociability (Riley and Foner, 1968; Neugarten, 1977a; Hunter et al., 1981–82; Schulz, 1982).

For most traits the evidence in favor of either age differences (cross-sectional studies) or age changes (longitudinal studies) is equivocal. Some scientists report differences between age groups or changes with age, while others are unable to demonstrate any differences or changes. Some of this uncertainty is related to research problems, including the definition and measurement of the traits (Lawton et al., 1980), the use of small or non-representative samples, or the failure to control for possible intervening factors (such as state of health, a significant life event, socioeconomic status, marital status, or race). However, despite the inconsistent findings there does appear to be sufficient evidence to conclude that the current cohort of older people are generally more conservative, cautious,[19] egocentric, introverted, passive, and less emotional than younger age groups. It is unclear whether these differences reflect lifelong characteristics, learned changes with age, or forced changes with age because of decreasing opportunities, stereotypes, or changing interaction patterns with younger cohorts.

In addition to the above factors, which are primarily internally determined, there are other personality dimensions that are more dependent on social learning and social interaction. These externally induced factors may be more likely to change with age. For example, consider the concept of self-esteem. This trait measures how people think and feel about themselves, and how they perceive others to view them. Self-esteem is a learned characteristic, a product of lifelong social interaction and social experiences. Most older people report a positive sense of self-esteem. However, the degree of self-esteem is related to such factors as higher socioeconomic status, a higher level of educational attainment, being white, having good health, and having an adequate income. Thus, it is not surprising that a loss in self-esteem may accompany the loss of a job, discrimination against the older worker, a decline in health, and a loss of independence. Moreover, withdrawal from or less frequent interaction with significant others may also reduce a person's level of self-esteem. Some personality dimensions are highly dependent on social learning and interaction, and when losses or changes occur in these areas, older persons, like younger persons, begin to question their worth and competence. This in turn can lower their level of self-esteem or change their self-concept, thereby leading to further changes in behavior and to changes in other personality dimensions.

In summary, while there appear to be some age differences and age changes in personality traits, these are not universal or inevitable. As in most social dimensions, there are individual differences in personality traits (within and between age cohorts) that are influenced by the social environment.

Personality Types

The identification of a number of personality types is the most definitive evidence that personality structures are relatively stable throughout adulthood. These types have been derived in an attempt to identify patterns of aging and to explain 'successful' aging or life satisfaction. Various labels or names have been assigned to the characteristic ways in which older individuals think and behave. This area of research has refuted the myth that there is one common personality structure for the aged. There is no evidence to support the usual derogatory stereotype of the elderly person as depressed, lonely, introverted, senile, conservative, aloof, or eccentric.

The first cross-sectional study of the personality structure of older people identified five personality types. These were derived from over one hundred personality traits that were found in eighty-seven white males between 55 and 84 years of age (Reichard et al., 1962). The 'mature' (stable, well-balanced, accepting of aging), the 'rocking-chair' (passive, somewhat dependent on others, voluntarily disengaged) and the 'armored' (rigid, disciplined, individualistic, active, highly independent) types were found to be well-adjusted and to be successfully adapting to the aging process. In contrast, the 'angry' (hostile, blaming others for declining abilities, unstable, fighting against social and physical signs of aging) and the 'self-hater' types (blaming themselves, depressed, isolated) were poorly adjusted.

Using data from the Kansas City Study of Adult Life, Neugarten et al. (1964) derived four personality types based on information from fifty-nine men and women aged 70 to 79. According to this classification scheme, the 'integrated' (mature, flexible, future-oriented, active, with high self-esteem) and 'armored or defended' (ambitious, achievement-oriented, fearful of aging, highly active, eager to maintain power and status) types were high in life satisfaction; the 'passive-dependent' types (dependent on others, disengaged, apathetic) expressed moderate levels of life satisfaction; and the small number of 'disorganized' types (unintegrated into society, depressed, angry, showing irrational behavior, unable to control emotions, with deteriorating cognitive processes) were low in satisfaction.

It is obvious that lifestyle factors as well as personality traits make up the personality type. Havighurst (1969) described eight lifestyle patterns of the elderly that were related to the four personality types outlined by Neugarten and her associates. For the integrated personality type, there are three associated lifestyles: (1) 'reorganizers' (engaged in a variety of roles and activities, replacing lost roles with new roles), (2) 'focused' (with interests centered on a few activities or roles); and (3) 'disengaged' (relatively uninvolved in social life). Associated with the armored or defended type are two lifestyles: (1) 'holding on' (attempting to continue midlife roles and activities), and (2) 'constricted' (fighting against aging by restricting social interaction to a few activities or roles). For the passive-dependent personality type, there are two hypothesized lifestyle patterns: (1) 'succorance-seeking' (dependent on attention and emotional support from others), and (2) 'apathetic' (passive, with little social involvement throughout life). Finally, the unintegrated personality type was associated with the 'disorganized' lifestyle pattern (unable to control emotions, behave consistently, or think clearly).

It must be stressed, again, that these personality types and lifestyle patterns are average patterns derived from a single study with a relatively small sample. Not every elderly person will demonstrate a particular type or lifestyle. Moreover, the evidence suggests that one's personality is relatively stable throughout life, and because of continuity in behavior, these later life patterns are probably similar to the personality and lifestyle of the earlier years.

In another study, Maas and Kuypers (1974) interviewed ninety-five women and forty-seven men when the subjects were in their 30s, and again when they were in their 70s. They described six lifestyles for the women (husband-centered, work-centered, group-centered, visiting, uncentered, and disabled-disengaged) and four for the men (family-centered, hobbyists, remotely sociable, and unwell-disengaged). The women demonstrated significant and sometimes dramatic changes in lifestyle over the forty-year period, especially those whose lives were work-centered. They moved from being 'husband-centered' to 'work-centered,' perhaps partly as a result of their personal experiences, but also as a result of changes in societal norms concerning the role of women with respect to family and work. For the men, continuity of lifestyle into the later years was the characteristic pattern. In short, women, especially if employed, may be more adaptive to changing conditions than men.

In addition to the lifestyle patterns, four personality types were identified for the women ('person-oriented,' 'fearful-ordering,' 'autonomous,' and 'anxious-asserting') and three for the men ('person-oriented,' 'active-competent,' and 'conservative-ordering'). Unlike the changes in lifestyle, which were more prevalent among women, changes in personality over the forty-year period were more pronounced for the men. Specifically, the 'conservative-ordering' males and the 'active-competent' males demonstrated the greatest degree of personality change in that they tended to become more conservative and less active with age. Based on the findings of this longitudinal study, Maas and Kuypers (1974:215) concluded that:

> ... for those small proportions in our study whose personalities and lifestyles seem problematic, it is not merely old age that has ushered in the dissatisfactions and the suffering. In early adulthood these men and women were in various ways at odds with others and themselves or too constricted in their involvements. Old age merely continues for them what earlier years have launched ... Different ways of living may be developed as our social environments change with time — and as we change them.

One other study that merits discussion is the combined longitudinal and cross-sectional research completed in West Germany by Thomae (1976) and his colleagues. They interviewed 220 men and women, born from 1890 to 1895 and from 1900 to 1905, at five different times from 1965 to 1973. At each point, the respondents were interviewed about their past, their present, and their future situations. The researchers found stability over time in such personality variables as rigidity, dogmatism, and attitudes toward the past, present, and future. Changes that were noted included a shift from an emphasis on extending personal contacts (new acquaintances) to an emphasis on maintaining existing social networks, an improved subjective view of health, and a more positive attitude toward others. As in other studies, there was a strong relationship between perceived health and general contentment with the present life situation. Thus, high degrees of life satisfaction may be a reflection of 'a balance between the individual's cognitive structure and his manner of coping with the present' (Grombach, 1976:66).

In recent years, the 'Type A' and 'Type B' behavior pattern proposed by Friedman and Rosenman (1964) has received much attention. Type A and Type B behaviors have an impact on health and lifestyle, and hence on the way in which individuals adapt to the aging process. To date, Type A and Type B behavior patterns have received relatively little attention from gerontologists. However, these patterns should be studied more intensely since there seems to be a strong relationship between the presence of Type A behavior and coronary heart disease among men (Siegler et al., 1980:607–8). For example, the most recent evidence suggests that the risk of coronary heart disease and atherosclerosis for Type A persons is about twice that for Type B persons (Brand, 1978). Both the incidence and the severity of attacks are likely to be greater among Type A people.

Using a longitudinal study of over 3,500 men, Rosenman and Friedman employed an interview schedule and the Jenkins Activity Survey (Jenkins et al., 1967) to identify those with Type A and Type B behavioral tendencies. Type A behavior is characterized by the presence of such behavioral traits as excessive competitiveness at work or play, a high need for recognition, rapid eating patterns, impatience with the slow pace at which events occur, thinking about or doing several tasks at the same time, feelings of hostility and aggressiveness, and a feeling of always struggling against time or the environment. Studies have found that those exhibiting Type A characteristics strive to control their environment and prefer to work alone while under stress (self mastery).

In contrast, Type B behavior is characterized by a relative absence of Type A predispositions, which suggests a different orientation to life. The Type B person can play to relax rather than to prove something to himself or others, can work calmly without self-imposed pressure, and can relax without feeling guilty.

At present there is little evidence as to how Type A or Type B behavior develops. While it is thought that heredity and family and work environment play a role, the influence of each factor is unknown. Moreover, it is unclear whether a Type A environment fosters Type A behavior, or whether Type A individuals seek out Type A environments in which to work and live. Both types of behavior only appear given the appropriate stimulus situation. That is, the striving, competitive, impatient Type A person will not demonstrate this behavior unless the demands of the job and personal lifestyle provide an opportunity to utilize this approach to work and living. Furthermore, the Type A and Type B patterns are not mutually exclusive, but rather represent the endpoints of a continuous dimension (Sparacino, 1979).

To date, few cross-sectional studies have examined the relationship between Type A behavior and age for men and women (Siegler et al., 1980:608). While most studies have found little or no relationship, a few have suggested that Type A behavior is more prevalent among younger subjects. However, because of the relative stability in personality structures, and the use of cross-sectional designs, it is likely that any differences between young and old adults in Type A behavior are more a reflection of cohort differences than of changes with age. Finally, although it appears to be difficult to modify Type A behavior, some success has been demonstrated among post-coronary patients who are between 45 and 65 years of age (Friedman, 1980).

In summary, personality types are established by early adulthood through the interaction of heredity, social involvement, and cultural and historical factors. As a result, individuals generally exhibit stable patterns of thought and behavior and relatively consistent lifestyles throughout the middle and later adult years, regardless of their social situation. However, older individuals may become more passive and show less concern for the external social system. They may also demonstrate more interest in the internal personal system (the self). These attitudes may be the result of cognitive or physical changes, or of the occurrence of significant personal life events that affect the individual's ability to cope with the social world. All of the foregoing assumes that an individual is in good health and free of chronic diseases. However, for a small percentage of adults the later years are characterized by serious declines in health that can lead to the development of psychological disorders. The next section briefly considers some of the changes in personality that result from the impact of declining physical and mental health on the psychological system.

Psychopathology

It is beyond the scope of this section to discuss in detail the causes and consequences of the many forms of abnormal personality processes.[20] Nevertheless, it is important that the reader recognize that with a decline in health as one ages,[21] individual behavior may change dramatically for a variety of reasons. These changes are reflected in abnormal emotional responses or in an inability to think clearly and consistently. Ultimately, the individual may be incapable of functioning as an independent person and will require nursing care, often in an institutional setting.

With a greater likelihood of experiencing social losses, physical disease, physiological changes, social isolation, nutritional deficiencies, a diminished self-esteem, and poverty, the elderly are more likely to be predisposed to both organic[22] (physical) and functional[23] (psychological) personality disorders. Functional disorders can be divided into the less serious neuroses (involving varying degrees of anxiety or fear) and the more disabling psychoses (where reality is distorted so that medication, psychotherapy, or institutionalization may be required). The most common neuroses are anxiety reactions to specific situations or stimuli, excessive concern about one's health (hypochondria), obsessions, and irrational fears or phobias. The more common psychoses are mild to severe depression (which can lead to suicide[24]), paranoid reactions, and schizophrenia.

Signs of forgetfulness or unusual behavior are often labelled as senility. However, only organic brain disorders, where there is deterioration in the brain cells because of disease, can be called senile brain disease (senile dementia). The onset of this disease state is reflected by confusion and disorientation with respect to time, people, and situations; loss of short- and long-term memory; poor judgment; inability to comprehend information; and emotional instability. The prognosis for this disease is not good; in most cases it eventually causes death, either directly or indirectly.[25] The other major organic disorder is cerebral arteriosclerosis. This is caused by a hardening of the arteries in the brain, reducing the blood flow and restricting the amount of oxygen and nutrients reaching the brain. The prognosis for cerebral arteriosclerosis is somewhat more optimistic since drugs are available to treat and retard the disorder.

In summary, few elderly persons experience personality dysfunctions. Most older people adapt, and do not suffer clinical levels of disturbance in the cognitive or emotional processes. That the majority do adapt is somewhat remarkable considering the crises and personal changes many people experience after about 60 years of age.

Summary and Conclusions

Just as there is in the physical system, there is inter- and intra-individual variation in intellectual performance and in personality structures throughout the life cycle. However, in the later years the degree of variation in intellectual functioning and personality adjustment increases, so that general norms are less likely to be applicable to the study of the elderly. Much of the observed variation is due to such personal factors as heredity, health, income, education, present or former occupation, and past and current lifestyle.

The first half of this chapter examined the relationship between aging and such cognitive processes as intelligence, learning, memory, thinking, problem solving, and creativity. In the second half, the focus was on the relationship between aging and personality processes. Specifically, the literature pertaining to personality traits, personality types, and psychopathology in the middle and later years was reviewed. Special attention was directed to the question of whether social behavior in the middle and later years is a function of personality traits or of the social situation, and to the question of whether one's personality remains stable or changes over the life cycle.

Based on this review of the relationship between aging and cognitive and personality processes, it can be concluded that:

1. The decline in cognitive processes may be less rapid and severe than the decline in sensorimotor or physical abilities.

2. Fluid intelligence, after reaching a peak during adolescence, declines with age. This loss may range from three to seven IQ units per decade between the age of 30 and 60.

3. Crystallized intelligence increases with age, at least until the individual is no longer interested in acquiring new information.

4. Individual differences in measured intelligence by age can be accounted for, not by chronological age per se, but rather by the interaction of biological and sensory losses with sociocultural, personal, and situational factors unique to a given individual.

5. The normal aging process does not significantly diminish the ability to solve problems.

6. The elderly can continue to learn if adequate personal and situational conditions are present. Since it might take them longer to learn and produce a required response, learning is more likely to occur if individuals can establish their own rate and speed of learning.

7. A progressive decline in memory performance is neither inevitable nor irreversible.

8. Older persons appear to be able to remember and recall distant events (reminiscence) more readily than recent events.

9. The ability to solve problems and engage in complex thinking may decline with age because of a general slowing of cognitive speed and verbal processes, and because of an unwillingness or an inability to utilize newer, more efficient strategies.

10. In general, creative potential peaks at about 40 years of age. However, there are individual differences by occupation, and given an appropriate environment and personal motivation, some elderly people are capable of highly creative work well into their later years.

11. Social behavior in the later years reflects a continuous interaction between the individual and the social situation. That is, an individual's personality influences the behavior and adaptation demonstrated in particular situations, while the situation itself influences what traits from the available repertoire will be expressed, and in what way.

12. According to cross-sectional studies, personality changes do occur beyond middle age; longitudinal studies suggest that after early adulthood personality characteristics are relatively stable.

13. Both personality traits and personality types are relatively stable across the life cycle. However, there are individual differences in thought and behavior that may be demonstrated in the later years as individuals become more passive and less concerned about normative constraints.

14. With a decline in physical health with advancing age, the elderly are more likely to be predisposed to organic or functional personality disorders. However, few elderly persons experience personality dysfunctions, and most older people do not experience any clinical level of disturbance in the cognitive or emotional processes.

Notes

1. Some tests are designed to assess the overall capacity or potential of the individual, and others are used to measure his or her ability at the time the test is completed. Similarly, some tests emphasize speed and performance, while others concentrate more on verbal skills.

2. One of the most frequently used intelligence tests is the Wechsler Adult Intelligence Scale (WAIS). This is based on materials originally used to test children and adolescents. The reliability and validity of this instrument for use with older adults is questionable since it is a general test that includes items that measure competence in situations rarely encountered by the middle-aged or elderly (Schaie, 1978).

3. Botwinick (1978:230) suggests that education may be more important than age in explaining individual differences in intelligence.

4. Individuals who have similar lifestyles also appear to experience similar patterns of cognitive functioning over time (Gribbin et al., 1980).

5. Many of the tasks in learning experiments are verbal and are not meaningful or relevant, especially to an older person. For example, paired-associate learning involves learning unrelated pairs of words in a list (fish-rainbow) and then responding with the second word in each pair when presented with the first word as the stimulus. The other most frequent learning task is serial learning, where a list of words or nonsense syllables are presented; then the list must be recalled in order (SCU, AXP, YYZ, DRU, MXE, FQI, NCP, etc.). It is generally found that older people perform poorly on both types of tasks. Moreover, women compared to men seem to be less proficient at all ages, but particularly in the later years, on tests involving nonverbal stimuli (Elias and Kinsbourne, 1974). Recent studies using meaningful and 'real' text materials have found that age-related differences are less prevalent (Hultsch and Pentz, 1980).

6. For example, university-level correspondence courses (where lectures are provided on tape and with printed learning aids) may be a more effective learning situation, not only for the elderly, but also for all adults who have been absent from formal schooling for many years. They can learn at their own pace without having to take notes in a classroom from a professor who speaks rapidly, and they can replay the tapes as many times as necessary.

7. Recall memory is thought to involve registration, storage, and retrieval of information, while recognition memory primarily involves registration and storage (Adamowicz, 1976).

8. This may be related to reminiscence, where significant events in the past have been frequently rehearsed.

9. Some of the more common theoretical approaches to the study of personality and its influence on human behavior are psychoanalytic theory, social learning theory, ego development theory, the personality-trait perspective, and the interactionist perspective.

10. While cross-sectional designs (the search for age differences) have been used almost exclusively, interest in both developmental psychology during adulthood and in social gerontology has led to the initiation of a few longitudinal or sequential-cohort (Siegler et al., 1979) studies (the search for age changes).

11. While most studies have focused on measures of one or more personality *traits* (for example, introversion, sociability, aggressiveness, egocentrism, achievement orientation, dependency, etc.), a few studies have used multidimensional scales to arrive at personality *types* (for example, integrated, passive-dependent, work-centered, active-competent, person-oriented, rocking chair, etc.). Moreover, a variety of instruments have been used to measure personality traits or types. These include clinical case studies obtained through interviews; personality inventories (the Cattell 16PF); projective techniques (the Thematic Apperception Test or the Rorschach Ink Blot Test); laboratory behavioral tests; and content analyses of life histories, diaries, memoirs, or autobiographies.

12. Gemeinschaft refers to a community or society where kinship bonds, tradition, informality, and friendship prevail as the major factors in social interaction. This type of society is often found in rural or primitive cultures with low degrees of industrialization.

13. Gesellschaft, the opposite of Gemeinschaft, refers to a society where social relationships are formal, impersonal, competitive, and utilitarian. This type of society is characterized by that found in modernized nations and in metropolitan regions.

14. See Levinson (1978) for a discussion of the hypothesized mid-life crisis for men, and Bardwick (1980) for a similar discussion concerning women.

15. Peskin and Livson (1981) stress the need for more longitudinal studies that will permit frequent measurements across the lifespan.

16. Gutmann (1969) suggested there is a shift in middle life from active to passive mastery. This involves a 'mellowing' process whereby people (men, according to Gutmann) are less active and more relaxed, passive, and reflective.

17. The instruments most frequently used are the Guilford-Zimmerman Temperament Survey; Cattell's 16 Personality Factor (16PF) Inventory; Eysenck's Personality Inventory; and the Minnesota Multiphasic Personality Inventory.

18. Sometimes the traits are measured as isolated characteristics; at other times they are measured in such a way that trait clusters are formed. For example, on the 16PF instrument, sociability, impulsiveness, and dominance combine to represent the personality factor of extraversion. Neugarten (1977a) questions whether it can be assumed that personality traits are independent of one another, or whether the traits are interrelated to create a personality structure (Costa and McCrae, 1976; 1977–78).

19. If cautiousness prevails, the stereotype of the older worker as being more cautious may result in a forced early retirement or in reassignment to lesser responsibilities if risk-taking situations exist on the job. It may also discourage the older worker who has been fired or retired from seeking new employment opportunities.

20. More comprehensive discussions can be found in Busse (1959), Langley (1975), and Pfeiffer (1977).

21. Pfeiffer (1977) estimated that about 15 percent of those over 65 in the United States experience some degree of psychopathology, with about 5 percent requiring institutionalization.

22. Organic disorders result from physiological changes and disease processes such as decreased or impaired blood flow to the brain (hardening of the arteries), brain tumors, or degenerative changes in the brain (senile brain disease).

23. Functional disorders are not related to physical causes and are a reflection of an individual's inability to cope with or adapt to the social environment.

24. In the United States elderly white men are the group most prone to suicide (Harris, 1978:159–60).

25. Alzheimer's disease is one common disorder that has received increased research attention in recent years. Although the cause of this disease is not known, it does not appear to result from a hardening of the arteries. The symptoms of Alzheimer's disease are a gradual loss of memory and learned skills (such as arithmetic and writing) that eventually progresses to a complete inability to utilize memory and judgment.

References

Adamowicz, J. 'Visual Short-Term Memory and Aging,' *Journal of Gerontology*, 31(1/1976), 39–46.

Alpaugh, P. 'Creativity in Adulthood and Old Age: An Exploratory Study,' *Educational Gerontology*, 8(2/1982), 101–16.

Arenberg, D. and E. Robertson-Tchabo. 'Learning and Aging,' pp. 421–49 in J. Birren and K.W. Schaie (eds.). *Handbook of the Psychology of Aging*. New York: Van Nostrand Reinhold, 1977.

Atchley, R. 'Selected Social and Psychological Differences Between Men and Women in Later Life,' *Journal of Gerontology*, 31(2/1976), 204–11.

Baltes, P. 'Life-Span Developmental Psychology: Some Converging Observations on History and Theory,' pp. 255–79 in P. Baltes and O. Brim (eds.). *Life-Span Development and Behavior*. Volume 2. New York: Academic Press, 1979.

Baltes, P. and S. Willis. 'Life-Span Developmental Psychology, Cognitive Functioning and Social Policy,' pp. 15–46 in M. Riley (ed.). *Aging From Birth to Death*. Boulder: Westview Press, 1979.

Bardwick, J. 'The Seasons of a Woman's Life,' in D. McGuigan (ed.). *Women's Lives: New Theory, Research and Practice*. Ann Arbor: University of Michigan Press, 1980.

Birren, J. and K.W. Schaie (eds.). *Handbook of the Psychology of Aging*. New York: Van Nostrand Reinhold, 1977.

Birren, J. et al. 'Behavioral Slowing with Age: Causes, Organization, and Consequences,' pp. 293–308 in L. Poon (ed.). *Aging in the 1980s: Psychological Issues.* Washington, D.C.: American Psychological Association, 1980.

Bolton, E. 'Cognitive and Noncognitive Factors That Affect Learning in Older Adults and Their Implications for Instruction,' *Educational Gerontology,* 3(4/1978), 331–44.

Botwinick, J. 'Intellectual Abilities,' pp. 580–605 in J. Birren and K.W. Schaie (eds.). *Handbook of the Psychology of Aging.* New York: Van Nostrand Reinhold, 1977.

Botwinick, J. *Aging and Behavior.* 2nd edition. New York: Springer Publishing Co., 1978.

Bowles, N. and L. Poon. 'An Analysis of the Effect of Aging on Recognition Memory,' *Journal of Gerontology,* 37(2/1982), 212–19.

Brand, R. 'Coronary Prone Behavior as an Independent Risk Factor for Coronary Heart Disease,' pp. 17–24 in T. Dembroski et al. (eds.). *Coronary Prone Behavior.* New York: Springer-Verlag, 1978.

Busse, E. 'Psychopathology,' pp. 364–99 in J. Birren (ed.). *Handbook of Aging and the Individual.* Chicago: University of Chicago Press, 1959.

Calhoun, R. and S. Hutchison. 'Decision-Making in Old Age: Cautiousness and Rigidity,' *International Journal of Aging and Human Development,* 13(2/1981), 89–98.

Cattell, R. 'Theory of Fluid and Crystallized Intelligence: A Critical Experiment,' *Journal of Educational Psychology,* 54(1/1963), 1–22.

Charness, N. 'Aging and Skilled Problem Solving,' *Journal of Experimental Psychology: General,* 110(1/1981), 21–38.

Cohen, D. and S. Wu. 'Language and Cognition During Aging,' pp. 71–96 in C. Eisdorfer (ed.). *Annual Review of Gerontology and Geriatrics.* Volume 1. New York: Springer Publishing Co., 1980.

Cole, S. 'Age and Scientific Performance,' *American Journal of Sociology,* 84(6/1979), 958–77.

Costa, P. and R. McCrae. 'Age Differences in Personality Structure: A Cluster Analytic Approach,' *Journal of Gerontology,* 31(5/1976), 564–70.

Costa, P. and R. McCrae. 'Age Differences in Personality Structure Revisited: Studies in Validity, Stability, and Change,' *International Journal of Aging and Human Development,* 8(4/1977–78), 261–67.

Costa, P. and R. McCrae. 'Still Stable After All These Years: Personality as a Key to Some Issues in Aging,' pp. 65–102 in P. Baltes and O. Brim (eds.). *Life-Span Development and Behavior.* Volume 3. New York: Academic Press, 1980.

Costa, P. and R. McCrae. *Still Stable After All These Years: Personality in Later Life.* Cambridge, Mass.: Winthrop Publishers Inc., forthcoming.

Costa, P. et al. 'Enduring Dispositions in Adult Males,' *Journal of Personality and Social Psychology,* 38(6/1980), 793–800.

Costa, P. et al. 'Personal Adjustment to Aging: Longitudinal Prediction from Neuroticism and Extraversion,' *Journal of Gerontology,* 36(1/1981), 78–85.

Coyne, A. et al. 'Adult Age Differences in Reflection-Impulsivity,' *Journal of Gerontology,* 33(3/1978), 402–7.

Craik, F. 'Age Differences in Human Memory,' pp. 384–420 in J. Birren and K.W. Schaie (eds.). *Handbook of the Psychology of Aging.* New York: Van Nostrand Reinhold, 1977.

Craik, F. and S. Trehub (eds.). *Aging and Cognitive Processes.* New York: Plenum Press, 1981.

Cunningham, W. 'Speed, Age, and Qualitative Differences in Cognitive Functioning,' pp. 327–31 in L. Poon (ed.). *Aging in the 1980s: Psychological Issues.* Washington, D.C.: American Psychological Association, 1980.

Cunningham, W. et al. 'Fatigue Effects on Intelligence Test Performance in the Elderly,' *Journal of Gerontology,* 33(4/1978), 541–45.

Elias, M. and P. Elias. 'Motivation and Activity,' pp. 357–83 in J. Birren and K.W. Schaie (eds.). *Handbook of the Psychology of Aging.* New York: Van Nostrand Reinhold, 1977.

Elias, M. and M. Kinsbourne. 'Age and Sex Differences in the Processing of Verbal and Nonverbal Stimuli,' *Journal of Gerontology,* 29(2/1974), 162–71.

Endler, N. and D. Magnusson. 'Toward an Interactional Psychology of Personality,' *Psychological Bulletin,* 83(5/1976), 956–74.

Epstein, S. 'The Stability of Behavior: I. On Predicting Most of the People Much of the Time,' *Journal of Personality and Social Psychology,* 37(7/1979), 1097–126.

Fisseni, H. 'Perceived Life Space: Patterns of Constancy and Change,' pp. 93–112 in H. Thomae (ed.). *Patterns of Aging.* New York: S. Karger, 1976.

Fozard, J. 'The Time for Remembering,' pp. 273–87 in L. Poon (ed.). *Aging in the 1980s: Psychological Issues.* Washington, D.C.: American Psychological Association, 1980.

Fozard, J. 'Person-Environment Relationships in Adulthood-Implications for Human Factors Engineering,' *Human Factors,* 23(1/1981), 7–27.

Friedman, M. 'Type A Behavior: A Progress Report,' *The Sciences,* 20(2/1980), 10, 11, 28.

Friedman, M. and R. Rosenman. *Type A Behavior and Your Heart.* New York: Knopf, 1964.

Goldstein, K. and S. Blackman. *Cognitive Style: Five Approaches and Relevant Research.* New York: Wiley-Interscience, 1978.

Granick, S. et al. 'Relationships Between Hearing Loss and Cognition in Normally Hearing Aged Persons,' *Journal of Gerontology,* 31(4/1976), 434–40.

Gribbin, K. et al. 'Complexity of Life-Style and Maintenance of Intellectual Abilities,' *Journal of Social Issues,* 36(2/1980), 47–61.

Grombach, H. 'Consistency and Change of Personality Variables in Late Life,' pp. 51–67 in H. Thomae (ed.). *Patterns of Aging: Findings from the Bonn Longitudinal Study of Aging.* New York: S. Karger, 1976.

Gutmann, D. *The Country of Old Men.* Detroit: Wayne State Institute on Gerontology, 1969.

Haan, N. '...Change and Sameness...,' *International Journal of Aging and Human Development,* 7(1/1976), 59–65.

Haan, N. and D. Day. 'A Longitudinal Study of Change and Sameness in Personality Development: Adolescence to Later Adulthood,' *International Journal of Aging and Human Development,* 5(1/1974), 11–39.

Harkins, S. et al. 'Memory Loss and Response Bias in Senescence,' *Journal of Gerontology,* 34(1/1979), 66–72.

Harris, C. (ed.). *Fact Book on Aging: A Profile of America's Older Population.* Washington, D.C.: National Council on the Aging, 1978.

Hartley, J. et al. 'Contemporary Issues and New Directions in Adult Development of Learning and Memory,' pp. 239–52 in L. Poon (ed.). *Aging in the 1980s: Psychological Issues.* Washington, D.C.: American Psychological Association, 1980.

Havighurst, R. 'Research and Development in Social Gerontology: A Report of a Special Committee of the Gerontological Society,' *The Gerontologist,* 9(4/1969), 1–90.

Hayslip, B. and H. Sterns. 'Age Differences in Relationships Between Crystallized and Fluid Intelligences and Problem Solving,' *Journal of Gerontology,* 34(3/1979), 404–14.

Hertzog, C. et al. 'Cardiovascular Disease and Changes in Intellectual Functioning from Middle to Old Age,' *Journal of Gerontology,* 33(6/1978), 872–83.

Hines, T. and J. Fozard. 'Memory and Aging: Relevance of Recent Developments for Research and Application,' pp. 97–120 in C. Eisdorfer (ed.). *Annual Review of Gerontology and Geriatrics.* Volume 1. New York: Springer Publishing Co., 1980.

Horn, J. 'Human Ability Systems,' pp. 211–56 in P. Baltes (ed.). *Life-Span Development and Behavior.* Volume 1. New York: Academic Press, 1978.

Horn, J. *Aging and Adult Development of Cognitive Functions.* Cambridge, Mass.: Winthrop Publishers Inc., forthcoming.

Horn, J. 'Apprehension, Memory and Fluid Intelligence Decline in Adulthood,' *Research on Aging,* 3(1/1981), 33–84.

Hoyer, W. and D. Plude. 'Attentional and Perceptual Processes in the Study of Cognitive Aging,' pp. 227–38 in L. Poon (ed.). *Aging in the 1980s: Psychological Issues.* Washington, D.C.: American Psychological Association, 1980.

Hultsch, D. 'Learning to Learn in Adulthood,' *Journal of Gerontology,* 29(3/1974), 302–8.

Hultsch, D. and F. Deutsch. *Adult Development and Aging: A Life-Span Perspective.* New York: McGraw-Hill, 1981.

Hultsch, D. and C. Pentz. 'Encoding, Storage and Retrieval in Adult Memory: The Role of Model Assumptions,' pp. 73–94 in L. Poon et al. (eds.). *New Directions in Memory and Aging: Proceedings of the G.A. Talland Memorial Conference.* Hillsdale, N.J.: Lawrence Erlbaum, 1980.

Hunter, K. et al. 'Characteristics of High and Low Self-Esteem in the Elderly,' *International Journal of Aging and Human Development,* 14(2/1981–82), 117–26.

Jenkins, C. et al. 'Development of an Objective Psychological Test for the Determination of the Coronary Prone Behavior Pattern in Employed Men,' *Journal of Chronic Diseases,* 20(6/1967), 371–79.

Kogan, N. 'Creativity and Cognitive Styles: A Life-Span Perspective,' pp. 146–78 in P. Baltes and K.W. Schaie (eds.). *Life-Span Developmental Psychology: Personality and Socialization.* New York: Academic Press, 1973.

Labouvie-Vief, G. and M. Chandler. 'Cognitive Development and Life-Span Developmental Theory: Idealistic Versus Contextual Perspectives,' pp. 181–210 in P. Baltes (ed.). *Life-Span Development and Behavior.* Volume 1. New York: Academic Press Inc., 1978.

Labouvie-Vief, G. and J. Gonda. 'Cognitive Strategy Training and Intellectual Performance in the Elderly,' *Journal of Gerontology,* 31(3/1976), 327–32.

Langley, G. 'Functional Psychoses,' pp. 326–55 in J. Howells (ed.). *Modern Perspectives in the Psychiatry of Old Age.* New York: Bronner/Mazel, 1975.

Laszlo, J. et al. 'Distracting Information, Motor Performance and Sex Differences,' *Nature,* 283(January, 1980), 377–78.

Lawton, M.P. et al. 'Personality Tests and Their Uses With Older Adults,' pp. 537–53 in J. Birren and R. Sloane (eds.). *Handbook of*

Mental Health and Aging. Englewood Cliffs, N.J.: Prentice-Hall, 1980.

Levinson, D. *The Seasons of a Man's Life.* New York: Ballantine, 1978.

Maas, H. and J. Kuypers. *From Thirty to Seventy.* San Francisco: Jossey-Bass, 1974.

Madden, D. and R. Nebes. 'Aging and the Development of Automaticity in Visual Search,' *Developmental Psychology,* 16(5/1980), 377–84.

Madden, D. and R. Nebes. 'Age Effects in Selective Attention During Visual Search,' paper presented at the annual meeting of the Gerontological Society of America, Toronto, November 1981.

McCrae, R. et al. 'Constancy of Adult Personality Structure in Males: Longitudinal, Cross-Sectional and Times of Measurement Analyses,' *Journal of Gerontology,* 35(6/1980), 877–83.

McLeish, J. *The Ulyssean Adult: Creativity in the Middle and Later Years.* New York: McGraw-Hill, 1976.

Murdock, B. 'Recent Developments in Short-Term Memory,' *Quarterly Journal of Experimental Psychology,* 18(3/1967), 206–11.

Neugarten, B. 'Personality and Aging,' pp. 626–49 in J. Birren and K.W. Schaie (eds.). *Handbook of the Psychology of Aging.* New York: Van Nostrand Reinhold, 1977a.

Neugarten, B. 'Personality and the Aging Process,' pp. 72–77 in S. Zarit (ed.). *Readings in Aging and Death: Contemporary Perspectives.* New York: Harper and Row, 1977b.

Neugarten, B. and D. Gutmann. 'Age-Sex Roles and Personality in Middle Age: A Thematic Apperception Study,' *Psychological Monographs,* 72(7/1958), 1–33.

Neugarten, B. et al. *Personality in Middle and Later Life.* New York: Atherton Press, 1964.

Parkinson, S. et al., 'An Analysis of Age Differences in Immediate Recall,' *Journal of Gerontology,* 37(4/1982), 425–31.

Peskin, H. and N. Livson. 'Psychological Health: Uses of the Past in Adult Development,' in D. Eichorn et al. (eds.). *Present and Past in Middle Life.* New York: Academic Press, 1981.

Peterson, D. and D. Eden. 'Cognitive Style and the Older Learner,' *Educational Gerontology,* 7(1/1981), 57–66.

Pfeiffer, E. 'Psychopathology and Social Pathology,' pp. 650–71 in J. Birren and K.W. Schaie (eds.). *Handbook of the Psychology of Aging.* New York: Van Nostrand Reinhold, 1977.

Plemons, J. et al. 'Modifiability of Fluid Intelligence in Aging: A Short-Term Longitudinal Training Approach,' *Journal of Gerontology,* 33(2/1978), 224–31.

Poon, L. and J. Fozard. 'Speed of Retrieval from Long-Term Memory in Relation to Age, Familiarity, and Datedness of Information,' *Journal of Gerontology,* 33(5/1978), 711–17.

Poon, L. et al. (eds.). *New Directions in Memory and Aging: Proceedings of the G.A. Talland Memorial Conference.* Hillsdale, N.J.: Lawrence Erlbaum, 1980.

Rabbitt, P. 'Changes in Problem Solving Ability in Old Age,' pp. 606–25 in J. Birren and K.W. Schaie (eds.). *Handbook of the Psychology of Aging.* New York: Van Nostrand Reinhold, 1977.

Rankin, J. and D. Kausler. 'Adult Age Differences in False Recognitions,' *Journal of Gerontology,* 34(1/1979), 58–65.

Reichard, S. et al. *Aging and Personality.* New York: John Wiley, 1962.

Riley, M. and A. Foner. *Aging and Society. Volume one: An Inventory of Research Findings.* New York: Russell Sage Foundation, 1968.

Rowe, A. 'The Retired Scientist: The Myth of the Aging Individual,' pp. 209–19 in J. Gubrium (ed.). *Time, Roles and Self in Old Age.* New York: Human Sciences Press, 1976.

Ryff, C. 'Self-Perceived Personality Change in Adulthood and Aging,' *Journal of Personality and Social Psychology,* 42(1/1982), 108–15.

Schaie, K.W. 'Age Changes in Adult Intelligence,' pp. 111–24 in D. Woodruff and J. Birren (eds.). *Aging: Scientific Perspectives and Social Issues.* New York: D. Van Nostrand Co., 1975.

Schaie, K.W. 'External Validity in the Assessment of Intellectual Development in Adulthood,' *Journal of Gerontology,* 33(5/1978), 695–701.

Schaie, K.W. and I. Parham. 'Stability of Adult Personality Traits: Fact or Fable?' *Journal of Personality and Social Psychology,* 34(1/1976), 146–58.

Schaie, K.W. and E. Zelinski. *Intellectual Functioning and Aging: A Selected Bibliography.* Los Angeles: Andrus Gerontology Center, University of Southern California, 1975.

Scheidt, R. and K.W. Schaie. 'A Taxonomy of Situations for an Elderly Population: Generating Situational Criteria,' *Journal of Gerontology,* 33(6/1978), 848–57.

Schulz, R. 'Emotionality and Aging: A Theoretical and Empirical Analysis,' *Journal of Gerontology,* 37(1/1982), 42–51.

Shanan, J. 'Personality,' chapter 6 in C. Eisdorfer (ed.). *Annual Review of Gerontology and Geriatrics.* Volume 3. New York: Springer Publishing Co., 1982.

Schonfield, A. 'Learning, Memory and Aging,' pp. 214–44 in J. Birren and R. Sloane (eds.). *Handbook of Mental Health and Aging.* Englewood Cliffs, N.J.: Prentice-Hall, 1980.

Siegler, I. et al. 'Cross-Sequential Analysis of Adult Personality,' *Developmental Psychology*, 15(3/1979), 350–51.

Siegler, I. et al. 'Health and Behavior: Methodological Considerations for Adult Development and Aging,' pp. 599–612 in L. Poon (ed.). *Aging in the 1980s: Psychological Issues*. Washington, D.C.: American Psychological Association, 1980.

Sills, R. et al. 'Age Norms: 1960s and 1980s Compared,' paper presented at the 33rd annual meeting of the Gerontological Society of America, San Diego, California, November 1980.

Sparacino, J. 'The Type A Behavior Pattern: A Critical Assessment,' *Journal of Human Stress*, 5(4/1979), 37–51.

Sprott, R. (ed.). *Age, Learning Ability and Intelligence*. New York: Van Nostrand Reinhold, 1980.

Taub, H. 'Memory Span, Practice and Aging,' *Journal of Gerontology*, 28(3/1973), 335–38.

Thomae, H. (ed.). *Patterns of Aging: Findings from the Bonn Longitudinal Study of Aging*. New York: S. Karger, 1976.

Thomae, H. 'Personality and Adjustment to Aging,' pp. 285–309 in J. Birren and R. Sloane (eds.). *Handbook of Mental Health and Aging*. Englewood Cliffs, N.J.: Prentice-Hall, 1980.

Troll, L. and E. Parron. 'Age Changes in Sex Roles Amid Changing Sex Roles: The Double Shift,' pp. 118–43 in C. Eisdorfer (ed.). *Annual Review of Gerontology and Geriatrics*. Volume 2. New York: Springer Publishing Co., 1981.

Tulving, E. 'Episodic and Semantic Memory,' pp. 382–403 in E. Tulving and W. Donaldson (eds.). *Organization of Memory*. New York: Academic Press, 1972.

Waugh, N. et al. 'Age-Related Differences in Serial Binary Classification,' *Experimental Aging Research*, 4(5/1978a), 433–42.

Waugh, N. et al. 'Retrieval Time from Different Memory Stores,' *Journal of Gerontology*, 33(5/1978b), 718–24.

Welford, A. 'Motivation, Capacity, Learning and Age,' *International Journal of Aging and Human Development*, 7(3/1976), 189–99.

Williams, R. and C. Wirths. *Lives Through the Years*. New York: Atherton Press, 1965.

Willis, S. and P. Baltes. 'Intelligence in Adulthood and Aging: Contemporary Issues,' pp. 260–72 in L. Poon (ed.). *Aging in the 1980s: Psychological Issues*. Washington, D.C.: American Psychological Association, 1980.

Winograd, E. 'Frame Representations in the Declarative/Procedural Controversy,' pp. 185–210 in D. Bobrow and A. Collins (eds.). *Representation and Understanding: Studies in Cognitive Science*. New York: Academic Press, 1975.

Winograd, E. et al. 'Aging and the Picture Superiority Effect in Recall,' *Journal of Gerontology*, 37(1/1982), 70–75.

Woodruff, D. and J. Birren. 'Age Changes and Cohort Differences in Personality,' *Developmental Psychology*, 6(2/1972), 252–59.

Woodruff, D. and D. Walsh. 'Research in Adult Learning: The Individual,' *The Gerontologist*, 17(5/1977), 424–30.

PART THREE

A Macroanalysis of Aging as a Social Process

In Part Three aging will be studied from a macrosociological perspective. Here, the focus is on how the social structure and related social processes influence aging and the status of the aged.

Chapter 7 contains a discussion of the way in which social structure influences the process of aging for age cohorts at the societal level of analysis, and for generations within the extended family. The chapter examines the relationship between social structure and such processes as cohort flow, socialization, stereotyping, attitude formation, ageism, and stratification. Other issues considered are the status of the elderly within the age structure; the extent to which the aged represent a unique minority, poverty, or political group; the issue of single versus multiple jeopardy; and the extent to which a generation gap exists in society and the extended family.

Chapter 8 looks at the influence of the physical environment on the aging process, with emphasis on interaction between personal and environmental systems. At the macro level of analysis, factors influencing the aging process such as rural versus urban living, age-integrated versus age-segregated housing, availability of transportation, criminal victimization of the elderly, fear of criminal victimization, and migration are considered. At the micro level, the type and quality of dwelling unit, institutionalization, and mobility and migration in the later years are discussed.

7

Aging: The Social Structure
and Social Processes

Chapters 5 and 6 dealt with changes within the organism that partially accounted for changing status and behavior during the life cycle; Chapters 7 and 8 will
examine the interaction between aging individuals and their external social and
physical environments. This chapter divides the complex phenomenon of social
organization into two major components – social structure and social process –
and discusses the interplay between structure, processes and social interaction as
an individual ages. The interaction between the individual, the age structure,
and the major social institutions (family, work, religion, and leisure) is
considered in Part Four of this book.

Throughout this chapter, the focus is on the influence of chronological age
and social age in the organization of society. Every society has a social structure
that is influenced by the age distribution of the population. This structure sets
boundaries for life chances and lifestyle by assigning people to age-appropriate
social roles. A culture evolves within this structure that defines, facilitates, or
prohibits particular forms of social behavior and self-perceptions at specific
stages in the life cycle. Through this complex interplay, an element of social
control is present within the society. For the individual, norms facilitate social
interaction and the transition between roles and stages in the life cycle.

As will be seen, however, the process and product of social interaction
between age cohorts is not as simple as suggested above. Rather, the process is
complicated by the following social factors:

1. A dynamic age structure that can change over time with respect to the size,
   composition, or social meaning of age groups;

2. Unique historical and social events that a specific generation may experience
   at a particular stage in life;

3. Perceived or real age-based inequalities that may lead to tension and conflict
   between age groups;

4. The relationship of age to other elements of social differentiation such as sex,
   race, ethnicity, and social class;

5. Individual differences within an age cohort or generation (generational
   units);

6. The presence of different age structures within a variety of social institutions
   such as the family, the economy, the polity, leisure, and religion;

7. The cross-cultural variations in the age structure of developing and
   developed nations.

It is necessary to distinguish between the structure and processes unique to age cohorts or generations at the societal level and those unique to aging within the extended family. For example, a generational difference or 'generation gap' may be revealed when studies randomly sample and compare unrelated 65, 45, and 25-year-olds. However, differences may or may not be perceived if the study compares the responses of those who are 65, 45, and 25 years of age within the same extended family. That is, differences between cohorts may be more pronounced at the societal level than at the micro level where the extended family is the unit of analysis.

The study of aging phenomena from a macro perspective is characterized by diverse conceptual and theoretical approaches. For example, many of the theories and concepts presented in chapter 4 (socialization theory, minority group theory, disengagement theory, and continuity theory) appear to be useful in studying the interaction between social structure, social processes, and aging phenomena. The remainder of this chapter introduces concepts and processes pertaining to birth cohorts and to generations at both the macro and micro structural levels of analysis, examines the influence on the aging process of the interaction between social structure and social processes from a macro level of cohort and generational analysis, and presents a micro-level analysis of lineage (family) interaction within and between generations in the kinship system. Included are a discussion of the structure of the kinship system and an analysis of the hypothesized generation gap or generational conflict assumed to exist within extended families.

The Social Structure and Aging

Introduction

In the absence of a social structure, chaos would prevail because of the lack of regular, persistent, and enduring patterns of social interaction. In order to function and survive, all social systems, from married couples to societies, require division of labor among the members. This horizontal separation of positions (husband, wife, friends, neighbors) occurs within all social institutions and is known as social differentiation.

The social positions found within each system are evaluated and ranked, and varying degrees of status are assigned to each position. As a result, a vertical dimension is added to the social structure. Certain positions are evaluated as having more or less status, power, or prestige than others. This vertical ranking may be based on the ascribed characteristics of the individuals who occupy the position (age, sex, race, ethnicity, socioeconomic status), or on the achievements of those who have occupied the position in the past (Foner, 1979). Generally, the greater the status of a position, the greater the social or monetary rewards given to the person who occupies the position.

Because specific ascribed or achieved characteristics are evaluated differently, not everyone has an equal opportunity to attain specific positions in the social structure. Some degree of inequality prevails in most social systems, and influences both the life chances and lifestyle of specific individuals. For example, within North American societies the institutionalized systems of stratification are generally based on age, sex, class, race, or ethnicity. As Tumin (1967:27) noted, one is generally considered better, superior, or more worthy if one is:

- White rather than black
- Male rather than female
- Protestant rather than Catholic or Jewish
- Educated rather than uneducated
- Rich rather than poor
- White-collar rather than blue-collar
- Of good family background rather than of undistinguished family origin
- Young rather than old
- Urban or suburban rather than rural-dwelling
- Of Anglo-Saxon origin rather than any other
- Native-born rather than of foreign descent
- Employed rather than unemployed
- Married rather than divorced

Like Rubik's Cube, the social structure of modern developed societies is a complex mosaic of intersecting horizontal and vertical dimensions representing a variety of social characteristics. In contrast, in preindustrialized societies a simple three-tiered structure often prevails: a group of elderly males who rule as a gerontocracy; all other adults; and children and adolescents who have not been declared 'adults' by some rite of passage.

The social structure represents an arrangement of positions or statuses within a number of social institutions (family, education, economy, polity, religion) in a given society. The status associated with each position is ascribed or achieved on the basis of such factors as age, race, sex, class, ethnicity, occupation, education, or religion. Associated with each position are roles that define the expected rights, obligations, and behavioral patterns of the individual who occupies the position. Social norms evolve that represent common agreement on how individuals should behave while occupying specific roles. These norms provide clues as to how others will interpret and react to the individual.

In short, the social structure represents the distribution of individuals according to various socially evaluated characteristics. These characteristics distinguish individuals from each other and influence the positions they occupy, both within a specific social system (such as the place of employment) and within the community or society at large. Thus, throughout one's life this 'assignment' to certain positions introduces inequality to the social system, influences the life chances and lifestyles,[1] and facilitates or inhibits social interaction within[2] and between the various strata of the social structure (Cain, 1964; Blau, 1974, 1975, 1980; Elder, 1975; Neugarten and Hagestad, 1976; Bengtson et al., 1977).

As already noted, there exist multiple structures that involve the differentiation of people on a number of horizontal and vertical dimensions. An individual may occupy different positions within a micro structure that primarily involves face-to-face interaction with others in the system (the same person may be a parent and a child in an extended family). The same individual will also occupy varying positions within different institutions in the macro structure of society. For example, Blau (1974) suggests that at the macro level, there is an age structure of the population, a kinship structure in the tribe or family, an age structure of occupations and jobs (Kaufman and Spilerman, 1982), a power structure within the community, and a class structure in the society.

It is this structural differentiation that facilitates or inhibits interaction and leads to the integration or isolation of individuals or groups within a social system. A middle-aged male may have relatively high status in the age structure, high status in the family, little authority or power in the place of employment and the community, and relatively low status because of his class background. With the interaction between substructures in mind, the remainder of this chapter will focus on the age structure of society and of a specific social institution (the family). We will also consider how these structures change over time and vary cross-culturally, and how various social structures influence social processes at the macro (societal) level and interaction at the micro (interpersonal) level.

Before turning to this analysis, it is important to clarify the meaning of three major concepts frequently used in this area of gerontology: 'cohort,' 'generation,' and 'generational unit.' The search for conclusive definitions of these concepts represents a continuing debate among social scientists and gerontologists (Mannheim, 1952; Eisenstadt, 1956; Ryder, 1968; Palmore, 1978; Rosow, 1978; McQuaide and Sauer, 1979; Troll and Bengtson, 1979; Kertzer, 1981, 1983; Marshall, 1981a). A 'cohort' is a group of individuals who were born within a given period. It is a general term that is based on a quantifiable difference between groups (one year or five years).

A 'generation' represents a grouping of individual or adjacent birth cohorts, where a large proportion of the members have experienced a significant sociohistorical event (a war, the baby boom, a depression) in a similar manner. This event subsequently influences their life chances (educational or occupational opportunities) or lifestyles. The term 'generation' represents a qualitative rather than a quantitative difference between groups of individuals. There may be subgroups within the same generation with different world views or with a unique group consciousness (for example, young adults who are college students versus age peers who are blue-collar workers). Each unique subgroup is defined as a 'generational unit.'

It is important to distinguish between cohort analysis, generational analysis, and lineage effects. The term 'cohort analysis' is in common use in demography, and refers to the analysis of quantitatively defined birth cohorts. 'Generational analysis' refers to a macro-level analysis of specific cohorts, or groups of cohorts, that are theoretically combined because of their common sociohistorical experiences. Generational analysis has also been used to examine differences between generations within the extended family. As Marshall (1981a) notes, however, the analysis of relationships within the kinship structure is more appropriately and commonly labelled 'lineage effects.' In this text, the use of 'cohort' and 'generational' analysis will be restricted to the macro level of analysis, while the term 'lineage effects' will be used at the micro level when examining the structure and social processes within the context of the extended family.

Age Cohorts and the Social Structure

Introduction.   Age, unlike attributes such as sex, race, or ethnicity, which have an impact only on certain individuals, is a universal factor in determining an individual's location and status in the social structure. One's entrance into and movement through a structure are inevitable and biologically determined. Every society has an age structure based on both chronological and social age. These factors determine which persons gain access to social positions, at what stage in life they gain access to or relinquish roles, how different cohorts interact with each other, what age-role expectations are demanded from the occupants of particular positions, and what status is attached to those of a particular chronological age. The following sections indicate how chronological and social age contribute to the creation of a social structure within society in general, and to an age structure within such institutions as the family, work, polity, and leisure.

Demographic factors and the age structure.   The discussion of demography in chapter 3 showed that age cohorts represent people born during the same period who age chronologically together. It was noted that there are local, regional, national, and international variations in the size and composition of the total population, as well as in the age cohorts or age strata that make up the population. Thus, a given society might be called 'young,' 'mature,' or 'old,' depending on the proportion of the population 65 years of age and over.

Whether a society has a high or low proportion of individuals of any given age depends on such demographic processes as fertility, mortality, and migration, and on the presence or absence of such historical events as technological revolutions, disasters, wars, or epidemics. Since new birth cohorts succeed one another over time, the size and composition of the population are subject to demographic changes, and the age structure of a local, regional, or national social system can change over time (Bengtson et al., 1977; Uhlenberg, 1977; Van Es and Bowling, 1978–79; Maddox, 1979; Stahura, 1980).

At the turn of the century, the age structure of a society generally consisted of a relatively simple age-graded system composed of infancy, adulthood, and old age. Today, most modern developed societies include as many as seven strata: infancy (birth to 2), childhood (3–12), adolescence (13–18), young adulthood (19–35), middle age (36–54), the young-old (55–75), and the old-old (76+).[3] There have been changes in the number of strata and in the shape of the age structure. There have also been changes in the relative prestige positions of the strata. For example, in premodernized societies the oldest male generally has the most prestige and power; in modern societies, which have more strata, the power shifts to the middle-aged group (Turner, 1975).

Demographic changes in the size and composition of the age structure may also lead to social changes in the society. A particular event may change the size of a cohort or the way in which a cohort ages. This in turn may lead to cohorts exhibiting different expectations, preferences, and behaviors. As a result, a particular cohort may interact differently with cohorts that precede or follow it through a particular stage in life. For example, the readiness of a particularly large birth cohort (such as the baby boom) to enter the labor force, or the onset of inflation and high unemployment among young adults, may put pressure on those over 60 years of age to retire early, thereby creating an unusually large cohort of economically dependent retired adults. At the same time, this situation may lead to conflict between unemployed youth and older adults over the allocation of programs and services geared to different age strata (financing job-creation programs versus expanding home-care programs).

Regardless of the demographic changes that may occur over time, chronological age structures are invariably present in most social institutions. These stratification systems serve to locate individuals and determine their status in the overall social structure. This location, in turn, influences when and how an individual will participate in particular institutions. Age serves as a criterion for entering and leaving positions, and for interacting with others (Cain, 1964). For example, the educational system is an elaborate age-graded system wherein chronological age is the basis for entrance, exit, and measurement of progress.

Similarly, in the labor force, codified norms based on chronological age determine when individuals are eligible for full-time employment, when they must retire and when they are eligible to receive age-related income tax or pension benefits (Smith, 1973).

In other areas of social participation, codified laws, based on chronological age, determine when one can vote, drive a car, or get married, be charged with a criminal offence as an adult, drink in public establishments, or attend certain movies. In this sense, chronological age has a significant impact on lifestyle and life chances. An individual is labelled as a member of a specific cohort located in a specific position within the age structure. However, chronological age is not a sufficient predictor of abilities, needs, achievement, social location, or interaction patterns, since chronological ages have varying social meanings depending on the culture and the historical period. For example, at one time those over 40 years of age were considered 'old,' yet early in this century people were not defined as 'old' until about 65 years of age. Therefore, social age may be a better predictor of social behavior than chronological age or membership in a particular birth cohort.

The age structure.   The process whereby age determines social location, roles, expectations, norms, and interpersonal relationships is known as age grading. This process results from a system of age stratification (Riley et al., 1972; Riley, 1976; Streib, 1976; Dowd, 1980) that is present not only within the society at large, but also within specific institutions. Age grades evolve within these systems to provide a cultural definition of the expected rights, behaviors, and responsibilities of an individual at a particular time in his or her life. These age grades become the basis for self-identification and for allocating positions within the society or institution. For example, while nothing in the law prevents one of your professors from being appointed president of your university, those under 40 years of age might be considered too young for such a position, however qualified they might be.

Within a system of age stratification, age is the criterion by which individuals are assigned to differently rewarded positions. Age strata, which are made up of members who are at different chronological stages in the life cycle, are interconnected, and there are varying degrees of interaction between them. As we will see in the next section, an individual's location often influences his or her behavior, attitudes, and values in a number of domains, and provides behavioral expectations for others with whom an individual might interact. Unfortunately, some of these age-related expectations become so institutionalized that they may lead to self-fulfilling prophecies and stereotypes that enhance the differences between strata. For example, retirees may be encouraged to 'relax' and not be concerned about productivity. However, for some the potential and desire to be creative and productive persists, and may go unfulfilled if they adhere to the socially induced age norm that says they are expected to 'take it easy' after they retire.

As noted earlier, social meanings are attached to chronological age spans, so that a hierarchical system emerges wherein one level differs from others on the basis of relatively clearly defined social expectations. As a result of this process of evaluation, age norms emerge that serve as a form of social control. These norms define socially appropriate behavior at different ages, they define status through ascription, they regulate social interaction, and they define when and in what order life events should occur (Hogan, 1978).

Two types of age norms are internalized to varying degrees, depending on the process of socialization to which an individual has been exposed at different stages in life. Ascriptive age norms are based on rules and constraints determined by a specific chronological age (retirement at 70, voting at 18, driving at 16). Consensual age norms provide an approximate age range in which specific roles or behavior are appropriate or relinquished (Neugarten and Datan, 1973). They define the approximate age for events such as leaving home and starting a career, getting married, having children, being promoted, or retiring. They also influence lifestyle factors such as appropriate dress or social participation. These age norms appear to exist in the minds of most people; they are learned through socialization, and they provide some degree of social control by constraining behavior (Neugarten et al., 1965). There appear to be few age-related norms that apply to acceptable and unacceptable behavior for older people (Havighurst and Albrecht, 1953; Rosow, 1974:68–69). In an early paper on social gerontology, Burgess (1960) suggested that the retired man and wife find themselves in a 'roleless role' whereby they have no vital function to perform. Similarly, Wood (1971) speaks of the ambiguity in the norms concerning behavior for older people. While general norms for the aged may be vague, incomplete, or nonexistent, age norms within an extended family are generally clear with respect to such roles as grandparent, parent, and wage earner (Rosow, 1974).

Where clearly defined norms for older adults are present, they often refer to behavior that should be avoided at a particular age (for those over 50, discos are 'out'; if one is over 60 and widowed, he or she should not cohabit with a member of the opposite sex). Obviously, age norms can change over time because of social change, and because of changes in socialization practices, societal values, or economic conditions. Furthermore, they may or may not be adhered to by all members of a particular age cohort. For example, those who are in their 20s today, some of whom may have lived with one or more friends of the opposite sex before marriage, may consider such behavior to be normative later in life if they become widowed or divorced. However, among those who are now over 65, this type of living arrangement generally invokes negative sanctions from the peer group.

As Neugarten (1980) recently noted, there now appear to be fewer age-related social norms for older persons than there were even a few years ago. Chronological age may be less relevant as a determinant of social behavior in the future. However, while some societies, or even segments of a particular society, may be placing less emphasis on age norms to guide behavior, it is unlikely that age will become irrelevant in allocating rewards and influencing social interaction and life chances. Rather, age norms will continue to impose some degree of order on the progression of events in the life cycle.

Where age norms are highly institutionalized, they serve to reinforce age grades, and to solidify age stratification to the point where age becomes a major element in social organization.[4] That is, age norms create order and some degree of predictability in life, and establish timetables and boundaries for acceptable behavior at successive stages (Neugarten and Hagestad, 1976). Furthermore, age status expectations provide a link between the personality system of individuals and their social system (Eisenstadt, 1956:32). Foner and Kertzer (1978) examined the process of life-course transitions in twenty-one African age-set societies. In these societies, people are assigned group membership on the basis of similarity in chronological age. Individuals proceed equally, at culturally prescribed intervals, from one age grade to another.[5] The age grade of an individual indicates his or her status and role relationships.

In contrast, modern societies are likely to have an age-stratification system wherein norms and status allocation processes are less clearly defined. In these societies, chronological age provides only a partial clue to an individual's social location. Other forms of differentiation such as class, race, sex, and education intersect with age stratification, thereby weakening age norms as the prime determinant of life chances and lifestyle. There is a greater likelihood of structured social inequality in societies where the age-stratification system is not the major form of differentiation.

Generations and the Social Structure

Introduction.   Earlier we saw that social structure comprises demographic factors (the size and composition of interrelated age cohorts) and the social meaning attached to chronological age or to particular stages in the life cycle (age grades, age status, age-related social roles). Age cohorts are heterogeneous groups, however, and there is intracohort differentiation in other relevant social characteristics, values, beliefs, and behaviors. Intercohort differences that occur over time may lead to continuity or change in the social structure because of such processes as generational differences, social conflict, and social change.

The concern of social scientists interested in generational analysis has been with social change, and the effect that each emerging age group may have on maintaining continuity (consensus) or introducing discontinuity (conflict) into the existing social order (Bengtson et al., 1974; Pampel, 1981; Tindale, 1981). In this section, the concept of 'generation' is introduced in order to provide a developmental and comparative perspective on the study of how location in the social structure impinges on processes at the societal level and on interaction at the individual level.

Generations, generational units, and social structure.   Philosophers, historians, and social scientists have long been interested in the impact that particular age groups, acting as a collective force, have on social, economic, and political changes in society. While a number of scholars have used the concept of generation, Mannheim (1952), Eisenstadt (1956), Troll (1970), Bengtson and associates (Bengtson and Lovejoy, 1973; Bengtson and Laufer, 1974a, 1974b; Bengtson et al., 1974; Bengtson and Cutler, 1976; Bengtson and Schrader, 1982), Graubard (1978) and Marshall (1981a) provided the necessary conceptual and empirical impetus that has led social gerontologists to use generational analysis in the study of aging phenomena (Dowd, 1979–80; Tindale, 1981; Bengtson et al., forthcoming; Hagestad, 1982).

Mannheim (1952) was the first to argue that a generation was more than a group of people (an age cohort) born during the same period. In his opinion, a generation was a unique group of individuals who were not only born during the same period, but who also experienced and reacted to particular political, social, or historical events in the same way. As a result, they developed a historical consciousness that gave a particular social meaning to their lives. This generational consciousness led them to think and behave in ways different from that of other generations, and often to become organized to initiate social change. Three unique generations that evolved in North America include those who had just entered, or were about to enter, the labor force when the Depression struck in 1929; the baby-boom generation born in the years following World War II; and the 'counterculture' and student protest youth generation of the 1960s.

These generations resulted from a merging and interaction of unique demographic facts and the social meaning of being at a particular chronological age when specific social, political, or historical events occurred. These events affected these generations throughout most of their lives, and a social or political consciousness evolved among them.[6] For example, the 'Depression generation' has generally been consistently willing to work hard for low wages. Similarly, the baby-boom cohort experienced crowded schools and now faces stiff intra- and intercohort competition for jobs; and the 'protest' generation may always be more outspoken and critical of political and economic conditions than preceding or subsequent generations.

Mannheim (1952) noted that the social construction of a generation will not occur among all age cohorts that emerge and pass through the stratification system. Mannheim (1952:304) further stated that because age strata are made up of individuals with heterogeneous characteristics and experiences, generations consist of subsets called 'generational units.' These subsets are made up of individuals who have unique characteristics, lifestyles, or beliefs, and who have enough common interests that they interact frequently. Thus, there may be a number of generational units within a given generation. For example, within the North American 'youth generation' of the 1960s, college students were the generational unit that was most radical, not working-class youth of the same age. In contrast, in Great Britain, youth from the working class tended to be the more radical and rebellious generational unit within the youth culture. In short, not only are there unique generational units within an age cohort, **but** the composition of the units may vary across cultures.

Generational units may be based on social characteristics such as class, race, or ethnicity; they may also be related to political or social perspectives such as liberalism, conservatism, or socialism. Furthermore, generations and generational units are stratified with respect to power, prestige, wealth, and authority. As a result, there may be many generational units within and between age cohorts. This may lead to different patterns of social behavior and needs among the elderly. For example, involuntary segregation (in inner cities or in institutions) or voluntary segregation (in retirement communities) of the aged may lead to the formation of an aging subculture and an emerging age-group consciousness. In contrast, those who are integrated into the community and who interact more frequently with other age groups may not be a generational unit. They may not even perceive themselves to be members of the 'older' generation. In fact, as Bengtson and Cutler (1976) noted, some elderly people over 70 deny their chronological age and identify with the middle-aged stratum rather than with their chronological age peers.

Eisenstadt's (1956) classic study sought to determine how generations interact to produce continuity or change in the social order. Eisenstadt was interested in how age strata are differentiated, how generations move from one age grade to another, and to what extent conflict develops between generations, particularly between younger and older members of society.

He hypothesized that social groups may be primarily or exclusively age-homogeneous rather than age-heterogeneous. He suggested that age-heterogeneous groups are prevalent in societies where the kinship system is the basic unit in the division of labor. In contrast, age-homogeneous groupings are characteristic of modern societies where patterns of interaction become segmented according to common age-related interests and needs. To illustrate this point, think of your own situation and keep a record for a week concerning how frequently you interact face-to-face with others who are at least five years older or younger than you are.

While most of the early interest in generations was concerned with the structural factors affecting the transition from youth to adulthood, more recently a developmental perspective has prevailed (Troll and Bengtson, 1979).[7] As a result, gerontologists have been interested in continuities and discontinuities in cohort flow; in intra- and intergenerational similarities and differences in values, attitudes, behavior, and interaction patterns; in generational cooperation and conflict; and in the formation of age-homogeneous political or social groups seeking social change.

As a result of this interest, scholars have begun to assess not only the effects of maturation (developmental age changes) and historical effects on age-related phenomena, but also the effect of cohort factors. For example, based on a review of generational differences in political beliefs and participation, Bengtson and Cutler (1976) concluded that in the United States generational differences rather than aging differences account for political-party affiliation; specific social or historical effects rather than aging or generational factors account for political alienation; and the effects of aging influence attitudes toward government involvement in specific areas such as health care. That is, within the general sphere of political participation, there are different explanations for different forms of involvement. The way in which generations influence social processes and interaction is presented in more detail later in this chapter.

Generations and family lineage.   Thus far we have been concerned with the societal level of analysis in our discussion of generations. However, the concept of 'generation' has also been used to refer to ranked descent within the extended family system (Troll, 1970, 1980; Bengtson, 1975; Troll and Bengtson, 1979; Marshall, 1981a). This ranking, although related to chronological age to some extent,[8] determines role allocation within the biological family unit on the basis of birth order, marital status, and the procreation patterns of succeeding generations. Thus, power, authority, and prestige within the extended kinship system are primarily based on ascribed characteristics; in society they are more likely to be based on achievement.

It is important to understand the structure of the family lineage system, which is parallel to but separate from the macro structure of society, since it too influences the interaction patterns within and between generations. Most kinship systems are made up of two (parents, children) or three (grandparents, parents, children) generations; because of increasing longevity in modern societies, the four-generation family (great-grandparents, grandparents, parents, children) is becoming more prevalent.[9] However, with zero population growth in some countries and an increase in childless marriages, a new type of two-generation family (parents, adult children) is appearing. In time, this last group will become one-generation families (old adults with no children), ultimately leading to the extinction of a particular kinship system.

Generational interaction operates on two separate but related levels — on the micro level within the family unit and on the macro level within the broader society. For example, aggregates of grandparents, parents, and children may interact on the societal level as members of particular generations or generational units. They will be exposed to particular societal processes (discrimination, stratification, socialization, conflict). At the same time, as members of an extended kinship system with varying degrees of filial bonding, they interact with other generations within the family. For some, particularly young adolescents, the socialization and social control process within this dual structure can create conflict and confusion, especially with respect to the transmission of values and other cultural characteristics from one generation to the next. The competing prestige of the parents and the peer group, who both seek to impose values and behaviors, can create role conflict for the adolescent and social conflict and change for the society.

It is necessary, then, to understand that the individual has generational links with both the family and society, and that there is a constant interplay (more at some stages in the life cycle than at others) between the family lineage structure and the societal age structure. This becomes even more complicated when the age structure within the labor force interacts with the class, racial, ethnic, or gender stratification systems. For example, when phenomena such as generational conflicts or 'generation gaps' are studied, it is essential to determine whether the observed generational differences (for example, in value orientations) are due to a societal cohort gap or to a familial lineage gap.

Age-related expectations for individuals may differ between the societal and family levels, resulting in varying degrees of conflict. For example, in recent years many older cohorts in society have held views of premarital sexual behavior that are at odds with those of teenagers and young adults. For some extended families, cohabitation and premarital sex on the part of adolescents or young adults has been the source of much family conflict and disharmony, because these practices are deemed contrary to cultural values. In other families, this practice has not been a cause of strain since the parents themselves may disagree with the prevailing values and attitudes of society, and thereby accept these practices. In summary, the analysis of generational phenomena must consider the societal and the family lineage structures, both of which intersect and interact with other stratification systems.

The Interaction of Social Structure and Social Processes: Macro-level Cohort and Generational Effects

Introduction

Although the social structure within a society is relatively static at specific times, it may change over the long term due to various dynamic social processes. Because of such changes, cohorts and generations age in different ways and introduce further cyclical changes into the society. As noted in the previous sections, both society at large and its institutions are characterized by social differentiation and stratification. These dynamic processes, along with the presence of ever-emerging age cohorts, result in a complex two-way interaction between social structure and process that can lead either to stability or to change in the social order. Given a particular social structure, stratification can lead to inequality. That is, structural barriers and 'gatekeepers' determine the processes and interaction to which cohorts and individuals, respectively, are exposed.

A chain of social processes may be initiated because of a particular social structure. In turn, these forces may ultimately lead to change in both the structure and processes that succeeding age cohorts experience. Given a particular social structure, with actual or perceived inequalities based on age, the socialization process and interaction patterns can lead to stereotyping of, and negative attitudes toward, the aged. These processes can also foster discrimination, segregation, and isolation of the aged. These in turn may lead to social conflict and to a change in the status and role of the elderly. Alternatively, where age-homogeneous groupings are prevalent, and where integration and support of the elderly are assured by law or social custom, little change in the status of the elderly will occur, and succeeding cohorts will age in a similar manner.

In this section we consider the influence of the interaction of social structure and processes on aging and the status of the aged from a cohort or macro perspective through generational analysis. Since cohort and lineage effects interact (Troll, 1980), the interaction of structure and processes across the life cycle at the micro level within the family system is discussed in the next major section. In the meantime, it is important to remember that there are similarities and differences in the aging structures and processes that operate on these two intersecting levels of analysis. Socialization, integration, ageism, isolation, and intergenerational relations function at the societal level for age cohorts or generations, and for the individual within specific social systems such as the family or the place of employment.

Social processes are institutionalized mechanisms that facilitate stability and change within a social system. They involve interaction at both the individual and cohort levels, and they provide some element of control by defining rights, power, and responsibilities; by allocating social positions; by facilitating or inhibiting interaction among certain individuals or groups; by integrating individuals and cohorts into the social structure; and by promoting conformity to the dominant values and norms within the social system. Not surprisingly, social processes can lead to a change in structure, while a change in structure can lead to a change in processes (Blau, 1980).

Before turning to an examination of the social processes that influence both the process of aging and the status of the aged, the issues and content of generational analysis need to be reviewed (Buss, 1974; Bengtson et al., 1974; Dowd, 1979–80). Generational analysis examines the impact of emerging age cohorts on the stability of the social structure, and considers the interaction patterns within and between members of age strata. More specifically, social scientists who have used generational analysis have been interested in:

1. Describing and explaining the degree, source, and outcome of social consensus or conflict resulting from intergenerational relations;
2. The form and amount of change that results from conflict within a society, and within intrasocietal social institutions;
3. The process and product of socialization wherein cultural characteristics and behaviors are transmitted from one generation to another;
4. The stability and long-term impact of generational units on behavior throughout the life cycle;[10]
5. The extent to which cohort solidarity or sub-group consciousness evolves within generational units and influences individual behavior and social change;[11]
6. The degree of inequality between age strata and the impact of stratification on the individual;
7. The extent to which age stratification interacts with other dimensions of social differentiation and how this has an impact on the individual; for example, the double standard with respect to sex, double or multiple jeopardy with respect to age, race, class, or sex (Bengtson et al., 1974; Foner, 1979).

These issues will be addressed in the following section, which focuses on social processes at the societal level, and in the last section, which discusses social processes within the kinship system.

Cohort Flow, Role Transition and Status of the Aged

Cohort flow: structural stability or changes.   Cohort flow is the process whereby a series of birth cohorts, varying in size and composition, succeed one another over time. This process ensures that there will be continuity in the social system, since departing cohorts are replaced by new ones. Each cohort, as it passes through the life course, experiences changes in its size and composition; it generally becomes smaller with age and comprises a larger percentage of females. While each cohort includes individuals with heterogeneous characteristics and experiences, all members of the cohort may experience similar events that make them different from members of other cohorts. This differentiation can lead to continuity or change in the social order. As a result of feedback and interaction with older cohorts that represent the dominant culture, each succeeding cohort makes 'fresh contact' (Mannheim, 1952) with the existing social order.

A cohort approaches adulthood, (a major transition point) seeking to develop its own independence and lifestyle. As a result, the existing social order may be perceived by the members of the cohort in a new way because of contemporary social, political, or economic conditions. Moreover, new cultural values or lifestyles may be initiated because of constant feedback between cohorts. For the most part these changes are so subtle that they are seldom noticed; if changes do occur they proceed via negotiation, compromise, and cooperation. Sometimes generational conflict and change is unavoidable, however. This is so because generations are at different stages of socialization, are born during unique historical periods that foster different values, or are faced with structural social inequalities.

Generational conflict may also arise because of cohort-centrism wherein all events are interpreted by members of the cohort in light of their own experiences, values, and needs (Riley, 1978; Foner, 1979). If these factors prevail, age-group consciousness and solidarity may develop, thereby leading to discontinuities or conflict between strata. Ultimately, this may lead to social change. However, there is little evidence that high levels of age-group consciousness exist (Bengtson et al., 1974; Bengtson and Cutler, 1976; Foner, 1979). In fact, even where there are dissimilarities in behavior or value orientations, there may not be generational conflict.

This lack of conflict occurs because differences may be minimal within the family lineage, even though value differences are present between age cohorts at the societal level. For example, Bengtson et al. (1974) reported that marijuana use by adolescents is more frequent among youths whose parents smoke, drink, or use drugs. That is, the actual behavior may be different, but the basic value system is similar (a dependence on stimulants). Hence, little intergenerational conflict develops. As Chellam (1980–81) recently reported, conflict between younger and older cohorts may be avoided because young adults and the elderly may be undergoing similar life experiences. Based on a study of forty young people aged 15 to 24 years and forty people aged 65 to 74 years, Chellam found that similar perspectives existed for the two groups with respect to goals of life, value priorities, satisfaction with life, and personal stresses and crises.

Through the process of socialization, interaction between age cohorts occurs, and the emerging cohorts accept or reject the goals and values of the dominant culture. New values or lifestyles may be considered as alternatives, but whether these will be adopted and will lead to social or cultural change depends on whether age-group consciousness develops to force a change, and on whether older age cohorts accept the new orientations as more appropriate for the times. In the former case, change could be characterized by conflict; in the latter case, the change would occur through negotiation and cooperation between age cohorts.

Role transitions.   Life consists of a sequence of societal roles (many of which interact with the family and work structure), which cohorts enter and then later leave (Rosow, 1976). This mobility is related to either chronological age (legal norms) or social age (social norms). This process of cohort replacement enables a cohort to move from one stage in life to another, thereby replacing the cohort that retires or dies. Some of these transitions are from school to work; from being single to being married; from work to retirement; from young adulthood to middle age; from middle age to old age; from parenting to an empty nest; from being married to being divorced or widowed; and from childhood dependence to adult independence to old-age dependence. For some of these transition points, rites of passage, such as the wedding ceremony or the retirement party, facilitate and legitimate the transition.

The process of cohort replacement is also facilitated by a normative ordering of life-cycle events. There exist relatively well-accepted normative beliefs as to the appropriate age and order for such events as completing an education, entering an occupation, marrying and forming a nuclear family, and retiring. In fact, there is usually social pressure from family and society to stay on schedule and in sequence, although there are subcultural differences in timing and sequence (Neugarten and Datan, 1973; Neugarten and Hagestad, 1976).

The normative regulations concerning the appropriate timing of each event may change for different cohorts. Those who follow the normative sequence generally achieve harmony between their own lifestyles and the social context (Hogan, 1978). However, as Hogan observes, because of military service, or college attendance by some into their late 20s, some events may be spaced more closely together and may occur out of sequence. This asynchronization may result in personal adjustment problems. For example, instead of following the normative order of completing an education, entering the first job, and marrying, Hogan found that males who marry, complete their educations, and then begin their first jobs seem to have higher rates of marital separation and divorce.

For other role transitions (to the empty nest, middle age, widowhood, or retirement), especially in the middle and later years when loss of roles is more usual than acquisition of roles, the transition can be stressful and can have a significant impact on some individuals (George, 1980). For example, much recent controversy has focused on the transition to middle age and the hypothesized 'midlife crisis.' This crisis is thought to be experienced primarily by males and to result from an interaction of changes and events in personal and social systems.

As males move into the middle years of life (35 to 55 years of age in North America) a number of physiological and psychological changes occur at the personal level. These may be accompanied by role losses or role ambiguity at work or home. According to some reports, middle-aged males experience a crisis that involves a loss or a questioning of identity; a preoccupation with death that is often precipitated by the death of an age peer; lowered self-expectations; marital and family dissatisfaction; depression and feelings of stagnation; and perception of a gap between career aspirations and attainments. These factors may lead to some changes in personality and lifestyle, with an accompanying identity crisis and increased anxiety about the present and future (Brim, 1980).

It has been suggested that there are two models to account for this crisis when and if it occurs (Perun and Del Vento Bielby, 1979). First, it has been argued that personal development in the middle years can not occur until a crisis occurs and is resolved. Therefore, the crisis is necessary and inevitable. The competing model argues that a crisis is an abnormal event within the life course and is not likely to occur for a majority of adults. The crisis phenomenon has primarily been noted among white, middle-class, professional males (Cytrynbaum et al., 1980). Yet, this stressful period, if it is perceived as such, can be experienced by both men and women, although women are more likely to experience physical as well as social symptoms (Robertson, 1978).

Despite the widespread belief that the midlife transition is characterized by a crisis, which would indicate that the crisis is a normative reaction in the middle years, scholars have suggested that there is little evidence to substantiate the view that this transition is really a crisis event.[12] Because of heterogeneity within cohorts, Rosenberg and Farrell (1976) suggest that four stereotypes evolve. These reflect individual adaptation to personal and role stresses associated with the transition to middle age. These four stereotypical groups include those who are satisfied with life, and either openly confront or openly deny the crisis, and those who are dissatisfied with life, and either openly confront or openly deny the crisis. In this fourfold typology there are degrees of reaction to entering the middle years of life. Hence, the onset of a generalized and inevitable male midlife crisis is not substantiated by scientific evidence (Rosenberg and Farrell, 1976; Brim, 1980; Marshall, 1980b).

In order to better understand the social stress and adaptation process induced when a role transition occurs in later life, George (1980:50–54) adapted House's (1974) model to explain adjustment to retirement, to widowhood, to community-based residential relocation, and to institutional relocation. This integrated model (see figure 7.1) considers the individual's status prior to the role transition; the aspects of the role transition that are potentially conducive to creating stress; the degree to which the transition is perceived as stressful (sense of loss, disruption of routine); the response to the stress (presence or absence of personal coping skills and social support); and the outcome in terms of personal identity and social adjustment. In addition, the entire model is influenced by personal resources, socialization experiences, and social status (marital status, income, occupation, health, class, race, sex, ethnicity).

Based on this social-stress model, it is argued that adjustment to major role transitions in later life is a process that is related not to the event itself, but to individual differences in the perception of stress associated with the transition. Adjustment is also related to individual differences in the ability to respond to the stress (that is, the impact of the stress on identity and social adjustment). Moreover, earlier socialization experiences, the personality structure and social demographic characteristics of the individual, and the social context in which the transition occurs also serve as mediating factors in this complex process of adjustment to transitions in later life.

Figure 7.1 Process of Adjustment to Role Transitions

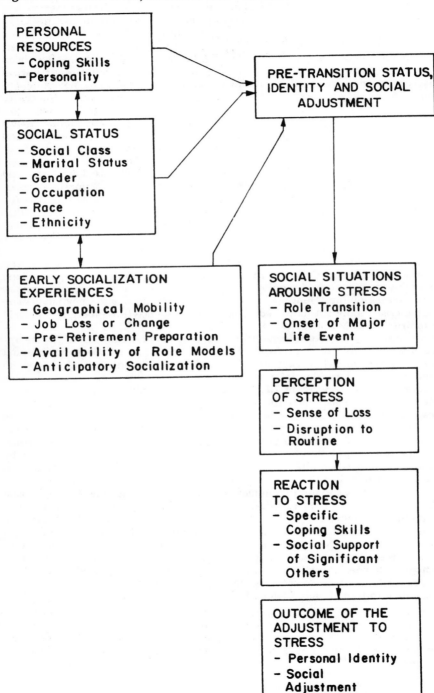

The status of the aged. The status of the elderly varies across cultures, and may change over time, especially in preindustrialized societies where the process of modernization may intervene. In preindustrial societies the social position and participation of the elderly is generally high in both the society at large and within the family unit. This is so because there is minimal role differentiation, because the elderly maintain power and status through control of family and community resources, and because most roles are ascribed rather than achieved.

With increasing modernization, social structure and processes change so that there is likely to be a separation of family and societal roles. This leads to a greater division of labor, with more dependence on achieved rather than ascribed roles. In addition, there is greater stratification within the social structure on the basis not only of age, but also of sex, race, ethnicity, education, occupation and social class. Moreover, social processes such as socialization, discrimination, segregation, stereotyping, and cohort centrism have an impact on the aging process and on the status of the aged. As in earlier times, the status of the aged in contemporary societies is determined by location in the social structure, as well as by the nature of the social processes that prevail.

In order to determine the status of the elderly at the societal level, a number of scholars have examined the processes of status attainment and maintenance across the adult life cycle (Rosow, 1967; 1974, 1976; Henretta and Campbell, 1976; Neugarten and Hagestad, 1976; Dowd, 1980). From the perspective of the middle class, and from that of middle-class researchers (Dowd, 1980:15), the transition from middle age to old age is thought to result in a loss or weakening of major social roles (through the empty nest, retirement, or widowhood) that were sources of status, power, and prestige. This 'role emptying' (Rosow, 1976) places the elderly in an unfavorable exchange position, and they are seen to have a devalued or marginal status.

This social loss is further enhanced by the onset of physical changes that make persons appear old to others, and by the presence of ascribed negative stereotypes that lead to unequal treatment or discrimination on the basis of age. Some elderly persons may begin to act 'old' because of social expectations, because a socialization process that provides a prescription for behavior is unavailable (Rosow, 1974), or because of the lack of adequate role models.

As noted previously, members of a given age cohort are not a homogeneous group, except with respect to chronological age. Thus, while the elderly lose some institutionalized roles, they do not abandon all social roles. For example, the recent widow may still be a mother, sister, friend, aunt, grandparent, employee, or volunteer. Therefore, while some role loss is inevitable because of declining involvement in some institutions, individual status may be retained within a more restricted social world, such as the family, even while the status of the age cohort declines. More important, however, is the need to consider the variation in norms and values by class, education, sex, and race. These interact with age to determine the status of a particular cohort. As a result, we cannot assume that loss of status permeates an entire age cohort. Rather, some elderly persons possess status characteristics (being male, white, or a member of the upper class, or having a higher level of education and occupational prestige) that enable them to retain power. This releases them from some of the constraints of aging imposed on others their age. They have resources[13] that give them power in social relationships, thereby enabling them to remain independent. For example, Henretta and Campbell (1976) reported that the higher the individual's social class, the greater the likelihood of maintaining status for a longer time. (The importance of this interaction between age and other stratification systems in determining the status of the aged is addressed later in this chapter.)

To summarize, the age stratification system may allocate unequal amounts of power, prestige, and privileges within and among different age cohorts. With increasing age, individuals may lose strength and attractiveness and may be excluded from occupying many institutionalized roles. They may be stigmatized, stereotyped, and discriminated against.

In their interaction with others, particularly with those in younger age cohorts, the elderly often have less power and occupy a weaker bargaining position. In this type of situation, it could be concluded that the aged have low status in society. However, within the elderly age cohort, individual differences in sex, race, education, and class background enable some members to be accorded higher status than others at all stages in the life cycle. Normally, they maintain this status well into their later years. Although the elderly were once a numerical minority, because of increasing longevity and declining birth rates they now have the potential to attain more power in the political process if they develop a sense of group consciousness and solidarity. While this might lead to social conflict with other generations, the process should increase the status of all members of future elderly age cohorts.

Socialization Through the Life Cycle: Integration and Segregation

The process of socialization.   Socialization is a complex developmental process that operates on two levels of analysis (Clausen, 1968; Inkeles, 1969; Bengtson and Black, 1973; Hagestad, 1982). From the societal perspective, the goal of socialization is to integrate each new cohort into the society by transmitting institutionalized behavior and values to ensure the continuity of the social system from one cohort to the next, thus ensuring that social control and social order are maintained. At this macro level of analysis, the social structure influences an individual's location and determines which facets of the culture he or she will have access to during socialization. In this way, the social structure impinges on the socialization process. At the same time, the socialization process, when it leads to conflict and change across cohorts, can result in cultural change or in a change to the social structure. This occurs because of changes in the institutional, stratification, or value systems developed by emerging cohorts.

At the micro level, socialization is the process of integrating the individual into specific institutions or positions within society. Generally, this involves two-way interaction or negotiation between a socializee (a child) and a socializer (a parent) within a given system such as the family or school (Inkeles, 1969; Dowd, 1980). For example, an adult is socialized into the status position of 'parent' by recalling his or her life as a child, as well as by actually being a parent.

Since the late 1960s, perhaps because of the changing demographic picture and the growth of gerontology, there has been increased interest in socialization as a process that prevails throughout the life cycle, not just during childhood and adolescence. For example, until recently in our own culture we acquired little valid knowledge about aging and being old until we reached middle age. Adult socialization is necessary because social mores change and because individuals enter new stages of the life cycle where role expectations vary from those of earlier stages. A growing interest in the later stages of socialization has increasingly dominated the literature since the 1960s (Brim and Wheeler, 1966;

Wright, 1967; Riley et al., 1969; Rosow, 1974; Albrecht and Gift, 1975; Marshall, 1975; Mortimer and Simmons, 1978; Rose, 1979; Bennett, 1980b; Dowd, 1980).

During childhood and adolescence, the socialization process is formal and goal-oriented. During adulthood the individual becomes more active in the process. There is a greater degree of self-determination in adulthood as to how and when socialization occurs. Because of social differentiation and stratification, and cross-cultural and subcultural variations, no individual is ever completely socialized into all of his or her culture. Much of the process in the middle and later years involves anticipatory socialization and resocialization in order to reduce ambiguity when entering new social positions (widow, retiree, institutionalized resident). Exchange theory and the symbolic interactionist perspective are increasingly being used to study the socialization process during adulthood (Dowd, 1980; George, 1980; Marshall, 1980a) because a process of bilateral negotiation based on values, power resources, and status is more conducive to adult socialization (Inkeles, 1969; Bengtson and Black, 1973; Dowd, 1980).

Although socialization occurs throughout the life cycle, the nature of the process varies from childhood to adulthood. During the adult years self-motivation becomes more important. As a result, the individual is more responsive to the demands of the self than to the demands of the social structure, although those cannot be completely ignored. For this reason, anticipatory socialization and resocialization are prevalent during the middle and later years. Regardless of the stage in life, the process involves social interaction and occurs at the societal level for age cohorts, and at the micro level for a given individual within a particular social context.

At the societal level, an age cohort may be socialized to, and conform to, relatively similar values, beliefs, and behaviors that make it unique. Yet even within this unique cohort there will likely be intracohort variations in the process. This occurs because of gender, class, racial, ethnic, religious, geographical, cultural, and educational differences that operate within the family, school, peer group, and neighborhood social systems. In fact, these variations greatly influence the extent to which attitudes toward aging and the aged are developed and perpetuated by means of socialization. These products of the socialization process are discussed next.

Stereotypes.   The outcome, or product, of the socialization process is evident on both the macro and micro levels of analysis. At the societal level, cohorts are socialized to existing cultural characteristics, and the society remains stable. If a particular cohort is socialized differently, conflict and social change may result when a new generation imposes its cultural system (beliefs, values, attitudes) on the existing social order.

Similarly, individuals are socialized by the family, school, peer group, and media to the normative behavioral pattern and values expected of persons occupying specific positions within a particular social structure. Those who are socialized less completely are labelled, to varying degrees, as deviants. They are either tolerated (the 35-year-old who continues to play the role of university student), stigmatized (the urban street panhandler), or incarcerated (the convicted criminal). There are many degrees of socialization and many outcomes of the process. In addition to the general socialization outcomes for cohorts or individuals per se, certain cultural by-products in the form of attitudes, beliefs, and stereotypes are often acquired during socialization. These by-products, as we will see in the following sections, can lead to the initiation and perpetuation of other social processes that have an impact on aging and on the aged.

Through social interaction with significant others, most of whom are not chronologically 'old,' and through exposure to particular cultural institutions (such as the mass media) and cultural artifacts (jokes, greeting cards, books, and popular magazines) individuals are exposed to a variety of attitudes and images pertaining to aging and the aged. While some of these are validly based on research evidence, many lack research support but are accepted as fact by at least some segments of the population. That is, they are myths, many of which create negative stereotypes about the aged (Hess, 1974). To illustrate, some common negative stereotypes portray the elderly as deficient in intelligence, or senile; as lonely; as unproductive and inefficient employees; as emotional and financial burdens to their children; as physically weak and in chronic ill health; and as having little interest in or capacity for sex. While some elderly people may experience some or all of these conditions, they do not represent the modal pattern for the elderly. In particular, they usually do not apply to the younger segment of the retirement cohort.

These stereotypes represent incorrect assumptions, faulty reasoning, and misperceptions. If accepted as fact, they influence our expectations about and reactions to the elderly, especially where there is lack of interaction. Once these views become institutionalized, they tend to be passed on to succeeding cohorts through the socialization process. Until questioned and disproven, they perpetuate and reinforce our attitudes and behavior toward the elderly.

Stereotypes may induce fear of aging among the young, and may also be accepted as fact by some elderly persons. This acceptance can lead to self-fulfilling prophecies where the elderly begin to think and behave as expected, thereby reinforcing the stereotypes. A societal norm may be internalized by an elderly person, and may subsequently influence his or her beliefs, behaviors, and self-concept (Miller, 1981).

This situation may lead to loss of self-esteem, disengagement, isolation, or labelling of oneself as 'old.' That is, the 'social breakdown' syndrome may be initiated (Kuypers and Bengtson, 1973). However, as Brubaker and Powers (1976) noted in a review of forty-seven studies related to attitudes toward old age, both positive and negative stereotypes exist. They hypothesized that the self-concept held before old age, along with personal objective indicators of old age, may determine whether an aging individual accepts the negative stereotype and develops a negative self-evaluation. That is, if one's self-concept has been positive throughout life, a positive self-concept will prevail in the later years.

Within the field of social gerontology, a number of studies using the research method of content analysis have sought to demonstrate the extent to which the aged are underrepresented or misrepresented, usually by negative stereotypes, in such cultural forms as literature, newspapers, humor, and television. Moreover, even where the elderly are portrayed as having a positive image they tend to be described stereotypically as altruistic, slow-moving, relaxed, excellent homemakers, and 'Mr. Fix-Its.'

It has been argued that since attitudes, beliefs, and values are acquired through socialization, these cultural forms serve to inculcate or perpetuate existing stereotypes of the aged. For example, in studies of elementary schoolbooks and children's literature (Ansello, 1977a, 1977b; Robin, 1977; Kingston and Drotter, 1981), adolescent fiction (Peterson and Karnes, 1976), poetry (Sohngen and Smith, 1978), and adult fiction (Spencer, 1979; Spencer and Hollenshead, 1980), it has been noted that the aged are seldom portrayed in illustrations; they are powerless, they are peripheral to the plot,[14] have limited abilities and behavioral capabilities, appear in passive rather than active roles, and are underrepresented in relation to their proportion in the 'real' population. Furthermore, women are underrepresented even though they comprise a higher proportion of the elderly population. Similarly, elderly minority-group members are seldom included, except in contemporary literature by and about blacks and native Americans (Spencer, 1979).

These studies suggest that readers acquire a misleading and stereotypical view of aging and the aged in our society. However, it has not been demonstrated that there is a causal relationship between the reading of books in which the elderly are ignored, underrepresented, or misrepresented and the acceptance of negative stereotypes or the formation of negative attitudes toward aging or the aged. A large inferential leap has been made that has yet to be substantiated. Furthermore, the content of school texts is often interpreted by teachers; some elementary school students may be more or less sensitized to aging issues, depending on the supplementary material presented by a particular teacher (Hauwiller and Jennings, 1981).

Few adolescents or adults read during their leisure time, and thus are not often exposed to literary stereotypes. Of those adolescents and adults who do read widely and frequently, many are part of the better-educated sector of society, and may therefore be more critical and discerning about the content of what they read. Caution is urged, therefore, when inferring that large segments of the population are socialized into internalizing negative stereotypes of aging and the aged by what they read. Certainly the content of children's literature contains stereotypical views of the elderly, but whether this leads to negative attitudes about aging has yet to be demonstrated. This type of research may be perpetuating yet another gerontological myth. More complete research is needed to provide links between reading and the adoption of stereotypical attitudes or behavior. One way to approach this problem, especially with respect to children's socialization, is to use participant observation to study the content and interaction of reading sessions in classrooms.

In a similar way, popular humor, as expressed in jokes (Palmore, 1971; Davies, 1977; Richman, 1977), cartoons (Smith, 1979; Sheppard, 1980, 1981), and humorous birthday cards (Andrews, 1981; Demos and Jache, 1981; Dillon and Jones, 1981) generally reflects a negative view of aging, especially with respect to women.[15] For example, some of the themes, of which between 26 and 66 percent present a negative view of aging,[16] are a reduction in physical, mental or sexual ability or performance, especially as it applies to men; lying about or concealing one's chronological age, especially by women; obsolescence and isolation; the 'freedom' of retirement; loss of physical attractiveness; and cultural expectations about age and aging.

However, as Weber and Cameron (1978) note, some of these studies are biased in that the samples represent edited joke books rather than everyday joking behavior. Furthermore, the way in which the intended humor is interpreted by the reader or listener is unknown; the relationship between the use of and response to humor and negative attitudes is untested. It is not known whether the intended messages or themes were perceived by the reader or listener as humorous. If they were, it is not known how this perception influences attitudes and behavior concerning aging and the aged. Moreover, there may be individual differences in the response to the stereotypes presented. Finally, Dillon and Jones (1981) raise the question as to whether the use of age-related humor is a defense mechanism (for the sender and receiver) to counteract age-related anxieties, or whether it reflects an acceptance of aging and a healthy adaptation to reality.

In an attempt to address these issues, two recent studies examined the relationship between cartoon images and attitudes toward aging among college students, and the degree of individual differences in the perception of old age as presented in cartoons. Based on disposition theory (Zillmann and Cantor, 1976), which suggests that the greatest humor appreciation occurs among individuals with both negative stereotypes and unfavorable attitudes toward aging, Sheppard (1980) found no relationship between appreciation of humor and attitudes toward aging. In the second study, Sheppard (1981) found that none of the fifty-two subjects ranked a series of cartoons in the same order (from a positive to a negative view of aging). Obviously, individuals vary in their perception of the meaning of humor. Furthermore, sex differences were noted in humor perception: male subjects thought the cartoons were funnier than did the females. Thus, the degree to which the humorous message or theme is interpreted and generalized appears to vary. We must be cautious in suggesting that humor contributes to negative attitudes toward the aged or to personal fears about aging.

It has also been suggested that negative stereotyping of the elderly is prevalent in the media, especially with respect to women (Hollenshead, 1982). However, print media do not appear to create, perpetuate, or reinforce negative stereotypes of the elderly. For example, a content analysis of *Time* magazine found that little age stereotyping was present (Kent and Shaw, 1980). Where negative age stereotyping did appear, it was usually in the form of references to young athletes or entertainers who were 'past their prime,' rather than to older persons. Similarly, an analysis of the portrayal of the elderly in two newspapers found that there were twice as many positive as negative images, and that a neutral image of the elderly was most prevalent (Buchholz and Bynum, 1982). Finally, a recent survey in the United States found that 53 percent of the total population believe that newspapers present a fair image of the elderly (Harris et al., 1981).

On television, aspects of the real world do appear to be selectively incorporated into game shows, drama and comedy series, and commercials. In fact, a recent survey (Harris et al., 1981) found that television commercials were faulted for making older people appear 'better' than they really are. For the purpose of entertainment, underrepresentation and misrepresentation[17] of aging and the aged may occur. For example, a number of studies (Francher, 1973; Arnhoff, 1974; Hess, 1974; Harris and Feinberg, 1977; Ansello, 1978; Greenberg et al., 1979) have all reported that the topics of aging and the elderly are generally ignored by the television industry.[18] Moreover, these studies suggest that when they are included, older men and women are treated in a humorous or negative way: older women are more likely to be underrepresented and overstereotyped;[19] men and women are rarely seen in positions of power or prestige except in a rural, extended-family setting; the aged are mainly included in plots that focus on intergenerational cooperation or conflict; and they are seldom used in commercials unless products specifically designed for the elderly are being advertised.

It has been indirectly suggested that material presented on television may lead to perpetuation of stereotypes and may result in succeeding generations being socialized to hold prejudices against the elderly. But as Greenberg et al. (1979) note, how can social learning really occur when so few older people are actually portrayed as role models on television? To date, research evidence has not supported the hypothesized linkage between viewing television and acquiring stereotypical attitudes about elderly persons.

Studies in these areas have also neglected to consider that attitudes and stereotypes can change over time because of shifts in cultural values and because of research evidence that refutes the myths. For example, in recent years older people have been portrayed in a wider variety of occupational or familial roles that more closely coincide with social reality. They have been depicted as independent influential citizens and family members, and as having something of value to offer to society. Therefore, they are less likely to be the butt of jokes. This more frequent positive view may be partly due to the changing demographic profile of society in general, and of television viewers in particular. It may also reflect pressure on the networks by an increasingly active and age-conscious cohort of elderly citizens.

As a result of these changes, the outcome of the socialization process for one generation may differ from that of a preceding generation. This may occur because of social change, particularly where direct attempts at social intervention seek to invalidate negative stereotypes, thereby leading to changes in attitudes and behavior. In fact, since the early 1970s there have been numerous direct attempts to criticize and dispel the negative stereotypes that evolved during the early part of this century (Tibbitts, 1979). This approach has provided research evidence to refute the myths and has promoted the potential of the elderly to contribute to society and to attain a better quality of life.

In conclusion, gerontologists have described and noted the outcomes of negative stereotypes about aging and the aged, particularly as they are represented and possibly inculcated through literature, popular humor, newspapers, and television. These studies have served a useful function by drawing attention to the problems experienced by some older citizens. In this sense, cultural forms may have contributed to changes in attitude and public-policy initiatives to improve the situation of the elderly.

If negative stereotypes are debunked, future cohorts should be provided with more factual information and more positive views about aging and the aged. It is hoped that ten years from now textbooks in this field will be able to treat the topic of negative stereotypes solely from a historical perspective. Negative stereotypes are still with us at present, however, and the next three subsections will focus on the social processes that evolve because of our acceptance of these stereotypes. Before discussing these processes in detail, it is necessary to examine attitudes toward and perceptions of aging and the aged. These attitudes and perceptions represent another outcome of the socialization process that may be internalized along with stereotypes.

Attitudes toward aging and age identification.   It is generally held that attitudes are derived, at least partially, from the prevalence of cultural stereotypes. In our culture, negative stereotypes about aging and growing old are inculcated through the socialization process. In turn, these stereotypes lead to the formation of attitudes and beliefs. In addition, attitudes are likely to form because of an institutionalized stratification process wherein there is differential ranking of status and opportunities by age.

As a result of these processes of attitude formation, negative societal and individual attitudes lower the status of older people in a society, decrease the frequency and quality of social interaction with them, and negatively affect their life chances, lifestyle, and quality of life. Negative attitudes may also decrease or inhibit the allocation of societal and personal resources to the elderly, or may lead to a self-labelling process where the elderly accept the negative stereotypes and attitudes. This results in negative self-evaluation and decreased self-esteem, which in turn can lead to disengagement and social isolation.

A large body of literature has examined the attitudes of various age groups toward aging and the aged, as well as the hypothesized effects of these attitudes on the elderly. This section presents a brief summary of the findings, and a detailed critique of the inherent weaknesses in this type of research. In short, the existing research evidence represents a mixture of conflicting findings, some of which can be attributed to the methodological, conceptual, and theoretical difficulties inherent in attitude research in general (Eagly and Himmelfarb, 1978), and to gerontological research concerning attitudes in particular (McTavish, 1971; Kogan, 1979; Lutsky, 1980; Green, 1981; Wingard et al., 1982).

Many criticisms have been raised about attitude research. The most serious pertain to concerns about definitions, sampling, measurement of the concept, the stability of attitudes, and the relationship between attitudes and behavior. There has been confusion over the terms 'attitudes' and 'beliefs.' 'Beliefs' represent knowledge (accurate or inaccurate) about an object; 'attitudes' connote an evaluative component wherein positive or negative feelings or dispositions are held toward an object or group. Attitudes are likely to result in a predisposition to behave in a positive or negative way toward individuals in a particular group. To illustrate, Kogan (1979), in a critique of attitude research in gerontology, indicated that the scale constructed by Tuckman and Lorge (1953), which is frequently used, is made up of a mixture of items that measure both attitudes and beliefs; Kogan's (1961) own scale measures only attitudes.

Although beliefs can be changed by an awareness of factual material, attitudes may not change even in the face of objective evidence because of the affective (emotional) component. Moreover, beliefs tend to be specific; attitudes, at least as commonly measured, are general. In short, where attitude scales include measurements of beliefs, any changes over time may reflect a change in knowledge rather than a change in attitudes.

Another concern with attitude research has been the long-standing debate as to the strength of the relationship between verbally expressed attitudes and actual behavior. To what extent is there congruency between what an individual feels about the elderly and the aging process, and how he or she actually behaves in face-to-face interaction with elderly individuals? The answer is that the relationship between attitudes and behavior is inconsistent at best. For example, the way in which a younger person behaves in a face-to-face situation with parents or grandparents may vary considerably from the behavior demonstrated toward elderly strangers in the supermarket, at work, or on a bus.

There also appears to be a discrepancy between the attitudes toward aging of the general population, and what the older person actually experiences. In the earliest studies by Tuckman and Lorge (1953), Kogan and associates (Kogan, 1961), Harris (1975) and Serock et al. (1977), it was generally found that the attitudes of a high percentage of respondents (50 percent in Harris, 1975) indicated that old age involves poor health, insufficient income, failing memory, and loneliness. However, the facts suggest that although some old people do experience these conditions to varying degrees, only a small percentage perceive these to be a problem in their lives.

A third criticism of this area of research relates to the question of whether attitudes can be measured on a single dimension or whether they represent a multidimensional concept. As recent research has suggested (Kogan, 1979; O'Connell and Rotter, 1979; Skoglund, 1979–80; Lutsky, 1980; Stier and Kline, 1980; Green, 1981), views of the elderly held by younger persons are situationally determined or are not consistent. For example, the child who sees an elderly transient begging or looking for food in a garbage pail might have an attitude different from that of a child whose major exposure to the elderly is playing catch with his grandmother or grandfather.

These attitudes also appear to be multidimensional; that is, complex phenomena are not determined by a single factor or a single meaning of 'old.' Rather, multiple meanings exist, shaped by experiences and by varying social or personality traits of the individual. Thus, positive attitudes toward old people are related to such factors as being female, being older, having a higher level of educational attainment, having a number of high-quality interpersonal relationships with older people, and attaining higher scores in measurements of such personality traits as affiliation and nurturance, and lower scores in dominance and aggression (Thorson and Perkins, 1980–81).

Like much research in psychology, attitudinal research in gerontology is frequently criticized because most of the tested subjects are college students (Ryan and Capadano, 1978; Sadowski, 1978; O'Connell and Rotter, 1979; Lutsky, 1980; Bassili and Reil, 1981; Thorson and Perkins, 1980–81). The attitudes of this group may not accurately represent the young adult population or the younger population in general.

Although most studies have used college students, in recent years many researchers have examined the attitudes of children and adolescents toward aging and the elderly through verbal instruments, drawings, or pictures (Jantz et al., 1976; Ivester and King, 1977; Seefeldt et al., 1977; Serock et al., 1977; Trent et al., 1979; Weinberger, 1979; Stier and Kline, 1980; Galper et al., 1980–81; Page et al., 1981; Burke, 1982; Fillmer, 1982). Similarly, a few studies have sought to document the attitudes of the general population (Harris, 1975) and of adults of various age ranges (Kilty and Feld, 1976; Skoglund, 1979–80; Lutsky, 1980). Surprisingly, relatively few studies have examined the attitudes of the elderly toward younger age groups, or toward unique generational units (those in the armed forces, those in college, those who are unemployed or unemployable) within the 16 to 25-year-old cohort (Cryns and Monk, 1973).

A final concern is the debate as to whether attitudes change and, if so, to what extent. Generally, it is agreed that attitudes, like beliefs, are not permanent, and can change or be changed over time. Attitudinal change may occur because of social change, because each new cohort is normally better educated than its predecessors, and because in some cases direct-intervention programs are designed to change attitudes. For example, Glass and Trent (1980), noting the generally negative views of children toward older persons, introduced a two-week study unit on aging to grade 9 students. Using the Kogan (1961) scale, they found small but positive changes in attitudes after the two-week course. While these changed attitudes persisted over a four-to-six-month period, there remains the question of the permanency of the change. Similarly, Seefeldt et al. (1981) found that a curriculum designed to foster positive attitudes toward the elderly among kindergarten to grade 6 children was successful.

In a more direct intervention program, Olejnik and LaRue (1981) observed changes in adolescents' perceptions of the aged after a two-month period during which forty persons 60 years of age and older were served lunch in a school cafeteria. They found that younger adolescents and female adolescents interacted more with the elderly guests and changed their perceptions to a greater extent. Most of the changed perceptions were related to misconceptions concerning the physical characteristics of older people. Unfortunately, this study did not determine whether there were changes in the older people's perceptions of the adolescents.

Despite methodological and theoretical limitations, much literature on attitudes and aging has been published (Lutsky, 1980) since the pioneering work by Tuckman and Lorge in the 1950s. Generally, three instruments have been used: the 137-item 'Attitudes Toward Old People' scale by Tuckman and Lorge (1953); the 34-item 'Old People' scale by Kogan (1961) (both of these are Likert-type scales that are reduced to a total score); and the 32-item semantic differential scale (Rosencranz and McNevin, 1969) that is reduced to three dimensions (instrumental-ineffective; autonomous-dependent; personal acceptability-unacceptability). More recently, Jantz et al. (1976) developed a test of children's attitudes toward the elderly.

This literature seems to indicate that, in general, children, adolescents, college students, and young adults hold negative attitudes, stereotypes, or perceptions about growing old, about the elderly, and about interacting with older people. These negative attitudes seem to center on the physical, psychological, and social conditions of growing old. However, the findings are inconsistent from study to study. For example, Lutsky (1980) concluded that there is an absence of a strong negative stereotype of elderly persons and old age, although negative attitudes tend to be more prevalent when subjects are asked to compare the elderly to some younger age group. Furthermore, attitudes seem to be affected by a number of intervening factors. For example, variation in age, sex, personality, and socioeconomic status of the respondents results in inconsistent findings; and those with more education consistently show more positive attitudes. In addition, there is some evidence that the later adults perceive the onset of middle age and old age, the more positive their attitudes toward aging.

Similarly, those who have frequent and meaningful interaction with elderly people, especially where there is a filial bond, have more positive attitudes (Sheehan, 1978; Ventis, 1981). Perhaps this occurs because the contact provides factual, personal knowledge to refute the myths about aging, and the individual is less likely to accept existing stereotypes. For example, Crockett et al. (1979) found that an older person who is alert, interesting, and involved in life is perceived as deviating from the stereotypes and is positively evaluated, even more so than a younger person who demonstrates these traits. They suggested that in the face of evidence, specific older persons may be viewed as unique, even though negative stereotypes of older people in general may still be retained.

Another problem in attitude measurement is that, from the researcher's perspective, it is uncertain whether the respondent is expressing an attitude with respect to a specific older individual known to him or her, or with respect to a generally held view of the elderly.

A final area of interest is the impact of negative stereotypes and attitudes on the elderly themselves. It has been suggested that the elderly perceive, accept, and internalize these negative views; they either deny they are aging and identify themselves to others and to themselves as younger than they are (Bengtson and Cutler, 1976; Bultena and Powers, 1978), or they accept the social label of 'old,' and either change their identity or become disengaged and isolated. Because of the perceived attitudes of others, old age is seen as a stigmatized attribute with negative meanings attached to the status (Ward, 1977).

This identification of the self as younger than actual chronological age is more likely to occur in women; in older respondents (Drevenstedt, 1976); in those of higher social classes; in whites; in those with better psychological functioning (Linn and Hunter, 1979); in those with higher levels of education; in those who are in good health and physically active; and in those who are still employed. Thus, it appears that societal attitudes toward the aged may lead to a change in an individual's subjective age-identification, which can have a subsequent impact on lifestyle and adaptation in the later years. Perceived age appears to be a function of demographic and lifestyle factors that influence how negative societal attitudes affect individuals. For some, these attitudes may be a threat to self-esteem. For others, however, old-age stereotypes may be functional in that the individuals may, in comparison to the stereotypes, appear to be better off than most elderly people. In this respect, negative stereotypes may enhance participation and satisfaction, especially among the better-educated (Kearl, 1981–82).

To summarize, a process of denial may be initiated to avoid being labelled as 'old,' or a process of acceptance may be initiated wherein the individual changes identity, disengages, and becomes isolated. For others, who are active, better educated, in good health, and part of a comparative reference group of age peers (Bultena and Powers, 1978), objective self-evaluations may lead to the adoption and reporting of a younger self-image.

Ageism: A Form of Discrimination

Stereotypes and attitudes about older adults often result from a socialization process that occurs within a society stratified by age. Through the interaction of an age-stratification system and the socialization process, negative attitudes and stereotypes are formed and perpetuated so that the elderly are viewed as a distinct and unique group. Many of these views are reinforced by the media, in programs and advertisements emphasizing the high value placed on looking, thinking, feeling, and acting young.

Where negative attitudes and stereotypes become pervasive and institution-alized in legal or moral codes (such as mandatory retirement), they represent a form of prejudice that may lead to discrimination against others on the basis of actual or perceived chronological age. Butler (1969) labelled this process 'ageism.' He suggested that older people are differentially discriminated against by virtue of their membership in a particular age cohort. These stereotypes are used, in turn, to justify such prejudicial and discriminatory social acts as elimination from the labor force at a particular chronological age, exclusion from social interaction, and denial of equal access to services in the public and private sectors (Barrow and Smith, 1979; Levin and Levin, 1980). In addition, ageism is perpetuated by the use of ageist terms when referring to the elderly. For example, Nuessel (1982) identifies eighty-five commonly used ageist terms.

Interestingly, like many other areas of social gerontology, ageism has been identified and studied primarily from the perspective of white members of the middle class. Since elderly members of racial or ethnic minority groups may or may not experience differential treatment based on subcultural values, attitudes, and stereotypes, the interaction of race, age, and class must be considered (Golden, 1976). This issue will be addressed later in the section on the interaction of stratification systems.

Having hypothesized that ageism exists, many social scientists have sought evidence to illustrate its psychological and social effects on the individual and on society. Unfortunately, definitive evidence is lacking for most of the hypotheses concerned with the outcome of ageism. While some studies have reported few perceived or actual acts of victimization (Kahana et al., 1977) or discrimination by age (Connor et al., 1978), others have reported perceived or actual age discrimi-nation in hiring (McCauley, 1977), promotion (Kasschau, 1976), and decision making (Rosen and Jerdee, 1976).

252 A MACROANALYSIS OF AGING

252   A MACROANALYSIS OF AGING

In a detailed overview of reactions to ageism, Levin and Levin (1980:97–114) suggest that older people may react to ageism by accepting or avoiding stereotypical labels and prejudicial interactions, or by becoming aggressive and attempting to alleviate the process by collective action. They suggest that acceptance of prejudice and discrimination is revealed by social or psychological disengagement (although few people actually disengage). More seriously, the elderly voluntarily or reluctantly accept the negative stereotypes and begin to behave as they are expected to behave (the self-fulfilling prophecy). This is what Kuypers and Bengtson (1973) refer to as the 'social-breakdown syndrome.' This process involves role loss, lack of socialization to old age (Rosow, 1974), lack of social norms, and social labelling based on negative and stereotypical views. As a result, older people in general are perceived and treated as if they are incompetent, obsolete, and poorly adjusted.

Kuypers and Bengtson argue that older persons internalize these external evaluations, perceive themselves to have these characteristics, and begin to behave as expected. This further reinforces societal stereotypes, which are then perpetuated. To date, little evidence exists that negative self-evaluation and self-labelling is a typical pattern for large numbers of older people. Furthermore, it has been suggested that acceptance of these 'labels' may result in voluntary age segregation in retirement communities. However, as we will see in chapter 8, only a small minority, many of whom are members of the upper-middle class, isolate themselves from the larger society.

Instead of accepting stereotypical labels, older people may avoid the social stigma of aging by a denial of old age. This occurs when individuals report that they themselves are not 'old,' when they conceal or lie about their age, or when they seek re-engagement in former roles (work after compulsory retirement, parenthood, or marriage to a younger person). Avoidance may be reflected in direct attempts to 'pass' as a younger person by means of cosmetics or plastic surgery, or by taking on social roles (becoming a college student) and engaging in social behavior (attending nightclubs for singles) more common during the earlier years of adulthood. In some situations this avoidance behavior may lead to serious psychological problems, and perhaps to alcoholism, drug abuse, or suicide.

Another type of reaction to ageism involves an unwillingness to accept the status quo, and participation in social and political activism aimed at changing society's views of the aged. In this situation, an age-group consciousness develops. This, in turn, may lead to the formation of advocacy groups (such as the Gray Panthers) who seek to end overt and covert discrimination against the elderly and to improve the economic and health status of those elderly people who need assistance (Pratt, 1974, 1976). Interestingly, some of these groups include not just the elderly, but individuals of all ages who seek to alleviate ageism.

It is largely through these action-oriented groups that an alternative view of aging has been presented to younger age cohorts and to policy makers. Hence, not only have policies been initiated or changed (the mandatory retirement age has been increased to 70 in the United States), but prevailing attitudes and stereotypes about the elderly have been questioned and discarded in the face of evidence. However, despite the introduction of legislation to reduce institutionalized age discrimination, despite the availability of research evidence that refutes many of the prevailing attitudes and stereotypes, and despite the visibility of highly active, creative, and intelligent people in their 70s or 80s, ageism still persists to varying degrees in many modern industrialized societies.

Ageist attitudes may be acquired in early childhood. Although ageism is primarily directed toward older persons outside the family unit, it may also influence behaviors within the family unit. As a social process, the prevalence of ageism may vary from one cohort to another. For example, there may have been little overt ageism early in this century, but with increasing industrialization and social differentiation the incidence has increased. However, ageism may now be declining because of increased age-consciousness and social and political activism by the elderly, and because of increased research dispelling the myths that perpetuate the stereotypes. The number of highly visible role models of active, successful elderly people is greater, and more educational programs relating to aging and the aged now exist.

Unfortunately, as with most forms of discrimination, it is difficult to obtain current, reliable, and valid research evidence to support the degree to which ageism is present in contemporary society. It may be that the degree of ageism is closely linked to prevailing demographic and economic factors in a society. For example, with a declining birth rate and increasing longevity, by the time the senior boom hits in the 2010s and 2020s, the skills and services of the elderly may be much needed in order to lower the dependency ratio and to meet the demands of the labor force. Incentives to continue working beyond the normal or mandatory retirement age may need to be introduced. The elderly may be a near-majority group in the social structure, and ageism may no longer be a social concern. It may be the case that ageism will be directed not toward the elderly, but rather toward the younger age cohorts.

Integration, Segregation, Isolation, Alienation, and Resocialization

Introduction.   The dynamics of an age-stratified social system interact with socialization, social interaction, and ageism to facilitate or inhibit other social processes in the later years. It is virtually impossible to separate the cause-and-effect order of the various processes, since they are highly interrelated in a feedback model. However, these secondary processes have an impact on some individuals as they age, and each process is briefly discussed in this subsection.

Integration versus segregation of the aged [20].   Because age strata exist within a society, social boundaries are established between age cohorts and can influence the nature of social relationships. Social scientists have frequently demonstrated the tendency for most social interaction outside the family to occur within age and class strata. This occurs because those within the age strata have encountered similar life experiences, are at a common stage in the life cycle, and probably have similar values and interests.

As a result of this tendency for intrastratum interaction, age groups may be segregated from each other to varying degrees. This can lead to differing values, infrequent cohort interaction, lack of access to social services, and overt conflict. The elderly may become self-segregated from society simply in order to cope (in age-segregated retirement communities and housing complexes), or they may experience forced segregation because of ageist stereotypes and attitudes.

In reality, most of the evidence suggests that despite societal ageism and self-segregation by some individuals, most older persons are integrated with other age strata (Rosow, 1967). On the individual level, relationships between age groups are influenced by perceived and desired social distance. For example, Kidwell and Booth (1977) found that adults of all ages felt more social distance between themselves and others when age differences were greater. Furthermore, respondents reported that they felt more socially distant from the elderly, regardless of their own age. Even the elderly themselves reported estrangement from the elderly. This social distancing is related to the stereotypes and ageism that lead to minimal or infrequent interaction with elderly persons outside the family unit. Moreover, as Kidwell and Booth (1977) reported, the less the social interaction, the greater the perceived social distance. Hence, a cycle is established wherein lack of social contact, the development of cohort-centrism, and the perpetuation of stereotypes interact. These in turn lessen the desire for, and the likelihood of, interaction with older persons.

Social isolation, resocialization, and alienation.   Although social isolation (deprivation of social contact) and loneliness (a psychological state) are frequently portrayed as normative and inevitable patterns for the elderly, few people actually experience either. While aging usually involves a constriction of social roles and the loss of role partners, this may not necessarily result in physical or social isolation. Even the status of widow or widower does not necessarily make loneliness or isolation an inevitable or typical reaction. In reality, there exists a continuum ranging from high social involvement in a variety of social networks to extreme isolation. This pattern holds for all age groups, not just the elderly.

    In order to understand the influence of isolation on an elderly person it is necessary to examine the degree of isolation across the life cycle, to determine the extent to which isolation is voluntary or involuntary in the later years, and to determine whether a confidant is available and used (Lowenthal and Robinson, 1976). For example, some people have been disengaged and isolated from social networks throughout their life cycles, while others have voluntarily or involuntarily moved between social involvement (living in a dorm at university) and isolation (living alone in a city apartment or in a rural setting). Bennett (1980a) has suggested that there may be four patterns of social involvement in the later years: (1) social integration over the life cycle; (2) isolation in early adulthood, with relatively more social activity in later years; (3) social activity in early adulthood, with involuntary isolation in later years; and (4) lifelong, voluntary isolation.

    At any stage, then, an individual may voluntarily or involuntarily withdraw from social networks. For those who withdraw voluntarily and remain isolated, most adjust quite satisfactorily and should not be perceived as a social problem. For those who become isolated involuntarily, this deprivation of social contact may affect their self-images, reduce their independence, and lead to institutionalization. This lack of social interaction can be prevented or reduced somewhat by having access to a confidant[21] with whom trivial or serious matters may be discussed on a regular basis.

    Isolation can also be reduced by participating in voluntary programs (such as 'Meals-on-Wheels') that involve daily visits, by continuing to read and keep up with current affairs, and by making use of alternatives to complete institutionalization (such as partial-care facilities that permit independent living within an environment where meals, security, and recreation are provided). Finally, for those who become totally isolated and who experience mental disorders, the effects may be reversible through resocialization. However, if this process is not initiated in time, isolation may lead to serious and irreparable cognitive, social, and emotional losses (Bennett, 1980b).

Alienation is another possible outcome of the interaction of various processes within a particular social structure. This can be measured along six dimensions: powerlessness, meaninglessness, normlessness, self-estrangement, social isolation, and cultural estrangement (Seeman, 1975). These feelings may lead to either psychological or social withdrawal, or to overt action to initiate social or political change.

The elderly may experience alienation when they become estranged from the prevailing value system; when they feel that political and economic institutions and policies are discriminating against the elderly; when they can no longer accept the dominant ideologies of a society; and when they feel powerless, isolated, and marginal in the social order (Cutler and Bengtson, 1974; Dowd, 1980). An elderly cohort, or a particular generational unit within an elderly cohort, may develop a group consciousness wherein they unite to redress inequity. This may result in withdrawal and the creation of age-segregated communities, or in the creation of political and social advocacy groups that use traditional (lobbying) or radical (withholding votes or taxes) methods to initiate change.

Alienation in the later years is a possible outcome of age differentiation, discrimination, segregation, lack of socialization for old age, isolation, or unacceptable dominant ideologies. Still, alienation is not widespread among the elderly. For example, Cutler and Bengtson (1974) found no evidence that the process of aging leads to political alienation. As Dowd (1980:94) concludes, 'this phenomenon is not the inevitable result of biological or physiological processes. It is, rather, a reaction to the loss of autonomy in our modern world.' Perhaps the major reason that alienation has not occurred to a greater extent is that many elderly people have not personally perceived or experienced a loss of autonomy. Furthermore, while the elderly might become alienated from the political process, and indeed may become cynical about their lack of power, few are alienated from family life and its social network.

The Aged as a Unique Social Group: Myth or Fact?

Introduction.   Since the 1960s there has been a continuing debate as to whether the elderly are a unique social group within modern societies. It has been argued that the aged do (or do not) constitute a subculture, a minority group, a poverty group, or a political group. Unfortunately, much of the evidence for or against each position has been based on inferential leaps from selective studies that include these concepts, rather than on empirical or theoretical studies designed to directly test the concepts themselves. To date, there is little evidence to suggest that the elderly are a subculture (chapter 4), a minority group (chapter 4) or a poverty group (chapter 10). In the following subsection evidence is presented to illustrate that the elderly are not, as yet, a political group. The overwhelming evidence indicates that the aged do not constitute a unique social group.

The aged as a political group.   In the field of gerontology there are three basic areas of interest with respect to aging and the political process: the political participation and attitudes of age cohorts across the life cycle, the extent to which the aged make up a political or power group, and the impact of government legislation and services for the aged (Eisele, 1974; Binstock and Levin, 1976; Hudson and Binstock, 1976; Hudson, 1981). In this section the extent to which the elderly have acquired, or will acquire, political power is discussed (political participation by the elderly is discussed in chapter 11). Unfortunately, as in many other areas of social gerontology, much of the literature contains assumptions or speculations rather than research evidence directly supporting the extent to which aging-based organizations can exercise power to the benefit of older individuals (Hudson and Binstock, 1976).

Although the number of persons over 65 years of age is increasing, and although they represent approximately 15 percent of the eligible voters in many nations, there is no evidence that they have voted, or will vote, as a bloc in national, regional, or local elections. Although the electoral impact of the elderly is questionable (Hudson and Binstock, 1976), politicians have increasingly become aware of the aged, some of whom are the peers of the political leaders. This awareness has been heightened by the formation of age-based associations, particularly in the United States, which provide group services for the elderly (such as prescription drugs, travel plans, or health care). Some examples of these organizations include the combined American Association of Retired Persons/National Retired Teachers Association; the National Caucus on the Black Aged; the National Council of Senior Citizens; and the Gray Panthers.[22]

Pratt (1976) views the formation of these age-based organizations as part of an evolving social movement designed to raise the consciousness of the elderly and other segments of society to the needs and concerns of the aging population. Binstock (1972), however, argues that these organizations are special-interest groups intended to enhance the power and advance the interests of the aged through conflict with other interest groups, including other age-based organizations.

Regardless of the orientation, the size of membership, or the methods of operation, these organizations have been effective in lobbying for legislative action. They have not been particularly effective as powerful political groups that can initiate social or political change. They have acted as catalysts in bringing the problems and concerns of the elderly to the attention of the public, but other groups have forced changes in health care, housing, income maintenance, and transportation policies. In short, these groups have not acquired the political power necessary to represent a force in local,[23] regional, national, or international politics.

Why have the aged not become a powerful political group? As noted earlier, there is little evidence that the aged form either a subculture or a minority group. While the potential for political action is present, there seems to be no strong age-group identity or consciousness that drives the elderly to act as a social group (Streib, 1976). The aged are a diverse group with great variation in needs, attitudes, values, and political opinions. As we have seen, old age is often perceived as a devalued status, and many of those over 65 years of age identify themselves as middle-aged rather than old (Cutler and Bengtson, 1974; Ragan and Davis, 1978), and thus do not exhibit much concern for issues relating to older people.

Furthermore, even where individuals do identify themselves as old, there seems to be a negative relationship between old-age identification and political participation. One study (Miller et al., 1980), based on 1972 and 1976 national surveys in the United States, found that the persons who identified themselves as old were not mobilized as a political group, even if they strongly identified with the status of their peers. The study suggested three alternative explanations for this lack of mobilization. First, the elderly person may have few socioeconomic resources and thus be denied effective participation in the political process. Second, because of stereotypes, the elderly feel incompetent and unable to become involved. Finally, on both personal and group levels, the elderly feel politically powerless, and assume that nothing they can do will be effective.

Another possible explanation is that there is little interstrata conflict, despite the inequality of access to political power. That is, the elderly are not forced to unite because of pressure from other groups. Foner (1974) suggests that this lack of conflict results from the fact that all members of society will eventually move into the older strata; in addition, many people have parents or grandparents in those strata. Furthermore, because of multiple group identification (with the family, work, voluntary associations) there is less commitment to a single age-based group.

Finally, on the individual level, Binstock (1974) suggests that there is continuity in political participation, and identification with one party or platform is likely to be reinforced by age. New political affiliations are seldom formed on the basis of age after the middle years. However, a small minority of the elderly may recognize that their life chances may be improved if group rather than personal resources are mobilized. Thus, as Trela (1972) suggested, making the decision to join an age-graded association reflects a concern with personal status. This concern may lead to a desire for change and a willingness to engage in collective political behavior. This act of joining may be especially important for members of the lower social classes in that it reduces or eliminates the impact of class-based interests in political involvement (Trela, 1977–78). That is, the lower-class individual who joins an age-based organization enters a generational group where age-based collective interests and concerns prevail over those that are class-based.

The Interaction of Stratification Systems: Single versus Multiple Jeopardy

Introduction.   As noted earlier, stratification systems evolve within most societies because of cultural values that result in a particular attribute being differentially evaluated. Thus, individuals possessing a particular attribute are differentially ranked, which inevitably results in variation in access to and acquisition of rewards. As a result of this ranking process, a social structure is created, where being upper- rather than lower-class, white rather than black, male rather than female, and young rather than old places one higher in the stratification system. Therefore, within each of the stratification systems (class, race, ethnicity, sex, and age), inequalities exist because strata are differentially valued.

While variation in life chances and lifestyle occurs between strata, there is also considerable heterogeneity within strata. Not all elderly people are ill or poor, and not all blacks are poor or socially disadvantaged. More important is the interaction between the stratification systems that can influence an individual's situation at a particular stage in the life cycle. This particularly applies to the age and class stratification systems where (unlike the sexual, racial, and ethnic systems) individuals can move between strata, either enhancing or reducing their life chances or lifestyles. Certainly everyone moves from one age stratum to another. But an elderly, black, lower-class woman experiences a different social situation from that of an elderly, white, upper-class woman. Although both women belong to the same age cohort, the influence of the social and racial stratification systems creates a different personal situation for each individual.

In the following subsections the interaction of age with social class, race, ethnicity, and sex is viewed as a social process with a potentially negative impact on the status of the elderly. This interaction is frequently referred to in the gerontology literature as double, triple, or multiple jeopardy. These conditions are assumed to exist when an elderly person has devalued status in two or more stratification systems. Consequently, the individual is more disadvantaged than the assumed 'average' member of a particular age cohort — that is, a white, middle-class male. Double jeopardy (Dowd and Bengtson, 1978; Posner, 1980) exists if an individual is old and poor, old and female, or old and a member of a racial or ethnic minority group; triple jeopardy exists if an individual is old and has two additional attributes such as being poor, female, or a member of a minority group (Palmore and Manton, 1973; Penning, 1981); multiple jeopardy involves being old, poor, female, and a member of a racial or ethnic minority group.

Alternatively, the relative disadvantages for women and ethnic group members may decrease with age. This is known as the 'age-as-leveler' hypothesis: prior social and economic distinctions become less important in determining the situation of the older female or ethnic-group member (Bengtson, 1979; Varghese and Medinger, 1979; Markides, 1981). The evidence for and against these competing hypotheses ('jeopardy' versus 'age-as-leveler') is presented in the following subsections.

Age and class stratification.   Most studies on aging have used middle-class subjects, and most have been written from the perspective of members of the middle class. Many of these studies have implied that all elderly people represent a social problem because they are or have become members of a lower-class poverty or minority group (Dowd, 1980:15–18). In reality, at all stages in the life cycle, within each cohort there is a range of class background that influences life chances, lifestyle, and attitudes toward aging. Those elderly people who, by nature of their past and present income and prestige are members of the upper class, generally have fewer negative attitudes toward aging, and are also more likely to be married. They are likely to have advantages over other members of their age cohort with respect to income, quality of housing, health, and access to health care. They live longer, and their quality of life may be higher. This is suggested by the fact that they have broader social networks, greater community involvement, higher levels of reported life satisfaction, better adaptation to retirement, greater opportunity for employment opportunities, greater mobility, and continuing power and prestige in economic and political institutions. In contrast, members of the middle class frequently lose power, prestige, and mobility after retirement; and members of the lower class, especially if they are not married, may be forced into ghettoes or institutions because of the loss of the few limited economic resources they once possessed.

In summary, the age and class stratification systems interact at all stages in the life cycle to create intracohort variation; the impact on a given individual, particularly a member of the lower class, can be most dramatic in the later years. Thus, the range of class backgrounds found throughout the life cycle continues to influence lifestyle in the later years (Marshall, 1981c). For members of the lower class, aging involves a significant loss of resources which, combined with poverty and poor housing, can significantly alter psychological, social, and physical adjustment, and, indeed, the ability to survive as independent individuals. Finally, because downward mobility is possible in most societies, being unemployed or unemployable in later life may mean a lowering of one's standard of living, especially if children are unable or unwilling to assist in the financial support of aging parents.

Age, racial, and ethnic stratification. Because of prejudice, stereotyping, and ethnocentrism, members of certain racial or ethnic groups have been discriminated against, and have been denied equal opportunity to gain access to the valued rewards of society. Thus, throughout their lives most (although not all) members of some racial and ethnic groups have had lower income, less education, and little power and prestige. This has had an impact on such lifestyle factors as employment patterns, marital stability, health, housing, community involvement, leisure patterns, access to health care and social services, and retirement benefits.

Although social class enhances the status of some members of a particular racial or ethnic group, most experience some degree of discrimination or racism throughout life. In addition to the lifelong stigma of race, as the individual becomes older he or she may be faced with the ageism experienced by many elderly people. If this occurs, double jeopardy exists.

To date, it has been argued either that the gap between minority and majority group members decreases from middle to old age (the age-as-leveler hypothesis); or that the problems of old age are compounded if one is a member of a minority group (the double-jeopardy hypothesis) (Dowd and Bengtson, 1978). The age-as-leveler hypothesis suggests that all elderly people are disadvantaged, but that because members of minority groups have been disadvantaged throughout life they have developed coping mechanisms that enable them to meet the demands of old age. In this way the impact of the aging process on the majority and minority groups is similar. In contrast, the double-jeopardy hypothesis proposes that not only are minority group members devalued on the basis of their ascribed characteristics, but they are further devalued because they are old, and their situation deteriorates even more as they age.

Only a few studies have directly addressed these competing hypotheses. Unfortunately, none of the studies employed a longitudinal analysis, which would have been the ideal design to answer these questions. Nevertheless, the results merit consideration. Dowd and Bengtson (1978) sampled over 1,200 middle-aged and older blacks, Mexican Americans, and whites, and found support for the double-jeopardy hypothesis with respect to objective indicators of income and health status. Older blacks and Mexican Americans were more disadvantaged than whites with respect to economic and health status. In a recent critique of this explanation, Markides (1981) argued that the reason for the apparent double jeopardy is that, beyond 65 years of age, blacks live longer than whites. Therefore, on the average, they are more likely to be in poorer health and in greater financial difficulty. The differences between the racial groups decreased with age for more subjective indicators (such as life satisfaction and frequency of contact with relatives). This suggests that the problems older people face are similar, regardless of racial or ethnic background. That is, support for the age-as-leveler hypothesis was found when subjective indicators of interaction and morale were employed to determine racial differences.

In a more recent study based on a national sample from the United States, Ward (1982) found little support for either explanation. There was little change with age by race in subjective health, income, social support or subjective well-being. Thus, as Henretta and Campbell (1976) suggest, the status of the aged may be determined more by a continuation of the impact of the class system than by the impact of the age or racial stratification systems. Furthermore, as Palmore and Manton (1973) indicated, age produces more income inequality than race, and thus all older people are similarly affected.

In summary, while the disadvantages of earlier life carry over into the later years for members of some racial or ethnic groups, there is little evidence that, except for income and health, the situation of the aged is made worse by minority-group status. Minorities enter old age with a cumulative disadvantage, but experience no more ageism per se than members of the majority groups. Their disadvantaged financial and health positions represent a residue of past experiences that accumulate and reach critical levels as they live longer, thereby enhancing the differences between minority and majority-group members. This situation is compounded further if members of a minority group experience greater longevity (Markides, 1981).

Age and gender stratification.   Despite the fact that women are not a numerical minority group (in fact, they make up a numerical majority in the later years), gender stratification[24] has resulted in discrimination against women (Dulude, 1978; Eichler, 1980). A woman's class position and social identity have generally been determined on the basis of her father's or husband's position (Posner, 1980). The older woman has few pension or government retirement benefits, other than those accumulated by her husband. In addition, compared to men, women have fewer opportunities to enter or re-enter the labor force at different stages in the life cycle; they traditionally have fewer opportunities to train for or enter a wide range of occupations; and physical attractiveness (particularly in the later years) has traditionally been thought to be more important to women than to men in social interaction.

As a result of this process of gender stratification, wherein women are less socially valued than men, it has been frequently suggested that there is a double standard of aging (Sontag, 1972; Payne and Whittington, 1976; Bell, 1980; Block et al., 1980; Fuller and Martin, 1980; Posner, 1980; Eichler, 1980). This double standard is reflected in conventional wisdoms: for example, chronological aging enhances a man but progressively destroys a woman because of the societal norm that physical attractiveness provides more social benefits for women than for men; a woman is expected to marry a man more or less her own age, but a man, especially if he is divorced or if he marries late in life, is almost encouraged to marry a younger woman; there is a negative connotation to the terms 'spinster' and 'old maid,' and there is a positive meaning attached to 'bachelor'; the use of cosmetic products by women to 'mask' old age is considered socially acceptable and, indeed, necessary; and social expectations and opportunities for employment and leisure for women are more restricted than for men.

This double standard varies cross-culturally; it may or may not be prevalent in some societies. The double standard also appears to vary by class background; for example, upper-middle-class and upper-class women are generally more anxious about the effects of individual aging. They may fight the cosmetic battle against aging more vigorously because they have more economic resources, and because physical attractiveness is more highly valued among the upper classes.

As a result of this double standard, a number of negative stereotypes evolve that persist into the later years. Like most stereotypes, these myths are false, misleading, and detrimental to social opportunities for women. Although the aging woman has generally been neglected by social science researchers, some recent studies have sought to refute the myths that the older women is passive, dependent, unskilled, and asexual (Dulude, 1978; Block et al., 1980; Fuller and

Martin, 1980). Studies by Chiriboga and Thurnher (1976) and Giesen and Datan (1980) of urban and rural older women respectively found that older women have developed competencies throughout the life cycle, and perceive themselves to be highly competent to interact with others and with the environment. In short, older women are socially competent, and this competence does not decline with age.

In addition to facilitating the perpetuation of stereotypes into the later years, the double standard of aging may ultimately lead to a double stigmatization — being female and being old (Posner, 1980). Just as the double-jeopardy hypothesis may apply to racial and ethnic group members, it may also apply to older women. Alternatively, greater equality or 'leveling' of the sexes may occur with age. In a test of these competing hypotheses, Chappell and Havens (1980) found support for the double-jeopardy hypothesis when an objective indicator of mental-health status was used to compare the situations of older men and women: there appear to be both age and sex inequities in the mental health of the elderly. However, when a subjective measure of perceived well-being was used, the double-jeopardy hypothesis was not supported. This suggests that even if double jeopardy does exist in an objective sense, women may be less likely than men to perceive or report a decrease in well-being, even where their subjective well-being may decrease relative to men.

In conclusion, older women may not express their perceived situations to the same extent as men (Dulude, 1978). They may suffer in silence even if they do perceive a decrease in subjective well-being; or they may be more accepting of their situation and may not perceive that their level of well-being is less than it was earlier, or less than that experienced by male age peers. While there are many more elderly women than men, the minimal evidence does not provide strong support for the double jeopardy hypothesis. Even though women may be devalued relative to men throughout life, the situation for most elderly women is not the result of a double stigmatization. Rather, since there are more elderly women, and since they do not form a homogeneous group, some may experience double jeopardy, but many will not.

Multiple jeopardy.   The existence of multiple jeopardy is related to the degree to which racism, sexism, and ageism interact to produce inequality among a cohort of older people. Again, as in many areas of gerontology, it is difficult to separate aging effects from cohort effects. While the elderly, black, lower-class female may be among the most impoverished of the elderly with respect to income, housing, and health, she is also likely to be the least educated and the one who has had the lowest income and the poorest health throughout life. Being female, poorly educated, and black has always been a disadvantage, and growing old may not significantly compound her problems.

Although some gerontologists speak of the problem of multiple jeopardy, it does not appear to be an aging event. Rather, it is a phenomenon that has been present throughout life for some lower-class women who are members of certain racial or ethnic groups. Penning (1981) recently found that while the older female member of an ethnic minority group in Canada is economically disadvantaged, differences were not apparent in subjective indicators such as perceived well-being, perceived economic security, and subjective health status. She concluded that there is no direct evidence to support the multiple jeopardy or the age-as-leveler hypotheses when subjective indicators of the quality of life are used in the research process. However, she did find support for the multiple-jeopardy hypothesis when an objective measure of income was utilized.

In short, there does not appear to be sufficient evidence as yet to argue that multiple jeopardy is a factor in the status of specific elderly individuals. Nevertheless, particular combinations of age, sex, and ethnicity may be important elements in the aging experiences of some members of society.

Intergenerational Relations: Micro-level Lineage Effects Versus Macro-level Cohort Effects

Introduction

In the previous section it was seen that interaction between social structure and social processes can lead either to continuity or to change in the social order. Each of these is influenced by a socialization process wherein successive age cohorts accept, redefine, or reject values, attitudes, beliefs, morals, and cultural patterns that older cohorts have sought to inculcate. This process is greatly influenced by the impact of social, political, and technological events on particular cohorts at specific periods in history. The end result of this interaction is either harmony or conflict between cohorts, and, ultimately, varying degrees of social order or social change.

The process of socialization also operates at the micro level, where it influences individuals within particular social institutions, such as the family and the school. This process of individual rather than societal socialization occurs through interaction in which there is a filial bond between the socializer and the socializee. In most societies, this interpersonal and individual socialization occurs within the nuclear and extended families.[25] This is known as a lineage relationship: there is a vertical linkage between generations based on biological and social ties.

The structure of the extended kinship system includes the family of orientation and the family of procreation (Glick, 1977). The extended-family system is created through marriage, grows as children are born, declines or dissolves through divorce or death, and may be re-created through remarriage. The structure of the extended family normally consists of four or five generations: grandchildren or great-grandchildren, a young couple with or without children, a postparental middle-aged couple, an older retired couple, and perhaps an 'old-old' widow or widower. As Marshall (1981b) recently noted, because of population aging and changes in demographic processes, lineages are becoming longer and thinner. In contrast, early in this century families of procreation were larger, people did not live as long, and the lineage was shorter and wider.

Because socialization involves a two-way process of interaction, negotiation, and feedback, the possibility for either cohesiveness or conflict between generations exists within a family. If conflict arises within the family, it is more likely to occur between parents and children during the critical years of identity formation and independence assertion. However, as Cohen and Gans (1978) noted, there is also 'the other generation gap' between adult children and aging parents. More will be said about this relationship in chapter 9.

Some degree of value and lifestyle differences exists among all generations within a family because of the influence of the media, because of historical events, and because of the different stages of maturation of family members. However, the existence and degree of conflict within the lineage system is often influenced by intergenerational conflict at the societal or cohort level. Thus, a complex linkage exists between the social structure and the socialization process at the societal and lineage levels (Bengtson and Cutler, 1976; Troll, 1980). The process of socialization within the family system is interdependent with the process of cohort socialization, and vice-versa. Each member in a specific lineage structure is also a member of an age cohort. Children are socialized by parents and others within the lineage network, and are also socialized by members of a peer group who are members of other lineage structures.

Troll and Bengtson (Troll, 1980:77) suggest that within each extended family there are 'family themes' of values, ideals, and behavior. These provide some degree of continuity and stability between the lineage generations. In contrast, at the societal level, 'keynote themes' distinguish succeeding cohorts from previous cohorts. These themes (such as premarital cohabitation or New Wave music) may or may not be adopted by all members of a particular cohort. However, if a keynote theme is compatible with a family theme, it is likely to be adopted and to cause little intergenerational conflict within the lineage system. If the two themes represent conflicting values or beliefs, and a keynote theme is adopted, then lineage or cohort conflict is likely to evolve.

The next section examines one facet of intergenerational relations[26] that has stimulated much discussion by social scientists, namely, the extent to which intergenerational relations are characterized by solidarity or conflict. In recent years this phenomenon, known as the generation gap, has received much attention because of the concern about real or imaginary generational differences in values, attitudes, and behaviors. The following section analyzes generational similarities and differences at the cohort and lineage levels of analysis.

Cohort and Lineage Generation Gaps: Fact or Fiction?

Intergenerational solidarity.   Before examining the research evidence for or against the existence of a generation gap, let us consider some of the potential conditions that might enhance or reduce intergenerational solidarity at the micro- and macro-structural levels. First, there is always likely to be some degree of strain and conflict between different age groups. This occurs because individuals are at different stages in the socialization process, because they are socialized during different historical periods, and because they may have different needs, interests, values, and lifestyles.

Nevertheless, social order rather than chaos is the norm, particularly within the extended family. Some social processes promote lineage solidarity. For example, Bengtson and his associates (Bengtson and Black, 1973; Bengtson and Cutler, 1976; Bengtson et al., 1976; Bengtson and Schrader, 1982; Marshall and Bengtson, 1983) suggest that the frequency of required interaction, the degree of intergenerational similarity in values because of socialization practices, and the degree of affection, bonding, or liking for family members are three processes that operate at the micro level in family relations. This bonding is revealed by the amount and frequency of helping, by the degree of consensus in beliefs or orientations, and by the frequency of interaction prevalent in family dynamics (Bengtson and Cutler, 1976; Troll, 1980).

As a result of the interaction of family bonding and socialization practices, differences between the lineage generations are minimized. Family members may share common experiences and discuss current events and issues. Moreover, children are dependent on parents for information and for gratification of needs, and the parents serve as role models for life-cycle events such as choosing an occupation, marriage, and child rearing. In short, from an exchange perspective, a bond and a debt is created during the early child-rearing years. This tends to minimize conflict and enhance lineage solidarity.

These processes are even more likely to be prevalent in the future, especially in North America, where each generation will have higher levels of educational attainment. Today, the grandparents may have completed elementary school, the parents high school, and the grandchildren university: in the future all three generations will have completed at least high school, and many extended families will have three or four generations that have completed university. Educational gaps between generations that foster differences in attitudes about the world will narrow, thereby eliminating one potential source of strain.

A final potential cause of conflict, which is also disappearing, pertains to cultural values among immigrant groups. In the past, second- or third-generation youth were socialized by parents or grandparents who were foreign-born. As a result, the younger generations were faced with accepting or rejecting traditional ethnic values and beliefs held by the family, as opposed to modern values and beliefs held by peers, the school, or the media. This was often a source of intergenerational strain and conflict. However, this strain disappears when second and subsequent generations, which have been socialized in North America, socialize their own children according to North American cultural norms. As structural and cultural assimilation occurs, differences narrow and disappear. At the same time, the level of immigration has recently fallen dramatically in Canada and the United States, and at present there is little variation in values based on cultural differences, either within extended families or between societal age cohorts.

When intergenerational strain arises, it reduces solidarity. To understand why this happens, some conditions at both the lineage and cohort levels must be examined. Bengtson and his associates (Bengtson, 1970, 1971; Bengtson and Black, 1973; Bengtson et al., 1976) looked at possible sources of strain. First, there may be some biological and physiological factors associated with advancing age that lead to changes in needs, perceptions, and cognitions, in responses to social stimuli, and in orientations to life.

Second, sociocultural and historical factors can create divisions between generations. For example, status (and hence power) in social institutions generally increases with advancing years, to a certain point; and the young and the old have less social and political power and influence than the middle generation. Also, age grading and stereotyping develop cohort consciousness and lead to intracohort solidarity and generational polarization. Historical events, such as high unemployment or a war (such as the war in Vietnam) that is perceived as unnecessary by one particular age cohort may lead to overt conflict. Finally, there is the phenomenon of fresh contact (Mannheim, 1952): each new generation perceives existing social institutions and social reality from its own perspective, which usually differs from the perspectives of older generations.

All of these factors taken together result in the older generation having a 'developmental stake' in the younger generation (Bengtson and Kuypers, 1970): they fear losing something that is valued. For example, the older generation has a stake in promoting the status quo and in maintaining the continuity of what they value. Therefore, they seek to inculcate similar values in younger generations. In contrast, young people seek to develop a lifestyle and a unique set of values by having the freedom to create and promote differences between the generations.

As a result of this dialectical process of negotiation between the generations, conflict may be perceived. However, the extent of the gap is seen differently by each generation. The older generation minimizes the gap and argues that apparent differences reflect differences in maturity. They also believe that these differences are temporary and will eventually disappear. In contrast, the younger generation exaggerates the differences and claims that the older generation interferes with their right to establish their own values, identity, and lifestyle.

In summary, a number of processes, particularly at the family level, promote intergenerational solidarity. However, at the macro level some social processes may foster real or imagined differences between generations. Yet, for the most part, social order prevails. In order to determine whether a significant generation gap exists, the next two subsections present some alternative hypotheses, examine some methodological problems in this area of study, and discuss the research evidence that supports or refutes the existence of a generation gap at the cohort and lineage levels.

Competing perspectives, alternative explanations, and methodological concerns. Three competing perspectives concerning the generation gap appear in the scientific and popular literature. The first holds that there is a great gap between the generations. The second suggests that the age gap is caused by other than generational factors, and is perpetuated by the media and by methodologically inferior research studies. The third position is that there are selective continuities and differences in the basic values, beliefs, and attitudes inculcated in succeeding generations. Thus, differences pertaining to political, sexual, or religious values and behaviors may arise to varying degrees among different generations at specific points in history. For example, it has been suggested that in periods of high unemployment intergenerational conflict may arise over a scarce resource, namely, jobs.

While these perspectives have been the stimulus for research studies that seek to support or reject a particular view, few researchers have considered alternative explanations for their findings; nor have they been able to eliminate a number of methodological problems. Most of the studies, at least in the early years, assumed that the gap existed at the lineage level primarily between adolescents and their parents, or at the cohort level between the young and the middle-aged. However, as some more recent studies have suggested, a gap may also exist between the elderly cohort and the youth cohort, or between the elderly and the middle-aged (Cohen and Gans, 1978), the so-called 'sandwich generation' (Miller, 1981b). Miller notes that some adults with elderly parents view their position in the extended family as stressful. This stress occurs because their own children are not yet totally independent, and their parents are becoming more dependent. As a result, they must share their resources with two other generations.

There appear to be three possible explanations for any lineage gaps. First, differences in values and attitudes may result from the generations being at different stages of development or maturation. In this situation, it is expected that young people will 'grow out' of their adolescent values, attitudes, and predispositions as they move into early adulthood, thereby narrowing or eliminating the gap. (This expectation is often expressed by parents with respect to the preferences in dress or music of adolescents.)

A second explanation is that the differences arise because of a generational or cohort effect, where members of a particular generation are socialized at a certain time in history and acquire behaviors, attitudes, and values that give them a unique view of the world. They subsequently demonstrate these differences during each stage of the life cycle. For example, adolescents who were socialized following the late 1960s and early 1970s may have acquired more liberal values and behaviors than those who were socialized as adolescents in the 1950s. The 1960s generation, which initiated openly liberated sexual practices, may continue to adhere to more liberal values and behaviors concerning most facets of life.

The third possible explanation for generational differences is a historical or period effect, where social or political events (such as an assassination, a war, or the fall of a corrupt government) can lead to dramatic changes in the behavior and beliefs of a specific generation. In this situation, even though the event has an impact on other generations, one generation is significantly more affected than others, and a gap is created. For example, those who were young adults during the Depression of the 1930s have always tended to be thrifty and more cautious in personal financial management.

While only one of the above explanations is normally proposed to account for the findings in a particular study, all three should be tested, since two or three may combine to explain the results. While some studies in recent years have sought to examine these competing hypotheses (Bengtson and Cutler, 1976:137–44), most have involved limited designs and data sets that prohibit such completeness. They have been content to describe rather than explain generational differences.

Another factor that interferes with the attempt to explain the existence of a generation gap at the cohort level of analysis is the failure to control for social variables such as occupation, class background, ethnicity, educational attainment, religion, sex, and place of residence. All of these, rather than age, may account for generational differences, since people who hold the same social position tend to share relatively the same world view, regardless of age. By including such control factors in the analysis of differences, an investigator might be able to demonstrate whether the generation gap is real or whether it is an illusion. For example, Fengler and Wood (1972) studied value differences among three-generation families. By controlling for variations by sex, education, religion, and place of residence they concluded that age consistently contributes to the explanation of generational differences in values and attitudes.

In contrast, Laufer and Bengtson (1974) suggested that demographic (cohort) groups should be divided into subcategories of generational units, since the position within the various stratification systems (class, race, ethnicity, sex) is a crucial factor in explaining generational differences when they exist. At the same time, Meddin (1975) found no support for a social differentiation model. Therefore, although intracohort variability may be a factor, further research is needed before it can be definitely concluded that a gap exists and that the gap is due to generational differences rather than to social stratification factors.

A final limitation[27] that should be addressed is the variety of attitudes, values, beliefs, norms, behaviors, and moral and religious tenets that are present in modernized societies. One should not conclude that a generation gap exists on the basis of studying only one of many factors. In fact, generational differences may be present on one value dimension, but not on others.

Similarly, there may be differences within a specific domain, such as politics. For example, there may be a gap with respect to party identification, but not with respect to political alienation or attitudes toward a particular government policy. Bengtson (1975) interviewed 2,044 members of 256 three-generation families to ascertain the extent to which intrafamily and intergeneration differences resulted from the process of value socialization. He did not find a 'great gap' in values between generations, although there was considerable intracohort variation. At the same time, he did not find much similarity between generations within an extended family. He suggested that any similarity between parents and youths may reflect a common social location rather than the direct transmission of values by socialization. He concluded that neither family (lineage) nor generation (cohort) effects consistently explain the variance in value orientations among social groups. He raised the concern that observed differences may vary according to the particular value dimension being used in a study; for example, there may be differences pertaining to sexual matters, but not to religious concerns; or there may be religious differences but not political differences.

Despite methodological limitations, the debate continues as to whether a generation gap is myth or fact, whether there is a cohort or lineage gap, and to what extent the gap, if it exists, leads to generational conflict or social disharmony. The current state of knowledge in these areas is summarized in the next subsection.

The generation gap: a summary of research evidence.   Based on the results of studies that have examined both cohort and lineage differences in three-generation families, most empirical evidence suggests that there is no significant gap at either level (Thomas, 1974; Bengtson and Cutler, 1976; Turner, 1975; Boxer, 1979). The generation gap is more imaginary than real, and there is more consensus than conflict among and between generations. For example, the recent survey by Harris et al. (1981) in the United States found no evidence of intergenerational conflict, especially over jobs.

The one exception, which stimulated much of the interest in and research into this question, is the value and behavioral gap that was observed among some generational units within the youth cohort of the late 1960s, and between this youth cohort and all other age cohorts. This conflict was even found within a number of extended families across the social spectrum. However, it is likely that this gap was a 'period effect' influenced by the war in Vietnam, a compulsory draft, a growing black-power movement, and the beginnings of the women's movement and the sexual revolution. Today, many of the so-called hippies, rebels, draft dodgers and bra burners are now middle-aged citizens with values similar to other 'liberal-oriented' members of their age cohort.

Where some studies do conclude that a generation gap exists, that gap tends to be more pronounced for specific values, beliefs, and behaviors, and to be more evident outside the extended family. That is, the gap shrinks dramatically when it becomes more personal. Bengtson and Cutler (1976:145) summarized this finding by reporting a common response of subjects: 'Yes, there is a generation gap, but not in my family.' One reason for fewer perceived differences within the family is that conflict resolution occurs through daily negotiation and compromise between parents and youth (Turner, 1975; Boxer, 1979; Troll and Bengtson, 1979; Troll, 1980). At the family level, individuals often coexist peacefully with respect to value differences. Tensions may develop over interpersonal and lifestyle issues rather than over political values and attitudes (Boxer, 1979). In fact, Troll and Bengtson (1979) suggest that political and religious beliefs and affiliations tend to be shared more by middle-aged parents and their young adult children than by middle-aged parents and their own parents. They further suggest that if differences appear between parent and child, they often persist only during such developmental periods as early or late adolescence.

Troll (1980) suggests that there is a shared value system within the family (the 'family theme') that provides a continuity in outlook across generations. This theme often interacts with 'keynote' themes at the societal level, so that new ideas or lifestyles are adopted throughout the extended family. For example, a youth raised in a family with a liberal set of values, where the parents have perhaps experimented with different lifestyles, may find that the recreational use of drugs creates less strain than it does in another family where more traditional, conservative lifestyles have prevailed over the generations.

Much of the reported gap may exist only in the eye of the beholder. As a result of possible misinterpretation or distorted perception, behavior and attitudes toward members of another generation may be altered. That is, the perception, even if biased or incorrect, can distort reality and can have consequences for intergenerational relationships. A member of the younger generation may perceive and exaggerate differences within the family, while parents and grandparents may perceive few differences and may exaggerate similarities.

At the societal level, the greatest differences may well be those between the youngest and the oldest generations, perhaps because of social and political change and the onset of historical events (Bengtson, 1971). Also, there is generally little communication or negotiation between these generations. In contrast, if differences exist between the youngest and the middle generations, the middle generation is likely to shift toward the views or beliefs of youth through negotiation, compromise, or identification (Troll, 1980). To illustrate, many middle-aged parents who were initially strongly opposed to children wearing jeans to school or social events, now wear jeans to social events themselves, perhaps to identify with younger age cohorts or to present a youthful figure.

In summary, the hypothesized generation gap is generally not supported by research evidence. This conclusion holds for both the lineage and cohort levels of analysis, but particularly for the lineage level, where solidarity rather than conflict is the norm. Where differences do exist, they tend to be related to a specific value or attitude and to lifestyle and developmental issues, many of which disappear as young adulthood is attained.

Summary and Conclusions

This chapter has introduced the reader to the importance of the social structure in the aging process. Based on a system of age stratification, with accompanying age norms and age grading, chronological and social age can create, stabilize, or change the structure within a society, or within a particular institution, such as the family. We saw how the social structure influences the process of aging at the societal level of analysis (through cohort analysis), and for generations within the extended family system (through generational analysis). The influence of the social structure and a number of social processes on aging and the status of the aged was considered from the cohort and generational analysis perspectives. Cohort flow, socialization, integration and segregation, resocialization, ageism, stereotyping, and attitude formation were seen to influence the aging process at the cohort level of analysis. In addition, special attention was given to how interaction among stratification systems affects the status of the elderly. Does the aging individual experience discrimination and limited life chances because of double, triple, or multiple jeopardy resulting from the interaction of age, gender, class, racial, or ethnic stratification? Or is age a leveling factor so that lifelong social or economic differentiation becomes less important in determining the situation and status of older women or minority-group members?

The final section focused on intergenerational relations at the cohort (societal) and lineage (family) levels of analysis. The literature on the existence of a cohort or lineage gap between generations was reviewed to determine whether intergenerational relations are characterized by solidarity or conflict.

Based on the literature reviewed, it can be concluded that:

1. Chronological age influences an individual's location and status in society and in the structures of specific social institutions.

2. Chronological age is a criterion for entering and leaving social positions. Codified laws based on chronological age influence life chances and lifestyles.

3. Within an age-stratification system, age grading occurs whereby age-based norms provide a cultural definition of expected rights, behaviors, and responsibilities of individuals at particular times in their lives. These norms regulate social interaction and define when life events should occur and in what order.

4. Few age-related norms pertain to the behavior of the elderly. Where norms are present, they usually relate to behavior to be avoided at or after a particular age.

5. The socialization process and social interaction patterns can lead to stereotyping of, and negative attitudes toward, the aged. They may also foster segregation and isolation of the aged.

6. There is little evidence that a high level of age group consciousness exists among the elderly, or among other age groups.

7. There is little evidence of the existence of the hypothesized 'midlife crisis,' for either men or women.

8. The aged tend to be underrepresented or misrepresented, usually through negative stereotypes, in such cultural forms as poetry, literature, humor, and television. Older women, despite their numerical majority, are underrepresented as major characters in most forms of literature and entertainment.

9. Although it has been hypothesized that negative or stereotypical views of the elderly in popular culture lead to the adoption of negative attitudes and behavior, this relationship has not been validated by research evidence.

10. Attitudes of younger people toward the elderly are influenced by interaction and experiences with older people, by the personality of the evaluator, and by the situation in which the evaluation occurs.

11. Most older persons do not evaluate or label themselves in negative terms.

12. Research evidence suggests that despite the presence of some degree of societal ageism, and despite self-segregation by some individuals, most older persons are integrated with other age strata.

13. Few older persons actually experience significant degrees of isolation, loneliness, or alienation.

14.   Research evidence indicates that the aged are not a unique social group within modernized societies. Older cohorts are heterogeneous and do not make up a subculture, a minority group, a poverty group, or a political group.

15.   The interaction of age with class, ethnic, racial, or gender stratification systems can influence the psychological, social, and physical adjustment of those at the lower end of the systems. With respect to income and health status, the situation of the elderly may be worsened by being female, a member of the lower class, or a member of a disadvantaged racial or ethnic group.

16.   Multiple jeopardy does not appear to be a factor in the status of elderly persons. That is, it is not an 'aging' event. Rather, the characteristics of multiple jeopardy have probably been present throughout life.

17.   The generation gap appears to be more imaginary than real. There is little empirical evidence to support the existence of a generation gap at either the societal (cohort) or family (lineage) levels of analysis.

18.   Where a perceived gap is noted, it tends to be at the societal level and to pertain only to certain specific values, beliefs, or behaviors. A generation gap, if it is perceived to exist, is more likely to be experienced by the younger of two or more age cohorts. Moreover, where generational differences are perceived, they are often related to lifestyle and developmental issues, many of which disappear with the transition to early adulthood.

Notes

1. For example, most people prefer interacting with others who have similar characteristics to themselves (race, age, socioeconomic status) or who live or work in close physical proximity (Blau, 1980).

2. Regardless of whether the process is voluntary or involuntary (segregation or discrimination), conscious or unconscious, generational homophyly exists. That is, individuals tend to associate most with those of their own generation (Cameron and Cromer, 1974).

3. The chronological ages in parentheses are merely approximate ranges for the social labels that have been applied to these different developmental stages. For a review of some of the many schema for defining age stages, see Cain (1964) and Fry (1976).

4. For example, in many cases age norms are formally institutionalized as laws (such as the minimum ages for voting, driving, drinking, and marrying). In other cases they are informal yet highly institutionalized, especially with respect to deference to older relatives in the family or to superiors at work.

5. The passage from one age status to another may involve rites of passage such as initiation rites into adulthood in primitive societies, Bar Mitzvahs or confirmation ceremonies, and retirement parties.

6. There may only be one generation throughout history that has any one of these labels. That is, the particular social or historical conditions may never occur again, and the size or composition of a specific cohort may vary little in the future.

7. In this sense 'generations' are seen as stages in a developmental sequence. That is, there will always be stages of infancy, youth, early adulthood, middle adulthood, and old age. While these are partially related to chronological age, the chronological boundaries and social meaning of each stage may vary over time or across cultures, but the stages (or generations) will persist in some form.

8. For example, grandparents are older than their children who are parents, and these parents are older than their own children. However, one could become a parent at 16 or 36 years of age, or a grandparent at 40 or 60

years of age. Thus, role rather than chronological age determines the power and prestige within the extended family.

9. The family life-cycle perspective of aging generally includes the following: child and grandchild, spouse and in-law, parent, grandparent, widow or widower.

10. For example, does the impact on society of a particular generational unit (such as the youth counterculture of the 1960s) have an influence at subsequent points in history, or does this particular unit mature and change so that it more closely resembles other middle-aged and elderly cohorts that have passed through the life course in recent years?

11. For example, do age-segregated living environments such as college campuses or retirement communities lead to the formation of high levels of group consciousness, which in turn may lead to age-group cohesiveness and social or political action?

12. Brim (1980:53) summarized the possible explanations for this crisis: endocrine changes that change the personality; a gap between aspirations and achievements, primarily related to one's the occupation; a resurgence of 'The Dream' of youth with goals to be attained; a conflict between stagnation and the need to grow despite declining physical energy; a fear of death; changing relationships within the family; and social status and role changes. These explanations range from the biological to the social-structural levels of analysis.

13. Dowd (1980:38) classified these resources into five categories: (1) personal characteristics such as beauty, strength, and knowledge; (2) material goods such as money or property; (3) relational characteristics such as influential friends or caring children; (4) authority by virtue of position or status in an organization or the family; and (5) generalized reinforcers such as respect and recognition from significant others.

14. One exception is the study by Sohngen (1977) that examined adult fiction wherein an elderly person was the main character. Even here, though, the main concerns of the elderly in the plot were retirement, reminiscing, and conflict with younger generations.

15. See Smith (1979).

16. See Richman (1977).

17. Hess (1980) suggests that a major dilemma facing the television industry is how to portray older people realistically.

18. For example, Arnhoff (1974) found less than 5 percent of the characters portrayed on television were elderly, while Ansello (1978) found that the elderly comprised only 6.3 percent of all characters on television.

19. Schuerman (1977) found that older characters in nine women's magazines were more likely to be portrayed positively than negatively.

20. This section will address the question of integration versus segregation on the social level only. In chapter 8, the impact of physical integration and segregation is discussed in more detail.

21. This confidant does not necessarily have to be a close friend or a blood relative. Service or voluntary personnel such as doormen, housekeepers, bartenders, or social workers can play this role, so that the older person has at least a minimal level of daily social contact.

22. Pratt (1974, 1976) describes the origins and organizational structure of these associations. He predicts that these organizations will increase in membership and influence because of better leadership, stability in membership and finances, and a political environment that is more aware of the concerns of the elderly.

23. Formal and informal organizations or coalitions for the elderly may be more effective at the local level where the social networks may easily facilitate political pressure. Also, at the local level there may be less differentiation within the older age cohorts, and more unanimity and commitment to action may be possible. To date, however, most studies have focused on the power of aging-based political groups at the national level.

24. 'Gender' is used rather than 'sex' since, as Tresemer (1975) notes, 'sex' refers to the physiological differences between males and females, whereas 'gender' refers to the psychological and cultural definitions of the dimensions of masculine and feminine which are learned roles.

25. The dynamics of family interaction as they pertain to adults in the middle and later years of life are discussed in chapter 9.

26. For a selected bibliography pertaining to intergenerational relations and aging, see Bengtson et al. (1975).

27. An additional methodological shortcoming is the failure and perhaps the inability of most studies to use a longitudinal design to analyze to what extent generational

differences at one time persist throughout later stages. To date, only one study has attempted such an analysis (Meddin, 1975).

References

Abu-Laban, S. and B. Abu-Laban. 'Women and the Aged as Minority Groups: A Critique,' pp. 63–79 in V. Marshall (ed.). *Aging in Canada: Social Perspectives*. Don Mills: Fitzhenry and Whiteside, 1980.

Albrecht, G. and H. Gift. 'Adult Socialization: Ambiguity and Adult Life Crises,' pp. 237–51 in N. Datan and L. Ginsburg (eds.). *Life-Span Developmental Psychology: Normative Life Crises*. New York: Academic Press, 1975.

Andrews, D. 'Work, Age and Retirement: Attitudes Reflected in Greeting Cards,' paper presented at the annual meeting of the Gerontological Society of America, Toronto, November 1981.

Ansello, E. 'Old Age and Literature: An Overview,' *Educational Gerontology*, 2(3/1977a), 211–18.

Ansello, E. 'Age and Ageism in Children's First Literature,' *Educational Gerontology*, 2(3/1977b), 255–74.

Ansello, E. 'Broadcast Images: The Older Woman in Television (Part I),' paper presented at the annual meeting of the Gerontological Society, Dallas, 1978.

Arnhoff, C. 'Old Age in Prime Time,' *Journal of Communication*, 26(4/1974), 86–87.

Barrow, G. and P. Smith. *Aging, Ageism and Society*. St. Paul: West Publishing Co., 1979.

Bassili, J. and J. Reil. 'On the Dominance of the Old-Age Stereotype,' *Journal of Gerontology*, 36(6/1981), 682–88.

Bell, I. 'The Double Standard,' pp. 134–46 in B. Hess (ed.). *Growing Old in America*. New Brunswick, N.J.: Transaction, Inc., 1980.

Bengtson, V. 'The Generation Gap: A Review and Typology of Social-Psychological Perspectives,' *Youth and Society*, 2(1/1970), 7–31.

Bengtson, V. 'Inter-Age Perceptions and the Generation Gap,' *The Gerontologist*, 11(1/1971), 85–89.

Bengtson, V. 'Generation and Family Effects in Value Socialization,' *American Sociological Review*, 40(3/1975), 358–71.

Bengtson, V. 'Ethnicity and Aging: Problems and Issues in Current Social Science Inquiry,' pp. 9–31 in D. Gelfand and A. Kutzik (eds.). *Ethnicity and Aging: Theory, Research and Policy*. New York: Springer Publishing Co., 1979.

Bengtson, V. 'Generation and Family Effects in Value Socialization,' *American Sociological Review*, 40(3/1975), 358–71.

Bengtson, V. and K. Black. 'Intergenerational Relations and Continuities in Socialization,' pp. 207–34 in P. Baltes and K.W. Schaie (eds.). *Life-Span Developmental Psychology: Personality and Socialization*. New York: Academic Press, 1973.

Bengtson, V. and N. Cutler. 'Generations and Intergenerational Relations: Perspectives on Age Groups and Social Change,' pp. 130–59 in R. Binstock and E. Shanas (eds.). *Handbook of Aging and the Social Sciences*. New York: Van Nostrand Reinhold, 1976.

Bengtson, V. and J. Kuypers. 'Generational Difference and the Developmental Stake,' *International Journal of Aging and Human Development*, 2(4/1971), 249–60.

Bengtson, V. and R. Laufer. (eds.). 'Youth, Generations and Social Change: Part I,' *Journal of Social Issues*, 30(2/1974a), 1–183.

Bengtson, V. and R. Laufer (eds.). 'Youth, Generations and Social Change: Part II,' *Journal of Social Issues*, 30(3/1974b), 1–209.

Bengtson, V. and M. Lovejoy. 'Values, Personality, and Social Structure: An Intergenerational Analysis,' *American Behavioral Scientist*, 16(6/1973), 880–912.

Bengtson, V. and S. Schrader. 'Parent-Child Relations: the Measurement of Intergenerational Interaction and Affect in Old Age,' in D. Mangen and W. Peterson (eds.). *Research Instruments in Social Gerontology*. Minneapolis: University of Minnesota Press, 1982.

Bengtson, V. et al. 'Time, Aging, and the Continuity of Social Structure: Themes and Issues in Generational Analysis,' *Journal of Social Issues*, 30(2/1974), 1–30.

Bengtson, V. et al. (eds.). *Intergenerational Relations and Aging: A Selected Bibliography*. Los Angeles: Andrus Gerontology Center, University of Southern California, 1975.

Bengtson, V. et al. 'The Generation Gap and Aging Family Members: Toward a Conceptual Model,' pp. 237–63 in J. Gubrium (ed.). *Time, Roles, and Self in Old Age*. New York: Human Sciences Press, 1976.

Bengtson, V. et al. 'The Impact of Social Structure on Aging Individuals,' pp. 327–54 in J. Birren and K.W. Schaie (eds.). *Handbook of the Psychology of Aging*. New York: Van Nostrand Reinhold, 1977.

Bengtson, V. et al. 'Aging, Generations, and Intergenerational Relations,' in R. Binstock and E. Shanas (eds.). *The Handbook of Aging and the Social Sciences*. 2nd Edition. New York: Van Nostrand Reinhold, forthcoming.

Bennett, R. 'The Concept and Measurement of Social Isolation,' pp. 9–26 in R. Bennett (ed.) *Aging, Isolation and Resocialization*. New York: Van Nostrand Reinhold, 1980a.

Bennett, R. (ed.). *Aging, Isolation and Resocialization.* New York: Van Nostrand Reinhold, 1980b.

Binstock, R. 'Interest-Group Liberalism and the Politics of Aging,' *The Gerontologist,* 12(3/1972), 265–80.

Binstock, R. 'Aging and the Future of American Politics,' *The Annals of the American Academy of Political and Social Science,* 415(September 1974), 199–212.

Binstock, R. and M. Levin. 'The Political Dilemmas of Intervention Policies,' pp. 511–35 in R. Binstock and E. Shanas (eds.). *Handbook of Aging and the Social Sciences.* New York: Van Nostrand Reinhold, 1976.

Blau, P. 'Presidential Address: Parameters of Social Structure,' *American Sociological Review,* 39(5/1974), 615–35.

Blau, P. (ed.). *Approaches to the Study of Social Structure.* New York: the Free Press, 1975.

Blau, P. 'A Fable About Social Structure,' *Social Forces,* 58(3/1980), 777–88.

Block, M. et al. *Women Over Forty: Visions and Realities.* New York: Springer Publishing Co., 1980.

Boxer, A. 'Intergenerational Conflicts in Three-Generation Families,' paper presented at the annual meeting of the Gerontological Society, Washington, D.C., November 1979.

Brim, O. 'Male Mid-Life Crisis: A Comparative Analysis,' pp. 147–63 in B. Hess (ed.). *Growing Old in America.* New Brunswick, N.J.: Transaction, Inc., 1980.

Brim, O. and S. Wheeler. *Socialization After Childhood.* New York: John Wiley, 1966.

Brubaker, T. and E. Powers. 'The Stereotype of 'Old': A Review and Alternative Approach,' *Journal of Gerontology,* 31(4/1976), 441–47.

Buchholz, M. and J. Bynum. 'Newspaper Presentation of America's Aged: A Content Analysis of Image and Role,' *The Gerontologist,* 22(1/1982), 83–88.

Bultena, G. and E. Powers. 'Denial of Aging: Age Identification and Reference Group Orientations,' *Journal of Gerontology,* 33(5/1978), 754–68.

Burgess, E. (ed.). *Aging in Western Societies.* Chicago: University of Chicago Press, 1960.

Burke, J. 'Young Children's Attitudes and Perceptions of Older Adults,' *International Journal of Aging and Human Development,* 14(3/1981–82), 205–22.

Bush, D. and R. Simmons. 'Socialization Processes over the Life Course,' pp. 133–64 in M. Rosenberg and R. Turner (eds.). *Social Psychology: Sociological Perspectives.* New York: Basic Books, 1981.

Buss, A. 'Generational Analysis: Description, Explanation, and Theory,' *Journal of Social Issues,* 30(2/1974), 55–71.

Butler, R. 'Ageism: Another Form of Bigotry,' *The Gerontologist,* 9(3/1969), 243–46.

Cain, L. 'Life Course and Social Structure,' pp.272–309 in R. Faris (ed.). *Handbook of Modern Sociology.* Chicago: Rand McNally, 1964.

Cameron, P. and A. Cromer. 'Generational Homophyly,' *Journal of Gerontology,* 29 (2/1974), 232–35.

Chappell, N. and B. Havens. 'Old and Female: Testing the Double Jeopardy Hypothesis,' *The Sociological Quarterly,* 157–71.

Chellam, G. 'Intergenerational Affinities: Symmetrical Life Experiences of the Young Adults and the Aging in Canadian Society,' *International Journal of Aging and Human Development,* 12 (1/1980–81), 79–92.

Chiriboga, D. and M. Thurnher. 'Concept of Self,' pp. 62–83 in M. Lowenthal et al. (eds.). *Four Stages of Life.* San Francisco: Jossey-Bass, 1976.

Christoffersen, T. 'Gerontology: Towards a General Theory and a Research Strategy,' *Acta Sociologica,* 17(4/1974), 393–407.

Clausen, J. *Socialization and Society.* Boston: Little, Brown & Co., 1968.

Cohen, S. and B. Gans. *The Other Generation Gap.* Chicago: Follett, 1978.

Connor, C. et al. 'Evaluation of Job Applicants: The Effects of Age Versus Success,' *Journal of Gerontology,* 33 (2/1978), 246–52.

Crockett, W. et al. 'The Effect of Deviations from Stereotyped Expectations upon Attitudes Toward Older Persons,' *Journal of Gerontology,* 34 (3/1979), 368–74.

Cryns, A. and A. Monk. 'Attitudes Toward Youth as a Function of Adult Age: A Multivariate Study in Intergenerational Dynamics,' *International Journal of Aging and Human Development,* 4 (1/1973), 23–33.

Cytrynbaum, S. et al. 'Midlife Development: A Personality and Social Systems Perspective,' pp. 463–74 in L. Poon (ed.). *Aging in the 1980's.* Washington, D.C.: American Psychological Association, 1980.

Cutler, N. and V. Bengtson. 'Age and Political Alienation: Maturation, Generation and Period Effects,' *The Annals of the American Academy of Political and Social Science,* 415 (September 1974), 160–75.

Davies, L. 'Attitudes Toward Old Age and Aging as Shown by Humour,' *The Gerontologist,* 17 (1977), 220–26.

Demos, V. and A. Jache. 'When You Care Enough: An Analysis of Attitudes Toward Aging in Humorous Birthday Cards,' *The Gerontologist,* 21 (1/1981), 209–15.

Dillon, K. and B. Jones. 'Attitudes Toward Aging Portrayed by Birthday Cards,' *International Journal of Aging and Human Development*, 13(1/1981), 79–84.

Dowd, J. 'The Problems of Generations and Generational Analysis,' *International Journal of Aging and Human Development*, 10(3/1979–80), 213–29.

Dowd, J. *Stratification Among the Aged*. Monterey: Brooks/Cole Publishing Co., 1980.

Dowd, J. and V. Bengtson. 'Aging in Minority Populations: An Examination of the Double Jeopardy Hypothesis,' *Journal of Gerontology*, 33 (3/1978), 427–36.

Drevenstedt, J. 'Perceptions of Onsets of Young Adulthood, Middle Age and Old Age,' *Journal of Gerontology*, 31 (1/1976), 53–57.

Dulude, L. *Women and Aging: A Report on the Rest of Our Lives*. Ottawa: Advisory Council on the Status of Women, 1978.

Eagly, A. and S. Himmelfarb. 'Attitudes and Opinions,' pp. 517–54 in M. Rosenzweig and L. Porter (eds.). *Annual Review of Psychology*. Volume 29. Palo Alto, California: Annual Reviews, Inc., 1978.

Eichler, M. *The Double Standard*. London: Croom Helm, 1980.

Eisele, F. (ed.). 'Political Consequences of Aging,' *The Annals of the American Academy of Political and Social Science*, 415 (September, 1974), 1–212.

Eisenstadt, S. *From Generation To Generation: Age Groups and Social Structure*. Glencoe: The Free Press, 1956.

Elder, G. 'Age Differentiation and the Life Course,' pp.165–90 in A. Inkeles et al. (eds.). *Annual Review of Sociology*. Volume 1. Palo Alto: Annual Reviews Inc., 1975.

Fengler, A. and V. Wood. 'The Generation Gap: An Analysis of Attitudes on Contemporary Issues,' *The Gerontologist*, 12 (2/1972), 124–28.

Fillmer, H. 'Sex Stereotyping of the Elderly by Children,' *Educational Gerontology*, 8(1/1982), 77–85.

Foner, A. 'Age Stratification and Age Conflict in Political Life,' *American Sociological Review*, 39 (2/1974), 187–96.

Foner, A. 'Ascribed and Achieved Bases of Stratification,' pp. 219–42 in A. Inkeles et al. (eds.). *Annual Review of Sociology*. Volume 5. Palo Alto: Annual Reviews Inc., 1979.

Foner, A. and D. Kertzer. 'Transitions Over the Life Course: Lessons from Age-Set Societies,' *American Journal of Sociology*, 83 (5/1978), 1081–104.

Francher, J. 'It's the Pepsi Generation...Accelerated Aging and the Television Commercial,' *International Journal of Aging and Human Development*, 4 (3/1973), 245–55.

Fry, C. 'The Ages of Adulthood: A Question of Numbers,' *Journal of Gerontology*, 31 (2/1976), 170–77.

Fuller, M. and C. Martin. *The Older Woman: Lavender Rose or Gray Panther*. Springfield, Ill.: Charles C. Thomas, 1980.

Galper, A. et al. 'The Child's Concept of Age and Aging,' *International Journal of Aging and Human Development*, 12(2/1980–81), 149–57.

George, L. *Role Transitions in Later Life*. Monterey: Brooks/Cole Publishing Co., 1980.

Giesen, C. and N. Datan. 'The Competent Older Woman,' pp. 57–72 in N. Datan and N. Lohmann (eds.). *Transitions of Aging*. New York: Academic Press, 1980.

Glass, J. and C. Trent. 'Changing Ninth-Graders' Attitudes Toward Older Persons,' *Research on Aging*, 2 (4/1980), 499–512.

Glick, P. 'Updating the Life Cycle of the Family,' *Journal of Marriage and the Family*, 39(1/1977), 5–13.

Golden, H. 'Black Ageism,' *Social Policy*, 7 (3/1976), 40–42.

Goslin, D. (ed.). *Handbook of Socialization Theory and Research*. Chicago: Rand McNally, 1969.

Graubard, S. (ed.). 'Generations,' *Daedalus*, 107 (4/1978), 1–203.

Green, S. 'Attitudes and Perceptions About the Elderly: Current and Future Perspectives,' *International Journal of Aging and Human Development*, 13(2/1981), 99–119.

Greenberg, B. et al. 'The Portrayal of the Aging: Trends on Commercial Television,' *Research on Aging*, 1 (3/1979), 319–34.

Hagestad, G. 'Problems and Promises in the Social Psychology of Intergenerational Relations,' in R. Fogel et al. (eds.). *Aging*. New York: Academic Press, 1982.

Harris, A. and J. Feinberg. 'Television and Aging-Is What You See What You Get,' *The Gerontologist*, 17 (5/1977), 464–68.

Harris, L. et al. *The Myth and Reality of Aging in America: A Study For the National Council on the Aging*. Washington, D.C.: National Council on the Aging, 1975.

Harris, L. et al. *Aging in the Eighties: America in Transition*. Washington, D.C.: National Council on the Aging, 1981.

Hauwiller, J. and R. Jennings. 'Counteracting Age Stereotyping with Young School Children,' *Educational Gerontology*, 7(2–3/1981), 183–90.

Havighurst, R. and R. Albrecht. *Older People*. New York: Longmans Green, 1953.

Henretta, J. and R. Campbell. 'Status Attainment and Status Maintenance: A Study of Stratification in Old Age,' *American Sociological Review*, 41(6/1976), 981–92.

Hess, R. 'Stereotypes of the Aged,' *Journal of Communication*, 24(4/1974), 76–85.

Hess, B. 'Dilemmas of TV Broadcasting: How To Portray Older People Realistically,' pp. 543–47 in B. Hess (ed.). *Growing Old in America*. 2nd Edition. New Brunswick, N.J.: Transaction Books, 1980.

Hogan, D. 'The Variable Order of Events in the Life Course,' *American Sociological Review*, 43(4/1978), 573–86.

Hollenshead, C. 'Middle Aged and Older Women in Print Advertisements,' *Educational Gerontology*, 8(1/1982), 25–41.

House, J. 'Occupational Stress and Coronary Heart Disease: A Review and Theoretical Integration,' *Journal of Health and Social Behavior*, 15 (1974), 12–27.

Hudson, R. (ed.). *The Aging in Politics: Process and Policy*. Springfield, Ill.: Charles C. Thomas, 1981.

Hudson, R. and. R. Binstock. 'Political Systems and Aging,' pp.369–400 in R. Binstock and E. Shanas (eds.). *The Handbook of Aging and the Social Sciences*. New York: Van Nostrand Reinhold, 1976.

Inkeles, A. 'Social Structure and Socialization,' pp. 615–32 in D. Goslin (ed.). *Handbook of Socialization Theory and Research*. Chicago. Rand McNally, 1969.

Ivester, C. and K. King. 'Attitudes of Adolescents Toward the Aged,' *The Gerontologist*, 17(1/1977), 85–89.

Jantz, R. et al. *Children's Attitudes Toward the Elderly: Final Report*. College Park: University of Maryland, 1976.

Kahana, E. et al. 'Perspectives of Aged on Victimization, Ageism and Their Problems in Urban Society,' *The Gerontologist*, 17 (2/1977), 121–29.

Kasschau, P. 'Perceived Age Discrimination in a Sample of Aerospace Employees,' *The Gerontologist* 16 (2/1976), 166–73.

Kaufman, R. and S. Spilerman. 'The Age Structures of Occupations and Jobs,' *American Journal of Sociology*, 87(4/1982), 827–51.

Kearl, M. 'An Inquiry into the Positive Personal and Social Effects of Old Age Stereotypes Among the Elderly,' *International Journal of Aging and Human Development*, 14(4/1981–82), 277–90.

Kent, K. and P. Shaw. 'Age in Time: A Study of Stereotyping,' *The Gerontologist*, 20(5/1980), 598–601.

Kertzer, D. 'Generation and Age in Cross-Cultural Perspective,' paper presented at the annual meeting of the American Association for the Advancement of Science, Toronto, January 1981.

Kertzer, D. 'Generation as a Sociological Problem,' in R. Turner (ed.). *Annual Review of Sociology*. Volume 9. Palo Alto: Annual Reviews, Inc., 1983.

Kidwell, J. and A. Booth. 'Social Distance and Intergenerational Relations,' *The Gerontologist*, 17(5/1977), 412–20.

Kilty, K. and A. Feld. 'Attitudes Toward Aging and Toward the Needs of Older People,' *Journal of Gerontology*, 31 (5/1976), 586–94.

Kingston, A. and M. Drotter. 'The Depiction of Old Age in Six Basal Readers,' *Educational Gerontology*, 6(4/1981), 29–34.

Kogan, N. 'Attitudes Toward Old People: The Development of a Scale and an Examination of Correlates,' *Journal of Abnormal and Social Psychology*, 62(1/1961), 44–54.

Kogan, N. 'Beliefs, Attitudes, and Stereotypes About Old People: A New Look at Some Old Issues,' *Research on Aging*, 1 (1/1979), 17–36.

Kuypers, J. and V. Bengtson. 'Social Breakdown and Competence: A Model of Normal Aging,' *Human Development*, 16(3/1973), 181–201.

Laufer, R. and V. Bengtson. 'Generations, Aging and Social Stratification: On the Development of Generational Units,' *Journal of Social Issues*, 30 (3/1974), 181–205.

Levin, J. and W. Levin. *Ageism: Prejudice and Discrimination Against the Elderly*. Belmont, Calif.: Wadsworth Publishing Co., 1980.

Linn, M. and K. Hunter. 'Perception of Age in the Elderly,' *Journal of Gerontology*, 34 (1/1979), 46–52.

Lowenthal, M. and B. Robinson. 'Social Networks and Isolation,' pp. 432–56 in R. Binstock and E. Shanas (eds.). *Handbook of Aging and the Social Sciences*. New York: Van Nostrand Reinhold, 1976.

Lutsky, N. 'Attitudes Toward Old Age and Elderly Persons,' pp. 287–336 in C. Eisdorfer (ed.). *Annual Review of Gerontology and Geriatrics*. Volume 1. New York: Springer Publishing Co., 1980.

Maddox, G. 'Sociology of Later Life,' pp. 113–35 in A. Inkeles et al. (eds.). *Annual Review of Sociology*. Volume 5. Palo Alto: Annual Reviews, Inc., 1979.

Mannheim, K. *Essays in the Sociology of Knowledge*. London: Routledge and Kegan Paul, 1952.

Markides, K. 'Letter to the Editor,' *Journal of Gerontology*, 36(4/1981), 494.

Marshall, V. 'Socialization for Impending Death in a Retirement Village,' *American Journal of Sociology*, 80(5/1975), 1124–44.

Marshall, V. 'No Exit: An Interpretive Perspective on Aging,' pp. 51–60 in V. Marshall (ed.). *Aging in Canada: Social Perspectives*. Don Mills: Fitzhenry and Whiteside, 1980a.

Marshall, V. *Last Chapters: A Sociology of Aging and Dying.* Monterey: Brooks/Cole Publishing Co., 1980b.

Marshall, V. 'Generations and Cohorts: A Generation Is a Cohort but a Cohort Is Not Necessarily a Generation,' paper presented at the 16th annual meeting of the Canadian Sociology and Anthropology Association, Halifax, May 1981a.

Marshall, V. 'Societal Toleration of Aging: Sociological Theory and Social Response to Population Aging,' pp. 85–104 in *Adaptability and Aging 1.* Paris: International Center of Social Gerontology, 1981b.

Marshall, V. 'State of the Art Lecture: the Sociology of Aging,' pp. 76–144 in J. Crawford (ed.). *Canadian Gerontological Collection III.* Winnipeg: Canadian Association on Gerontology, 1981c.

Marshall, V. and V. Bengtson. 'Generations: Conflict and Cooperation,' in U. Lehr (ed.). *Aging in the 80s and Beyond.* New York: Springer Publishing Co., 1983.

McCauley, W. 'Perceived Age Discrimination in Hiring: Demographic and Economic Correlates,' *Industrial Gerontology,* 4 (1/1977), 21–28.

McQuaide, M. and W. Sauer. 'The Concept of Cohort: Its Utility for Social Gerontology,' *Sociological Symposium,* 26(1/1979), 28–41.

McTavish, D. 'Perceptions of Old People: A Review of Research Methodologies and Findings,' *The Gerontologist,* 11 (2/1971), 90–101.

Meddin, J. 'Generations and Aging: A Longitudinal Study,' *International Journal of Aging and Human Development,* 6 (2/1975), 85–101.

Miller, A. et al. 'Age Consciousness and Political Mobilization of Older Americans,' *The Gerontologist,* 20 (6/1980), 691–700.

Miller, R. 'The Elderly's Stereotypes of Aging: A Social Psychological Analysis,' paper presented at the Southwestern Social Science Meetings, Dallas, March 1981.

Miller, D. 'The Sandwich Generation: Adult Children of the Aging,' *Social Work,* 26(5/1981b), 419–23.

Mortimer, J. and R. Simmons. 'Adult Socialization,' pp.421–54 in R. Turner et al. (eds.). *Annual Review of Sociology.* Volume 4. Palo Alto: Annual Reviews, Inc., 1978.

Morris, R. and R. Murphy. 'A Paradigm for the Study of Class Consciousness,' *Sociology and Social Research,* 50(3/1966), 297–313.

Neugarten, B. 'Age Groups in American Society and the Rise of the Young-Old,' *The Annals of the American Academy of Political and Social Science,* 415(September 1974), 187–98.

Neugarten, B. 'Acting One's Age: New Rules for Being Old,' *Psychology Today,* 14(1980), 66–80.

Neugarten, B. and N. Datan. 'Sociological Perspectives on the Life Cycle,' pp. 53–69 in P. Baltes and K.W. Schaie (eds.). *Life-Span Developmental Psychology: Personality and Socialization.* New York: Academic Press, 1973.

Neugarten, B. and G. Hagestad. 'Age and the Life Course,' pp. 35–55 in R. Binstock and E. Shanas (eds.). *Handbook of Aging and the Social Sciences.* New York: Van Nostrand Reinhold, 1976.

Neugarten, B. et al. 'Age Norms, Age Constraints and Adult Socialization,' *American Journal of Sociology,* 70(6/1965), 710–17.

Northcott, H. 'Too Young, Too Old – Age in the World of Television,' *The Gerontologist,* 15(2/1975), 184–86.

Nuessel, F. 'The Language of Ageism,' *The Gerontologist,* 22(3/1982), 273–76.

O'Connell, A. and N. Rotter. 'The Influence of Stimulus Age and Sex on Person Perception,' *Journal of Gerontology,* 34 (2/1979), 220–28.

Olejnik, A. and A. LaRue. 'Changes in Adolescents' Perceptions of the Aged: the Effects of Intergenerational Contact,' *Educational Gerontology,* 6(4/1981), 339–51.

Page, S. et al. 'Children's Attitudes Toward the Elderly and Aging,' *Educational Gerontology,* 7(1/1981), 43–47.

Palmore, E. 'Attitudes Toward Aging as Shown by Humor,' *The Gerontologist,* 3 (3/1971), 181–86.

Palmore, E. 'When Can Age, Period and Cohort be Separated?' *Social Forces,* 57(1/1978), 282–95.

Palmore, E. and K. Manton. 'Ageism Compared to Racism and Sexism,' *Journal of Gerontology,* 28(3/1973), 363–69.

Pampel, F. *Social Change and the Aged.* Lexington, Mass.: D.C. Heath and Co., 1981.

Payne, B. and F. Whittington. 'Older Women: An Examination of Popular Stereotypes and Research Evidence,' *Social Problems,* 23(4/1976), 488–504.

Penning, M. 'Multiple Jeopardy: Age, Sex and Ethnic Variations,' paper presented at the annual meeting of the Canadian Association on Gerontology, Toronto, November 1981.

Perun, P. and D. Del Vento Bielby. 'Midlife: A Discussion of Competing Models,' *Research on Aging,* 1(3/1979), 275–300.

Peterson, D. and E. Karnes. 'Older People in Adolescent Literature,' *The Gerontologist,* 16(3/1976), 225–31.

Posner, J. 'Old and Female: The Double Whammy,' pp.80–87 in V. Marshall (ed.). *Aging in Canada: Social Perspectives.* Don Mills: Fitzhenry and Whiteside, 1980.

Pratt, H. 'Old Age Associations in National Politics,' *The Annals of the American Academy of Political and Social Science,* 415 (September 1974) 106–19.

Pratt, H. *The Gray Lobby.* Chicago: University of Chicago Press, 1976.

Ragan, P. and W. Davis. 'The Diversity of Older Voters,' *Society,* 15 (5/1978), 50–53.

Richman, J. 'The Foolishness and Wisdom of Age: Attitudes Toward the Elderly as Reflected in Jokes,' *The Gerontologist,* 17(3/1977), 210–19.

Riley, M. 'Age Strata in Social Systems,' pp. 189–217 in R. Binstock and E. Shanas (eds.). *Handbook of Aging and the Social Sciences.* New York: Van Nostrand Reinhold, 1976.

Riley, M. 'Aging, Social Change and the Power of Ideas,' *Daedalus,* 107(1/1978), 39–52.

Riley, M. et al. 'Socialization for the Middle and Later Years,' pp. 951–82 in D. Goslin (ed.). *Handbook of Socialization Theory and Research.* Chicago: Rand McNally, 1969.

Riley, M. et al. *Aging and Society. Volume 3: A Sociology of Age Stratification.* New York: Russell Sage Foundation, 1972.

Robertson, J. 'Women in Midlife: Crises, Reverberations, and Support Networks,' *The Family Coordinator,* 27(4/1978), 375–82.

Robin, E. 'Old Age in Elementary School Readers,' *Educational Gerontology,* 2(3/1977), 275–92.

Rose, P. (ed.). *Socialization and the Life-Cycle.* New York: St. Martins Press, 1979.

Rosen, B. and. T. Jerdee. 'The Influence of Age Stereotypes on Managerial Decisions,' *Journal of Applied Psychology,* 61 (4/1976), 428–32.

Rosenberg, S. and M. Farrell. 'Identity and Crisis in Middle Aged Men,' *International Journal of Aging and Human Development,* 7 (2/1976), 153–70.

Rosencranz, M. and T. McNevin. 'A Factor Analysis of Attitudes Toward the Aged,' *The Gerontologist,* 9 (1/1969), 55–59.

Rosow, I. *Social Integration of the Aged.* New York: The Free Press, 1967.

Rosow, I. *Socialization to Old Age.* Berkeley: University of California Press, 1974.

Rosow, I. 'Status and Role Change Through the Life-Span,' pp.457–82 in R. Binstock and E. Shanas (eds.). *Handbook of Aging and the Social Sciences.* New York: Van Nostrand Reinhold, 1976.

Rosow, I. 'What Is a Cohort and Why?' *Human Development,* 21(2/1978), 65–75.

Ryan, E. and H. Capadano. 'Age Perceptions and Evaluative Reactions Toward Adult Speakers,' *Journal of Gerontology,* 33 (1/1978), 98–102.

Ryder, N. 'Cohort Analysis,' pp.546–50 in *International Encyclopedia of the Social Sciences.* Volume 2. New York: The Free Press, 1968.

Sadowski, B. 'Attitude Toward the Elderly and Perceived Age Among Two Cohort Groups as Determined by the AAAT,' *Educational Gerontology,* 3 (1/1978), 71–77.

Schuerman, L. et al. 'Older People in Women's Periodical Fiction,' *Educational Gerontology,* 2(3/1977), 327–51.

Seefeldt, C. et al. 'Using Pictures To Explore Children's Attitudes Toward the Elderly,' *The Gerontologist,* 17(6/1977), 506–12.

Seefeldt, C. et al. 'Healthy, Happy and Old: Children Learn About the Elderly,' *Educational Gerontology,* 7(1/1981), 79–87.

Seeman, M. 'Alienation Studies,' pp. 91–123 in A. Inkeles et al. (eds.). *Annual Review of Sociology.* Volume 1. Palo Alto: Annual Reviews Inc., 1975.

Serock, K. et al. 'As Children See Old Folks,' *Today's Education,* 66(2/1977), 70–73.

Sheehan, R. 'Young Children's Contact with the Elderly,' *Journal of Gerontology,* 33 (4/1978), 567–74.

Sheppard, A. 'Individual Differences in the Perception of Old Age in Cartoons,' paper presented at the annual meeting of the Gerontological Society of America, San Diego, November 1980.

Sheppard, A. 'Response to Cartoons and Attitudes Towards Aging,' *Journal of Gerontology,* 36 (1/1981), 122–26.

Skoglund, J. 'Attitudes Toward the Elderly in Sweden: Correlates and Age Group Comparisons,' *International Journal of Aging and Human Development,* 10 (1/1979–80), 47–62.

Smith, J. 'Age and Occupation: The Determinants of Male Occupational Age Structures – Hypothesis H and Hypothesis A,' *Journal of Gerontology,* 28 (4/1973), 484–90.

Smith, M. 'The Portrayal of Elders in Magazine Cartoons,' *The Gerontologist,* 19 (4/1979), 408–12.

Sohngen, M. 'The Experience of Old Age as Depicted in Contemporary Novels,' *The Gerontologist,* 17 (1/1977), 70–78.

Sohngen, M. and R. Smith. 'Images of Old Age in Poetry,' *The Gerontologist,* 18(2/1978), 181–86.

Sontag, S. 'The Double Standard of Aging,' *Saturday Review,* 55(39/1972), 29–38.

Spencer, B. 'Images of Older Men and Women in Contemporary Black and Native American Literature.' paper presented at the annual meeting of the Gerontological Society of America Washington, D.C., November 1979.

Spencer, B. and C. Hollenshead. 'Fictional Portrayals of Family Dynamics: Older Women Compared to Older Men,' paper presented at the annual meeting of the Gerontological Society of America, San Diego, November 1980.

Stahura, J. 'Ecological Determinants of the Aging of Suburban Populations,' *The Sociological Quarterly*, 21(1/1980), 107–18.

Stier, D. and D. Kline. 'Situational Determinants of Attitudes Toward the Elderly,' *Research on Aging*, 2 (4/1980), 489–98.

Streib, G. 'Social Stratification And Aging,' pp. 160–85 in R. Binstock and E. Shanas (eds.). *Handbook of Aging and the Social Sciences*. New York: Van Nostrand Reinhold, 1976.

Thomas, L. 'Generational Discontinuity in Beliefs: An Exploration of the Generation Gap,' *Journal of Social Issues*, 30 (3/1974), 1–22.

Thorson, J. and M. Perkins. 'An Examination of Personality and Demographic Factors on Attitudes Toward Old People,' *International Journal of Aging and Human Development*, 12 (2/1980–81), 139–48.

Tibbitts, C. 'Can We Invalidate Negative Stereotypes of Aging,' *The Gerontologist*, 19 (1/1979), 10–20.

Tindale, J. 'Social Class, Social Closure, and the Role of the State in Generational Analysis,' paper presented at the annual meeting of the Canadian Association on Gerontology, Toronto, November 1981.

Tindale, J. and V. Marshall. 'A Generational-Conflict Perspective for Gerontology,' pp. 43–50 in V. Marshall (ed.). *Aging in Canada: Social Perspectives*. Toronto: Fitzhenry and Whiteside, 1980.

Trela, J. 'Age Structure of Voluntary Associations and Political Self-Interest Among the Aged,' *Sociological Quarterly*, 13(2/1972), 244–52.

Trela, J. 'Social Class and Political Involvement in Age Graded and Non-Age Graded Associations,' *International Journal of Aging and Human Development*, 8 (4/1977–78), 301–10.

Trent, C. et al. 'Changing Adolescent 4-H Club Members' Attitudes Toward the Aged,' *Educational Gerontology*, 4(1/1979), 33–48.

Tresemer, D. 'Assumptions Made About Gender Roles' in M. Millman and R. Louter (eds.). *Another Voice: Feminist Perspectives on Social Life and Social Science*. New York: Anchor Press, 1975.

Troll, L. 'Issues in the Study of Generations,' *International Journal of Aging and Human Development*, 1(3/1970), 199–218.

Troll, L. 'Intergenerational Relations in Later Life: A Family System Approach,' pp. 75–91 in N. Datan and N. Lohmann (eds.). *Transitions of Aging*. New York: Academic Press, 1980.

Troll, L. and V. Bengtson. 'Generations in the Family,' pp. 127–61 in W. Burr et al. (eds.). *Contemporary Theories About the Family*. Volume 1. New York: the Free Press, 1979.

Tuckman, J. and I. Lorge. 'Attitudes Toward Old People,' *Journal of Social Psychology*, 37 (1953), 249–60.

Tumin, M. *Social Stratification*. Englewood Cliffs, N.J.: Prentice-Hall, 1967.

Turner, J. 'Patterns of Intergenerational Exchange: A Developmental Approach,' *International Journal of Aging and Human Development*, 6 (2/1975), 111–15.

Uhlenberg, P. 'Changing Structure of the Older Population of the USA During the Twentieth Century,' *The Gerontologist*, 17(3/1977), 197–202.

Van Es, J. and M. Bowling. 'A Model For Analyzing the Aging of Local Populations: Illinois Counties Between 1950 and 1970,' *International Journal of Aging and Human Development*, 9(4/1978–79), 377–87.

Varghese, R. and F. Medinger. 'Fatalism in Response to Stress Among the Minority Aged,' pp. 96–116 in D. Gelfand and A. Kutzik (eds.). *Ethnicity and Aging: Theory, Research and Policy*. New York: Springer Publishing Co., 1979.

Ventis, D. 'Contact with the Aged and Attitude Change,' paper presented at the annual meeting of the Gerontological Society of America, Toronto, November 1981.

Ward, R. 'The Impact of Subjective Age and Stigma on Older Persons,' *Journal of Gerontology*, 32 (2/1977), 227–32.

Ward, R. 'The Stability of Racial Differences Across Age Strata,' *Sociology and Social Research*, 67(forthcoming, 1982).

Weber, T. and P. Cameron. 'Humor and Aging -- A Response,' *The Gerontologist*, 18 (1/1978), 73–75.

Weinberger, A. 'Stereotyping of the Elderly: Elementary School Children's Responses,' *Research on Aging*, 1 (1/1979), 113–36.

Wingard, J. et al. 'The Effects of Contextual Variations on Attitudes Toward the Elderly,' *Journal of Gerontology*, 37(4/1982), 475–82.

Wood, V. 'Age-Appropriate Behavior For Older People,' *The Gerontologist*, 11 (4/1971), 74–78.

Wright, C. (ed.). 'Adult Socialization,' *Sociological Inquiry*, 37(Winter 1967), 3–128.

Wrong, D. 'The Oversocialized Conception of Man in Modern Sociology,' *American Sociological Review*, 26(2/1961), 183–93.

Zigler, E. and I. Child. 'Socialization,' pp.450–589 in G. Lindzey and E. Aronson (eds.). *The Handbook of Social Psychology*. 2nd Edition. Volume 3. Reading, Mass.: Addison-Wesley, 1969.

Zillman, D. and J. Cantor. 'A Disposition Theory of Humour and Mirth,' in T. Chapman and H. Foot (eds.). *Humour and Laughter: Theory, Research, Applications*. New York: John Wiley and Sons, 1976.

8

Aging: The Physical Environment and Social Processes

Introduction

In this chapter we will examine the interaction among aging individuals, aging cohorts, and the changing macro- and micro-physical environments (region, neighborhood, residence). More specifically, we will see how characteristics of past and present physical environments interact with aging individuals and aging cohorts to influence their social behavior and quality of life.

In order to answer the question of how the physical environment influences the aging process, information has been drawn from gerontological research and various disciplines and perspectives:

1. Demographers have studied the spatial distribution of older age groups (percentage and population mix) at the local, regional, and national levels, and local mobility and interregional migration by the elderly.

2. Psychologists have examined the influence of the environment on the quality of life, life satisfaction, and subjective well-being of older individuals; the perceived meaning of the environment; and the ability of older individuals to interact with the environment in the face of perceptual, sensory, or cognitive changes or losses.

3. Sociologists have been interested in environmentally induced changes in lifestyles (such as institutionalization); in the impact of environment on networks, interaction, social support, and access to services; in rural/urban differences in the aging process; and in the impact of age-segregated and age-integrated residential living environments on social interaction, lifestyle, and life satisfaction.

4. Planners, architects, and social workers have been concerned with developing housing that meets the needs of older individuals.

5. Criminologists have focused on the incidence and type of victimization by the elderly, along with the incidence and impact of fear of crime.

6. Urban and regional planners have studied the present and future need for housing, transportation, and social services for the elderly, especially in light of population aging.

7. Environmentalists, ecologists' and geographers have been concerned with the nature and quality of the living environment in the home, neighborhood, community, region, and nation.

As a result of this diversity of interests, the environment has become an important psychosocial variable in the study of the aging process at both the micro (individual) and macro (societal) levels of analysis (Rapoport, 1973; Kahana, 1975; Windley and Ernst, 1975; Lawton, 1977, 1980a, 1980b, 1982; Howell, 1980a, 1980b; Fozard, 1981; Lawton et al., 1982; Rowles and Ohta, 1982). However, this disciplinary diversity has created conceptual problems with respect to what constitutes 'environment,' and the way in which the environmental-behavioral interaction can be analyzed, both qualitatively and quantitatively. A number of social and physical components have been studied under the heading of 'environment,' and their effects have been related to such dependent variables as life satisfaction, subjective well-being, quality of life, happiness, security, coping ability, adaptation to changes in environment (relocation), lifestyle, social interaction, number of active social roles, and number of friendships. The following list illustrates some of the components of 'environment' that have been used in studies:

1. The type, variety, and quality of housing.
2. The place of residence.
3. The degree and type of institutionalization.
4. The availability of and access to social networks, transportation, social services, and health services.
5. The physical characteristics, spatial configuration, and size of the living area at the micro (home) and macro (region, neighborhood) levels.
6. The age, ethnic, and racial composition of the neighborhood.
7. The amount of actual or imagined crime in the neighborhood.
8. The size and quality of private space, especially within institutionalized settings.
9. The objective indicators and subjective meaning of the quality of the environment.
10. The availability and use of sensory, perceptual, and cognitive resources to influence what stimuli are received and how they are used to influence behavior.
11. The degree and rate of urban renewal.
12. The mobility and migration patterns of the elderly.
13. The degree of familiarity with the physical environment.
14. The degree of physical danger in the environment (poor lighting, deteriorating buildings).
15. The degree of personal control, autonomy, and freedom within the home and community.
16. The degree of choice in relocation of the place of residence.
17. The degree of actual or perceived change in the local physical and social environment over time.

The factors listed above have been used in a number of studies on the adaptation of aging individuals or cohorts to changing physical and social environments. The question of adaptation is complicated by the prevalence of individual differences among the elderly in health and economic status, and in personal coping skills. These factors influence the ability to maintain or change living environments and lifestyles.

As will be seen throughout this chapter, there is a need for a continuum of environments to meet the needs of a heterogeneous aging population. These environmental dimensions may range from completely independent to completely dependent lifestyles, living arrangements, and support networks; from completely self-supported to publicly or privately supported medical, nursing, social, transportation, and recreational services; from age-segregated to age-integrated living environments; from voluntary to involuntary relocation; from very large to very small personal space; and from high-quality to low-quality personal space.

Individuals change throughout their lives; towns and neighborhoods change; and older people are voluntarily or involuntarily relocated (Lawton, 1980b). Each new environment presents not only a foreign physical milieu, but also the possibility of new social networks, depending on the nature of the housing setting and the distance of the move. A new environment may increase or decrease the amount of personal space, the personal satisfaction with the available space, and the barriers to mobility. These, in turn, can influence the style and frequency of social participation.

The two-way interaction of these environmental and interpersonal changes, which may be initiated by the individual or by others, can influence one's adaptation to the aging process and the way in which a society is affected by population aging. Much of the research in this area has been motivated by the search for optimal patterns of aging wherein the elderly select or are placed in environments suited to their needs and abilities. Environment, however defined, is thought to influence quality of life, lifestyle, life satisfaction, and subjective well-being. Much less emphasis has been placed on changing the society or the physical environment to meet the needs of the elderly.[1] Because of the diversity within and between aging cohorts, ideal or even typical patterns are difficult to identify. Therefore, a variety of environments must be available to facilitate adaptation to aging by a heterogeneous population.

This chapter includes a description and explanation of environment-behavior interaction with respect to the macroenvironment, the microenvironment, and mobility and migration. The remainder of the first section focuses on models and theories that seek to explain the interaction between environment and behavior. The second section examines the regional and local living patterns of the elderly; the need for and the problems associated with private and public transportation; the incidence of victimization and fear of crime among the elderly; and differences between urban and rural lifestyles. In the third section, the type and quality of housing and the degree and impact of institutionalization are discussed. The last section focuses on the patterns and problems associated with local mobility and distant migration.

Interaction of the Personal and Environmental Systems: Theories and Models

In chapter 4, the construction of environmental theories of aging was seen to be a relatively recent development. In an early statement concerning the need for models of man-environment relations, Rapoport (1973) said that the following concerns must be accounted for: the meaning of space; the issues of territoriality, crowding, and privacy; environmental preferences; and the effects of environments on specific groups. With the initiation of research in this area, many additional issues and concerns have been identified as essential in understanding the complex interaction between aging individuals and their environments.

The first theory in social gerontology to explicitly consider the impact of the social environment on the elderly was developed, tested, and applied by Gubrium (1972, 1973, 1975). Not satisfied with the existing theoretical explanations for the social and personal adjustment of the elderly, Gubrium (1975:3–27) argued that both activity and disengagement theory offer incomplete explanations of the process of aging in the later years. In fact, these theories perpetuate the myth that old age represents 'the golden years.' He developed an alternative theory which proposed that there is a strong interrelationship between individual characteristics (the personal system) and the sociocultural environment (the social system) with respect to the attitudes and behavior of the aged. Gubrium began with the symbolic interactionist premise that individuals attach different meanings to similar social events, and thus may respond differently. He was interested in the impact of the physical and social milieu on the meaning older people attach to life, and in how this meaning influences their social interaction and morale.

Gubrium (1973:28–59) suggests that the environment in the later years includes 'individual' and 'social' contexts that interact to determine social interaction and hence well-being. The individual context involves the possession, to varying degrees, of three types of resources: good health, financial solvency, and continuing social support from friends and peers. These personal resources, if present, permit flexibility in behavior, and enable people to 'satisfactorily adjust' to local age-related norms. Those who lack one or more of these three resources have less flexibility and are adversely affected by local normative demands.

The 'social' context, according to Gubrium, provides activity norms that influence behavioral expectations. The meaning of being old is related to the degree of involvement in age-concentrated environments. For example, in age-homogeneous environments group-consciousness norms are likely to be age-linked; there is little variety in the experiences and events an individual encounters, and little role flexibility is required. In contrast, in an age-heterogeneous environment a variety of experiences and demands are likely, and these require greater role flexibility in order for the individual to adapt to them. Thus, personal and social resources interact with different normative situations to influence behavioral interaction and morale. Adjustment is most likely to be successful when there is congruency between what people expect of themselves and what is expected of them by others.

Gubrium's socioenvironmental theory of aging sought to predict behavior and adjustment in the later years. It was based on the activity norms in specific age-linked environments, on the activity resources of the individual, and on the degree of congruency between these two factors. It is predicted that those who have high morale will be either those who have high activity resources and live in an age-heterogeneous social context, or those who have low resources and live in an age-homogeneous environment. It must be recognized that these general patterns of adaptation reflect not only the present status of the elderly person, but also the cumulative experiences of adapting to various environments at earlier stages in the life cycle.

A second theory, introduced by Kahana (1975), argued that the environment is unique to an individual. According to this 'person-environment congruence' model, individuals change their environment or alter their needs via adaptive behavior in order to maximize the fit, or congruence, between their needs and the specific environment. Where congruence exists, the individual perceives a high level of subjective well-being. When there is a deviation from congruence, in either a positive or a negative direction, a change in needs or environment is necessary to reduce the deviation and to restore congruence. To illustrate: an environment can be overstimulating and create anxiety and tension, or it can be so unstimulating that apathy and low levels of arousal prevail. In either of these situations, individuals, depending on their personal needs, might adapt by reducing or augmenting personal tension, thereby moving toward a higher degree of person-environment congruence. To date, this theory has primarily been tested within institutionalized settings. For example, Kahana et al. (1980), in a study of 124 residents in three homes for the aged, found a positive relationship between person-environment fit, as measured by the dimensions of impulse control, congregation and segregation, and well-being.

A theory proposed by Schooler (1975) focuses on the cognitive interpretation of external stimuli with respect to the amount of threat they pose to the individual or to the environment. If a threat is perceived, a stress reaction is induced that leads to individual coping behavior or to a change in environment. This in turn can result in positive or negative morale, health, and life satisfaction. If no threat is perceived, behavior and environmental interaction continue as in the past. This model stresses the individual's perception of the meaning of the environment, and the adoption of appropriate coping behavior to change the environment and reduce the stress.

The most comprehensive theory relating the individual, the environment, and aging has been proposed by Lawton and his associates (1973, 1977, 1980a). Whereas the Gubrium theory represents a sociological approach and emphasizes interaction within the social structure, Lawton's theory represents a psychological approach. This theory emphasizes the macroenvironments where older people live, and the various microenvironments to which they may voluntarily or involuntarily move.

After years of research on older people living in a variety of housing environments, Lawton and his associates developed an 'ecological model of adaptation and aging' in order to enable gerontologists and policy makers to identify, create, or select the best environment for specific individuals. The theory is based on the premise that a person's behavioral and psychological state can be better understood with knowledge of the context in which the person behaves (Lawton, 1980a:2). Thus, adaptation depends on the interaction of two basic elements — individual competence and environmental press.

An individual has a theoretical upper limit of capacity in health, sensorimotor functioning, perception, cognitive skill, and ego strength. This multidimensional concept, known as 'individual competence,' is measured by observable behavior that reflects the presence of these states and abilities. In addition, external factors such as loss of income, forced retirement, loss of spouse, or ageism may be experienced in such a way that they reflect reduced competence.

As noted earlier, the concept of 'environment' has many meanings. Lawton (1980a:17–18) suggests that it is made up of five components:

1. The personal environment, consisting of significant others, such as parents, spouse, children, and friends.

2. The group environment, which provides social norms and reference groups.

3. The suprapersonal environment, or the average characteristics of individuals in the immediate neighborhood (homogeneity or heterogeneity in age, race, ethnicity).

4. The social environment, which includes cultural values, institutions, and economic cycles.

5.   The objective physical environment, whether it be small (one room) or large (a metropolitan area).

Each of these environments makes varying behavioral demands on individuals; that is, they exert 'environmental press.'

   In addition to the objective environment, the perceived environment is also important. For example, the perception of a safe community or an unfriendly city depends on the individual's subjective judgment based on his or her own knowledge and experience. Subjective experiences may influence behavior in addition to, and independent of, either the person or the 'objective' environment. An elderly couple whose money is stolen from their hotel room may perceive the city environment to be dangerous, even if they were the only guests who had been victimized in recent years.

   An examination of the ecological model (figure 8.1) indicates that the level of individual competence may range from low to high, while the degree of environmental press may range from weak to strong.

Figure 8.1 An ecological model of aging (adapted from Lawton and Nehemow 1973:661)

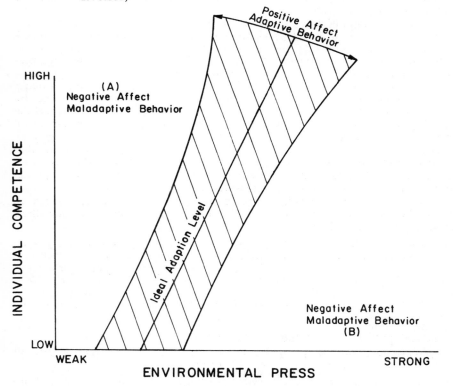

In this model, the outcome of the competence/environment interaction leads to varying degrees of adaptive behavior and affect (emotional or mental state), with the slope representing ideal behavioral adaptation and positive affect. Point A represents maladaptive behavior and negative affect. This is illustrated by the situation where highly competent people experience sensory deprivation (such as solitary confinement). Point B represents a low level of competence and strong environmental press. This situation leads to maladaptive behavior and negative affect, and is illustrated by the elderly person in a northern region who spends the winter months in a skid-row environment in a large city.

The slightly fan-shaped curve indicates that the more competent the individual, the greater the ability to tolerate higher levels of environmental press. The less competent the individual, the greater the impact of environmental factors on him or her (Lawton, 1980a:14). The combinations of individual competence and environmental press are compounded by individual differences in needs and in the extent to which environments vary in their ability to satisfy these needs. Where competence and press are in balance, congruence and a positive mental state occur. A lack of balance suggests person/environment incongruence and a negative mental state (Kahana, 1975).

This model has been tested and supported by examining the meaning to older individuals of living in non-institutionalized macro- and microenvironments, as well as in institutions for the elderly (Lawton, 1980a). In later life, individual competence may decline because of losses in the cognitive or sensory-motor functions and general health. These psychological and physical losses are compounded by social hardships such as retirement, loss of income, widowhood, and ageism. As a result, the aging individual experiences a reduced capacity to cope with environmental press, which may occur in such forms as the deteriorating physical condition of the home, or a forced move to an institution.

Two other psychological models have recently been proposed to explain how an elderly individual demonstrates competence. These models stress the continuous reciprocal interaction between the internal personal system and the social, physical, and psychological components of the external environment. In the first model, Windley and Scheidt (1980), employing a dialectical perspective, present a taxonomy, or hierarchical list, of environmental attributes that contribute to the dynamic interaction between individuals and their environments. These attributes pertain to the content of the environments (lighting, size, privacy), rather than to the different environments per se.

Windley and Scheidt (1980) suggest that the following attributes can be assessed objectively (measured on a scale) and/or subjectively (in terms of their meaning to an individual):

1. Amount of sensory stimulation (the quantity and intensity of, for example, light or sound needed to compensate for age changes).

2. Degree of legibility (clarity and order in the environment to facilitate cognition and orientation).

3. Feelings of comfort (temperature, illumination, and sound all influence the level of task performance in the environment).

4. Amount of privacy (controls outside visual or auditory stimuli).

5. Degree of adaptability (whether the setting can be rearranged to accommodate different patterns of behavior).

6. Amount of control or territoriality (whether an individual can express himself or herself through the display of such things as pictures, furniture, and decoration).

7. Degree of sociality (the extent to which the environment facilitates or inhibits social interaction).

8. Degree of accessibility (whether there are physical or social barriers that prevent interaction and receipt of services).

9. Density (the extent to which the space is crowded with other people).

10. Meaning (the degree to which a setting holds attachment for an individual through memories or a sense of family history).

11. The quality of the environmental setting (the perceived aesthetic appeal to the inhabitant or user).

All of these attributes can be used to determine how well older people are functioning in a specific setting. In this way, the well-being of the elderly might be improved by changing particular attributes of the environment, or by providing environments with a range of attributes. It is increasingly being proposed (Green et al., 1980; Fozard, 1981) that intervention strategies be used to facilitate the personal and social transitions occurring in later life. Interventions such as one-story housing to eliminate stairs, brighter lighting, or larger printing on signs can improve the perception of information from the environment and can promote interaction between people and their environment. As a result, the older person is encouraged to continue living independently and can enjoy mobility in safe and interesting surroundings.

The second model also stresses the reciprocal, interactive nature of personal and environmental characteristics. Parr (1980) suggests that personal characteristics (abilities, desires, health, and economic resources) and environmental characteristics (physical barriers, availability of services, privacy, incidence of crime) interact through mediating factors (such as perception of the environment, expectancies based on previous experience, and knowledge of the environment) to influence the behavior of the elderly person in using or modifying the environment. Because reciprocal interaction is possible, an individual's behavior may in turn act on the environment and on the person. This model stresses that four classes of variables operate simultaneously when person-environment interaction is studied: personal characteristics, environmental characteristics, mediating factors, and individual behaviors. Parr also emphasizes that the number of variables in each component must be limited, and that interdisciplinary research in this area is necessary in order to better understand person-environment interaction throughout the life cycle.

In summary, a number of models or theories have been proposed to help explain the way in which characteristics of individuals and environments interact to influence behavior and well-being at different stages in life. While these models have served to guide research or to explain findings after a study is completed, a comprehensive theory to account for the many factors related to personal and environmental characteristics is not yet available, nor is one likely to appear soon, given the interdisciplinary approach necessary to this area of scientific inquiry and the many social, psychological, and environmental factors that would need to be included. Thus, while the theories and models described above may serve as preliminary conceptual frameworks, they are unlikely to account for all of the possible interactions between the person and the environment.

The Macroenvironment and Aging

Introduction

The macroenvironment is made up of the geographical region, the community,[2] and the neighborhood where an individual resides (Lawton, 1977, 1980; Rowles, 1978; Golant, 1979a; Warnes, 1982). Gerontologists have been interested in the impact on an individual's behavior and well-being of such factors as climate; rural-urban differences in services and lifestyle; availability of neighborhood support networks; access to social, recreational, and health services; size of the community; the age, race, and class composition of the community; and access to private and public transportation.

The Suprapersonal Environment: Distribution and Composition of the Elderly Population

According to Lawton (1977) the dominant characteristics of the people living in a particular region, community, or neighborhood form the suprapersonal environment. The aggregate characteristics of a geographical environment can change rapidly because of permanent[3] in-migration or out-migration of individuals with particular social characteristics, but generally the geographical location of the elderly remains relatively stable.

In the United States, the western North Central states have the highest proportion of residents over 65, followed by New England and the Middle Atlantic region, the eastern North Central states, the Pacific states, and the Mountain states (Harris, 1978; Lawton, 1980a:23). Florida has the largest proportion of elderly persons (16 percent in 1975), because of in-migration to its warm climate; Arkansas, Iowa, Nebraska, Missouri, South Dakota, Kansas, and Oklahoma are next (12–13 percent), because of the out-migration of the young. A relatively recent pattern is the increased migration by the elderly to nonmetropolitan areas (Lichter et al., 1981; Longino, 1982; Burley, 1982), which can suddenly place unexpected demands on the social, health, and recreational services in these areas.

In Canada, most elderly people live in the three largest provinces (Ontario, Quebec, and British Columbia). The highest proportion of elderly people is found in the Atlantic provinces. This geographical area is characterized by low incomes and a high old-age dependency ratio, primarily because the young migrate to other provinces in search of employment (Statistics Canada, 1979).

Although a high percentage of the elderly live in an urban environment (about 75 percent in the United States and Canada), many of the residents of small towns are elderly. In the United States, of those living in large urban centers, over 60 percent live in the central core, with the proportion of elderly residents decreasing as the distance from the center of the city increases (Kennedy and DeJong, 1977; Cowgill, 1978). Many older people prefer to 'age in place'; that is, to remain in a familiar environment where they have established roots (Lichter et al., 1981). They also remain in city centers because they do not have the economic resources to pay for housing in newer areas.

In some older cities that have already experienced urban renewal, there is less segregation of the elderly in the central core. This is because they have been dislodged, sometimes through destruction and reconstruction of housing, sometimes because they have been forced out by increasing housing costs. In the latter situation, the proportion of the elderly living in the central core decreases because of the process of 'gentrification' (Henig, 1981). This involves the gradual resettlement of inner-city neighborhoods by younger, highly educated professionals who wish to live close to the central business district. As a result, less rental housing is available, rents increase for the remaining accomodation, and older residents who live on fixed incomes are displaced or bought out. Henig (1981) found that in-migration by young professionals was associated with out-migration of retirees in 967 census tracts across nine cities. Gentrification poses a threat to the elderly and represents a facet of the urbanization process that may change the spatial distribution of the elderly in the future.

Another pattern in urban location that may soon begin to appear is the 'graying of the suburbs.' During the accelerated suburbanization of large metropolitan regions in the 1950s and 1960s, many young married couples moved to these neighborhoods. When these couples retire they will be living in large 'empty nests.' Since an automobile is usually required to reach shopping and medical services, if they become unable to drive living in a suburban location may create environmental press.

Although it is difficult to define the borders of a 'neighborhood,' it may include a small section of the city, a census tract, or a single block. This geographical area facilitates relations with neighbors, provides services and resources, and fosters a sense of community identity. The neighborhood represents a microcommunity within the larger community. The suprapersonal environment can influence interaction, lifestyle, and well-being, depending on the age, racial, and class composition of the neighborhood residents (Pampel and Choldin, 1978).

Residential age segregation can occur both within a broader neighborhood and within a particular housing complex. At the neighborhood level, age segregation often results from people of about the same age and life cycle stage moving into a neighborhood at about the same time. They age in place in the later years, voluntarily or involuntarily because of roots, familiarity, or low income. They may remain because they are satisfied with neighborhood safety, housing, interaction with neighbors, and recreational, social, and health services (Toseland and Rasch, 1978). As they age, they may become increasingly less mobile and more and more restricted to their house or block. As a result, they become even more reliant on the local area to supply physical, social, and emotional resources.

Within most stable neighborhoods, especially in low-income areas, there is a high degree of homogeneity with respect to age, race, ethnicity, and class. This homogeneity facilitates the development of a network of neighbors who are willing to provide mutual support and assistance if necessary. In many cases, this quality and frequency of neighborly interaction promotes person-environment congruence (Ward, 1979; Ward et al., 1981). However, as Ward et al. (1981) found, individuals prefer to rely on their children for assistance if possible. Nevertheless, where the neighborhood age structure is homogeneous, neighbors do provide instrumental support, especially to those who live in apartments, who have functional impairments, or who are new arrivals to the neighborhood. As people become less competent, they depend more on neighborhood services and resources, and are more likely to make use of these if the neighborhood age structure is homogeneous.

Rural and Urban Environments

The environment of the rural aged has not been studied to the same extent as that of the urban aged (Youmans, 1963, 1977; Lozier and Althouse, 1975; Dillman and Tremblay, 1977; Ansello, 1980; Ansello and Cipolla, 1980; Montgomery et al., 1980; Kim and Wilson, 1981). Rather, inferences have been drawn from urban studies as to how the rural environment differs from the urban, and what impact these differences have on the aging rural resident. When rural environments or residents are studied, a complete definition of 'rural' is seldom provided. Does the term refer only to those who live on farms, or does it refer to those who live in rural communities isolated from larger population centers?

Obviously, the lifestyle of a self-employed farmer differs from that of a businessman or a mechanic in a small town or village. The farmer's life may be more structured, with less leisure time, and he may not retire until his health declines (Keating and Marshall, 1980). A further distinction must be drawn between impoverished, traditional, and subsistence rural settings (Gardner, 1981), such as might be found in the Appalachians or in eastern Canada, and the more modernized, wealthy rural areas of the midwestern and western United States and Canada.

Based on descriptive reports of rural environments, the following are some objectively assessed characteristics of rural milieus compared to urban areas:

1. Fewer institutionalized recreational, social, or health care services are available.

2. The distance to shopping and services is greater, and public transportation is usually unavailable.

3. The crime rate is lower.

4. The average per-capita income is lower.

5. The level of health status is generally lower, perhaps because the average age of residents is higher.

6. The distance from children who have migrated is greater, and there is less face-to-face contact with children.

7. There are more rural widows.

8. The quality of housing is lower because the homes are older.

9. The population density of the surrounding community is lower, and therefore interaction is more frequent and occurs with a greater proportion of neighbors.

10. Neighbors live at greater physical distances.

11. Fewer alternative forms of housing are available (such as apartments or retirement homes) for those who wish to relocate (Youmans, 1963, 1977; Lawton, 1977; Ansello, 1980).

Despite these objective facts, the apparent disadvantages of the rural milieu may not be perceived as such by people who live in rural areas. The objective limitations may be irrelevant to perceived life satisfaction and quality of life. Some recent studies have examined this disparity between self-reported satisfaction and objective indicators that suggest a lower quality of life. Lee and Lassey (1980) found that when comparing objective and subjective indicators of the quality of life, rural residents were clearly at a disadvantage with respect to objective socioeconomic status, health status, availability of services, and quality of housing. However, on subjective indicators of morale, neighborhood satisfaction, and well-being, they scored as high as or higher than urban residents.

Similar results were reported by Fengler and Jensen (1981) with respect to rural-urban differences in life satisfaction. These differences were attributed to a greater frequency and quality of interaction with friends and neighbors, to a lower incidence and fear of crime, to a smaller community size, and to more informal support by neighbors. The rural elderly may perceive and experience relatively less economic deprivation than younger age groups, because they live in an environment that has a lower average income per capita, and a lower cost of living. The relative dissatisfaction expressed by some of the urban elderly may stem from their real or imagined economic deprivation compared to younger age groups who live in more affluent urban areas.

Rowles (1980) suggests that the values and meanings attached to everyday experiences may be different in rural environments. A study of twelve elderly residents in an Appalachian mountain community found that, despite a deteriorating physical setting, the residents were reluctant to be relocated. This reluctance may have occurred for three reasons. First, there was a special meaning attached to the community that had evolved from physical familiarity and social bonding. Second, the residents were part of the local history. Third, they had created a 'society of the old,' with a status hierarchy based on past and present contributions and chronological age. They were surrounded by others who shared in the evolving history of the community.[4] For 'insiders' in this unique subculture, the locale acquires special meaning, and the attachment increases with time. This intensification of attachment would be much less likely to develop in large communities where anonymity is greater, and where the rate of social and physical change in the surrounding environment is more rapid.

Finally, Windley and Scheidt (1982) interviewed 989 elderly residents in small rural towns (with fewer than 2,500 residents) to identify the impact of three domains of environmental variables (ecological/architectural, psychosocial, and personal) on mental health. They found that lack of perceived environmental constriction (physical and social barriers), satisfaction with dwelling features, and satisfaction with the community were the most important factors contributing to the mental health of older rural residents.

In summary, there appear to be both physical and social differences in the rural environment that create unique aging experiences for residents. Specifically, they appear to be faced with a lower quality of environment as measured by objective indicators, but they do not perceive these factors to be barriers to their quality of life or life satisfaction. The objective factors are ignored or considered less important than the quality of social relationships and the meaning of the social milieu.

Private and Public Transportation in the Community

In order for older individuals to maintain independent lifestyles and engage in social interaction in a variety of settings (visiting friends, children, shops, church, clubs), transportation must be available and accessible (Wachs, 1979). In fact, among the elderly there is a very strong and consistent relationship between access to transportation and life satisfaction (Cutler, 1972, 1975; Carp, 1980). This relationship is even stronger when private rather than public transportation is available. As long as their health permits, people will frequently walk to their neighborhood destinations. But walking may not be feasible if distances are great, if the streets are unsafe because of crime or poor lighting, if sidewalks are rough and uneven, if traffic-light cycles are short (Wilson, 1981), or if the weather is inclement.

The elderly individual who lacks access to a car or public transportation has limited mobility and a restricted lifestyle. For most adults, owning a car is essential, especially in rural or suburban areas. An elderly person's limited or fixed income may prohibit owning or operating an automobile. In addition, declining perceptual skills, information processing, and response rate may reduce driving ability. Stirner (1978) found that less than 50 percent of those over 65 drive cars; however, this percentage may increase, because more women in the middle and younger cohorts now drive and own their own cars, and will likely continue to do so in their later years.

If they are unable to drive, the elderly depend on public transportation to move about the community on their own, or are restricted by the schedules of friends and relatives. Unfortunately, public transportation is generally only available in urban centers, and therefore those living in rural areas who are unable to drive are even more likely to be housebound and dependent than those in urban areas. Moreover, isolation in the rural areas is increasing because train and bus schedules between rural communities and urban centers are being reduced or eliminated owing to operating costs or lack of use.

The transportation needs of elderly members of minority groups, especially those living in rural areas, have received little attention (Karafin et al., 1981). Because of their disadvantaged economic position, they may be less likely to own and maintain automobiles, and are therefore totally dependent on public transportation. For some who are isolated on the fringes of metropolitan areas, or for others such as Indians living on a reservation, all forms of transportation may be unavailable. This situation contributes to poor health, because they must be transported many miles for treatment or because they fail to seek transportation to obtain needed health care. For Indians who are hospitalized many miles from the reservation, visits from friends and relatives may be virtually impossible. At present, little is known about the transportation needs or capabilities of the elderly in minority groups; but it is likely that lack of transportation is a major concern for them. For those whose children have automobiles, the problems may be less serious, although if they are geographically isolated from needed services they are still dependent on others for mobility.

Finally, where public transportation does exist, routes needed by the elderly may not be available or convenient, the fare may be too expensive unless there are reduced fares for senior citizens, and psychological barriers (such as fear of crime on the subways) and physical barriers (such as fear of large crowds or long flights of stairs) may discourage the elderly from using the system. Partly because of these concerns, shuttle buses and Dial-A-Ride programs have been initiated for the elderly and the handicapped in many communities.

In summary, the elderly must often cope with a decrease in the availability of and access to various modes of transportation. If private or public transportation is not available, the elderly become isolated, alienated, and housebound, and they suffer social and physical resource deprivation. Public transportation must try to compensate for individual physical losses with age, such as loss of visual acuity and slower response rate. It must also overcome structural barriers, such as the height of stairs or poor lighting, psychological barriers, such as large crowds and petty crime, and economic barriers, such as the cost of fares. Clearly, more research and policy analysis is needed in this area in order to facilitate the transportation needs of the elderly.

Incidence of Crime and Fear of Victimization

Introduction. In recent years gerontologists and criminologists have become increasingly interested in the incidence of crime by and against the elderly (Goldsmith and Goldsmith, 1976; Hindelang et al., 1978; Lawton and Yaffe, 1979; Malinchak, 1980; Lester, 1981).[5] Much of this interest has been stimulated by news reports of savage crimes and swindles against elderly persons, and by the increasing number of elderly persons who report a fear of being victimized. In some cases this fear is so great that they become prisoners in their own homes because they are afraid to walk in their neighborhoods at any time of the day. As a result, lifestyle, life satisfaction, and well-being are influenced by a real or imagined unsafe environment. In order to determine the prevalence and consequences of actual victimization, as well as fear of victimization, a number of studies using local, regional, and national samples have been completed in the United States in recent years. These are summarized in the next two subsections in order to separate fact and myth concerning victimization and fear of crime.

Elderly crime, victimization rates, and the consequences for the elderly. Although significantly fewer crimes are committed by the elderly than by members of other age groups, the rate does appear to be increasing, at least in the United States. In fact, recent estimates suggest that as many as 100,000 Americans over 65, and 400,000 over 55 years of age, may be arrested every year. Among males, the most common offenses are drunkenness and driving while legally intoxicated, while older females are more likely to be charged with petty theft for shoplifting food, clothing, or some consumer good they cannot afford. The stolen items generally are worth less than $50.

In addition to theft motivated by necessity, criminologists have recently observed a pattern of increasing 'elderly delinquent' crime. This type of crime may be motivated by boredom, by a need for stimulation, or by resentment against the private or public sector. For example, recent arrests have included an 80-year-old bald man who stole a hairbrush, and an 82-year-old woman who stole birth-control pills. In most of these cases of 'senior delinquency,' the individual is seldom incarcerated or fined. Rather, he or she receives a warning, is placed on probation, or is required to enter an intervention or educational program designed to prevent reoccurences. In many cases these intervention programs involve voluntary work in the community to provide a meaning and structure in the elderly person's forced life of leisure.

It is difficult to obtain complete statistics on crimes against the elderly. Victims may not report crimes because they are afraid of retaliation, because they may be perceived by children or friends as no longer being able to take care of themselves, or because they are embarrassed to admit they were exploited by a fraudulent investment scheme. In addition, published crime statistics seldom include the age of the victim, or the time of day when the crime was committed. Thus, even though this information may be available in the original police report, it seldom reaches the aggregate level of statistical tables from which secondary analyses of victimization are usually drawn.

Despite these difficulties, relatively consistent patterns of victimization have been found (Antunes et al., 1977; Cook et al., 1978; Harris, 1978; Balkin, 1979; Lawton and Yaffe, 1980; Pollack and Patterson, 1980; Cohen et al., 1981; Dowd et al., 1981; Liang and Sengstock, 1981; Ollenburger, 1981; Morello, 1982). All of these studies indicate that, contrary to popular myth, the elderly as a group are victimized less than other age groups, except for larceny-with-contact crimes such as purse snatching and pickpocketing,[6] and property crimes such as burglary. The elderly are also more likely to be victims of fraud, confidence games, and medical or health care quackery.[7] In general, the elderly are more likely to experience financial loss or property damage than personal assault (Liang and Sengstock, 1981). Unfortunately, being the victim of personal larceny, property loss, or fraudulent crime has a significant impact on the elderly person, because the loss represents a larger percentage of financial resources than it does for a younger person (Cook et al., 1978). Such crimes can also generate fear and anxiety about the security of their environment.

Although the elderly as a group appear to be victimized less than the general population, the possession of certain social, physical, demographic, and environmental facts predispose some segments of the elderly population to a higher risk of victimization. It has been found that victimization rates are higher for males, blacks, and the poor; for those who live alone; for those who live in urban (especially the central core in large cities) rather than suburban or rural areas; for those who are single; for those who live in age-integrated[8] neighborhoods or public-housing developments; for those who are less physically mobile; and for those who lack social support systems.

Having identified some patterns of victimization, how can they be explained? First, the elderly may be victimized less than younger people because they are less mobile; because they avoid high-crime environments such as parks or dark streets, especially at night;[9] and because the lifestyles of the young more frequently expose them to environments or situations conducive to crime. Or, the elderly may simply be less likely to report a crime. Finally, those elderly people who run a higher risk of victimization are often those who are more socially disadvantaged. That is, they live in or near neighborhoods with high crime rates; they are more dependent on walking and on public transportation than on their own automobiles, which increases the chances of street assault; and they live or walk alone. The likelihood of personal victimization is related to environment and lifestyle. Where people live, how much time they spend away from their homes and in the streets, and where they travel in the streets influences their vulnerability (Hindelang et al., 1978).

In summary, despite the myth of the vulnerable elderly person, the elderly experience less general criminal victimization than the total adult population. However, they are more vulnerable to personal larceny and property crimes than younger age groups. Moreover, considering that they spend less time away from their homes, the rate of victimization per minute in the external milieu may be disproportionately high. Finally, the rates of larceny and burglary involving the elderly are increasing. This has led to the creation of special social support systems, including such programs as special police units in neighborhoods where there is a high percentage of middle- and low-income elderly, voluntary escort services, Dial-A-Bus services, and neighborhood home-watching services. Because of the increase in certain types of victimization, greater publicity about crime against the elderly, and the creation of special support systems to prevent or inhibit crime, it is not surprising that fear of victimization has become a major factor in further restricting the mobility and lifestyles of some segments of the elderly population.

Fear of victimization.   Although the elderly are actually victimized less than other age groups, a large number (as many as 50 percent in some studies) express fear and indicate that fear of crime is one of their most serious personal problems (Clemente and Kleiman, 1976; Sundeen and Mathieu, 1976; Antunes et al., 1977; Harris, 1978; Braungart et al., 1980; Lawton and Yaffe, 1980; Yin, 1980; Ollenburger, 1981; Lee, 1982). In fact, in a recent national survey in the United States, fear of crime was mentioned as a serious personal problem by 25 percent of those over 65 years of age (Harris et al., 1981). This fear is more frequently reported by women,[10] the poor, blacks, and central urban residents;[11] by those who live alone; by those who live in high-crime neighborhoods; by those who live in subsidized age-heterogeneous or racially heterogeneous housing complexes (Sherman et al., 1976); by those who have been victimized or on whom an attempt has been made;[12] by those with physical disabilities that inhibit their defensive reactions; and by those who use public transportation, especially at night and when adolescents are dismissed from school.[13] Cutler (1979–80) found that while the fear of walking alone at night increased among all age cohorts over an eleven-year period, the increase was greater among older cohorts.

The ecology of a particular environment may also influence the incidence and level of fear. Fear may be aroused or increased where the level of illumination is low, where the pedestrian traffic volume is low, where police surveillance is minimal or absent, or where minority youth congregate. Thus, fear of crime is related to a combination of social factors (demographic characteristics, previous victimization experiences, availability of social support networks), psychological factors (the perceived seriousness of the event and the perceived ability to recover from a criminal act), physical factors (degree of mobility) and ecological factors (actual and perceived safety of the physical and social environments).

For the elderly, fear of crime is a reality. Paradoxically, while they experience less victimization, they have higher levels of fear than younger age cohorts. This fear of crime usually has a greater impact on social behavior and well-being than crime itself, it may lead to self-imposed restrictions on social mobility and participation in the community. As a result of a real or perceived threat in the external environment, elderly persons may restrict their movement and become housebound (Norton and Courlander, 1982). In this way, their lifestyles are altered and they become isolated from the larger community even further. In fact, a cycle of fear, restricted mobility, and isolation may escalate to the point that some elderly persons, especially if they lack a social support network, may become self-exiled prisoners in their own homes. While this behavioral pattern reduces the incidence of victimization, it also decreases social and psychological well-being and dramatically lowers the quality of life (Balkin, 1979).

Although most of the elderly are not personally victimized, the effect on those who are victimized indirectly influences a number of their age peers who subsequently modify their behavior because of fear (Dowd et al., 1981:351).[14] For example, Godbey et al. (1980) found that 33 percent of the elderly users of public parks were likely to fear the possibility of being victimized while using the park. However, it should also be determined how many never use public parks, or other social or recreational facilities, because some elderly persons have been victimized en route to or in the facility.

In summary, the incidence of fear of crime among the elderly is higher than actual victimization rates, especially for women, blacks, and those who live in city centers. Fear appears to restrict mobility and social interaction in the community, thereby detracting from life satisfaction and the quality of life in the later years. As a result, policies and programs are needed, not only to reduce victimization rates, but also to reduce and overcome the real or imagined environmentally induced fear that is felt by many elderly persons, especially those living in urban areas.

The Microenvironment: The Dwelling Unit

Introduction

The quality, type, size, location, and design of the dwelling unit interacts with health status and economic resources to influence the lifestyle, life satisfaction, and quality of life of the elderly person. Personal satisfaction with housing is an important factor in behavior and social interaction in the later years (Lawton, 1980c; Lawton and Hoover, 1981). This is so because the home is a major social center for the elderly person. Thus, it is necessary to consider the interaction of the personal and social systems with environmental factors, especially in light of the numerous housing alternatives available to a heterogeneous elderly cohort.

Most of the elderly live in houses or apartments where they have resided for many years.[15] In fact, approximately 70 percent of the elderly population own their own homes[16] (Lawton, 1980a; Stone and Fletcher, 1980:49–78). The home is a major asset, one that assists the retired or widowed person in coping with a reduced income. However, it can also become a liability because of increased operating costs or because, with declining health, the individual is unable to perform regular maintenance requirements. Because the homes of the elderly are often older,[17] and therefore susceptible to deterioration, a high percentage of the owner's fixed income may be required for maintenance. Similarly, with inflation, those who rent (unless they are subsidized by the government) are usually paying an increasingly higher proportion of their fixed income for shelter.

Despite these economic concerns, most older people prefer to live in an independent dwelling and in a setting that provides a secure and familiar environment. For those who do not or cannot live in their own homes or apartments because of economic, health, or lifestyle factors, a number of alternative forms of housing are possible. These alternatives range from independent housing to semi-institutionalized congregate housing[18] to completely institutionalized settings, and from age-segregated to age-integrated housing environments. It is this variation in type, needs,[19] and quality of housing that has stimulated much of the research into the impact of housing on the social behavior and well-being of the elderly person (Carp, 1976; Cohn, 1979; Keith, 1979; Lawton and Hoover, 1981; Wigdor and Ford, 1981).

These studies have primarily examined the type and quality of housing available to the older person, the meaning of the housing environment, and the impact of type of housing on social interaction, well-being, life satisfaction, or morale. Typically, surveys or participant observation ethnographies, alone or in combination, have been used to examine the relationship between housing environment and social behavior. Some of the major studies have examined the following topics:

1. The short- and long-term effects of moving or not moving to planned housing for the elderly (Carp, 1966. 1978–79).

2. The impact on the individual of living in age-segregated versus age-integrated apartment buildings (Rosow, 1967. Keith, 1979).

3. The lifestyle of elderly blue-collar residents in a mobile-home park (Johnson, 1971).

4. The development of a sense of community in a small apartment complex inhabited primarily by elderly widows (Hochschild, 1973).

5. Adjustment to living in an affluent retirement community in the southwestern United States (Jacobs, 1974).

6. The environment, structure, and meaning of long-term care institutions (Tobin and Lieberman, 1976; Brody, 1977; Hendricks, 1980).

7. Adjustment to living in a retirement residence for construction workers in France (Ross, 1977).

8. The subjective value of the home (familiar environment, familiar memories, the status of owning a home, low housing cost) and its impact on housing satisfaction (O'Bryant, 1981).

9. The autonomous lifestyle and background of the elderly occupants of single-room occupancy (SRO) hotels in the central core (on or near 'skid row') of large cities (Tindale, 1974, 1980; Erikson and Eckert, 1977; Goode et al., 1979; Lally et al., 1979).

Although most studies have been concerned with the type and location of the dwelling unit and with the behavior and characteristics of the inhabitants, some descriptive studies have focused on the problems arising from the quality of the unit and its design and structural limitations. The quality of the unit can usually be assessed (Struyk, 1977; Harris, 1978; Lawton and Nehemow, 1979) by such objective indicators as appearance (paintwork, deteriorating plaster or bricks); age of the structure; amount of personal space and privacy per resident; quality of the cooking, heating, lighting, and plumbing facilities; and the number of safety hazards (lack of bannisters, unsafe stairs, faulty appliances, or unsafe furniture). Generally, studies in this area indicate that the elderly live in older structures that are of lower quality than other dwellings in the area. For example, Struyk (1977) found that a significant proportion of the elderly live in dwellings with five or more structural defects. Others (Harris, 1978, 1981; Lawton, 1980c; Hoover, 1981) have found that housing quality is even lower for the elderly who are black, who are single, who rent, and who live in rural areas.

Quality of housing can be assessed subjectively by asking residents to comment on their satisfaction with their particular housing as it is, as they would like it to be, or in comparison to alternative environments. In general, studies indicate that there is wide variation in the subjective assessment of the quality of housing for the elderly. Those who are single, who are black, or who rent generally report the lowest degree of satisfaction. Clearly, for some individuals low-quality or substandard housing is often combined with poverty and poor health. These factors may have been present for years and may reflect a traditional lifestyle. For others, deterioration in the quality of housing may reflect the advancing years of both the resident and the dwelling unit, which may then have a compounding effect on the physical safety, health, and subjective well-being of the individual. Ultimately, it may lead to an involuntary relocation to a safer environment (an apartment, a home for the aged, or a nursing home), but at the cost of the emotional loss that is suffered in giving up one's home with its memories and familiar environment (O'Bryant, 1981).

In addition to the quality of the physical structure, factors such as structural design (high-rise versus low-rise), environmental configurations (arrangement of furniture, number and type of stairs), type of furniture (contemporary low seating with cushions versus more traditional chairs with well-supported backs), and interior design (height of storage cupboards, traffic patterns) can all influence safety and mobility within the unit (Raschko, 1982). These factors can also influence satisfaction with the personal environment. Devlin (1980) compared the degree of satisfaction of residents in high-rise buildings with that of residents of those in townhouses or court apartments. The high-rise structure was perceived to provide greater security and better recreational opportunities, although it also generated fears associated with height, fire, and elevators. A high-rise can also create disorientation because of the uniform appearance of floors and apartment doors. Devlin found that elderly residents of both high-rise and low-rise buildings preferred that high-rises not be constructed in the future. According to the residents, the ideal environment would be townhouse units with a centrally located community center. However, this model, which provides lower-density housing and higher satisfaction, is generally not a viable economic alternative.

Even if the quality of the physical structure is poor, the presence of a personally designed interior environment that permits mobility and is familiar and nonthreatening is favored over an impersonal, institutionalized setting. As a result, efforts have been directed toward personalizing institutional rooms by permitting residents to bring objects from their homes to decorate and furnish their living areas, and by providing more environmental stimulation (bright colors, music, color codes, signs and symbols to identify floors or corridors) (Schwartz, 1975).

Type of Housing Environment

Introduction. The location and type of housing environment influences the social interaction patterns and well-being of the elderly, and determines what services are available to the elderly within the neighborhood. Housing for the elderly generally lies along two dimensions: independent to dependent, and age-integrated to age-segregated. These dimensions are illustrated in figure 8.2, and the various types of housing are noted in the appropriate quadrant. In quadrant A, the dwelling unit is age-integrated within the city, suburb, or town, and consists of either privately owned or rented dwellings or subsidized low-rent, age-heterogeneous housing. This latter type of housing provides low-cost shelter, but social services and assistance programs are seldom available. Generally, residents in these dwellings are high in social interaction and life satisfaction because they are independent. Where the quality of the neighborhood has deteriorated or undergone a change in the population mix, there is still potentially a high degree of independence, although it may not be maximized because of fear of crime. In addition, in deteriorating or changing neighborhoods life satisfaction may be low and there may be little, if any, interaction with neighbors. For those who live in single-room occupancy (SRO) hotels, social interaction may be low, but life satisfaction may be high because the hotel provides a major source of support and a sense of security.

Quadrant B represents two types of housing that combine age integration with partial institutionalization. The type of housing varies according to the services offered and the rules imposed on the residents. The type of congregate housing that falls into this category is illustrated by the two-generational high-rise residence adjacent to Syracuse University. Here, one high-rise tower houses university students, the other low-income retirees. The two residential towers are joined by a community center and a cafeteria where residents of the two age

Figure 8.2 Housing alternatives for the elderly

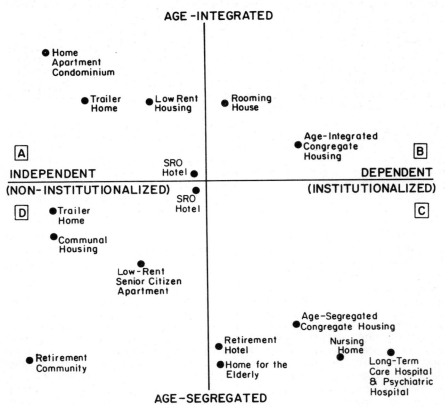

AGE -INTEGRATED

● Home
Apartment
Condominium

● Trailer   ● Low Rent   ● Rooming
Home   Housing   House

                                          Age-Integrated
[A]   ● Congregate   [B]
                         SRO   Housing
INDEPENDENT   Hotel ●   DEPENDENT
(NON- INSTITUTIONALIZED)   ●   (INSTITUTIONALIZED)
[D]   ● Trailer   SRO   [C]
         Home   Hotel

       ● Communal
         Housing

            ●
         Low - Rent
         Senior Citizen
         Apartment

                                          Age–Segregated
                                          ● Congregate Housing

                           ● Retirement   Nursing
                             Hotel   Home
  ● Retirement   ●   ●
    Community   ● Home for the   Long-Term
                            Elderly   Care Hospital
                                                            & Psychiatric
            AGE–SEGREGATED   Hospital

groups are encouraged to interact. Similarly, a home for the aged might be situated adjacent to an orphanage so that 'foster grandparents' can interact with children. Neither of these two types of housing is widely available, and not many have been successful, perhaps because they require the continuing leadership of full-time personnel to encourage intergenerational social interaction.

Quadrants C and D represent housing that is totally age-segregated and that involves varying degrees of dependency. These settings, with the exception of SRO hotels, represent planned housing for the elderly in which direct attempts have been made in the structure and interior design to enhance person-environment compatibility. Many of these housing units provide facilities and programs that can satisfy the needs of the elderly who previously lived in integrated, independent settings such as a home, an apartment, or a trailer park. Planned housing of this nature expands the lifestyle opportunities for the elderly and generally has a positive influence on their well-being (Carp, 1978–79; Harel and Harel, 1978; Carp and Carp, 1980; Ehrlich et al., 1982). The options in quadrant C range from minimal services such as maid service and security in retirement hotels, to homes for the aged and congregate housing providing meals and other services, to nursing homes where all services are provided, to total dependency in long-term and psychiatric hospitals for geriatric patients. For those who are mentally and physically healthy, most of these environments generally foster high levels of social interaction and life satisfaction.

Quadrant D represents noninstitutionalized, segregated housing and independent lifestyles. These range from age-segregated affluent retirement communities, to communes where a group of elderly persons form a family (Streib and Streib, 1975), to trailer parks and subsidized senior-citizen housing, to SRO hotels that cater to elderly men and women. In short, there are a variety of forms of housing for the elderly, but not all forms are equally available or personally satisfying to all elderly people.

Age-segregated versus age-integrated housing. Because the elderly are a heterogeneous group with differences in past experiences and current needs, a range of viable options with respect to housing must be provided. However, research evidence suggests that the elderly generally prefer age-segregated housing. Even here, however, there is wide variation in the definition of age-segregated housing, which can range from inner-city, SRO hotels to affluent suburban or rural retirement communities in the sunbelt areas of the United States (such as Fun City in Arizona (Jacobs, 1974) or Leisure World in California[20]).

Gerontologists have long been interested in the advantages and disadvantages of segregated and integrated housing, in why a particular environment is preferred, and in how a specific environment is selected. The origin of the debate concerning segregated versus integrated housing can be traced indirectly to the proponents of disengagement theory, who argued that age segregation was the preferred mode of housing in the later years, and to the proponents of activity theory, who argued that an age-integrated environment was more conducive to adaptation. A direct stimulus to the debate was the classic study by Rosow (1967) of older apartment dwellers in Cleveland. He found that older people in age-segregated apartment buildings had more friends and engaged in greater interaction with neighbors. As a result, they were seen to have higher levels of satisfaction and well-being. Similar findings have been reported for different types of age-segregated housing environments, including trailer parks (Johnson, 1971), private or public housing complexes (Carp, 1966; Hochschild, 1973; Conner and Powers, 1975; Sherman, 1975; Ross, 1977; Teaff et al., 1978; Howell, 1980b), retirement communities (Jacobs, 1974), and SRO hotels (Erikson and Eckert, 1977; Lally et al., 1979).

Although a definitive explanation for the selection of, and satisfaction with, age-segregated housing environments has yet to be accepted, a number of alternative explanations have been proposed:

1. The environment is voluntarily selected by those who need a social support network of age-peers, especially those who lack or do not need family interaction and support; by those who seek a new ecological environment; and by those who prefer to remain close to public transportation (LaGory et al., 1980, 1981).

2. The environment is not voluntarily selected. Younger cohorts, including family members, have left the neighborhood. In this situation, the elderly may report satisfaction with this environment because they have no alternatives, or because they prefer that which is familiar and has a high degree of personal meaning. They are unable to move to a more suitable housing situation, or they refuse to move because of a nostalgic attachment to the family home (the aging-in-place phenomenon).

3. Age segregation is generally associated with greater social interaction with neighbors, greater mobility within the neighborhood, a greater sense of security or safety, a higher level of morale, greater satisfaction with the housing unit, greater mutual assistance among neighbors, fewer negative stereotypes about aging (at least to the 'insiders' or residents of these segregated environments), easier access to needed services or facilities (shopping, medical, and recreational services are often part of the planned development of an age-segregated environment), and quieter surroundings.

4. Satisfaction and well-being in an age-segregated environment result from a sense of identity or community created when interaction and interdependence among residents evolve, when emphasis is on personal relations and not on status, when leadership skills are available and utilized effectively, and when shared values, symbols, and norms take priority in the lifestyles of residents (Ross, 1977; Perkinson, 1980).

As Chevan (1982) recently noted, there are both micro and macro theories to explain age segregation. From the macro perspective, individuals respond to urban processes such as availability of housing at a specific stage in the life cycle. Thus, age segregation may occur because newly created neighborhoods attract people with similar characteristics, one of which may be age.

From the micro perspective, individual differences in decision making concerning the choice of neighborhood and type of housing can lead to age segregation (Pampel and Choldin, 1978). Age segregation is the end product of a process whereby families with similar location and housing preferences, who are often at the same stage in the life cycle and of the same economic and social background, move into the same neighborhood (Chevan, 1982). Except for later life decisions concerning age-segregated apartments or retirement communities, most housing decisions are not based on a conscious decision or a desire to live with or apart from a specific age group.

The following disadvantages of age-segregated housing have been noted:

1. It creates physical and social boundaries that foster and promote age grading and stereotyping in the larger community.

2. It implies discrimination, rejection, and abandonment of the elderly.

3. This environment may not foster social interaction unless the segregation is structured so that residents have a common racial, educational, and class background (Perkinson, 1980).

4. Interaction among neighbors may not be facilitated unless there is a common social or recreational center with programs that can foster interaction.[21]

5. There is little likelihood of new ideas or experiences from the community or society at large being diffused into and throughout the segregated housing environment; this inhibits cognitive stimulation and change.

6. Some retirement communities (such as Fun City) are isolated in that they lack public transportation and are far from medical, cultural, shopping, and entertainment centers.

In summary, age-segregated housing appears to be preferred by much of the elderly population. This applies to those who are affluent and wish a change in environment, as well as to those in the low-income category who have the opportunity to move into new housing that will improve their physical and psychological environment. Still, as noted earlier, most elderly people prefer to remain in their own homes as long as possible. For most, this involves living in an age-integrated neighborhood. Some elderly homeowners in the inner cores of large cities are restricted in their housing options for economic reasons, and may see their area become age-segregated because of the out-migration of younger residents. In short, the elderly, being a heterogeneous group, may encounter a variety of age-integrated environments. The type of housing in which one resides in the later years often depends on personal resources and previous life history.

Institutionalization as a Housing Alternative

The nature and quality of institutions.   Although less than 10 percent of the elderly population may be institutionalized at any one time, it has been estimated that anywhere from 25 to 75 percent are housed in an institutional setting for some part of their later years.[22] This probability increases beyond the mid-70s, and is higher for women because they live longer. Approximately 20 percent of all deaths occur in an institutionalized setting.

Those most likely to be voluntarily or involuntarily institutionalized are those who no longer have a sufficient degree of physical or mental competence to continue living independently in the community; those who are very old; those who have no families or whose families are unable or unwilling to care for them; those who live where community-based support services are unavailable or inaccessible; those who are financially or socially disadvantaged; and those who are white. Not surprisingly, people with good economic resources and a supportive family tend to enter institutions that provide a higher quality of health care and whose personnel demonstrate greater concern for the residents. At the other extreme of the social spectrum, elderly members of minority ethnic or racial groups may experience discrimination in gaining admission to an institution. Furthermore, once institutionalized, they may become isolated because of language and cultural barriers between themselves, the staff, and other residents. They may also receive less attention and care from staff (Carp, 1976). This suggests that racial and ethnic minorities may have to provide facilities to meet the special institutional needs of the elderly members of the group.

The number of institutionalized elderly may be increasing for a variety of reasons. First, it has become more culturally acceptable to have elderly parents admitted to an institution, rather than caring for them in the home. At the same time, the increasing size of the elderly population has led to an increase in the number and variety of institutions that are available. These are established with funds from either the private or public sector, and most receive government subsidies of some type. Few institutions for the elderly are still operated by religious or voluntary groups, largely because of increasing expenses.

Most facilities for the elderly are now operated as profit-oriented enterprises. As a result, the nature of the physical and psychological environments and the quality of care[23] can vary greatly from institution to institution. A major factor that determines the quality of care is accountability. If the resident or a relative is paying the total daily cost, and if the resident receives regular visits from nonresidents who can check on the quality of care, the resident has a degree of assurance that the care he or she receives will be of reasonably high quality. In contrast, where government subsidies are high, where few friends or relatives visit, and where government regulations with respect to standards and inspections are weak or absent, the environment and quality of care in the institution can be less than adequate. The status of the resident can also influence the quality of care. Generally, blacks, members of other minority groups, and the poor receive lower-quality care. Moreover, in communities with a shortage of institutionalized space, overcrowding often results. This further lowers the quality of care, and the number of viable housing alternatives decreases, except for the most financially and socially advantaged elderly who can pay for better care in private housing.

In order to provide housing, services, and treatment for those who are partially or totally unable to care for themselves, a variety of institutionalized settings have evolved. In many cases the type of institution that evolves is related to the availability of government funding and to the government regulations in a particular locale. There seem to be three general categories of institutionalized settings for the elderly (Tobin and Lieberman, 1976; Brody, 1977; Hendricks, 1980; Lawton, 1980a; Tobin, 1980). First, there is the personal care home, or home for the aged, which generally caters to those with some physical disability. Nursing or medical care may not be available on the site, and the institution may or may not offer social or recreational programs. The second type of institution is the nursing home, where on-site medical and nursing care is provided. Here, the residents are usually very old, and many are confined to bed. The third type is the psychiatric or geriatric hospital, for those who are unable to function in the community or in a personal care or nursing home. The supervision offered by these various institutions ranges from a minimal level in a personal care home to total supervision in a psychiatric hospital. The personal care and nursing homes are increasingly likely to be operated as proprietary or profit-making enterprises, while hospital settings are almost exclusively heavily subsidized or operated by government agencies.

Adjustment to institutionalized living.   Relocation from independent, private living to a form of institutionalization in the later years represents a complete change in lifestyle. While preparation for the first move to an institution can lessen the shock, most people have difficulty adjusting to the lack of privacy and personal space. This section summarizes some of the literature pertaining to the impact of relocation on the individual. Because many facilities are operated as private enterprises, owners frequently will not permit research personnel to study the residence or the residents. As a result, most studies in this area involve non-profit institutions, or, less frequently, those where the residents are affluent and pay high fees. Unfortunately, from a research perspective, these are often atypical institutions in that the environment and the quality of care are generally superior to that of ordinary profit-oriented institutions, which are oriented to the survival and growth of the institution. Institutions operated by voluntary organizations or religious groups tend to be more person-oriented and less bureaucratic.

When an individual is institutionalized, he or she may experience great stress, especially if the relocation is an involuntary move. The loss of one's home or apartment entails a loss of privacy and personal possessions, disrupts well-established lifestyles, and symbolizes rejection, deterioration, and the imminence of death. In fact, being institutionalized is often perceived as the penultimate stage in life. Unless the move is voluntary, or the individual is well prepared for the move, the social, emotional, and psychological needs of the individual are seldom satisfied in the bureaucratic, depersonalized environment. This is reflected in declining health and an increased chance of dying within a year, especially if the individual is subsequently relocated to an extended-care facility (Gutman and Herbert, 1976). At present, the literature is equivocal concerning the relationship between the onset of institutionalization and mortality. Those who die soon after being institutionalized appear to be those who have not been prepared for the move, who experience a significant loss of functional competence, who are passive and have lost a sense of awareness, or who have experienced a significant degree of environmental change (for example, in moving from their own homes to psychiatric hospitals).

In a limited longitudinal study of the effects of initial institutionalization on individual adjustment in a long-term care facility, Tobin and Lieberman (1976) studied eighty-five elderly people before admission, two months after admission, and one year after admission. At all three stages they measured physical health, cognitive functioning, affective responsiveness, emotional states, and self-perception. Prior to admission the respondents had a low level of personal adjustment that was attributed to a declining physical or mental state. This suggests that the factors leading to institutionalization may be as important in the process of adjustment as the onset of institutionalization itself. During the first months in the extended-care facility, residents exhibited signs of depression and anxiety and greater passivity than they had prior to admission. After two months their behavior patterns became more like their preadmission patterns. By the end of the first year, about 50 percent of those who were institutionalized had died. There was little statistical difference between the groups studied and the control group who remained in the community. In short, Tobin and Lieberman (1976:126) concluded that 'institutionalization is a consequence of adaptive problems as well as a cause of them.' Some individuals who experience physical or mental deterioration will be poorly adjusted whether they remain in the community or whether they are institutionalized.

In general, the stress of relocation to an institution can be reduced by preparation for the move, by moving to a similar or better environment, and by ensuring that contact is maintained as long as possible with the community and the family (George, 1980). On the individual level, there appears to be better adjustment by those who have physical and cognitive resources, particularly the traits of assertiveness and aggressiveness (Tobin, 1980); for those who have social support from friends and relatives; for those who move voluntarily; for those who have been social isolates in the community; and for those who are given some control over their daily lives within the institution. In fact, for some, depending on the institution, activity levels and life satisfaction increase following institutionalization — at least for residents in personal care homes (Myles, 1979).

Given that so many of the elderly are institutionalized, and that a large number do not satisfactorily adjust to this type of living environment, viable alternatives have been sought for assisting the elderly who become increasingly dependent on others (Brody, 1977; Chappell and Penning, 1979; Hendricks, 1980; Lawton, 1980a; Neysmith, 1980; Penning and Chappell, 1980; Schwenger and Gross, 1980). Researchers stress the need for alternative services and environments to reduce institutionalized care and to help the elderly maintain some degree of independence in the community. Some of the proposed alternatives include foster homes for elderly people without families; government assistance to encourage families to care for their elderly relatives at home; professional home-care visitations by social workers and medical personnel; vacation relief for children who regularly care for their elderly parents; providing treatment at day hospitals so that the elderly can return to their homes at night; and day-care centers for the elderly.

In short, there is a need for a more efficient and personalized health care delivery system, for increased social and recreational services in the community, and for more economical and psychologically satisfying housing alternatives. Even where the cost per day is no lower than that of traditional institutions, there still may be an improvement in the quality of life for the elderly person who can remain in the community with friends and relatives. However, with the onset of severe physical and mental impairment, a time may finally arrive when it is best for the individual and the family that extended-care institutionalization occur. Until this time arrives, however, premature institutionalization should be avoided if at all possible. For both humanitarian and economic reasons, institutionalization is a costly step that could be avoided or delayed in many situations if viable alternatives were available in the community.

In summary, a variety of options are necessary to retain and support the elderly in the community as long as possible. This community living permits a higher quality of life than that found within many nursing home or extended-care facilities. Persons living in institutions are often stigmatized because they are treated as invalids or as children by an impersonal, bureaucratic staff, because they have little or no control over their ritualized lives, and because they have little contact with those in the larger community. It is essential that a greater effort be directed 'to increasing the fit between the individual and the environment' (Marshall, 1980:246). This involves a two-way process wherein the individual must fit the environment, and the social and physical environments must be changed to meet the needs, capacities, and interests of the aging individual.

Mobility and Migration in the Later Years

Introduction

In the later years of life an individual has two general alternatives with respect to living arrangements: to age in place in the residence and the community that have provided shelter for most of the adult years, or to age in a new place, either in a new residence in the same neighborhood or community, or in an entirely new neighborhood, community, or geographical region. Except for institutionalization very late in life, aging in place was the more common pattern until the 1960s; today there is a greater likelihood that those over 60 years of age will either voluntarily or involuntarily change their place of residence. The change may involve local mobility within the community or region, or migration to a new geographical region. The increase in mobility and migration rates has resulted from such factors as:

1. Enforced moves because of urban renewal or gentrification.

2. Availability of a greater variety of specialized housing for the elderly.

3. Changing norms and values that allow children to place their aging parents in institutionalized settings.

4. A greater likelihood of children living at some distance from their parents, and dependent parents being institutionalized in their own community rather than moving into the children's home.

5. Increased longevity and affluence, which makes it possible for the retired, particularly couples, to make a seasonal or permanent migration to a warmer climate.

6. Deteriorating housing or increased crime in a neighborhood.

As a result of the increase in the rates of local mobility and regional migration, two areas of study have evolved on two different levels of analysis. At the micro level, social gerontologists and psychologists have been interested in the characteristics of those who move versus those who stay in place, and in the adjustment and satisfaction of those who relocate in the later years. This area of study has been characterized primarily by surveys or participant observations of elderly people after they have voluntarily or involuntarily changed their place of residence. Unfortunately, there have been few longitudinal studies wherein observations or interviews have been conducted at various times before and after a move.

The other major area of study is more recent and reflects the work of demographers or gerontologists interested in demography. Here, the focus has been on the macro-level patterns and effects of migration rates from one geographic region to another. These studies, which are primarily based on 1970 U.S. census data[24] (Rives, 1980), have examined the characteristics and motivations of migrants and the changing composition of the population in the communities or regions they leave and enter. The next two subsections will briefly review the literature on the patterns and outcomes of local (mobility) and distant (migration) moves by the elderly population, and the characteristics and motivations of those who move compared to those who stay in place.

Patterns of Local and Distant Moves by the Elderly

Most older people are satisfied with the residences that have been their homes for many years (Ferraro, 1981), and unless they are forced to move by declining personal competence or by a changing external environment, they have little desire to move. However, it has recently been noted that about one out of six people over 65 changed his or her place of residence at least once in the previous four years (United States Bureau of the Census, 1980). Recent studies of relocation patterns among the elderly in the United States[25] indicate that while most residential change occurs within or between metropolitan areas (Golant, 1979b; Wiseman, 1979; Longino, 1980; Stahura and Stahl, 1980), there is an increasing trend among young and old alike toward movement to nonmetropolitan areas (Heaton et al., 1980; Longino, 1980, 1982; Clifford et al., 1981–82; Aday and Miles, 1982). This trend may reflect a search for lower housing and subsistence costs, a safer environment, or lower-density housing conditions. Alternatively, the trend may be explained by a decline in intrastate migration by the elderly into metropolitan regions (Longino, 1982).

Most moves are within the same county; of those people who migrate outside their county, most settle in the sunbelt or coastal regions that have temperate climates and well-developed retirement communities (Chevan and Fischer, 1979; Flynn, 1979; Biggar, 1980; Bowles, 1980; Rives and Serow, 1981). In a sample of 14,197 people over 60, Biggar (1980) found that 10,650 had not changed their residences between 1965 and 1970. Of the 3,547 'movers,' 2,324 moved within the county and 1,223 moved to another county or state.

It has been argued that much of the interstate migration among the elderly reflects a return to the state of birth or childhood. However, only about 20 percent of all older migrants return to their state of birth (Serow, 1978). Furthermore, it is primarily the southern and coastal states that attract these return migrants (Longino, 1979a). That is, older adults are more likely to return to the state of birth if the state is attractive in itself to a large percentage of older migrants.

While most migration studies have described the absolute number of elderly people who move to a particular region, increasing attention is being directed to the size of the migration flow (or stream) between given areas, the distance between origin and destination, and the impact of net migration on the age composition of the state. Rives and Serow (1981) found that only about 2 percent of all migrant flows involve more than 5,000 persons, while almost 50 percent of the flows involve fewer than 100 people. The majority of the large flows are to Florida, Arizona, and California from the highly populated states in the Northeast.

Not surprisingly, the flow sizes decrease with age, since most long-distance moves tend to be made by people between 55 and 70 years of age. Similarly, the migration streams are dominated by female movers, and this pattern, as expected, increases with age (Clifford et al., 1981–82). Finally, Rives and Serow (1981) note that states that experience a large in-migration of older people have a younger population of elderly people, while those states that experience a large out-migration of older people are left with a considerably older population. This places excessive and sudden demands on the economic, social, and health services of the states where the very old remain (such as New York, Pennsylvania, and Ohio), and it delays or lessens the demand for these services to some extent in the states populated by a larger percentage of the healthier and younger members of the elderly cohort (such as Arizona, Arkansas, and Florida).

In summary, in recent years there has been considerable interest in studying the local mobility and migration patterns of the elderly. Research studies (Golant, 1980; Longino and Jackson, 1980) have examined the motivations, characteristics, and adjustment of elderly movers. A review of these findings appears in the following subsections.

Motivations, Characteristics, and Adjustment of Movers

Introduction.   Most studies of those who move involve cross-sectional rather than longitudinal designs, and basic information about the mover at specific points prior to and following the move is not usually available. It is difficult, therefore, to determine the impact of the move itself on the satisfaction and well-being of the respondent, and to determine whether the process of adjustment to the move varies according to the time elapsed since the move.

There do appear to be some general factors that can influence adaptation to a local or long-distance move. These include such things as the amount of personal control or involvement in the decision to move; the amount of anticipatory planning for the move; the amount of improvement or change in the environment as a result of the move (Schulz and Brenner, 1977); the degree of fit between the needs of the individual and how well the environment meets those needs; and the extent to which one's lifestyle is altered by the move. Regardless of the nature or distance of the move, a relocation in the later years is often precipitated by a transition point in the life cycle (such as an empty nest, retirement, widowhood, physical or mental disability, and decreasing independence), by a decrease in the safety and security of the housing or neighborhood environment, or by a change in the structure of the environment (such as urban renewal or gentrification). In this respect, a move, whether voluntary or involuntary, represents a way to adjust to or cope with a change in personal competence, needs, opportunity, or lifestyle.

Local movers. A number of elderly people may desire to change their local residence. However, few actually move as long as they have sufficient economic and physical resources to maintain their current shelter. As they grow older they may not have the social or economic resources necessary to make a move (Yee and Van Arsdol, 1977). Local moves are more likely to be involuntary and to represent a move to a setting that is less expensive or that provides more security or care. Three types of local moves represent decreasing independence and an increasing degree of environmental change: from a house to an apartment, from a home or an apartment to an institution, and from an institution to another institution (Schulz and Brenner, 1977). Those most likely to make a local move are those who are single, separated, widowed, or divorced; those who rent; those who have low incomes and little education; those who have a history of mobility; those who are black; those who are still employed; those who are in good health; and those who are becoming dependent on others because of declining physical or mental skills.

Conversely, those who remain in place ('stayers') are more likely to live with a spouse, to own their own home, to have strong emotional, ethnic, or racial ties to the neighborhood, and to be in poorer health but not yet dependent on others. For local moves (Wiseman, 1980), environmental characteristics may operate as push factors (declining safety and security, urban renewal, gentrification) or as pull factors (provision of economic or health assistance, higher-quality shelter).

The pattern and degree of adjustment to a local move depends primarily on whether the move is voluntary or involuntary (Beaver, 1979), and on the nature of the new housing environment. Among those who voluntarily move from a house to an apartment, to planned housing, or to a home for the aged, adjustment is made in a relatively short time. Carp (1966) found that residents of the planned housing environment of Victoria Plaza were higher in happiness, activity levels, number of friends, self-rated health, and optimism about the future than those who had not been admitted to the project. Similarly, among low-income elderly, Ferraro (1981) found that while most people are satisfied with their housing and do not wish to move, those who are experiencing environmental press or financial stress are most likely to desire and adapt well to a local move.

Despite the findings of these two studies, George (1980:107) notes that the available evidence concerning the impact of voluntary moves on adjustment is inconclusive. While some studies report an increase in health, life satisfaction, and morale, other studies report either no change or a decrease. In short, people react in different ways to a move, and what may be stressful for one individual may not be for another. George also concluded that those who adjust more satisfactorily to a move tend to have higher social, economic, and health status; to have a higher level of education; to have the ability to seek and create new relationships outside the family; and to perceive the change as an improvement over the previous housing environment.

In contrast, involuntary moves, especially to a less desirable physical environment or to an institution, can lead to maladjustment. An involuntary move can occur when individuals are evicted from their dwellings because of urban renewal projects, gentrification, an inability to continue payments, because of an unsafe physical structure, or because they are no longer able to care for themselves. In these situations, unless there is adequate preparation, relocation can be a traumatic and stressful event. Lawton (1980a:143) refers to this reaction as 'transplant shock' and, as he and others have noted, it may be related to higher mortality rates among those who are involuntarily moved to an institution or involuntarily moved from one institution to another.

Migrants.   Migration represents a change of residence across political boundaries (outside the county, state, or province). Whereas those in the labor force migrate to seek employment or an improvement in socioeconomic status, those over 65 are not likely to migrate in search of employment. Rather, migration tends to represent a voluntary move that may be made for one or more of the following reasons:

1. To improve person-environment congruence, especially in a sunbelt or rural area.

2. To seek a leisure lifestyle different from that adopted during the working years.

3. To reduce the cost of living.

4. To obtain subsidized housing, which is more available in metropolitan areas.

5. To move closer to relatives.

6. To move from a changing or deteriorating neighborhood.

7. To begin a new stage in life in order to facilitate the process of adjustment to retirement.

8. To move to an area that may assist the individual in adapting to, or coping with, a deteriorating health status (Patrick, 1980).

9. To return to the place of childhood residence (Longino, 1979a; Murphy, 1979; Wiseman and Roseman, 1979; Lee, 1980; Wiseman, 1980; Heaton et al., 1981).

Thus, while both push and pull factors stimulate migration in the later years (Lee, 1966), the pull factors tend to be more influential in the decision to migrate to seek an alternative or higher-quality lifestyle. Moreover, it appears that noneconomic factors are relevant in determining who migrates and to what regions (Heaton et al., 1980). Finally, as Marshall (1982) points out, there is a need for research concerning both the seasonal migratory worker and the political refugee. Political refugees often experience aging in a foreign land deprived of contact with their extended family, including their own aging parents. They also often lack the economic security to help them survive in the later years.

Although some individuals move during their final years in the labor force to the area where they wish to spend their retirement years, most migration by the elderly occurs within the first ten years of retirement. Contrary to the popular myth that many of the elderly migrate outside their state, only about 15 percent of all residential change by the elderly involves an interstate move (Longino, 1979b). For most elderly persons who migrate, the decision has been reached after visits to the area and after knowing people who have lived in the area (Longino, 1980). Those who migrate primarily for lifestyle reasons are more likely to have higher economic resources;[26] to be married; to have previously migrated during adulthood; to have a higher level of education; to be white; to be in the first few years of retirement; and to be in good health, especially since the distance of the migration is related to the state of health. Those seeking a leisure-oriented retirement tend to be highly independent individuals, especially with respect to their children.

By comparison, migrants who return to the region of their birthplace are closely linked emotionally and psychologically with their children; (Longino, 1979a) are less likely to be married and well-educated; have fewer economic resources; are more likely to be female and widowed; and are more likely to have lived in older, poorer-quality housing prior to migration. This pattern of return migration is becoming more common among older blacks, who return to the southern United States because race relations have changed for the better since their childhood (Longino, 1979a).

While some elderly people migrate to a new area or return to the region where they spent their childhood, most maintain a residence within the county where they resided during the preretirement years. For some, the decision to stay in place is based on the fact that they are trapped by a low economic or health status that discourages or prevents migration. For others, remaining in place may be the appropriate mechanism for maintaining a balance between environmental press and personal competence.

In an effort to summarize and conceptualize the migration process, Wiseman (1980) developed a conceptual model that includes four stages in the decision-making process. First, there are push and pull 'triggering mechanisms.' These include a personal crisis or transition point; environmental stress; environmental attractions; friends or kin already relocated in the region; or a desire for a change in lifestyle. Second, the decision to move is realistically assessed in light of such personal factors as health, community ties, economic resources, and former migration experiences, and in light of such environmental factors as the nature of the housing market and the cost of living in the receiving area. At the completion of this stage a decision to migrate or not to migrate is made. A large number of potential migrants become involuntary stayers at this stage because they realize that they lack the personal resources or experience to engage in migratory behavior, either permanently or seasonally. For those who decide to move, the third step is to determine whether the move will be permanent or seasonal. Finally, the destination must be selected on the basis of previous experience, knowledge of alternative locations, preference for climate and entertainment opportunities, location of friends or kin, and inducements from local government or private sector entrepreneurs (such as facilities and services provided to senior citizens by towns and cities, or as part of the residence contract in retirement communities). Having selected a community, the retiree must then select the neighborhood, type of dwelling, and living arrangements that will be equal to or better than the present housing situation. Wiseman's model seeks to explain the process whereby individuals become either migrants or voluntary or involuntary stayers during the early retirement years. It focuses on the interaction between motivations to migrate, personal resources, perception of environmental stress in the present location, and perception of and experience with environmental opportunities in the proposed destination.

In summary, those who are married, in good health, and with sufficient economic resources are those who are most likely to migrate to a new region following retirement. In general, however, the migration rates for the elderly are lower than for all other age groups. For those who do migrate, a major motivation is the desire to reside in a region that provides a temperate year-round climate and age-appropriate recreational programs and facilities (Wiseman, 1980; Heaton et al., 1981). For others, migration occurs because they seek support from kin, or they wish to return to the area where they were born. In contrast, those who engage in short-distance local moves are more likely to be seeking improved or more appropriate (in cost or size) housing.

Summary and Conclusions

This chapter has focused on the interaction between the physical environment and the aging process. The first section introduced theories and models that seek to explain the influence of the physical environment on aging individuals, as well as a number of objective and subjective indicators of environmental impact on the elderly. The second section involved an analysis of the suprapersonal or macroenvironment, including the spatial distribution and characteristics of older people in rural, urban, age-integrated, or age-segregated neighborhoods; the availability of and need for private and public transportation; the incidence of crime by and against the elderly; and the extent and consequences of fear of victimization.

In the third section, the reader was introduced to the impact of the quality, type, size, location, and design of the dwelling unit on the lifestyle and life satisfaction of the aging individual. It was noted that the type of housing in the later years varies along two intersecting dimensions: independent to dependent, and age-integrated to age-segregated. A number of advantages and disadvantages of each type of housing were set out. This section also considered institutionalization as a housing alternative in the later years by examining the type and quality of institutions, the process of adjustment to institutionalization, and some alternatives to early and complete institutionalization of the elderly. The final section considered patterns of local mobility and distant migration in the postretirement years. In addition, the characteristics and motivations of those who move, compared to those who age in place, were reviewed.

Based on current research evidence concerning the physical environment and aging, it can be concluded that:

1. While a number of models or theories have been developed to explain the relationship between factors in the physical environment and the aging process, a comprehensive and definitive theory is not yet available.

2. About 75 percent of the elderly in North America live in an urban environment.

3. A high proportion of the residents of small towns are elderly because they age in place, and because younger cohorts migrate to larger urban centers.

4. At present, of the elderly who live in large cities in the United States, over 60 percent live in the central core. This proportion decreases when they are forced out by urban renewal and gentrification.

5. In the future, the elderly will be increasingly located in the 'graying' suburbs where they settled in the 1950s and 1960s.

6. Within most stable neighborhoods, there is a high degree of homogeneity with respect to the age, class, racial, or ethnic composition of the residents.

7. The environment of the rural elderly has seldom been studied. Where it has been studied, there appears to be an often-reported discrepancy between the quality of life as measured by objective and subjective criteria. That is, whereas objective indicators indicate a generally lower quality of life in rural areas, subjective indicators suggest a higher perceived quality of life.

8. Availability of private or public transportation is essential in maintaining independence and a higher quality of life and life satisfaction in the later years.

9. For public transportation to be effective in meeting the needs of the elderly, a number of physical, structural, psychological, and economic barriers must be reduced or eliminated before the elderly will use the system.

10. Although the rate of crime committed by the elderly is significantly less than for younger age groups, the incidence is increasing. While some of this criminal activity involves theft to meet personal wants or needs, it may also be motivated by boredom or by rebellion against the private or public sectors.

11. The elderly are victimized less than other age groups, except for larceny-with-contact crimes (such as purse snatching) and crimes against the place of residence (burglary).

12. The elderly are victimized less than younger people because they are less mobile and because they avoid high-crime environments. They may also appear to be victimized less because they are less likely to report a crime.

13. The elderly who are most likely to be victimized are those who are economically and socially disadvantaged (women, the poor, blacks, and inner-city residents).

14. Although they are actually victimized less than other age groups, the elderly frequently say that fear of crime is one of their most serious personal problems. This fear tends to be greater among those who are most economically and socially disadvantaged.

15. Fear of crime often leads to self-imposed restrictions on travel and social participation within the neighborhood and community. In fact, the elderly individual may become housebound rather than walk in the streets.

16. Most older people prefer to live in an independent dwelling.

17. Approximately 70 percent of the elderly people own their own homes.

18. The quality, type, size, location, and design of the dwelling unit interacts with health and economic status to influence lifestyle, life satisfaction, and the quality of life in the later years.

19. As measured by objective indicators, the quality of housing is generally lower for the elderly who are black, who are single, who rent, and who live in rural areas.

20. Because the elderly are a heterogeneous group, a variety of housing alternatives should be provided in every community (independent to dependent, age-integrated to age-segregated, single-family dwelling to high-rise).

21. The elderly seem to prefer to reside in age-segregated housing units and neighborhoods.

22. Three general categories of institutionalized housing for the elderly include the personal care home or home for the aged; the nursing home; and the psychiatric or geriatric hospital.

23. The stress associated with institutionalization is high, but can be reduced by preparation for the move, by moving to a similar or higher-quality environment, and by ensuring that contact is maintained with the family and community.

24. While most residential change in the postretirement years occurs within and between urban metropolitan regions, there is an increasing trend toward longer moves and toward migration to nonmetropolitan areas.

25. In the United States, about 75 percent of all residential change by the elderly involves an interstate move.

26. In the United States, about 20 percent of older migrants to another state are those who return to their state of birth, although this primarily applies to those who were born in the warmer southern or coastal states.

27. Migration streams in the later years are dominated by widows, by married couples, by those in good health, and by those with higher economic resources.

28. Local moves are more likely to be involuntary (for example, because of forced institutionalization or urban renewal projects), whereas distant moves to another county or state are more likely to be voluntary, for the purpose of establishing an alternative or higher-quality lifestyle.

29. It is essential to match the aging individual with a compatible environment in order to enhance life satisfaction and the quality of life.

Notes

1. This point is raised by Marshall and Tindale (1978–79) in their plea for a radical gerontology. They argue that more research needs to be conducted from the perspective of the elderly themselves. If this is so, there should be a greater attempt to adjust society to the aging individual, rather than requiring individuals to adjust to the ongoing social order.

2. In this section, the term 'community' refers to a geographical unit such as a town, city, or metropolitan area situated on a rural-urban continuum of size and lifestyle. In the third section of this chapter, 'community' will be used as a sociological concept that refers to a group of individuals who share a similar territory and thereby interact with some degree of interdependence (an apartment complex, a retirement community, a home for the aged).

3. Seasonal migrations from north to south in the winter and from south to north in the summer are considered temporary moves and are not normally included in migration statistics.

4. Yet, surprisingly, they were not physically or cognitively isolated from the larger world since they watched television regularly and frequently travelled great distances from the community to visit relatives.

5. Relatively few elderly persons engage in criminal behavior. Among those most likely to engage in criminal behavior are those older males who have lived or are living on the streets. Among members of this subculture, the use of alcohol and drugs may precipitate criminal behavior (Pottieger and Inciardi, 1981).

6. These crimes are especially frequent at the end of the month when pension and social security checks are cashed, and are often classified as 'predatory' crimes wherein the elderly are randomly attacked by unarmed young black males (Antunes et al., 1977).

7. Some of these schemes include the purchase of products to retard the biological process of aging, or the appearance of aging; the purchase of land or a home as a retirement investment without visiting the site; or the withdrawal of savings from a bank under some pretext.

8. This is most likely to occur in low-rental public housing units where there is an age and race mix of black youth and elderly white people (Lawton and Yaffe, 1980).

9. Cohen (1981) suggests that given the relatively brief time the elderly are exposed to risk each day, their victimization rate is actually quite high. That is, although the elderly expose themselves or their property less often to risk of victimization, their relative rates are considerably higher than other age groups who are exposed much more frequently each day.

10. This statistic may partially reflect the tendency for men to be less willing to admit fear because of social norms that equate bravery with masculinity. Also, with advancing age there is a higher ratio of women to men.

11. Like rates of victimization, fear of crime is directly related to type of environment. The greatest fear is expressed by those who live in the center core of large cities. Fear decreases concentrically from this core as one moves to the suburbs of large cities, to smaller cities, towns and farms, and to segregated retirement communities with elaborate security systems (Sundeen and Mathieu, 1976). For example, the Leisure World retirement community in Laguna Hills, California, is surrounded by six-foot walls and sentry posts.

12. Dowd et al. (1981) recently reported that elderly people who have been victimized are more likely to approve of police violence against the criminal than are younger people. They disapprove of citizen violence against the criminal, whereas younger people approve of it.

13. For example, Godbey et al. (1980) found that senior citizens in large cities express almost as much fear for the hours when school is dismissed as they do after darkness sets in. That is, they fear the predatory crimes and verbal abuse of teenagers, and they avoid walking in the streets and shopping plazas during noon hour and after school.

14. Although there appears to be a relationship between fear, decreased mobility, and less victimization, it is not at all clear that lower rates of victimization will reduce the incidence or frequency of fear among the elderly (Yin, 1980). Even the reporting by the media, or by neighbors, of a single violent or nonviolent crime against an elderly person may be sufficient to arouse or heighten the level of fear among the elderly population, not only in the neighborhood where the event took place, but also across community, regional, and national boundaries.

15. While only between 5 and 10 percent of the elderly reside in institutionalized settings at any one time (Lesnoff-Caravaglia, 1978–79; Schwenger and Gross, 1980), Kastenbaum and Candy (1973) suggest that this statistic promotes a fallacy that the rest of the population is noninstitutionalized throughout the later years. As they note, perhaps as many as 25 percent of the elderly spend at least some part of their later years in an institutionalized setting. Therefore, as age increases and health declines, the chance of being institutionalized increases.

16. However, the increasing number of divorced and never-married individuals may increase the demand for rental housing for single elderly persons in the future. This housing will be required prior to age 65, not only in the 70s or 80s when declining health and widowhood require a relocation to an apartment (Miron, 1981).

17. Many older homes are located in the central and older residential areas of towns and cities. However, by the end of the century this problem of maintaining older residences will more frequently be found among suburban residents who reside in homes built after 1950.

18. Congregate housing provides a semi-independent living arrangement wherein each individual or couple has an independent living unit (an apartment or room) with bathroom facilities, and which may or may not have cooking or laundry facilities. Thus, in addition to shelter, the unit provides services that may include one to three meals per day, laundry and maid service, private transportation, security service, minor health care, and recreational programs. The congregate concept usually means that the residents eat at the same time in a common dining area (Lawton, 1980a:81).

19. For example, needs change if children leave the home, if income and social interaction decrease, if health declines and the individual has less mobility, if daily and annual maintenance requirements grow burdensome, if the dwelling is vacant for part of the year while time is spent in a second residence, or if a spouse is institutionalized or dies.

20. It has recently been reported that retirement homes in Leisure World are being sold for more than $350,000.

21. For example, Merrill Court (Hochschild, 1973) had a common meeting place, whereas Fun City (Jacobs, 1974) did not have this structural stimulus to facilitate social interaction. As a result, a sense of 'community' evolved in Merrill Court, while Fun City was characterized by empty streets and very little community or neighborly interaction. In fact, only about five hundred of the 6,000 residents participated in planned activities. That is, although there were enough residents to enable programs to be successful, there was no focal point to facilitate the delivery of the programs or to foster social interaction.

22. The percentage of the elderly population that is institutionalized varies by country, and is largely determined by the degree of government subsidization for the care of the elderly. The percentage of those over 65 years of age who are institutionalized in England, the United States, and Canada varies from 5.1 percent to 6.3 percent to 8.4 percent respectively (Schwenger and Gross, 1980:251).

23. It must be recognized that the evaluation of quality in an institution can result in varying assessments, depending on whether the evaluation is made by the resident, a relative, the staff, or a government inspector. Included in these evaluations are such concerns as amount of personal space and degree of privacy; safety of the physical structure; type, availability, and quality of health and medical care; degree of emotional interest in and concern for the residents on the part of staff; the availability and variety of social, recreational, and therapeutic programs; the variety and nutritional quality of the food; and the willingness of the institution to meet the needs and interests of residents with respect to sex, alcohol, and tobacco.

24. Exceptions are the study by Cribier (1980), which includes an extensive bibliography on migration patterns in France and Great Britain, and the article by Murphy (1979), which includes information about Europe and Australia.

25. Among Canadians, a few migrate to British Columbia because of the more temperate coastal climate, although only those who are most affluent have the economic resources to make such a move. Older migrants in Canada tend to make a seasonal move to the southern United States, or, if they have been previously employed in a large metropolitan area, a permanent move to a smaller, rural community.

26. It is generally the wealthy who initiate migration trends. These people are motivated by a search for an alternative or higher-quality lifestyle. Clearly, the search for a higher quality of life is a factor in relocation to a rural or sunbelt environment.

References

Aday, R. and L. Miles. 'Long-Term Impacts of Rural Migration of the Elderly: Implications for Research,' *The Gerontologist*, 22(3/1982), 331–36.

Ansello, E. 'Special Considerations in Rural Aging,' *Educational Gerontology*, 5(4/1980), 343–54.

Ansello, E. and C. Cipolla (eds.). 'Rural Aging and Education: Issues, Methods and Models,' *Educational Gerontology*, 5(4/1980), 343–47.

Antunes, G. et al. 'Patterns of Personal Crime Against the Elderly: Findings from a National Survey,' *The Gerontologist*, 17(4/1977), 321–27.

Balkin, S. 'Victimization Rates, Safety and Fear of Crime,' *Social Problems*, 26(3/1979), 343–58.

Beaver, M. 'The Decision-Making Process and Its Relationship to Relocation Adjustment in Old People,' *The Gerontologist*, 19(6/1979), 567–74.

Biggar, J. 'Who Moved Among the Elderly, 1965 to 1970: A Comparison of Types of Older Movers,' *Research on Aging*, 2(1/1980), 73–91.

Bowles, G. 'Age Migration in the United States,' *Research on Aging*, 2(2/1980), 137–40.

Braungart, M. et al. 'Age, Sex and Social Factors in Fear of Crime,' *Sociological Forces*, 13(1/1980), 55–66.

Brody, E. *Long-Term Care of Older People*. New York: Human Sciences Press, 1977.

Burley, D. 'Occupation as a Motivating Factor in Retirement Migration: An Extreme Case Study,' *The Gerontologist*, 22(4/1982), 435–37.

Carp, F. *A Future for the Aged: The Residents of Victoria Plaza*. Austin: University of Texas Press, 1966.

Carp, F. 'Housing and Living Environments of Older People,' pp. 244–71 in R. Binstock and E. Shanas (ed.). *Handbook of Aging and the Social Sciences*. New York: Van Nostrand Reinhold, 1976.

Carp, F. 'Effects of the Living Environments on Activity and Use of Time,' *International Journal of Aging and Human Development*, 9(1/1978–79), 75–91.

Carp, F. 'Environmental Effects upon the Mobility of Older People,' *Environment and Behavior*, 12(2/1980), 139–56.

Carp, F. and A. Carp. 'Person-Environment Congruence and Sociability,' *Research on Aging*, 2(4/1980), 395–415.

Chappell, N. and M. Penning. 'The Trend Away from Institutionalization: Humanism or Economic Efficiency?' *Research on Aging*, 1(3/1979), 361–87.

Chevan, A. 'Age, Housing Choice, and Neighborhood Age Structure,' *American Journal of Sociology*, 87(5/1982), 1133–49.

Chevan, A. and L. Fischer. 'Retirement and Interstate Migration,' *Social Forces*, 57(4/1979), 1365–80.

Clemente, F. and M. Kleiman. 'Fear of Crime Among the Aged,' *The Gerontologist*, 16(3/1976), 207–10.

Clifford, W. et al. 'Residential Mobility and Living Arrangements Among the Elderly: Changing Patterns in Metropolitan and Nonmetropolitan Areas,' *International Journal of Aging and Human Development*, 14 (2/1981–82), 139–56.

Cohen, L. et al. 'Social Inequality and Predatory Criminal Victimization: An Exposition and Test of a Formal Theory,' *American Sociological Review*, 46(5/1981), 505–24.

Cohn, J. 'Alternatives in Housing for Older Parents,' pp. 221–36 in P. Ragan (ed.). *Aging Parents*. Los Angeles: University of Southern California Press, 1979.

Conner, K. and E. Powers. 'Structural Effects and Life Satisfaction Among The Aged,' *International Journal of Aging and Human Development*, 6(4/1975), 321–27.

Cook, F. et al. 'Criminal Victimization of the Elderly: the Physical and Economic Consequences,' *The Gerontologist*, 18(4/1978), 338–49.

Cowgill, D. 'Residential Segregation by Age in American Metropolitan Areas,' *Journal of Gerontology*, 33(3/1978), 446–53.

Cribier, F. 'A European Assessment of Aged Migration,' *Research on Aging*, 2(2/1980), 255–70.

Cutler, S. 'The Availability of Personal Transportation, Residential Location and Life Satisfaction Among the Aged,' *Journal of Gerontology*, 27(3/1972), 383–89.

Cutler, S. 'Transportation and Changes in Life Satisfaction,' *The Gerontologist*, 15(2/1975), 155–59.

Cutler, S. 'Safety on the Streets: Cohort Changes in Fear,' *International Journal of Aging and Human Development*, 10(4/1979–80), 373–84.

Devlin, A. 'Housing for the Elderly: Cognitive Considerations,' *Environment and Behavior*, 12(4/1980), 451–66.

Dillman, D. and K. Tremblay. 'The Quality of Life in Rural America,' *The Annals of the American Academy of Political and Social Science*, 429(January, 1977), 115–29.

Dowd, J. et al. 'Socialization to Violence Among the Aged,' *Journal of Gerontology*, 36(3/1981), 350–61.

Ehrlich, P. et al. 'Congregate Housing for the Elderly: Thirteen Years Later,' *The Gerontologist*, 22(4/1982), 399–403.

Erikson, R. and K. Eckert. 'The Elderly Poor in Downtown San Diego Hotels,' *The Gerontologist*, 17(5/1977), 440–46.

Fengler, A. and L. Jensen. 'Perceived and Objective Conditions as Predictors of the Life Satisfaction of Urban and Non-urban Elderly,' *Journal of Gerontology*, 36(6/1981), 750–52.

Ferraro, K. 'Relocation Desires and Outcomes Among the Elderly: A Longitudinal Analysis,' *Research on Aging*, 3(2/1981), 166–81.

Flynn, C. et al. *Aged Migration in the United States, 1965–70: Final Report*. Washington, D.C.: National Institute on Aging, 1979.

Fozard, J. 'Person-Environment Relationships in Adulthood: Implications for Human Factors Engineering,' *Human Factors*, 23(1/1981), 7–27.

Gardner, M. 'Caring and Sharing,' *Perspective on Aging*, X(January/February, 1981), 4–7.

George, L. *Role Transitions in Later Life*. Monterey: Brooks/Cole Publishing Co., 1980.

Godbey, G. et al. *The Relationship of Crime and Fear of Crime Among the Aged to Leisure Behavior and Use of Public Leisure Services*. Washington, D.C.: NRTA-AARP, Andrus Foundation, 1980.

Golant, S. (ed.). *Location and Environment of the Elderly Population*. Washington, D.C.: V.H. Winston and Sons, 1979a.

Golant, S. 'Central City, Suburban and Nonmetropolitan Migration Patterns of the Elderly,' pp. 37–54 in S. Golant (ed.). *Location and Environment of the Elderly Population*. New York: John Wiley and Sons, 1979b.

Golant, S. 'Future Directions for Elderly Migration Research,' *Research on Aging*, 2(2/1980), 271–80.

Goldsmith, J. and S. Goldsmith (eds.). *Crime and the Elderly*. Lexington, Ky.: D.C. Heath Inc., 1976.

Goode, C. et al. *Elderly Hotel and Rooming-House Dwellers*. Philadelphia: Philadelphia Geriatric Center, 1979.

Green, B. et al. (eds.). 'Old Age: Environmental Complexity and Policy Interventions,' *The Journal of Social Issues*, 36(2/1980), 1–192.

Gubrium, J. 'Toward a Socio-Environmental Theory of Aging,' *The Gerontologist*, 12(3/1972), 281–84.

Gubrium, J. *The Myth of the Golden Years: A Socio-Environmental Theory of Aging*. Springfield, Ill.: Charles C. Thomas, 1973.

Gubrium, J. *Living and Dying At Murray Manor.* New York: St. Martin's Press, 1975.

Gutman, G. and C. Herbert. 'Mortality Rates Among Relocated Extended-Care Patients,' *Journal of Gerontology*, 31(3/1976), 352–57.

Harel, Z. and B. Harel. 'On-Site Coordinated Services in Age-Segregated and Age-Integrated Public Housing,' *The Gerontologist*, 18(2/1978), 153–57.

Harris, C. (ed.). *Fact Book on Aging: A Profile of America's Older Population.* Washington, D.C.: National Council on the Aging, 1978.

Harris, L. et al. *Aging in the Eighties: America in Transition.* Washington, D.C.: National Council on the Aging, 1981.

Heaton, T. et al. 'Changing Patterns of Retirement Migration: Movement Between Metropolitan and Nonmetropolitan Areas,' *Research on Aging*, 2(1/1980), 93–104.

Heaton, T. et al. 'Temporal Shifts in the Determinants of Young and Elderly Migration in Nonmetropolitan Areas,' *Social Forces*, 60(1/1981), 41–60.

Hendricks, J. (ed.). *Institutionalization and Alternative Futures.* Farmingdale, N.Y.: Baywood Publishing Co., 1980.

Henig, J. 'Gentrification and Displacement of the Elderly: An Empirical Analysis,' *The Gerontologist*, 21(1/1981), 67–75.

Hindelang, M. et al. *Victims of Personal Crime: An Empirical Foundation for a Theory of Personal Victimization.* Cambridge, Mass.: Ballinger Press, 1978.

Hochschild, A. *The Unexpected Community.* Englewood Cliffs, N.J.: Prentice-Hall, 1973.

Hoover, S. 'Black and Spanish Elderly: Their Housing Characteristics and Housing Quality,' in M.P. Lawton and S. Hoover (eds.). *Community Housing Choices for Older Americans.* New York: Springer Publishing Co., 1981.

Howell, S. 'Environments and Aging,' pp. 237–60 in C. Eisdorfer (ed.). *Annual Review of Gerontology and Geriatrics. Volume 1.* New York: Springer Publishing Co., 1980a.

Howell, S. 'Environments as Hypotheses in Human Aging Research,' pp. 424–32 in L. Poon (ed.). *Aging in the 1980s.* Washington, D.C.: American Psychological Association, 1980b.

Jacobs, J. *Fun City: An Ethnographic Study of a Retirement Community.* New York: Holt, Rinehart and Winston 1974.

Johnson, S. *Idle Haven.* Berkeley: University of California Press, 1971.

Kahana, E. 'A Congruence Model of Person-Environment Interaction,' in P. Windley and G. Ernst (eds.). *Theory Development in Environment and Aging.* Washington, D.C.: Gerontological Society, 1975.

Kahana, E. et al. 'Alternative Models of Person-Environment Fit: Prediction of Morale in Three Homes for the Aged,' *Journal of Gerontology*, 35(4/1980), 584–95.

Karafin, S. et al. 'Minority Elderly Transportation Research: the State of the Literature,' paper presented at the National Conference on Transportation for the Elderly and Handicapped, Sarasota, October 1981.

Kastenbaum, R. and S. Candy. 'The Four Percent Fallacy: A Methodological and Empirical Critique of Extended Care Facility Population Statistics,' *International Journal of Aging and Human Development*, 4(1/1973), 15–21.

Keating, N. and J. Marshall. 'The Process of Retirement: the Rural Self-Employed,' *The Gerontologist*, 20(4/1980), 437–43.

Keith, J. (ed.). 'The Ethnography of Old Age,' *Anthropological Quarterly*, 52(1/1979), 1–69.

Kennedy, J. and G. DeJong. 'Aged in Cities: Residential Segregation in 10 USA Central Cities,' *Journal of Gerontology*, 32(1/1977), 97–102.

Kim, P. and C. Wilson. *Toward Mental Health of the Rural Elderly.* Lanham, Md.: University Press of America, 1981.

LaGory, M. et al. 'Explanations of the Age Segregation Process in American Cities,' *Urban Affairs Quarterly*, 16(1/1980), 59–80.

LaGory, M. et al. 'Patterns of Age Segregation,' *Sociological Focus*, 14(1/1981), 1–13.

Lally, M. et al. 'Older Women in Single Room Occupant (SRO) Hotels: A Seattle Profile,' *The Gerontologist*, 19(1/1979), 67–73.

Lawton, M.P. 'The Impact of the Environment on Aging and Behavior,' pp. 276–301 in J. Birren and K.W. Schaie (eds.). *Handbook of the Psychology of Aging.* New York: Van Nostrand Reinhold, 1977.

Lawton, M.P. *Environment and Aging.* Monterey: Brooks/Cole Publishing Co., 1980a.

Lawton, M.P. 'Environmental Change: the Older Person As Initiator and Responder,' pp. 171–93 in N. Datan and N. Lohmann (eds.). *Transitions of Aging.* New York: Academic Press, 1980b.

Lawton, M.P. 'Housing the Elderly: Residential Quality and Residential Satisfaction,' *Research on Aging*, 2(3/1980c), 309–28.

Lawton, M.P. and S. Hoover (eds.). *Community Housing Choices for Older Americans.* New York: Springer Publishing Co., 1981.

Lawton, M.P. and L. Nahemow. 'Ecology and the Aging Process,' pp. 619–74 in C. Eisdorfer and M.P. Lawton (eds.). *The Psychology of Adult Development and Aging.* Washington, D.C.: American Psychological Association, 1973.

Lawton, M.P. and L. Nahemow. 'Social Science Methods for Evaluating Housing Quality for Older People,' *Journal of Architectural Research*, 7(1/1979), 5–11.

Lawton, M.P. and S. Yaffe. *Victimization of the Elderly and Fear of Crime.* Philadelphia: Philadelphia Geriatric Center, 1979.

Lawton, M.P. and S. Yaffe. 'Victimization and Fear of Crime in Elderly Public Housing Tenants,' *Journal of Gerontology*, 35(5/1980), 768–79.

Lawton, M.P. et al. (eds.). *Aging and the Environment.* New York: Springer Publishing Co., 1982.

Lee, E. 'A Theory of Migration,' *Demography*, 3(1/1966), 47–57.

Lee, E. 'Migration of the Aged,' *Research on Aging*, 2(2/1980), 131–36.

Lee, G. 'Residential Location and Fear of Crime Among the Elderly,' *Rural Sociology*, 47(4/1982), 655–79.

Lee, G. and M. Lassey. 'Rural-Urban Differences Among the Elderly: Economic, Social and Subjective Factors,' *Journal of Social Issues*, 36(2/1980), 62–74.

Lesnoff-Caravaglia, C. 'The Five Percent Fallacy,' *International Journal of Aging and Human Development*, 9(2/1978–79), 187–92.

Lester, D. (ed.). *The Elderly Victim of Crime.* Springfield, Ill.: Charles C. Thomas, 1981.

Liang, J. and M. Sengstock. 'The Risk of Personal Victimization Among the Aged,' *Journal of Gerontology*, 36(4/1981), 463–71.

Lichter, D. et al. 'Components of Change in the Residential Concentration of the Elderly Population: 1950–1975,' *Journal of Gerontology*, 36(4/1981), 480–89.

Longino, C. 'Going Home: Aged Return Migration in the United States, 1965–1970,' *Journal of Gerontology*, 34(5/1979a), 736–45.

Longino, C. 'Intrastate Migration of the Elderly,' in C. Flynn et al. (eds.). *Aged Migration in the United States: Final Report.* Washington, D.C.: National Institute on Aging, 1979b.

Longino, C. 'Residential Relocation of Older People: Metropolitan and Nonmetropolitan,' *Research on Aging*, 2(2/1980), 205–16.

Longino, C. 'Changing Aged Nonmetropolitan Migration Patterns, 1955 to 1960 and 1965 to 1970,' *Journal of Gerontology*, 37(2/1982), 228–34.

Longino, C. and D. Jackson (eds.). 'Migration and the Aged,' *Research on Aging*, 2(2/1980), 131–280.

Lozier, J. and R. Althouse. 'The Rural Old: Retirement to the Porch in Rural Appalachia,' *International Journal of Aging and Human Development*, 6(1/1975), 7–15.

Malinchak, A. *Crime and Gerontology.* Englewood Cliffs, N.J.: Prentice-Hall Inc., 1980.

Marshall, V. (ed.). *Aging in Canada: Social Perspectives.* Don Mills: Fitzhenry and Whiteside, 1980.

Marshall, V. and J. Tindale. 'Notes for a Radical Gerontology,' *International Journal of Aging and Human Development*, 9(2/1978–79), 163–75.

Miron, J. 'Household Formation Among the Elderly,' pp. 23–30 in B. Wigdor and L. Ford (eds.). *Housing for an Aging Population: Alternatives.* Toronto: University of Toronto Press, 1981.

Montgomery, J. et al. 'The Housing Environment of the Rural Elderly,' *The Gerontologist*, 20(4/1980), 444–51.

Morello, F. *Juvenile Crimes Against the Elderly.* Springfield, Illinois: Charles C. Thomas, 1982.

Murphy, P. 'Migration of the Elderly: A Review,' *Town Planning Review*, 50(2/1979), 195–200.

Myles, J. 'Institutionalization and Disengagement Among the Elderly,' *Canadian Review of Sociology and Anthropology*, 16(2/1979), 171–82.

Neysmith, S. 'Marginality and Morale,' pp. 281–85 in V. Marshall (ed.). *Aging in Canada: Social Perspectives.* Don Mills: Fitzhenry and Whiteside, 1980.

Norton, L. and M. Courlander. 'Fear of Crime Among the Elderly: The Role of Crime Prevention Programs,' *The Gerontologist*, 22(4/1982), 388–93.

O'Bryant, S. 'The Value of Home to Older Persons and Its Relationship To Housing Satisfaction,' paper presented at the annual meeting of the Gerontological Society of America, Toronto, November 1981.

Ollenburger, J. 'Criminal Victimization and Fear of Crime,' *Research on Aging*, 3(1/1981), 101–18.

Pampel, F. and H. Choldin. 'Urban Location and Segregation of the Aged: A Block Level Analysis,' *Social Forces*, 56(4/1978), 1121–39.

Parr, J. 'The Interaction of Persons and Living Environments,' pp. 393–406 in L. Poon (ed.). *Aging in the 1980s.* Washington, D.C.: American Psychological Association, 1980.

Patrick, C. 'Health and Migration of the Elderly,' *Research on Aging*, 2(2/1980), 233–41.

Penning, M. and N. Chappell. 'A Reformulation of Basic Assumptions About Institutions for the Elderly,' pp. 269–80 in V. Marshall (ed.). *Aging in Canada: Social Perspectives.* Don Mills: Fitzhenry and Whiteside, 1980.

Perkinson, M. 'Alternate Roles for the Elderly: An Example from a Midwestern Retirement Community,' *Human Organization*, 39(3/1980), 219–26.

Pollack, L. and A. Patterson. 'Territoriality and Fear of Crime in Elderly and Non-Elderly Home-Owners,' *The Journal of Social Psychology*, 111(1980), 119–29.

Pottieger, A. and J. Inciardi. 'Aging on the Street: Drug Use and Crime Among Older Men,' *Journal of Psychoactive Drugs*, 13(2/1981), 199–209.

Rapoport, A. 'An Approach to the Construction of Man-Environment Theory,' pp. 124–35 in W. Preiser (ed.). *Environmental Design Research*. Volume 2. Stroudsburg, Pa.: Dowden, Hutchinson and Ross, 1973.

Raschko, B. *Housing Interiors for the Disabled and Elderly*. New York: Van Nostrand Reinhold, 1982.

Rives, N. 'Researching the Migration of the Elderly: Sources of Statistical Information,' *Research on Aging*, 2(2/1980), 155–63.

Rives, N. and W. Serow. 'Interstate Migration of the Elderly: Demographic Aspects,' *Research on Aging*, 3(3/1981), 259–78.

Rosow, I. *Social Integration of the Aged*. New York: Free Press, 1967.

Ross, J. *Old People, New Lives*. Chicago: University of Chicago Press, 1977.

Rowles, G. *Prisoners of Space? Exploring the Geographical Experience of Older People*. Boulder: Westview Press, 1978.

Rowles, G. 'Growing Old 'Inside': Aging and Attachment to Place in an Appalachian Community,' pp. 153–70 in N. Datan and N. Lohmann (eds.). *Transitions of Aging*. New York: Academic Press, 1980.

Rowles, G. and R. Ohta. *Aging and Milieu: Environmental Perspectives on Growing Old*. New York: Academic Press, 1982.

Schooler, K. 'Response of the Elderly to Environment: A Stress-Theoretic Perspective,' in P. Windley and G. Ernst (eds.). *Theory Development in Environment and Aging*. Washington, D.C.: Gerontological Society, 1975.

Schulz, R. and G. Brenner. 'Relocation of the Aged: A Review and Theoretical Analysis,' *Journal of Gerontology*, 32(3/1977), 323–33.

Schwartz, A. 'Planning Micro-Environments for the Aged,' pp. 279–94 in D. Woodruff and J. Birren (eds.). *Aging: Scientific Perspectives and Social Issues*. New York: D. Van Nostrand Co., 1975.

Schwenger, C. and J. Gross. 'Institutional Care and Institutionalization of the Elderly in Canada,' pp. 248–56 in V. Marshall (ed.). *Aging in Canada: Social Perspectives*. Don Mills: Fitzhenry and Whiteside, 1980.

Serow, W. 'Return Migration of the Elderly in the USA: 1955–1960 and 1965–1970,' *Journal of Gerontology*, 33(2/1978), 288–95.

Sherman, E. et al. 'Patterns of Age Integration in Public Housing and the Incidence and Fears of Crime Among Elderly Tenants,' pp. 67–93 in J. Goldsmith and S. Goldsmith (eds.).

Crime and the Elderly: Challenge and Response. Lexington, Mass.: Lexington Books, 1976.

Sherman, S. 'Patterns of Contacts for Residents of Age-Segregated and Age-Integrated Housing,' *Journal of Gerontology*, 30(1/1975), 103–7.

Stahura, J. and S. Stahl. 'Suburban Characteristics and Aged Net Migration,' *Research on Aging*, 2(1/1980), 3–22.

Statistics Canada. *Canada's Elderly*. Ottawa: Ministry of Supply and Services, 1979.

Stirner, F. 'The Transportation Needs of the Elderly in a Large Urban Environment,' *The Gerontologist*, 18(2/1978), 207–11.

Stone, L. and S. Fletcher. *a Profile of Canada's Older Population*. Montreal: Institute for Research on Public Policy, 1980.

Streib, G. and R. Streib. 'Communes and the Aging,' *American Behavioral Scientist*, 19(2/1975), 176–89.

Struyk, R. 'The Housing Situation of Elderly Americans,' *The Gerontologist*, 17(2/1977), 130–39.

Sundeen, R. and J. Mathieu. 'The Fear of Crime and Its Consequences Among The Elderly in Three Urban Communities,' *The Gerontologist*, 16(3/1976), 211–19.

Teaff, J. et al. 'Impact of Age Integration on the Well-Being of Elderly Tenants in Public Housing,' *Journal of Gerontology*, 33(1/1978), 126–33.

Tindale, J. 'Old and Poor: Old Men on Skid Row,' master's thesis, Department of Sociology, McMaster University, 1974.

Tindale, J. 'Identity Maintenance Processes of Old Poor Men,' pp. 88–94 in V. Marshall (ed.). *Aging in Canada: Social Perspectives*. Don Mills: Fitzhenry and Whiteside, 1980.

Tobin, S. 'Institutionalization of the Aged,' pp. 195–211 in N. Datan and N. Lohmann (eds.). *Transitions of Aging*. New York: Academic Press, 1980.

Tobin, S. and M. Lieberman. *Last Home for the Aged: Critical Implications of Institutionalization*. San Francisco: Jossey-Bass, 1976.

Toseland, R. and J. Rasch. 'Factors Contributing to Older Persons' Satisfaction with Their Communities,' *The Gerontologist*, 18(4/1978), 395–402.

United States Bureau of the Census. 'Geographical Mobility: March, 1975 to March, 1979,' in *Current Population Reports*, Series P–20, No. 353. Washington, D.C.: Government Printing Office, 1980.

Wachs, M. *Transportation for the Elderly*. Berkeley: University of California Press, 1979.

Ward, R. 'The Implications of Neighborhood Age Structure for Older People,' *Sociological Symposium*, 26(1/1979), 42–63.

Ward, R. et al. 'Neighborhood Age Structure and Support Networks,' paper presented at the annual meeting of the Gerontological Society of America, Toronto, November 1981.

Warnes, A. (ed.). *Geographical Perspectives on the Elderly.* New York: John Wiley and Sons, 1982.

Wigdor, B. and L. Ford (eds.). *Housing for an Aging Population: Alternatives.* Toronto: University of Toronto Press, 1981.

Wilson, J. 'Walking Out of Doors: the Plight of the Elderly,' *Canadian Journal of Applied Sport Sciences,* 6(4/1981), 179–81.

Windley, P. and G. Ernst (eds.). *Theory Development in Environment and Aging.* Washington, D.C.: Gerontological Society, 1975.

Windley, P. and R. Scheidt. 'Person-Environment Dialectics: Implications for Competent Functioning in Old Age,' pp. 407–23 in L. Poon (ed.). *Aging in the 1980s.* Washington, D.C.: American Psychological Association, 1980.

Windley, P. and R. Scheidt. 'An Ecological Model of Mental Health Among Small-Town Rural Elderly,' *Journal of Gerontology,* 37(2/1982), 235–42.

Wiseman, R. 'Regional Patterns of Elderly Population Concentration and Migration,' in S. Golant (ed.). *Location and Environment of the Elderly Population.* New York: John Wiley and Sons, 1979.

Wiseman, R. 'Why Older People Move,' *Research on Aging,* 2(2/1980), 141–54.

Wiseman, R. and C. Roseman. 'A Typology of Elderly Migration Based on the Decision-Making Process,' *Economic Geography,* 55(4/1979), 324–37.

Yee, W. and M. Van Arsdol. 'Residential Mobility, Age and the Life Cycle,' *Journal of Gerontology,* 32(2/1977), 211–21.

Yin, R. 'Fear of Crime Among the Elderly: Some Issues and Suggestions,' *Social Problems,* 27(4/1980), 492–504.

Youmans, E. *Aging Patterns in a Rural and Urban Area of Kentucky.* Lexington: University of Kentucky Agricultural Experiment Station, 1963.

Youmans, E. 'The Rural Aged,' *The Annals of the American Academy of Political and Social Science,* 429 (January, 1977), 81–90.

PART FOUR

Aging and Participation in Social Institutions

Social institutions are an enduring aspect of cultural life. They meet essential needs by providing value orientations, norms, and a structure for interaction within specific contexts in our daily lives. In preindustrial societies, the family and the tribe (and perhaps religion) were the major institutions; today a number of social institutions affect our lives. These are often divided into three types: socializing, regulative, and cultural.

Socializing institutions include the family, the peer group, and the educational system. These institutions normally have the greatest impact on our lives during childhood, adolescence, and early adulthood, when we learn the prerequisites of the general and specific social roles we will play throughout life. During adulthood, the family continues to be an important institution, although the perspective changes as we enter and leave the roles of spouse, parent, or grandparent.

Regulative institutions include the economic, legal, military, and political systems. During adulthood, the economic system most significantly determines our life chances and lifestyle, both in terms of our earnings from employment and the effect of changes in the economy generally.

Cultural institutions include the arts, the media, religion, voluntary associations, recreation, sport, and science. They usually claim our involvement during leisure time.

As will be seen throughout this section, involvement in social institutions varies by stage in the life cycle. As we age we acquire and lose positions within the various institutions. These transitions may have a subsequent impact on social interaction and adjustment to the aging process. The individual participates in and is affected by a number of institutions. The connection between the family, work, and leisure creates different lifestyles. This institutional interaction also creates unique coping strategies resulting from status passages or role transitions. For example, a 30-year-old career woman with no children finds the experience of widowhood to be markedly different from that of a 30-year-old woman with two young children and no career, or a 70-year-old woman who has adult children and a social network of age peers who have also been widowed in recent years. In short, the adjustment to potentially traumatic status passages such as divorce, widowhood, or retirement can be affected by existing life chances and the degree of social support available.

Part Four of this book will focus on the changing patterns of social participation, and the impact of transitions or status passages on the individual. For most adults, the family, the labor force, the economy, and leisure are the major institutions that create and maintain social interaction at all stages of the life cycle. Individuals voluntarily or involuntarily acquire and relinquish specific roles at particular stages in life. These transitions can lead to significant social pressures to maintain or change existing social behavior patterns, often without the assistance of clear normative guidelines or role models. Furthermore, some transition points, such as the empty nest, divorce, retirement, or widowhood, have the potential to create personal crises that require adjustment and a change in lifestyle. Chapter 9 focuses on aging and family dynamics such as inter- and intragenerational relations and marital satisfaction over the life cycle, and the impact of divorce, the empty nest, retirement, and widowhood on the family as a basic social unit. In chapter 10, the effect of economic and employment history on social interaction during the middle and later years of life is discussed, and the process of retirement is examined in detail. Finally, in chapter 11, leisure is viewed as a cultural institution and varying patterns of social participation throughout the life cycle are described and explained, particularly with respect to religion, politics, education, the media, and voluntary associations.

9

Aging and Family Dynamics

Introduction

The family is both a biological unit and a social unit, and is the basic institution in virtually every society. As a primary social group it provides an environment for the addition of new members, for child care and socialization, for affection and social bonding throughout the life cycle, and for emotional, social, economic, and health support in old age. Until recently, most research focused on the young nuclear family (Henderson, 1981). There was much less interest in the interaction between nuclear families within an extended-family system, or in the dynamics of the family in the later part of the life cycle.

With increased life expectancy and the appearance of three-, four- or even five-generation families, and the increasing necessity to provide support for aging family members, scholars in demography, sociology, psychology, social gerontology, and family studies[1] have increasingly studied the dynamics of interaction in the extended kinship system.[2] This research has focused on changes in kinship structure over time, on the status of the elderly within the family in various societies,[3] on marital relations over the family life cycle, on the adjustment to the aging process within the family context, and on the onset and adjustment to family-related role transitions such as the empty nest and widowhood. Researchers have also examined the dynamics of interaction between adult children and aging parents, and between grandparents and grandchildren.[4] These relationships are influenced by residence location, frequency of communication, amount and type of mutual support, class, gender, ethnicity, health, and living arrangements. To date, much of this research has described rather than explained the structure and processes that pertain to the family life cycle.

This chapter will focus on social structure and interpersonal interaction at the micro level of analysis within the nuclear and extended family kinship system. For the most part, the evidence is presented from the perspective of the older members of the extended family. However, the perspectives of grandchildren and adult children must also be considered, since their views influence attitudes toward the elderly, the amount and type of support given, and the frequency and quality of intergenerational interaction.

Kinship Structure and Social Change

One individual may occupy many positions within the extended family structure. A man can be a son, brother, grandson, husband, son-in-law, brother-in-law, father, uncle, grandfather, or widower. As a result, few people reach the later stages of life with no surviving kin.[5] At various stages in life some kinship positions are more salient than others, although the positions of child, parent, and spouse are always central. Interaction with kin may vary throughout the life cycle. For example, the frequency and type of interaction between an 8-year-old grandson and his 60-year-old grandfather may change dramatically by the time they are 18 and 70 respectively.

The most basic unit within the kinship system is the nuclear family, which, at least initially, consists of a mother, a father, and children. This unit is known as the family of procreation. After marriage, this unit becomes more salient to the young married couple than the family of orientation (their parents and siblings), although the ties to the family of orientation persist, and create the extended family. Because of greater life expectancy, extended families may now include as many as four or five generations, whereas the three-generation extended family was the norm in previous centuries. Thus, the kinship system may consist of infants and young children (Generation 5 or G5), a young married couple with or without children (G4), a postparental middle-aged couple (G3), an older retired couple (G2), and a very old widow or widower (G1).

It has often been suggested that in the nineteenth century and earlier, three generations frequently lived within the same household, thereby ensuring care and security for the elderly. However, this pattern has recently been questioned (Laslett, 1971; Dahlin, 1980; Synge, 1980).[6] Laslett (1971) argued that not many people in those days lived to an old age; the norm of independence during young adulthood prevailed as it does today; young people in the United States often moved from the east to seek new opportunities in the west; and there was no compulsory retirement to create sudden economic hardships. In fact, even where children created their own nuclear families and remained on the farm, they usually resided in a separate household. Thus, the three generation household was the exception rather than the norm. As a result, it is likely that parents moved in with their adult children, or vice versa, only when declining health and economic status created a loss of independence.

The current extended family structure, which consists of three or four generations of separate households, was in existence earlier than is commonly believed. This network consists of separate families, related by marriage and intermarriage, which interact to varying degrees through visiting and by exchanging assistance as needed. Within many extended families, one particular individual usually takes on the role of kinkeeper and serves as a communications center whereby family members can indirectly keep in touch with each other. According to the recent 'Generational Relations and Succession Project' (Rosenthal et al., 1980, 1981a, 1981b), this leadership role is normally occupied by a female who is often a sibling in the middle generation. The role of kinkeeper involves telephoning, writing, and visiting in order to keep the extended family together.

Although separate homes for the extended family are the norm, in some cultures the elderly still live in the households of their children. Some examples include elderly Japanese (Palmore, 1975), and Pueblo (Rogers and Gallion, 1978) and Sioux (Murdock and Schwartz, 1978) Indians in the United States. Also, as we will see later, some social classes and ethnic groups are more likely to adhere to a cultural norm wherein the elderly are taken into the home of one of the adult children, usually a daughter. However, for the most part, the elderly in most modernized societies prefer not to live with their adult children or with other relatives. They retreat or disengage into the family of procreation only if they are very old or in poor health, if they have inadequate financial resources, or if they are widowed, unmarried, or divorced and can no longer live alone.

Although the modified extended family is still an important supportive system for the elderly person, because of social and demographic changes it is less viable as a source of social, emotional, and economic support than it was in the past. With the combination of increased life expectancies and decreased birth rates, there are fewer children per family; child rearing, if it happens, is completed earlier; and the married couple live as a postparental childless unit for a significantly larger portion of their adult life. Child launching and grandparenting have become middle-age rather than old-age phenomena (Troll, 1971; Troll et al. 1979). At the same time, because of the decrease in family size there are fewer offspring to assist or care for elderly parents should they need assistance (Singh and Williams, 1981). For those who are childless and unmarried, social support seems to be available from other relatives and friends when it is needed; for the childless married couple, the main source of support is each other (Johnson and Catalano, 1981). This may create problems if both members become ill and dependent at about the same time.

In addition to these demographic changes, a number of social changes have also influenced the current pattern of intergenerational interaction and support. First, each succeeding generation has enjoyed increasing economic independence, so that adult offspring have fewer financial obligations to repay. However, this financial independence may decrease in the next few years if high inflation and high unemployment rates continue. That is, acceptance of support from parents or in-laws may be necessary. Second, subsequent generations have been both geographically and socially more mobile than their parents or grandparents. As a result, children may not live close to their parents. A third factor is the increasing presence of women in the labor force, either by necessity or by choice. For example, some middle-aged women may be grandmothers, and may also work full-time or part-time. This prevents them from offering services or performing caretaking roles for grandchildren or aging parents (Treas, 1979). Finally, in many countries the state provides a number of social services for the elderly to offset the loss of familial assistance (Tobin and Kulys, 1980), perhaps resulting in more formal, bureaucratic, and impersonal care.

The appearance of these social and demographic changes has led many professionals and lay people to assume that the elderly are being rejected and neglected by their families. This argument is further supported when statistics indicate that many of the elderly widowed live alone: the myth of the lonely, alienated elderly person is created and perpetuated. While this belief has led to the improvement of the social and health care delivery systems for the elderly in many nations, research evidence does not support it. Rather, the evidence indicates that many of those over 65 live within a one-hour drive of at least one adult child. Furthermore, visiting, communicating by mail or telephone, and helping are part of the normative pattern for all social classes. In a recent review of the research evidence Shanas (1979a:8) concludes that 'the belief that old people are alienated from their families, particularly their children, is a myth, not a truism.' She further notes that 'where old people have no children, a principle of family substitution seems to operate and brothers, sisters, nephews and nieces often fulfill the roles and assume the obligations of children' (Shanas, 1979a:4).

In summary, while the elderly who live alone may have less daily contact with family members than in the past, most are not neglected by the extended family. Therefore, they are not dependent on impersonal social service bureaucracies for their survival, as is commonly assumed. Only those who have no living kin, and those who have lost touch with kin because of past family conflicts or dissolution will be totally dependent on public social services for their care and survival in the later years. In short, the idea that the elderly are isolated and kinless is a myth.

The Family Life Cycle

Some attention should now be given to the developmental process whereby individuals move from one status to another within the family life cycle. We saw earlier that on the macro level, cohorts pass through developmental stages of the life cycle from infancy to old age. Similarly, within the family context, individuals enter and exit from different stages (Glick, 1977). These passages involve changes in role and status, some of which are cause for joyous celebration by the extended family (births and marriages), others of which bring grief and adjustment problems to the individual and to the family (widowhood and divorce).

Generally, the cycle begins when a new family of procreation is created through marriage. Then, at various intervals some or all of the following stages may occur: (1) the birth of the first child and the beginning of parenting and grandparenting; (2) the birth of subsequent children and the last child; (3) the departure of the last child from the family of orientation and the onset of the empty nest or postparental stage; (4) the death of a parent or grandparent; (5) the retirement of one or both members of the couple; and (6) the death of one spouse, which normally occurs during the later years but which may occur during middle adulthood for some. In addition, separation, divorce, unemployment, or retirement can create a traumatic situation to which members of the family must adjust. The following sections present some of the more common transitions that influence both personal adjustment and inter- and intragenerational interaction in the middle and later years of life.

Social Factors Influencing Family Dynamics

Introduction.   The patterns of interaction within and between generations of the extended family and within the nuclear family are known as 'lineage relationships' (Bengtson and Cutler, 1976:134). These are seldom homogeneous within or between societies. Rather, a number of structural, process, and personal variables affect the quantity and quality of interpersonal attraction and interaction within the kinship system (Troll, 1971; Troll et al., 1979:32–33; Atchley and Miller, 1980). These factors influence the type and amount of economic, social, and emotional resources that are available to be shared between members of the extended family. Although these will be discussed in more detail later in the chapter, they are briefly noted below, since many studies of the aging family fail to consider them.

Structural variables.   First, relatives must be available, and the more there are, particularly adult children, the greater the likelihood that the older generation will interact with them. However, the nature of the interaction and the type of assistance given and received often depends on residential propinquity — that is, how close the relatives live to each other. Today, in addition to face-to-face interaction, the telephone plays a major role in maintaining relations between generations (Synge et al., 1981). However, the greater the distance between relatives, the less frequent the face-to-face or telephone interaction. In this situation it is likely that mutual support will be in the form of money or gifts rather than in services rendered.

While most elderly persons appear to live within a one-hour drive of at least one child, this may more likely be the case for those who live in urban areas. Children raised in rural areas are more likely to move to a larger city that is more than one hour away. In this situation, relatives outside the family of procreation and neighbors tend to form the social and health support system for the elderly in the rural community.

Another structural factor influencing social support and interaction between parents and adult children is the greater opportunity for young and middle-aged women to enter and remain in the labor force throughout their adult lives. This pattern used to be more common among lower- or working-class families, where it was an economic necessity. However, changing social norms and values now encourage and provide opportunities for middle-class women to begin careers early in life, or to renew careers in midlife once children are in school. Hence, fewer middle-aged daughters or daughters-in-law are available for daily interaction, or to provide care for the elderly within the family (Horowitz, 1981).

Stratification variables. As will be seen, the frequency and quality of interaction and support tend to be stronger along the mother-daughter line than along the son-parent line. This pattern is partially related to the fact that women are generally more concerned and involved in expressive rather than instrumental relationships at all stages of the life cycle. Although sons can act as caregivers in the absence of daughters, they seem to provide less direct support. Thus, parents without a daughter may be at a disadvantage in the later years when they need assistance, especially in terms of the quality of assistance. For example, they may receive financial aid from a son to hire a homemaker or nurse, but they will miss the personalized care that might be provided by a daughter.

Social class is another stratification variable that has an impact on family dynamics. A common pattern observed is that members of the middle class interact more with friends and colleagues outside the family, whereas those in the working class generally have stronger and more frequent interaction with kin. Furthermore, values pertaining to expected social and geographic mobility and economic independence are more prevalent among the middle class. A move to another city to further one's career during early and middle adulthood is viewed as necessary and acceptable both by aging middle-class parents and by their adult children, even if it means a lessening of contact.

A third stratification variable is ethnic or racial diversity. While it is relatively easy to accept stereotypical images of the structure and dynamics of particular racial or ethnic groups (for example, the older black matriarch as the family leader and anchor point), care must be taken not to generalize findings or images to all members of the group (Jackson, 1972). As noted elsewhere, there are differences between groups and within groups due to class, sex, ethnic, racial, and historical differences in values, opportunities, and emotional bonds.

The social situation of the elderly varies within ethnic groups in the United States (Mindel and Habenstein, 1976). In order to understand these differences both the cultural heritage and the degree of assimilation of the elderly within each racial or ethnic group must be examined. Studies of the Japanese in North America (Kiefer, 1974; Kobata, 1979) have noted how immigration laws and patterns have influenced family dynamics. The Issei, or oldest generation in North America, were born in Japan and emigrated between 1885 and 1924; the Nisei were born in North America between 1910 and 1945 and never had contact with their grandparents; while the Sansei, or the third generation, were born after 1945, have had contact with their grandparents, and have begun to intermarry with North Americans. Despite these historical and cultural differences, including language difficulties, strong intergenerational and ethnic ties provide social support for the elderly. Those Issei who have no surviving kin are usually cared for by Japanese community groups or religious institutions.

In another study of several ethnic groups, Woehrer (1978) found differences in visiting patterns and in primary support systems for the elderly. For example, the number who visited their parents at least once a week ranged from 75 percent for Italian Americans to 65 percent for Polish Americans to 39 percent for those of English or Scandinavian descent. While some of this variation might be accounted for by cultural heritage, it may also reflect residential propinquity. That is, the more recent immigrant groups may still live close to their parents because they have had less opportunity for social or geographic mobility than those of British or Scandinavian descent. Woehrer (1978) also found that the family is the main source of support for the elderly among Italian, Mexican, Polish, and Jewish Americans; that friends and colleagues are a more salient source for Irish Americans; and that some ethnic groups, such as the Scandinavians, use ethnic social organizations to care for the elderly. This dependence on ethnic organizations rather than family may occur because of greater geographical mobility of adult children, and the acceptance of cultural values derived from a homeland where state-supported services are widely available.

Many studies have examined the situation of elderly blacks, who comprise the largest minority group in the United States. Although relatively little is known about aging within this unique group which lives in a predominantly white culture, it is clear that the structure and dynamics of the black family vary by education, class, birthplace, and place of residence (Jackson, 1971, 1972; Yelder, 1979). There is a high incidence of poverty and deprivation among blacks, with many living close to or below the poverty line. These families tend to be headed by a woman because of higher frequencies of desertion, legal separation, or divorce. At higher income levels, the proportion of black families headed by males is similar to that of white families with comparable income.

The one clear pattern that emerges from most studies of black families is the strong kinship ties and the greater dependence on family for social, housing, and economic support, not only in the later years but throughout the life cycle. Perhaps because of minority-group status and cultural values, a closely knit family unit is the primary resource, rather than friends or social organizations. Of course, if cultural values are weakened by greater assimilation, the primary resource for the elderly could change from the family to friends or social agencies.

Personal variables.   In addition to the foregoing structural and process variables, the dynamics of nuclear and extended families are influenced by personal variables unique to the individuals within particular families. For example, whether people are married, widowed, or divorced influences where they fit within the kinship structure and with whom they are likely to interact. Health status determines not only their ability to interact, but also how others in the family perceive them as recipients of affection and interaction. For the individual in poor health, some relationships with other family members may cease (for example, with siblings or grandchildren), while others will continue because of a sense of obligation on the part of the closest relatives (spouse or adult children).

The quality and type of interaction within the family unit is also influenced by personality, by affectional bonds built over time among specific members, and by values pertaining to the role of family in the lifestyle. For example, women and members of the lower class are generally more expressive in their interpersonal interaction, while men and members of the middle class are generally more instrumental in their interaction patterns. As a result, older widowers, unlike older widows, may lack the skills and support network necessary to foster a suitable adjustment to single status in the later years.

In summary, there is no typical family structure, nor are there modal patterns of interaction within and between the generations. Rather, there is some variation in structure and great variation in frequency, type, and quality of interaction. These differences can be partially accounted for by demographic and sociohistorical variables; by structural variables in the larger society; by the processes of gender, racial, and class stratification; and by individual differences in health status, personality, and values among members of specific families.

Theoretical Perspectives on the Aging Family

Although many of the theoretical perspectives presented in chapter 4 could be applied to the study of family dynamics at different stages in the life cycle, much family research has been atheoretical, thereby resulting in a description rather than an explanation of family phenomena. Because role transitions and status passages influence and regulate patterns of social interaction within the extended family, both a structural-functionalist and an interactionist perspective may be useful in accounting for the behavior of family members within the kinship structure (George, 1980:1–6). The structural perspective explains the process whereby an individual acquires, via socialization, the behavioral rights and duties held by society to be associated with particular familial roles. This process is more passive and involves 'role taking' (Turner, 1962).

In contrast, the interactionist perspective applies to the micro level of analysis (that is, within a particular extended family structure) and accounts for individual interpretation and negotiation of role relationships. This process is more active and involves 'role making' (Turner, 1962) as the individual adapts to and modifies his or her unique family situation as it changes throughout the life course. For example, some children, regardless of age, will always accept a subordinate, submissive role relationship with their parents; others will interpret and negotiate changes in the relationship as they mature. As a result, from the perspective of the child, the child-parent relationship may pass through stages of subordination, equality, and dominance. The latter relationship may occur if the parents experience a serious loss of health or economic status in the later years, thereby necessitating a reversal to a childlike, dependent status.

A third perspective that has application to family dynamics is exchange theory (Mindel and Wright, 1982). As family members pass through various developmental stages and acquire or lose roles, role relationships need to be renegotiated. During this process of negotiation and exchange, the goal is to attain a mutually satisfying relationship characterized by cooperation rather than conflict. An attempt is made to balance the perceived costs and the rewards of the relationship. Similarly, exchange characterizes the process whereby a potentially supportive relationship is negotiated between adult children and their elderly parents, and between members of a married couple throughout the marriage. However, in some instances (such as the divorce of an adult child) conflict between the generations may prevail. In some family situations, and at some stages in the family life cycle, a conflict rather than an exchange perspective may be more appropriate for the study of changing family relationships.

The above perspectives apply to the dynamics of both the nuclear and the extended family; the developmental approach applies mainly to the nuclear family as it expands and contracts across the family life cycle (Troll et al., 1979:21–22). One example of such an approach is the developmental model proposed by Duvall (1977) in which she identifies developmental tasks that must be accomplished in ten behavioral categories at seven stages in the life cycle. Unfortunately, these normative tasks represent an ideal sequence and permit little individual variation if family or social situations differ. While this developmental perspective serves as a general descriptive model, it fails to explain the onset of developmental stages in alternative forms of family structure (for example, communes or single parenthood). It also does not explain family dynamics where there are individual differences in the personal or social status of family members (differences in personality, values, race, gender, class, or culture).

In summary, while a number of theoretical perspectives might be employed to increase the level of explanation, few studies of the aging family have used a theoretical framework to guide research. As a result, while many descriptive facts and patterns are available, we do not really understand why they exist or why they may change over time. The following sections present the current state of knowledge with respect to intragenerational relations, intergenerational relations, and transition points within the extended family during the middle and later years of life.

Intragenerational Family Relations

Marital Satisfaction and Adjustment Through the Life Cycle

Methodological concerns.   Most first marriages[7] are between individuals who were born at about the same time. Thus, the marriage cohort is usually made up of members of a generation who are at similar stages in the life cycle. They often have relatively similar backgrounds with respect to religion, social class, and education, and hence are often members of a generational unit. In this section, some of the patterns and correlates of marital satisfaction are discussed, with particular emphasis being given to the marital relationship during the postparental and retirement years.

Like many areas in social gerontology, the literature on marital satisfaction lacks a consistent and conclusive empirical and theoretical base, primarily because of inconsistent conceptualization and methodology. For example, marriage is a dynamic process of interpersonal exchange involving interaction, feelings, and shared responsibilities across many years of adulthood. Yet, with a few exceptions (Pineo, 1961; Paris and Luckey, 1966), the evidence is based primarily on cross-sectional rather than longitudinal studies.[8] Cross-sectional studies often include subjects who are both within and outside lineage generations, who are at different chronological ages, and who are at different stages in the marriage and career. Furthermore, these studies seldom control for possible confounding variables such as class, ethnicity, race, religion, education or cohort-historical effects.[9] As a result, it is difficult to compare findings and cumulative evidence when one study defines middle-aged couples as those between 30 and 55, another defines them as those with adolescent children, and a third defines them as being in the postparental stage of life but not yet retired.

Another methodological shortcoming pertains to the theoretical and operational definition of the concept of 'satisfaction.' First, the study of marital relations has focused on such parameters as satisfaction, adjustment, success, or happiness. These may have different meanings for respondents, and each concept may be measured in a variety of ways by different investigators.

Both single and multiple dimensions have been used to measure the specific concept being studied, although unidimensional scales have prevailed. This use of unidimensional scales is surprising, since, as Gilford and Bengtson (1976, 1977) suggest, the marital relationship involves an emotional dimension (feelings or sentiments about the partner) and a behavioral dimension (companionship and interaction in common activities). Similarly, Medley (1977) suggests that there are four major dimensions of marital adjustment: (1) the relative degree of positive self-esteem or self-worth of each member; (2) the degree of commitment on the part of each member to maintain the marriage; (3) the availability of resources such as financial security, health, effective and mature communication skills, rational cognitive and behavioral skills, and socioemotional support from friends, colleagues, and family outside the family of procreation; and (4) a degree of consensus on short- and long-term goals for the members, both individually and as a couple. As a result of these diverse conceptual and methodological approaches, the literature on marital satisfaction lacks definitive conclusions.

Patterns of marital satisfaction over the life course. At present there appears to be a relationship between number of years of marriage and marital satisfaction.[10] While there may be cycles of enchantment and disenchantment with marriage, there are generally two different patterns of satisfaction across the marriage career (see figure 9.1). Based on longitudinal studies, Pineo (1961) and Paris and Luckey (1966) suggest that there is a gradual and linear decline in marital satisfaction across all stages of the marriage cycle (pattern A). The alternative pattern, based on cross-sectional studies, suggests that the relationship is curvilinear (pattern B). At present, the curvilinear pattern has the greatest support in the research literature (Stinnett et al., 1972; Rollins and Cannon, 1974; Atchley and Miller, 1980; George, 1980:80).

However, some studies have failed to demonstrate either a linear or a curvilinear relationship (Spanier et al., 1975), while others have found that the pattern of the relationship varies according to the dependent variable that is measured. For example, Gilford and Bengtson (1976) found a curvilinear relationship across the marriage for satisfaction with companionship experiences, and a linear pattern of decline in satisfaction for negative feelings about the spouse. That is, negative feelings influenced the level of marital satisfaction more in the earlier years of marriage than in the later years.

Individual variations in the base of the curve and in the height of the curve in the later years have been observed. Curve B1 suggests that the low point occurs when children are adolescents; B2 suggests that it occurs when the last child leaves home; and B3 suggests that it occurs just prior to, or at, the husband's retirement. At these transition points both husbands and wives may experience a redefinition of their marital roles. For example, when the children leave home there may be a shift in focus from the children to each other, or to a greater commitment to other interests. Similarly, at retirement, the presence of the husband in the wife's daily routine and responsibilities can be either a

Figure 9.1 Four possible patterns of marital satisfaction over the life course.

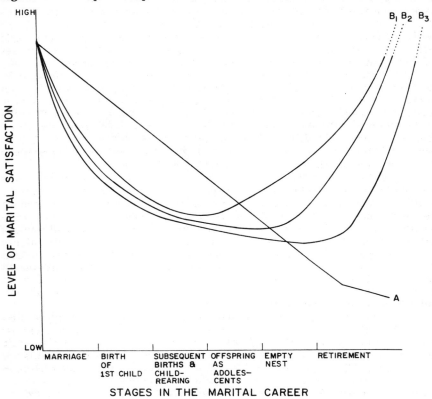

source of increasing companionship or a source of conflict if her domestic role is partially usurped. This stage may also require that her daily routine be changed to meet the husband's schedule. There is a continuing debate as to whether the level of satisfaction is actually higher in the later years than it is during the honeymoon and in the years before children arrive. This hypothetical pattern is reflected by the extension upward (dotted lines) of the three curvilinear paths.

Another pattern may show the relationship reaching a low point at either the empty-nest stage or the retirement stage, and then either declining or beginning to increase. Both of these transition points provide the opportunity either for a renewal of the marriage and increasing marital satisfaction, or for dissatisfaction on the part of one or both partners. In this latter situation, the disharmony is often resolved by separation and divorce when the child-rearing or occupational responsibilities have been completed.

A final pattern concerns sex differences in the perception of marital satisfaction at different stages in the marriage. Generally, middle-aged women express the most dissatisfaction with marriage (Lowenthal et al., 1975; Thurnher, 1976).[11] However, few men or women express dissatisfaction beyond the retirement stage. The one exception that may lead to loss of morale in general, and to an increasing dissatisfaction with the marital state, occurs when one spouse (usually the wife) is faced with the long-term care of a disabled partner. This situation often leads to loneliness, isolation, economic difficulties, and role overload (Fengler and Goodrich, 1979). In short, except during the middle-aged years for women, and the later years when a spouse is disabled, there are few sex differences in the perception of marital satisfaction at any one stage.

Given that the curvilinear pattern of marital satisfaction appears to be prevalent, how can this pattern be explained? While a definitive answer is not available, Troll et al. (1979:55–60) and Abu-Laban (1980) have suggested that the peaks of satisfaction at the early and later stages of the marriage reflect the similar lifestyles of the two partners. Both stages are adult-centered and child-free, both partners have time to engage in activities together, household responsibilities can be shared, and the level of income (and thus expectations and needs) is lower than in the intervening period.

The decline in marital satisfaction during the middle years often results from strain created by child-rearing responsibilities and demands on parental time; by occupational strain, especially for upwardly striving men or women; by the onset of personality, value, or behavioral changes in one member but not in the other; by the declining health of one member, which restricts the lifestyle of both members; by the wife entering the labor force; and by the general tendency for the interpersonal attraction in any relationship to decline with time (Zube, 1982). Thus, for a variety of reasons, the initially high level of satisfaction declines until late in the middle years or until retirement, when it begins to increase again, perhaps even rising to higher levels as the meaning of the marriage changes for some couples.

High levels of marital satisfaction may be expressed by different types of relationships. Medley (1977) suggests that in the postretirement years there are three types of conjugal relationships: (1) the husband-wife relationship, wherein the respective marital roles are central to the couple's life and other relationships are secondary; (2) the parent-child relationship, wherein one member assumes the role of protective and dominant parent when the other member experiences a decline in health and becomes more dependent on the other; and (3) the associate relationship, wherein the members are friends but the central focus of each of them is outside the marital relationship.

To date, research evidence is lacking to determine whether couples adopt one of these lifestyles after both spouses are retired, or whether they develop one of these patterns as their social situation changes. While it is quite possible that the parent-child relationship may evolve if both members of the dyad survive well into the later years of life, it is likely that the husband-wife or the associate relationship, both of which represent opposite ends of a continuum, have been in existence for years. That is, because of continuity in lifestyle, the style of marriage adopted in the earlier years is likely to be followed in the later years, especially if the style has led to a marital relationship that is at least minimally satisfactory for both partners.

Another type of marital relationship occurring in the later years is referred to as the 'married widow' or 'married widower,' wherein one partner is institutionalized because of chronic illness. The spouse who remains in the community, while married, has a lifestyle similar to that of a widow or widower. Yet, this individual must cope with two conflicting roles: (1) he or she is the spouse of an institutionalized partner, and (2) he or she is a spouse who is single within the community. An identity crisis may develop because of this marginal status. The healthy partner must share the care of the spouse with the institutional employees, who have the final say on disputed issues; in the community, he or she is not free to establish new sexual relationships or to start a new life. While this type of marital relationship has seldom been studied, Brandwein et al. (1979) interviewed eighteen 'community spouses' and concluded that this situation creates stress and requires unique adjustments to the marital role in two very different social situations.

Sibling Interaction in the Later Years

Sibling relationships during infancy, childhood, and adolescence have been studied extensively (Sutton-Smith and Rosenberg, 1970). However, relatively little attention has been devoted to relationships during the middle and later years of life (Troll et al., 1979:121–24; Weishaus, 1979; Atchley and Miller, 1980; Cicirelli, 1980). This is surprising in that this relationship is normally egalitarian (little power or conflict is present) and persists from infancy to death. In fact, between 75 and 90 percent of the older population have at least one surviving sibling (Harris et al., 1975; Atchley and Miller, 1980; Cicirelli, 1980). Despite the extensive literature concerning the differences between first- and later-born children, differences by birth order, if any, during the middle and later years of life have yet to be identified or studied.

The general life-cycle pattern of sibling relationships involves three stages: (1) frequent interaction during childhood and adolescence until departure from the family of orientation; (2) a drifting apart to varying degrees[12] after entrance into the labor force and marriage; and (3) a renewal of more frequent interaction in the later years. This renewal may increase when the children leave home, when they jointly contribute to the care of an ailing parent, or upon the death of one or both parents.[13] However, contact is unlikely to be renewed if the past relationship was characterized by rivalry and conflict, if one or both of the respective in-laws are perceived as incompatible, if settlement of the parent's estate has created conflict, or if distance or health prohibits regular visiting.

Gender, cultural, marital status, and chronological age differences also appear to influence sibling relationships in the later years. First, as at all stages of life, the female linkage within a family tends to be strong and pervasive: among older people, sister-sister ties are stronger than sister-brother relationships (Troll, 1971). Moreover, older sisters may provide economic and social security for a brother who is a widower or a bachelor. In effect, the sister may begin to serve as a surrogate wife or mother for the brother (Cicirelli, 1977; Lee and Ihinger-Tallman, 1980).

Cultural values and historical tendencies may also influence the quantity and quality of sibling interaction among members of some racial or ethnic groups. Within cultural groups where a high value is placed on family solidarity and mutual assistance (for example, the Japanese), sibling links will be more likely to exist in the later years, especially if one of the siblings is widowed and experiences a decline in health or economic status. Regardless of ethnic heritage, marital status may influence sibling links in later life. Research studies generally find that the never-married, the widowed, and the divorced have more frequent interaction with their siblings than those who are married. Finally, and not surprisingly, even though interaction with siblings may be greater for some older people than during midlife, there is a decline in frequency among the very old as health and mobility decrease.

In summary, little theoretical or empirical work has been completed on the quantity, quality, or nature of sibling relationships during the middle and later years. However, it does appear that siblings may be the next-best resource after children in the later years, especially among sisters and for those who are widowed or were never married. In fact, older female siblings may unite to create a household in the later years in order to provide each other with social, emotional, and economic support. Unfortunately, with declining family size this resource may be less readily available in the future. Considerable research is needed to enable us to better understand the nature of sibling relationships, particularly with respect to their quality and meaning during the later years of life.

Intergenerational Family Relations

Parent and Adult Child Interaction

Introduction.   Being a parent involves reciprocal interaction with children throughout the life cycle. This lineage interaction can vary in frequency, quality, and type depending on the age, interests, and needs of the two generations. For example, during early childhood the relationship is constant and largely unidirectional, in that the children are highly dependent on the parents for support. During adolescence, the interaction declines in frequency and becomes more reciprocal as both generations influence each other. The relationship at this time may be characterized by conflict over values, beliefs, and behaviors (Alpert and Richardson, 1980). As children leave home and eventually establish their own nuclear families, and begin to experience interaction from the parental perspective, the relationship with their own parents may decrease further in quantity and quality as new demands are placed on them. Finally, as the children enter midlife[14] and the parents grow old, interaction may increase, especially if an elderly parent becomes more dependent on an adult child. In this situation the relationship once again becomes primarily unidirectional, but in the opposite direction from that of childhood.[15] More help is given to the parent, especially with respect to health care. However, there may be a continuing economic exchange in both directions, although whether the direction is parent-to-child or child-to-parent may depend on the socioeconomic status of the two generations.

It has frequently been suggested that dependent elderly parents experience role reversal and enter a second childhood; this is another myth that lacks research support (Brody, 1979). The onset of varying degrees of dependency does, however, introduce the possibility of a shift in power from the parent to the child. Depending on the quality of the relationship during the earlier years, the onset of dependency can provide an opportunity to reward the parent for past debts, or to seek revenge for real or imagined parental injustice during childhood or adolescence. For example, in recent years there has been an increase in the reported cases of what has been referred to as 'granny bashing.' That is, elderly parents may be verbally, physically, emotionally, or sexually abused by their children, who imprison, neglect, or harass them.

The theme of parent-child conflict during adulthood has recently been examined by Steinman (1979). She suggests that transitions such as illness, the death of one parent, financial difficulties for the elderly person, or a divorce or financial crisis on the part of the offspring[16] can increase parent-child interaction and dependency during middle adulthood. These transitions can lead to three types of conflict: (1) continuing conflict, wherein the underlying tension has always been present in questions of lifestyle, values, morals, friends, or religion; (2) new conflict, wherein parents and adult children disagree on their respective roles in caring for the surviving parent or in the raising of the third generation; and (3) reactivated conflict, which was present and unresolved before the child left home, and which reappears because of renewed or increased interaction. This reactivated conflict is frequently based on differing perceptions of the degree of independence each should experience, and of the extent to which the child perceives himself or herself as being accepted or rejected by the parent throughout life.

Steinman (1979) proposed four possible patterns of behavior in response to reactivated conflict. First, the 'overzealous approacher' devotes excessive energy and resources to minimizing the conflict by helping the parent to the exclusion of personal needs, interests, and responsibilities. This approach can lead to stress and interpersonal problems with the spouse or children, who may feel neglected. The 'active avoider' resolves the conflict by avoiding interaction and hires others (such as nurses or institutions for the aged) to care for the aging parent. This pattern often creates guilt. The third pattern is that of a 'vacillator,' whose overzealousness and subsequent stress are followed by avoidance and subsequent guilt, which then leads to overzealous involvement and a repetition of the cycle of vacillation. Finally, the 'constructive approacher' seeks external assistance from friends or professional counselors in an attempt to reduce conflict and improve the frequency and quality of interaction. While these types of reaction have yet to receive empirical support, they suggest how adult children might react to parent-child conflict in midlife.

Although the possibility of overt conflict and high dependency exists within the parent-child relationship, the prevailing evidence suggests that the role relationship is not usually characterized by conflict, nor are most of the elderly abandoned by or alienated from their families. Rather, as the following subsection illustrates, the immediate family is still the predominant institution for the provision of physical, emotional, and economic support to the elderly, and the extended family is the major source of social interaction within the community (Shanas, 1979b). For example, Marshall et al. (1981) noted that three dimensions of health care are provided to parents by adult children. These include concern about and monitoring of the parents' health; provision of care in a crisis situation; and long-term, routine health care of the very old parent.

Aging parent and adult child exchange relationships.   Recent demographic changes such as decreased family size, childless marriages, and fewer single adult daughters, combined with an increasing number of middle-aged women in the labor force, have led to a decrease in the availability and opportunity of children to care directly for aging parents (Horowitz, 1981). As a result, more social and health care support services are provided by the private and government sectors (Treas, 1977; Brody, 1978; Kaplan, 1979; Remnet, 1979). Nevertheless, in most societies the family is the first and major resource for the elderly, of whom less than 10 percent are ever institutionalized. Also, as Mindel (1979) noted, movement into a multigenerational family household is often an intervening stage between independent living and institutionalization.

When economic status or health deteriorates, the role of primary caregiver is assumed, in rank order, by the spouse, then by an adult child, then by another relative (Horowitz and Shindelman, 1981). This process normally represents a 'substitution' model wherein only one of the possible caregivers intervenes at a time. In contrast, an ideal model is one of shared responsibility, where a number of caregivers are available and willing to assist and interact with the older person at the same time. For older widows, one or more of the adult children usually intervenes, first to provide assistance, then to serve as the mediator between the parent and the formal organizations that provide partial assistance, and finally to negotiate on behalf of the parent when some degree of institutionalization appears to be the only solution. In short, social exchange patterns continue throughout the family life cycle, and the middle family unit eventually acquires increasing power in the exchange relationship (Turner, 1975; Sussman, 1976; Dowd and La Rosa, 1982; Mindel and Wright, 1982).

Within the family there are physical, emotional, economic, and social resources that can be exchanged in a serial or reciprocal manner, depending on the needs and stage in life.[17] Serial exchanges tend to be prevalent, and generally represent a downward flow of assistance from the older generations to the younger generations because of a sense of responsibility and affection (Moore, 1966). Reciprocal exchange, or a two-way flow, is most common among the middle and oldest generations, especially among the middle class. Johnson and Bursk (1977) found that 93 percent of the elderly in their study who had adult children engaged in reciprocal patterns of exchange.

This process of exchange usually involves services such as babysitting, nursing, counseling, shopping, and household maintenance; gifts such as money, clothes, appliances, or air or train tickets for visits; or interaction in the form of face-to-face visits, telephone calls, or letters (Hill, 1965; Synge et al., 1981). The form and frequency of exchange varies greatly among families and is influenced by a number of social factors. These include residential propinquity, social class, children's sex, race, ethnicity, age of the middle and oldest generations, and the degree of 'filial maturity' (that is, a growing concern about parents in the middle years: Blenkner, 1965.) The greater the extent to which elderly parents live in close proximity to children, the greater the likelihood of visiting and exchanging goods or services. In fact, many elderly parents report weekly face-to-face visits with at least one child. This occurs especially among members of the working class who, because of cultural ties and lower levels of social mobility, live in closer proximity to each other.

Class differences in frequency and type of exchange have been found in many studies (Troll and Bengtson, 1979; Neugarten, 1979; Lacy and Hendricks, 1980). For example, Shanas (1967), in a study of family help patterns among approximately 2,500 people over 65 in Britain, Denmark, and the United States, found that members of every social class engaged in reciprocal assistance. However, since size of family, living arrangements, family values, and economic position vary by social class, the amount, form, and frequency of mutual aid also varies. Studies have shown that working-class parents are more likely to receive more help and to live with their children; that the middle class is more likely to exchange money and gifts, and the working class is more likely to exchange services; that the middle class is more likely to exhibit patterns of serial exchange from the oldest to youngest generations, while reciprocity is more common among the working class; and that there is more face-to-face interaction among the working class, and more telephoning and letter writing among the middle class because of greater social and geographical mobility.

Some racial and ethnic minority groups often have stronger family ties and cultural norms of family assistance than others. For example, even though there may be social mobility and cultural assimilation among members of second- and third-generation Japanese Americans, the cultural heritage of group goals and respect for elders persists (Osako, 1979). This results in a high frequency of mutual aid to conserve and share resources, especially if the group live in poor social or economic conditions.

There are also sex differences in familial exchange relationships, and these interact with class and racial factors. For example, sons often perceive assisting older parents as an instrumental act resulting from an obligation to repay a past debt. In contrast, daughters, because of long-standing, expressive lineal mother-daughter ties, see assistance as an expressive act which they want to or need to perform. As a result, sons generally provide more financial assistance and make more decisions about the care of the parents. Daughters seem to be the primary caregivers (Horowitz, 1981). This may occur because women are more likely to play the traditional nurturant role, because they have more time, or because the mother-daughter relationship is strengthened during the adult years, especially after the daughter has become a mother (Fischer, 1981). Marshall et al. (1982) found that daughters worry more about parental health than do sons, and that the health of the father generates more concern and worry than that of the mother.

These sex differences in types of assistance may also reflect the resources of each child. A daughter, if she is a housewife, may not have personal economic resources to share with her own parents; a son is more likely to. With increasing numbers of women entering the labor force, this pattern may be altered in the future. Working daughters may not have the time to offer services, but will have their own economic resources to share with their parents.

In general, daughters interact more frequently with elderly parents and are more likely to take aged parents into their homes. Similarly, when they are unable to live alone, widows are more likely to move in with a child, usually a daughter, than are older widowers.

From the perspective of elderly parents, it appears that they primarily offer financial assistance to sons, and services to daughters. However, there are great interfamily variations, depending on class and on the individual interests of the parents. For example, if they are still employed, younger grandparents may have neither the time for nor the interest in performing babysitting or other service roles. As a result, they may replace this personal assistance with loans or gifts of money.

Another factor influencing the type and frequency of interaction and assistance is filial responsibility, or filial maturity. This represents the extent to which adult children feel obligated to meet the basic needs of their aging parents. While the family is an important source of aid and support for the elderly, the expectations of the parents and children as to what should be done may or may not coincide. For example, the chronological age of the children may determine their desire or ability to assist or interact with their parents. Adult children with very old parents may also be retired and have their own economic and health concerns. Therefore, they may be less able or willing to assist their aging parents and may abdicate some of their filial responsibility to public or private social service agencies (Gelfand et al., 1978).

From the perspective of the aging parents, expectations for filial responsibility seem to be higher with increasing age among females and among the widowed or divorced, if they have few economic resources, if health fails, and if their general level of morale or life satisfaction is low (Seelback, 1977, 1978; Seelback and Sauer, 1977). In short, the perception of filial responsibility may intervene to decrease or increase child-parent interaction patterns in the later years. Where expectations differ, family solidarity is weakened, overt conflict may occur, and public or private social agencies may be required to fill the void for visiting, health, and household services.

Up to this point in our discussion of family relationships, most of the emphasis has been on the type and frequency of interaction, and on the factors influencing familial relationships later in life. Quantity rather than quality has been the central concern. We have seen that there is a high degree of contact and mutual helping in most families, although this may primarily be a monitoring, ritualistic function and may not necessarily imply a meaningful relationship characterized by positive feelings, shared values and beliefs, respect, trust, and deep affection (Hess and Waring, 1978).

It has often been assumed that a high-quality relationship exists because of the oft-quoted theme, 'intimacy at a distance' (Rosenmayr and Kockeis, 1963). This suggests that the process of social and economic exchange between the generations is based on mutual understanding. The elderly recognize the right of their adult children to live independently, as they themselves did; they wish to continue to help them if they are able; they seek to interact but remain independent as long as possible; and they expect to receive assistance when and if it is needed. Employing a different interpretation of 'intimacy at a distance,' Blau (1981) suggests that this theme does not reflect an ideal, voluntary situation but rather reflects the marginal status of the elderly within the extended family. She states that they would actually prefer more frequent and meaningful interaction with their children. However, recognizing that this is unlikely to occur, the elderly say that they prefer intimacy at a distance in order to rationalize and maintain at least a minimal amount of interaction.

This second interpretation suggests that more research should be directed toward understanding the quality of the relationship between elderly parents and adult children. Unfortunately, to date only a few studies have examined this question. Noting that the process of aging can be stressful both for older parents and for their children, Johnson and Bursk (1977) and Johnson (1978) found that the quality of the relationship is influenced by the health, economic, and housing situation of the elderly, and by attitudes to their personal aging experience. The level of affect was higher when the parents were in good health and held positive feelings about their personal aging process. They also noted that there was more quality interaction in the relationship when parents were socially active outside the extended family. In a more detailed examination of the quality of mother-daughter relationships, Johnson (1978) found that a higher-quality relationship was likely to exist if the mother had a positive attitude toward her personal aging experience, and if she was satisfied with her living environment.

Finally, although the mother-daughter link persists throughout life, Weishaus (1979) suggests that the quality of the relationship decreases over time. This occurs because by the time the daughter reaches 40 the mother has become less important in the daughters' life, even though the mother still perceives the daughter as highly salient in her life. This decrease in the affective feelings for the mother may be the result of too many competing alternatives in her own lifestyle. These include the launching and marriage of her own offspring; an involvement in the labor force; a changing marital relationship after child launching; and the declining health of an aging mother, which makes care and assistance, rather than meaningful verbal or social interaction, the major focus of the role relationship.

In summary, little attention has been directed toward studying the quality of parent-adult child relationships. However, it appears from the research completed to date that the quality may change over time, even if the frequency of interaction continues in some form. Specifically, it seems that the quality can deteriorate when competing alternatives for the children prevail, and when the morale and health of the elderly parent decline. These factors are clearly interrelated, and more research is needed to explain when and why a change in the quality of the parent-child relationship occurs. There is a need to examine more closely and directly the relationship between the quantity of interaction and the quality of the relationship. In many respects this linkage represents the classic chicken-and-egg situation: which event occurs first? Does quantity decline because the quality ebbs, or does the quality decline as the frequency decreases?

Grandparent and Grandchild Interaction

Introduction.   The likelihood of a grandchild interacting with a grandparent increases with the longevity of the grandparent, and is greater the earlier children are born to a couple. Today, over 90 percent of all children in North America have at least one living grandparent at age 10, while approximately 75 percent have one living grandparent at age 20. Yet, because of a declining birth rate (as reflected in smaller families and childless marriages), surviving grandparents have fewer grandchildren than in the past. With an increasing incidence both of divorce and of the number of children that never marry, many older persons never become grandparents. Also, because of increased geographical mobility in this century, face-to-face contact is less frequent than it was in the past, at least in North America. Finally, although grandparenting has become more common among the middle-aged because of marriage at an earlier age, it is still likely that most grandparents are approaching the retirement years when they acquire the role.

Although the role of grandparent exists in most extended families, relatively little research has been completed concerning this ascribed status. This lack of interest may reflect the marginal status of the elderly within society and within families, and the fact that grandparent and grandchild relations are infrequent and peripheral to other social and family roles. It may also indicate that the role is not clearly defined, and is primarily an expressive rather than an instrumental role. Nevertheless, studies of the role within the family have revealed that grandparenthood is a complex phenomenon. Kahana and Kahana (1971) suggest that it can be analyzed on at least five levels: as a social role; as an emotional state for the individual; as a process of interaction between two generations within a family; as a part of the intergenerational relationships within the extended family; and as a symbol of age, wisdom, experience, and independence. To date, most research on grandparenthood has focused on the definition and meaning of the role (from the perspective of society and the individual) and on the interaction and meaning of the relationship from the perspective of both the child and the grandparent (Troll et al., 1979; Troll, 1980b; Kivnick, 1982).

The role of grandparent.   Unlike most other familial roles, the role of grandparent is acquired involuntarily. The individual subsequently enacts the role in varying ways. The extent and style of the enactment, at least in the early stages, are greatly influenced by three factors: residential proximity (Gronvold, 1981); the extent to which parents act as mediators between the grandparents and the grandchildren by providing opportunities for the first and third generations to be socialized into their respective roles (Robertson, 1975); and the lifestyle, personality, and employment status of the older generation. The meaning and satisfaction attached to the role often depends on the degree of interest or commitment on the part of an individual. In this sense, the role of grandparent is more a personal experience than an institutionalized role with specific rights, responsibilities, or norms. In fact, like retirement, it has been labelled a 'roleless' role because there are no definitive responsibilities or rights attached to it. It has also been labelled a 'sexless' role, in that there is often little role differentiation between grandmothers and grandfathers.[18] Both can engage in child care, teaching, and friendship with one or more of their grandchildren.

The stereotypical lifestyle of a grandparent has often been portrayed as involving child care, baking cookies and preparing large family meals at holidays, sitting on the front porch in a rocking chair, serving as a fishing companion for a grandchild, or acting as 'Mr. Fix-It' for the extended family and neighbors. In reality, however, the image and style of grandparenting is very different. The way in which the role is played may vary with class and subculture. Because of the earlier onset of grandparenthood, the larger number of middle-aged women in the labor force, and increased longevity, grandmothers are more likely to be employed and to have little time or interest in surrogate parenting. Grandfathers may not retire as early as they did in the past, and may not have time to play the role until the grandchildren are into middle or late adolescence.

In recent years, grandparents have been more likely to be older couples, with their own interests and lifestyles, than widows or widowers. In addition, a surviving grandparent is less likely to enter an offspring's household until after the grandchild has left the home. Moreover, with increased longevity, a grandmother in an extended family may be required to direct her energy and resources to caring for her own elderly mother. Social and demographic changes have altered the style of grandparenting; it has also been greatly influenced by the personalities of the grandparent and the grandchild, and by the particular needs, interests, and affections of each generation at varying life stages.

With respect to social, racial, or ethnic differences in grandparenting, there appear to be different interpretations of the role, given that there are few institutionalized norms to guide behavior. In one of the few studies on the influence of social class on grandparenting, Clavan (1978) found differences between the middle and lower classes. In the middle class, the role is more peripheral, perhaps because more grandmothers are employed and have different sex-role definitions; there is little differentiation between grandmother and grandfather; financial aid is given more frequently than services; and the role is more symbolic and ritualistic (that is, it is expressed during family celebrations at confirmations, Bar Mitzvahs, Thanksgiving, Christmas, or Easter).

Within the working class, Clavan (1978) found that the grandparents, especially the grandmother, are more likely to be integrated into the family and to play a functionally central role in child rearing.[19] This occurs because the grandparents are more likely to live close to their offspring, because both parents are more likely to work, and because there may be a higher incidence of single-parent families and a need for a surrogate mother or father. In short, grandparenting among the working class, and within racial and ethnic subcultures that are largely made up of working-class members, is more likely to be a 'real' role that involves functional integration into the daily life of the extended family.

Institutionalization is another factor that influences the role of grandparent. In most instances, the role ceases, like many others, when an older person enters an institution. At this transition point opportunities and ability to play the role are usually lost. In order to compensate for this loss, a foster-grandparent program has been initiated in many communities. This program provides emotional and psychological support for young children who do not have grandparents, or for orphaned or foster children who may have little or no contact with adults other than foster parents or social workers. For elderly people who are totally or partially institutionalized, the adoption of a foster grandchild may enhance their self-esteem and morale, and decrease their feelings of loneliness. In some communities, the elderly are hired to play a surrogate teaching and caring role for an institutionalized child who is emotionally, socially, or intellectually deprived. This arrangement provides a modest source of income for elderly people, and permits them to engage in necessary and meaningful social work (Saltz, 1971). Finally, in order to provide companionship for preschoolers and the elderly, day-care centers have been located within or adjacent to senior citizen homes or adult drop-in centers. Elderly volunteers teach or play with preschoolers, thereby acting as surrogate teachers, grandparents, or simply older friends.

Grandchildren's perceptions of grandparents.   Although the role relationship between grandparents and grandchildren has been examined mainly from the perspective of the grandparent, a few studies have dealt with the perceptions and experiences of the grandchildren (Kahana and Kahana, 1970; Robertson, 1976). These studies reveal that children who interact with grandparents have fewer prejudices about the elderly and growing old; that the parents play a significant mediating role in the quantity and quality of interaction; that as the grandchildren grow older, they feel a responsibility toward their grandparents; that granddaughter-grandmother ties are stronger than grandfather-grandchildren ties; and that perceptions and interactions vary by the age of the grandchild. The following expresses the view of one third-grader who responded to a teacher's request to define a grandmother (Huyck, 1974:77):

A grandma is a lady who has no children of her own, so she likes other people's little boys and girls.

A grandfather is a man grandmother. He goes for walks with the boys and they talk about fishing and things like that.

Grandmas don't have to do anything except be there. They're so old they shouldn't play hard. It is enough if they drive us to the supermarket where the pretend horse is and have lots of dimes ready.

Or, if they take us for walks, they should slow down past things like pretty leaves or caterpillars. And they should never say, 'Hurry up!'

Usually they are fat, but not too fat. They wear glasses and funny underwear. They can take their teeth and gums off.

They don't have to be smart, only answer questions like why dogs hate cats, and how come God isn't married.

They don't talk baby talk like visitors do because it is hard to understand.

When they read to us they don't skip words and they don't mind if it is the same story.

Grandmas are the only grownups who have got time — so everybody should have a grandmother, especially if you don't have television.

(This definition was written a number of years ago; contemporary third-graders may speak of quarters and Pac-Man instead of dimes and pretend horses.)

Kahana and Kahana (1970) found that younger grandchildren (4 to 5 years old) valued grandparents for their willingness to play, to give them toys, and to idolize them; the middle group (8 to 9 years) saw them as active partners to have fun with; the oldest group (11 to 12 years) reported that they were more distant from their grandparents. It was concluded that social and emotional barriers increase with age. Yet, as studies of college students have shown, grandchildren visit, have affection for, and feel responsible for their grandparents (Robertson, 1976). Therefore, it may be that the bond is strong through childhood, declines during early adolescence when self-interests prevail and the peer group becomes the primary reference point, and is renewed in early adulthood when grandchildren are independent and free to visit with or without their parents. Role reversal may occur from childhood to early adulthood; the child, who was the recipient of gifts and affection, becomes a donor as he or she enters adult life. In fact, children may assist their parents by sharing some of the responsibilities for the social or economic needs of the oldest generation.

Grandparents' perceptions of their role. As noted earlier, involvement in the grandparent role is affected by residential propinquity, by the personal needs and interests of the grandchildren and grandparents, by the involvement of the parents, and by social class and subcultural variations. Few studies have examined the meaning and style of grandparenthood as perceived by the grandparent. In one study of seventy middle-class grandparents, Neugarten and Weinstein (1964) found that almost 30 percent felt remote from their grandchildren, and that the role had little or no influence on their lives. Of those who felt the role had some meaning, most said that it involved the continuity of the family name and biological renewal, or renewed feelings of youth and vigor. A second commonly expressed statement was that the role provided emotional fulfillment. Surprisingly, a higher percentage of grandfathers than grandmothers reported this feeling.

In another part of this early study, Neugarten and Weinstein identified five styles of grandparenting, listed in order of prevalence: (1) a formal style, wherein there is no interference with child rearing; (2) a fun-seeking style, wherein the grandparents serve as playful companions during leisure time; (3) a distant-figure style, wherein they have little influence on the grandchildren and primarily serve a symbolic, ritualistic function during family celebrations; (4) a parent-surrogate style that involves direct assistance with child care, especially by grandmothers; and (5) a reservoir-of-family-wisdom style, wherein family history, knowledge, and skills are passed on, especially by grandfathers.

As in any typology, elements of the various styles may be found within one individual. The style that is adopted may vary with the age of the grandparent. For example, the authors found that the formal style was more prevalent among those over 65, and that the fun-seeking style was more commonly reported by those under 65. Whether these differences in style can be attributed to cohort effects or to aging effects remains to be determined by longitudinal or cohort analysis. However, it does seem that the saliency of the role may decline as both the grandchild and the grandparent age. Again, it is not clear whether this saliency decreases because as the grandparents age they are less able to interact, or whether it is because the grandchildren, as they mature, become more independent of their family ties and increase their involvement in nonfamilial relationships.

Another major study of grandparenting style was undertaken by Wood and Robertson (1976) and Robertson (1977). They saw the role as having a social or normative dimension that meets the needs of society, and a personal dimension that meets the needs of the individual. Based on interviews with 125 grandmothers and 132 grandfathers from a working-class sample, they developed a fourfold typology of role meaning by cross-classifying the high and low responses on the social and personal dimensions. The four styles included: (1) the 'apportioned' type, who attached high meaning to both the social and the personal roles in their own situations; (2) the 'symbolic' type, who had low personal involvement in the role but who attached high importance to the role in society generally; (3) the 'remote' type, who perceived little meaning in the role personally or from a societal perspective; and (4) the 'individualized' type, who did not perceive the role to have much meaning in society, but for whom the role held a high degree of personal significance.

Not surprisingly, when control variables were introduced, some social characteristics were common to each type. First, there were no significant sex differences, reinforcing the earlier statement that the role is not significantly differentiated by gender. However, those who were high in personal meaning (the 'apportioned' and 'individualized') were generally older and less well educated, were less likely to be employed, and interacted more frequently with their grandchildren. Those in the 'remote' category (low on both dimensions) had the lowest level of interaction with grandchildren. Finally, those in the 'symbolic' category (low on the personal dimension and high on the normative dimension) were generally younger and more involved in community rather than family matters.

Most recently, Kivnick (1982) noted that the meaning of grandparenthood evolves from people's own experience as grandchildren, their experience as parents, and ultimately their own experience in the role of grandparents. These resulted in a multidimensional view of the meaning of grandparenthood that included five elements: (1) grandparenthood is central to the lifestyle of the grandparent; (2) grandparenthood means being a valued elder and serving as a resource center; (3) grandparenthood assures the immortality of the family name; (4) grandparenthood provides an opportunity to spoil and indulge grandchildren; and (5) grandparenthood provides an opportunity to become reinvolved with one's own history and that of the family.

Although there appear to be some distinct styles of grandparenting, it is not clear whether the style adopted by a given individual is related to the lifestyle of the grandparent that was present before the third generation is born, whether it is influenced by the mediation style of the parents, or whether it evolves and changes through interaction with one or more specific grandchildren. Since grandparents sometimes have a preferred grandchild, it may be that the meaning and style adopted varies according to the partners involved in a specific grandchild-grandparent relationship.

In summary, most children in North America have at least one living grandparent with whom they have some degree of interaction. From the perspective of the grandparent, the role has different meanings, and different styles of involvement can be adopted. At present, especially for middle-aged grandparents, the role is not highly salient. It does seem to be more salient for the working class, for widows, for those who are less educated, for those who are older, for those who are unemployed or retired, and for those who are not involved in community affairs. Those who fall into the above categories find the extended family to be a major source of interest and social interaction, and are more likely to seek active involvement in legitimate familial roles such as grandparenting, especially if their own children encourage this involvement.

Role Transitions and Status Passages Within the Family

Introduction

In contrast to role change, which involves a change in role requirements and expectations with no change in status, (for example, the behavioral expectations for a son or daughter at different stages in the life cycle), role transitions occur when status is gained or lost (by marriage, parenthood, retirement, widowhood, divorce) (George, 1980:6–7). For some, the process of role transition and status passage is voluntary, expected, and can be planned for as part of the developmental process of aging (in the case of marriage, parenthood, or remarriage). Adjustment to the transition and to the new status is relatively satisfactory. Other transitions may represent a discontinuous and traumatic event (for example, widowhood, retirement, an empty nest). As a result, a crisis can occur suddenly, and there may be little opportunity or willingness to be socialized for the new status. This situation can be stressful and can result in an inadequate transition and an uncertain identity in the acquired status.

In order to explain the reaction and adjustment to role transitions in later life, the model outlined earlier in figure 7.1 has been developed and supported by presenting research evidence concerning such role transitions as retirement, the empty nest, grandparenthood, widowhood, remarriage, and residential relocation (George, 1980). This model indicates that with the onset of the role transition, the individual must adjust to new patterns of social interaction and to a change in identity. Some may perceive the transition as stressful; if so, their response and subsequent degree of adjustment will be influenced by their coping resources, personal skills, social status variables, and socialization experiences. These same factors can serve a preventive function by inhibiting the onset of stressful responses to the role exit or role entrance. The following subsections will consider the impact of family-based transitions and status passages.[20]

The Empty Nest

With the departure of the last child from the home, child rearing is completed and the parents are said to live in an 'empty nest.' Early in the century, this situation usually did not occur until the parents were in their late 50s or early 60s. Increasingly, however, this has become a middle-aged phenomenon, because of earlier marriages and earlier completion of childbearing owing to more closely spaced births and fewer children. Furthermore, with increased longevity, married couples can expect to live in this empty-nest state for a much longer time than did their parents (Glick, 1977).[21]

In recent years, problems associated with the empty-nest syndrome have been described by the media and, to a lesser extent, by social scientists. This interest has arisen because of apparently conflicting patterns of adjustment, especially for mothers. While the transition represents a release from the many domestic chores associated with child rearing and a reduction in economic and parental responsibility, it also represents a change in lifestyle that can be either satisfying or traumatic. For example, it has been hypothesized that the transition represents a loss of the 'mothering' role. It is argued that women become depressed and disenchanted because their major source of responsibility and satisfaction is no longer available. In contrast, the transition also represents more freedom to pursue new roles outside the home, perhaps full- or part-time employment, volunteer work, a hobby, or school. Harkins (1978) found more positive psychological well-being among empty-nest mothers than among mothers who had children at home.

Similarly, the departure of children can improve the quality of the marriage because the couple have more time to focus on their leisure interests and on each other rather than on the children (Lowenthal et al., 1975). Conversely, the empty-nest state also has the potential to magnify existing dissatisfactions. While the transition may not be the direct cause of a divorce (Atchley and Miller, 1980), it may provide the opportunity to resolve long-standing differences. Divorce may now be perceived as a realistic alternative to a stressful marriage since it is no longer necessary to 'stay together for the sake of the children.' Today, many of these post-empty-nest separations or divorces, especially within the middle class, are initiated by women who seek a higher-quality relationship, or who wish to have more freedom from domestic responsibilities to pursue their own occupational lifestyle. From the perspective of the husband, role strain and dissatisfaction may result if the wife obtains full-time employment and neglects what are perceived to be her traditional domestic responsibilities. The marriage may also be disrupted by the individual growth or change in one partner that has evolved throughout the middle years. In that case, the empty nest may represent an appropriate opportunity to resolve these differences by divorce.

Unfortunately, little research has been completed concerning adjustment to the empty-nest transition. The transition is not usually a traumatic experience, except for those women whose entire focus in life has centered on child rearing, often at the expense of developing personal interests and skills. This is more likely to be the case in lower-class families, where the mother's identity is closely linked to domestic responsibilities, and perhaps among those women who were divorced early in the marriage and were solely responsible for child rearing. But for most, the transition is not traumatic, although it draws symbolic attention to the personal aging process.

The empty nest is an expected event (Neugarten and Datan, 1974). It is generally known when the transition will occur, and it is normatively expected that children will establish their own identities and nuclear families. For the parents, the transition is gradual since not all children leave home at the same time. Anticipatory socialization for the transition occurs during childhood, when children spend a month at camp; later, it occurs when children leave home to attend college, perhaps only returning for weekends or vacations.

In many cases the departure of the last child coincides with a new status being acquired by the child through marriage or a first job, or by one or both of the parents taking a new job or moving to a new location. When their children leave home, parents not only have more freedom, but also acquire a new resource in adult children (and eventually grandchildren). In fact, a survey of parents of college students found that parents see child launching as a time when a more equal and reciprocal role relationship is established with their children (Hagestad and Snow, 1977). These parents reported that they felt they had gained a resource, since their children could now give rather than take, especially if the children were daughters.

In summary, although it is frequently assumed to be a traumatic role transition, the onset of the empty-nest stage in life is generally not disruptive to the individual or to the married couple. However, for a mother whose identity is almost exclusively based on her children, and for some married couples with a long-standing underlying strain between them, the transition may create adjustment problems and lead to other changes. Although the transition to the empty-nest stage has been occurring earlier in the life cycle in North America, at least in middle- and upper-class families, it may be delayed in the near future because of a changing economy. With high mortgage rates and housing shortages, more adult children may remain in the 'nest,' at least until marriage. Interestingly, the empty-nest phenomenon is not experienced or discussed to the same extent outside North America. In many countries, it is common for children, even if they are married with children of their own, to live in the parents' household, or to live in a small unit attached to the parent's home.

Retirement

The onset of retirement has an influence not only on the individual, but also on family and married life. To date, this phenomenon has been considered almost exclusively as a male transition point wherein the husband experiences a major role loss and enters the wife's domain on a full-time basis. This transition may result in the loss of status for the spouse and a possible reduction in the standard of living for the couple because of a decline in income. Retirement brings about the possibility of a merging of household responsibilities and a change in sex-role differentiation with respect to these responsibilities. This represents a potential source of conflict, but few empirical studies have examined this question.

In general, it has been found that the onset of retirement results in an increase in marital satisfaction, especially on the part of the husband; an opportunity to play more fully the role of grandparent; and a freedom to adopt a new lifestyle, possibly one that includes a summer and a winter residence. Most research on this role transition has focused on the process, and on the effect on the individual (primarily the male) and on society from a psychological and economic perspective (see chapter 10). The influence of the transition on the marital dyad and on the extended family has seldom been studied.

Widowhood

Introduction.   Although widowhood is experienced at some point by one member of every still-married couple, the role exit or role loss is most likely to be experienced by women, and particularly by women over 60. For example, in North America, among older women the ratio of widows to widowers is approximately 5:1, or approximately 12 percent of the adult female population in the United States. As a result, most studies of this role transition have focused on older women (Lopata, 1970, 1973, 1979; Morgan, 1979; Harvey and Bahr, 1980; Matthews, 1980; Anderson, 1981). Much less is known about the phenomenon from the perspective of widowers at any age (Berardo, 1970; Kohn and Kohn, 1979; Vinick, 1981), or from that of young and middle-aged widows (Glick et al., 1974).[22]

Much of the early research focused on the immediate problems and behavior associated with the status of widowhood. This status has seldom been viewed as a process that requires short- and long-term personal adjustments and modifications in lifestyle. As a result, cross-sectional retrospective studies have been more common than longitudinal studies. Moreover, few studies controlled for such possible confounding factors as social class, racial or ethnic background, rural versus urban residence, or age at widowhood. Finally, most studies have focused on the personal level of analysis rather than on the societal level.

At the personal level, the major topics of interest have been the use of personal coping skills associated with the initial grief; the pattern and degree of adjustment as determined by morale or life satisfaction; the amount of social participation within the family and community; and the loss of, or change in, self-concept and identity. At the societal or social structural level, the major interests have centered on the normative roles of widows in various cultures; the economic and employment status of widows and widowers; the availability and reaction of family and community support groups; the living arrangements and location of widows; the process of anticipatory socialization for widowhood; and variations in adjustment patterns and problems by sex, class, age, and place of residence.

The following subsections examine the transition to widowhood by focusing on the process and problems of adjustment from the dual perspective of the individual and society. This approach is taken because there is a great deal of interaction between the two levels. Greater emphasis is placed on long-term adjustment than on the short-term grief management and mourning stage (Glick et al., 1974; Ball, 1976–77). Unless otherwise noted, the information presented pertains to older widows, with exceptions for widowers and younger widows being noted where research evidence is available.

The initial process of adjustment.   For most people, the onset of widowhood occurs suddenly and unexpectedly. There is little opportunity for anticipatory socialization for the transition from spouse to widow. It is only in situations where the deceased spouse was very old, or had been ill for a period of time, that any degree of direct anticipatory socialization occurs. Even here, the process tends to relate to pragmatic matters such as financial and household management, living on a reduced income, and declining social interaction as a couple with friends and relatives. The grief is not diminished, but the process may be of shorter duration and the long-term adjustment may be more satisfactory (George, 1980).

Some degree of indirect anticipatory socialization or anticipatory grief may occur if the widow is older and is among the last of her social peers to experience widowhood. In this situation, she will have had face-to-face interaction with role models whom she may have assisted through the transition. In addition, unlike those who are among the first in a friendship group to be widowed, she will have an established peer group or social network of widows who can provide emotional and social support.

For young widows, this lack of opportunity for anticipatory socialization and the unavailability of a network of widows, plus the suddenness of the transition, makes the initial adjustment more traumatic. The adjustment process is often compounded by the responsibilities of being a single parent with dependent children, by the lack of adult children to turn to for support, and by the need to meet mortgage payments and daily living costs for the family. As a result, the process of adjustment is often longer and more difficult, and involves a pattern different from that for older widows.

After a time, the younger widow may no longer be perceived as a 'widow,' but rather as a single person who has remarriage and career opportunities not available to the older widow. Once she is perceived as a 'single,' previous friendships with married couples may cease, either because of a change in lifestyle by the young widow, or because married female friends may perceive her as a threat to their own marriages. In the long term, many women who are widowed before 55 remarry, and the likelihood increases the earlier they are widowed. However, this pattern may occur less in the future now that it has become more socially acceptable to be single throughout the adult years. Young widows may opt for some combination of a career, single parenthood, or cohabitation, rather than for the more traditional married lifestyle.

For widows of any age, initial adjustment can often last until after the first 'anniversary reaction' (Bornstein and Clayton, 1972). This period is often stressful, and is characterized by varying individual differences in level and duration of shock, disbelief, numbness, yearning, questioning, depression, anger, and guilt. Physiological problems such as insomnia, irritability, and weight loss may occur (George, 1980:89–90; Lopata, 1980:103–5), and the widowed person is susceptible to deteriorating health in the first few years after a spouse's death (Vachon, 1979).

It is during this mourning stage that the widow needs the greatest emotional support. In some cultures there are rituals and beliefs related to the process of adaptation. These range from formal periods of mourning and ritualistic practices, including the wearing of mourning clothes, to requirements concerning dependent living arrangements with relatives or other widows, to the extreme rituals of self-sacrifice. In contrast, in modern societies even the wearing of traditional mourning clothes is no longer encouraged, and the suddenly independent widow is soon left to her own social support network. This potential family and community support system can provide varying degrees and types of emotional, social, service, and economic support in both the short and the long term (Lopata, 1979; Anderson, 1981).

As Silverman (1972) and Lopata (1978) have noted, there are few formalized transition rituals or community resources in modern societies to assist the widow in adapting to a new status identity and to a 'single' lifestyle. This problem is compounded by the geographic dispersion of children who sooner or later must return to their own families and careers, thereby physically abandoning the recently bereaved parent. For this reason, voluntary, formalized, 'widow-to-widow' programs (Silverman, 1972) have been established. These programs provide emotional support from a role model who has experienced and survived the transition.

The volunteer service worker can also serve as a source of advice on financial and legal issues, and can be of assistance in interpreting societal expectations with respect to the mourning period, subsequent social interaction, and remarriage. It is for this reason, particularly, that it is important to match the recently widowed person with an individual similar in age, class, parental status, and economic status. The volunteer must understand the social situation and lifestyle of the new widow and should be a credible role model. Not surprisingly, these programs seldom include widowers. This is because there is a smaller cohort available to provide assistance, because men are more likely to assert independence and to be reluctant to share emotional experiences with a confidant, and because men usually do not need assistance in coping with financial and legal matters resulting from the death of a spouse.

The long-term process of adjustment.   Once the immediate and acute period of grief and mourning begins to subside, the process of reconstructing a new identity and lifestyle must begin. Just as the adjustment to living with a partner occurs early in marriage, so too must resocialization occur to the new status of being a widow or widower. This process of resocialization operates on two interacting levels, and involves personal changes as well as changes in social roles and participation.

On the personal level, the recently widowed person must learn to cope with loneliness, with no longer having someone to care for, and with the loss of companionship, especially at mealtimes and at times when ideas, thoughts, or feelings need to be shared. If the marriage was not a satisfactory experience, if the individual has been able to cope with or enjoy being alone, or if the nursing of a disabled spouse was viewed as a burden, then relief rather than loneliness may be the reaction (Fengler and Goodrich, 1979). Some widows must learn to cope with a change in identity from one closely linked to the husband's status and occupation to one of single independence. This sudden, enforced independence can be traumatic if the widow has been highly or totally dependent on the spouse for decision making in financial and social matters, or if she does not have a meaningful parental or occupational role. This identity crisis is less likely to occur for widowers, unless widowhood occurs at about the same time as retirement. In that case, the widower, or widow, experiences a loss of the occupational role and the major companion role at the same time (Berardo, 1970).

These psychological adjustments can be more difficult and traumatic if the older widow is placed in a vulnerable economic situation because the husband's pension benefits are inadequate for her survival, or because she is unemployable or underemployed. In one of the few longitudinal studies of older widows (58 or 59 years of age when first interviewed), Thompson (1980) concluded that the economic status of widows is directly related to employment status. Those widows who do not have a high-school education or who have had little work experience are unable to obtain work when it is necessary, or they remain unemployed for a long time, or they accept low-paying positions with little potential for advancement.

For those who have been employed during middle age, the employment and economic status at widowhood is influenced by level of education and by the amount of time and experience in the labor force. Even if they are unemployed when widowhood occurs, those with previous experience in the labor force are more likely to be employable, and at a higher level, should they need or desire to work after the death of the spouse. Atchley (1975) argued that widows experience more difficulty than widowers because lack of money decreases their mobility; this in turn results in low levels of social participation, which can cause psychological problems related to loneliness and anxiety.

The recently widowed may also experience real or imagined physical and mental health problems. Loneliness, in combination with these types of health problems, often results in death by illness and suicide within two years of the death of a spouse. Among the very old, the physical health problems may be the natural result of physiological aging, although the onset may be hastened by caring for a dying spouse (Marshall, 1980:147–51) and by a change in lifestyle initiated by widowhood. Inadequate nutrition, increased alcohol consumption, and deteriorating sanitary conditions in the home may contribute to declining health. These conditions seem to occur more frequently among widowers, perhaps because they are forced to play domestic roles in which they have little experience or interest. This need for assistance with household tasks, along with greater opportunities for men to marry younger women, may be a factor in the higher remarriage rates of older widowers. Older widows who survive the first few years of widowhood can expect to live much longer than earlier cohorts of widows. Widows also generally live longer in this situation than widowers, since widowhood for males generally occurs much later in the life cycle.

Closely linked to increased loneliness and declining health is a decrease in morale or life satisfaction that is often reported by widows and widowers (Berardo, 1970; Morgan, 1976; Kohn and Kohn, 1979). Few of these studies, however, have controlled for the possible influence of age, social class, length of widowhood, economic status, and health. Thus, it may not be the transition to widowhood per se that results in lower levels of reported morale and well-being, but rather the social, health, and economic changes that result from the unexpected transition. These changes are more likely for women in the middle and lower class who, compared to men, experience greater economic difficulties. They are also generally older and in poorer health than their male peers. While most widows and widowers eventually adjust to the personal and psychological problems associated with widowhood, the duration and pattern of adjustment may vary across social groups.

The widowed person must also make decisions concerning where and how to live as a single adult, and whether to seek employment or not. The decision to work is usually based on economic necessity, age at widowhood, employment status at widowhood, and the psychological need for a new focus in life and a new social network. With marginal increases in social security and private pension benefits, the economic status of the older widow is improving somewhat, at least for those in the middle and upper classes. Within younger cohorts, where the concept of careers for women is more socially acceptable, the likelihood of a younger widow continuing employment or returning to the labor force is much greater than it was in the past.

Most older widows live alone in their own homes. Approximately 50 percent of the older widows in Lopata's study (1973:75–76) reported that they preferred to live alone. In this way they avoided potential conflict situations with children. It seems that only the very poor, the very old, the poorly educated, and those with strong ethnic and cultural ties are likely to share a household with a relative in either an equal or a dependent relationship.

At the social structural level of analysis, adjustment to widowhood involves role changes, changing patterns of interaction with friends and relatives, and striving to meet societal norms concerning widowhood. The result of this process is a reconstructed social life as a single person, including modifications to lifestyle and friendship networks.

The transition to widowhood also involves role changes that may occur to varying degrees (Gibbs, 1978; Lopata, 1980:112–14). The major change is the loss of the role of spouse, and the assumption by the widow of the role of head of the household with full responsibility for home maintenance and financial obligations. The widow generally maintains the same degree of role involvement in the role of mother, although it may increase if the children are young and she is a single parent, or if she is older and moves in with one of her children. For many widows, role conflict may arise out of the desire to demonstrate that they are coping as independent adults. Yet, internally they need the emotional and social support of a companion. The widow or widower often experiences the loss of friends who continue to socialize as 'couples.' In fact, widows often report feeling like a 'fifth wheel' at social events (Gibbs, 1978:24).

While returning to work represents one option for widows, increased involvement in voluntary associations may also compensate for the loss of the role of spouse[23] This is especially likely to occur where the widow was at least minimally involved in voluntary organizations before the transition. However, where that involvement was primarily related to the husband's membership or activity, widowhood may lead to a decreased role involvement.

A member of the opposite sex may become a partner for some social events, although this occurs more often for widowers than for widows. Social norms concerning the initiation of heterosexual relationships are more restrictive for women, since they are often expected to play the role of grieving widow for a longer period of time. This type of relationship may pose some difficulties at family events, since children and siblings may be critical and disapproving. The decision to resume dating, and the possibility of cohabitation or remarriage, may create anxiety for the widowed person who may desire such a relationship, but who may lack the social skills and attitudes that facilitate such events. Most studies (Lopata, 1970) have found that widows report little desire to remarry. They do not wish to give up their independence, especially if it means playing the role of housekeeper and eventually nurse. In addition, they may lose the economic support provided by the pension of the first spouse and remarriage may jeopardize social and emotional support from children. Finally, they may reject remarriage simply because their experiences during the first marriage were such that they have no desire to repeat them.

If social interaction outside the extended family decreases, the widowed person may experience some degree of social isolation. This social isolation is less pronounced among those with sufficient economic and health resources, among the employed or employable, among those with higher levels of education, and among those living in smaller towns (Arling, 1976). In contrast, elderly widows in rural areas may be more lonely and isolated because their children may have moved from the region. In addition, they are often geographically isolated from health, recreation (for example, senior-citizen centers), and social services (Kivett, 1978). For the rural widow, lack of public transportation and physical distance from services create physical barriers to a social reconstruction of the elderly widow's lifestyle. Although not yet supported by research, it has been suggested that the hypothesized isolation of the rural widow may be offset by higher quality relationships with neighbors.

Summary.   While the initial process of adjustment is difficult for all recently widowed persons, the majority do adjust, although there are many possible patterns of adaptation and lifestyles. While the status of widowhood per se may not be traumatic for most in the long term, the indirect effects of losing a spouse may be traumatic. Women may lose financial security, and men are apt to lose social services and social support. Clearly, the study of widowhood must be analyzed by age and sex since there are many differences in the process between and among widows and widowers. For example, males are generally older and in poorer health, yet they often have better financial resources and greater opportunities to remarry if they wish. Widowers are more likely to be isolated from, or have fewer close emotional ties with their families; widows become closer to their children, especially daughters. They may also, in the later years, form a new household with a sister, who also may be widowed. This shared living arrangement may provide economic, social, and emotional support for the widowed siblings late in life. Another difference between widows and widowers is that widows often have an available peer group of other widows who can provide social and emotional support. In contrast, widowers do not have nearly as large a peer group, and men are generally less willing to relate to a male confidant. With respect to younger widows and widowers, there are fewer sex differences, although it is often easier and more acceptable for the young widower to remarry. Regardless of age, it is likely that sex differences will narrow in the future since older women will have higher levels of education, greater experience in the labor force throughout marriage, more independent coping skills, greater financial knowledge and resources, and more liberal norms concerning marriage, remarriage, and cohabitation. At the same time, men may now be taking more responsibility for household tasks during marriage, especially when both partners have careers. As widowers, they may be less likely to remarry to acquire domestic assistance.

Remarriage in the Later Years

For the older widow, widower, or divorcee, a number of living arrangements are possible. These include living alone, with adult children, with another relative, in a communal or congregate unit,[24] cohabitation in a heterosexual or homosexual relationship, or remarriage. While most tend to live alone, especially women, an increasing number remarry. Those most likely to remarry are whites rather than nonwhites, the divorced rather than the widowed, and men rather than women.[25] These patterns are partially accounted for by higher levels of income and health among whites, by a greater number of eligible women, and by the lesser stigma attached to remarriage among men and the divorced. The time until remarriage is half as short for men (1.7 years) as it is for women (3.5 years), and is shorter for whites than for blacks (Cleveland and Gianturco, 1976).

Although those 65 years of age and older comprise only about 1 percent of all brides and 2 percent of all grooms (Glick, 1979), over 35,000 'older' marriages take place each year in the United States. Almost 80 percent of these later life marriages involve the remarriage of a widow to a widower (Treas and Van Hilst, 1976). Remarriage probabilities decrease rapidly for a widow after 35 years of age, and only about 5 percent of those widowed after age 55 ever remarry (Cleveland and Gianturco, 1976). This occurs because men tend to remarry younger women, and because the number of eligible widowed, divorced, or never-married men of about the same age declines rapidly with age.

Given the possibility of remarriage in the later years, why does it happen, how does it happen, and how successful is the transition from widowhood or being divorced to a new marital relationship? First, a high percentage of these 'autumn loves' (Treas and Van Hilst, 1976) are perceived as successful by both partners (McKain, 1972; Vinick, 1978). The rate of success and satisfactory adjustment is closely linked to the motivation to remarry, to the process whereby the relationship evolves into marriage, and to the support of adult children and friends.

Most older brides and some older grooms report that they never had any intention or desire to remarry. For men, the transition often occurs because they have difficulty adjusting to widowhood and remarriage appears to be a viable alternative. Men often have less involvement in family and friendship roles, and they seek companionship. They are often faced with the loss of both the work and spouse roles at about the same time, and therefore tend to seek emotional support. In addition, older widowers often have limited experience with and little interest in domestic responsibilities, and may remarry in order to have someone care for them. For older widows, the need for companionship and intimacy, especially if their adult children are not close, may be a motivating factor. Cohabitation rather than marriage may result if there is a financial penalty[26] for remarriage, or if adult children either refuse to sanction or actively discourage a marriage.[27]

Although economic, social, legal, and demographic factors may discourage or prevent remarriage among older persons, a number of other factors increase the probability and the success rate of remarriage (Stryckman, 1981). First, neither adult children nor aging parents are likely to encourage the entrance of the widowed parent into the home of one of the children. Yet, the older person needs daily companionship in a family unit, and in many cases sexual intimacy. Therefore, remarriage becomes a socially acceptable and viable alternative to living alone, especially for widowers who can marry younger women and who have the economic resources and health to create a new household. Research indicates that partners in a remarriage were either introduced by a mutual friend or relative, or knew each other when one or both were previously married. In some cases, retirement communities and adult recreation centers have served as the social context for the initiation of a new relationship that leads to remarriage.

Successful remarriage in the later years seems to be related to six general conditions (McKain, 1972): (1) both partners have known each other for many years prior to widowhood; (2) friends and relatives approve of the marriage (if not initially, then eventually when the relationship is seen to be successful and in everyone's interest);[27] (3) both partners have previously adjusted well to the empty nest, retirement, and widowhood; (4) the remarried couple move into a residence that neither had lived in prior to the marriage, thereby removing old memories and possible conflict as to who is the head of the household; (5) they have an adequate income and common agreement on the inheritance to be left to children; and (6) the partners have a number of similar interests and values, and their major focus is on the marriage rather than on raising children or being responsible for an adult child.

In summary, while little research has been concerned with the characteristics or processes associated with remarriage in the later years, this transition represents an increasingly viable alternative for older persons. At present it is more likely that men will exercise this option, but if the financial penalty of lost pensions is reduced or removed, it may become equally attractive to women. In contrast, remarriage may be less likely to occur in the future if alternative models of cohabitation evolve because of changing values and norms. For example, living together in a heterosexual relationship may become as normative in the later years as it is during young adulthood. For those who do remarry the success rate appears to be high and to fulfill a need for a family relationship, especially where older persons are not invited to move into the home of an adult child. Furthermore, contrary to popular opinion, there appears to be little alienation or intergenerational family conflict when a widowed or divorced older parent remarries. In fact, remarriage may relieve the adult child of the burden of daily care and companionship for the elderly parent (Vinick, 1980).

The Never-Married and the Divorced in Later Life

Those older persons[28] who have never married (approximately 5 to 10 percent of the adult population in North America) eventually lose most familial ties unless a close relationship is established with a sibling. For these individuals, family relationships in the later years tend to be minimal or nonexistent. A frequent concern raised by gerontologists is the extent to which the never-married (compared to widows) report loneliness and dissatisfaction in the later years. It is assumed that they are or become socially isolated because they lack family ties. Ward (1979), in a study of the never-married in later life, reported that they are not as happy as those who are married, but are slightly happier than the widowed or divorced.

The never-married do not experience the trauma and grief of widowhood (Gubrium, 1975), but neither do they have access to extended family networks for social, emotional, or economic support in the later years. Having lived alone for most of their adult life, they are able to cope with independent living more successfully, at least until a loss of health or income reduces their independence. It is at this stage that lack of access to familial networks may generate dissatisfaction and lead to greater dependence on social service agencies. Clearly, more information is needed concerning this segment of the older population, especially since their numbers may increase in the future. In the past, the never-married were likely to have never been involved in a heterosexual relationship; future cohorts of the never-married may include both those who did and did not engage in marriage-like relationships (cohabitation) with one or more partners.

The recently divorced is another category of older persons that has grown in number. As noted earlier, the empty nest and retirement represent a transition that may provide an opportunity to dissolve an unsatisfactory marriage. At present, approximately 1 percent of those over 65 in North America become divorced, while between 10 and 13 percent of those over 65 have experienced an earlier divorce (Uhlenberg and Myers, 1981). The percentage of elderly people who have been divorced at least once may increase in the future for the following reasons (Uhlenberg and Myers, 1981): (1) the trend toward higher divorce rates after age 65 will continue; (2) higher divorce rates in the early and middle years will continue, and there is a likelihood that subsequent remarriages will end in divorce; (3) future cohorts are more likely to view divorce as a viable and socially acceptable solution to an unhappy marriage; (4) women will have greater financial independence with their own pensions, savings, and equity; and (5) increased longevity will decrease the probability that a marriage will be terminated by the death of one spouse, and divorce may be seen as a viable alternative to an unhappy marriage, even after the age of 60.

Although the divorce rate may increase for the elderly, it will likely always be less than that for younger adults. Nevertheless, a divorce in later life may have social or economic implications for the elderly in the future (Chiriboga, 1982). For men, this role transition can be especially traumatic if they also lose the work role at about the same time. Divorced women over 65 experience financial hardship because they lose pension benefits paid to the former spouse. In addition, they experience the social stigma associated with divorce among their age cohort. Although both members of the formerly married couple experience a dramatic change in their relationships with children and grandchildren, women seem to be more affected because of their greater involvement in kinship relationships. Unfortunately, relatively little is known at present about the impact of later-life divorce on family dynamics.

Similarly, relatively little is known about the impact on the extended family when an adult child is divorced. That is, what impact does a divorce have on the quantity and quality of the relationships between parents and adult children, and between grandparents and grandchildren? Do these earlier life events influence the type, amount, and quality of support an older person can expect from a divorced versus a married child? Do the elderly experience decreased satisfaction in later life because they have little or no access to grandchildren who may live with the former son- or daughter-in-law?

The answers to these questions are not available, but the minimal evidence suggests that divorced sons and daughters may be less able to support aging parents because of personal financial burdens or time commitments to a new relationship and family. Older mothers, particularly, experience stress when a child divorces (Johnson, 1981), and some grandparents lose contact with their grandchildren, especially paternal grandparents (Ahrons and Bowman, 1981; Fisher, 1981; Johnson, 1981; Sprey and Matthews, 1981; Wilson and DeShane, 1982).[29] A further source of strain may arise when members of the oldest generation are required to play the role of grandparent for a stepgrandchild when a son or daughter remarries. In summary, little evidence is available concerning how the divorce of an adult child affects older parents. The preliminary evidence, however, suggests that the divorce of a child is often a traumatic experience for the older mother or grandmother, and therefore merits further research.

Summary and Conclusions

In this chapter the literature pertaining to the dynamics of aging within the context of the extended family has been reviewed. The first section presented some of the structural, stratification, and personal factors that influence intragenerational and intergenerational relations. Some of the theoretical perspectives that have been used to study intergenerational lineage relations were briefly outlined. The second section focused on intragenerational family relations by examining marital satisfaction across the life cycle and sibling interaction in the later years. In the third section, which was concerned with intergenerational relations in the later years, the relationships between parents and adult children and between grandparents and grandchildren were reviewed from the perspective of both partners in each intergenerational relationship. Finally, the last section reviewed the reaction and adjustment of the individual to personal role transitions within the family context (such as the empty nest, retirement, widowhood, divorce, and remarriage), along with the impact of an adult child's divorce on parent-child and grandparent-grandchild role relationships.

Based on the literature reviewed in this chapter, it can be concluded that:

1. Kinship interactions vary in quantity and quality throughout the life cycle.
2. Child launching and grandparenting were once considered as events unique to the later years of life. Increasingly, however, at least in modernized societies, these events have become middle-aged phenomena.
3. Research indicates that many of those over 65 live within a one-hour drive of at least one adult child. This would seem to refute somewhat the myth of the lonely, alienated elderly person.
4. Residential propinquity influences the type and quality of interaction between generations within the extended family.
5. With increasing labor-force participation by middle-aged and older women, fewer daughters or daughters-in-law provide daily care and services for the eldest members of the extended family.
6. The frequency and quality of interaction tends to be stronger between mothers and daughters than between sons and parents.
7. Sons who provide assistance to older parents are more likely to provide financial assistance than personal care.
8. Intergenerational lineage relationships and care are often stronger and more frequent among members of the working class, and within ethnic and racial groups.
9. Much of the research on the family and aging has been descriptive and atheoretical. Hence, many of the observed patterns of behavior are not well understood.
10. Research concerning marital satisfaction across the life cycle suggests that the relationship may be curvilinear or negatively linear with advancing age. However, based primarily on cross-sectional evidence, most studies suggest that the relationship is curvilinear, with the highest point occurring during the honeymoon stage. Thereafter, there is a decline in satisfaction until a low point is reached. This low point may occur when children are adolescents, when the last child leaves home, or at the time of retirement. After this low point, there appears to be an increase in satisfaction into the later years.
11. Interaction between parents and adult children varies in frequency, type, and quality across the life cycle.
12. Contrary to popular myths, the relationship between generations within families is not characterized by conflict, nor are most of the elderly abandoned by or alienated from their family.
13. The form and frequency of communication and assistance between adult children and aging parents is influenced by such factors as residential propinquity, social class, sex of the child, race, ethnicity, age and health of the two generations, and the degree of filial responsibility felt by the children.
14. Most research has focused on the type and frequency of interaction between aging parents and adult children. Quantity rather than quality has been the central concern.

15. Studies of the quality of the relationship between parents and adult children have indicated that the relationship is strongly influenced by the health, economic, and housing status of the elderly parent, by the attitudes of the aging parent to their personal aging experience, and by the competing interests and demands of the adult children.

16. Over 90 percent of all children in North America have at age 10 at least one living grandparent.

17. Children who interact with grandparents have fewer prejudices about the elderly and about growing old.

18. The frequency of interaction between grandchildren and grandparents is normally high during childhood. It often decreases during adolescence and increases again during early adulthood.

19. The role of grandparent is not a highly salient role for most, at least until the later years of life. The role tends to be more meaningful for members of the working class, for widows, for those who are less educated, for those who are retired or unemployed, and for those not involved in voluntary associations or community affairs.

20. The transition to the empty-nest stage is not a traumatic experience for most parents, although it may be for women whose major interest in life has been child rearing.

21. In North America, the ratio of widows to widowers is approximately five to one. Whereas the initial stage of adjustment to this new status is often difficult, most adjust satisfactorily, although there are many possible patterns of adjustment and lifestyles.

22. The widows who are most likely to experience financial difficulties are those who are unemployable or underemployed.

23. Men and those who have been divorced rather than widowed are most likely to remarry in the later years.

24. To date, little research has been completed concerning the changing relationships between parents and adult children and between grandparents and grandchildren when an adult child is divorced. Preliminary evidence suggests that this event affects the quality and quantity of intragenerational interaction and may be especially traumatic for the older mother or grandmother.

Notes

1. Studies of aging and the extended family from the perspective of family studies are often published in *The Family Coordinator* or *The Journal of Marriage and the Family.*

2. Some general review articles include: Streib, 1970; Troll, 1971; Berardo, 1972; Adams, 1975; Treas, 1975; Brubaker and Sneden, 1978; Lewis, 1978; Ragan, 1979; Troll, 1979; Abu-Laban, 1980; George, 1980; Atchley and Miller, 1980; Tobin and Kulys, 1980; Troll, 1980a; and, Blau, 1981; Fogel et al., 1981; and Lovas, 1982.

3. See chapter 2 for a detailed discussion of the status of the elderly in various societies.

4. Intergenerational conflict was discussed in chapter 7 and will not be discussed further here.

5. A higher percentage of the institutionalized elderly are kinless, and may, in fact, be institutionalized because they have no surviving relatives to take care of them.

6. See Decker (1980:201–8) for a brief historical overview of aging and the family in the United States from early colonial times to the twentieth century.

7. Second and subsequent marriages often involve an older man marrying a woman who may be ten to fifteen years younger than he (especially if the first marriage ended in divorce during the early and middle years).

8. For example, unsuccessful marriages are frequently terminated by separation and divorce. As a result, studies of older married couples include only those whose marriages have survived, and who are therefore likely to have maintained at least a minimal degree of harmony in the relationship.

9. Cohort and historical effects need to be controlled since particular marital values, beliefs, or mores may account for differences between marriage cohorts. For example, divorce as an alternative to an unsuccessful or unhappy marriage was not a viable option, for legal and moral reasons, to most members of your parents' and grandparents' generation.

10. Although most studies suggest the relationship is between age and marital satisfaction, it is more likely a reflection of the number of years a couple has been married and the stages in the marriage career that have been completed.

11. For example, only two-fifths of the middle-aged women in the extensive Lowenthal et al. (1975) study evaluated their spouse positively.

12. This degree of drifting depends on such factors as residential propinquity, relations with in-laws, and career or lifestyle differences.

13. Until the death of one or both parents, siblings may maintain indirect contact with each other by communicating through the parents. However, upon the death of a parent, and particularly the mother, there may be a need to increase direct communication, thereby renewing the relationship.

14. Schwartz (1979) and Miller (1981) describe adult children between 40 and 60 years of age as being members of the 'sandwich generation.' That is, they are caught between the demands of completing the launching of their own children and caring for their elderly parents, and at the same time they face personal concerns about their own future. Similarly, Cohen and Gans (1978) identified

the 'other generation gap' between parents and adult children. They suggest that a major concern in midlife is the potential inner conflict derived from relief at being free from child rearing and regret at having to accept responsibility for the care of a very old parent.

15. When parents support the children during childhood and adolescence, and when the adult children as adults later support the aging parents, 'serial reciprocity' (Sussman, 1976) occurs.

16. Peterson (1979) suggests that with the rising incidence of divorce among the middle-aged, especially if the mother wins custody of young children, the intimate relationship with parents and grandparents may dramatically increase or decrease. In fact, the divorcee may become dependent on his or her parents for emotional and financial support.

17. Streib (1972) identified five family types based on the resources available. These ranged from the 'strong and organized' family that has an abundance of all four resources to share with each other to the 'weak and disorganized' family that lacks the basic resources, and thereby usually leads to the institutionalization of the aged relative. He further suggests that family financial or health problems can lead to three responses: (1) the family has resources and uses them to rebound; (2) the family may or may not have the resources and may or may not use them, and never recovers fully; and (3) an incomplete recovery is made and new problems may compound earlier problems.

18. Perhaps because of stereotypes and the greater number of surviving women, most studies of grandparenthood have assumed that it is a female role, or have included only grandmothers (Robertson, 1977; Troll et al., 1979).

19. The pattern of functional centrality may partially explain why grandfathers are often ignored in research studies, especially where middle-class researchers and subjects are concerned. Because they are employed and may not retire until the grandchildren are adolescents, they are minimally involved, if at all, in the maternal, child rearing aspects of grandparenting. However, they may indirectly play a significant functional role by providing economic assistance. Therefore, their contribution and involvement should not be neglected.

20. See Lewis (1978) for an extensive bibliography concerning child launching (the empty nest), retirement, widowhood, and remarriage.

21. Couples with childless marriages live their entire married life in the empty-nest state.

22. Glick and associates (1974) interviewed eighty-five widows 45 years of age and younger with respect to their patterns of adjustment to widowhood. They identified five common patterns for young widows: (1) a disorganized and chaotic lifestyle; (2) an independent lifestyle with no close relationships; (3) a lifestyle centered on relatives, usually the children; (4) an intimate relationship with a man, but no remarriage; and (5) remarriage. The independent lifestyle and remarriage were the most common patterns among these young widows. In contrast, Lopata (1973), in her study of older widows, identified three patterns of adjustment. The 'traditional' pattern was more common to ethnic and racial subcultures. Those in this pattern experienced little or no change in identity or lifestyle and pursued activities similar to those that had existed before the loss of the spouse. The 'modern' type of widow experienced a brief mourning period but later built a new independent lifestyle. Finally, the 'social isolate' pattern was common among those with less education and income who did not have a great deal of social or economic support.

23. For example, because of their popularity, senior-citizen clubs often become subcultures of widows, in many cases to such a degree that widowers are reluctant to become involved.

24. Streib (1978) described the 'Share-A-Home' program in Florida wherein a 'family' of related older adults share a household by pooling their resources and skills to share tasks and gain companionship. This type of living arrangement provides an alternative to living alone, to living with another person, or to living in an institutionalized nursing home.

25. Treas and Van Hilst (1976) report that, based on United States data from 1974, the marriage rates per 1,000 males and (females) over 65 years of age is 3.4 (1.1) for the never-married, 19.4 (2.3) for the widowed, and 23.6 (6.1) for the divorced.

26. For example, until 1979 in the United States, a widow who remarried was no longer eligible for social security benefits earned by her first husband. Similarly, many private pension plans revoke benefits to a widow if she remarries. As a result of these rules, some older persons live together without remarrying to maximize their economic resources.

27. It has been argued that adult children oppose a remarriage because it suggests loss of respect and love for the deceased spouse, or because it may deprive them of their share of the estate when the surviving parent dies. On the other hand, remarriage removes some of the daily concern and responsibility of the adult child since the parent no longer lives alone. In this respect it has been considered somewhat more socially acceptable for a widower to remarry since he will be properly cared for. However, if a mother remarries it is often thought that she will become a nurse and housemaid for another man who will eventually become ill or disabled and die.

28. Those most likely to never marry are highly educated women (Ward, 1979), and those for whom psychological characteristics, physical attractiveness, or social values and opportunities were less conducive to marriage.

29. In fact, Ahrons and Bowman (1981) note that in Wisconsin, grandparents have the right to petition the court for visitation rights. According to Wilson and DeShane (1982), grandparents may be awarded visitation rights, or even adoption rights, if it is in the best interest of the child to do so, or if the grandparents contribute to the financial support of the child.

References

Abu-Laban, S. 'The Family Life of Older Canadians,' pp. 125–34 in V. Marshall (ed.). *Aging in Canada: Social Perspectives.* Don Mills: Fitzhenry and Whiteside, 1980.

Adams, B. 'Aging and the Family in the United States,' pp. 315–34 in B. Adams (ed.). *The Family: A Sociological Interpretation.* 2nd edition. Chicago: Rand McNally, 1975.

Ahrons, C. and M. Bowman. 'Changes in Family Relationships Following Divorce of Adult Child: Grandmother's Perceptions,' in E. Fisher (ed.). *Impact of Divorce on the Extended Family.* New York: Haworth Press, 1981.

Alpert, J. and M. Richardson. 'Parenting,' pp. 441–54 in L. Poon (ed.). *Aging in the 1980s.* Washington, D.C.: American Psychological Association, 1980.

Anderson, T. 'Widowhood as a Life Transition: Its Impact on Kinship Ties,' paper resented at the annual meeting of the Midwest Sociological Society, Minneapolis, April 1981.

Arling, G. 'Resistance to Isolation Among Elderly Widows,' *International Journal of Aging and Human Development*, 7(1/1976), 67–86.

Atchley, R. 'Dimensions of Widowhood in Later Life,' *The Gerontologist*, 15(2/1975), 176–78.

Atchley, R. and S. Miller. 'Older People and Their Families,' pp. 337–69 in C. Eisdorfer (ed.). *Annual Review of Gerontology and Geriatrics*. Volume 1. New York: Springer Publishing Co., 1980.

Ball, J. 'Widow's Grief: The Impact of Age and Mode of Death,' *Omega*, 7(4/1976–77), 307–33.

Bengtson, V. and N. Cutler. 'Generations and Intergenerational Relations: Perspectives on Age Groups and Social Change,' pp. 130–59 in R. Binstock and E. Shanas (eds.). *Handbook of Aging and the Social Sciences*. New York: Van Nostrand Reinhold, 1976.

Berardo, F. 'Survivorship and Social Isolation: The Case of the Aged Widower,' *The Family Coordinator*, 19(1/1970), 11–25.

Berardo, F. (ed.). 'Aging and the Family,' *The Family Coordinator*, 21(1/1972), 3–115.

Blau, Z. *Aging in a Changing Society*. 2nd edition. New York: Franklin Watts, 1981.

Blenkner, M. 'Social Work and Family Relationships in Later Life with Some Thoughts on Filial Maturity,' pp. 46–59 in E. Shanas and G. Streib (eds.). *Social Structure and the Family: Generational Relations*. Englewood Cliffs, N.J.: Prentice-Hall, 1965.

Bornstein, P. and P. Clayton. 'The Anniversary Reaction,' *Diseases of the Nervous System*, 33(4/1972), 470–71.

Brandwein, C. et al. 'The Married Widow(er): A New Role,' paper presented at the annual meeting of the Gerontological Society, Washington, D.C., November 1979.

Brody, E. 'The Aging of the Family,' *The Annals of the American Academy of Political and Social Science*, 438(July 1978), 13–26.

Brody, E. 'Aged Parents and Aging Children,' pp. 267–87 in P. Ragan (ed.). *Aging Parents*. Los Angeles: University of Southern California Press, 1979.

Brubaker, T. and L. Sneden (eds.). 'Aging in a Changing Family Context,' *The Family Coordinator*, 27(4/1978), 301–476.

Chiriboga, D. 'Adaptation to Marital Separation in Later and Earlier Life,' *Journal of Gerontology*, 37(1/1982), 109–14.

Cicirelli, V. 'Relationship of Siblings to the Elderly Person's Feelings and Concerns,' *Journal of Gerontology*, 32(3/1977), 317–22.

Cicirelli, V. 'Sibling Relationships in Adulthood: A Life Span Perspective,' pp. 455–62 in L. Poon (ed.). *Aging in the 1980s*. Washington, D.C.: American Psychological Association, 1980.

Clavan, S. 'The Impact of Social Class and Social Trends on the Role of Grandparent,' *The Family Coordinator*, 27(4/1978), 351–57.

Cleveland, W. and D. Gianturco. 'Remarriage Probability After Widowhood: A Retrospective Method,' *Journal of Gerontology*, 31(1/1976), 99–103.

Cohen, S. and B. Gans. *The Other Generation Gap*. Chicago: Follett, 1978.

Dahlin, M. 'Perspective on the Family Life of the Elderly in 1900,' *The Gerontologist*, 20(1/1980), 99–107.

Decker, D. *Social Gerontology*. Boston: Little, Brown, 1980.

Dowd, J. and R. La Rossa. 'Primary Group Contact and Elderly Morale: An Exchange/Power Analysis,' *Sociology and Social Research*, 66(2/1982), 184–97.

Duvall, E. *Family Development*. 5th edition. Philadelphia: J.B. Lippincott, 1977.

Fengler, A. and N. Goodrich. 'Wives of Elderly Disabled Men: The Hidden Patients,' *The Gerontologist*, 19(2/1979), 175–83.

Fisher, E. (ed.). *Impact of Divorce on the Extended Family*. New York: Haworth Press, 1981.

Fischer, L. 'Transitions in the Mother-Daughter Relationship,' *Journal of Marriage and the Family*, 43(5/1981), 613–22.

Fogel, R. et al. (eds.). *Aging: Stability and Change in the Family*. New York: Academic Press, 1981.

George, L. *Role Transitions in Later Life*. Monterey: Brooks/Cole Publishing Co., 1980.

Gelfand, D. et al. 'Two Generations of Elderly in the Changing American Family: Implications For Family Services,' *The Family Coordinator*, 27(4/1978), 395–403.

Gibbs, J. 'Role Changes Associated with Widowhood Among Middle and Upper-Class Women,' *Mid-American Review of Sociology*, 3(2/1978), 17–33.

Gilford, R. and V. Bengtson. 'Marital Satisfaction in Three Generations: Positive and Negative Dimensions,' paper presented at the 29th Annual Scientific Meeting of the Gerontological Society, New York, October 1976.

Gilford, R. and V. Bengtson. 'Correlates of Marital Satisfaction in Old Age,' paper presented at the 30th Annual Scientific Meeting of the Gerontological Society, San Francisco, November 1977.

Glick, I. et al. *The First Year of Bereavement*. New York: John Wiley and Sons, 1974.

Glick, P. 'Updating the Family Life Cycle,' *Journal of Marriage and the Family*, 39(1/1977), 5–13.

Glick, P. 'The Future Marital Status and Living Arrangements of the Elderly,' *The Gerontologist*, 19(3/1979), 301–9.

Gronvold, R. 'Spatial Distance and the Quality of Communication: An Intergenerational Analysis Among Grandparents and Grandchildren,' paper presented at the annual meeting of the Gerontological Society of America, Toronto, November 1981.

Gubrium, J. 'Being Single in Old Age,' *International Journal of Aging and Human Development*, 6(1/1975), 29–41.

Hagestad, G. and R. Snow. 'Young Adult Offspring as Interpersonal Resources in Middle Age,' paper presented at the annual meeting of the Gerontological Society, San Francisco, November 1977.

Harkins, E. 'Effects of Empty Nest Transition on Self-Report of Psychological and Physical Well-Being,' *Journal of Marriage and the Family*, 40(3/1978), 549–56.

Harvey, C. and H. Bahr. *The Sunshine Widows*. Lexington, Mass.: Lexington Books, 1980.

Harris, L. et al. *The Myth and Reality of Aging in America*. Washington, D.C.: National Council on the Aging, 1975.

Henderson, R. *Parent-Child Interaction: Theory, Research and Prospects*. New York: Academic Press, 1981.

Hess, B. and J. Waring. 'Changing Patterns of Aging and Family Bonds in Later Life,' *The Family Coordinator*, 27(4/1978), 303–14.

Hill, R. 'Decision Making and the Family Life Cycle,' pp. 113–39 in E. Shanas and G. Streib (eds.). *Social Structure and the Family: Generational Relations*. Englewood Cliffs, N.J.: Prentice-Hall, 1965.

Horowitz, A. 'Sons and Daughters as Caregivers to Older Parents: Differences in Role Performance and Consequences,' paper presented at the annual meeting of the Gerontological Society of America, Toronto, November 1981.

Horowitz, A. and L. Shindelman. 'Reciprocity and Affection: Past Influences on Current Caregiving,' paper presented at the annual meeting of the Gerontological Society of America, Toronto, November 1981.

Huyck, M. *Growing Older*. Englewood Cliffs, N.J.: Prentice-Hall, 1974.

Jackson, J. 'Sex and Social Class Variations in Black Aged Parent-Adult Child Relationships,' *International Journal of Aging and Human Development*, 2(1/1971), 96–107.

Jackson, J. 'Marital Life Among Aging Blacks,' *The Family Coordinator*, 21(1/1972), 21–27.

Johnson, C. and D. Catalano. 'Childless Elderly and Their Family Supports,' *The Gerontologist*, 21(6/1981), 610–18.

Johnson, E. 'Good Relationships Between Older Mothers and Their Daughters: A Causal Model,' *The Gerontologist*, 18(3/1978), 301–6.

Johnson, E. 'Older Mothers' Perceptions of Their Child's Divorce,' *The Gerontologist*, 21(4/1981), 395–401.

Johnson, E. and B. Bursk. 'Relationships Between the Elderly and Their Adult Children,' *The Gerontologist*, 18(3/1978), 301–6.

Kahana, B. and E. Kahana. 'Grandparenthood from the Perspective of the Developing Grandchild,' *Developmental Psychology*, 3 (1/1970), 98–105.

Kahana, E. and B. Kahana. 'Theoretical and Research Perspectives on Grandparenthood,' *Aging and Human Development*, 2(3/1971), 261–68.

Kaplan, B. 'An Overview of Interventions to Meet the Needs of Aging Parents and Their Families,' pp. 190–205 in P. Ragan (ed.). *Aging Parents*. Los Angeles: University of Southern California Press, 1979.

Kiefer, C. *Changing Cultures, Changing Lives*. San Francisco: Jossey-Bass, 1974.

Kivett, V. 'Loneliness and the Rural Widow,' *The Family Coordinator*, 27(4/1978), 389–94.

Kivnick, H. 'Grandparenthood: An Overview of Meaning and Mental Health,' *The Gerontologist*, 22(1/1982), 59–66.

Kobata, F. 'The Influence of Culture on Family Relations: The Asian American Experience,' pp. 94–106 in P. Ragan (ed.). *Aging Parents*. Los Angeles: University of Southern California Press, 1979.

Kohn, J. and W. Kohn. *The Widower*. Boston: Beacon Press, 1979.

Lacy, W. and J. Hendricks. 'Developmental Models of Adult Life: Myth or Reality,' *International Journal of Aging and Human Development*, 11(2/1980), 89–110.

Laslett, P. *The World We Have Lost*. London: University Paperbacks, 1971.

Lee, G. and M. Ihinger-Tallman. 'Sibling Interaction and Morale: The Effects of Family Relations on Older People,' *Research on Aging*, 2(3/1980), 367–91.

Lewis, R. 'Transitions in Middle-Aged and Aging Families: A Bibliography from 1940 to 1977,' *The Family Coordinator*, 27(4/1978), 457–76.

Lopata, H. 'The Social Involvement of American Widows,' *American Behavioral Scientist*, 14(1/1970), 40–56.

Lopata, H. *Widowhood in an American City*. Cambridge, Mass.: Schenkman Publishing Co., 1973.

Lopata, H. 'The Absence of Community Resources in Support Systems of Urban Widows,' *The Family Coordinator*, 27(4/1978), 383–88.

Lopata, H. *Women as Widows: Support Systems.* New York: Elsevier, 1979.

Lopata, H. 'The Widowed Family Member,' pp. 93–118 in N. Datan and N. Lohmann (eds.). *Transitions of Aging.* New York: Academic Press, 1980.

Lovas, P. 'The Aging and Family Relationships,' *Educational Gerontology*, 8(2/1982), 209–14.

Lowenthal, M. et al. *Four Stages of Life.* San Francisco: Jossey-Bass Publishing Co., 1975.

Marshall, V. *Last Chapters: A Sociology of Aging and Dying.* Monterey: Brooks/Cole Publishing Co., 1980.

Marshall, V. et al. 'The Family as a Health Service Organization for the Elderly,' paper presented at the annual meeting of the Society For the Study of Social Problems, Toronto, August 1981.

Marshall, V. et al. 'Concerns About Parental Health,' in E. Markson (ed.). *Women and Aging.* Lexington, Mass.: Lexington Books, 1982.

Matthews, A. 'Women and Widowhood,' pp. 145–53 in V. Marshall (ed.). *Aging in Canada: Social Perspectives.* Don Mills: Fitzhenry and Whiteside, 1980.

McKain, W. 'A New Look at Older Marriages,' *The Family Coordinator*, 21(1/1972), 61–69.

Medley, M. 'Marital Adjustment in the Post-Retirement Years,' *The Family Coordinator*, 26(1/1977), 5–11.

Miller, D. 'The 'Sandwich Generation': Adult Children of the Aging,' *Social Work*, 26(5/1981), 419–23.

Mindel, C. 'Multi-Generational Family Households: Recent Trends and Implications For the Future,' *The Gerontologist*, 19(5/1979), 456–63.

Mindel, C. and R. Habenstein. *Ethnic Families in America: Patterns and Variations.* New York: Elsevier, 1976.

Mindel, C. and R. Wright, Jr. 'Satisfaction in Multigenerational Households,' *Journal of Gerontology*, 37(4/1982), 483–89.

Moore, W. 'Aging and the Social System,' pp. 23–41 in J. McKinney and F. DeVyver (eds.). *Aging and Social Policy.* New York: Appleton-Century-Crofts, 1966.

Morgan, L. 'A Reexamination of Widowhood and Morale,' *Journal of Gerontology*, 31(6/1976), 687–95.

Morgan, L. 'Problems of Widowhood,' pp. 66–82 in P. Ragan (ed.). *Aging Parents.* Los Angeles: University of Southern California Press, 1979.

Murdock, S. and D. Schwartz. 'Family Structure and the Use of Agency Services: An Examination of Patterns Among Elderly Native Americans,' *The Gerontologist*, 18(5/1978), 475–81.

Neugarten, B. 'The Middle Generations,' pp. 258–66 in P. Ragan (ed.). *Aging Parents.* Los Angeles: University of Southern California Press, 1979.

Neugarten, B. and N. Datan. 'The Middle Years,' pp. 592–608 in S. Arieti (ed.). *American Handbook of Psychiatry.* Volume 1. 2nd edition. New York: Basic Books, 1974.

Neugarten, B. and K. Weinstein. 'The Changing American Grandparent,' *Journal of Marriage and the Family*, 26(2/1964), 199–204.

Osako, M. 'Aging and Family Among Japanese Americans: The Role of Ethnic Tradition in the Adjustment to Old Age,' *The Gerontologist*, 19(5/1979), 448–55.

Palmore, E. 'The Status and Integration of the Aged in Japanese Society,' *Journal of Gerontology*, 30(2/1975), 199–208.

Paris, B. and E. Luckey. 'A Longitudinal Study of Marital Satisfaction,' *Sociology and Social Research*, 50(2/1966), 212–23.

Peterson, J. 'The Relationships of Middle-Aged Children And Their Parents,' pp. 27–36 in P. Ragan (ed.). *Aging Parents.* Los Angeles: University of Southern California Press, 1979.

Pineo, P. 'Disenchantment in the Later Years of Marriage,' *Marriage and Family Living*, 23(1/1961), 3–11.

Ragan, P. (ed.). *Aging Parents.* Los Angeles: University of Southern California Press, 1979.

Remnet, V. 'Alternatives in Health Care Services,' pp. 206–20 in P. Ragan (ed.). *Aging Parents.* Los Angeles: University of Southern California Press, 1979.

Robertson, J. 'Interaction in Three Generation Families. Parents as Mediators: Toward a Theoretical Perspective,' *International Journal of Aging and Human Development*, 6(2/1975), 103–10.

Robertson, J. 'Significance of Grandparents: Perception of Young Adult Grandchildren,' *The Gerontologist*, 16(2/1976), 137–40.

Robertson, J. 'Grandmotherhood: A Study of Role Conceptions,' *Journal of Marriage and the Family*, 39(1/1977), 165–74.

Rogers, C. and T. Gallion. 'Characteristics of Elderly Pueblo Indians in New Mexico,' *The Gerontologist*, 18(5/1978), 482–87.

Rollins, B. and K. Cannon. 'Marital Satisfaction Over the Family Life Cycle: A Reevaluation,' *Journal of Marriage and the Family*, 36(3/1974), 271–83.

Rosenthal, C. et al. 'The Succession of Lineage Roles as Families Age,' *Essence*, 4(3/1980), 179–93.

Rosenthal, C. et al. 'The Head of the Family: Authority and Responsibility in the Lineage,' paper presented at the annual meeting of the Canadian Association on Gerontology, Toronto, November 1981a.

Rosenthal, C. et al. 'Maintaining Intergenerational Relations: Kinkeeping,' paper presented at the annual meeting of the Canadian Association on Gerontology, Toronto, November 1981b.

Rosenmayr, L. and E. Kockeis. 'Propositions for a Sociological Theory of Aging and the Family,' International Social Science Journal, 15(3/1963), 410–26.

Saltz, R. 'Aging Persons as Child-Care Workers in a Foster-Grandparent Program: Psychosocial Effects And Work Performance,' Aging and Human Development, 2(3/1971), 314–40.

Schwartz, A. 'Psychological Dependency: An Emphasis on the Later Years,' pp. 116–25 in P. Ragan (ed.). Aging Parents. Los Angeles: University of Southern California Press, 1979.

Seelback, W. 'Gender Differences in Expectations For Filial Responsibility,' The Gerontologist, 17(5/1977), 421–25.

Seelback, W. 'Correlates of Aged Parents' Filial Responsibility Expectations and Realizations,' The Family Coordinator, 27(4/1978), 341–50.

Seelback, W. and W. Sauer. 'Filial Responsibility Expectations and Morale Among Aged Parents,' The Gerontologist, 17(6/1977), 492–99.

Shanas, E. 'Family Help Patterns and Social Class in Three Countries,' Journal of Marriage and the Family, 29(2/1967), 257–66.

Shanas, E. 'Social Myth as Hypothesis: The Case of the Family Relations of Old People,' The Gerontologist, 19(1/1979a), 3–9.

Shanas, E. 'The Family as a Social Support System in Old Age,' The Gerontologist, 19(2/1979b), 169–674.

Silverman, P. 'Widowhood and Preventive Intervention,' The Family Coordinator, 21(1/1972), 95–102.

Singh, B. and J. Williams. 'Childlessness and Family Satisfaction,' Research on Aging, 3(2/1981), 218–27.

Spanier, G. et al. 'Marital Adjustment over the Family Life Cycle: The Issue of Curvilinearity,' Journal of Marriage and the Family, 37(3/1975), 263–75.

Sprey, J. and S. Matthews. 'The Impact of Divorce on Grandparenthood,' paper presented at the annual meeting of the Gerontological Society of America, Toronto, November 1981.

Steinman, L. 'Reactivated Conflicts with Aging Parents,' pp. 126–43 in P. Ragan (ed.). Aging Parents. Los Angeles: University of Southern California Press, 1979.

Stinnett, N. et al. 'Older Persons' Perceptions of Their Marriages,' Journal of Marriage and the Family, 34(6/1972), 665–70.

Streib, G. 'Old Age and the Family,' American Behavioral Scientist, 14(1/1970), 25–39.

Streib, G. 'Older Families and Their Troubles: Familial and Social Responses,' The Family Coordinator, 21(1/1972), 5–20.

Streib, G. 'An Alternative Family Form for Older Persons: Need and Social Context,' The Family Coordinator, 27(4/1978), 413–20.

Stryckman, J. 'The Decision to Remarry: The Choice And Its Outcome,' paper presented at the annual meeting of the Canadian Association on Gerontology, Toronto, November 1981.

Sussman, M. 'The Family Life of Old People,' pp. 218–43 in R. Binstock and E. Shanas (eds.). Handbook of Aging and the Social Sciences. New York: Van Nostrand Reinhold, 1976.

Sutton-Smith, B. and B. Rosenberg. The Sibling. New York: Holt, Rinehart and Winston, 1970.

Synge, J. 'Work and Family Support Patterns of the Aged in the Early Twentieth Century,' pp. 135–44 in V. Marshall (ed.). Aging in Canada: Social Perspectives. Don Mills: Fitzhenry and Whiteside, 1980.

Synge, J. et al. 'Phoning And Writing as Means of Keeping in Touch in the Family of Later Life,' paper presented at the annual meeting of the Canadian Association on Gerontology, Toronto, November 1981.

Thompson, G. 'Economic Status of Late Middle-Aged Widows,' pp. 133–49 in N. Datan and N. Lohmann (eds.). Transitions of Aging. New York: Academic Press, 1980.

Thurnher, M. 'Midlife Marriage: Sex Differences in Evaluation and Perspectives,' International Journal of Aging and Human Development, 7(2/1976), 129–35.

Tobin, S. and R. Kulys. 'The Family and Services,' pp. 370–99 in C. Eisdorfer (ed.). Annual Review of Gerontology and Geriatrics. Volume 1. New York: Springer Publishing Co., 1980.

Treas, J. 'Aging and the Family,' pp. 92–108 in D. Woodruff and J. Birren (eds.). Aging: Scientific Perspectives and Social Issues. New York: D. Van Nostrand Co., 1975.

Treas, J. 'Family Support Systems for the Aged: Some Social and Demographic Considerations,' The Gerontologist, 17(6/1977), 486–91.

Treas, J. 'Intergenerational Families and Social Change,' pp. 58–65 in P. Ragan (ed.). Aging Parents. Los Angeles: University of Southern California Press, 1979.

Treas, J. and A. Van Hilst. 'Marriage and Remarriage Rates Among Older Americans,' The Gerontologist, 16(2/1976), 132–36.

Troll, L. 'The Family of Later Life: A Decade Review,' *Journal of Marriage and the Family*, 33(2/1971), 263–90.

Troll, L. 'Intergenerational Relations in Later Life: A Family System Approach,' pp. 75–91 in N. Datan and N. Lohmann (eds.). *Transitions of Aging*. New York: Academic Press, 1980a.

Troll, L. 'Grandparenting,' pp. 475–81 in L. Poon (ed.). *Aging in the 1980s*. Washington, D.C.: American Psychological Association, 1980b.

Troll, L. and V. Bengtson. 'Generations in the Family,' pp. 127–61 in W. Burr et al. (eds.). *Contemporary Theories About the Family*. New York: The Free Press, 1979.

Troll, L. et al. *Families in Later Life*. Belmont, Calif.: Wadsworth Publishing Co., 1979.

Turner, J. 'Patterns of Intergenerational Exchange: A Developmental Approach,' *International Journal of Aging and Human Development*, 6(2/1975), 111–15.

Turner, R. 'Role-Taking: Process Versus Conformity,' pp. 20–40 in A. Rose (ed.). *Human Behavior and Social Processes: An Interactionist Approach*. Boston: Houghton Mifflin, 1962.

Uhlenberg, P. and M. Myers. 'Divorce and the Elderly,' *The Gerontologist*, 21(3/1981), 276–82.

Vachon, M. 'Identity Change over the First Two Years of Bereavement: Social Relationships and Social Support,' Ph.D. dissertation, Department of Sociology, York University, 1979.

Vinick, B. 'Remarriage in Old Age,' *The Family Coordinator*, 27(4/1978), 359–63.

Vinick, B. 'Intergenerational Relations And the Remarriage of the Older Parent,' paper presented at the annual meeting of the Gerontological Society, San Diego, November 1980.

Vinick, B. 'Three Years After Bereavement: Lifestyles of Elderly Men,' paper presented at the annual meeting of the Gerontological Society of America, Toronto, November 1981.

Ward, R. 'The Never-Married in Later Life,' *Journal of Gerontology*, 34(6/1979), 861–69.

Weishaus, S. 'Aging Is a Family Affair,' pp. 154–74 in P. Ragan (ed). *Aging Parents*. Los Angeles: University of Southern California Press, 1979.

Wilson, K. and M. DeShane. 'The Legal Rights of Grandparents: A Preliminary Discussion,' *The Gerontologist*, 22(1/1982), 67–71.

Woehrer, C. 'Cultural Pluralism in American Families: The Influence of Ethnicity on Social Aspects of Aging,' *The Family Coordinator*, 27(4/1978), 329–39.

Wood, V. and J. Robertson. 'The Significance of Grandparenthood,' pp. 278–304 in J. Gubrium (ed.). *Time, Roles, and Self in Old Age*. New York: Human Sciences Press, 1976.

Yelder, J. 'The Influence of Culture on Family Relations: The Black American Experience,' pp. 83–93 in P. Ragan (ed.). *Aging Parents*. Los Angeles: University of Southern California Press, 1979.

Zube, M. 'Changing Behavior and Outlook of Aging Men and Women: Implications For Marriage in the Middle and Later Years,' *Family Relations*, 31(1/1982), 147–68.

10

Work, Retirement, Economic
Status, and Aging

Introduction

Although the process of retirement is the major phenomenon dealt with in this chapter, it cannot be studied in isolation, or on one level of analysis. Retirement is a social process and a social institution (Atchley, 1982) related to the work history of the individual and the labor-force needs of society; to the economic status of the individual and the state; and to the health status of the individual and the health care services provided by the society. In addition, retirement as a social process is related to the leisure interests of the individual and to the social and leisure services provided by the public and private sectors; to the type and degree of support provided by the family and by societal norms; and to individual decisions about when to retire and to public- and private-sector retirement policies.

Furthermore, personal factors (sex, marital status, work or retirement status of the spouse, class background, widowhood, or age), demographic factors (fertility rates, migration rates, and patterns or longevity), societal factors (trends toward early retirement, 'gray power' movements), and historical factors (wars or depressions) influence the process as well. Throughout adulthood, work and retirement are interrelated with the family life cycle (chapter 9) and with leisure lifestyles (chapter 11). In short, the study of retirement must involve an analysis of both individual and population aging throughout the middle and later years. Therefore, although most retirement research has been completed at the individual (micro) level of analysis, wherever possible in this chapter a societal (macro) perspective is taken, especially with respect to retirement policies, economic concerns, and the societal consequences of retirement.

Retirement is a social invention found in most industrialized societies.[1] Conceptually, it can be viewed as a social process wherein an individual withdraws from the labor force sometime after 55 or 60 years of age and enters a new stage in life. In return for this voluntary or involuntary withdrawal, the individual receives economic benefits in the form of social security from the government, or pensions from the public or private sector.[2] In addition, the elderly individual is usually eligible for varying levels of subsidized health care (drugs, hospitalization, or long-term care), as well as certain subsidized social services (housing, transportation, or leisure). For most people, retirement represents a major transition from the status of being employed and earning an income to the status of being retired, or unemployed (George, 1980:55–76). This transition is accompanied by a reduced income — a pension — awarded on the basis of past contributions to one or more employers, or as a form of social welfare, regardless of work history.

Early conceptualizations of retirement described the phenomenon (and indeed all of the postretirement years) as a 'roleless' role (Burgess, 1960:20). This view held that the retired individual (usually a man) and his spouse were faced with an ambiguous social status and a lack of purpose and meaning in their lives. As a result of this perspective, many of the early studies of retirement were motivated by the unchallenged assumption that the transition to retirement is stressful and creates adjustment problems for many individuals and couples. However, the research evidence generally supports the finding that most men and women adjust successfully to retirement and experience little stress in adapting to their new social status and lifestyle (Havighurst et al., 1969; Streib and Schneider, 1971; Atchley, 1976a; Irelan et al., 1976; Sheppard, 1976; Parnes et al., 1979; George, 1980; Foner and Schwab, 1981; McCluskey and Borgatta, 1981; Parnes, 1981; Parker, 1982).[3] The retirement role is not viewed as a 'problem' by most retirees. Most older people seem to tolerate and adjust to the role, even if it does appear ambiguous in the preretirement years (Streib and Schneider, 1971). In fact, recent research suggests that many people look forward to retirement, and some even plan for retirement and decide to retire before the mandatory age (Barfield and Morgan, 1970, 1978a; McPherson and Guppy, 1979; Clark and Barker, 1981).

As a result of research that refuted the myth of retirement as an ambiguous, stressful event, retirement is now viewed as an institutionalized social process (Atchley, 1976a, 1982) that is related to the stability, prestige, and type of career, and to health and economic status. To date, there appear to be at least five retirement patterns: (1) voluntary retirement as soon as it is financially feasible; (2) acceptance of compulsory retirement; (3) reluctance to accept compulsory retirement; (4) retirement following a period of unemployment; and (5) involuntary or forced retirement because of declining health (Atchley, 1979).

The retirement process is made up of many stages and involves adaptive strategies by the individual and by society. For example, Atchley (1976a:63–71) suggests that for some the process involves two stages prior to retirement and five stages following the actual event. The preretirement stage includes a 'remote' phase, wherein the individual recognizes that retirement will occur someday and that savings and pension plans are needed. This phase may also involve some informal anticipatory socialization through observation of the way in which parents or neighbors adapt to retirement. The 'near' phase includes formal and informal preretirement planning initiated by the individual or by the employer.

The initial or 'honeymoon' phase of the postretirement stage is characterized by involvement in a variety of self-selected activities (visiting, reading, travelling, hobbies). The second postretirement phase is characterized by 'disenchantment': the reality of poor economic and health status or the lack of meaningful and satisfying activities may lead to depression and perhaps to fear of the future. This phase is followed by a 'reorientation' phase, in which a realistic plan of alternatives is developed. If this phase results in a satisfactory reorientation, then a period of 'stability' follows, in which a satisfying routine for the retirement years is established.

The final 'termination' phase involves coping with illness and the loss of many activities because of declining health or financial resources. At this stage illness or disability may prevail and the individual may become dependent on others, often to the extent that institutionalization is necessary. Thus, the seven stages of retirement range across the life cycle from middle age to near death. However, it is important to recognize, as Atchley (1976a:71) notes, that these seven stages represent an ideal conceptual model rather than social reality. That is, not everyone experiences every phase, and those that are experienced may occur in a different sequence (for example, 'disenchantment' may come before the 'honeymoon' stage) or at different chronological ages.

The adaptive strategies initiated by the individual following retirement generally involve adjustments to the loss of job and friends, to a perceived loss of job prestige and identity, to loss of income, to increased 'free' time, to declining health, and to increased interaction with the spouse. From the perspective of society, mandatory retirement can deprive the labor force of experienced, loyal, and reliable workers; it can initiate population shifts because of migration; and it can create economic stress, especially if large numbers of people opt for early retirement and withdraw social security or pension funds sooner and faster than projected. In this situation, alternative strategies must be developed to maintain the financial solvency of pension and social security systems (such as higher taxation of those in the labor force, reduced benefits to retirees, and incentives to retain older workers on staff).

In short, the constant interplay between individual and population aging is illustrated by the process of retirement. For example, the phenomenon can be viewed as a process of either abandonment or liberation of the elderly (Baum and Baum, 1980:102–45). This view varies within and across societies depending on the personal situation of the elderly individual, and on societal policies and institutionalized norms pertaining to retirement. As a result, the meaning and experience of retirement may vary within and between cohorts. Just as the retirement situation experienced by your parents may differ from that of your grandparents, so too may your situation differ from that reported in current literature.

Similarly, as with other aging phenomena, it must be remembered that the elderly at any point in history comprise a heterogeneous cohort influenced by stratification variables and personal characteristics. The following section examines the relationship between retirement and work patterns and attitudes in the middle years. Later, the process of retirement and the relationship between retirement and the financial resources of the individual and the society are considered. Throughout, special attention is directed to the recent and emerging literature concerning women in the work force, women and retirement, and the disadvantaged economic status of older women.

Work Patterns and Attitudes Toward Retirement in the Preretirement Years

Introduction

Most individuals exhibit continuity in attitudes, behaviors, values, and interests across the life cycle. Therefore, it is important to understand the meaning and function of work to an individual, the preretirement work history, and the attitudes toward retirement while working in order to explain why and how particular retirement decisions and adjustments are made.[4] It is also necessary to examine the many myths concerning the incompetence of the older worker. If these stereotypes persist, they may result in forced or voluntary early retirement for some workers. Finally, variations by sex in careers must be understood in order to comprehend the retirement decisions and adjustments of women in the labor force.

Work Patterns During Adulthood

To date, most research on the middle-aged and older worker has focused on white males, although increasing attention has been directed to the career patterns of women and to members of minority groups. This inherent male bias has been based on the demographic fact that until the last few decades, few women were permanent full-time workers, and on the false assumption that retirement was a 'male' phenomenon and a 'male' problem. However, as later sections indicate, both men and women participate in the labor force, and both are involved in the retirement process.

For most adults, work is a central focus in life, although it may not be the only or major life interest. Work is of primary concern because it influences life chances, income, social status, lifestyle, and friendships. Most adults generally hold jobs that are related to their education and early occupational socialization. That is, they follow a career line that involves a sequence of jobs within a particular field of work (education, civil engineering, the automotive industry, real estate, etc.), or a sequence of jobs with similar skill requirements that involve different occupational fields (selling autos, homes, computers, or sporting goods).

Throughout the early and middle years of adulthood, individuals generally have a stable work pattern. A worker is employed continuously after leaving school by one or more organizations, accumulates pension benefits, and may or may not develop feelings of loyalty and commitment to the job or the organization. For example, those with a continuous work history derive a sense of security from their work, gain an identity and a social network of colleagues and enjoy the benefits of a stable position at work and in the community.

The job also has the potential to provide life satisfaction or dissatisfaction, although this varies by the type of job. For example, those in high-prestige positions, those in decision-making positions, and those in the professions generally report high levels of intrinsic job satisfaction. In contrast, blue-collar workers are more likely to report lower levels of job satisfaction, greater alienation from the work and the organization, and less commitment to the job. Part of this dissatisfaction and lack of commitment is because of low income, the repetitive and unchallenging nature of the job, impersonal employee-employer relations, and an earlier attainment of the highest position (the career peak) they can achieve in their career (Ward, forthcoming). Also, those in the lower occupational levels tend to be more concerned throughout their careers about security, income, and friendships with colleagues than with the meaning and satisfaction derived from the job per se. Regardless of work orientation, both blue-collar and white-collar workers who have had a continuous and stable work history generally face retirement with a positive attitude. Those most likely to express reservations are those concerned about economic security rather than about loss of identity or friendship networks.

In contrast, different orientations toward work are held by those who have had an unstable or interrupted work history. This pattern is characterized by cyclical periods of full-time employment, unemployment, part-time employment, or underemployment. As a result, commitment to a job or organization is seldom developed, a lifetime of job uncertainty and economic insecurity prevails, and work is only salient as a means of survival. Hence, there is little subjective attachment to work at any stage of adulthood. As a result, retirement for these individuals may be viewed either as 'more of the same' or as a form of relief, since they will at least be assured of a minimal income, depending on the credits they accumulated whenever they were employed. However, some individuals with an irregular work history will arrive at retirement with few accumulated benefits, often because pensions are not 'portable' from one job or field to another.

A third, but atypical, pattern is the truncated career. This is a pattern found among professional athletes and dancers who are forced to retire in their late 20s or early 30s because of declining physical skills (Loy et al., 1978:244–48; McPherson, 1980); by those whose employment depends on public acceptance and demand (singers, rock musicians, comedians, or actors); and by fashion models whose physical attractiveness is the primary prerequisite for employment. In all of these occupations the chosen career can end suddenly, either voluntarily or involuntarily. Many of these individuals find themselves 'retired' in the prime of life. Unfortunately, they often lack the skills necessary to make a successful transition to a more stable or traditional career. Moreover, some are so ego-identified with their former 'public' life that they are unable to accept living a 'private' life where they are not idolized. They often show a pattern of unstable employment with many job changes in a number of fields. While most eventually settle in one job, the intervening period can be traumatic; there may be a high incidence of depression, alcoholism, and divorce.

Previous work patterns and orientation to work can thus influence when an individual retires, how the individual adjusts, and whether he or she returns to work on a full-time or part-time basis. Although most older workers are not alienated from their work (Meier and Kerr, 1976; Sheppard, 1976; Meltzer and Stagner, 1980), the meaning of work and orientation to work can change with age. For example, there may be a decline in intrinsic work satisfaction during the later stages of labor-force participation (Cohn, 1979). As a result, individuals may accept mandatory retirement because they have lost interest in the job, or because it no longer represents a a major life interest. While this loss of interest and meaning occurs earlier and more frequently for blue-collar workers, regardless of whether they have a stable or an unstable career, dissatisfaction has recently become more evident among white-collar workers in the professions and in the corporate sector. The problem is often resolved by a midlife career change (rather than by a job change within a similar occupational field), or by early retirement.

In order to counteract this 'burn-out' or 'plateauing,' which appears to be a social psychological rather than a biological phenomenon, organizations have introduced 'flextime' and 'sabbatical' and 'reduced-load' policies to provide alternative work patterns. Flextime can take many forms and generally represents an attempt to meet the lifestyle needs of employees, as well as the business and production demands of the employer. Employees may begin and end each workday at their own selected hour within a set range (for example, they may begin work at any time between 7 and 9 a.m. and, having worked the required number of hours, leave work at any time between 4 and 6 p.m.); or they may work their own hours to a daily or weekly required maximum (a four-day week is possible under this option). Moreover, it is often possible within this system to accumulate extra credit hours to provide time off in addition to regular vacation periods.

The sabbatical option permits individuals to obtain fully or partially paid leave for professional or personal development; the reduced-load policy enables an older individual to opt for a three-quarter or half-time appointment at a proportionately reduced salary. Both of these plans permit people to pursue alternative leisure or career interests. One major attraction of the reduced-load approach is that individuals receive full pension benefits when they retire, despite not working full-time for a few years prior to normal retirement age. From the perspective of the organization, the reduced-load policy permits new employees to be hired, especially in an inflationary period characterized by high unemployment.

The reduced-load policy is currently being adopted by a number of universities. Senior faculty can reduce their load and pursue other interests; the university, faced with declining enrollments, saves money because of the reduced salaries, and may use the savings to provide an opportunity for young Ph.D.s with new skills and ideas to enter the labor force. In short, work patterns and the meaning of work to the individual throughout adulthood, along with the availability of alternative work patterns in the later years, can have a significant bearing on the process of retirement.

Atypical Work Patterns: Midlife Career Changes

Some occupations encourage or require a midlife career change. For example, commercial pilots may be grounded if they fail to pass a rigid medical exam, or they may be forced out by an early compulsory retirement age. Similarly, the armed forces often encourage personnel to 'opt out' after about twenty years of service by providing a large pension immediately upon retirement, regardless of age. In this way, the salary component of the budget is reduced and opportunities are created for the promotion of younger personnel. For individuals leaving the armed forces, the adjustment to another career is usually orderly and satisfactory since they often enter an occupation where their existing skills are utilized to a great extent. For many, this transition is more a job or organization change than a career change where unique retraining is required.

There are, however, an increasing number of individuals who opt for a career change rather than a job change during middle age. Although it is not known how many make this transition, it has primarily been a male phenomenon to date,[5] and has occurred mainly among those in the middle or upper class who are financially independent and well educated. These individuals may be either married or single, although a large number tend to be divorced or never-married and without dependents. Many of these changes involve a shift from a profession (lawyer, engineer, or professor) or business position (executive or accountant) to a more independent, less structured occupation such as that of author, craftsman, or self-employed businessman. In some situations, people may pass through the intervening stage of being career 'dropouts' where they are voluntarily unemployed and make no attempt to re-enter the labor force. During this period they exist on savings, investments, or consultation fees as they search for a higher quality of life or new challenges.

For most, the exit from the labor force appears to be carefully planned and often results from a basic dissatisfaction with the work or living environment. In short, most people are motivated by a desire for a change in lifestyle, not by a search for more money. In fact, many move to careers with less prestige and income, but which have greater personal freedom and intrinsic satisfaction.

Although some career changes are preceded by a dropout stage, many are planned so that the individual moves directly or indirectly (after returning to school for formal training) into the new career path. Again, most of these career changes are motivated by social and psychological factors rather than economic factors, and are voluntary rather than forced transitions (Parnes and King, 1977; Wiener and Vaitenas, 1977; Roberts, 1980).[6] Forced transitions result from direct factors such as declining health, which inhibits or prevents performance on the job, or from being laid off or fired. For those who are well educated and have some degree of financial stability, these circumstances may influence the individual to consider following a more enjoyable or secure career path. However, many individuals who are laid off or fired have low-level job skills and little education or training, and a career change may be impossible because of these limitations.

In addition to the direct stimuli noted above, there may be a number of 'push' and 'pull' incentives that operate at the personal and structural levels. Some of the internal push factors include an inability to resolve a conflict between the values, goals, and policies of the employer and those of the individual, or boredom and loss of motivation if the position or task is no longer challenging ('plateauing'). Push factors external to the individual may result from family pressures to improve or save a marriage, or from an illness or disability in the family. External push factors at the structural or organizational level may involve a company move to another community, or being continually overlooked for a promotion.

Among the internal pull factors are financial independence, lack of dependents, or having a potentially lucrative or intellectually challenging outside interest that requires a full-time commitment (for example, art or writing). Some of the structural pull factors include the availability of new occupations that are more relevant and challenging and the presence of former work associates who have successfully changed careers and who serve as role models.

In summary, an increasing number of middle- and upper-class individuals are voluntarily changing careers in midlife in order to attain a higher quality of life, new challenges, or greater meaning in their work. If these goals are attained, increased job and life satisfaction may influence the retirement decision. That is, the individual may choose to continue working in the 'new' career, opt for early retirement, retire and start a third career, or elect to remain 'unretired' by volunteering his or her expertise to voluntary or corporate organizations. Unfortunately, valid information is not yet available about 'career changers' as they approach or enter the normal retirement years. It may be that the midlife career change provides some experiences and develops some strengths that carry over into the retirement phase of the life cycle.

Female Work Patterns

The labor-force participation rate of women has risen dramatically in the last two decades; approximately 30 to 40 percent of the adult work force in North America (and about 20 percent worldwide) is made up of women (Semyonov, 1980). In fact, Harris (1981) recently reported that in the United States nearly one-half of all married women now work outside the home. However, after 65 years of age the proportion of elderly women in the labor force declines to about 9 percent in the United States (Harris, 1981) and to about 5 percent in Canada (Statistics Canada, 1979); for men in both countries, the figure is between 18 and 20 percent.[7]

Although an increase in labor-force participation by women was one of the significant social changes that followed World War II, the study of female occupational patterns and problems was a neglected area of research until the onset of the women's movement in the 1970s. When women were studied, the focus was usually on their reaction to the retirement of the spouse, rather than on their role as workers. A stereotypical view was held that women's major role was that of homemaker, and that work was mainly an instrumental (to earn money) rather than an expressive (to give meaning to life) role.

In recent years, however, increasing research attention has been directed to issues pertaining to labor-force participation and withdrawal by women. Researchers have looked at such topics as rates and patterns of participation; personal and structural factors influencing participation rates; attitudes toward work; the meaning of work; sex-based inequalities or discrimination in salary, mobility, and access to specific occupations; attitudes and adjustment to retirement; the relationship between work history and economic status in the later years; and the need for an adequate pension system for women, regardless of their history of labor-force participation (Kline, 1975; Atchley, 1976b, 1976c; Blaxall and Reagan, 1976; Jaslow, 1976; Payne and Whittington, 1976; Fox, 1977; Barnett and Baruch, 1978; Feldberg and Glenn, 1979; Fischer et al., 1979; McCarthy, 1979; Wolf and Fligstein, 1979; Block, 1980; Semyonov, 1980; Kasworm and Wetzel, 1981; Prothero, 1981).

The results of the research to date suggest that there are few, if any, significant sex differences in the importance of work to the individual (Atchley, 1976b), and that work is a serious, meaningful, expressive, and satisfying role for women. In short, work has become a central life interest for many women; for them, as for men, it is a source of personal satisfaction, prestige, identity, and power. Prothero (1981) suggests that for some older women the work role may be more salient than it is for older men, especially if the women entered the labor force late in life, or only recently approached or attained their 'career peak.'

Labor-force participation rates among women vary considerably from country to country. Semyonov (1980), in a comparative study of sixty-one countries, found that the percentage of women in the labor force varied from 11 percent in Syria to 46 percent in Poland and Finland. He explained this cross-cultural variation by noting that the rate at which females participate in the labor force is positively related to the level of economic development. That is, with industrialization and increased technological development, there is an increase in the number of service and white-collar occupations. This increases the demand for female laborers. The supply may not, at least initially, match the demand if fertility rates are high and family commitments take precedence over labor commitments. However, with increasing industrialization, fertility rates decline and more women are available for, and seek, labor-force involvement.

Although the onset of industrialization and a decrease in fertility rates are important factors in women's labor-force participation, the most important structural or social factor is the shape of the stratification system. Where sexual and income inequality is low, women are less likely to experience occupational discrimination and to be blocked from entering the labor force. Sexual inequality is most likely to be high in high-status occupations. When women compete for these positions they may experience discrimination. Moreover, even where women are actively recruited to the labor force, they may be segregated in low-status, poorly paid occupations that offer little chance for upward mobility.

Semyonov (1980) found that on an average there were about half as many women as men in high-status occupations (professional, managerial, or administrative). He attributed this apparent discrimination to fertility rates and to the number of women in the labor force. High-status positions require a degree of career commitment that low-status occupations (in the clerical or service sectors) do not, and childbearing, at least until recent years, imposed constraints on that commitment. Thus, where fertility rates are high, women may not have the time to devote to a career and may be excluded from high-status occupations. Furthermore, he argued that where the number of women in the labor force is small, a woman has a greater relative chance of attaining a high-status position. Semyonov stressed the importance of social structural variables in determining the rate and type of labor-force participation by women. Moreover, it can be seen that the rates vary cross-culturally because of variation in such structural factors as level of economic development (industrialization), fertility rates, the nature of the stratification system, and the degree of occupational discrimination.

At the personal level of analysis, a number of factors influence the frequency and pattern of labor-force participation by women in the middle and later years of life. First, marital status has a significant effect. Women who are single, separated, divorced, or widowed are more likely to need to work. However, married women at all ages are increasingly entering the labor force to satisfy personal social and psychological needs, as well as the economic needs or desires of the family. Health status and age of children also play an important role for those women who are able to choose whether or not to participate in the labor force,[8] as do such factors as education, socioeconomic status, religion, and race. For those who do become involved, it appears that the quality of the job is more important than any personal or demographic background variables in developing and maintaining a high degree of positive work orientation and commitment (Atchley, 1976c).

With the growing participation of women in the labor force, a number of new work patterns have evolved (Fischer et al., 1979). These patterns have been labelled as follows: (1) 'nonentry,' where the woman is never employed regularly (full-time) after leaving school; (2) 'delayed,' where entry into the labor force occurs relatively late in life (at the empty-nest stage); (3) 'truncated,' where a career is interrupted (by a late marriage or childbirth) and not resumed; (4) 'interrupted,' where the woman temporarily leaves the work force (perhaps to raise a child) and then returns to resume the career path; and (5) 'full employment,' or the 'dual career,' where the woman works full-time for her entire working life, and may or may not play the role of spouse concurrently. In the full-employment pattern neither the domestic role nor the work role predominates; both are equally important.

In summary, regardless of the pattern, it is clear that an increasing percentage of women want to work, that between 30 and 40 percent of women do work, that work is no less meaningful for women than it is for men, and that a variety of work patterns have evolved to enable women to participate in the labor force to a greater extent. Moreover, they have been assisted in achieving this goal by legislation that inhibits income and occupational discrimination, by social services (such as community or company-sponsored day care centers) that facilitate participation, and by increasing recognition that women can acquire and use occupational skills previously assumed to be the exclusive domain of men (for example, as engineers, business executives, pilots, or law-enforcement officers).

The Aging Worker

Contrary to prevailing myths and stereotypes about the deficiencies of the older worker, research evidence indicates that general job performance rarely declines, and that there are individual differences in work-related skills among the elderly, just as there are among younger workers (Meier and Kerr, 1976; Sheppard, 1976; Schwab and Heneman, 1977; Baugher, 1978; Meltzer and Stagner, 1980; Foner and Schwab, 1981:13–28; Yolles et al., 1982). Negative myths about incompetence and declining productivity have been present throughout most of the post-World War II era. However, they appear more frequently during periods of high unemployment when there is intense competition for fewer jobs, and during periods of slow economic growth where personnel managers are pressured to reduce the size of the payroll by eliminating jobs or highly paid workers.

Most recently, the myths reappeared during the discussions that led to the raising of the mandatory retirement age to 70 in the United States (McConnell and Morgan, 1979), and to the abolition in Canada of forced retirement before the mandatory age unless an employer can prove that older workers cannot do the job satisfactorily. During the hearings, some employers argued that the older worker does not have the productivity, strength, stamina, and competence of the younger or middle-aged employee.

Unfortunately, most of the evidence comparing the work performance of younger and older workers is based on cross-sectional rather than longitudinal studies. That is, variation in specific and general aptitudes within and between cohorts is usually overlooked, and job experience is seldom considered as a factor in performance. Moreover, the creation and perpetuation of stereotypes are often based on subjective measures of performance, capacity, or potential, rather than on valid and reliable objective measures of productivity or performance. The stereotypes may also be a function of the age of the evaluator: younger evaluators may assess older workers less favorably ('they are less productive or creative than my age peers'), while older evaluators may evaluate them more favorably ('older people like myself are loyal, efficient, and experienced workers'). Where negative stereotypes exist, the older worker may experience discrimination in opportunities for promotion or simply in retaining the existing job. These views may also result in the internalization of a negative self-image, which in turn can lead to a loss of interest and motivation or to an indirectly forced early retirement to escape an unpleasant work environment.

Recognizing that there are individual differences within and between age cohorts in experience and education, and that individual variations may be related to the nature of the job or to familiarity with the test situation, the research evidence pertaining to the older worker generally refutes prevailing myths by indicating that:

1. There is relatively little decline in productivity with age.

2. There is some loss of muscular strength and endurance.

3. Reaction time slows with age (see chapter 6), but experience at the task may offset the losses.

4. There is little decline in intelligence affecting job performance (see chapter 6).

5. Older workers are generally more satisfied with their jobs (Janson and Martin, 1982) and are less likely to leave an organization for another job (perhaps because they have few alternatives).

6. Decremental changes in job-related aptitudes or skills do not occur at the same rate (for example, a hearing loss may not be accompanied by a slower reaction time or by a loss of visual acuity), and those that do occur may be compensated for by experience.

7. Declining cognitive or physical skills can be overcome by a willingness to resort to coping strategies (such as a reliance on co-workers for assistance, taking work home).

8. Older workers are absent less often and have fewer accidents than younger workers.

In short, prevailing stereotypes or myths about the older worker are not supported by research evidence.

For those individuals who experience personal losses that begin to affect job performance, alternative work patterns or job redesign may provide a solution. For example, workers can be moved laterally to a new job that falls within their range of abilities (a job that is less physically demanding, that requires fewer reaction-type tasks, or that requires less travel); or the existing job can be redesigned to meet the worker's capabilities (more concrete stimuli are provided, telephone contacts with clients are encouraged rather than personal visits, self-paced instructions are provided).

A number of alternative general work patterns are also available to meet the interests and potential of older workers (for example, flextime, job sharing, or longer vacations leading to a phased-in retirement). Thus, by redesigning the job or providing alternative work patterns, the worker may retain a high level of motivation and satisfaction, and the organization will retain a loyal and experienced employee. Rather than perpetuating stereotypes about the older worker, employees and co-workers must recognize that there are individual differences in the rate and type of age-related losses, and must consider whether, and how, a specific job or work pattern can be altered to compensate for these changes.

Preretirement Attitudes Toward Retirement

Attitudes toward retirement can be assessed at three general stages: at some point prior to retirement, on the day of retirement, and at some point after retirement. Attitudes expressed during the first two stages represent perceived views that are often based on anticipatory socialization. Attitudes expressed in the postretirement stage are based on actual experiences. Unfortunately, some studies of attitudes toward retirement fail to identify whether the attitudes were recorded during the pre- or postretirement stage, or how long before or after the actual event they were assessed. Furthermore, it is often not clear whether respondents were asked about their specific attitudes toward retirement as it applies to them (are you looking forward to retirement?), or whether they were asked about their attitudes toward retirement in general (is retirement a valued stage in life?). Finally, most studies in this area are based on samples of white, urban males, and little information is available about the pre- or postretirement attitudes of women,[9] rural residents, or members of minority groups who have been in the labor force for many years.

Most studies have found that as many as 75 to 80 percent of the respondents report favorable attitudes toward retirement prior to the event (Glamser, 1976); but the degree to which the attitude is positive is related to a number of factors. Generally, positive attitudes toward retirement during the preretirement stage are associated with high levels of health, income, and education, and with a high degree of support from significant others in the family and at work concerning the approaching event (Goudy et al., 1975; Glamser, 1976; Cox and Bhak, 1978–79; McPherson and Guppy, 1979). Also, the younger the age at which the respondent is queried, the more favorable the attitude is. This may occur because the event is further away, because retirement and early retirement are becoming more socially acceptable, and because pension plans may be perceived as more satisfactory than those available to previous retirees.

In contrast, negative attitudes are related to a fear of financial difficulties in retirement (Prothero, 1981), and a high commitment to or satisfaction with work, such that work is the major or only life interest (Glamser, 1981b). To these individuals, retirement is perceived to be a traumatic event that is to be avoided. Finally, the research evidence to date suggests that there is not a consistent relationship, either positive or negative, between work satisfaction and attitudes toward retirement (Goudy et al., 1975, 1980). In summary, most individuals appear to have favorable attitudes toward retirement during the preretirement years.

The Process of Retirement

Introduction

Retirement is both a legal right and a social act prevalent in most modernized nations. The process of retirement involves a partial or total withdrawal from the labor force sometime between about 55 and 70 years of age. In most countries the mandatory retirement age is 65 or 70 years of age, with only the self-employed or a small percentage of those in organizations being able to continue working beyond that age. In return for this mandatory withdrawal, individuals receive social security benefits and other services designed to provide direct or indirect medical, social, or economic assistance in the later years.

In the more highly developed countries, only about 8 to 20 percent of the men[10] and about 5 to 10 percent of the women[11] continue working beyond 65 years of age. In contrast, in the less developed regions of the world, as many as 53 percent of the men and 17 percent of the women may continue working beyond 65 years of age (International Labour Office, 1978). However, as retirement becomes a more institutionalized process, and as social security systems and private pension plans develop in a nation, the percentage of those who continue working beyond age 65 will decrease during the remainder of this century, and the percentage of those who retire early will increase. For example, from 1950 to 1975 there was a decrease in the number of workers 55 to 64 years of age in the United States labor force from 87 to 75 percent (Anderson, 1981). In fact, even where the mandatory retirement age has been increased (to age 70 in the United States as of 1979), the median age at retirement is declining. This decline in labor-force participation after about age 50 is influenced by labor market policies (layoffs or firings), by discrimination against older workers (transfer to other jobs or cities late in life, unwillingness to hire older workers), by physical disabilities that prevent working, by insufficient incentives to continue working, by economic or other incentives to retire early,[12] and by the increasing number of workers who perceive that it is socially acceptable not to work and to seek an alternative lifestyle in the later years (Fisher, 1975; Clark and Spengler, 1980:85–119; Anderson, 1981; Foner and Schwab, 1981:45–66).

The outcome of this trend toward early retirement, combined with the demographic patterns of increased longevity and decreased fertility, is an increase in the proportion of dependent elderly people. When the aged dependency ratio increases, a greater economic burden is placed on a smaller labor force (Anderson, 1981). The economic ramifications of retirement, from an individual and societal view, are discussed later in this chapter. The remainder of this section examines the process of retirement by considering conceptual perspectives, preretirement preparation, the decision with respect to voluntary (early or late) and mandatory retirement, adjustment to retirement, retirement by women, and working beyond or in lieu of retirement. In the next chapter, the relationship between leisure and work and retirement is examined.

The Process of Retirement: Conceptual Perspectives

Introduction.   One of the major topics of interest among gerontologists has been the assumed problems associated with adjusting to mandatory retirement. This social event has been viewed as a major transition stage (primarily for adult men) with the potential to precipitate adjustment problems for the retiree. It is not surprising, therefore, that much of the early work in social gerontology (using the three major theoretical frameworks) sought to explain how men adjusted to retirement.

Disengagement theory argued that society expected individuals to give up the work role, and that they did so voluntarily and with relief. According to this theory, no attempt is made to compensate for the role loss, and the overall level of activity decreases as the individual disengages. Activity theory, in contrast, suggested that the work role is replaced with other roles so that the postretirement level of activity remains at about the same level as during the preretirement stage. Finally, continuity theory argues that although the work role is lost, the individual compensates by increasing his or her involvement in existing roles. Thus, the overall level of activity may remain about the same, may decrease slightly, or may increase depending on the postretirement level of involvement in preretirement nonwork roles.

Since the early 1970s, a number of conceptual models or frameworks have been proposed to explain the retirement process. As yet, however, a definitive theory accounting for all or part of the process has yet to be supported. The following discussion represents a brief review of some of the proposed conceptual frameworks that have appeared in the literature. They are presented to illustrate the range of approaches to understanding this complex process, which most adults in the labor force ultimately experience. While many of the earlier models were problem- or adjustment-oriented and focused on the individual and social psychological variables, more recent models have focused on elements of the process and have considered structural as well as social psychological variables (Calasanti, 1981; Foner and Schwab, 1981).

An analytical model of retirement.   From the premise that retirement is not a negative, crisis-generating event, Sussman (1972) argued that retirement represents a social psychological process that is experienced in relation to societal, biological, and environmental factors. These factors limit the options available to the individual. According to this model, societal and social psychological constraints influence the options available to an individual prior to, at, and following the act of retirement. More specifically, structural variables (such as class, retirement income policies, or preretirement preparation) and individual variables (such as lifestyles, value orientations, health, income, or competence) in the preretirement years influence the perception of retirement.

This perception is also colored by prevailing societal constraints (for example, norms concerning retirement as an event, the health of the economy, private and public retirement policies, and the presence or absence of intergenerational conflict). The retiree's perceptions and the degree of support or opposition from family, friends, and colleagues all interact in influencing the retiree's decision about how the retirement years will be spent. Will these years include another career, leisure pursuits, or volunteer work? The goal of this selection process is to develop competence in choosing options suited to the needs of the individual and to the specific social, biological, and environmental situation in which the individual is located.

Adjustment to retirement: substitution or accommodation.   According to Shanas (1972), the study of the transition to retirement involves two alternative assumptions: (1) the individual finds substitutes for lost roles or satisfaction provided by the job, or (2) the individual adapts to retirement by accommodating his or her lifestyle to changes in health and income status, and to changes in daily routine resulting from an increase in free time. Operating on the social psychological level, Shanas reviewed the literature and concluded that adjustment to retirement involves an ongoing process of accommodation or adaptation to changing personal and structural situations.

Adjustment to retirement: intervention models.   Eisdorfer (1972) viewed the loss of work as an event that precipitates a need for social psychological adaptation to a new situation or status. He, like many others, assumed that this transition had negative consequences for elderly persons. He argued that adaptation could be facilitated by intervention strategies to improve both the process of retirement and the ultimate quality of life. He proposed three models of adjustment, which include significant variables in the process of retirement. The 'crisis' model argues that retirement creates an emotional crisis to which the individual must respond, often with the help of significant others or professional counseling. The 'reinforcement' model suggests that in order to understand the adaptation of an individual to retirement, factors that were considered important to the individual during work must be identified and understood. Thus, if the loss of friends at work is considered traumatic, then efforts to enable the individual to retain the friendship links should be initiated. Salient interests or values from the work stage need to be reinforced in the retirement stage.

The third model suggests that an individual may adapt to the approaching retirement by developing a new 'motivational style' — fear of failure and a conservation-of-energy style may emerge to protect the ego of the retiree. This style may influence subsequent behavior in that the individual avoids failure situations and conserves energy in social interactions. He or she may withdraw, and may need help from significant others or professional counselors to change the motivational style so that a successful adaptation to retirement results.

Adjustment to retirement: internal compromise and interpersonal negotiation.   Atchley (1976a:113–22) proposed that the central processes of adjustment to retirement involve 'internal compromise' and 'interpersonal negotiation.' Internal compromise occurs when individuals perceive that retirement represents a significant change in their lives. In order to adjust to this transition, the individual must make a decision about altering his or her hierarchy of personal goals to fit the reality of the new status. If the retirement event is not viewed as a significant change, then the hierarchy of goals is not altered. For example, where one's job was never high in the ranking of personal goals, retirement poses few adjustment problems and the personal hierarchy does not need to be altered. However, where the job has been high on the list of personal goals and interests, and where few other goals exist, the loss of the job can pose serious adjustment problems. If the individual has the health, wealth, and ability to change the hierarchy of goals, then the adjustment may be satisfactory. However, if the individual does not have these personal resources, it may not be possible to alter the hierarchy of goals, and the only solution may be withdrawal from social interaction.

This process of internal compromise does not operate in isolation; a second process of negotiation with significant others provides reinforcement and feedback. Changes in the personal hierarchy of goals after retirement are carried out only if the individual gains approval from others, or receives advice from others that the goals need to be altered.[13]

Retirement: a systems perspective.   Kimmel (1978) suggests that the retirement decision involves interaction between variables representing three levels of analysis. These include the individual (occupation, health, finances, attitudes), the institutional (employer policies and benefits, employer-sponsored preparation programs), and the sociocultural-environmental (demographic factors, cultural values, government policies and benefits) levels. The retirement decision, in turn, has a subsequent impact on the individual (for example, on satisfaction, attitudes, or income), on the institution from which the person retired (for example, the loss of an experienced worker), and on the sociocultural environment (another 'dependent' person is created, and a consumer is lost). Thus, a feedback loop develops within the social system: factors influencing the retirement decision of a given individual may be altered or reinforced as a result of earlier events and the experiences of already-retired workers. In short, this approach recognizes the interaction between individual and structural variables.

A multivariate model of retirement research.   After a five-day seminar in 1977, eleven scholars generated a conceptual model of retirement research, a list of variables affecting the decision to retire, and a list of research questions concerning the process of retirement (Atchley, 1979). The following interrelated factors were thought to be important in retirement research: employer and government retirement policies; labor market conditions; personal characteristics of the retiree; personal and structural factors influencing retirement decisions; physical, social, and psychological effects of retirement on individuals and married couples; and economic and labor-force effects of retirement on work organizations, the community, and other institutions in society.

The researchers proposed a model that included the following variables: social system pressures to retire; personal desire to retire; perceived need to continue working; availability of information about retirement; personality, attitudes, and beliefs of the retiree; economic and psychological rewards of employment; physical and mental demands of the job versus perceived capacities; and financial need versus financial resources.

While these conceptual models do not represent a theory, they do provide a comprehensive framework for studying the phenomenon of retirement. Moreover, they raise research questions and suggest variables that need to be included in future research studies. In short, they represent the beginning of an agenda for future research in this area.

A dual-economy model of retirement. In a recent critique of the atheoretical nature of retirement research, Calasanti (1981) argues that a structural model is needed as a viable alternative to most of the above perspectives, which are based on the functionalist paradigm. This is particularly important when historical changes in the process are to be studied, since changes in the socioeconomic structure can influence individual behavior.

The dual-economy model is based on the assumption that historical changes in the nature of the capitalist economy have occurred in the United States. Basically, the structure of the economy moved from local, small-business capitalism (for example, a family-owned motel or grocery store) to a large, monopolistic, corporate capitalism (for example, a large multinational food or hotel chain) that sought national and international markets (Edwards et al., 1975; Edwards, 1979). This led to employment being based in either core (large national) or peripheral (small local) firms; that is, the dual-economy structure (Averitt, 1968). Thus, the work histories of individuals, which are important factors in the process of retirement, are determined by their places in either core or peripheral organizations. The place in the work structure, in turn, influences how micro-level variables (education, occupation, marital status, income, and health) will have an impact on a given individual. For example, those with higher educational attainment are more likely to be found in core organizations, and therefore may have better pensions and more options concerning when and how to retire. In short, the impact of individual factors on the retiring individual is influenced by the structure of the economic system. Therefore, the process of retirement may differ for retirees depending on whether they were employed in core or peripheral work organizations throughout their career. In fact, it is assumed that there is little if any movement between the two levels.

In summary, the dual-economy approach suggests that retirement is a dynamic process involving interaction between individual and societal factors. Therefore, further efforts to explain the theoretical process of retirement must consider both levels of analysis, and particularly the interaction between the two levels. The dual-economy model is proposed as one approach to a more complete analysis of adaptation to retirement at the individual and social structural levels.

Preparation for Retirement

Preretirement preparation represents a form of anticipatory socialization: the individual acquires knowledge about the postretirement stage and makes some tentative plans for this new phase in life. Planning should facilitate a smooth transition and reduce the stress created by the economic, social, and psychological uncertainty often associated with retirement (Cox and Bhak, 1978–79). Although many people agree that planning is important, very few make concrete plans on their own, or participate in formal programs (Glamser and DeJong, 1975; Kalt and Kohn, 1975; McPherson and Guppy, 1979).[14]

Most retirement preparation involves some type of financial planning to ensure economic security in the later years. Yet even this is difficult, because it must begin early in life even though the individual is unable to predict such factors as his or her work pattern and income levels, when the individual or spouse will die, what the retirement needs or lifestyle will be, the state of health, the date of retirement, the state of the economy, and the availability and impact of changes in retirement policies and benefits. This does not imply that retirement planning is useless, only that it is extremely difficult to accurately account for the many possible situations that any one person might experience in the future.

In order to assist people in preparing for and adjusting to retirement, many formal preretirement programs have been initiated by employers, by individuals, or by private entrepreneurs (Kelleher and Quirk, 1974; Rosencranz, 1975; Peavy, 1980; Foner and Schwab, 1981a; Glamser, 1981a; Olson, 1981b; Migliaccio and Cairo, 1981). These programs have ranged from a brief conversation about retirement benefits between the retiree and the personnel officer during the last week of work to comprehensive programs that begin a number of months or years prior to the retirement date. These programs involve testing and discussion about finances, health, leisure, travel, housing, legal matters, the marital relationship, postretirement employment options, and availability of community resources.

Programs that are largely concerned with disseminating facts and information are usually offered to a large group through lectures or printed material. Those programs that focus on providing assistance in personal adjustment are offered in small discussion groups or in individual counseling sessions.[15] In general, these formal programs are more readily available to white-collar men (who are usually well prepared financially for retirement), are voluntary, do not involve the spouse, and do not involve continuing contact with the individual after retirement. Furthermore, as Migliaccio and Cairo (1981) noted, there is often a gap between what research personnel recommend as the ideal structure and content of these programs and what is actually included in them.

Some programs involve alterations to the preretirement work pattern. Employees approaching retirement are permitted to taper off their work commitments by taking longer vacations or by working shorter days or weeks. In this way, the individual experiences increasing amounts of nonwork time in a progressive sequence leading up to retirement, and actually 'learns by doing' how to cope with suddenly available free time. To date, however, these transitional programs have usually only been available to upper-management white-collar or professional workers.

Although it has been demonstrated that preretirement planning via informal or formal programs is an important factor in the initial adjustment to retirement,[16] many employers have been reluctant to become involved in providing this type of service to their employees. However, in response to increasing demands from unions and employees for enhanced benefits, a growing number of employers are offering preretirement programs. These employers are becoming involved in order to enhance the corporate image as a socially responsible organization, and to improve employee relations (Peavy, 1980).

In summary, since few individuals engage in preretirement planning on their own,[17] organized programs are a necessary mechanism for facilitating adjustment to the early stages of retirement. These programs should offer both information and discussion, should include the spouse, and should consider individual differences in health and income status and in preretirement lifestyle, especially in the leisure domain.[18] A single recipe to be used by everyone in the preretirement years will not guarantee postretirement adjustment or satisfaction. Moreover, the formal programs should be made available to all workers, not just to those in high-status positions. In addition, since few people voluntarily prepare for retirement, a minimal compulsory program needs to be initiated to provide essential information concerning finances, legal and health matters, and the use of free time. Finally, the following principles may be useful in preparing for and adjusting to retirement: plan early, maintain flexibility in interests and social roles, remain physically and socially active, plan for a gradual transition from work to retirement, provide for a 'trial run' before a final commitment is made to a new residence or lifestyle, and consult with spouse, friends, and children about short- and long-term retirement plans.

The Retirement Decision

Voluntary versus involuntary retirement. The retirement decision is an essential intervening stage between the planning and adjustment phases of the retirement process. Historically, mandatory retirement has been the norm, and for many the only option; happily, flexible, voluntary retirement policies and options are becoming increasingly available to workers. Where the decision is voluntary rather than imposed, the individual feels that he or she has more control over the decision. As a result, the voluntary retiree, compared to the involuntary retiree, often engages in more planning for retirement; has a higher retirement income; reports better health; perceives a higher level of adjustment to and satisfaction with retirement; and in general has more favorable attitudes toward retirement (Kimmel et al., 1978).

Until 1979, the mandatory retirement age in North America for most workers was 65. However, people such as airline pilots, professional athletes, and dancers were exceptions; they could be forced to retire at any age if medical or physical limitations affected job performance. In addition, the self-employed worker was not subject to mandatory retirement legislation. Apart from these specialized categories of worker, most of the labor force was required to retire at age 65.

As of January 1, 1979, the Age Discrimination in Employment Act in the United States raised the age limit for most occupations to 70 years.[19] While this type of legislation has yet to be passed in Canada, there are cases before the courts in which mandatory retirement at age 65 is being cited as an example of age discrimination that violates human rights. Depending on the outcome of this litigation, the age of mandatory retirement may be raised, or automatic mandatory retirement at any age might be declared unconstitutional. If the latter ruling was handed down, each occupation or organization might be required to introduce aptitude tests and physical examinations that would ascertain, at regular intervals beyond a certain age, whether an employee was competent to continue full- or part-time employment in that occupation or organization (Walker and Lupton, 1978). Raising the mandatory retirement age may increase discrimination against older workers who belong to minority groups: they are often in poor health, and some are unable to work even until age 65 because of the physical demands of many jobs (McFadden et al., 1981).

Most workers retire voluntarily, and with relief, at or before the mandatory age. Relatively few workers are reluctant or unwilling retirees, although many of those who are members of minority groups are forced to retire early because of poor health, or an inability to obtain full- or part-time employment (McFadden et al., 1981).

The increase in voluntary retirement prior to or at the mandatory age is related to the fact that retirement is no longer viewed as a socially stigmatized stage in life. This pattern of early retirement is also related to the improved financial status provided by social security and private pension plans, and to the initiation of company incentive plans to encourage early retirement with a reasonable pension for long-term employees. However, with growing rates of unemployment or underemployment, and with the presence of double-digit inflation, many of those who might voluntarily retire early or at the mandatory age may now have to continue working for economic survival. Moreover, where formerly a younger spouse who was employed often retired voluntarily when the older spouse reached mandatory retirement age, there may be increasing economic pressure for the younger worker to remain in the labor force until mandatory retirement age.

Faced with the two competing alternatives of mandatory versus voluntary retirement, the public and private sectors have engaged in a long-standing debate as to which policy should be the norm.[20] To date, many rational and irrational arguments for each case have been presented. Some of the more rational and frequently used arguments are listed below. Generally, proponents of a flexible and voluntary retirement policy have argued that:

1. Mandatory retirement is discriminatory, and violates human rights.
2. It forces an experienced and skillful worker out of the labor force, and society is the loser, as well as the individual.
3. It increases the national debt because most of those beyond the mandatory age must be supported by social security payments.
4. It contributes to the alienation, isolation, and dissatisfaction of the elderly.
5. Because of individual differences, chronological age is an inaccurate predictor of work capabilities in the later years of life.

Not surprisingly, these arguments are supported by legal, empirical, or experiential evidence.

In contrast, advocates of mandatory retirement at a specific chronological age counter these arguments by stating that:

1. In the absence of valid and reliable tests of competency, all individuals are treated equally with respect to the timing of their exit from the labor force.
2. Less competent or less motivated workers are not forced to submit to competency tests, thereby revealing weaknesses prior to, or at, the retirement age. Hence, older workers are protected against being forced out of the labor force prior to the mandatory age.
3. Mandatory retirement is a major mechanism for promoting mobility within the labor force, since middle-aged workers can be promoted and young workers can enter.
4. It provides stability in pension systems because the demand for increased payments in a given year can be more accurately predicted.

To date, few of the claims for mandatory retirement can be supported by research evidence. Despite the prevailing evidence in favor of flexible and voluntary retirement policies, there is increasing support for a compromise: mandatory retirement would be abolished, but a periodic review of performance would be required for workers over a specific age. In some occupations and industries, incentives have been offered for early retirement (for example, the 'thirty-years-and-out' policy in the automotive industry, or the policy of the teaching profession that permits early retirement when the sum of age plus number of years of teaching equals ninety).

Early versus late retirement.   As we saw earlier, only about 18 percent of the men and 7 percent of the women in North America continue to work after 65 years of age. Among those most likely to continue working are those in good health; self-employed professionals; those who are highly educated; those whose major life interest has been work (especially those who are single); blue-collar workers with few pension credits; rural farm workers; and workers employed in an occupation or industry characterized by a labor shortage. The individual who decides to continue working has four basic options: retire and obtain a part-time position with the same employer or a new employer; continue in the same job; begin a second career in a new field; or become engaged in full- or part-time volunteer work wherein the work pattern represents a nonsalaried career.

In some situations the decision to continue working beyond the normal retirement age may be a mutually beneficial one for the employee, the employer, and the government. For example, in Japan, where the mandatory retirement age is 55, many workers continue to work beyond age 55 to meet a labor shortage, to maintain some degree of economic security, and to relieve pressure on the government pension system (Sodei, 1981). To facilitate this continued involvement in the labor force, Japanese workers are either re-employed in a smaller company or are permitted to remain with their original employer. In both situations the worker is hired for a one- to five-year period at a reduced salary, and usually in a less prestigious position.

Until recent inflationary times, only about 65 percent of men 60 to 64 years of age in the United States were still in the labor force by age 65 (Schulz, 1980). Some of those who became unemployed prior to age 65 were victims of age discrimination in hiring, job obsolescence, the closing or reduction in size of manufacturing plants, a history of unemployment, or an inability to work because of declining motivation, skills, or health. This pattern of involuntary early retirement is especially prevalent among members of some minority groups who have historically had higher levels of unemployment, lower incomes, and a higher incidence of health problems (McFadden et al., 1981). In recent years, it has also become more common among middle-management workers whose positions are suddenly discontinued five to ten years before their normal retirement age.

In recent years a number of studies have sought to identify and explain the factors influencing the decision to retire voluntarily before the normal mandatory age (Parnes et al., 1975; Irelan et al., 1976; Barfield and Morgan, 1978a; Kell and Patton, 1978; McPherson and Guppy, 1979; Price et al., 1979; Clark and Spengler, 1980:85–119; Ekerdt et al., 1980; Hardy, 1980; Anderson, 1981; Clark, 1981; Foner and Schwab, 1981; McFadden et al., 1981; Prothero, 1981; Hardy, 1982; Palmore, 1982). The decision to retire early appears to be influenced by personal factors unique to an individual, and by institutional or structural factors impinging on an individual after about 55 years of age. Both push and pull factors operate within each of these categories to encourage an early retirement.

At the institutional or structural level, the voluntary decision to retire early is influenced by:

1. A labor market characterized by high unemployment at all ages. In this situation it may be more economically advantageous to retire early and to receive retirement benefits than to continue on welfare, or to continue searching for full- or part-time work.

2. Policies that permit partial or total old age security and pension payments to be received before 65 years of age.

3. A lowering or elimination of the fixed limit on earnings above which old-age security benefits may not be claimed. This enables an individual to retire with a private pension and still remain eligible to receive old-age security payments (even if he or she works part-time and earns a salary).

4. Raising the mandatory retirement age so that more workers opt out of the labor force between 60 and 69 years of age.

5. A forced horizontal or downward move, or a reclassification to a lower job category within the organization.

6. The presence of societal norms that make an 'early' retirement socially acceptable.

7. Union demands for a ceiling on the number of years of employment (for example, 'thirty and out').

The personal factors that have been found to influence the decision to retire early include:

1. Being financially secure enough to support the retiree and the spouse for an unknown number of years (no mortgage, few dependents, sufficient savings, a large pension).

2. A decline in health that cannot be compensated for by a change to a more suitable job.

3. A desire for a change in lifestyle that can be accommodated by savings, equity in a home, and the availability of private pension benefits to ensure an acceptable standard of living.

4. A positive attitude toward retirement, and an expectation that retirement will be a satisfying stage in life.

5. A supportive spouse and family (Chown, 1977).

6. Being single or having few dependents.

7. Being a disadvantaged member of a minority group with a low level of education, an irregular employment history, and poor health.

8. Having a low level of education.

9. Being employed in a physically demanding job.

10. Making early and concrete plans for retirement.

11. Being dissatisfied with the job while at the same time having some degree of economic security.

The most significant personal factors in the retirement decision are financial security and the state of health. If the individual has sufficient financial resources and is in good health there is a higher probability of early retirement. The actual age at which the retirement occurs may depend on other factors such as pension policies, age and employment status of the spouse, leisure lifestyle, physical and mental demands of the job, level of job satisfaction, life-long attitudes toward work, or societal norms pertaining to early retirement. For the individual who is in poor health, early retirement may occur suddenly, regardless of financial status. Those who are forced to retire early because of deteriorating health may be eligible for financial assistance in the form of long-term disability pensions.

Partial versus full retirement.   For some individuals the transition to full retirement is preceded by a period of partial withdrawal from the labor force. This pattern is more common among the self-employed than among wage and salary workers. For example, Quinn (1981) found that among respondents in the Social Security Retirement History Study in the United States, only 5 percent of the wage and salary workers were partially retired, whereas 12 percent of the self-employed (especially among those aged 58 to 63) were partially retired. One reason for this higher rate is that the self-employed are exempt from such institutional constraints as company pension policies and discrimination in hiring older workers.

At present, partial retirement is not a widely available option. However, with increasing inflation, with a higher age for mandatory retirement, and with the initiation of policies promoting job sharing and reduced work loads, partial retirement may become more prevalent in the future. In fact, Quinn (1981) suggests that a greater number of wage and salary workers might select a transitional period of partial retirement if more part-time positions were available.

Adjustment to Retirement

The study of reactions to retirement has generated a large body of literature in the field of social gerontology. Much of this work is based on the assumption that being retired is a traumatic event, and that many elderly men do not adjust to the new status of retiree. Many articles have sought to describe and explain the 'crises,' the 'despair,' the 'losses,' and the 'changes' that accompany or are initiated by retirement.

This literature was further expanded by the long-standing interest of researchers in accounting for the life satisfaction, well-being, or morale of the elderly (Larson, 1978). Just as widowhood was seen as a significant transition point for women, the onset of retirement was thought to be a significant event for men in the later years. As a result of this interest in the impact of retirement on the individual, it has been hypothesized that retirement represents a roleless role fraught with uncertainty, fear, dissatisfaction, and loss of identity. Moreover, it has also been argued that retirement leads to declining health or an early death (Haynes et al., 1978), to marital disharmony, to decreased levels of social interaction and activity, and to the onset of economic hardship and poverty.[21]

Clearly, the onset of retirement represents a major transition point that has the potential to alter the lifestyle and life chances of the former worker and his or her spouse. However, recent evidence suggests that the majority of male respondents (70 to 90 percent) report few problems in adjusting to retirement (Friedman and Orbach, 1974; Atchley, 1975; Darnley, 1975; George and Maddox, 1977; Barfield and Morgan, 1978b; Matthews and Brown, 1981a; Foner and Schwab, 1981; Mutran and Reitzes, 1981; Hendrick et al., 1982; Beck, 1982).[22] This pattern seems to hold true both during the 'honeymoon' phase and in the long run (Ekerdt et al., 1981).[23]

The major problems reported during the retirement stage pertain to loss of income, declining health, nostalgia for the job, and the death of the spouse. Only the loss of income and the perceived social and psychological losses accompanying the loss of a job are related to the retirement event per se. Even here (at least until the recent period of double-digit inflation) most individuals seemed to be able to adjust to changes in their financial status by lowering their expectations or by altering their consumption patterns (Atchley, 1979).[24]

Given the apparent variation in the degree and quality of adjustment to retirement, a number of studies have sought to identify the factors that facilitate a satisfactory transition from the role of worker to that of retiree. Generally, the transition is less traumatic and more satisfying for those with higher perceived levels of health and economic status;[25] for those who have a harmonious marriage and social support from a spouse and family (Krauss, 1981); for those who continue to participate in social activity and interaction at about the same level and in about the same type or form as earlier (Foner and Schwab, 1981:40; Matthews and Brown, 1981a); for those who have lost interest in work and who have a positive orientation to and interest in leisure; for those who have an accurate perception of retirement, a positive attitude toward retirement, and who have engaged in realistic preretirement planning; for those who remain in their own home rather than moving to an apartment or institution; and for those who retire with adequate pensions at a period in history that is not characterized by excessive and rapid inflation.

In summary, in 1900, about 6 percent of the life cycle was spent in retirement; by 1980, that figure had risen to about 17 percent (Best, 1979). While some men do not adjust well to retirement, and either return to the work force or remain dissatisfied, the majority do adjust well in both the short and long terms. This pattern has been prevalent until recently. With the recent rapid rise in the rate of inflation, the number of retirees reporting dissatisfaction or adjustment problems may be increasing, even though an intervening stage of decreased expectations has likely occurred. This increased dissatisfaction is probably most prevalent among those with inadequate pensions, savings, and equity. The commonly held view that retirement leads to serious physical or psychological deterioration is not supported for most retired individuals. In fact, if those who retire because of poor health are not included in studies, there are few differences between the elderly who are retired and those who continue working. Moreover, the trend toward early retirement[26] seems to suggest that older workers are less apprehensive about retirement. Most look forward to retirement and find that leaving the stress or boredom of work brings a new meaning and enjoyment to life. However, there is some evidence (Beck, 1982) that those who retire earlier than they expected to are less satisfied than men who are still in the labor force. It may be that the unexpected retirement is undesired and therefore lowers the level of life satisfaction.

Women and the Retirement Process

Just as the study of the impact on men of widowhood has been neglected, so too has the impact of retirement on women been understudied. At first, the concern of researchers was primarily with how a wife reacted to the retirement of her husband (Keating and Cole, 1980), how retirement affected the marital relationship (Blieszner and Szinovacz, 1979), and how the adjustment of the husband could be facilitated by a supportive wife (Fengler, 1975). Generally, these studies have found that the wife's reaction can influence the adjustment of both the husband and the marital dyad (Fengler, 1975). However, retirement by the husband can create stresses in the wife's daily life, especially if she has not been involved in preretirement planning. For example, a recent study found that the wives of retired teachers perceived that the retirement of the spouse led to a loss of independence and privacy. Furthermore, the wives reported that there was often a need to reduce their social network and to restructure their normal pattern of daily activities to accommodate the retired spouse (Keating and Cole, 1980). Thus, there is a need to consider the wife in the retirement process, especially when only the husband has been employed.

There is also a growing need to study the retirement process as it influences the increasing number of older women, both single and married, in the labor force. The pattern of women's work history across the life cycle must be examined in order to better understand the retirement process. As noted earlier, many women have had a cyclical pattern of participation in the labor force; have received lower salaries than men (unequal pay for equal work or level of job responsibility); have been employed in low-skill positions; and have generally not been eligible for high pension or old-age security payments because of these factors. Those who are married and who are younger than their husbands may retire early, voluntarily or involuntarily, to coincide with the husband's retirement. If retirement is involuntary, marital conflict may result (Prothero, 1981). Some widowed or divorced women may retire later because of economic necessity (Sheppard, 1976), or because they fear they will lose their major social network (Prothero, 1981). In general, having children and delaying entry into a career may mean reduced pension benefits and therefore may lead to a decision to delay retirement. In contrast, where an adequate pension is available, declining health, remarriage, or widowhood may lead to an early retirement by older women (O'Rand and Henretta, 1982).

A majority of white-collar working women think about retirement, look forward to it, and feel that they will make a satisfactory adjustment (Prentis, 1980); but the actual evidence concerning the adjustment of women to retirement is contradictory. Some studies have shown that retired older women are less well-adjusted than working older women, although both groups are more satisfied than homemakers who have not worked (Jaslow, 1976; Atchley, 1976b; Fox, 1977; Blieszner and Szinovacz, 1979; Block, 1980). Others have found that there are few sex differences in overall well-being in retirement, or in attitudes toward retirement (Levy, 1980–81; Schnore and Kirkland, 1981). However, women may require a longer period of adjustment (Atchley, 1976b), especially if they have had negative attitudes toward retirement and if they have retired involuntarily (Levy, 1980–81).

Despite the uncertainty about the attitudes of women toward retirement, objective data indicate that a greater number of retired women than men live in poverty, are in poor health, and live longer. Furthermore, as with men, the degree of satisfaction may vary according to the individual's health, economic, and marital status, and type of career. Some single women may be more likely to resist retirement and to continue working so as to avoid losing income and their major life interest (Ward, 1979; Matthews and Brown, 1981a). Older women, regardless of marital status, who have followed a continuous career with high levels of achievement, may report higher levels of life satisfaction after retirement, because they see their lives as more complete than those of the homemaker or intermittent worker (Block, 1979; Holahan, 1981).

In summary, there is variation in the willingness and the ability of women to adjust to retirement. While most retire voluntarily and adjust satisfactorily, those who are economically disadvantaged (for example, the widowed, the divorced, and the intermittent worker) may adjust less satisfactorily. Those who are both self-dependent and economically disadvantaged are more likely to want to, and to need to, continue working up to (and beyond) the normal retirement age.

Retirement and Economic Status

Introduction

In recent years economists, actuaries, and gerontologists interested in economics, have become increasingly concerned about the impact of retirement on the economic status of an individual and of a society (Kreps, 1976; Sebastian, 1976; Schulz, 1976, 1980; Clark et al., 1978; Clark and Spengler, 1978, 1980; Herzog, 1978; Cowgill, 1979; Grad and Foster, 1979; Stone and MacLean, 1979; Muller, 1980; Powell and Martin, 1980; Clark, 1981; Harris, 1981; Olson, 1981a; Tindale, 1981; Grimaldi, 1982; Myles, forthcoming). Most of this interest has focused on the diminished and disadvantaged economic status of the elderly individual or couple.

Because of rapid inflation, early retirement, and an increasing old-age dependency ratio, concern has also been expressed concerning the insufficiency of payments to older individuals, and the diminishing resources of old-age security funds and public and private pension plans. As a result, attention is being directed toward the impact of retirement policies, mandatory retirement age, fertility and mortality rates, and social (early retirement) and economic (inflation and high unemployment) changes on the ability of a society to meet the needs of the elderly, and at the same time maintain a near-balanced budget.

Retirement Policy and Societal Economic Stability

Social security[27] and private pension plans are not universal phenomena, but they are present in most industrialized societies (Fisher, 1978).[28] Pension systems were originally established at a time when inflation and fertility rates were reasonably predictable, and when it was assumed that retirement would not occur until at least 65 years of age. On the basis of these assumptions it was relatively easy to project the amount of income needed over the years to provide payments to the members of each cohort as they entered retirement. However, some observers have expressed a fear that the old-age security system will be faced with potential bankruptcy when the baby-boom cohort approaches retirement around 2010, if not earlier. Moreover, the public pension system may be threatened now because of the decreased fertility rates of the past fifteen years: fewer workers are contributing to the pension system, and the old-age dependency ratio is increasing. The system is also threatened during periods of high unemployment, since contributions to the system are reduced accordingly. This problem is further compounded by the recent trend toward early voluntary retirement, a pattern that reduces the projected amount of contributions even further. Old-age security and private pension funds are depleted, since early retirees begin to withdraw monies from them earlier than projected. Furthermore, because security payments are tied to the Consumer Price Index, the recent rapid rise in inflation has necessitated an almost monthly increase in the amount of payments, thereby further weakening the solvency of the system. Finally, the costs of supporting older dependents are rising because they live for a longer period in retirement, because the cost of health care for the elderly is escalating rapidly, and because more former workers are eligible for benefits than in the past.

In order to maintain solvency in the social security system, a number of revisions in retirement policies and payments have been initiated or proposed (Sheppard and Rix, 1977; Clark, 1980; Ragan, 1980; Foner and Schwab, 1981:83–117; Clark et al., 1982). First, when the mandatory retirement age was raised to 70 years of age in the United States, it was thought that this policy would increase the number of contributors to the system and would delay payments for about five years. Although it is still too soon to determine whether this will occur, early trends suggest that a large number of workers are not remaining employed until 70 years of age. Second, in some countries social security payments before a specified age are reduced by the amount of income a person earns. Older workers are discouraged from seeking employment, especially if they are eligible to receive benefits from a private pension plan. Hence, they retire at or before the mandatory age and remain unemployed so as not to lose the benefits they feel are owed them for a lifetime of work and contributions.

Other alternatives to keep the system viable include increasing the social security contributions of those in the labor force; reducing the amount of benefits paid to retirees; increasing personal and corporate income tax so that old-age security is paid in part from general income tax revenues; delaying the retirement age; raising the minimum age of eligibility, regardless of when the individual retires; imposing income taxes on one-half of social security benefits; and permitting individuals to opt out of the social security system (Fox, 1979; Schulz, 1980; Foner and Schwab, 1981).

While some or all of these proposals might solve the economic problem in either the short or long term, they also have the potential to create social problems. For example, with an increasing old-age dependency ratio, increased income taxes or social security contributions place a greater burden on a smaller number of workers. This could lead to intergenerational conflict. Also, by using general taxes to supplement a depleted social security system, funds may be shifted from other crucial areas such as national defense, education, welfare, health care, or other programs.

In short, the economic viability of the old-age security system may be in jeopardy, and viable solutions have yet to be found. As we move toward an era of greater drain upon the system with fewer workers making regular contributions, bankruptcy seems to be a possibility. With declining fertility rates and changing social norms, more women enter and remain in the labor force, and make contributions to social security and private pension funds. However, while these contributions help to maintain a balance in the pension system at present, many of these female contributors will be eligible for benefits at some time in the future. As a result, the size of payments needed for a specific retiring cohort may be greater than projected, thereby reducing the fund dramatically during a given period of time (Clark and Spengler, 1978).

Retirement and Individual Economic Stability

This subsection focuses on factors influencing the sources, amounts, and adequacy of income in the retirement years. Retirement income comes from three sources: (1) government-based minimum and supplementary social security payments, tax benefits, and in-kind benefits (non-money benefits such as subsidized medical care, housing, transportation, food, social and recreational services); (2) private pension plans; and (3) personal resources (for example, savings, investments, equity in a home, earnings after retirement, gifts, or assistance from relatives). Table 10.1 indicates the 1976 median income from various sources for those over 65 years of age in the United States. Again, these figures are generally lower for blacks, for women, and for the very old who are less likely to have access to a private pension plan that can supplement social security payments.

Table 10.1 Median income from various sources for 55-year-olds in the United States during 1976. Adapted from Grad and Foster (1979).

Social security	$2870
Private pensions	1860
Personal assets (savings, bonds, stocks)	870
Salary (full-time or part-time work)	2530

For all three sources, the individual's pattern of employment, place of employment, and level of earnings influences the amount of income after retirement.[29] Monthly payments from social security and private pensions and amount of savings and investments are closely related to annual income during the working years (Tindale, 1981). This level of income is especially critical for private pension plans where the amount of annual benefits is often based on the average earnings during the last five to ten years of employment. Therefore, the higher the salary near the end of the career, the higher the pension.[30]

Although there has been a dramatic increase in the number of individuals eligible for a private pension, this benefit is still not available to all workers. Those with irregular patterns of employment, the self-employed, and those employed in small organizations may not have access to employer-sponsored pension plans. For those who are enrolled in a private plan, contributions are usually paid by both the employee and the employer. Under this system, the workers must be protected if they are fired, if they leave the company, or if they retire early. Many private pension plans are 'portable': paid-in contributions can be transfered to a plan in another company. This ensures that the benefits paid at retirement are similar to those that would have been paid had the place of employment not changed.

Similarly, the plan should provide for 'vesting,' so that those who are fired or quit before retirement receive all or part of the benefits that have been earned prior to leaving the organization. Normally, an individual must remain at least five to ten years with the company before vesting occurs. In addition, the benefits are seldom adjusted upward to keep pace with inflation after the individual leaves the organization. A viable private pension plan should also include 'survivor's benefits' so that the spouse will be protected during widowhood. Finally, the plan should provide 'reduced benefits' for those who opt to retire before the mandatory age.[31]

We have seen that the economic status of the retired individual or couple can range from poverty to great wealth, depending on past earnings and assets and on the eligibility for retirement benefits. From the perspective of society, there has been great concern expressed about the need to ensure 'adequate' retirement incomes or wealth for the elderly, especially for older widows and members of minority groups who have had an irregular work history. However, these objective, external assessments of adequacy have seldom identified the standard to which 'adequate' is compared. If the income of the current cohort aged 65 and over is compared to those who retired ten or fifteen years ago, their relative status is adequate; a larger percentage of each retiring cohort is eligible for private pension plans, and they receive larger social security payments. The members of more recently retired cohorts also receive greater tax concessions and in-kind benefits.

Generally, various occupational groups are able to maintain their relative position in the income hierarchy and to maintain their relative standard of living in retirement (McAllister, 1981; Myles, 1981; Hurd, 1982).[32] However, if the economic status of the recently retired is compared to their preretirement status, to the status of those in their occupational group who remain in the labor force, or to age peers who continue to work in any occupation, then their objective economic status is inferior (Myles, 1981). For some, this reduced income may create some hardships; for others, it may be totally inadequate and lead to poverty and to dependence on welfare or family assistance.

Although the objective indicators provide aggregate information about the relative economic status of retired cohorts, individual responses to the loss of income must also be assessed, especially when considering the relationship between economic status and well-being. The perception of financial 'adequacy' by a given individual or couple may be more relevant than the objective economic situation as viewed by outsiders (Peterson, 1972; Harris, 1975; Liang and Fairchild, 1979; Liang et al., 1980; Brown and Matthews, 1981). Many individuals are aware of their own needs, priorities, resources, and debts, and are able to establish personally satisfying, albeit lower, standards of living in the retirement years.

Nevertheless, about 24 percent of the elderly in the United States report that inflation, the high cost of living, and high prices are the greatest problems facing the elderly (Harris, 1981). Not surprisingly, 42 percent of blacks and 52 percent of Hispanics 65 years of age and over reported that not having enough money to live on is a very serious personal problem. For many, then, inflation may be traumatic, especially if their assets depreciate in value (for example, if they suffer losses in stocks or bonds or own a house in a deteriorating real estate area), if transfer payments (pensions or social security) lag behind inflation, and if inflationary prices affect items (such as food or medical care) that comprise a large proportion of the retired person's budget (Schulz, 1980:42–46). In contrast, Grimaldi (1982) argued that on the basis of data collected in the United States from 1973 to 1981, the elderly do not experience higher inflation rates than the general population. In fact, he suggests that the aged may have been overcompensated for inflation via higher social security benefits. These higher payments have resulted from the rapid increase in home-ownership costs since 1977, an increase not experienced by many of the elderly who already owned their homes. Thus, while receiving higher payments, they did not have to assign a part of these payments to mortgage costs.

The perceived adequacy of economic status in retirement is usually based on a comparison with the individual's past lifestyle and with the status of the peer group. In short, the definition of the economic situation in retirement is based on perceptions about relative deprivation (self now versus self in the past; self versus others). For example, Liang and Fairchild (1979) and Liang et al. (1980) tested this relative-deprivation model with a national sample for each year from 1972 to 1977. They found that feelings of relative deprivation and perceived distributive justice (where past investments or past efforts are balanced by present rewards) do influence financial satisfaction in the later years. Specifically, those with lower preretirement incomes were found to be less dissatisfied, probably because there was little perceived change or deprivation in their financial status.

In contrast, those with high preretirement incomes expressed greater dissatisfaction with their postretirement financial status because they had experienced the greatest loss in income. Yet, they are also likely to have the largest discretionary income, and they should therefore be more able to cope with any required adjustments. However, they have seldom had to make adjustments in their lifestyle, and even the slightest reduction in their standard of living may be perceived as unsatisfactory or traumatic. Brown and Matthews (1981) found that both men and women were more satisfied with their financial situation in retirement if they were content to retire and leave work, if they voluntarily retired at a time when they wanted to retire, and if they had high social status.

Many of the retired elderly do view their economic situation as satisfying; one possible explanation for this pattern may be a change in consumption or expenditure patterns.[33] However, it is not clear whether expenditures decline because income declines after retirement, or because actual needs and wants decrease in the later years. On the one hand, expenses are lower because the retirees do not have to support children, because they have fewer work-related expenses (such as clothes and transportation), because they have few or no mortgage obligations, and because they are eligible for senior-citizen discounts. On the other hand, medical, energy, food, and home-maintenance costs increase with age and because of inflation. For example, food costs represent about 20 percent of the family budget (Mason and Bearden, 1978), and the elderly spend approximately 70 percent more on medical care than the younger population. In addition, medical costs escalate more rapidly (by approximately 30 percent) than prices in general (Borzilleri, 1978).

Because a larger percentage of the retiree's reduced economic resources is allocated to food and medical costs, Borzilleri (1978) advocated the creation and use of a separate Consumer Price Index for older persons in order to make adjustments in social security and pension payments. Rising pensions and increased savings do increase the amount of discretionary income available. At the same time, the elderly comprise an ever-increasing proportion of the total population. Thus, there has been a growing awareness on the part of the business sector that a 'maturity market' may be on the horizon, especially if inflation and interest rates are reduced. As a result, there has been and will continue to be increased advertising and increased development of products designed to meet the needs and wants of middle-aged and older persons who have larger discretionary incomes (for such things as clothes, travel, food, cosmetics, leisure products, music, and movies).

In summary, the circumstances leading to perceived adequacy of the financial situation in retirement appear to be related not only to the relative deprivation from the preretirement income levels, but also to social status, education, race, expenditure and consumption patterns, inflation, and the specific circumstances of the retirement. As Liang and Fairchild (1979) indicate, there is a need to maintain the financial status of the retired in line with their preretirement situation and that of their reference group of age peers. This appears to be especially relevant to higher-wage earners who may have higher expectations for the retirement lifestyle and who may be less willing or able to make compromises in their standard of living. In short, both the absolute and relative economic positions of the elderly must be understood prior to establishing or implementing policies.

Economic Status of Retired Women and Housewives

As noted earlier, the work history of women often represents an intermittent pattern; they tend to voluntarily enter and leave the labor force more frequently than males. They also are more likely to engage in part-time work, to leave the labor force after childbirth, and to remain at home at least until their children reach school age. Moreover, during the time they are in the labor force they frequently occupy low-prestige, low-income positions, and seldom seek or receive the opportunity to advance to high-status, high-paying positions. Finally, many women remain homemakers throughout their adult life and receive no direct salary for this work and responsibility.

As a result of these work-related factors, and because they live longer, older women often have fewer financial resources than men after the mandatory age of retirement, and especially after they are widowed (Dulude, 1978; Women and Poverty, 1979; Burks, 1980; Schulz, 1980; Thompson, 1980). This disadvantaged economic status is a result of their intermittent work history; they may not have worked long enough to be eligible for private pension plans or higher social security payments. Even where they have been employed long enough to meet eligibility requirements, low wages or fewer years of participation may result in relatively small pensions, since the amount is based on earnings and contributions while employed. Furthermore, some social security and private pension payments may be reduced or eliminated when the spouse dies.

Many women, especially divorcees and widows, become economically disadvantaged to some degree at some point in their lives. For example, until recently pensions were not considered family assets to be shared in a divorce settlement. Although this is no longer the case in some jurisdictions, further reforms are needed to improve the social security and pension eligibility of women who have been full- or part-time workers in the labor force. These reforms should permit interruptions in employment and should take into account part-time work with reduced earnings and contributions (Dulude, 1981; Kahne, 1981).

Life-long homemakers who have not participated in the labor force since they were married or since the birth of the first child are especially likely to be poor. It has recently been argued that the responsibilities of homemakers constitute unpaid labor. Homemakers should be eligible for increased social security payments in recognition of their labor in the home (Dulude, 1981).[34] It has also been suggested that women who spend a portion of their adult life raising children should be eligible for higher social security payments because of their contribution to society.[35] In addition, it has been recommended that pension credits accumulated during the years of marriage should be shared between spouses after age 65 in order to improve the economic status of the divorced and widowed. The funds for these increased benefits to older women might be paid by the husband during his working years, by higher contributions from all workers, or by funds from general tax revenues.

Not surprisingly, some observers argue that homemakers should not be eligible for special considerations if it increases the burden on current workers, or if it increases the national debt. They claim that women who remain permanently at home do so voluntarily, often because they feel that they do not need to work for economic reasons. Why should their economic position be any different in retirement? Moreover, it is argued that women who have decided to remain out of the labor force to perform a service for their husbands should receive retirement benefits from the spouse rather than from society. In summary, while social security and pension reforms are needed to improve the economic status of older women, especially the widowed and divorced, the procedures and policies by which this goal can be realized have yet to be firmly established.

Summary and Conclusions

This chapter has examined the relationship between work, retirement, and economic status in the later years of life. The first major section considered work patterns during the adult years, the competence of the older worker, and preretirement attitudes toward retirement. In the second section, the literature pertaining to various facets of the retirement process was reviewed. The reader was first introduced to a number of conceptual perspectives that included some of the personal and social structural variables thought to be important in the retirement process. Following this section on conceptual frameworks, evidence was presented from the literature concerning preretirement preparation, the nature of the retirement decision, the process of adjustment to retirement, and the retirement process for women. The final section of the chapter considered the present and future structure and stability of public and private pension systems, the actual and perceived economic status of elderly persons, and the disadvantaged economic status of retired women and housewives.

Based on the literature pertaining to work, economic status, and retirement in the later years of life, it can be concluded that:

1. Most men and women adjust to retirement and experience little stress in adapting to the new social status and lifestyle.

2. Previous work patterns and orientation to work influence when an individual retires, how he or she adjusts, and whether he or she returns to work on a full-time or part-time basis.

3. Women comprise approximately 30 to 40 percent of the adult work force in North America.

4. There are few significant sex differences in the importance of work to the individual. Work is a serious, meaningful, expressive, and satisfying role for most women, as it is for most men.

5. The general job performance of older workers rarely declines. However, there are individual differences in work-related skills among older workers, just as there are among younger workers.

6. There is relatively little decline in work productivity with age, providing that a high level of motivation is present.

7. Declining cognitive or physical skills can be compensated for by experience and by utilizing coping strategies.

8. Older workers are absent less and have fewer accidents than younger workers.

9. Most individuals have favorable attitudes toward retirement during the preretirement years. These positive attitudes are related to having high levels of health, income, and education, and to perceived support from significant others in the family and at work.

10. In the more developed countries of the world, between 8 and 20 percent of the men and between 5 and 10 percent of the women work beyond the age

of 65. In the less developed countries approximately 53 percent of the men and 17 percent of the women continue working beyond age 65.

11. While many individuals believe that preretirement planning is important, very few make concrete plans or participate in formal programs.

12. Most workers retire voluntarily at the mandatory retirement age. An increasing number (at least until the recent period of inflation) are opting to retire voluntarily before the mandatory age.

13. Involuntary early retirement is more prevalent for members of minority groups, and for those in poor health.

14. Partial retirement is not a common option except for the self-employed.

15. Many women have had an irregular or cyclical work history wherein they have occupied low-skill positions with low wages and few benefits. As a result, at retirement age many women are not eligible for a complete or partial pension, and they may be entitled to fewer social security benefits than men who have been regularly employed throughout adulthood.

16. Divorced or widowed women in the labor force may retire later than other women because of economic necessity. Furthermore, because they are economically disadvantaged they may adjust less satisfactorily to retirement.

17. The economic status of older women is further compounded by the fact that they live longer than men, and therefore must support themselves for a longer period of time.

18. The economic viability of public and private pension systems may be in jeopardy in the future as a result of decreased fertility rates and high unemployment; early retirements; and an increase in middle-aged and older female workers.

19. Private pension earnings after retirement are related to the individual's pattern of employment, place of employment, and level of earnings during the working years.

20. Private pension benefits are significantly lower or nonexistent for those who are self-employed, for those employed by small organizations, and for those with irregular patterns of employment.

21. Those with high preretirement incomes may express greater dissatisfaction with their postretirement financial status because they usually experience larger absolute and relative decreases in income. Therefore, a greater adjustment in lifestyle may be necessary unless they use their savings to maintain a standard of living similar to that of the preretirement years.

Notes

1. The concept of retirement as a societal institution was first formalized in Germany in 1888 (Hudson and Binstock, 1976). Legislation permitted workers to leave the labor force at 70 years of age with a degree of guaranteed economic support. This age criterion was later reduced to 65 years of age. A national retirement policy was initiated in the United States in 1935. In Canada, a Pension Act was enacted in 1918 for war veterans only; in 1927 Parliament passed the Old Age Pension Act, which applied to all citizens over 65 years of age.

2. For a historical analysis of how retirement policies and the institution of retirement grew in the United States, see Atchley (1976a:10–21); Baum and Baum (1980:102–45); Graebner (1980); Ragan (1980); Foner and Schwab (1981:83–87); and Hendricks and Hendricks (1981:280–87). For an analysis of the situation in England, see Parker (1982).

3. The studies by Streib and Schneider (1971), Irelan et al. (1976), Parnes et al. (1979), and Parnes (1981) are longitudinal studies; the evidence reported by most other authors is based on retrospective interviews or questionnaires.

4. It is also important to understand the relationship between work and leisure during the adult years. The relative weighting of each in an individual's hierarchy of values can greatly influence whether early retirement will be elected and how the individual will make use of free time during retirement. This relationship between work and leisure is discussed in more detail in chapter 11.

5. There are an increasing number of housewives who re-enter the educational system, often after child rearing is nearly or fully completed, and then begin a career in their 40s. For those who enter business or the professions, this transition may be considered a midlife career change, especially if the new occupation becomes the major life interest.

6. In fact, it has been suggested that from the perspective of a society or an organization, these career changes are threatening; the investment in training the individual for the first career has been lost. Also, if one person in an organization initiates a career change, a role model for others is created, thereby leading to possible further personnel losses. In order to counteract these organizational losses, some companies have attempted to improve the work situation by offering their staffs new challenges, alternative work patterns, sabbatical leaves, and greater autonomy.

7. These percentages may increase after the next census report in the United States because the mandatory retirement age was raised to 70 years in 1979. It is not known how many people will continue working to age 70 and whether there will be sex, class, racial, regional, or occupational differences in those choosing to remain in the labor force until 70 years of age.

8. Surprisingly, little research attention has been directed to those women who are unable or unwilling to enter the labor force. Is this attitude or inability a result of lack of opportunity, lack of motivation, or other factors?

9. Prentis (1980) found that 73 percent of the white-collar professional and clerical women in her study had favorable preretirement attitudes toward retirement.

10. The percentages of men over 65 working in Canada and the United States are approximately 18 and 20 percent respectively (Statistics Canada, 1979; Harris, 1981).

11. The percentages of women over 65 working in Canada and the United States are approximately 5 and 9 percent respectively (Statistics Canada, 1979; Harris, 1981).

12. One hypothesized reason, besides the civil rights issue, for the raising of the mandatory retirement age in the United States was to delay social security payments and thereby reduce the risk of the social security system becoming bankrupt. In spite of this opportunity to continue working, many individuals, especially males, choose to retire before age 65, thereby increasing the aged dependency ratio.

13. Atchley et al. (1981) initiated a test of this model. In their preliminary findings they found that 75 percent of those who rated their jobs as unimportant retained the same hierarchical goal ordering after retirement. That is, retirement did not require adjustment for those for whom the job was of little importance. Hence, they did not need to change their goals after retirement either by internal compromise or by interpersonal negotiation.

14. Although the evidence pertains mostly to men in white-collar occupations, Beutner and Cryns (1979) found that professional women in the labor force may be more likely to plan for retirement, and to have different needs in planning from men.

15. Glamser and DeJong (1975) found that group discussion was more effective than individual briefings in changing attitudes, behavior, and knowledge about retirement.

16. Glamser (1981b) recently suggested that retirement preparation programs may be most effective for the early stages of retirement. It was found that three to four years after retirement there was no significant difference in life satisfaction, attitudes toward retirement, or feelings of job

deprivation between individuals who did not participate in a preretirement program and those who participated in either an individual or a group program.

17. Keating and Marshall (1980) indicate that self-employed farmers tend to be highly aware of the need to plan for their voluntary retirement. They also noted that farmers, more frequently than urban workers, engage in joint discussion about retirement planning with their spouses, possibly because their occupation has always been viewed as a joint undertaking.

18. There is some support for the continuity theory of aging when preretirement and postretirement lifestyles are examined. That is, early and middle-life leisure interests and experiences probably influence postretirement lifestyles. For example, the individual who has never travelled or engaged in extensive volunteer work is unlikely to find these leisure patterns satisfying in retirement (McPherson and Guppy, 1979).

19. In contrast, while North American societies are promoting later retirement (yet at the same time providing incentives to retire early), many other countries have lowered or are considering lowering the age to 60 or 55. This is especially likely to occur where unions demand a lower retirement age with full or partial pensions immediately upon retirement.

20. See Palmore (1972) for an early summary of the points for and against mandatory retirement.

21. There are a number of methodological limitations in many of these studies that must be considered. First, those who are dissatisfied with retirement may have returned to work, and thus may not be included in a particular sample. Second, those in poor health may die before or just after the information is collected. Third, the age of the sample may vary to include adjacent cohorts who have had different life experiences. Finally, 'adjustment' and 'satisfaction' involve qualitative and quantitative changes, and both can be assessed by subjective and objective indicators (Matthews and Brown, 1981b). Therefore, more sophisticated, multivariate instruments are needed to obtain valid information about satisfaction with and adjustment to retirement (Brown et al., 1981; Valasek, 1981a).

22. For many people, retirement is perceived as a reward and is accepted with relief. In fact, some may be cognitively and emotionally retired from the job long before they retire officially.

23. There may be less dissatisfaction with retirement and fewer problems of adjustment reported by respondents in more recent studies, since retirement is now generally considered to be more socially acceptable than in the past. Moreover, those who have retired in recent years have generally received higher pensions and have had more opportunity to plan for the event (Valasek, 1981b).

24. For example, less money may be spent on discretionary items such as clothing, household furnishings, and entertainment.

25. Larson (1978) suggests that the frequently observed relationship between activity and a sense of well-being may be a spurious relationship that is really accounted for by the strong relationship between higher health and economic status and high levels of activity among the elderly. That is, it is the higher health and economic status and not the higher activity level that accounts for the sense of well-being.

26. Less than 5 percent of those in the automotive industry who are eligible to retire after thirty years of employment elect to continue working until 65 years of age.

27. In most systems social security is financed by payments from both the worker and the employer. Benefits are based on the employee's past earnings and contributions over the years. In the United States, benefits paid to eligible retirees and their surviving spouse include a basic benefit, a minimum benefit, a dependent benefit, a survivor's benefit, disability benefits, hospital insurance and supplementary medical insurance (Medicare), a medical assistance program (Medicaid), and a supplemental security income for the needy aged (Schulz, 1980:94–122). In Canada, social security includes all hospital and medical care plus a retirement income system, which includes a basic benefit plus a Guaranteed Income Supplement and a Spouse's Allowance both based on total income (Powell and Martin, 1980).

28. Hendricks and Hendricks (1981:273–87) provide a descriptive overview of the pension systems in a number of countries.

29. Private pension plans and social security payments are also influenced by inflation. Most plans are indexed: monthly payments are increased as the cost of living increases.

30. McAllister (1981) argues that financial adequacy in the retirement years is strongly related to the individual's position in the 'dual economy.' If individuals are employed in a 'central' firm (such as the insurance or automotive industry) rather than in a 'peripheral' firm (such as a company with fewer than twenty-five employees that manufactures some obscure product in small numbers), they will receive higher wages and more fringe benefits throughout the working and retirement years. The employee of a peripheral firm may lack a private pension and may be more dependent on supplementary security payments and other forms of government welfare. Thus, regardless of the human potential of an individual, if the career is spent in a 'central' firm, greater retirement benefits will accrue than if the career had been spent in a 'peripheral' firm.

31. See Schulz (1980:83–148) for a detailed discussion of the content and problems of social security and private pension systems.

32. In fact, Myles (1981) notes that pension income cannot reduce intracohort differences in retirement, largely because better-educated, higher-income retirees have more investment income, which if anything, widens the gap during the retirement years.

33. Some of the characteristics of the older consumer that have been identified by market researchers include: relatively little tendency toward impulse buying; a preference for retail outlets that offer senior-citizen discounts; less money spent on 'physical' forms of leisure (such as hiking, boating, or skiing); a shift in expenditures to basic needs in response to a reduced discretionary income; and a dependence on advertising and an increase in comparison shopping.

34. For example, the Dulude (1981) report recommends that the level of the social security old-age payment be based on 50 percent of the average wage of women in the labor force.

35. The pension plan operated by the Canadian province of Quebec gives special consideration to women during the years they drop out of the labor force to raise children. They are eligible for some partial payments based on the time they were out of the labor force.

References

Anderson, T. 'The Dependent Elderly Population: A Function of Retirement,' Research on Aging, 3(3/1981), 311–24.

Atchley, R. 'Adjustment to Loss of Job at Retirement,' International Journal of Aging and Human Development, 6(1/1975), 17–27.

Atchley, R. The Sociology of Retirement. Cambridge, Mass.: Schenkman Publishing Co., 1976a.

Atchley, R. 'Selected Social and Psychological Differences Between Men and Women in Later Life,' Journal of Gerontology, 31(2/1976b), 204–11.

Atchley, R. 'Orientation Toward the Job and Retirement Adjustment Among Women,' pp. 199–208 in J. Gubrium (ed.). Time, Roles and Self in Old Age. New York: Human Sciences Press, 1976c.

Atchley, R. 'Issues in Retirement Research,' The Gerontologist, 19(1/1979), 44–54.

Atchley, R. 'Retirement as a Social Institution,' in R. Turner et al. (eds.). Annual Review of Sociology. Volume 8. Palo Alto: Annual Reviews, Inc., 1982.

Atchley, R. et al. 'Evaluation of a Theory of Adaptation to Loss of Job at Retirement,' paper presented at the annual meeting of the Gerontological Society of America, Toronto, November 1981.

Averitt, R. The Dual Economy. New York: W.W. Norton and Co., Inc., 1968.

Barfield, R. and J. Morgan. Early Retirement: The Decision and the Experience. Ann Arbor: University of Michigan, Institute of Social Research, 1970.

Barfield, R. and J. Morgan. 'Trends in Planned Early Retirement,' The Gerontologist, 18 (1/1978a), 13–18.

Barfield, R. and J. Morgan. 'Trends in Satisfaction with Retirement,' The Gerontologist, 18 (1/1978b), 19–23.

Barnett, R. and G. Baruch. 'Women in the Middle Years: A Critique of Research and Theory,' Psychology of Women Quarterly, 3(2/1978), 187–97.

Baugher, D. 'Is the Older Worker Inherently Incompetent?,' Aging and Work, 1(4/1978), 243–50.

Baum, M. and R. Baum. Growing Old: A Societal Perspective. Englewood Cliffs, N.J.: Prentice-Hall, 1980.

Beck, S. 'Adjustment to and Satisfaction with Retirement,' Journal of Gerontology, 37(5/1982), 616–24.

Best, F. 'The Future of Retirement and Lifetime Distribution of Work,' Aging and Work, 2(3/1979), 173–81.

Beutner, G. and A. Cryns. 'Retirement: Differences in Attitudes, Preparatory Behavior and Needs Perception Among Male and Female University Employees,' paper presented at the annual meeting of the Gerontological Society of America, Washington, D.C., November 1979.

Blaxall, M. and B. Reagan (eds.). *Women and the Workplace: The Implications of Occupational Segregation.* Chicago: University of Chicago Press, 1976.

Blieszner, R. and M. Szinovacz. 'Women's Adjustment to Retirement,' paper presented at the annual meeting of the Gerontological Society, Washington, D.C., November 1979.

Block, M. 'Work Pattern as a Correlate of Satisfaction with Retirement Among Women,' paper presented at the annual meeting of the Gerontological Society of America, San Diego, November 1980.

Borzilleri, T. 'The Need for a Separate Consumer Index for Older Persons,' *The Gerontologist,* 18(3/1978), 230–36.

Brown, K. and A. Matthews. 'Changes in Economic Well-Being at Retirement,' paper presented at the annual meeting of the Canadian Association on Gerontology, Toronto, November 1981.

Brown, K. et al. 'Crisis Assessment Scale: Response to Retirement – An Example,' paper presented at the annual meeting of the Canadian Sociology and Anthropology Association, Halifax, Nova Scotia, May 1981.

Burgess, E. *Aging in Western Societies.* Chicago: University of Chicago Press, 1960.

Burks, J. 'Economic Crises for Women: Aging and Retirement Years,' pp. 455–66 in J. Quadagno (ed.). *Aging, the Individual and Society.* New York: St. Martin's Press, 1980.

Calasanti, T. 'Is Retirement Research Atheoretical?' paper presented at the annual meeting of the Gerontological Society of America, Toronto, November 1981.

Chown, S. 'Morale, Careers and Personal Potentials,' pp. 672–91 in J. Birren and K.W. Schaie (eds.). *Handbook of the Psychology of Aging.* New York: Van Nostrand Reinhold, 1977.

Clark, R. (ed.). *Retirement Policy in an Aging Society.* Durham: Duke University Press, 1980.

Clark, R. 'Aging, Retirement, and the Economic Security of the Elderly: An Economic Review,' pp. 299–319 in C. Eisdorfer (ed.). *Annual Review of Gerontology and Geriatrics.* Volume 2. New York: Springer Publishing Co., 1981.

Clark, R. and D. Barker. *Reversing the Trend Toward Early Retirement.* Washington, D.C.: American Enterprise Institute, 1981.

Clark, R. and J. Spengler. 'Changing Demography and Dependency Costs: The Implications of Future Dependency Ratios and Their Composition,' pp. 55–89 in B. Herzog (ed.). *Aging and Income.* New York: Human Sciences Press, 1978.

Clark, R. and J. Spengler. *The Economics of Individual and Population Aging.* New York: Cambridge University Press, 1980.

Clark, R. et al. 'Economics of Aging: A Survey,' *Journal of Economic Literature,* 16(3/1978), 919–62.

Clark, R. et al. 'A Symposium on Pension Policy,' *The Gerontologist,* 22(6/1982), 473–92.

Cohn, R. 'Age and the Satisfactions from Work,' *Journal of Gerontology,* 34(2/1979), 264–72.

Cowgill, D. 'Demographic Aging and Economic Dependency,' pp. 303–5 in H. Orimo et al. (eds.). *Recent Advances in Gerontology.* Amsterdam: Excerpta Medica, 1979.

Cox, H. and A. Bhak. 'Symbolic Interaction and Retirement Adjustment: An Empirical Assessment,' *International Journal of Aging and Human Development,* 9(3/1978–79), 279–86.

Darnley, F. 'Adjustment to Retirement: Integrity or Despair,' *The Family Coordinator,* 24(2/1975), 217–26.

Dulude, L. *Women and Aging: A Report on the Rest of Our Lives.* Ottawa: Advisory Council on the Status of Women, 1978.

Dulude, L. *Pension Reform with Women in Mind.* Ottawa: Canadian Advisory Council on the Status of Women, 1981.

Edwards, R. *Contested Terrain: The Transformation of the Workplace in the Twentieth Century.* New York: Basic Books, 1979.

Edwards, R. et al. (eds.). *Labor Market Segmentation.* Lexington, Mass.: D.C. Heath and Co., 1975.

Eisdorfer, C. 'Adaptation to Loss of Work,' pp. 245–65 in F. Carp (ed.). *Retirement.* New York: Human Sciences Press, 1972.

Ekerdt, D. et al. 'Concurrent Change in Planned and Preferred Age for Retirement,' *Journal of Gerontology,* 35(2/1980), 232–40.

Ekerdt, D. et al. 'Adapting to Retirement: Is There a Honeymoon?' paper presented at the annual meeting of the Gerontological Society of America, Toronto, November 1981.

Feldberg, R. and E. Glenn. 'Male and Female: Job versus Gender Models in the Sociology of Work,' *Social Problems,* 26(5/1979), 524–38.

Fengler, A. 'Attitudinal Orientations of Wives Toward Their Husband's Retirement,' *International Journal of Aging and Human Development,* 6(2/1975), 139–52.

Fischer, J. et al. 'Life-Cycle Career Patterns: A Typological Approach to Female Status

Attainment,' Technical Bulletin 8, Center for the Study of Aging, University of Alabama, March 1979.

Fisher, P. 'Labor Force Participation of the Aged and the Social Security System in Nine Countries,' *Industrial Gerontology*, 2(1/1975), 1–13.

Fisher, P. 'The Social Security Crisis: An International Dilemma,' *Aging and Work*, 1(1/1978), 1–14.

Foner, A. and K. Schwab. *Aging and Retirement*. Monterey: Brooks/Cole Publishing Co., 1981.

Fox, A. 'Earnings Replacement Rates of Retired Couples: Findings from the Retirement History Study,' *Social Security Bulletin*, 42(January 1979), 17–39.

Fox, J. 'Effects of Retirement and Former Work Life on Women's Adaptation in Old Age,' *Journal of Gerontology*, 32(2/1977), 196–202.

Friedman, E. and H. Orbach. 'Adjustment to Retirement,' pp. 609–47 in S. Arieti (ed.). *The Foundations of Psychiatry*. Volume 1. New York: Basic Books, 1974.

George, L. *Role Transitions in Later Life*. Monterey: Brooks/Cole Publishing Co., 1980.

George, L. and G. Maddox. 'Subjective Adaptation to Loss of the Work Role: A Longitudinal Study,' *Journal of Gerontology*, 32(4/1977), 456–62.

Glamser, F. 'Determinants of a Positive Attitude Toward Retirement,' *Journal of Gerontology*, 31(1/1976), 104–7.

Glamser, F. 'The Impact of Pre-Retirement Programs on the Retirement Experience,' *Journal of Gerontology*, 36(2/1981a), 244–50.

Glamser, F. 'Predictors of Retirement Attitudes,' *Aging and Work*, 4(1/1981b), 23–29.

Glamser, F. and G. DeJong. 'The Efficacy of Preretirement Preparation Programs for Industrial Workers,' *Journal of Gerontology*, 30(5/1975), 595–600.

Goudy, W. et al. 'Work and Retirement: A Test of Attitudinal Relationships,' *Journal of Gerontology*, 30(2/1975) 193–98.

Goudy, W. et al. 'Changes in Attitudes Toward Retirement: Evidence from a Panel Study of Older Males,' *Journal of Gerontology*, 35(6/1980), 942–48.

Grad, S. and K. Foster. *Income of the Population 55 and Older, 1976*. Washington, D.C.: U.S. Department of Health, Education and Welfare, Social Security Administration, 1979.

Graebner, W. *A History of Retirement: The Meaning and Function of an American Institution, 1885–1978*. New Haven: Yale University Press, 1980.

Grimaldi, P. 'Measured Inflation and the Elderly, 1973 to 1981,' *The Gerontologist*, 22(4/1982), 347–53.

Hardy, M. 'Age-Linked Variations in the Retirement Behavior of Older Workers, 1969–1975,' paper presented at the annual meeting of the Gerontological Society of America, San Diego, November 1980.

Hardy, M. 'Social Policy and Determinants of Retirement: A Longitudinal Analysis of Older White Males, 1969–75,' *Social Forces*, 60(4/1982), 1103–22.

Harris, C. *Fact Book on Aging: A Profile of America's Older Population*. Washington, D.C.: National Council on the Aging, 1978.

Harris, L. *The Myth and Reality of Aging in America*. Washington, D.C.: National Council on the Aging, 1975.

Harris, L. et al. *Aging in the Eighties: America in Transition*. Washington, D.C.: National Council on the Aging, 1981.

Havighurst, R. et al. *Adjustment to Retirement: A Cross-National Study*. Assen, Netherlands: Van Gorcum and Co., 1969.

Haynes, S. et al. 'Survival After Early and Normal Retirement,' *Journal of Gerontology*, 33(3/1978), 269–78.

Hendrick, C. et al. 'Social and Emotional Effects of Geographical Relocation on Elderly Retirees,' *Journal of Personality and Social Psychology*, 42(5/1982), 951–62.

Hendricks, J. and C. Hendricks. *Aging in Mass Society*. 2nd edition. Cambridge, Mass.: Winthrop Publishers, Inc., 1981.

Herzog, B. (ed.). *Aging and Income: Programs and Prospects for the Elderly*. New York: Human Sciences Press, 1978.

Holahan, C. 'Lifetime Achievement Patterns, Retirement and Life Satisfaction of Gifted Aged Women,' *Journal of Gerontology*, 36(6/1981), 741–49.

Hudson, R. and R. Binstock. 'Political Systems and Aging,' pp. 369–400 in R. Binstock and E. Shanas (eds.). *Handbook of Aging and the Social Sciences*. New York: Van Nostrand Reinhold, 1976.

Hurd, M. and J. Shoven. 'Real Income and Wealth of the Elderly,' *The American Economic Review*, 72(2/1982), 314–18.

Irelan, L. et al. *Almost 65: Baseline Data from the Retirement History Study*. Washington, D.C.: U.S. Department of Health, Education and Welfare, Social Security Administration, 1976.

Janson, P. and J. Martin. 'Job Satisfaction and Age: A Test of Two Views,' *Social Forces*, 60(4/1982), 1089–102.

Jaslow, P. 'Employment, Retirement and Morale Among Older Women,' *Journal of Gerontology*, 31(2/1976), 212–18.

Kahne, H. 'Women and Social Security: Social Policy Adjusts to Social Change,' *International*

Journal of Aging and Human Development, 13(3/1981), 195–208.

Kalt, N. and M. Kohn. 'Pre-Retirement Counseling: Characteristics of Programs and Preferences of Retirees,' *The Gerontologist,* 15(2/1975), 179–81.

Kasworm, C. and J. Wetzel. 'Women and Retirement: Evolving Issues for Future Research and Education Intervention,' *Educational Gerontology,* 7(4/1981), 299–314.

Keating, N. and P. Cole. 'What Do I Do with Him 24 Hours a Day? Changes in the Housewife Role After Retirement,' *The Gerontologist,* 20(1/1980), 84–89.

Keating, N. and J. Marshall. 'The Process of Retirement: The Rural Self Employed,' *The Gerontologist,* 20(4/1980), 437–43.

Kell, D. and C. Patton. 'Reaction to Induced Early Retirement,' *The Gerontologist,* 18(2/1978), 173–80.

Kelleher, C. and D. Quirk. 'Preparation for Retirement: An Annotated Bibliography of Literature, 1965–1974,' *Industrial Gerontology,* 1(3/1974), 49–73.

Kimmel, D. et al. 'Retirement Choice and Retirement Satisfaction,' *Journal of Gerontology,* 33(4/1978), 575–85.

Kline, C. 'The Socialization Process of Women,' *The Gerontologist,* 15(6/1975), 486–92.

Krauss, I. 'Individual Differences in Reactions to Retirement,' paper presented at the annual meeting of the Gerontological Society of America, Toronto, November 1981.

Kreps, J. 'The Economy and the Aged,' pp. 272–85 in R. Binstock and E. Shanas (eds.). *Handbook of Aging and the Social Sciences.* New York: Van Nostrand Reinhold, 1976.

Larson, R. 'Thirty Years of Research on the Subjective Well-Being of Older Americans,' *Journal of Gerontology,* 33(1/1978), 109–25.

Levy, S. 'The Adjustment of the Older Woman: Effects of Chronic Ill Health and Attitudes Toward Retirement,' *International Journal of Aging and Human Development,* 12(2/1980–81), 93–110.

Liang, J. and T. Fairchild. 'Relative Deprivation and Perception of Financial Adequacy Among the Aged,' *Journal of Gerontology,* 34(5/1979), 746–59.

Liang, J. et al. 'Financial Well-Being Among the Aged: A Further Elaboration,' *Journal of Gerontology,* 35(3/1980), 409–20.

Loy, J. et al. *Sport and Social Systems.* Reading, Mass.: Addison-Wesley Publishing Co., 1978.

Mason, J. and W. Bearden. 'Profiling the Shopping Behavior of Elderly Consumers,' *The Gerontologist,* 18(5/1978), 454–61.

Matthews, A. and K. Brown. 'Economic and Social Welfare of the Recently Retired: Factors Which Contribute to the Perception of Crisis,' paper presented at the twelfth International Congress of Gerontology, Hamburg, West Germany, July 1981a.

Matthews, A. and K. Brown. 'Retirement and Change in Social Interaction: Objective and Subjective Assessments,' paper presented at the annual meeting of the Canadian Association on Gerontology, Toronto, November 1981b.

McAllister, C. 'An Alternative Perspective on Retirement Benefits: A Dual Economic Approach,' paper presented at the annual meeting of the Gerontological Society of America, Toronto, November 1981.

McCarthy, M. 'Women's Economic Roles, Problems and Opportunities,' pp. 186–223 in M. Richmond-Abbott (ed.). *The American Woman.* New York: Holt, Rinehart and Winston, 1979.

McCluskey, N. and E. Borgatta (eds.). *Aging and Retirement: Prospects, Planning, and Policy.* Beverly Hills: Sage Publications, 1981.

McConnell, S. and L. Morgan. *The Older Worker: A Selected Bibliography.* Los Angeles: Andrus Gerontology Center, University of Southern California, 1979.

McFadden, M. et al. 'Dimensions of Retirement Among Minority Elderly,' paper presented at the annual meeting of the Gerontological Society of America, Toronto, November 1981.

McPherson, B. 'Retirement from Professional Sport: The Process and Problems of Occupational and Psychological Adjustment,' *Sociological Symposium,* 30(Spring, 1980), 126–43.

McPherson, B. and N. Guppy. 'Pre-Retirement Life-Style and the Degree of Planning for Retirement,' *Journal of Gerontology,* 34(2/1979), 254–63.

Meier, E. and E. Kerr. 'Capabilities of Middle-Aged and Older Workers: A Survey of the Literature,' *Industrial Gerontology,* 3(3/1976), 147–56.

Meltzer, H. and R. Stagner. 'The Social Psychology of Aging in Industry,' *Professional Psychology,* 11(3/1980), 436–44.

Migliaccio, J. and P. Cairo. 'Preparation for Retirement: A Selective Bibliography, 1974–1980,' *Aging and Work,* 4(1/1981), 31–41.

Muller, C. 'Economic Roles and the Status of the Elderly,' pp. 17–41 in E. Borgatta and N. McCluskey (eds.). *Aging and Society.* Beverly Hills: Sage Publications, 1980.

Mutran, E. and D. Reitzes. 'Retirement, Identity and Well-Being: Realignment of Role Relationships,' *Journal of Gerontology,* 36(6/1981), 733–40.

Myles, J. 'Income Inequality and Status Maintenance,' *Research on Aging*, 3(2/1981), 123–41.

Myles, J. *Political Economy of Pensions*. Cambridge, Mass.: Winthrop Publishers Inc., forthcoming.

Older Workers: Work and Retirement. Report 6(1). Geneva: International Labour Office, 1978.

Olson, L. et al. *The Elderly and the Future Economy*. Lexington, Mass.: Lexington Books, 1981a.

Olson, S. 'Current Status of Corporate Retirement Preparation Programs,' *Aging and Work*, 4(3/1981b), 175–87.

O'Rand, A. and J. Henretta. 'Delayed Career Entry, Industrial Pension Structure, and Early Retirement in a Cohort of Unmarried Women,' *American Sociological Review*, 47(3/1982), 365–73.

Palmore, E. 'Compulsory Versus Flexible Retirement: Issues and Facts,' *The Gerontologist*, 12(4/1972), 344–45.

Palmore, E. et al. 'Predictors of Retirement,' *Journal of Gerontology*, 37(6/1982), 733–42.

Parnes, H. *Work and Retirement: A Longitudinal Study of Men*. Cambridge, Mass.: MIT Press, 1981.

Parker, S. *Work and Retirement*. London: George Allen and Unwin, 1982.

Parnes, H. and R. King. 'Middle-Aged Job Losers,' *Industrial Gerontology*, 4(2/1977), 77–96.

Parnes, H. et al. *The Pre-Retirement Years*. Volume 4. Manpower Research and Development Monograph, No. 15. Washington, D.C.: U.S. Government Printing Office, 1975.

Parnes, H. et al. *From the Middle to the Later Years: Longitudinal Studies of the Preretirement and Postretirement Experiences of Men*. Columbus: Ohio State University, Center for Human Resources, 1979.

Payne, B. and F. Whittington. 'Older Women: Examination of Popular Stereotypes and Research Evidence,' *Social Problems*, 23(4/1976), 488–504.

Peavy, N. (ed.). 'Retirement Preparation: Growing Corporate Involvement,' *Aging and Work*, 3(1/1980), 1–26.

Peterson, D. 'Financial Adequacy in Retirement: Perceptions of Older Americans,' *The Gerontologist*, 12(4/1972), 379–83.

Powell, B. and J. Martin. 'Economic Implications of Canada's Aging Society,' pp. 204–14 in V. Marshall (ed.). *Aging in Canada: Social Perspectives*. Don Mills: Fitzhenry and Whiteside, 1980.

Prentis, R. 'White-Collar Working Women's Perception of Retirement,' *The Gerontologist*, 20(1/1980), 90–95.

Price, K. et al. 'Retirement Timing and Retirement Satisfaction,' *Aging and Work*, 2(4/1979), 235–45.

Prothero, J. 'Retirement Expectations and Intentions of Older Workers: Male and Female, Married and Unmarried,' paper presented at the annual meeting of the Gerontological Society of America, Toronto, November 1981.

Quinn, J. 'The Extent and Correlates of Partial Retirement,' *The Gerontologist*, 21(6/1981), 634–43.

Ragan, P. (ed.). *Work and Retirement: Policy Issues*. Los Angeles: University of Southern California Press, 1980.

Roberts, B. *Middle-Aged Career Dropouts*. Cambridge, Mass.: Schenkman Publishing Co., 1980.

Rosencranz, H. (ed.). *Pre-Retirement Education: A Manual for Conference Leaders*. Storrs, Conn.: University of Connecticut, 1975.

Schnore, M. and J. Kirkland. 'Sex Differences in Adjustment to Retirement,' paper presented at the annual meeting of the Canadian Association on Gerontology, Toronto, November 1981.

Schulz, J. 'Income Distribution and the Aging,' pp. 561–91 in R. Binstock and E. Shanas (eds.). *Handbook of Aging and the Social Sciences*. New York: Van Nostrand Reinhold, 1976.

Schulz, J. *The Economics of Aging*. 2nd. edition. Belmont, Calif.: Wadsworth Publishing Co., 1980.

Schwab, D. and H. Heneman. 'Effects of Age and Experience on Productivity,' *Industrial Gerontology*, 4(2/1977), 113–17.

Sebastian, C. *The Economics of Aging: Toward 2001*. Detroit: University of Michigan-Wayne State University Institute of Gerontology, 1976.

Semyonov, M. 'The Social Context of Womens' Labor Force Participation: A Comparative Analysis,' *American Journal of Sociology*, 86(3/1980), 534–50.

Shanas, E. 'Adjustment to Retirement: Substitution or Accommodation?' pp. 219–44 in F. Carp (ed.). *Retirement*. New York: Human Sciences Press, 1972.

Sheppard, H. 'Work and Retirement,' pp. 286–309 in R. Binstock and E. Shanas (eds.). *Handbook of Aging and the Social Sciences*. New York: Van Nostrand Reinhold, 1976.

Sheppard, H. and S. Rix. *The Graying of Working America: The Coming Crisis in Retirement Age Policy*. New York: The Free Press, 1977.

Sodei, T. 'A Description of Mandatory Retirement in Japan,' *Aging and Work*, 4(2/1981), 109–14.

Statistics Canada. *Canada's Elderly*. Ottawa: Ministry of Supply and Services Canada, 1979.

Stone, L. and M. MacLean. *Future Income Prospects for Canada's Senior Citizens.* Montreal: Institute for Research on Public Policy, 1979.

Streib, G. and C. Schneider. *Retirement in American Society.* Ithaca: Cornell University Press, 1971.

Sussman, M. 'An Analytic Model for the Sociological Study of Retirement,' pp. 29–73 in F. Carp (ed.). *Retirement.* New York: Human Sciences Press, 1972.

Thompson, G. 'Economic Status of Late Middle-Aged Widows,' pp. 133–49 in N. Datan and N. Lohmann (eds.). *Transitions of Aging.* New York: Academic Press, 1980.

Tindale, J. 'Income Source Trends and the Nature of State Initiatives In Income Maintenance Programmes for the Canadian Aged,' paper presented at the annual meeting of the Canadian Association on Gerontology, Toronto, November 1981.

Valasek, D. 'Predicting Retirement Satisfaction Using a Multifaceted Questionnaire,' paper presented at the annual meeting of the American Psychological Association, Los Angeles, August 1981a.

Valasek, D. 'Retirement Satisfaction: Is There a Young/Old — Old/Old Difference,' paper presented at the Gerontological Society of America Annual Meeting, Toronto, November 1981b.

Walker, J. and D. Lupton. 'Performance Appraisal Programs and the Age Discrimination Law,' *Aging and Work,* 1(1/1978), 73–83.

Ward, R. 'The Never Married in Later Life,' *Journal of Gerontology,* 34(6/1979), 861–69.

Ward, R. 'Occupational Variation in the Life Course: Implications for Later Life,' in N. Osgood (ed.). *Life After Work: Retirement, Leisure, Recreation and the Elderly.* New York: Praeger Press, forthcoming.

Wiener, Y. and R. Vaitenas. 'Personality Correlates of Voluntary Midcareer Change in Enterprising Occupations,' *Journal of Applied Psychology,* 62(6/1977), 706–12.

Wolf, W. and N. Fligstein. 'Sex and Authority in the Workplace: The Causes of Sexual Inequality,' *American Sociological Review,* 44(2/1979), 235–52.

Women and Poverty. Ottawa: National Council on Welfare, 1979.

Yolles, S. et al. *The Aging Employee.* New York: Human Sciences Press, Inc., 1982.

11

Aging and Leisure Involvement

Introduction

With the transition from primitive to industrial to postindustrial societies, dramatic changes have occurred in the quantity, meaning and form of leisure (Dumazedier, 1972). There has been a shift from little personal freedom in lifestyle and little formal leisure time to freedom in selecting a range of lifestyles and the initiation of formal, structured periods of leisure (such as vacations or mandatory retirement). As a result, leisure is no longer the exclusive right of the upper class, nor is it viewed as the 'leftovers of life' after work and maintenance responsibilities have been met.

Leisure is no longer restricted to the childhood, adolescent, and postretirement stages of life. Because of changing social structures (for example, an increase in the number of age and class strata), social values (reduced adherence to the work ethic), social processes (increasing democratization in opportunities and access to social participation), and laws (the introduction of mandatory retirement), leisure has become an attainable goal at all stages for most segments of modernized societies. Age, gender, race, occupation, education, or income are no longer barriers to leisure, although these factors still influence the number, type, and quality of specific leisure experiences of a given individual. A linear life cycle of play, education, work, and leisure (in retirement) is no longer the normative pattern. Instead, some form of leisure is integrated at all stages in the life cycle into all facets of contemporary lifestyles, including work.

With the reduction in the length of the work week, and the availability of labor-saving devices in the home, the amount of free time has gradually increased in most modernized nations. In turn, personal and societal decisions have had to be made concerning how to make use of this free time. The choices may involve additional work, some form of leisure activity, or simply rest.

Accompanying these social and technological changes is a lessening of the value or importance of work, and an increase in the significance of leisure to personal identity and the quality of life. Moreover, the relative importance of work, family, and leisure in our daily lives seems to vary at different stages in the life cycle. The way in which time is used for obligatory and discretionary activities represents a conscious decision reflecting the characteristics of individual and societal lifestyles across the life span (Gordon and Gaitz, 1976). However, not all people are able to spend their leisure time exactly as they wish: there is often a lack of congruence, for a variety of real or imagined reasons, between actual and desired use of time. This has implications for the degree of life satisfaction and for the quality of life of given individuals. For example, Seleen (1982) found that older adults who were spending their time as they desired were more satisfied with life than those who were not. Similarly, recognizing that the use of time influences the meaning of old age, Ward (1981–82) noted that older people need a variety of nonwork opportunities for the creative and expressive use of time.

As a result of the changing values and meanings of work, time, and leisure, it is not surprising that scholars in the social sciences and humanities have demonstrated increasing interest in understanding the phenomenon of leisure in contemporary society. This interest is reflected in a growing body of literature, much of it written only in the past 30 years, that seeks to define, conceptualize, and measure leisure-related phenomena. To date, most of this scholarly work has concentrated on searching for the meaning of leisure per se, on defining the characteristics or types of leisure, and on describing the patterns of leisure activities pursued by various strata of the population (for example, males versus females, young versus old, lower-class versus upper-class). Relatively few of these studies have been devoted to patterns or meanings of leisure across the life cycle (Kleemeier, 1961; Havighurst, 1972; Huet, 1972; Kaplan, 1972; Long and Wimbush, 1979; Schmitz-Scherzer, 1979; Teague, 1980), although interest in the leisure patterns of the retiree has increased in recent years (Born, 1976; Schmitz-Scherzer, 1976; Lawton, 1978; Dangott and Kalish, 1979; Kaplan, 1979; Ray, 1979a; Osgood, 1982).

This chapter begins with a brief discussion of the definitions of 'leisure' and examines the relationship between leisure and other social institutions (the family, work, and retirement) at varying stages in the life cycle. In the next two subsections patterns of involvement by age are described for a variety of leisure experiences, including voluntary associations, the media, and education. Where information is available, the leisure involvement of those beyond 60 or 65 years of age is highlighted. In addition to the information presented in this chapter, the reader should refer to chapter 5 for a disussion of patterns of involvement across the life cycle in physical activity as a form of leisure.

Leisure and Aging: Conceptual and Methodological Issues

In Search of a Definition of Leisure

From a historical perspective, interest in the study of leisure was initially the domain of philosophers and religious leaders. At varying periods throughout history, the ethics and value of leisure were debated, usually in comparison to work and often in relation to family, church, or state responsibilities. The outcome of these philosophical and religious debates was that leisure in general, or a specific type of leisure activity, was 'judged' as either appropriate or inappropriate, good or evil, productive or nonproductive, constructive or destructive, re-creative or dissipative. As a result, the opportunity to engage in leisure, or in certain types of leisure, was seldom a personal decision or a matter of right. Rather, the role of leisure in individual lifestyles was determined by religious and societal leaders, many of whom issued proclamations labelling leisure as a stigmatized form of social behavior to be avoided.

   With the rise of industrialization and the accompanying social, political, and economic changes, leisure continued to be defined in relation to work. However, the onset of shorter work weeks, formal vacation periods, mandatory retirement, and voluntary early retirement led to an increase in discretionary free time, and leisure became an acceptable, worthwhile, and necessary facet of contemporary lifestyles. The individual acquired the freedom to choose how, when, and where he or she would make use of increased discretionary time and income. Leisure time became more available, more socially acceptable, and more institutionalized, and scholars (psychologists, sociologists, economists, anthropologists, philosophers, and recreation personnel) sought to define and measure the meaning, characteristics, and patterns of leisure in general and for particular subgroups in society (Dumazedier, 1967; Parker, 1976, 1981; Purohit et al., 1976; Fontana, 1977; Csikszentmihalyi, 1979, 1981; Zuzanek, 1979; Gunter and Gunter, 1980; Kleiber and Kelly, 1980; Wilson, 1980, 1981; Keating and Spiller, 1981; Kelly, 1981; Neulinger, 1981; Roadburg, 1981).

   Not surprisingly, a universally accepted definition of 'leisure' has so far been unattainable, partly because needs and experiences concerning work and leisure are extremely personal and heterogeneous. Moreover, many of the definitions have been related to the meaning of work,[1] which also has acquired a multitude of definitions within and between occupations and at various stages in the life cycle.[2] Difficulties in arriving at a comprehensive definition have persisted because leisure is a multidimensional concept,[3] because activities may have a variety of meanings or functions for an individual at different times,[4] and because individuals can engage in more than one leisure activity at a time.[5] Furthermore, some leisure activities fall into overlapping categories,[6] and the concept of 'leisure' is used at both the individual and societal level of analysis (Parker, 1981). Finally, and perhaps most important, there is a lack of research to validate or refute the various hypothesized definitions of the concept, largely because few reliable measures of these dimensions have been derived.[7]

   The meaning of leisure, as a form of social participation for a given individual or social group, is also influenced by cultural and subcultural norms, values, experiences, and opportunity sets. These cultural parameters are unique to individuals or groups differentiated by age, sex, race, education, ethnicity, socioeconomic status, religion, or place of residence. More specifically, the form of leisure that is selected by a given individual is influenced by a variety of factors, such as health, climate, access to transportation, and quality of the neighborhood.

   Despite the many problems outlined above, some definitions of leisure have been set forth. Although it is beyond the scope of this section to provide a comprehensive review, the following list identifies many of the hypothesized components of leisure. Leisure is thought to be made up of, or to represent:

• A state of mind or attitude

• Nonwork

• Freedom of choice in selecting activities

• Free or discretionary time

• Relaxation and diversion from work and personal maintenance activities

• Playfulness or play

• Voluntary activity

• Expressive activities (internal satisfaction, or an emphasis on the process rather than the end product)

- Instrumental activities (external rewards, with an end product as the goal)
- Spontaneity
- Utilitarian and meaningful activities
- A state of being
- Active and passive activities
- Social (group) and individual (solitary) activities
- Expensive and inexpensive pursuits
- Intellectual (cognitive), social, and physical pursuits
- Intrinsic and extrinsic rewards
- Creativity
- High culture and mass culture

Although many of these characteristics are often viewed as dichotomous scales (i.e., either/or), in reality they represent continua.[8] That is, individuals may change their position on a particular scale with age, with transitions in work or family, with the time of year, when moving to a new neighborhood or region, or with changes in cultural or subcultural values or norms. Moreover, the dimensions are not discrete entities; many of the scales intersect, so that there are many permutations and combinations of types and meanings of leisure involvement. For example, the same individual may participate equally in a structured, expressive, physical activity (such as a dance class), and in an unstructured, instrumental, passive activity (the acquisition of a complete set of stamps for a specific country). Similarly, as Csikszentmihalyi (1981) argues, no event is ever entirely instrumental, even work. He suggests that individuals are searching for pleasure and expressive experiences within the instrumental roles of society (for example, in work or parenthood).

Finally, a distinction is seldom drawn between the quantity and the quality of leisure, either as a whole or with respect to a particular dimension. Research studies have generally been more concerned with the number or variety of leisure activities available to or pursued by an individual of group; the quality of the experience has seldom been considered. However, increasing attention is being paid to the quality of the leisure experience, regardless of the amount of leisure time available or the number of activities pursued. In short, meaningless or unsatisfying free-time activities may not constitute true leisure, and may fail to meet the leisure needs of the individual.

Leisure, like life, cannot be categorized into discrete entities. For this reason, some scholars believe that any attempt to define leisure is a futile exercise. If it were, so too would be the search for cures for degenerative diseases. Rather than abandoning the search for an understanding of leisure, more creative approaches and more sophisticated conceptualization and methodologies are needed. This search for understanding is especially important now, because individuals are living longer in retirement, because many experience periods of unemployment during the adult years, and, most important, because the value of leisure as a salient component of contemporary lifestyles is increasing. For some people, the importance of work is declining, the time spent on household and other routine chores is decreasing, and a greater concern with using leisure time productively and meaningfully is emerging. These developments have combined to increase the amount of discretionary time available and to enhance the relative importance of leisure for the quality of life at all stages in the life cycle. Nevertheless, despite individual and societal shifts in values, the quantity and quality of leisure is still dependent on the nature of the work situation. The next subsection presents a brief review of the literature pertaining to the relationship between work and leisure.

The Relationship Between Work and Leisure

Introduction.   Upon the completion of formal schooling and the subsequent entrance into the labor force in early adulthood, the type and frequency of leisure changes. This change results from a limited availability of free time; a new lifestyle because of the nature and demands of the job, and, for most, because of marriage, home ownership, and child rearing. These demands and responsibilities usually change as one passes through the stages of the work and family career, and the meaning, form, and frequency of leisure may also change. However, most evidence indicates that while the amount of free time may increase or decrease at varying stages, the types of leisure pursuits favored are relatively constant, once patterns are established in the early and middle years of adulthood.

The development of a leisure lifestyle in the adult years is thought to be highly influenced by the type of occupation and by the role requirements of a specific job. There has been a growing interest in the relationship between work and leisure, between class and leisure,[9] and between career and lifestyle.

Initially, those who were interested in describing or explaining how work affects the use of nonwork time made selective observations or inferential leaps from everyday situations. 'Few attempted to explicate the relationship or to research it systematically' (Kando and Summers, 1971:310). Moreover, the research studies rarely isolated the effects of possible confounding variables such as age, sex, race, ethnicity, health, income, or educational attainment. Nevertheless, a number of conceptual approaches have been derived in an effort to better understand the relationship between the nature and meaning of work and leisure.

The initial attempts to explain leisure involvement during adulthood focused on the relationship between class background and the type and number of leisure pursuits. For example, a number of studies, controlling for occupation, found that those employed in high-prestige occupations engaged in different leisure activities at different rates from those in low-prestige occupations (Lundberg et al., 1934; Riessman, 1954; White, 1955; Clarke, 1956; Kahl, 1961; Wippler, 1970; Noe, 1974; White, 1975). These studies were based on the assumption that norms and values unique to a particular class are acquired through socialization, so that individuals adopt certain leisure activities and exclude others.

Some researchers have posited a more direct link between work and leisure, arguing that the two spheres are not really separate from each other. In Wilensky's (1960:545) words, 'a man's work routine places a hand on his routine of leisure.' A large body of literature has appeared since the 1960s that focuses on the way in which specific occupations and work environments are related to particular forms and types of leisure involvement (Smigel, 1963; Parker, 1965, 1972, 1975, 1981; Meissner, 1971; Kelly, 1972, 1976; Haworth and Smith, 1975; White, 1975; McPherson, 1978; Colley, 1979; Keith et al., 1979; Staines, 1980; Weiner and Hunt, 1981; Andrew, 1982; and, Ward, 1982). For example, Gerstl (1961) and Jordan (1963) argued that while social class was important in determining leisure behavior, the specific nature of an occupation (for example, salesman versus teacher) may demand different leisure lifestyles. Even though occupations may fall within the same general social class, the leisure patterns related to those occupations may vary. They found that people within common occupational groupings demonstrated differences in the pattern of normal leisure pursuits. They concluded that the crucial explanatory factor linking occupation and leisure is the occupational milieu, including such factors as the nature of the work setting and the norms derived from the occupational reference groups.

More specifically, it has been suggested that the relationship between work and leisure is the result of work contacts and work experiences (Wilensky, 1964), the degree of physical and mental involvement in one's occupational role, and the degree to which the work role is person-oriented rather than concept- or thing-oriented (Bishop and Ikeda, 1970). Furthermore, the leisure pattern is influenced by the technical and social constraints of a job (Meissner, 1971), and by the degree of involvement in the decision-making process at work (Hagedorn and Labovitz, 1968a, 1968b). In short, the nature of the work and the amount of power and involvement associated with the job, rather than its prestige, determine the form and frequency of leisure involvement. In order to explain this observed relationship between work and leisure, three general hypotheses have been proposed and tested to varying degrees. These are outlined in the following subsection.

Work-leisure hypotheses.   A basic tenet of the Protestant work ethic is that work is an essential and valued life interest. As such, it influences other domains of social life so that adult lifestyles are largely determined by the type of occupation and by the demands of the job. Not surprisingly, work has been defined as the independent variable that is hypothesized to determine the amount of time and energy available for leisure, as well as the appropriate types of leisure pursuits.

The feedback between the domains of work and leisure has seldom been tested, even though the degree of importance attached to leisure may have a significant effect on work. For example, if a particular leisure lifestyle becomes highly salient for an individual, he or she may refuse to accept a promotion that involves a move to a new community or region; or may search for a job in a region where the salient leisure lifestyle can be pursued (for example, a community with easy access to skiing). The individual might seek a change in career in order to pursue leisure interests, or perhaps decide not to work at all.[10] Finally, little attention has been directed to the possibility that there is leisure in work (expressive needs are met in instrumental tasks); that work may be a major source of leisure and pleasure for some individuals; or that the relative influence and value of the two domains may vary by age, sex, ethnicity, career stage, or employment history.[11]

Despite the methodological and conceptual limitations in the hypothesized linkage between work and leisure, scholars do argue that there are two or three general hypotheses or alternative explanations for the relationship (Wilensky, 1960; Kando and Summers, 1971; Parker, 1972, 1975, 1981; Kabanoff and O'Brien, 1980; Staines, 1980; Wilson, 1980; Lambert and White, 1981; Andrew, 1982; Ward, 1982). Arguing from the premise that work rather than leisure is the central life interest (Dubin, 1956), those who adhere to a holistic perspective maintain that work and leisure are integrated, congruent, or fused aspects of the lifestyle, that there is no distinction between work and leisure in meaning or form, and that each facet affects the other. According to this 'congruence' hypothesis, the type of leisure activities selected by an individual represent a 'spillover' from the job. For example, those employed in intellectually rigorous occupations with a substantial decision-making component are likely to engage in serious reading, to attend high-cultural events, to play 'intellectual' games, and to participate in fewer physical activities during their leisure time. People in this category are also, as Stone (1955:93) suggested, likely to 'work at our play and play at our work.' That is, leisure is used for self-development (Parker, 1972), and there may be little perceived difference between work and leisure.

In contrast, those who argue from the segmentalist perspective believe that work and leisure represent opposite extremes of a bipolar scale. Lifestyles are composed of two distinct and separate entities, work and leisure. Some degree of leisure is seen as being necessary for recuperation and relaxation from work. The 'compensatory' or 'contrast' hypothesis proposes that leisure activities are deliberately chosen because they are unlike work activities. Moreover, some proponents of this view regard the job as at best a necessary evil.[12]

The compensatory hypothesis suggests that individuals seek in their leisure what is lacking in their jobs. For example, a desk-bound executive might choose leisure activities involving physical labor (gardening) or physical activity (squash), while the laborer might prefer to engage in decision making (as a little-league coach), intellectual (self-study), or artistic activities. A recent study by Lambert and White (1981) found that the physical demands of a job influence the type of leisure involvement. They found that those in less physically demanding occupations were more likely to engage in physically active leisure pursuits.

To date, the research evidence is supportive of the spillover hypothesis: statistically significant and substantive correlations have consistently been obtained between the types of activities engaged in at work and at leisure (Staines, 1980; Wilson, 1980). However, there are subgroup variations. For example, the spillover relationship does not appear to be supported for physically demanding jobs, especially where the workers have low levels of education. Moreover, some studies support the compensatory or contrast hypothesis (Lambert and White, 1981), while other studies do not support either hypothesis. Similarly, there are case studies showing that individuals with non-creative jobs engage in creative leisure, while others show that those with highly creative jobs report that their leisure lacks meaning and satisfaction. Thus, it appears that a definitive and complete explanation for the hypothesized relationship between work and leisure is not yet available (Kabanoff and O'Brien, 1980).

The lack of a definitive explanation has led to a third hypothesis, namely the 'neutrality' hypothesis. Proponents of this view argue that there is little attachment to work, and that there may or may not be a linkage and overlap between work and leisure. Leisure activities are usually different from work activities, but not intentionally so (as in the 'compensatory' process). That is, there is a detachment from work, and work style has little bearing on leisure pursuits. Moreover, there tends to be a slightly greater interest in leisure than in work by individuals who adhere to this philosophy of work and leisure.

Perhaps a major reason for the inability to provide an adequate explanation of the hypothesized relationship between work and leisure has been the failure of scholars to recognize that the question is not as simple as originally stated. That is, the adoption of a particular work or leisure style may be influenced not by work-related factors, but rather by a number of personal and social situational factors such as personality, family status, previous leisure experiences, economic status, career stage (Ward, 1982), place of residence (Keith et al., 1979), or reference group norms.

Since job and family responsibilities and goals change with age, the relationship between work and leisure may vary by age. For example, Kelly (1976) suggested that with the departure of children from the home, and the establishment and plateauing of the career, there is a change in the relative meaning and value attached to work and leisure. He found that with increasing age there was a greater chance of leisure being viewed as compensatory. Similarly, Ward (1982) indicated that the compensatory pattern may become more salient as the value and meaning of work change. However, possible cohort or period effects also need to be considered, and caution must be exercised when interpreting the presence of a compensatory pattern until longitudinal or cohort analysis studies are completed.

Another confusing factor in the interpretation of the work-leisure relationship is the tendency to examine that relationship on an individual rather than a societal level of analysis. In reality, there is an interaction between the two levels that must be considered. For example, where societal norms hold that leisure is an extension of work (the spillover effect), it is more difficult for an individual to adopt a segregated (compensatory) lifestyle. Before a definitive explanation can be provided at the individual level, a thorough analysis of societal norms concerning work and leisure is required (Parker, 1972).

Finally, from another perspective, the onset of retirement means the end of the work-leisure relationship. Yet, leisure patterns persist and do not appear to be greatly altered by retirement. For example, Roadburg (1981) found that in the absence of work, leisure is perceived more in terms of pleasure than in terms of freedom, and that those who retire voluntarily see leisure in terms of the enjoyment it can provide. This indirect evidence suggests that the meaning of leisure is somewhat related to work, and that in the absence of work the meaning of leisure may be altered, although the type of leisure activities may change relatively little.

In summary, two major alternative explanations have been proposed for the relationship between work and leisure. Both argue that type or style of work influences the adoption of particular leisure lifestyles. While much of the evidence suggests that the spillover hypothesis is a valid explanation, longitudinal studies to investigate possible changes with age have yet to be undertaken. Similarly, studies seldom control for the personal or societal characteristics that might influence the relationship between work and leisure. Therefore, while it is generally agreed that work and leisure interact to influence lifestyle, there is as yet no definitive explanation of why or how this linkage occurs.

Leisure and Aging: The Early and Middle Years

The type of activities pursued during leisure time[13] and the meaning and function of these activities often vary from one stage in the life cycle to the next. Since leisure involves the utilization of discretionary time and income, an individual's (or cohort's) leisure lifestyle depends on the financial and social constraints accompanying specific stages in life. The varying demands and responsibilities of family, school, and work influence the amount of time available, and personal characteristics such as marital status, class, education, place of residence, and health status influence the selection and meaning of specific activities.

A large number of descriptive studies have identified the leisure interests or activities of individuals at a particular stage in life, or at a particular chronological age. Although some inferences and general patterns across the life cycle can be derived from these cross-sectional studies, longitudinal studies are lacking, and patterns observed across the life cycle may reflect aging, cohort, or period effects. In fact, some leisure pursuits are fads that influence one age cohort but not others (a period effect).

The adoption of a specific type of activity at one stage in life may significantly influence leisure involvement throughout the life cycle. For example, dancing was a craze in the 1920s; for many who were in late adolescence or early adulthood at that time, dancing is still a major leisure interest that has special meaning for many members of that generation. Similarly, those who were preadolescents, adolescents, and young adults in the 1970s were exposed to the 'fitness boom,' and many adopted some form of physical activity as part of their lifestyle. It may be that these cohorts will demonstrate relatively higher levels of physical activity involvement than earlier or later cohorts at all subsequent stages in the life cycle. Or, it may be that this emphasis will persist for only a few years, and the pattern of involvement will reflect that of earlier cohorts at the same stage in life (a maturation effect).

Although it is not possible to identify a single leisure pattern across the life cycle, or to indicate a definitive pattern for a specific activity, some general findings based on conceptual and empirical studies from a life-cycle perspective can be summarized (Rapoport and Rapoport, 1975; Harris, 1975; Gordon and Gaitz, 1976; Parker, 1976; Kelly, 1977; Kaplan, 1979; Zuzanek, 1979; Kleiber and Kelly, 1980; McPherson and Kozlik, 1980; Wilson, 1980).

Figure 11.1 illustrates various patterns of leisure involvement across the life cycle. The curves represent life-cycle involvement in sport (A), visiting (B), political participation through active membership in a political party (C), reading for pleasure (D), travel or solitary activities (E), or home-centered activities (F). However, leisure involvement is not as orderly as these smooth curves suggest. There may be minor or major peaks and valleys at various stages in the life cycle because of institutional (family, school, or work) or cultural constraints.[14] Moreover, for a given activity (such as reading), all six patterns in figure 11.1 may apply to six different individuals or six different cohorts.

Despite these complex individual differences, there are some general and relatively predictable leisure patterns at different stages in the life course. These patterns are determined by transitions within the family or work careers that require a continuous process of adaptation. During childhood and early adolescence, a variety of leisure experiences are pursued in the family or school settings. Many of these are encouraged by parents, peers, and teachers, and most are voluntarily selected by the individual. During middle and late adolescence, the influence of the family decreases, and the peer group, the media, and the youth culture become more influential in determining lifestyles (and particularly for fads and fashions). In addition, the individual may enter the labor force on a part-time basis, thereby experiencing a reduction in discretionary time and an increase in discretionary income. Constraints begin to affect decision making concerning the type, meaning, and function of leisure experiences.

The next major transition occurs at the time of leaving school and entering the labor force. This stage may also be accompanied by marriage, home ownership, and the birth of a child. The commitment of time to establishing a career and family may dramatically restrict or change leisure patterns during the early years of adulthood, when leisure activities tend to be home and family-centered, and often less important in the hierarchy of values.

Figure 11.1 Possible patterns of leisure involvement across the life cycle

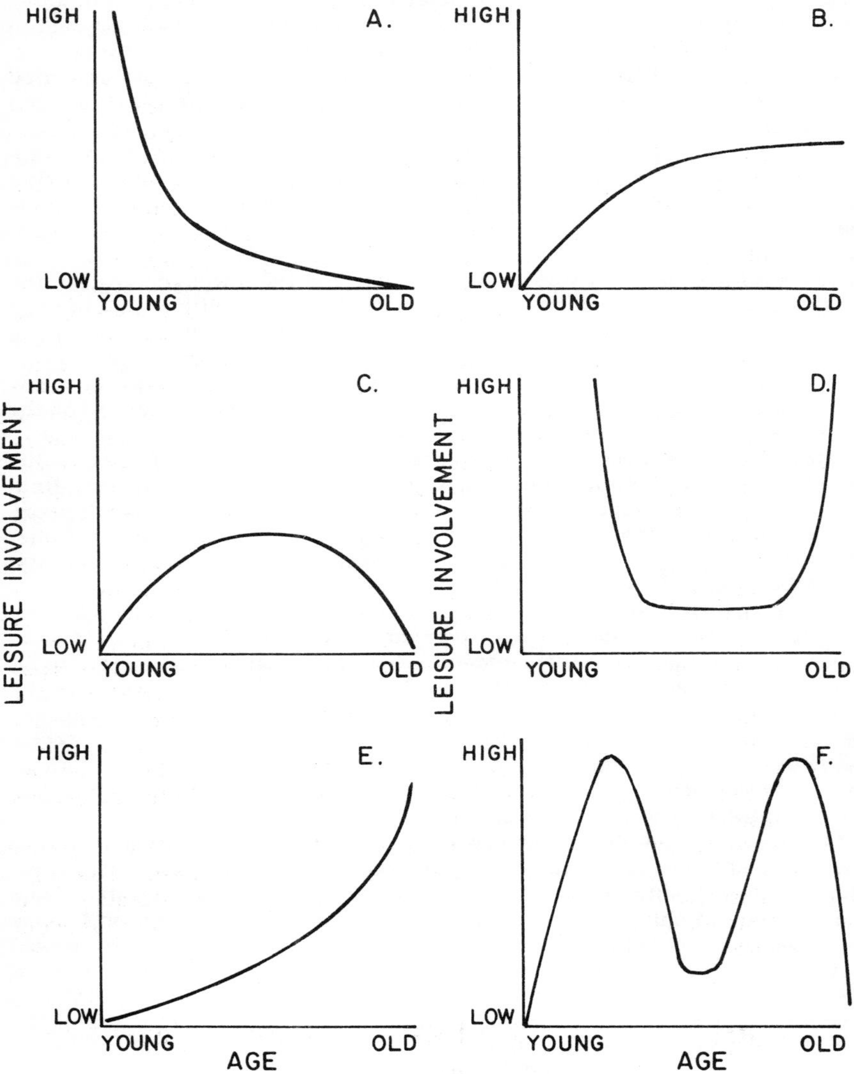

By middle age, one's career is usually well established, the children are leaving home, more time and money are available, and leisure may become more salient in the lifestyle. However, this may also be the stage at which women enter or re-enter the labor force, thereby reducing the time available for leisure. As a result, a couple may develop or pursue individual interests, and may compress leisure time spent together into weekends and vacation periods. Generally, the pattern established by the middle years continues into the preretirement stage, and often into the postretirement stage (Atchley, 1971;

Yoesting and Burkhead, 1973; Kleiber and Kelly, 1980). Because of this pattern of continuity, it is important to be aware of patterns of leisure behavior during the middle years in order to better understand the use of time in the postretirement years.

In summary, it appears that many patterns of leisure involvement are possible in the early and middle years of adulthood. Individual differences in these patterns are related to class[15] and type of occupation;[16] to regional differences in opportunity and values; to variations in the family life course; and to cultural variation by gender, race, and ethnicity. Moreover, societal changes in ethics, values, and norms affect the amount, meaning, and function of leisure over time. For example, if there is a decline in the importance of the work ethic, there may be a concomitant increase in the importance of leisure. A national survey in Canada in 1978 found that a typical working adult spends fifty hours a week in leisure activities, compared with fewer than forty hours in the workplace. Or, expressed on a weekly basis, Canadians spent almost a billion hours in leisure-time activities, and about a third of this amount as members of the labor force.

Yet, a decrease in the work week (to under forty hours or to four days) has not necessarily increased leisure involvement across all strata (Conner and Bultena, 1979). That is, fewer hours spent at the primary job may provide an opportunity to 'moonlight' at a second job to increase income. This pattern is most prevalent among those in the lower and middle income strata. Similarly, the increasing entrance of women into the labor force changes and restricts opportunities for leisure.

In short, the meaning and availability of leisure may change across the life cycle in response to personal needs, interests, and abilities; to institutional (work and family) demands; and to cultural change. For this reason chronological age is a weak predictor of leisure behavior. For example, a 24-year-old male may be attending university or be employed full time; he may be a member of the upper or lower socioeconomic strata; and he may be married or not married, with or without children. Similarly, the leisure patterns of 45-year-old women may vary by class, marital status, or employment status (Zuzanek, 1979). Thus, when attempting to identify and explain leisure patterns in the early and middle years of the life cycle, a variety of personal, social, cultural, and environmental factors must be considered.

In the next section, leisure in the later years is discussed. It will be seen that the meaning of leisure may change if family and occupational constraints are reduced or eliminated. However, class, gender, ethnicity, race, education, and previous lifestyles still influence the leisure patterns selected by older individuals and cohorts.

Leisure and Aging: The Postretirement Years

Introduction: A General Pattern

With the onset of partial or complete retirement, the amount of unstructured free time increases dramatically. This time can be filled by continuing some form of work, by expanding the time used to complete daily personal tasks, or by leisure activities. While it has often been suggested that the leisure role is the major role in the retirement years, relatively few people adopt new patterns or pursuits after retirement, or increase the number or frequency of activities. Most studies indicate that there is continuity between the work and retirement leisure styles, although the number of activities and frequency of involvement decrease at various rates with age (Harris, 1975; Gordon and Gaitz, 1976; Schmitz-Scherzer, 1978; Statistics Canada, 1978; Long and Wimbush, 1979; McAvoy, 1979; McPherson and Kozlik, 1980; Teague, 1980; Wilson, 1980; Bosse and Ekerdt, 1981; Moss and Lawton, 1982).

While there may be some initial experimentation with new leisure activities immediately following retirement (Peppers, 1976), most individuals restrict their range of activities as retirement goes on. This restriction occurs for a variety of reasons, including loss of interest in some activities, declining health and energy for physical activities, loss of mobility and transportation, lack of opportunity, widowhood, declining economic resources, lack of social norms and reinforcement that encourage continued involvement, and moving to an institutionalized setting.

As a result of these confounding factors, the leisure patterns of the elderly are quite heterogeneous. Moreover, they vary in frequency and type for the younger and older segments of the retired cohort, by class, by gender, by region, by actual or perceived level of crime in the neighborhood (Godbey et al., 1980), by type of housing environment (Moss and Lawton, 1982), by education, by place of residence (Gunter, 1979; Strain and Chappell, forthcoming), and by racial or ethnic group. Moreover, environmental intervention may lead to changes in leisure opportunities and involvement. For example, moving to an age-segregated apartment or to a retirement community, or migrating for the winter to a warmer climate where there is a large population of older people may permanently or temporarily increase the leisure activity levels of the elderly (Bultena and Wood, 1970; Sherman, 1974; Carp, 1978–79; Morgan and Godbey, 1978).[17] Similarly, institutionalization may deprive the elderly person of lifelong leisure experiences, and thereby lead to a decrease in the quantity or quality of leisure.

The leisure activities most frequently reported by those over 65 years of age are socializing with friends and relatives, watching television,[18] gardening, reading newspapers, and sitting and thinking (Harris, 1975, 1981; Statistics Canada, 1978; Schmitz-Scherzer, 1979; Moss and Lawton, 1982). Most activities take place indoors and are home-based rather than community-based.[19] Many elderly people, especially the very old, are involved in solitary rather than group activities. For example, Moss and Lawton (1982) found that among lower-middle-class urban dwellers who lived in their own homes, 64 percent of the day was spent alone, 75 percent of the day was spent inside the home, and 34 percent of the day was spent on obligatory personal or household activities. This finding coincides with the perception of retirees that there is an increase in their solitary activities after retirement (Bosse and Ekerdt, 1981).

Most research has focused on the quantity of the retiree's leisure activities rather than on the quality or meaning of the leisure experience. It is important to examine not only the number and frequency of leisure experiences, but also their meaning and quality. For example, rather than determining how many hours per day an individual spends watching television, a researcher should find out what programs are watched; with whom, if anyone, the programs are watched; and what function the programs serve. Similarly, it is more interesting and useful to note changes in meaning over time rather than whether a decrease or increase has occurred. For example, a hike in the mountains may have been perceived at one stage in life as primarily a form of physical exercise in an aesthetically pleasing setting; later in life this same activity may be perceived as a providing an opportunity to study plants and animals in their natural environment, or to develop photographic skills. In fact, the activity of hiking may serve all three purposes at the same time, and at the same stage in the life cycle.

In addition to the need to assess the quality of the leisure experience in the later years, there is also a need to examine the influence of the quantity and quality of leisure on other facets of life. Some studies have examined the relationship between leisure activity patterns and such factors as marital satisfaction (Orthner, 1975), adjustment to retirement (Fly et al., 1981), and life satisfaction or successful aging (Atchley, 1971; De Carlo, 1974; Peppers, 1976; Ray, 1979b, 1981; Cutler, 1981–82). Most of these studies have found that individuals who are involved in leisure activities report higher levels of satisfaction or adjustment. However, before definitive conclusions can be drawn about the value and importance of leisure activities in the later years, it must be recognized that being highly satisfied or adjusted may lead to greater involvement in all forms of social participation. Thus, the chicken-and-egg dilemma is raised again. Nevertheless, there does appear to be a complex and not well understood relationship between the frequency, type, and quality of leisure participation and such global measures of adjustment as life satisfaction, successful aging, morale, and quality of life.

Volunteerism and Voluntary-Association Participation

Introduction.   This subsection presents an analysis of volunteerism and of the patterns of participation by the elderly in voluntary associations. From adolescence on, much of our social behavior during leisure occurs within the context of voluntary associations such as labor unions, professional associations, fraternal and church-affiliated groups, sport and service clubs, and cultural, hobby, and political groups. These associations serve a variety of expressive or instrumental functions for society and for the individual.

On the basis of cross-sectional studies, the general life-cycle pattern of involvement in voluntary associations is curvilinear (see figure 11.1), especially for those associations that pertain to the job or to children's activities (Smith, 1975; Cutler, 1976a, 1977; Trela, 1976; Hoyt and Lockwood, 1981).[20] The peak of involvement is likely to occur within about ten years before or after retirement, although this peak varies by type of association. Moreover, involvement is more likely to be part of the lifestyle of those who have higher levels of education and income, who are in good health, and who are members of the higher social classes.

Not surprisingly, there are distinct sex differences in the type of memberships: women are more involved in church, school, cultural, and hobby groups, and men more involved in job-related, fraternal, sport, veterans', and service associations. Men belong to larger and more essential organizations (such as service or fraternal groups) that are likely to be related to economic institutions, while women belong to smaller and more peripheral organizations (such as Block Parents or quilting groups) that are focused on domestic or community affairs (McPherson and Smith-Lovin, 1982). Women generally belong to a greater variety of associations, and attend meetings and activities more frequently. However, with the increase in labor-force participation by women, their type and pattern of voluntary-association involvement is becoming more similar to male involvement, especially for career women. Also, the variety and frequency of involvement by women may decline in conjunction with a reduction in discretionary time because of work demands (Harris, 1981). Finally, although members of racial or ethnic groups constitute a numerical minority in all voluntary association memberships, they represent a proportionately higher percentage in voluntary associations, and they have higher rates of attendance (Clemente et al., 1975; Hoyt and Babchuk, 1981).

With the exception of specifically age-based organizations, most association memberships are age-heterogeneous, although they tend to be homogeneous in class composition. In general, membership in a voluntary association may enable an individual to contribute to society, to help others, to advance a personal interest, to acquire new skills, or to interact with others who have similar interests. In addition, members of voluntary associations are able to play a leadership role, use their free time in a meaningful way, or enhance their sense of identity.

From the societal perspective, voluntary associations and volunteerism can promote social integration and assimilation (ethnic associations), foster conflict and change (political groups or labor unions), and provide social services (service and fraternal groups). It has been estimated that voluntary activities accounted for about 3 percent of Canada's gross national product in 1981. This figure translates into about 374 million person hours per year, and represents a significant unsalaried human resource within a nation.

Throughout the life cycle, voluntary associations serve expressive, instructional, and instrumental purposes for individuals and for the society. However, membership is not universal or inevitable: rather, it appears that there is a pattern of stability and continuity across the life cycle. Those who are 'joiners' early in life tend to remain involved when they are older, and those who are 'nonjoiners' early in life tend to remain uninvolved. This same pattern appears to hold for volunteerism (for example, canvassing for a local charity or daily telephoning of an older neighbor).

Voluntary associations and the retirement years.   Although the results of cross-sectional studies suggest that voluntary-association involvement decreases with age, there appears to be a growth in the number of age-based associations for older people,[21] and an increase in volunteerism[22] (Cutler, 1973, 1976b; Payne, 1977; Babchuk et al., 1979; Bull and Payne, 1979; Ward, 1979). This increase in joining behavior, which is especially likely for women, and for those with a history of past involvement, may result from better health, better education, earlier retirement, greater economic security, more discretionary time and income, and a desire to maintain continuity in lifestyle. It may also result from a greater opportunity set, a need to compensate for role losses, a need to enhance life satisfaction, or a need to acquire a new social support system after retirement. This greater involvement by the elderly represents a significant contribution to the economy in the form of free labor and expertise.

As retirement approaches, older individuals often become less involved in leadership roles. In addition, they may shift their involvement from instrumental to expressive associations, they may still belong to a group but participate less frequently, and they may become more involved in age-homogeneous groups, either because they feel a need to affiliate with age peers for personal or political gains or because they are directly or indirectly discouraged from continued participation in age-heterogeneous associations. Similarly, for the white elderly of ethnic origin, ethnic clubs can be a source of security and can act as a support system. This affiliation with the ethnic group continues, even though younger people are less likely to join an ethnic association as they become increasingly assimilated into mainstream society (Hoyt and Babchuk, 1981).

Although a majority of older people do not become involved in senior-citizen organizations, these clubs or centers do serve a number of functions. They provide information and educational services, serve as social centers and support networks, offer leisure opportunities at lower costs, and act as political advocacy groups for the rights and needs of older persons. Those who are most likely to join are women, those in good health, those who have easy access to public or private transportation, those who have always been 'joiners,' those who are from middle- and lower-middle-class backgrounds, and those with a strong attachment to the community (Maeda, 1975; Taietz, 1976; Trela, 1976; Cuellar, 1978).

Regardless of the earlier life pattern of involvement in voluntary associations, volunteer involvement ultimately decreases because of declining health, loss of energy, loss of interest, lack of mobility and transportation (Cutler, 1974), and fear of crime. However, this decline can be at least partly prevented or delayed through community social services (Dial-A-Ride transportation), or by moving to age-segregated retirement housing where clubs and associations are organized on the premises by and for the residents. Clearly, effective leisure services for the elderly require an integration of housing, health care, transportation, and leisure policies (Rapoport and Rapoport, 1975).[23]

Political Participation

In chapter 7 the political power of elderly cohorts was discussed in relation to their position in the social structure. Here, the emphasis is on the political participation of the elderly person with respect to political attitudes and orientation, voting behavior, and involvement in political leadership roles. In effect, political participation represents a form of leisure behavior within[24] and outside voluntary associations. Most individuals have the right to vote, to affiliate with political parties, or to hold political office, although not all choose to become interested or involved in the political process. In recent years, largely because of the increasing proportion of elderly people in the population, interest in describing and explaining patterns of political participation across the life cycle has increased (Cutler and Schmidhauser, 1975; Binstock and Levin, 1976; Hudson and Binstock, 1976; Pratt, 1976, 1979, 1981; Brotman, 1977; Trela, 1977–78; Estes, 1979; Hudson, 1981; Williamson et al., 1981; Binstock, forthcoming). As a result, certain patterns of political participation have been noted, especially in the United States where party affiliation and interest in the political process tends to be high and relatively consistent across the life cycle.

Based on conclusions drawn from U.S. studies, interest in political matters appears to increase with age and is closely related to level of educational attainment, type of occupation, and being male. The degree of political interest or knowledge at any one time is related to past views and experiences, to social change, to particular attitudes about general issues (indifference or opposition to increases in education or foreign trade expenditures) or specific issues (positive support for pensions, housing, or health care policies), and to the type and degree of party affiliation.

Changes in political interest or attitudes across the life cycle may represent maturational changes, cohort effects or period effects. For example, although cross-sectional studies suggest that elderly persons as a group are more conservative than other age cohorts, this does not imply that they have become more conservative with age. Rather, they may have been politically socialized at a period in history when conservatism prevailed.[25] They may also appear conservative relative to younger cohorts because of dramatic changes in values and social norms over a twenty- to thirty-year period (for example, the rise of the women's movement, youthful political activism, and recreational drug use). In fact, based on a cohort analysis, Glenn (1974) concluded that Americans have actually become less conservative with age because of value changes in society. He found that people in their 50s and 60s were generally more liberal than they were in their 30s and 40s. Cutler et al. (1980) examined cohort differences in attitudes towards legalized abortion. They found that attitudes toward legal abortions became considerably more liberal across all age cohorts between 1965 and 1973. However, the older cohorts were slower to change their attitudes: the process takes longer for them than for younger persons, and there may be greater intracohort variability with respect to a specific attitude or political opinion.

As is usual with social science data, caveats must be introduced. There are wide regional and class variations across cohorts with respect to political matters; for example, the values and lifestyles of those who live in the southern United States or in the eastern Canadian provinces have, regardless of age, traditionally been more conservative than those of persons living in other regions. This regional variation is partly related to the presence of prevailing subcultural norms and values, which in turn are related to the distance from the decision-making processes of the political and economic centers of the nation. The regional difference is also related to generally lower levels of educational attainment, which, combined with isolation, restrict access to new information. Similarly, members of the lower classes in all geographical regions tend to be less educated, to have less access to new ideas, and to be more likely to adhere to childhood and adolescent values throughout life.

In short, political interest and orientation can change with age, particularly on issues related to one's changing personal situation (health care, pensions, housing). However, the rate of change may be slow and it may not affect all members of a given age cohort, especially those who live in certain regions of a country or who have a particular class background.

Even if political interest and orientations do change in the later years, actual participation in the political process through voting may not occur. Most cross-sectional studies indicate that voting participation increases with age until some point in the 60s and then declines. During the middle years of life people are generally better informed, have more free time, and are well integrated into a community or region. The decline in voting in the later years has been attributed not to chronological age per se, but rather to declining health and to lack of mobility or transportation. In addition, because women vote generally less often than men at all ages, and because women comprise an increasingly larger proportion of the population, there are fewer voters in total among the older age cohorts. Finally, older cohorts have generally been composed of a larger proportion of ethnic and racial minority groups. Until recently, these groups have tended to be less informed, less interested, and less active in the political process of a community or nation (Torres-Gil and Becerra, 1977). However, with declining immigration rates and growing political involvement by minority groups, this pattern may be less apparent among future elderly cohorts.

The elderly are, of course, also eligible to hold political office. In fact, many elderly persons are elected because of their perceived stability and experience, and because they serve as a symbol of wisdom. In both business (Warner and Abegglen, 1955) and politics (Lehman, 1953; Schlesinger, 1966) it has been found that a large percentage of the elites, or leaders, are over 60 years of age. Lehman

(1953), in a study of the ages of political leaders in Great Britain, France, Canada, and the United States from 1900 to 1930, reported that there has been an upward shift in age across time. This trend seems to occur even more frequently as the importance of the leadership position increases. It is also more likely to occur where legislation does not limit the term of office. Incumbents often age in office (for example, the late Mayor Richard Daley in Chicago, Prime Minister Pierre Trudeau in Canada, Supreme Court justices, the late President Leonid Brezhnev, the Pope), so that the elderly are overrepresented in political positions. In the future, elderly people may be even more likely to hold office because an increasingly larger proportion of the electorate will be their age peers.

In summary, as the population ages, older age cohorts will be better educated, and may recognize the extent of their potential influence through bloc voting. This recognition may lead to shifts in political interests and orientation across the life cycle, including the possibility of politically based conflict or cooperation between age strata. In addition, the number of elderly persons involved in the political process will probably increase, especially since women are becoming more involved at younger ages. It is partly for this reason that an increasing number of women are being elected to political offices at all levels of government.

Religious Participation

As a cultural institution, organized religion has a symbolic and functional role in most societies; it has the potential to provide a sense of security, a readily available social group, and a social role for the older individual. Religious belief can also assist in coping with grief and death, especially among older persons. Because of these apparent functions, gerontologists have been interested in the patterns of religious behavior during the middle and later years of life (Bahr, 1970; Wingrove and Alston, 1971; Moberg, 1972; Blazer and Palmore, 1976; Alston and Alston, 1980; Payne and Brewer, 1980; Payne, 1981).

As with other forms of social participation, it is important to distinguish between age differences, the outcome of aging, and period effects with respect to adherence to religious beliefs or attendance at religious events. Moreover, it is important to differentiate between attitudes or beliefs and behavior. Religious attitudes and beliefs may persist until death; church or temple attendance (behavior) may decrease as health or access to transportation declines. For example, Mindel and Vaughan (1978) found that about 60 percent of the elderly people in their study, who seldom or never attended religious services, did listen to or watch religious services on radio or television, prayed at home, or read the Bible on their own. For them, religion was a private, subjective experience, and although they were disengaged organizationally, they were engaged in a nonorganizational sense.

Stereotypes and myths concerning the religious behavior of older people have been perpetuated by conflicting hypotheses and evidence (Bahr, 1970; Blazer and Palmore, 1976; Payne and Brewer, 1980). There appear to be at least five possible patterns of religious involvement, which are usually measured by attendance: (1) attendance increases with age; (2) attendance is cyclical, and is related to the stage in the family life cycle;[26] (3) attendance begins to decrease after middle age; (4) the pattern is stable across the life cycle; (5) regardless of the pattern earlier in life, attendance increases in the later years.[27]

To date, most studies have found that attendance at religious ceremonies remains stable across the life course, or that there is a withdrawal in the middle and later years. However, these patterns vary by religious affiliation, by sex, by education, and by place of residence: women, Catholics, the less educated, and those who live in rural areas seem to attend services more frequently at all ages.

It has generally been found that religion is a more important element in the life of the elderly person, and that older age cohorts report stronger religious beliefs than younger age cohorts. However, it has not been determined whether these findings reflect cohort or aging effects. Wingrove and Alston (1971) argued that patterns of religious attendance at any age reflect the 'mood of the times'; that is, period effects influence attendance patterns. For example, at present there is a heightened interest, especially among adolescents and young adults, in nontraditional religious beliefs and practices.[28] Is this a passing fad, or will these cohorts remain committed, in the same form and to the same degree, at all stages in the life cycle?

In short, religious participation can vary in form and frequency across the life cycle for any one cohort, and between cohorts as values, norms, needs, and interests change over time. Moreover, it appears that some degree of continuity prevails from one stage in life to another. Thus, those elderly persons who were religious early in life are likely to exhibit some form of religious behavior late in life, even if attendance at religious services declines because of failing health or lack of mobility.

The Media and the Elderly

The media are made up of printed (newspapers, magazines, and books) and electronic (radio, television, and movies) communication systems designed to reach a large and diverse audience. As an increasingly salient social institution, the media serve a number of functions: they entertain, disseminate information, promote social integration, provide an escape from the realities of everyday life, select and perpetuate specific cultural norms, and educate the masses (De Fleur, 1970). In addition, the media may provide the elderly with indirect contact with the social world, and may help to counteract loneliness by presenting characters and situations with which they can identify.

As age increases, people may read fewer books and newspapers and see fewer films because of financial constraints, declining vision, and loss of interest in the content. However, the amount of television viewing increases until about age 70, before a modest decline begins (Kubey, 1980). This greater television usage may be an aging effect rather than a cohort effect. However, a recent study in the United States found that television viewing by those 65 and over declined from 36 to 31 percent between 1974 and 1981, while reading as a leisure pursuit increased from 36 to 39 percent (Harris, 1981). These changes may reflect a higher level of educational attainment for recent retirees, or it may be the result of changing leisure patterns among older age cohorts in the United States. Nevertheless, television is the medium most frequently selected by the elderly for entertainment and information.[29] (Davis, 1975, 1979; Dimmick and McCain, 1979; Dimmick et al., 1979; Swank, 1979; Young, 1979; Kubey, 1980). This use of television may occur because more time is spent at home, because more leisure time is available, and because the elderly have fewer links with the community. Television is also more accessible to those with failing vision or hearing than either a newspaper or the radio, since television transmits both picture and sound.

Television became widely available only after the late 1940s, and many of the current cohort of older persons were first exposed to television during early adulthood. Television viewing was not inculcated during childhood and has not been a lifelong habit as it is for many younger age cohorts. Nevertheless, the elderly (especially older women, the less educated, and those with lower incomes) are regular and avid viewers of quiz shows, news programs, soap operas, and variety shows.

Although there is still a debate as to whether media consumption is a substitution or compensation for a lack of face-to-face interpersonal relations, it does appear that television may provide surrogate company for some elderly persons. Also, television viewing can provide a structured daily schedule for older people: mealtimes, chores, and going to bed are regulated by the television programs that are watched on a given day. In short, the higher rates of television consumption (three to four hours per day) may not only 'kill time,' but may also impose a schedule or routine, thereby serving a functional role.

While most of the research relating to television and the older person has focused on participation rates and the types of programs viewed, few studies have examined how the elderly are depicted on television, or the potential uses of television for the elderly. With respect to the image presented, older people are often portrayed in a negative and stereotypical manner in television serials and comedy shows, or appear in news items presented to create sympathy (for example, a widow cheated of her life savings), humor, or amazement (at a man fathering a child at age 75 or a grandmother who singlehandedly flies around the world). Compared to the general population, the aged as a group are underrepresented as television characters, although older men are overrepresented compared to older women. In short, television often fails to provide an accurate representation of older people (see chapter 7).

Although television seldom provides intellectual stimulation for individuals at any age, the use of the medium to present educational programs for the aging (such as PBS's 'Over Easy' and CBC's 'From Now On') is increasing. Cable television and pay television services, particularly those that provide two-way interactive videotext systems (Telidon), have a great potential to provide learning experiences, intellectual stimulation, and social and commercial services for adults of all ages.

Education and the Elderly

It was once believed that an individual's education was completed in late adolescence; today, continuing education during adulthood has become necessary or desirable because of rapid technological and social change. Learning has become a lifelong necessity, as well as an accepted leisure pursuit whereby an individual can 'learn for the sake of learning' regardless of chronological age or stage in life. Although it was once thought that an older person lacked the ability to learn, recent evidence suggests that, given the opportunity, encouragement, and sufficient time, an older person can acquire new skills through formal and informal educational systems (see chapter 6).

Changing social norms, along with research evidence relating to the learning and ability of older people, have made it possible for them to pursue an education in the home via cassette tapes and television, in off-campus centers in the community, and on college campuses[30] (Peterson, 1978; Johnson et al., 1980; Perkins and Robertson-Tchabo, 1981; Heisel et al., 1981). Not surprisingly, there is a higher participation rate in these programs by whites, by members of the upper and middle classes, by those who completed their early schooling in North America, by those in good health, by those who are mobile, and by those with few vision or hearing problems. It appears that this pattern of pursuing an educational program as a form of leisure is increasing for those in the postretirement years. For example, Harris (1981) found that enrollment in educational courses by those over 65 years of age increased from 2 percent to 5 percent between 1974 and 1981. Not surprisingly, a large percentage of those enrolled had already earned a college degree. This pattern of growing enrollment in educational programs is likely to continue if tuition fees are waived or reduced significantly, if recruitment and counselling programs for the mature student are available, if admission standards are flexible, if courses are offered off-campus in convenient locations, if both credit and noncredit programs are available,[31] and if examination situations are not perceived to be stressful. In short, education has become an increasingly salient leisure pursuit for middle-aged and elderly persons, especially during the early years of retirement when high rates of health, mobility, and discretionary time and income are present.

Summary and Conclusions

In this final chapter we have looked at leisure as a form of social participation that is an important facet of contemporary lifestyles at all stages in the life cycle. In the first section a number of conceptual and methodological issues concerning leisure as a social concept were introduced, and alternative explanations for the relationship between the type of work and the amount, form, and meaning of leisure were discussed. The remainder of the chapter described patterns of leisure involvement in the middle and later years of adulthood, especially with respect to volunteerism, voluntary-association involvement, religious and political participation, continuing education, and the media.

Despite the relatively small body of literature pertaining to aging and leisure involvement, the following conclusions appear to be warranted:

1. A generally accepted definition of 'leisure' has yet to be derived, perhaps because leisure is a personal experience, because a number of inherent methodological and conceptual matters have yet to be resolved, and because there are a variety of cultural and subcultural variations in norms and values concerning work and leisure.

2. To date, relatively few cross-sectional or longitudinal research studies have examined the pattern or meaning of leisure involvement across the life cycle.

3. The quality of leisure, compared to the quantity of leisure, is seldom considered in analyses of leisure involvement at any stage in the life cycle.

4. While the amount of free time and frequency of leisure involvement may increase or decrease at varying stages in the life cycle, the type of leisure pursuits are relatively constant once patterns are established in the early and middle years of adulthood.

5. Although there appears to be evidence that there is a relationship between type of work and type of leisure, a definitive explanation for this relationship is not available. Rather, three major hypotheses have been proposed and tested. The 'spillover' or 'congruence' hypothesis argues that there is

little difference between work and leisure, and that therefore the leisure activities selected are similar to the job. The 'compensatory' or 'contrast' hypothesis argues that individuals seek in their leisure what is lacking in their work, and that leisure activities tend to be unlike work activities. The 'neutrality' hypothesis argues that there is little attachment to work; therefore, the nature of work has little bearing on leisure pursuits and there may or may not be a linkage between work and leisure activities.

6. To date, the research evidence is supportive of the 'spillover' hypothesis, although the relationship between work and leisure in one's lifestyle may vary by age and by stage in the family life cycle. The personal and cultural characteristics that might influence the relationship have seldom been considered.

7. During the working years, personal characteristics, the demands and responsibilities of the family and work, and social and technological change all influence the selection of leisure activities and the meaning these activities have for the individual. Chronological age per se is an incomplete predictor of leisure behavior.

8. The leisure patterns of the elderly are heterogeneous. However, regardless of the pattern, leisure activities generally become constricted in frequency and type as the number of years beyond retirement increases. Declining health, income, and energy, a lack of opportunity, and a loss of mobility and transportation can dramatically alter the leisure patterns in the later years of life.

9. The most frequently reported leisure activities by those over 65 years of age are socializing with friends and relatives; watching television; gardening; reading newspapers; and sitting and thinking. In short, most activities are indoor, home-based, and solitary, especially for the very old segment of the retired population.

10. Studies have found that older individuals who are more involved in leisure activities report higher levels of satisfaction or adjustment. However, the causal direction of this relationship has yet to be established, although it is probably a two-way process of interaction.

11. The general life-cycle pattern of volunteerism and involvement in voluntary associations is curvilinear, with the peak of involvement generally occuring within the ten years prior to or following retirement.

12. Membership in voluntary associations is not a universal or inevitable pattern. Those who are 'joiners' early in life tend to join and participate in the middle and later years.

13. A majority of older people do not become involved in senior-citizen organizations, even where the groups are known and available to older residents. Those who are most likely to join are women; those in good health; those with access to transportation; those who have been 'joiners' throughout life; those who are members of the lower-middle or middle class; and those with a strong attachment to the neighborhood or community.

14. Interest in political matters and voting increases with age until health and mobility decline in the later years. However, there are class, sex, educational, regional, cultural, and subcultural variations in political interest and participation at all ages.

15. Changes in political interest or attitudes across the life cycle may represent maturational changes, cohort effects, or period effects. The explanation may depend on the salience of a particular topic or issue at a particular stage in the life cycle of an individual or a cohort, or at a particular period in history.

16. Many older persons hold political office. The number may increase in the future since the older segment of the population will comprise a larger proportion of the voting population.

17. Most studies have found that attendance at religious ceremonies remains stable across the life course, or is characterized by a withdrawal in the middle or later years. Some who withdraw return later if there is a concern with the nearness and consequences of death.

18. While attendance at religious services may decline in the later years, continuity in religiosity may prevail. That is, those who were religious early in life may continue to be involved through reading or by watching or listening to religious services on television or radio.

19. As age increases, the use of movies and the print media may decrease because of cost, declining vision, and loss of interest in the content. However, the amount of television viewing generally increases until about 70 years of age. Among the elderly population, the most regular and avid viewers of quiz shows, news programs, soap operas, and variety shows are women, the less educated, and those with the fewest economic resources.

20. With increasing opportunities to pursue credit and noncredit educational programs, a larger percentage of the elderly population is enrolling in educational courses as a form of leisure in the pre- and postretirement years.

Notes

1. Interestingly, there appear to be some commonalities in meaning between work and leisure, even though they are often viewed as bipolar opposites. Both provide the individual with a sense of worth, an identity, a milieu in which to initiate and maintain social interaction, a source of prestige and status, and an outlet for expressive and instrumental needs.

2. For example, the emphasis attached to work (the work ethic) by a society and by individuals varies historically: that is, within the hierarchy of values of a society or an individual, the status of work and leisure shifts over time (Dumazedier, 1972).

3. Some of the more common dimensions are expressive-instrumental; free choice-constrained involvement; low involvement-high involvement; active-passive; individual-group; home centered-community centered; institutionalized- noninstitutionalized; inexpensive-expensive; mass culture-high culture; creative-noncreative;

spontaneous-planned; structured-unstructured; work-nonwork; and, physical-nonphysical.

4. For example, reading as a leisure activity may be pursued to improve the mind, to learn a skill, to study for a degree, or simply to pass the time.

5. An individual is able to listen to music while reading, to watch television while visiting with others, or to play darts or backgammon while drinking.

6. An example of an activity in an overlapping category is watching television. The activity can be categorized as educational or recreational or as a solitary or group activity, depending on the situation in which the activity takes place.

7. Some recent attempts to measure various dimensions of leisure have been made by McKechnie (1975), Yoesting and Burdge (1976), Gordon and Gaitz (1976), Dangott and Kalish (1979:160), Beard and Ragheb (1980), Gunter and Gunter (1980), Kabanoff and

O'Brien (1980), Pierce (1980a, 1980b), Yu and Mendell (1980), Moss and Lawton (1982).

8. For example, Gordon and Gaitz (1976:314) illustrate that the intensity of expressive involvement in leisure can vary in the cognitive, emotional, and physical dimensions across the following five levels: (1) very high (sexual activity, competitive games and sport); (2) medium high (creative activities such as music and art); (3) medium (attending cultural events, reading for learning, recreational sport or exercise); (4) medium low (watching television, attending spectator sports, hobbies, reading for pleasure); and (5) low (solitude, resting, 'killing time').

9. Class is often measured by occupational prestige or type of occupation.

10. For example, Lefkowitz (1979) presents an analysis of one hundred individuals who chose not to work unless absolutely necessary for survival. They represent a modern-day 'leisured' class.

11. For example, in recent years some individuals have experienced periods of voluntary or involuntary unemployment; this has led to their acceptance of leisure in the absence of work, and to the use of leisure to escape jobs that are characterized by tension, triviality, or boredom.

12. This view is represented by those who barely tolerate their '9-to-5' existence, and who adhere-to-the TGIF (Thank Goodness It's Friday) philosophy.

13. Kaplan (1979:137–200) identified eight general types of leisure experiences possible during adulthood: aesthetic, civic, intellectual, mass media, physical, social, spiritual, and tourism.

14. Some specific events that can alter leisure are marriage, the birth of a child, a promotion, the empty nest, entrance of the spouse into the labor force, retirement, death of the spouse, or divorce.

15. For example, those in lower-status occupations generally engage in more home-centered leisure; those in higher-status occupations become more involved in community-centered activities such as service groups and private clubs.

16. For example, a store owner, a physician, and a professor, although all members of the upper-middle class, generally have different work styles and career demands. The store owner may work six days and two evenings a week; the physician may work five days a week and be on call at certain times; and the professor may work five to seven days a week and in the evenings in order to read and write papers or books. Time demands vary from occupation to occupation and greatly influence the amount and style of leisure.

17. Those who live in age-segregated apartments or condominiums spend less time on obligatory home maintenance than those who live in houses.

18. The Harris (1975) survey found that those aged 65 to 69 averaged 2.4 hours per day, while those aged 70 to 79 averaged 2.2 hours per day. These averages were higher for blacks and for lower income and education groups.

19. Kaplan (1979) indicates that there is a low level of leisure involvement by the elderly in parks, planned communities, senior-citizen centers, nursing homes, and libraries.

20. The curvilinear pattern may reflect cohort effects rather than aging effects, since older cohorts are generally less educated, have had fewer opportunities to join associations, and are more likely to be members of the lower class.

21. Some of these include the American Association of Retired Persons, senior-citizen centers, and Widow-to-Widow programs.

22. The retired person can volunteer to be a foster grandparent, a teacher, or an executive in a community association or a developing country.

23. Some recent sources of information on leisure programming for the elderly are Dangott and Kalish (1979), Moran (1979), Weiss (1979), Schiff (1980), and Shivers and Fait (1980), and Wapner (1981). A monthly publication of the National Geriatrics Society in the United States entitled *Aging and Leisure Living* also provides information on leisure programming.

24. Many age-based organizations for the elderly have been created in the United States to lobby for and promote the needs and interests of the elderly (Pratt, 1981). These include the American Association of Retired Persons, the National Retired Teachers Association, and the National Council on Aging. To date, these organizations have had little significant influence on the overall political process or structure, largely because there has been little evidence of the development of a national age-group consciousness (Ragan and Dowd, 1974), or of bloc voting by

the elderly (except on some issues at the local level).

25. In the United States there is generally continuity in party affiliation across the life cycle. Moreover, older people are more likely to be affiliated with the conservative party (Republican) because they were socialized to this view of the political world at a young age. That is, affiliation with a particular party may represent historical experiences rather than age-related conservatism, and therefore significant shifts in party affiliation are unlikely to occur later in life.

26. One pattern for adults is shown in a peaking of religious participation when children are involved in Sunday school, and a decline when the children leave home; another is shown in an increase until late adolescence, a decline from 18 to 35 years of age, and then an increase until the later years when it decreases again (Bahr, 1970).

27. This pattern is sometimes referred to as the 'just-in-case' phenomenon: religious behavior increases and remains high in the later years 'just-in-case' judgment will be delivered upon the individual after death.

28. Most readers will be familiar with the existence of sects such as the 'Moonies' and the Hare Krishna adherents; in addition, some individuals refer to themselves and others as 'born-again Christians,' and religious groups of all types are thriving on college campuses.

29. Although three to four hours of viewing per day may be the average reported by the elderly, many self-reports underestimate the actual viewing time. Moreover, some studies ask only whether a television set is on or off, not whether a program is being watched. From this perspective, the average number of 'viewing' hours may be an overestimate.

30. Higher education for the elderly is discussed in *Educational Gerontology* and at the annual meetings of the Association For Gerontology in Higher Education.

31. Many older persons may initially lack the confidence to enter a degree program, or may not be motivated to obtain sufficient credits for a degree. As a compromise, many institutions offer a certificate for completing a specified number of university courses.

References

Alston, L. and J. Alston. 'Religion and the Older Woman,' pp. 262–78 in M. Fuller and C. Martin (eds.). *The Older Woman: Lavender Rose or Gray Panther.* Springfield, Ill.: Charles C. Thomas, 1980.

Andrew, E. *Closing the Iron Cage: The Scientific Management of Work and Leisure.* Toronto: Black Rose Books, 1982.

Atchley, R. 'Retirement and Leisure Participation: Continuity or Crisis?' *The Gerontologist,* 11(1/1971), 13–17.

Babchuk, N. et al. 'The Voluntary Associations of the Aged,' *Journal of Gerontology,* 34(4/1979), 579–87.

Bahr, H. 'Aging and Religious Disaffiliation,' *Social Forces,* 49(1/1970), 59–71.

Beard, J. and M. Ragheb. 'Measuring Leisure Satisfaction,' *Journal of Leisure Research,* 12(1/1980), 20–33.

Binstock, R. *Aging: Politics and Policies.* Belmont, Calif.: Wadsworth Publishing Co., forthcoming.

Binstock, R. and M. Levin. 'The Political Dilemmas of Intervention Policies,' pp. 511–35 in R. Binstock and E. Shanas (eds.). *Handbook of Aging and the Social Sciences.* New York: Van Nostrand Reinhold, 1976.

Bishop, D. and M. Ikeda. 'Status and Role Factors in Leisure Behavior of Different Occupations,' *Sociology and Social Research,* 54(2/1970), 190–209.

Blazer, D. and E. Palmore. 'Religion and Aging in a Longitudinal Panel,' *The Gerontologist,* 16(1/1976), 82–85.

Born, T. 'Variables Associated with the Winter Camping Location of Elderly Recreational Vehicle Owners in Southwestern Arizona,' *Journal of Gerontology,* 31(3/1976), 346–51.

Bosse, R. and D. Ekerdt. 'Change in Self-Perception of Leisure Activities with Retirement,' *The Gerontologist,* 21(6/1981), 650–54.

Brotman, H. 'Voter Participation in November 1976,' *The Gerontologist,* 17(2/1977), 157–59.

Bull, N. and B. Payne. 'Volunteering as an Alternative to Leisure in Old Age,' pp. 99–103 in R. Ray (ed.). *Leisure and Aging.* Madison: Recreation Resources Center, University of Wisconsin, 1979.

Bultena, G. and V. Wood. 'Leisure Orientation and Recreational Activities of Retirement Community Residents,' *Journal of Leisure Research,* 2(1/1970), 3–15.

Carp, F. 'Effects of the Living Environment on Activity and Use of Time,' *International Journal of Aging and Human Development,* 9(1/1978–79), 75-91.

Clarke, A. 'Leisure and Occupational Prestige,' *American Sociological Review*, 21(3/1956), 301–7.

Clemente, F. et al. 'The Participation of the Black Aged in Voluntary Associations,' *Journal of Gerontology*, 30(4/1975), 469–72.

Colley, L. 'Work Occupation and Leisure Patterns of Self-Supporting Women in the Pre-Retirement Years,' pp. 470–78 in E. Avedon et al. (eds.). *Contemporary Leisure Research: Proceedings of the Second Canadian Congress on Leisure Research*. Toronto: Ontario Research Council on Leisure, 1979.

Conner, K. and G. Bultena. 'The Four-Day Work Week: An Assessment of Its Effects On Leisure Participation,' *Leisure Sciences*, 2(1/1979), 55–70.

Csikszentmihalyi, M. *The Value of Leisure: Towards a Systematic Analysis of Leisure Activities*. Waterloo: University of Waterloo Research Group on Leisure and Cultural Development, 1979.

Csikszentmihalyi, M. 'Leisure and Socialization,' *Social Forces*, 60(1/1981), 332–40.

Cuellar, J. 'El Senior Citizens Club: The Older American in the Voluntary Association,' pp. 207–30 in B. Myerhoff and A. Simic (eds.). *Life's Career-Aging*. Beverly Hills: Sage Publications, 1978.

Culture Statistics, Recreational Activities, 1976. Ottawa: Statistics Canada, 1978.

Cutler, N. 'Voluntary Association Participation and Life Satisfaction: Replication, Revision, and Extension,' *International Journal of Aging and Human Development*, 14(2/1981–82), 127–37.

Cutler, N. and J. Schmidhauser. 'Age and Political Behavior,' pp. 374–406 in D. Woodruff and J. Birren (eds.). *Aging: Scientific Perspectives and Social Issues*. New York: D. Van Nostrand Co., 1975.

Cutler, S. 'Voluntary Association Participation and Life Satisfaction: A Cautionary Research Note,' *Journal of Gerontology*, 28(1/1973), 96–100.

Cutler, S. 'The Effects of Transportation and Distance on Voluntary Association Participation Among the Aged,' *International Journal of Aging and Human Development*, 5(1/1974), 81–94.

Cutler, S. 'Age Profiles of Membership in Sixteen Types of Voluntary Associations,' *Journal of Gerontology*, 31(4/1976a), 462–70.

Cutler, S. 'Membership in Different Types of Voluntary Associations and Psychological Well-Being,' *The Gerontologist*, 16(4/1976b), 335–39.

Cutler, S. 'Aging and Voluntary Association Participation,' *Journal of Gerontology*, 32 (4/1977), 470–79.

Cutler, S. et al. 'Aging and Conservatism: Cohort Changes in Attitudes About Legalized Abortion,' *Journal of Gerontology*, 35(1/1980), 115–23.

Dangott, L. and R. Kalish. *A Time to Enjoy: The Pleasures of Aging*. Englewood Cliffs, N.J.: Prentice-Hall, 1979.

Davis, R. 'Television Communication and the Elderly,' pp. 315–35 in D. Woodruff and J. Birren (eds.). *Aging: Scientific Perspectives and Social Issues*. New York: D. Van Nostrand Co., 1975.

Davis, R. 'Television, Society and the Older Audience,' pp. 55–67 in B. O'Brien (ed.). *Aging: Today's Research and You*. Los Angeles: Ethel Percy Andrus Gerontology Center, University of Southern California, 1979.

De Carlo, T. 'Recreation Participation Patterns and Successful Aging,' *Journal of Gerontology*, 29(4/1974), 416–22.

De Fleur, M. *Theories of Mass Communication*. Second Edition. New York: David McKay, 1970.

Dimmick, J. et al. 'Media Use and the Life Span,' *American Behavioral Scientist*, 23(1/1979), 7–31.

Dimmick, J. and T. McCain (eds.). 'Use of Mass Media: Patterns in the Life Cycle,' *American Behavioral Scientist*, 23(1/1979), 3–136.

Dubin, R. 'Industrial Worker's World: A Study of the 'Central Life Interests' of Industrial Workers,' *Social Problems*, 3(3/1956), 131–42.

Dumazedier, J. *Toward a Society of Leisure*. New York: The Free Press, 1967.

Dumazedier, J. 'Cultural Mutations in Post-Industrial Societies: Implications for the Role of Leisure in the Specific Style of Life of People in the Third Age,' pp. 11–34 in J. Huet (ed.). *Leisure and the Third Age*. Paris: International Center of Social Gerontology, 1972.

Estes, C. 'Toward a Sociology of Political Gerontology,' *Sociological Symposium*, 26 (1/1979), 1–27.

Fly, J. et al. 'Leisure Activity and Adjustment to Retirement,' *Sociological Spectrum*, 1(2/1981), 145–57.

Fontana, A. *The Last Frontier: The Social Meaning of Growing Old*. Beverly Hills: Sage Publications 1977.

Gerstl, J. 'Leisure, Taste and Occupational Milieu,' *Social Problems*, 9(1/1961), 56–68.

Glenn, N. 'Aging and Conservatism,' *The Annals of the American Academy of Political and Social Science*, 415(September 1974), 176–86.

Godbey, G. et al. *The Relationship of Crime and Fear of Crime Among the Aged to Leisure Behavior and Use of Public Leisure Services*. Washington, D.C.: Andrus Foundation, 1980.

Gordon, C. and C. Gaitz. 'Leisure and Lives: Personal Expressivity Across the Life Span,' pp. 310–41 in R. Binstock and E. Shanas (eds.).

Handbook of Aging and the Social Sciences. New York: Van Nostrand Reinhold, 1976.

Gunter, B. and N. Gunter. 'Leisure Styles: A Conceptual Framework for Modern Leisure,' *The Sociological Quarterly,* 21(3/1980), 361–74.

Gunter, P. 'The Rural Aged and Leisure Activities: Problems and Issues,' pp. 115–32 in R. Ray (ed.). *Leisure and Aging.* Madison: Recreation Resources Center, University of Wisconsin, 1979.

Hagedorn, R. and S. Labovitz. 'Participation in Community Associations by Occupation: A Test of Three Theories,' *American Sociological Review,* 33(2/1968a), 272–83.

Hagedorn, R. and S. Labovitz. 'Occupational Characteristics and Participation in Voluntary Associations,' *Social Forces,* 47(1/1968b), 16–27.

Harris, L. et al. *The Myth and Reality of Aging in America.* Washington, D.C.: National Council on the Aging, 1975.

Harris, L. et al. *Aging in the Eighties: America in Transition.* Washington, D.C.: National Council on the Aging, 1981.

Havighurst, R. 'Life Styles and Leisure Patterns: Their Evolution Through the Life Cycle,' in J. Huet (ed.). *Leisure and the Third Age.* Paris: International Center of Social Gerontology, 1972.

Haworth, J. and M. Smith (eds.). *Work and Leisure.* London: Lepus Books, 1975.

Heisel, M. et al. 'Participation in Organized Educational Activities Among Adults Age 60 and Over,' *Educational Gerontology,* 6(2–3/1981), 227–40.

Hoyt, D. and N. Babchuk. 'Ethnicity and the Voluntary Associations of the Aged,' *Ethnicity,* 8(1/1981), 67–81.

Hoyt, D. and W. Lockwood. 'Age-Associated Patterns of Membership in Voluntary Groups,' paper presented at the annual meeting of the American Sociological Association, Toronto, August 1981.

Hudson, R. and R. Binstock. 'Political Systems and Aging,' pp. 369–400 in R. Binstock and E. Shanas (eds.). *Handbook of Aging and the Social Sciences.* New York: Van Nostrand Reinhold, 1976.

Hudson, R. (ed.). *The Aging in Politics: Process and Policy.* Springfield, Ill.: Charles C. Thomas, 1981.

Huet, J. (ed.). *Leisure and the Third Age.* Paris: International Center of Social Gerontology, 1972.

Johnson, H. et al. (eds.). 'Foundations for Gerontological Education,' *The Gerontologist,* 20(3, Part II/1980), 1–61.

Jordan, M. 'Leisure Time Activities of Sociologists, Attorneys, Physicists and People at Large from Greater Cleveland,' *Sociology and Social Research,* 47(3/1963), 290–97.

Kabanoff, B. and G. O'Brien. 'Work and Leisure: A Task Attributes Analysis,' *Journal of Applied Psychology,* 65(5/1980), 596–609.

Kahl, J. *The American Class Structure.* New York: Holt, Rinehart and Winston, 1961.

Kando, T. and W. Summers. 'The Impact of Work on Leisure: Toward a Paradigm and Research Strategy,' *Pacific Sociological Review,* 14(3/1971), 310–23.

Kaplan, M. 'Implications for Gerontology from a General Theory of Leisure,' pp. 49–63 in J. Huet (ed.). *Leisure and the Third Age.* Paris: International Center of Social Gerontology, 1972.

Kaplan, M. *Leisure: Lifestyle and Lifespan: Perspectives for Gerontology.* Philadelphia: W.B. Saunders Co., 1979.

Keating, N. and L. Spiller. 'Retired Women's Definitions of Leisure,' paper presented at the annual meeting of the Canadian Association on Gerontology, Toronto, November 1981.

Keith, P. et al. 'Work-Nonwork Orientations Among Older Men in Nonmetropolitan Communities,' *Sociological Symposium,* 26 (2/1979), 83–100.

Kelly, J. 'Work and Leisure: A Simplified Paradigm,' *Journal of Leisure Research,* 4(1/1972), 50–62.

Kelly, J. 'Leisure as a Compensation for Work Restraint,' *Society and Leisure,* 8(1/1976), 73–82.

Kelly, J. 'Leisure Socialization: Replication and Extension,' *Journal of Leisure Research,* 8(2/1977), 121–32.

Kelly, J. 'Leisure Interaction and the Social Dialectic,' *Social Forces,* 60(1/1981), 304–22.

Kleemeier, R. (ed.). *Aging and Leisure.* New York: Oxford University Press, 1961.

Kleiber, D. and J. Kelly. 'Leisure, Socialization, and the Life Cycle,' pp. 91–137 in S. Iso-Ahola (ed.). *Social Psychological Perspectives on Leisure and Recreation.* Springfield, Ill.: Charles C. Thomas, 1980.

Kubey, R. 'Television and Aging: Past, Present and Future,' *The Gerontologist,* 20(1/1980), 16–35.

Lambert, R. and P. White. 'Work Activity and Participation in Physical Recreation among Employed Canadian Males,' paper presented at the annual meeting of the North American Society for the Sociology of Sport, Fort Worth, November 1981.

Lawton, M.P. 'Leisure Activities for the Aged,' *The Annals of the American Academy of Political and Social Sciences,* 438(July/1978), 71–80.

Lefkowitz, B. *Breaktime.* New York: Elsevier-Dutton, 1979.

Lehman, H. *Age and Achievement.* Princeton: Princeton University Press, 1953.

Long, J. and E. Wimbush. *Leisure and the Over 50s.* Edinburgh: Tourism and Recreation Research Unit, University of Edinburgh, 1979.

Lundberg, G. et al. *Leisure: A Suburban Study.* New York: Columbia University Press, 1934.

McAvoy, L. 'The Leisure Preferences, Problems, and Needs of the Elderly,' *Journal of Leisure Research*, 11(1/1979), 40–47.

McKechnie, G. *Leisure Activities Blank Manual.* Palo Alto: Consulting Psychologists Press, 1975.

McPherson, B. 'The Influence of Intra-Organizational Parameters on the Leisure Pursuits of Adult Men,' pp. 35–50 in M. Maldague and C. Westland (eds.). *First Canadian Congress on Leisure Research.* Quebec: University of Laval Press, 1978.

McPherson, B. and C. Kozlik. 'Canadian Leisure Patterns by Age: Disengagement, Continuity or Ageism?' pp. 113–22 in V. Marshall (ed.). *Aging in Canada: Social Perspectives.* Don Mills: Fitzhenry and Whiteside, 1980.

McPherson, J. and L. Smith-Lovin. 'Women and Weak Ties: Differences by Sex in the Size of Voluntary Associations,' *American Journal of Sociology*, 87(4/1982), 883–904.

Maeda, D. 'Growth of Old People's Clubs in Japan,' *The Gerontologist*, 15(3/1975), 254–56.

Meissner, M. 'The Long Arm of the Job: A Study of Work and Leisure,' *Industrial Relations*, 10(3/1971), 239–60.

Mindel, C. and C. Vaughan. 'A Multidimensional Approach to Religiosity and Disengagement,' *Journal of Gerontology*, 33(1/1978), 103–8.

Moberg, D. 'Religion and the Aging Family,' *The Family Coordinator*, 21(1/1972), 47–60.

Moran, J. *Leisure Activities for the Mature Adult.* Minneapolis: Burgess Publishing Co., 1979.

Morgan, A. and G. Godbey. 'The Effect of Entering an Age-Segregated Environment upon the Leisure Activity Patterns of Older Adults,' *Journal of Leisure Research*, 10(3/1978), 177–90.

Moss, M. and M.P. Lawton. 'Time Budgets of Older People: A Window on Four Lifestyles,' *Journal of Gerontology*, 37(1/1982), 115–23.

Neulinger, J. *To Leisure: An Introduction.* Boston: Allyn and Bacon, 1981.

Noe, F. 'Leisure Life Styles and Social Class: A Trend Analysis, 1900–1960,' *Sociology and Social Research*, 58(3/1974), 286–94.

Orthner, D. 'Leisure Activity Patterns and Marital Satisfaction over the Marital Career,' *Journal of Marriage and the Family*, 37(1/1975), 91–102.

Osgood, N. *Life After Work: Retirement, Leisure, Recreation and the Elderly.* New York: Praeger Publishers, 1982.

Parker, S. 'Work and Non-Work in Three Occupations,' *Sociological Review*, 13(1/1965), 65–75.

Parker, S. *The Future of Work and Leisure.* London: Paladin Books, 1972.

Parker, S. 'Work and Leisure: Theory and Fact,' pp. 23–35 in J. Haworth and M. Smith (eds.). *Work and Leisure.* London: Lepus Books, 1975.

Parker, S. *The Sociology of Leisure.* London: George Allen and Unwin, 1976.

Parker, S. 'Change, Flexibility, Spontaneity, and Self-Determination in Leisure,' *Social Forces*, 60(1/1981), 323–31.

Parker, S. and M. Smith. 'Work and Leisure,' pp. 37–64 in R. Dubin (ed.). *Handbook of Work Organization and Society.* Chicago: Rand McNally, 1976.

Payne, B. 'The Older Volunteer: Social Role Continuity and Development,' *The Gerontologist*, 17(4/1977), 355–61.

Payne, B. 'Religiosity and Religious Participation,' in D. Mangen (ed.). *Handbook of Social Gerontology.* Minneapolis: University of Minnesota Press, 1981.

Payne, B. and E. Brewer. 'Religion and Everyday Life of the Elderly: A Theoretical Model,' paper presented at the annual meeting of the Gerontological Society of America, San Diego, November 1980.

Peppers, L. 'Patterns of Leisure and Adjustment to Retirement,' *The Gerontologist*, 16(5/1976), 441–46.

Perkins, H. and E. Robertson-Tchabo. 'Retirees Return to College: An Evaluative Study at One University Campus,' *Educational Gerontology*, 6(2–3/1981), 273–87.

Peterson, D. 'An Overview of Gerontology Education,' pp. 14–26 in M. Seltzer et al. (eds.). *Gerontology in Higher Education: Perspectives and Issues.* Belmont: Wadsworth Publishing Co., 1978.

Pierce, R. 'Dimensions of Leisure. I: Satisfactions,' *Journal of Leisure Research*, 12(1/1980a), 5–19.

Pierce, R. 'Dimensions of Leisure. II: Descriptions,' *Journal of Leisure Research*, 12(2/1980b), 150–63.

Pratt, H. *The Gray Lobby.* Chicago: University of Chicago Press, 1976.

Pratt, H. 'Politics of Aging: Political Science and the Study of Gerontology,' *Research on Aging*, 1(2/1979), 155–86.

Pratt, H. 'Foundations of Age-Based Political Organization in Three Western Countries,' paper presented at the annual meeting of the Gerontological Society of America, Toronto, November 1981.

Purohit, S. et al. 'A Synthesis of Activity, Substitution and Identity Crisis Theories: Toward Some Assumptions for Constructing a Theory of Aging and Leisure,' *Society and Leisure*, 8(4/1976), 153–69.

Ragan, P. and J. Dowd. 'The Emerging Political Consciousness of the Aged: A Generational Interpretation,' *Journal of Social Issues*, 30(3/1974), 137–58.

Rapoport, R. and R. Rapoport. *Leisure and the Family Life Cycle*. Boston: Routledge and Kegan Paul, 1975.

Ray, R. (ed.). *Leisure and Aging*. Proceedings of the National Recreation and Park Association annual meeting, 1979. Madison: Recreation Resources Center, University of Wisconsin, 1979a.

Ray, R. 'Life Satisfaction and Activity Involvement: Implications for Leisure Services,' *Journal of Leisure Research*, 11(2/1979b), 112–19.

Ray, R. 'The Development of Adult Leisure Behaviors: An Exploratory Inquiry,' paper presented at the annual meeting of the Gerontologica,l Society of America, Toronto, November 1981.

Riessman, L. 'Class, Leisure and Social Participation,' *American Sociological Review*, 19(1/1954), 74–84.

Roadburg, A. 'Perceptions of Work and Leisure Among the Elderly,' *The Gerontologist*, 21(2/1981), 142–45.

Schiff, M. *Assessing Recreation Services for Older Adults in Small Communities*. Toronto: Ministry of Culture and Recreation, 1980.

Schlesinger, J. *Ambition and Politics: Political Careers in the United States*. Chicago: Rand McNally, 1966.

Schmitz-Scherzer, R. 'Longitudinal Change in Leisure Behavior of the Elderly,' pp. 127–36 in H. Thomae (ed.). *Patterns of Aging: Findings from the Bonn Longitudinal Study of Aging*. New York: S. Karger, 1976.

Schmitz-Scherzer, R. 'Ageing and Leisure,' *Society and Leisure*, 2(2/1979), 377–93.

Seleen, D. 'The Congruence Between Actual and Desired Use of Time by Older Adults: A Predictor of Life Satisfaction,' *The Gerontologist*, 22(1/1982), 95–99.

Sherman, S. 'Leisure Activities in Retirement Housing,' *Journal of Gerontology*, 29(3/1974), 325–35.

Shivers, J. and H. Fait. *Recreational Service for the Aging*. Philadelphia: Lea and Febiger, 1980.

Smigel, E. (ed.). *Work and Leisure: A Contemporary Social Problem*. New Haven: University of Connecticut Press, 1963.

Smith, D. 'Voluntary Action and Voluntary Groups,' pp. 247–70 in A. Inkeles et al. (eds.).

Annual Review of Sociology. Volume 1. Palo Alto: Annual Reviews Inc., 1975.

Staines, G. 'Spillover Versus Compensation: A Review of the Literature on the Relationship Between Work and Nonwork,' *Human Relations*, 3(1/1980), 111–29.

Stone, G. 'American Sports: Play and Dis-play,' *Chicago Review*, 9(3/1975), 83–100.

Strain, L. and N. Chappell. 'Outdoor Recreation and the Rural Elderly: Participation, Problems and Needs,' *Therapeutic Recreation Journal*, forthcoming.

Swank, C. 'Media Uses and Gratifications Among the Elderly,' *American Behavioral Scientist*, 23(1/1979), 95–117.

Taietz, P. 'Two Conceptual Models of the Senior Center,' *Journal of. Gerontology*, 31(2/1976), 219–22.

Teague, M. 'Aging and Leisure: A Social Psychological Perspective,' pp. 219–57 in S. Iso-Ahola (ed.). *Social Psychological Perspectives on Leisure and Recreation*. Springfield, Ill.: Charles C. Thomas, 1980.

Tedin, K. 'Age and Social Composition Factors as Explanations for Cleavages In Socio-Political Values,' *International Journal of Aging and Human Development*, 9(4/1978–79), 295–303.

Torres-Gil, F. and R. Becerra. 'The Political Behavior of the Mexican-American Elderly,' *The Gerontologist*, 17(5/1977), 392–99.

Trela, J. 'Social Class and Association Membership: An Analysis of Age-Graded and Non-Age-Graded Voluntary Participation,' *Journal of Gerontology*, 31(2/1976), 198–203.

Trela, J. 'Social Class and Political Involvement in Age Graded and Non-Age Graded Associations,' *International Journal of Aging and Human Development*, 8(4/1977–78), 301–10.

Wapner, E. *Recreation for the Elderly: A Leadership, Theory and Source Book*. Great Neck, N.Y.: Todd and Honeywell, 1981.

Ward, R. 'The Meaning of Voluntary Association Participation to Older People,' *Journal of Gerontology*, 34(3/1979), 438–45.

Ward, R. 'Aging, the Use of Time, and Social Change,' *International Journal of Aging and Human Development*, 14(3/1981–82), 177–87.

Ward, R. 'Occupational Variation in the Life Course: Implications for Later Life,' in N. Osgood (ed.). *Life After Work: Retirement, Leisure, Recreation, and the Elderly*. New York: Praeger Press, 1982.

Warner, W. and J. Abegglen. *Occupational Mobility in American Business and Industry, 1928–1952*. Minneapolis: University of Minnesota Press, 1955.

Weiner, A. and S. Hunt. 'Retirees' Perceptions of Work and Leisure Meanings,' *The Gerontologist*, 21(4/1981), 444–46.

Weiss, C. 'Leisure Planning Programs,' *Perspective on Aging*, (1/1979), 18–22.

White, P. 'Social Class Differences in the Use of Leisure,' *American Journal of Sociology*, 61(2/1955), 145–50.

White, T. 'The Relative Importance of Education and Income as Predictors in Outdoor Recreation Participation,' *Journal of Leisure Research*, 7(3/1975), 191–99.

Williamson, J. et al. *The Politics of Aging: Power and Policy*. Springfield, Ill.: Charles C. Thomas, 1981.

Wilensky, H. 'Work, Careers and Social Integration,' *International Social Science Journal*, 12(4/1960), 543–60.

Wilensky, H. 'Mass Society and Mass Culture: Interdependence or Independence?' *American Sociological Review*, 29(2/1964), 173–97.

Wilson, J. 'Sociology of Leisure,' pp. 21–40 in A. Inkeles et al. (eds.). *Annual Review of Sociology*. Volume 6. Palo Alto: Annual Reviews Inc., 1980.

Wilson, R. 'The Courage to Be Leisured,' *Social Forces*, 60(2/1981), 282–303.

Wingrove, C. and J. Alston. 'Age, Aging and Church Attendance,' *The Gerontologist*, 11(4/1971), 356–58.

Wippler, R. 'Leisure Behavior: A Multivariate Approach,' *Sociologica Neerlandica*, 1(1/1970), 51–67.

Yoesting, D. and D. Burkhead. 'Significance of Childhood Recreation Experiences on Adult Leisure Behavior: An Exploratory Analysis,' *Journal of Leisure Research*, 5(1/1973), 25–36.

Yoesting, D. and R. Burdge. 'Utility of a Leisure Orientation Scale,' *Iowa State Journal of Research*, 50(5/1976), 345–56.

Young, T. 'Media Use by Older Adults,' *American Behavioral Scientist*, 23(1/1979), 119–36.

Yu, J. and R. Mendell. 'The Development and Utility of a Leisure Behavior Index,' *Research Quarterly for Exercise and Sport*, 51(3/1980), 553–58.

Zuzanek, J. 'Leisure and Cultural Participation as a Function Of Life-Cycle,' paper presented at the annual meeting of the Canadian Sociology and Anthropology Association, Saskatoon, June 1979.

Appendix A

How to Read a Statistical Table or Figure

Throughout this text, and particularly in journal articles, information is often presented graphically in tables or figures. It is important that you learn to read and to interpret this information accurately and completely, so that you gain a more thorough understanding of the relationships or trends being discussed. A thorough analysis of a table or figure involves three main stages: (1) reading to acquire an overview of the information presented; (2) analyzing the numbers in the body of the table; and (3) interpreting the information.

An Overview

The first step involves a careful reading of the title of the table or figure, which should tell you the specific topic and content of the material; what variables are included; whether the information is presented by subcategories such as age, sex, or region; and how the information is presented (in raw numbers, means, percentages, correlations, or ratios). It should also indicate whether the information is purely descriptive (percentages), or whether it illustrates a relationship between variables (a cross-classification of variables or a correlation matrix for a number of variables). Next, you should read the labels for each vertical column and horizontal row to determine what data appear in the table. Similarly, in a graph or figure you should read the labels on the vertical and horizontal axes. You should also examine any footnotes to determine the source of the data (the year, the country, or region), the definitions of variables, and whether data are missing.

If the table is related to a causal analysis, the final step in the overview involves identifying the independent (cause), control (factors such as sex, race, social class or age that can alter or influence the initial relationship), and dependent (outcome) variables. For example, consider a table presenting information about relationships between age, income, and race: obviously, income does not cause or influence age or race. Therefore, the dependent variable is income. It must then be determined whether the major independent variable is age, with race as the control variable in the relationship between age and income, or whether race is the independent variable and age the control variable. In most tables and figures the independent and dependent variables are identified in the title.

An Analysis of the Numbers or Plots

The first step in the analysis is to determine the size and type of units that are used (raw numbers or percentages, hundreds or millions, inches or centimeters, etc.). Next, look at the overall totals, and at the highest, lowest, and average figures. These should be compared with other data in the table, and trends and deviations should be noted. In a table the figures in the lower right-hand corner usually give the overall total or average for the entire population in the study. If the percentages total 100 in the columns, then the table should be read across the rows to determine group differences or patterns.

The third step involves determining the range or variability of the information (ages 20 to 60; income $5,000 to $50,000, etc.). Next, look at the totals, averages, or percentages for each subgroup, or examine the patterns exhibited by subgroups in a figure where the data are plotted. Is the pattern linear (as height increases, weight increases) or curvilinear (strength increases with age to a maximum and then declines with age)? Does the pattern increase, decrease, remain stable, or fluctuate in any observable pattern with age or over time? The next step involves identifying unexpected irregularities or findings (for example, males over 65 reporting higher income than 55-year-olds), and searching for a valid explanation of these atypical patterns.

Interpreting the Information

After you have become thoroughly familiar with the descriptive information, the relationships between variables, and the observable patterns and irregularities, you will interpret this information to arrive at valid conclusions and explanations. In many cases the author will present an interpretation in the text. However, it is possible that there might be an equally valid alternative interpretation. In addition to becoming more familiar with the data from which conclusions are drawn, this search for alternative explanations is a major reason for you to analyze and interpret graphic information carefully and thoroughly. Do not automatically accept the author's interpretation as the only one.

In order to interpret the data, begin by attempting to explain patterns and irregularities in the data and decide whether this explanation agrees with previous information cited in other sources. If it does not, question the validity of the explanation by considering whether the interpretation is spurious — that is, whether the relationship is due solely to the fact that a variable happens to be associated with another variable. For example, an observed relationship between a large number of storks in a certain area and a high birth rate could be interpreted to mean that storks deliver babies. However, this interpretation is spurious since a greater number of storks inhabit rural areas, and the rural birth rate is higher than the urban birth rate. Tables and graphs must be analyzed carefully in order to fully understand the evidence on which a conclusion is based, and to determine if a misleading or unlikely explanation has been presented. Finally, remember to note whether different patterns or results occur by social categories such as age, sex, race, class, education, nationality, religion, ethnicity, geographical region, or place of residence.

Index